The Land of Scholars

Two Thousand Years
of Korean Confucianism

The Land of Scholars

Two Thousand Years of Korean Confucianism

Kang Jae-eun

Translated by Suzanne Lee

HOMA & SEKEY BOOKS
Paramus, New Jersey

FIRST AMERICAN EDITION

This book is published with the support of the Korea Literature Translation Institute in commemoration of Korea being the Guest of Honor at the Frankfurt Book Fair 2005.

Library of Congress Cataloging-in-Publication Data

Kang, Jae-eun, 1926-
The Land of Scholars: Two Thousand Years of Korean Confucianism /
by Kang Jae-eun ; translated from the Korean by Suzanne Lee. -- 1st ed.
p. cm.   Includes index.
ISBN 1-931907-30-7 (hardcover) -- ISBN 1-931907-37-4 (pbk.)
1. Philosophy, Confucian--Korea--History. 2. Confucianism--Korea--
History. 3. Korea--Civilization--Confucian influences. I. Lee, Suzanne. II. Title.
B5253.C6K355 2006
181'.119--dc22   2005019692

Homa & Sekey Books
3rd Floor, North Tower
Mack-Cali Center III
140 E. Ridgewood Ave.
Paramus, NJ 07652

Tel: 800-870-HOMA, 201-261-8810
Fax: 201-261-8890, 201-384-6055
Email: info@homabooks.com
Website: www.homabooks.com

Edited by Larry Matthews
Printed in U.S.A.
1 3 5 7 9 10 8 6 4 2

Table of Contents

A Word from the Author

How Did the Confucians in Each Period
Respond to the Historical Tasks They Faced?

Korea is viewed by Japan as "the honor student of Confucianism" or "heavily tinged with Confucianism" in general. But very little of the specific content of Korean Confucianism is known to the Japanese.

The contents of this book were originally published as a series titled "The Ethos of Joseon Confucian" from May 1997 to May 2000 in *Korean Culture*, compiled under the supervision of Korea Cultural Center in Japan. The contents were reorganized and the title changed to the easier one of *The Land of Scholars: Two Thousand Years of Korean Confucianism*.

I celebrated my 70th birthday in October of 1996. That was when I was contacted by the editorial department of *Korean Culture* with the question of whether there was something to print serially. I had just finished publishing a five-volume book entitled *Gangjae-eon jeojakseon* (Selected Works of Kang Jae-eun) in 1996 in which research on the history of modern Korean thought has been set to rest in my own way. But then a vague idea of finding the thread of the Confucian ethos deeply rooted in the political culture of Korea and connecting it to the history of modern thought came to me. But it would be a daunting task for an individual of only ordinary and mediocre ability such as I, and it seemed to be a risky venture at best and lacking good sense when my age is also taken into consideration. After pondering over this issue for a while, I came to the conclusion that "it would not be out of order to take on this daunting task before my life's breath leaves my body."

It goes without saying that the mainstream of Korean Confucianism is in Korea. But I have always felt a bit of disharmony in the research trend in Korean Confucianism. This shows up in agreeing with the Learning of Master Zhu as the only scholarship without criticism, the disproportionate emphasis on the study of the principle of human nature, and especially the moralistic evaluation of the Sarim Faction. As described in the book, the history of Joseon politics changed into a history of the factional struggles since the latter half of the 16th century when the Sarim Faction was in power. In addition, the dispute was far removed from the original responsibility of "statecraft on providing for the people" which Confucians must be in charge of in Confucian politics. The general trend has been to enthusiastically welcome the emergence of the Sarim Faction as if a "revolution" was brought to Joseon Confucianism. Jeong Yagyong, who lived during the turbulent times around 1800, describes what the scholarship of a "true Confucian" should be in "Sogyuron" (俗儒論, On Confucian Customs).

> The scholarship of a true Confucian originally involves capabilities in managing to defeat barbaric enemies, make available goods plentiful, and be accomplished in both literary as well as military arts to govern the nation and provide security to its people.... Mencius told the rulers of Zhai and Liang of virtue and righteousness only in an effort to modify putting too much value on combat. Later Confucians called anything beyond virtue and righteousness or the principle and material force as miscellaneous studies because they did not know the original meaning of the sage.

The excerpt above can be said to be a brief frontal criticism of the Confucian perspective of the Sarim Faction. In short, the Sarim Faction disdained the military but emphasized scholarship to politely shun military affairs and the economy as "miscellaneous learning," while incurring an endless cycle of political confusion by uniting the debates on "benevolence and righteousness" or "the principle and material force" that are not related to reality with factional disputes.

The motive for writing this book was to attempt to organize the Confucian history grounded on what the Confucians searched for and how they responded to the historical tasks they confronted in each period. Therefore I wrote this as a way of throwing a rock at the Confucian historical narrative centered around "benevolence and righteousness" and "the principle and material force" by revealing my honest heterodox opinion.

In addition, the following books on the comprehensive history of Confucianism are available and in print. In my opinion, *Joseon yugyo yeonwon* (The Origin of Confucianism in Joseon, 1922, Hoedong Seogwan) by Jang Ji-yeon is the most pioneering of its kind; it is sometimes quoted in this book. Other books published in South Korea subsequent to *The Origin of Confucianism in Joseon* are sequentially as follows:

Hyeon Sang-yun, *Joseon yugyosa* (History of Joseon Confucianism), 1949, Minjungseogwan.

Bae Jong-ho, *Hanguk yugyosa* (History of the Study of Korean Confucianism), 1974, Yonsei University Press.

Yu Seung-guk, *Hangugui yugyo* (Confucianism of Korea), 1976, Gyoyang Guksa Chongseo. A Chinese translation of this book was published by Fu Jigong in 1988 under the title of *Hanguo rujiaoshi* (韓國儒敎史) by the Commercial Press in Taiwan.

Lee Byeong-do, *Hanguk yuhaksa* (History of the Study of Confucianism), 1987, Asea Munhwasa.

Choe Yeong-seong, *Hanguk yugyo sasangsa* (The History of the Idea of Korean Confucianism), 5 volumes total, 1994-1997, Asea Munhwasa.

Korean Association for Studies of Philosophical Thought ed., *Nonjaenguiro bon hanguk cheolhak* (Korean Philosophy through Disputes), 1995, Yemun Seowon.

Hanguk Sasangsa Yeonguhoe ed., *Joseon yuhagui jehakpa* (The Jehak Faction in the Study of Joseon Confucianism), 1996, Yemun Seowon.

The following books were published in North Korea:

Chung Chin Suk, Chung Sung Chul, and Kim Chang Won, *Joseon cheolhaksa* (History of Joseon Philosophy) I, 1962, Gwahak-won Press. This book was translated into Japanese by Song Ji-hak and published by Kobundo under the title of *Chosen tetsugakushi* (朝鮮哲學史, History of Joseon Philosophy).

Choi Bong Ik, *Joseon cheolhak sasangsa yeongu — godae-geunse* (A Study of the History of the Ideas of Joseon Philosophy — Antiquity to Modern Times), 1975, Social Sciences Press.

The two books published in North Korea reflect the transformation in the chaotic ideological conditions from 1962 to 1975. The difference between the two books is that the former is a history of the ideas of Marxism but the latter is that of the so-called *juche* ideology of Kim Il Sung. The heading for each chapter of the latter book states: "The *juche* ideology as the revolutionary thought of our Great Leader Kim Il Sung is the only leading guide for the study of the history of the idea of Joseon philosophy." It is likely that the former was discontinued from publication and the latter was published in its stead to wash away its ideological "poison."

The following book is published in the Yanbian Korean Autonomous Prefecture of Jilin Province:

Ju Hong-seong, Lee Hong-sun, and Ju Chil-seong, *Chaoxiàn zhexue sixiangshi* (朝鮮哲學 思想史, History of Thought of Joseon Philosophy), 1989, Yanbian People's Publishing House.

There are so many other research results and papers categorized by different periods, figures, and/or issues in addition to the ones mentioned above, and they contain such diverse opinions, that I became more confused the more I read them. It was impossible for me to gather and organize all available information.

It was my intention to write this book with the idea of outlining the entire image of Korean Confucianism from a visibly macro perspective of what is "Korean" among the Confucian culture of East Asia based on the classics.

Changes in publishers and managing editors have occurred in the three years since I began serially publishing my manuscript in *Korean Culture*. There are many memories involved in the process, but it is the support of the readers of the serial publication that made this book possible. I can only remember and be grateful to the fortuitous luck that led to the publication of this book at the advent of the 21st century.

Kang Jae-eun
June 2003

A Word from the Translator
(Japanese to Korean)

History of Korean Confucianism from a New Perspective

It is not that simple a task to take a bird's-eye view of the history of Korean Confucianism. This is because the task cannot be performed without comprehensive knowledge not only of thought but also of Korean history as well, since the history of Korean Confucianism is closely related to the historical reality of Korea throughout all periods. Thus only a distinguished scholar who is knowledgeable in history and philosophy can do this.

A comprehensive history of Korean Confucianism thus far includes, among others: *The Origin of Confucianism in Joseon* by Jang Ji-yeon (1922), *History of Joseon Confucianism* by Hyeon Sang-yun (1949), *History of the Study of Korean Confucianism* by Bae Jong-ho (1974), *Confucianism of Korea* by Yu Seung-guk (1976), *History of the Study of Confucianism* by Lee Byeong-do (1987), and *The History of the Idea of Korean Confucianism* by Choe Yeong-seong (5 volumes total, 1997).

All the books contain strong and weak points. In general, books written by philosophers are elaborate on tenets and logic but are somewhat distant from historical reality and remain focused on the history of hollow disputes. Historians, on the other hand, show a decided limitation in analyzing the contents of subtle disputes and delicate differences among Confucians due to lack of knowledge of Confucian thought itself.

This book proposes a new perspective that is in contrast to the existing comprehensive history of Confucianism. Prof. Kang Jae-eun is a historian, and therefore this book stresses the social function of Confucianism rather than the philosophical analysis or enumeration of doctrines on Confucianism. The author has shown a superlative view on the major flow in history by linking thought and movements together. Flashes of the historical perspective as well as original arguments stand out in this book.

Information on the author may assist in better understanding this book. I would like to introduce a section from an article I wrote on "Naega bon gangjae-eon — Hyeonsil mosun oemyeon anneun silcheonjeok jiseon" (Kang Jae-eun as I See Him — Practicing Intellect Who Does Not Avoid the Contradictions in Reality) in *Gyosu sinmun*, September 2000.

Kang Jae-eun was a hero to students who studied history in Korea in the late 1970s. We could not keep from feeling an admiration for and being impressed by his novel claims and clear reasoning as his Japanese manuscripts were secretly copied and read in turn. His manuscripts that described modern history after opening of the ports resolved a difficult issue with incisiveness and strength by linking thought and movements. I first met the "idol" of my graduate days in Osaka, Japan, in 1985. But contrary to my preformed image of a man with sharp and strong eyes, he was a very open-hearted and mellow person. I was immediately reminded of the image of Kim Sak-kat as I saw him throw his bag on his back like a vagabond's bundle and leave after a drink. I had several other opportunities to meet with him, but he did not change all that much from the first impression I had of him.

Diverse aspects can be seen in Prof. Kang Jae-eun, just as his life story is full of vicissitudes, but his achievements as a scholar can be broadly divided into three categories.

First is the study of the modern history of Korea. The study of modern Korean history which began with the presentation of "Joseon bonggeonchejeui haechewa nongminjeonjaeng" (The Dissolution of the Joseon Feudal System and the Peasants' War) in 1954 was expanded to the anti-Japanese Righteous Army movements and the partisan movements of the 1930s to resist Japan. He has presented many works on modern Korean history since the early 1970s, but he focused on finding "the artery of thought of modern Joseon" that was the basis of the movements rather than stopping at just the history of various movements. This is why his works are superior; they raised the standard on the study of the modern history of Korea one level up. Thereafter his research on the history of the ideas moved back in time to the era of practical learning and reached into the research of Dasan (Jeong Yag-yong), whom he had adored in his mind. His

xiii

works on the history of the ideas of modern Korea are contained in the 1996 publication entitled *Gangjae-eon jeojakseon* (Selected Works of Kang Jae-eun, 5 volumes total).

Second are the theoretical research and education activities to resolve the issues of Zainichi Koreans in Japan.

He has been the editor for 22 years of *Samcheolli* (Three Thousand *Li*) and *Cheonggu* (Korea), quarterly magazines that act as a forum and compass for Korean residents in Japan. He encompassed the various contradictions of the Zainichi Korean society and did his best to resolve issues as a practicing intellectual.

Third is his attempt to contribute to improving the relationship between Japan and Korea and unification between North and South Korea as a mediator. He changed distorted images about Korea by introducing true aspects of Korea to the Japanese society as well as presenting the history of relations between the two nations and prospects for their future. *Hanil gyoryusa* (The History of Exchange between Japan and Korea), *Gyogwaseo-e sseuyeojin joseon* (Joseon in the Textbooks), and *Hanilgwangyeui heosanggwa silsang* (False and True Images of the Relationship between Japan and Korea) are a part of such efforts. Prof. Kang's research is avant-garde in all fields and is highly acknowledged academically. Thus he can be said to be one of the historians who led Japanese academia after the liberation of Korea.

As the author confessed in "How did the Confucians Respond to the Historical Tasks Confronted in Each Period?" this book was a challenge and written with a passion during his remaining life. He was desirous of organizing "a comprehensive history of Korean Confucianism" into the history of modern thought of Korea that he had been studying throughout his life. His opinions are clearly and strongly expressed in this book, and they raise some fundamental questions on existing doctrines. I have arbitrarily organized the unique features and contributions made by this book as follows.

First, this book presents a model of delineating the history of the idea. The author pursued meaning within the cultural and social space of Korean society rather than approaching from within the Confucian theory. In other words, he emphasized social background, functions, and transfiguring aspects rather than tenets or textual

xiv

debates. Chapters 19 and 20 are so rich with a historical approach that they may be confused for delineation of modern Korean history. This book is the result of widening the horizons and of cultivating diversity for understanding the history of Korean Confucianism.

Second, this book provides a bird's-eye view of the history of Korean Confucianism from an East Asian perspective through comparing the exchange of China, Japan, and Korea without limiting the perspective of Korean history. Although this book was originally written with Japanese readers in mind, usage of many excerpts from Japanese historical texts is beneficial to Korean readers in that Korean thought is compared to Japanese thought. Historical texts from China are also frequently introduced. The merit of this book is due to the wide appreciation for history of the author. This book is expected to contribute to comparative studies on Chinese and Japanese Confucianism needed to understand the characteristics of Korean Confucianism.

Third, the contents of this book are presented in a lecture style for the refined audience rather than an academic style. As such, the book is written simply but the flowing and broad contents provide an appreciation for the deliberate historical perspective of an old master. The author's extensive knowledge as well as his unhesitatingly wandering spirit that crosses the boundary between history and philosophy can be felt.

Fourth, most memorable in this book should be a sharp criticism of the consciousness that became common in Korean academia. For example, several issues are raised such as "Is the Period of Military Regime the Dark Age?" or "Is Serving Two Dynasties Impossible?" The sentences are in a questioning form, but the author provides answers to them. In that respect, the historical perspective and philosophy of the author as well as his distinctive personality and human touch are clearly reflected in the book, rather than it being solely an objective organization of the history of Korean Confucianism. It is hoped that readers will appreciate these points when reading this book.

It is easy to see that the author's strong critical consciousness is in general from extreme awareness of issues over reality rather than the past history of the ideas. It denies the doctrine of the unity of cultures and the Learning of Master Zhu as the only scholarship, and fundamentally revolts against the history of Korean Confucianism centered around the ruling class, traditions, mainstream, and the Sarim Faction. He projects his opinion to the Koreans of today through such claims.

Below are the claims in the book emphasized by the author.

First is a strong criticism against dogmatization of thought. The author dislikes the Learning of Master Zhu as the only scholarship of the Sarim Faction and the "religiousness of thought" led by Song Si-yeol in the 17th century. This comes from the unique historical awareness of the harmful influence brought on by the "religiousness of thought" on top of discerning the entirety of the history of Korean thought. At the same time, I think this is related to his life that was full of fight for freedom of thought and civil rights through experiencing cruel contemporary history as a Korean residing in Japan. Could it be that he desired to emphasize that ideological dogma or philosophical rigidity in any form will ruin history and culture?

Second is the criticism against conceptualization of the Sarim Faction that ignored practicality, ideology that was estranged from reality, and the custom of "encouraging learning and disdaining military arts." His criticisms of the dogmatism and unrealistic emphasis on justification of the Sarim Faction are stern. He does not stop at criticizing the Confucians toward the end. An inquiry is made into the core thought of Jo Gwang-jo, the leader of the "early Sarim Faction" and the idol of politics judged by Confucian morals.

The author has stated achieving "enriching and strengthening a country" is more difficult than "the way of benevolence and righteousness." This is a direct reversal of the words of Jo Gwang-jo: "...enriching and strengthening a country is easy but the way of benevolence and righteousness is difficult." Further, the fact that "politics by Confucian morals" as emphasized by the Sarim Faction is contrary to the original Confucian thought is pointed out. The Imjin War and the Manchu invasion of Korea in 1636 resulted from governing in the kingly way. A question is raised as to whether governing in the kingly way is in fact the right way to govern and to be adopted by Confucians. He almost seems to rebuke it for glossing over the total failure of national administration with abstract words.

The author not only denies the orthodox teachings of Confucius and Mencius of the Sarim Faction but criticizes the basic political philosophy of the Sarim Faction as well. I am also critical of the existing concept of orthodox teachings centered around the Sarim Faction. In short, this is because explaining the history of Confucianism of the Joseon period with the concept of orthodox teachings is very difficult without considering Jeong Do-jeon of early Joseon and Jeong Yag-yong of late Joseon. But there was no other book prior to this one to clearly and emphatically raise this issue. Others have criticized Jo Gwang-jo, the Sarim Faction, and Song Si-yeol, but with such extreme radical reasoning to be called a self-admitted "heretic verdict." This book comes as a shock in that such issues were raised for the first time since the Joseon period and after liberation in the history of Confucian thought today. Contrasting theories are thus proposed in this book to provide an impetus for vehement debates. If such debates can be productively held, then that in itself justifies the translation and publication of this book.

Third is the rigid worship of the greater and national characteristics that are also objects of criticism. Serving the greater as a policy is acknowledged, but the original pure functions will disappear and contrary functions will remain if serving the greater becomes distant from reality or becomes dogmatic or rigid due to other political designs. The main point of his criticism on this issue is also the rigidity and dogmatization of thought. He severely criticizes almost to the point of anger the unrealistic justification of "pro-Ming and anti-Qing" advocated by the Seoin Faction that instigated King Injo's Restoration of Rectitude. Moreover, "the northern expansion policy" led by Song Si-yeol was refuted as being nothing more than logic based on ethnic prejudice. The author frontally assaults the irresponsibility of the northern expansion policy as being nothing more than an outrageous opinion when a detailed historical comparison is made between the national and military power of China and those of Joseon at the time.

Fourth is the difference in the relative defense of the Hungu Faction in comparison to the Sarim Faction from the viewpoint of orthodox teachings of the Joseon period, which is totally different from the general awareness of today. The fact that the period of military regime was not the cultural Dark Age, and instead safeguarded the sovereignty by defying the Mongol invasions as the function of the military regime, is highly evaluated. Attention should be paid to reevaluation of historic figures. Historical "restoration" is attempted by reinterpreting Jeong Do-jeon, Sejo, Shin Suk-ju, and Gwanghae-gun.

An essay titled "Nanggaegui sinnyeonmanpil" (Jottings of an Unreliable Person in the New Year) written by Danjae Shin Chae-ho, a nationalistic historian of the period of the Great Han Empire, and published in the January 2, 1925, edition of the *Dong-A Ilbo* (Donga Daily News) came to mind as I read the issues raised strongly by the author.

To questions of whether morality and the principles arise from interests or right and wrong, Danjae answered that they arise from interests. He adamantly stated, "Thus mankind is all about interests. Sakyamuni, Confucius, Christ, Marx, and Kropotkin were born to resolve the issue of interests." On the other hand, absolute universality of the standard for the relationship of interests was seen as nonexistent because it differs according to various periods and nations. The transfiguration of thought dependent on the era and region is acknowledged as a matter of course through his statement, "Sakyamuni of China is different from that of India, Confucius of Japan is different from that of China, and Marx is different from Kautsky's Marx, Lenin's Marx, China's Marx, and Japan's Marx."

But what was the condition of the custom of thought in Joseon? Danjae indicated as follows:

> We Joseon people always attempt to find truth in something other than interests; Joseon becomes Joseon of Sakyamuni rather than Sakyamuni of Joseon when Sakyamuni is introduced into Joseon; Joseon becomes Joseon of Confucius rather than Confucius of Joseon when Confucius is introduced into Joseon; and whatever principle attempts to become Joseon of the principle

rather than the principle of Joseon when a principle is introduced into Joseon. Thus Joseon for morality and principle exists, but morality and principle for Joseon do not exist. Alas! Is this the distinct characteristic of Joseon? It could be considered a distinct characteristic, but that of a slave. I will lament for the morality and principle of Joseon.

The essay is truly like the nationalist Danjae. The custom of the world of Korean thought which easily leans toward universalism that buries the self and morality that has idealistic tendencies are accurately and sharply pointed out. The fact that the cause of the emergence and function of thought lay within interests rather than morality or right and wrong is a factor of materialistic viewpoints which greatly influenced him in those days, but it may be the result of clear-sightedness in staring directly at the reality of loss of national sovereignty and the international society in which imperialism was rampant. Danjae severely criticized the tendency toward "doctrinal" thought of the times and the Joseon period which was not concerned with reality as "the characteristics of a slave."

Danjae and Kang Jae-eun are almost in total agreement in their extreme dislike of moralism and dogmatism. The author consistently emphasizes "Korean Confucianism" rather than "Confucian Korea" as well as "Confucianism that helped Korea" from the beginning to the end of this book. This is where the doctrine of Learning of Master Zhu is the only scholarship as well as the Sarim Faction that wholeheartedly supported governing in the kingly way and ignored the policy of enriching and strengthening a country and practical learning are positioned. Confucianism that would help the reality of Korea was what he deemed necessary, not the distinction between governing in the kingly way and governing with might or between the study of the principle of human nature and practical learning. All historic figures, schools, and events are evaluated based on this standard. Both Kang Jae-eun and Danjae pointed out the fundamental fact that thought originates and functions within interests rather than morality or principle.

On the other hand, the author is similar to Dasan Jeong Yag-yong in his emphasis of practicality and utility. He defined "the study of practicality and utility" as the new learning toward which Dasan was inclined by quoting from "On Confucian Customs" by Dasan in "A Word from the Author."

Dasan called Confucians who neglected economic issues that were of assistance in everyday life in favor of focusing on fancy useless words and disdained practical studies as devotees of miscellaneous learning; they were "Confucians ignorant of the true state of affairs" or "secularized Confucians." "Confucians who were ignorant of the true state of affairs" are ideological dogmatists. Dasan criticized them as needing to be the target of a purge along with corrupt bureaucrats, the so-called "rotten Confucians." The claim was that national reform would not be achieved with them in official posts.

Then what is the scholarship advocated in contrast to the "Confucians ignorant of the true state of affairs," "secularized Confucians," and "rotten Confucians"? Dasan defines the scholarship of "a true Confucian" as follows in "On Confucian Customs":

> The scholarship of a true Confucian is applicable in governing the nation and making the people feel secure, fighting off the barbarians, strengthening the national economy, and cultivating the literary and military arts capabilities. How can it be said that writing by copying prose from people of the olden days, commenting on insects or fish, or becoming familiar with propriety while wearing wide-sleeved clothing can be called learning?

In one word, the scholarship of a true Confucian is statecraft and practical learning. To be more specific, it is the study to become a rich and strong nation. Dasan revealed that the goal of the reform is the promotion of enriching and strengthening a country in the "Preface" of *Bang-lae chobon* (邦禮草本, rough draft of *Design for Good Governance*), a book that contains his thoughts on reform. He also affirmed that the worldly greed of a person can become the motivation for development and achievement in economic development. Application of this to the national polity is an affirmation of the policy toward enriching and strengthening a country. Practicality and rationality, two characteristics of modernism, are in fact related to utilitarianism. Secularism and acknowledgment of greed are necessary to do so, and the primary goal of national policy can only be enriching and strengthening a country.

Dasan claimed in *Noneo gogeumju* (論語古今註, Ancient and Contemporary Commentaries on the Analects of Confucius) that King Shun, Gija, Guan Zhong, and Mencius all adopted economic measures first, after which they became concerned about education Especially requiring attention is the interpretation about Guan Zhong, who had so far been judged to be a lesser scholar by Confucian scholars because of being an advocate of enriching and strengthening a country. Dasan rated Guan Zhong as a scholar who practiced the ways prescribed by the ancient kings as much as Mencius did by introducing the positive evaluation made by Confucius.

Those who carefully read this book will know that the claim made by the author in affirming the policy of enriching and strengthening a country while advocating for a new rating of Guan Zhong is the same as that of Dasan. The former is emphasized repeatedly in this book as the "theory of pursuing riches before education" by the author, and the latter is the support for Guan Zhong. The author did not quote words of Dasan in this book because the goals and consciousness of issues of the two are superbly in tune. Jo Gwang-jo, the spiritual mainstay of the Sarim Faction, could be a "Confucian ignorant of the true state of affairs" from this standard.

The theory of enriching and strengthening a country is the core policy of modernization. The author can be viewed as a "modernist" in that he uses it as the standard for judgment and brings attention to its pure function. Postmodern discourse is the fashion in Korea in these days when globalization and the information revolution are the current of the times. It is almost to the point where one feels behind the times without one word of criticism against characteristics of modern life in the form of nationalism and utilitarianism. But is not enriching and strengthening a country by increasing economic power and military power the saving grace of a statesman?

Nationalism and modernism have consistently been the two supreme issues to the Korean people in the 20th century. Nationalism is valid for the Korean people who have not been able to build a "whole nation of one ethnic group" until the unification of the two

Koreas, even if globalization is the general tide of today and one cannot go against it. As well, I think modernism is a value still applicable in Korean society. To insist on redressing the past without attaining rationality is to go against history, which will incur a cost at some time later. The denial and deconstruction of "the modern" should be restricted to the negative aspects such as imperialism or environmental corruption, while positive elements should be inherited and developed. Discussion should be first held on the issue of deconstruction for whom and for what purpose. Without this clarification, Korea will be swept away amidst the interests of the advanced nations and result in unilaterally forced disarmament. There is a need to listen attentively to what Dasan, Danjae, and Kang Jae-eun point out.

Limitations to the arguments presented in this book may exist. But the first feeling one gets when reading this book is that the plans presented by the author can become schematized. In other words, viewing the Learning of Master Zhu = premodern, morality, and conservative while antithesis of the Learning of Master Zhu = inclined toward the modern, realism, and progressive can be seen as an overgeneralization.

The book does neglect the development of domestic diversity in some way by simplifying the mainstream Confucianism in the Joseon period of the Learning of Master Zhu as the only scholarship. This is due to the likelihood of conforming to the conclusion reached by the study by imperial Japanese scholars of the history of the idea during the colonial period which states that the history of Confucianism of the Joseon period is not diverse or rich and rather standardized and lacking, which is contrary to the intention of the author.

I hope the publication of this book will bring about an opportunity for active discussions on the history of Korean Confucianism and the history of Korean thought, especially including various viewpoints in this book. That is the wish of this translator.

Finally, I would like to express my heartfelt gratitude to President Kim Eon-ho of Hangilsa for publishing this book in spite of difficult conditions, as well as Kang Ok-sun, Seo Sang-mi, and Jeon Sang-hui who assisted in making it such an elegant production.

June 4, 2003
Ha Woo-bong

A Note from the Translator
(Korean to English)

This book by Prof. Kang Jae-eun contains a vast amount of knowledge, not only on the history of Korean Confucian thought but on Chinese and Japanese history, as well as background information on the transmission of Buddhism, Confucianism, and Christianity in Korea. The book is very informative in that the perspective of the author is somewhat different from what I am used to. He is not blindly patriotic toward Korea as is often the case with Korean scholars, nor is he blindly accepting of the situation. He can be very critical on occasion about his motherland. However, he seems to be more critical of different aspects of Korea as compared to Korean scholars, and I have also noticed that he praises things and people criticized by some Korean scholars. For example, Prof. Kang seems to distinguish "the study of the principle of human nature" from Neo-Confucianism, whereas most Confucian scholars tend to link the two together. The term "Neo-Confucianism" is equated with "new Confucianism," and "the Learning of Master Zhu" with "the Zhu Xi School" in this book in an effort to mark this difference. Moreover, Korean politics governed by Confucian scholar-officials is seen by Prof. Kang as having been dominated by factional disputes waged over ideological justification and not related to national polity for most of the Joseon period until the late Joseon period. National polity became linked to factional disputes (or "political party" struggles, as Bak Yeong-hyo claimed) in the late Joseon period. This changed the political map of Korea.

Perhaps his "unique" perception of Korea can be attributed to the fascinating and often chaotic life he had led in his younger days as well as the fact that he lives abroad. Although born in Korea, Prof. Kang has lived in Japan for many years. He became involved in the Communist activities in Korea as a student when it was taking its "baby steps." Due to his involvement in what was perceived as "anti-government" thought at the time, he often had to hide from the police; he ultimately stole away to Japan to avoid them. His life in

Japan was probably not easy. I attribute his life experiences to his ability to voice his opinions about his motherland without reservation. This book was refreshing because it contains a well-balanced mixture of criticism and admiration for the history, historic figures, and thought of Korea. Korean thought, and especially Confucian thought in Korea, is viewed from a different perspective, a historical perspective. I hope the readers will enjoy this book as much as I did.

Other points I planned on mentioning are included in Prof. Ha Woo-bong's note, so I will not tire the reader by another rendition of the same thought. Instead, let me take a few moments to briefly explain about the translation in this book. First and foremost, I followed the guidelines of the Revised Romanization of Korean as put forth by the Korean Ministry of Culture and Tourism. Names of people from countries that put the last name before the first and middle names are denoted in that order without a comma separating the last name from the first name. I made some exceptions, of course, especially with Korean last names. "Kim," "Shin," "Kang," and "Ahn" are used to denote the last names rather than "Gim," "Sin," "Gang," and "An," respectively, for the simple reason that Kim as a last name is widely used, and the other last names would look strange by themselves. An attempt has been made to follow the *pinyin* system used in China for denoting Chinese words.

I would like to take this time to recognize the paramount role Prof. Han Hyong Jo (Dept. of Philosophy & Ethics, The Academy of Korean Studies) played in this book being translated into English. If not for him, I would not have had the privilege of getting to know this vastly informative book. I would also like to recognize the effort of Harvey E. Schmidt (Duksung Women's University) for his assistance in proofreading, Jongryul Choi (Dept. of Sociology, Keimyung University) for his assistance in translating, and Homa & Sekey Books for their cooperation and assistance in publishing this book.

Suzanne Lee
June 15, 2005
Bundang, South Korea

Preface

History is ultimately created by man.
— while writing this book

I belong to a generation born and raised during Korea's colonial period. I have always wondered why Korea deteriorated into a colony by failing to achieve autonomous modernization, and this questioning spirit has never left my consciousness. Indeed, I believe this attitude has affected my attempts to explore and systematize the conflict between conservatism and progress during the collapse of the Joseon dynasty (also known as Chosŏn and Chosun) and the circumstances surrounding it from the perspective of the history of thought. Moreover, an interest in an ideological approach to comparing Korea with Japan, which has succeeded in modernization, has always followed. I can still recall reading a shocking article during this course of events involving an excerpt from *Ildonggiyu* (日東記游, Record of a Journey to Japan), a private memoir written by Kim Gi-su (金綺秀) during his first visit to Japan as the Joseon ambassador to Japan in April of 1876. This was when Japan succeeded in coercing Joseon to sign the Treaty of Ganghwa Island between Joseon and Japan. Below is the excerpt from a conversation between Kim Gi-su and Kuki Ryuichi, Japan's Minister of Culture:

> Minister Kuki Ryuichi of the Ministry of Culture and Science greeted me with courtesy. He asked me the following question when we were sharing a drink.
>
> "Does your country only revere the scholarship of Zhu Xi [Chû Hsî]? Or are there other scholars who are revered as well?"
>
> "The scholarship of my country has recognized only Zhu Xi for the past 500 years. Those who go against Zhu Xi are treated as rebels. Those who write about Buddhism or the words of Lao-zi (老子) in the civil service exam are sent into exile and not for-

given for their transgressions. Everyone knows only of Zhu Xi because the national law is very strict. Mistakes are not made at different crossroads in life and tricks cannot dazzle, because the way (道, *dao* in Ch.) of Confucius and Mencius is consistently followed by the sovereign and the subject, father and son, between brothers, and husband and wife."

Kuki Ryuichi nodded his head and stood up after he finished his tea.

> • "Mundapguchik" (問答九則),
> *Record of a Journey to Japan*, Vol. 2

The year 1876 was only eight years after the Meiji Restoration. Japan was focusing efforts on "civilization and enlightenment," whereas Joseon scholarship in those days was exclusively supportive of the Learning of Master Zhu ("Sokhak 24chik" 俗學二十四則, Twenty-Four Items of Secular Learning, Vol. 2).

Weeds flourished in the shrines and monks fell into a deep abyss in Japan after Japan began to communicate with westerners. The Japanese people did not have the leisure to think about these things, because they were so busy studying to become a rich nation with a strong army. Neo-Confucian writings were all said to be impractical writings and not useful in reality... A child was educated to read both the national language and Chinese characters by the age of eight. When the child finished learning Chinese characters, he did not read the scriptures; rather, he preferred writings on agriculture, military tactics, astronomy, geography, medicine, and forestry. Thus wives, daughters, and even children of merchants understood astrology and pointed at the earth when an order was shouted. But they only blinked their eyes and stared when asked what kind of person Confucius or Mencius was, because they did not understand the question. Names of schools varied from Tokyo Kaisei School, girls' schools, English schools, to Japanese language schools. Teachers were polite and professors diligent, but the learning was no more than utilitarian. Their excellence was far-reaching and others could not compare to their diligence, because they put all of their efforts into learning night and day. Their precise calculations and elaborate standard of value would put even Shangyang (商鞅) of Qin (秦) dynasty China to shame and Jinggong (荊公, 王安石) of Song (宋) dynasty China would have adjusted the folds of his clothes and paid homage.

In other words, the mainstream opinion in 1876 was that the scholarship of Korea was "impractical learning" and that of Japan "practical learning." People ultimately create history. What shocked me was the huge difference in educational contents between Korea and Japan from the beginning of modernity.

Then what ideological background defines backwardness in the modernization of Korea?

To be honest, I have always felt a great resistance toward the study of Confucian history in Korea wherein the statement of "Zhu Xi [Chû Hsî, 朱子] is the greatest scholar" is affirmed without criticism from time immemorial. A paragraph on this has been mentioned in section two of Chapter 1 in *Hangugui gaehwa sasang* (Enlightened Thought of Korea), published in 1981 by Bibong Chulpansa.

When the Hungu Faction (or the Clique of the Meritorious and the Conservative, *hungupa* in Kr.) lost power and the Sarim Faction (*sarimpa* in Kr.) came into real power in politics and academics in the latter half of the 16th century, scholarly differences in opinion turned into a self-consuming party strife.[1] This was followed by Korean Confucianism becoming dominated by the Learning of Master Zhu, and especially toward the study of the principle of human nature (性理學, *seongnihak* in Kr.) within the Learning of Master Zhu, which favors reality (the Learning of Master Zhu is not equivalent to the study of the principle of human nature).[2]

---

[1] Hungu Faction and Sarim Faction are two of the four political factions in the reign of Sejo. (S. Lee)

[2] This view is unique in that most Neo-Confucian scholars equate the study of the principle of human nature with Neo-Confucianism or the Learning of Master Zhu. In this book, the term "Neo-Confucianism" will be differentiated from "the Learning of Master Zhu" in that the former will

A natural result of a value system becoming standardized is the loss of flexibility in the way of thinking. Diverse views on value become divided into "orthodoxy" and "heterodoxy," and they confront each other. The claim that the spiritual climate of "orthodoxy" in forming a liaison with power and charging the opposition of being "heterodoxy" produces stagnation in thought and scholarship is a valuable teaching that can be seen in the history of Korean Confucianism centered on the Sarim Faction. "Zhu Xi is the greatest scholar" is just such a singular system of thought.

There is no need to explain this book in detail at this point. Perhaps it may seem that this book contains quite a bit of heterodox opinions in evaluating the people and thought from the viewpoint of Sarim Faction. I am only a scholar with a short time remaining on this earth, but I would like to think about reconstructing Confucian history in Korea by listening to the frank opinions of readers.

Hangilsa published another book of mine entitled *Hangugui geundae sasang* (Modern Korean Thought) in 1995. I would like to express my gratitude to President Kim Eon-ho (金彦鎬) of Hangilsa for publishing this second book as well. I have requested Prof. Ha Woobong (河宇鳳) in the Dept. of History at Chonbuk University to translate this book from Japanese to Korean, because he has profound knowledge of Korean and Japanese language and culture. He went through much trouble to translate very difficult contents in this book from Japanese to Korean, and I would like to take this time to express my gratitude to him.

Kang Jae-eun
May 2003
Osaka, Japan

---

refer to "new Confucianism" and the latter to the Zhu Xi School. (S. Lee)

1

What Is Confucianism?

Confucianism Is a Political and Ethical System of Thought

The spiritual climate of Korea, like that of China and Japan, was influenced most by Buddhism and Confucianism. Buddhism (translated into Chinese characters) and Confucianism, of course, are considered to have originated in China, but they became "Koreanized" under a different geographic climate, primitive religions, and way of life in Korea.

The Joseon dynasty (1392-1910) advocated Confucianism and especially the Learning of Master Zhu as the foundation of politics and education, while putting forth the ruling ideology of "putting value on Confucianism and devaluing Buddhism." Confucianism has been deeply engrained in the spiritual climate, way of life, and interpersonal relations of Koreans since the fall of the Joseon dynasty, the Japanese colonial period (August 1910 to August 1945), and the divided Koreas of today.

This book attempts to examine the types of transfiguration Confucianism underwent and the role performed in each period, beginning with its introduction, while considering the relevance to China and Japan. Just as the relationship between capitalism and Protestantism in the shape of religious reform received attention in the West, the relationship of economic development to Confucian cultures including Korea, Japan, and Taiwan is receiving global attention today.

Generally, Confucianism is called the study of "governing others after self-cultivation." In other words, Confucianism contains two aspects that are simultaneously and indivisibly connected: "Self-cultivation" (or ethics) and "governing others" (or politics). Further,

1

Confucianism can be said to be a system of thought that integrates politics and ethics insofar as a scholar should attain "self-cultivation" to later "govern others." Due to this fundamental characteristic, the metaphysical features of both the philosophical and the realistic exist in Confucianism.

Emphasis is inevitably put on the "governing others," i.e., political ideology, of Confucianism in each stage of the historical development in order to closely examine its role within each period; an explanation of the philosophical factor is also included.

It goes without saying that the Confucian tinge is deeply rooted in the thought and habits of the way of life of the Korean people today as a direct influence of 500 years of the Joseon dynasty. Many pages of this book are dedicated to describing the Joseon dynasty concisely and simply.

Prior to going into the main discourse of this book, the background of the establishment of Confucianism in China will be briefly outlined.

Confucius Roams the Chaotic World

After it was founded by King Wu (武王), Zhou established its capital in Hao-jing (鎬京) west of Xian (西安) and governed the basin of the Yellow River (黃河). King Wu also felled King Zhou (紂王), the last despotic ruler of Yin (殷) China, in 11th century BC.

The capital of Zhou China remained the same for about 800 years but relocated to Luo-yang (洛陽) in 770 BC due to continued revolts led by the feudal lords from the 9th century BC. Using this as the crossroad, the former Zhou dynasty is called West Zhou and the latter East Zhou. The East Zhou period is further divided into the Age of Spring and Autumn and the period of the Warring States (403 BC-221 BC).

The power of the Zhou dynasty declined further and became disordered during the East Zhou period; the royal family did exist but may as well not have. The Age of Spring and Autumn originated from the fact that Confucius wrote *Spring and Autumn Annals* (*Chunqiu* in Ch.), a history of the 12 dukes [or *gong*, 公] who lived during the period of 250 years in Lu (魯) dynasty China, from Yingong (隱公) to Aigong (哀公). This was done in order to leave a good justification for future generations, because Confucius was concerned that the legitimacy of the Zhou dynasty might become uncertain in later times. The Age of Spring and Autumn and the period of the Warring States prior to Emperor Shi of Qin (秦) China unifying China is called the pre-Qin period, and Confucianism of this period is referred to as pre-Qin Confucianism, or original Confucianism.

Lu China was established as a state in the region south of today's Shandong (山東省) during the Zhou dynasty. King Wu of Zhou destroyed the tyrannical King Zhou of Yin China and appointed his younger brother Zhou Gonggan (周公旦, Duke of Zhou) to govern this area. Lu China was the birthplace of Confucianism. It was a small state without a flourishing state of affairs, but it is known for having best succeeded Zhou China's culture of studying propriety from the time of Zhou Gonggan.

Confucius (552 BC–479 BC) lived during the Age of Spring and Autumn (770 BC–476 BC) when Zhou (or Châu, 周) China fell into a decline and many local military leaders competed with each other for power. Confucianism with the teachings of Confucius at the center became a great system of thought because successive Confucians were able to expand on these teachings in later times.

The real name of Confucius was Qui (丘), and his additional name was Zhongni (仲尼). He was born in Changpingxiang Zouyi (what is currently Qufu in Shandong) of Lu China. Confucius was proud to have been born in Lu China, a state that had succeeded the culture of Zhou in studying propriety.

> Châu had the advantage of viewing the two past dynasties. How complete and elegant are its regulations! I follow Châu.
>
> • "Ba Yi" (or Pâ Yih, 八佾), *Analects of Confucius* (論語)

3

The culture of the Zhou dynasty in studying propriety contained the best elements insofar as it accepted the strengths and modified the weaknesses of the two previous Xia and Yin dynasties. Music made up a large part of the rituals for worshipping heaven and ancestors in Zhou China. Confucius was strongly interested in perfecting human nature to be in harmony with music and in recovering social order through rituals.

Confucianism, which developed a culture on studying the propriety of Zhou dynasty, began in the neighboring state of Zhai (齊). The founder of Lu was Zhou Gonggan, the younger brother of King Wu and respected by Confucius. Zhai China was the state wherein Tai Gongwang (太公望) Lushang (呂尚: Jiang Taigong, 姜太公) was appointed to serve in return for his support in founding the Zhou dynasty by King Wu as a military leader. The royal family of East Zhou was related to the Jiang clan of Zhai dynasty, and a custom of taking brides from Zhai dynasty developed in East Zhou. Thus it was natural for Zhai to inherit the Zhou dynasty culture of studying propriety. Gonggan created the foundation for a system of propriety in Zhou China by acting as the regent for young King Cheng (成王) after King Wu died.

The Dream of Confucius

There are many biographies written of Confucius, some of which overly glorify him as a sage. "Biography of Confucius" (孔子世家) in *Historical Records* (史記, *Shiji* in Ch.) was written by Sima Qian (145 BC-86 BC) in the pre-Han dynasty period, 400 years after the death of Confucius. This is the biography written closest to the actual period wherein Confucius had lived. Therefore some of its contents are not related to historical fact, but it does include the most realistic image of him.

Sima Qian completed writing 130 volumes of a comprehensive historical record of antiquity in *Historical Records*. Sima Qian used a new descriptive method of annalistic and biographical style (紀傳體)

rather than the more traditional chronological style (編年體) used by Confucius in *Spring and Autumn*. This new method was also introduced in the writings of *Historical Records of the Three Kingdoms*.

Historical Records is divided into the following chapters: "Benji" (本紀, imperial biographies of the rulers/emperors), "Shijia" (世家, biographies of the houses of the feudal lords and of eminent people), and "Liezhuan" (列傳, biographies of ordinary persons and collective biographies of empresses, officers, etc. as well as reports of foreign countries). Confucius is categorized as one of the "Shijia" despite not having been a feudal lord ("Biography of Confucius," No. 17) because of Sima Qian's evaluation of Confucius.

> Taishigong (Sima Qian) said, it is written in the odes for "high mountains to be looked at and big roads to be traveled." This refers to the mind yearning for it although it is not reachable. I read the works of Confucius and imagined his character; I went to Lu and saw Zhongni's tomb, cart, clothes, and utensils used in rituals, and saw Confucians train in propriety at the house of Confucius.[1] I stopped at this place while wandering and could not leave. There were many figures from the lord of all to wise men, but they only had glory for a moment in that no one asked about them after their death. Confucius was a scholar who did not hold a government position, but his way was passed on for ten generations, and his way was adopted by scholars as the foundation and fundamental principle. He cannot fail to be called a great sage, because those who speak of the six subjects of learning, including sons of Heaven (emperors), kings, and princes, all accept the standard of the Master (Confucius) and adjust their behaviors accordingly.

Sima Qian was an unparalleled wanderer. In today's terms, he wrote *Historical Records* by verifying documented records through field surveys. When he visited the hometown of Confucius and saw the continuation of the virtue of the deceased, he was moved to write the above comment.

---

[1] Cart and clothes combined symbolized propriety. (S. Lee)

Confucius reflected on his scholarship in his later years and reminisced as follows:

> At fifteen, I had my mind bent on learning. At thirty, I stood firm. At forty, I had no doubts. At fifty, I knew the decrees of Heaven. At sixty, my ear was an obedient organ *for the reception of truth*. At seventy, I could follow what my heart desired, without transgressing what was right.

- "Wei Zheng" (or Wei Chăng, 爲政), *Analects of Confucius*

Confucius was determined to devote himself to scholarship when he was 15. Scholarship in those days consisted of "propriety and music" (禮樂). As previously mentioned, "propriety" is the regulation for recovering social order, and "music" is the harmony for completing the character of each individual. He considered regulation based on "propriety" and harmony based on "music" to be the two pillars for overcoming turbulent times.

He burned with political aspirations to apply scholarship in the real world, but he was 51 when appointed to the post of a *zhongdouzai* (中都宰, a government official of a province) by Dinggong (定公) of Lu, and he did not hold any other higher position than the ones of Sikong (司空, Minister of the Ministry of Construction) and Sikou (司寇, Minister of the Judicial Branch and the Ministry of Foreign Affairs) during the short period before he left Lu China at the age of 55.

From the age of 55 to 68, he lived a life of a wandering traveler with his disciples after he left Lu China. When he and his disciples did not have any place to stay in the faraway state of Zheng (鄭), people likened him to "a dog at a house of death" (i.e., a beggar that goes from one house of death to another to eat). How must he have felt when he reached the end of his wandering days?

> With coarse rice to eat, with water to drink, and my bended arm for a pillow; — I have still joy in the midst of these things. Riches

and honours acquired by unrighteousness are to me as a floating cloud.

- "Shu Er" (or Shû R, 述而), *Analects of Confucius*

Confucius may have been unlucky in politics due to his assertions being too exalted and far removed from reality. He desired to find a post in Zhai China. Jinggong (景公), the ruler of Zhai, was desirous of appointing Confucius as his vassal after the two met and held a question-and-answer session on politics. However, Yanying (晏嬰), premier to Jinggong, adamantly opposed it and said as follows:

Zhou dynasty was already in decline after the death of wise men such as King Wu and Duke of Zhou, and much time has passed since propriety and music have been maintained. But now Confucius expands on appearances and adornments, and makes moderation in decorum complicated. This does not assist learning in future generations, and it is impossible to ascertain propriety. The thought of adopting this to change the folk customs of Zhai is not a matter of urgency in saving the poor.

- "Biography of Confucius" (孔子世家),
  Historical Records (史記)

This strict statement of Yanying was in fact felt keenly by the Confucians who served under Confucius. The point Yanying was making was that changing the customs of the Zhai people by appointing Confucians to magnify propriety and music and thus increase the financial burden of the people would not save the poor of Zhai. Instead, Confucius was a great educator who cultivated disciples and left everlasting doctrines for future generations.

As Sima Qian pointed out, "Confucius was a scholar who did not hold a government position, but his way was passed on to ten generations and adopted by scholars as the foundation and fundamental principle." *Analects of Confucius* is the memoir of Confucius and his disciples; the disciples organized and made them everlasting for future generations. Also, Confucius taught poetry, writing, propriety, and music to more than 3,000 students according to the "Biography of Confucius" in the *Historical Records*, and among them 72 disciples became well versed in the six subjects of learning: propriety, music, archery, animal husbandry, writing, and mathematics.

The ideals of Confucius were not accepted during his time, but his greatness as an educator can be seen in that his disciples were commissioned to achieve his dream. His educational thought was that "in teaching there should be no distinction between classes" (Wei Ling Kung, *Analects of Confucius*). In other words, he claimed that "the thing that differentiates one man from another is the existence or nonexistence of refinement; originally, there is no distinction of rank among men." Therefore, it is against the teachings of Confucius to evaluate man based on one's origin of birth or on being wise or foolish.

Emperor Wu of Han China (漢武帝) Establishes Confucianism as the State Religion

Qin China ended the period of the Warring States by unifying "all under heaven" in 221 BC. Before the unification, Qin was one of the seven Warring States; the others that fought for supremacy were Yan (燕), Zhao (趙), Zhai (齊), Han (韓), Wei (魏), and Chu (楚). The king of Qin who had unified all under heaven contrived for a title that would surpass that of kings of all states and so proclaimed himself "Emperor" for the first time in China's history. This may have been patterned after the three sovereigns and five emperors of the legendary period. Successive generations of sovereigns of China did not permit other kings to use the term emperor.

Qin China collapsed in 206 BC, and Xiang Yu (項羽) of Chu and Liu-bang (劉邦) of Han dynasty fought for supremacy. Liu-bang unified all of the states in 202 BC and became the founder of Han dynasty.

Han dynasty was interrupted by the reign of Wang Mang (王莽) of Xin (新) China for approximately 15 years, but Former Han and Later Han dominated China for a total of 400 years before and after

Xin. The period before Qin unified all under heaven can be described in a positive way as a period wherein freedom of speech abounded, but also negatively as an ideologically confusing time. Evidence of this is the "Hundred Schools of Thought."

The first emperor of Qin implemented a strong system of central government and strict control of thought grounded on the legalism of Li Si (李斯), a disciple of Xun-zi (or Hsün-tzu, 荀子). He also created a standardization that was worthy of a unified dynasty. Confucians who advocated the doctrine of governing with virtue as opposed to legalism were met with a reign of terror called *"fenshu kengru"* (焚書坑儒), during which time all books except those on medicine, fortunetelling, and agriculture were destroyed; Confucian scholars were killed to prevent political criticism. It is not clear whether the first emperor was an enemy of Confucians, but the significance of unifying the ideographic style to seal characters (篆書) is noteworthy in the history of culture.

In contrast to the first emperor, Emperor Wudi (武帝) of Han China adopted the measure for the worthy and the virtuous as proposed by Dong Zhongshu (董仲舒, 176-104 BC). Ideologies of the Hundred Schools of Thought were forbidden, and Confucianism was established as the state religion. The following is an excerpt from the question-and-answer session between Dong Zhongshu and Emperor Wudi.

> Solidarity was praised in the *Spring and Autumn Annals* (春秋), because that is the proper way of the heaven and earth as well as what is right and proper throughout the ages. You are taking a different path now, people have differing opinions, and various schools propose different policies. Solidarity cannot be maintained by people in high positions because the intent of various teachings differs, and people in lower positions do not know what to follow because the legislation changes frequently. It is recommended that subjects that do not correspond to the six subjects of learning or to the scholarship of Confucius should be severed and not followed. Then vicious and biased talk will disappear, and

solidarity can be realized, etiquette will become clear, and the people will become devoted.

- Ban Gu (班固), "Dong Zhongshu" (董仲舒), A Series of Biographies in the *History of the Han Dynasty* (漢書)

Sima Qian lived in the Former Han period. His evaluation of Confucius as "a great sage" and the creation of the "Biography of Confucius" in *Historical Records* were due to the fact that Confucianism had become the state religion.

A school based on the Learned of the Five Confucian Classics was founded since the time of Emperor Wudi of the Former Han period, and those who aspired to become bureaucrats were made to learn Confucianism only. The Learned of the Five Confucian Classics refers to Confucians who had mastered the Confucian classics of the *Book of Changes* (周易, *Yijing* in Ch.), *Book of Documents* (書經, *Shujing* in Ch.), and *Maoshi* (毛詩, one of the woodblock-printed chapters of the *Book of Poetry*). Many scholars have thereafter added annotations and supplements to annotations to the Five Confucian Classics. In 640, Chancellor Kong Yingda (孔穎達) of the Imperial University (Guozi Jijiu, 國子祭酒) was commanded to compile *Interpretation of the Five Confucian Classics*, which became the national textbook used at the Imperial University during the reign of Emperor Taizong of Tang China.

After it became the state religion, Confucianism dominated all of politics in the history of China for close to 2,000 years until the end of Qing (淸) China. Joseon dynasty, which lasted for over 500 years, also made Confucianism the state religion. Furthermore, Confucian culture expanded into Japan and Vietnam, creating additional regions of Confucian culture.

Mencius Succeeds Confucius

The achievements of Mencius contributed greatly to Confucius being evaluated as superior among the Hundred Schools of Thought and to Emperor Wudi of Han China appointing Confucianism as the state religion. This is why Confucianism is called "the Scholarship of Confucius and Mencius" (孔孟之學), Confucius as a "sage," Mencius as a "wise man," Confucianism sometimes as "the Scholarship of the Sage and the Wise Man" (聖賢之學), and Confucians as "the Way of the Sage and the Wise" (聖賢之徒).

The original name of Mencius (372-289 BC) is Ke (軻) and, like Confucius, he was born in Xouxian (鄒縣) in Lu China. He lived during the period of the Warring States, about 100 years after the death of Confucius.

In contrast to the convention of his times, Confucius was raised by his mother, Yan Zhizai (顏徵在). She was a common-law wife, and there was a big age gap between Confucius and his father Shu Liang-he (叔梁紇); the father passed away when Confucius was young. As his reminiscence states, it is supposed that he had to apply himself to various tasks due to poverty: "I am capable of performing many menial tasks, because I am of humble origin" ("Tsze Han," 子罕, *Analects of Confucius*). Thus he was not assigned a specific tutor, but he had humility enough to be able to learn the merits of others because he was born in the state of Lu, where cultural importance was attached to the propriety and music of Zhou dynasty.

> When I walk along with two others, they may serve me as my teachers. I will select their good qualities and follow them, their bad qualities and avoid them.
>
> - "Shu Er" (or Shû R, 述而), *Analects of Confucius*

Mencius also lost his father when young, but the tale of how "the mother of Mencius thrice changed her residence on his account" from near a cemetery to a commercial center and finally to a school neighborhood due to her great desire to educate Mencius is very well known. Mencius succeeded to orthodox Confucian thought by studying under a disciple of Zisi (or K'ung Chî, 子思), the grandson of Confucius. The orthodox teachings of Confucianism is Confucius → Zengzi (or Tsăng, 曾子) → Zisi (子思) → Mencius.

Mencius also promoted his ideals to King Xuan (宣王) of Zhai China as well as to King Hui (惠王) of Liang (梁, Wei 魏) dynasty among others so that he would not lag behind the Hundred Schools of Thought, but no one would receive him. Sima Qian evaluated Mencius as follows:

> But Mencius only preached about the virtues of the three sovereigns of the idyllic peace in the history of China; he was not accepted wherever he preached, because his words were so remote from the requirements of the times. Thus he retired and expounded on the *Book of Poetry* and the *Book of Documents* with disciples such as Mozhang (萬章), and wrote seven volumes of *The Works of Mencius* by describing the so-called intentions of Zhongni.

- "Sun-qing" (筍卿) and "Mencius" (孟子) in *Liezhuan* of *Historical Records* (史記)

"Tangyu sandai" (唐虞三代) refers to the three generations of idyllic peace in the history of Xia (夏), Yin (殷), and Zhou (周) China during which time ideal sovereigns Yao (堯, family name of Yaotang 陶唐), Shun (舜, family name of Youyu 有虞), and Yu (禹) ruled. Mencius advocated the lofty idea of the "ways prescribed by the ancient kings," but this was not accepted because it was too far removed from reality. Therefore, Mencius wrote *The Works of Mencius* (孟子) for future generations by delineating the teachings of Confucius (the sayings of Confucius were "communicated exactly without exaggeration").

Confucius and Mencius Who Taught Men

The ideals of Confucius are contained in the *Analects of Confucius*. This was not written directly by Confucius but is a chronicle of the

12

questions and answers between his disciples and himself. The *Analects* was organized into the present condition 400 years after the death of Confucius.

Central to the thought of Confucius is "benevolence" (仁). He thought to recover peace by putting "benevolence" at the center of morality and politics, because he considered the source of turbulent times to be the struggle for supremacy with force.

> The superior bends his attention to what is radical. That being established, all practical courses naturally grow up. Filial piety and fraternal submission: — are they not the root of all benevolent actions?

- "Xue Er" (or Hsio R, 學而), *Analects of Confucius*

The doctrine of governing the people with virtue is to bring peace to all under heaven by gradually expanding the familial love that begins with filial duty between father and son and fraternity between brothers to the state and all under heaven.

> Fan Ch'ih (樊遲) asked about benevolence. The Master said, "It is to love *all* men." He asked about knowledge. The Master said, "It is to know *all* men."

- "Yan Yuan" (or Yen Yüan, 顏淵), *Analects of Confucius*

Unraveling of the word benevolence reveals exactly what the Chinese character portrays; the character represents the personal relations and love between two people. But that love is a differentiating love containing hierarchy; it begins with people closest to one and gradually diminishes with distance. It is not an undifferentiating love. Rather, order based on propriety that corresponds to each individual's role is established in differentiating love. This is the reason for attacking as heresy the doctrine of universal love advocated by Mozi (or Mo Ti, 墨子), compassion by Buddhism, and philanthropy by Christianity.

13

To Confucius who had defined benevolence as "loving all men" and knowledge as "knowing all men," problems faced by man in everyday life were central to his thought. Thus he avoided discussions on issues related to non-everyday life. Confucius met and answered questions from Zilu (or Tsze-lû, 子路) as follows:

> Chî Lû [季路, Tsze-lû 子路] asked about serving the spirits *of the dead.* The Master said, "While you are not able to serve men, how can you serve their spirits?" Chî Lû added, "I venture to ask about death?" He was answered, "While you do not know life, how can you know about death?"

- "Xian Jin" (or Hsien Tsin, 先進), *Analects of Confucius*

In other words, Confucius responded by stating, "You cannot serve men, so how can you serve their spirits?" or "You do not know life, so how can you know about life and death?" Spirits or deaths are of the world of the unknowable. This corresponds to the attitude of "The subjects on which the Master did not talk were — extraordinary things, feats of strength, disorder, and spiritual beings" ("Shu Er," *Analects of Confucius*). This is the very reason that I cannot agree with the recent argument on Confucianism being a "religion." In particular, Confucians were in charge of politics in the 500-some years of the Joseon dynasty established in 1392, and Confucianism was the political thought of Korea.

Confucius lived in a period of unity of church and state in which ghosts and man were not differentiated. Confucius differentiated man from the spiritual world and examined man itself. However, man must realize that there is a limitation to achieving his dreams. That is the "decrees of Heaven," and Confucius himself reminisced that "At fifty, I knew the decrees of Heaven."

However, disliking the non-virtuous (不仁) is also part of loving during turbulent times when its is difficult to reinstitute order. "It is only the (*truly*) virtuous man who can love, or who can hate, others" ("Le Jin" 里仁, *Analects of Confucius*). Thus there must be a relentless

14

spirit to dislike the non-virtuous in order to express such virtue consistently.

> The Master said, "The determined scholar and the man of virtue will not seek to live at the expense of injuring their virtue. They will even sacrifice their lives to preserve their virtue complete."
>
> - "Wei Ling Gong" (or Wei Ling Kung, 衛靈公),
>   *Analects of Confucius*

The *Analects of Confucius* is the model for *The Works of Mencius*, but the tone of the latter is sharper and more argumentative. The core thought contained in the *Analects of Confucius* is "virtuous" as viewed thus far. In comparison, *The Works of Mencius* emphasizes governing in the kingly way through "benevolence and righteousness" in the very first question-and-answer session with King Hui of Liang as soon as the book is opened: "Why must your Majesty use that word 'profit?' What I am provided with are *counsels to* benevolence and righteousness, and these are my only topics."

As stated above, *The Works of Mencius* is said to have delineated the teachings of Confucius, but the content did not stop there. For instance, governing in the kingly way as advocated by Mencius is associated with the theory of revolution based on governance of the people.

> Mencius said, "The people are the most important elements *in a nation*; the spirits of the land and grain are the next; the sovereign is the lightest. Therefore to gain the peasantry is the way to become sovereign; to gain the sovereign is the way to become a prince of a State; to gain the prince of a State is the way to become a great officer. When a prince endangers the altars of the spirits of the land and grain, he is changed, and another appointed in his place.
>
> - "Jin Xin, Part II" (or Tsin Sin, 盡心章句 下),
>   *The Works of Mencius*

Even if a sovereign, he must accept the will of Heaven and win the sentiments of the people; he is nothing more than an ordinary man if that is lost. It must be known that the ruler is not omnipotent and the virtue of a ruler is achieved through strict self-control based on the decree of Heaven. If that is lost, then it must be reinstituted or he must be replaced. I cannot say that this is not a strong statement.

This is the reason that Japan did not adopt *The Works of Mencius* and considered it dangerous when serving an emperor of "a dynasty that will rule for 10,000 years" from the Edo period to immediately before World War II. For example, Yoshida Shoin, who was an advocate of the thought of respecting the royal family and excluding all foreigners in the late Bakufu period, responded to the above excerpt from *The Works of Mencius* during his lecture to prisoners at the Yasanok (野山獄) of Hagi as below:

> The rulers and the people of our country have not been divided since the creation of the nation. Therefore people exist because there is a ruler, and people cannot exist when a ruler does not exist. Also, a ruler exists when people exist, and a ruler cannot exist when his people do not exist. I am afraid people will neglect the national polity by rattling on about this verse without knowing such meaning through copying foreign barbarians, saying that "all under heaven is not one person's world but all under heaven is the world of the people."

In other words, putting relative value between the ruler and his people, such as "people are important and rulers are not important," is criticized as "aping the sayings of foreign barbarians" because the national polity of Japan after the founding is that the ruler and his people are one.

The Doctrine of Innate Evilness of Xun-zi and the Doctrine of Innate Goodness of Mencius

The thought of Confucius is about the study of man, which elucidates "love of man and knowledge of man in everyday life." This was intensified by the debate between Mencius and Xun-zi.

Xun-zi was born later than Mencius, but they were both follow-ers of Confucius and lived in the period of the Warring States. On the nature of man, Xun-zi criticized the doctrine of innate goodness by Mencius and advocated the doctrine of innate evilness. The two pillars of the teachings of Confucius were originally "virtue" and "propriety." The way of thinking between Mencius and Xun-zi divides at the point where the doctrine of innate goodness by Mencius puts emphasis on "virtue," and the doctrine of innate evilness by Xun-zi puts emphasis on "propriety."

Confucius advocated "learning much and being proper at all times" (博文約禮), or "learning widely and regulating the body with propriety." "Propriety" can easily be defined as societal standards based on distinction of rank and role. Thus "propriety" is a step immediately below "the law." It was not by chance that Prime Minis-ter Li Si (李斯) of Qin China adopted the doctrine of governing the people with law after he stopped learning from Xun-zi's teachings. Xun-zi's view on the nature of man is clear as follows:

> The nature of man is evil; the good which it shows is factitious. There belongs to it, even at his birth, the love of gain, and as ac-tions are in accordance with this, contentions and robberies grow up, and self-denial and yielding to others are not to be found.

  • "That the Nature Is Evil" (性惡), *The Philosopher Hsün*

The character "*wei*" (偽) used here can easily be misunderstood; "*ren wei*" (人偽) means to cultivate. According to this, the essence of the nature of man is evil, but *ren wei* cultivates it to become beautiful.

> Wherein they [the sages] agree with all other men and do not dif-fer from them, is their nature; wherein they differ from and ex-ceed other men, is this artificial work.

  • "That the Nature Is Evil" (性惡), *The Philosopher Hsün*

In other words, the nature of a sage and a common man is the same, but a sage transforms his nature through cultivation. Mencius also states in the education theory that the nature granted by Heaven must be cultivated and practiced, but Xun zi claims that the evil nature is corrected through the "cultivation of law."

Mencius was very optimistic about the nature of man. A man would instinctively save a child who has fallen into the well although the child is not a relative. Mencius referred to sympathy for the pain of others as "the feeling of commiseration." Mencius holds that this feeling of commiseration implies the principle of benevolence; the feeling of shame and dislike the principle of righteousness; the feeling of reverence and respect the principle of propriety; and the feeling of approving and disapproving the principle of knowledge in "the four beginnings." Therefore benevolence, righteousness, propriety, and knowledge are the manifestations of the inherently good nature of man.

> Benevolence, righteousness, propriety, and knowledge are not infused into us from without. We are certainly furnished with them. *And a different view* is simply owing to want of reflection.
>
> - "Gao Zi, Part I" (or Kâo Tsze, 告子章句 上),
>   *The Works of Mencius*

Mencius was the one who was endowed with legitimacy in the debate over the nature of man by future generations. In late Tang China, Han Yu (or Han Yü, 韓愈, 768-824) stated in "Yuan dao" (原道) that the uninterrupted genealogy from Yao and Shun to Confucius and Mencius was severed at the death of Mencius, and Xun-zi was eliminated from the genealogy.

The Color Blue Comes from Indigo

Although Mencius may be the acknowledged successor to the orthodox teachings of Confucius, the weakness in the doctrine of

18

innate goodness as pointed out by Xun-zi was not resolved. Xun-zi indicated Mencius when this was pointed out.

> Mencius said, "Man has only to learn, and his nature appears to be good"; but I reply, — It is not so. To say so shows that he had not attained to the knowledge of man's nature; nor examined into the differences between what is natural in man and what is factitious. The natural is what the constitution spontaneously moves to — it needs not to be learned, it needs not to be followed hard after. Propriety and righteousness are what the sages have given birth to — it is by learning that men become capable of them, it is by hard practice that they achieve them. That which is in man, not needing to be learned and striven after, is what I call natural; that in man which is attained by learning, and achieved by hard striving, is what I call factitious. This is the distinction between those two.

- "That the Nature Is Evil" (性惡), *The Philosopher Hsün*

Xun-zi was the underclassman of Mencius. Xun-zi criticized the doctrine of innate goodness as advanced by Mencius by stating that the doctrine makes vague the distinction between that which is natural in man and that which is factitiously attained by learning and striving. The famous phrase, "the color blue comes from indigo, but it is bluer than indigo," of "Quan xue" (勸學) in *The Philosopher Hsün* emphasizes the importance of the student, who is the color blue, learning and "surpassing the fame of one's master," who is indigo.

Criticism of the doctrine of innate goodness by the doctrine of innate evilness is a difficult issue that still remains unresolved. The School of the Cheng Brothers and Zhu Xi presented a solution to this issue by dividing the nature of man into two types. In other words, the doctrine of innate goodness proposed by Mencius refers to the "original nature" of man, and the doctrine of innate evilness proposed by Xun-zi refers to the "physical disposition" of man.

Zhu Xi explains this in "Dao-ti" (道體) of *Reflections of Things at Hand* (近思錄) by comparing it to the flow of water. Indeed, "the originally clean stream (original nature) becomes more impure as it travels downstream (physical disposition). Thus one must continue to build "the piety of governing with a pure mind" and overcome the evil in "physical disposition" in order to return to "original nature."

Scholars of the Learning of Master Zhu followed Han Yu's opinion and eliminated Xun-zi from the orthodox teachings of Confucius by linking Confucius → Cheng-zi (程子) to the orthodox teachings of Mencius → Zhu Xi.[2] This is determined to be the genealogy of orthodox Confucianism. As mentioned later, the unique characteristic and at the same time the limitation of the Sarim Faction in Joseon dynasty is the acknowledgment of this Confucian orthodoxy as the only "righteous" one and the rest as "unrighteous."

Viewed from the starting point of Confucius in Confucianism, however, Xun-zi cannot be excluded from being called a follower of Confucius. However, he was treated as one who did not conform to Confucianism by later Confucians, because Li Si, who studied to "become a good emperor" under Xun-zi, gave counsel to the Emperor of Qin as prime minister and a politician of the school that advocates governing the people with law. He created and executed policies. He was a great politician who contributed much to establishing an autocratic state, such as the system of localized administration, unification of the alphabet, and weights and measures. However, he also incurred the ill will of Confucians because of his militaristic suppression of ideological confusion arising from the dispute among various schools.

---

[2] Cheng-zi and Zhu Xi are also referred to as Master Cheng and Master Zhu, respectively. (S. Lee)

2

Did Gija Joseon Really Exist?

How Are Residual Events of the Three Kingdoms and Historical Records of the Three Kingdoms Different from Each Other?

Confucian scholars of Korea from old would bring up the fact that Gija (箕子, Ji-zi in Ch.) was vested with a fiefdom of Joseonhu (朝鮮侯) at the end of Yin dynasty and beginning of Zhou dynasty China when they desired to brag of Korea as "a state of man of virtue in the East" with a culture homogeneous to that of China. This legend of Gija coming east can be seen in China's historical documents; among the ancient historical documents of Korea this event is briefly mentioned in the *Residual Events of the Three Kingdoms* (三國遺事) but not at all in the *Historical Records of the Three Kingdoms* (三國史記). These two ancient historical documents have different characteristics, which will be briefly explained below.

"The Three Kingdoms" refer to Goguryeo (or Koguryŏ, 高句麗), Baekje (or Paekche, 百濟), and Silla (or Shilla, 新羅), but these two historical documents were compiled during the Goryeo (Koryŏ) period. While these two books each have advantages and disadvantages, because ancient historical materials used during their compilation have not been passed down to the present, they cannot be omitted from the study of ancient Korean history. This is comparable to the relative weight given to Japan's *Kojiki* (古事記, 712) and *Nihonshoki* (日本書紀, 720).

Historical Records of the Three Kingdoms was completed in 1145 after Kim Bu-sik (Kim Pu-sik, 金富軾, 1075-1151) was put in charge of the compilation by the edict of Injong (仁宗, r. 1122-1146), the 17th monarch of Goryeo. The writing style of this book is an official history using an annalistic and biographical style copied from the delineating method used by Sima Qian in the *Historical Records*. What was the impetus behind the writing of this historical document?

> Scholars and great officials of today are well versed in the Five Confucian Classics and All Masters, or the historical records of Qin and Han periods, but it is lamentable that they are rather ignorant about our own historical records and do not know about the beginning and the end. But both the *History of the Han Dynasty* by Fenye (范曄) and *Tangshu* (唐書) by Songqi (宋祁) contain biographies about the Three Kingdoms, because there was frequent interaction with China as a courtesy at the time when the Three Kingdoms of Silla, Goguryeo, and Baekje were founded. However, the state of affairs of China is depicted in detail (in the historical records of China) but foreign affairs are abridged or omitted. As well, ancient records [of the Three Kingdoms period] such as "Haedong gogi" (海東古記, Old Record of Korea), "Samhan gogi" (三韓古記, Old Record of the Three Hans), and "Silla gogi" (新羅古記, Old Record of Silla) exist, but sentences are crude and awkward and missing some historical records. Thus they are inappropriate to manifest as authority and warning of right and wrong to a ruler concerning loyalty and deceitfulness, welfare of the state, and order and disorder of the people. By all means, an attempt is made to attain the three virtues necessary to become a historian (talent, knowledge, and discernment), complete the history of a family, and leave it for all the ages in order to make it as bright as the sun and the stars.

> - Kim Bu-sik, "Table of the Three Kingdoms"
> (進三國史表)

Thus the goal of this officially compiled historical document was to urge and admonish politicians based on Confucian morality, which led to the deliberate omission of irrational superstitions, legends, and vulgar folk songs of the common people. Omitted were "extraordinary things, feats of strength, disorder, and spiritual beings" mentioned by Confucius

Iryeon (一然, 1206-1289), on the other hand, the monk who was put in charge of compiling the *Residual Events of the Three Kingdoms*, was especially discontent with these omissions as can be seen below.

The sages of old did not talk about extraordinary things, feats of strength, disorder, and spiritual beings because they brought prosperity to their states through propriety and music, and they gave instructions based on benevolence. But when a sovereign attempts to establish a nation, he differs from ordinary men because he embraces the will of heaven and receives a *dorok* (圖錄, a list of contents depicted as drawings or pictures), after which he would accomplish his goals by taking advantage of an opportunity arising from a great upheaval. Thus a sage emerged as pictures of Hetu from the Yellow River and dots on the back of a turtle from the Luoshui River came out... It would not be strange, therefore, to say that all of the founders of the Three Kingdoms of our state originated from Sini.

- "Giijaseo" (紀異自敍, Autobiography of Strange Events), *Residual Events of the Three Kingdoms*

The strange and mysterious myth of the founding of Korea was omitted in the *Historical Records of the Three Kingdoms* compiled by a Confucian scholar. In the *Residual Events of the Three Kingdoms* compiled in 1280 by Iryeon, however, descriptions of valuable vestiges passed down through the ages abound — such as the myth of the founding of Korea as well as old folk songs and folk tales. According to records, the monk Iryeon had written over 100 works on Buddhism in addition to the *Residual Events of the Three Kingdoms*. Iryeon himself may have desired to transmit writings related to Buddhism to the future generations, but the *Residual Events of the Three Kingdoms* is the only thing remaining today.

According to the "Dongmyeongwang pyeon seomun" (東明王篇序, Introduction to the Saga of King Dongmyeong)

23

written by Yi Gyu-bo (李奎報, 1168-1241), unbiased writing of the history of Korea in the form of *Gu samguksa* (舊三國史, Older Version of the History of the Three Kingdoms) existed as follows:

> The exploits of King Dongmyeong Sini (神異) were well-known throughout the secular world, and even men and women who are not learned talk about his deeds. I heard them of old and said with a smile, "the old master Zhongni did not talk about extraordinary things, feats of strength, disorder, and spiritual beings. This is because it is not appropriate to talk about absurd and strange things." This is also mentioned in *Book of Northern Wei* (魏書, *Weishu* in Ch.) and *History of Institutions* (通典, *Tongdian* in Ch.) briefly and not in detail. This is probably due to the desire to write one's own affairs of state in detail but briefly of affairs occurring in foreign states. The accomplishments of Sini were the ideal discussed by all in the "Dongmyeongwang bongi" (Imperial Biography of King Dongmyeong) of the *Older Version of the History of the Three Kingdoms* but considered a ghost or an illusion and not believable at first. The book was repeatedly read thrice and the origin examined, and the illusion turned out to be something holy and the ghost a divine spirit. How can an absurdity be transmitted in the national history (*Older Version of the History of the Three Kingdoms*) when it is an unbiased writing? The accomplishments of Sini were overly abridged when Kim Bu-sik rewrote the National History. His intention in abridging the National History was perhaps due to the fact that he did not consider it proper to transmit great accomplishments of Sini to future generations, because the purpose of the book is to correctly deliver national history.

Yi Gyu-bo wrote the above paragraph before Iryeon's *Residual Events of the Three Kingdoms* was introduced to the world. However, the opinion of Yi Gyu-bo and Iryeon on "Sini" during the period of founding a nation coincides exactly: they were both critical of Kim Bu-sik's *Historical Records of the Three Kingdoms*. However, there seemed to be a difference in historical perspectives. From Yi Gyu-bo's historical perspective, "Sini" must also be dealt with in "a book of unbiased writing" such as the *Older Version of the History of the Three*

Kingdoms, but Kim Bu-sik deleted the accomplishments of "Sini" and turned the book into a book of corrections for future generations. In spite of this, it is unavoidable that the *Historical Records of the Three Kingdoms* and *Residual Events of the Three Kingdoms* became basic historical materials of ancient Korea due to the fact that the *Older Version of the History of the Three Kingdoms* was destroyed and has not been passed on to the present.

Dan'gun the Son of a Bear and Gija the Wise of Yin China

A summary of the founding myth of Gojoseon (Wanggeom Joseon) as it appears in the *Historical Records of the Three Kingdoms* is as follows:

> A long time ago, there lived Hwanung (桓雄), one of the sons of the Lord of Heaven (天帝) by the name of Hwanin (桓因) and a concubine. Because Hwanung always had a deep interest in the happenings of the human world below, Hwanin gave him three heavenly seals and sent him down to rule the human world.
>
> Hwanung landed under Sindansu (神檀樹, a divine-altar tree) at the summit of the Taebaek Mountain with 3,000 vassals and called the spot Sinsi (神市, Divine City). Pungbaek (風伯), Usa (雨師), and Unsa (雲師) were in charge of grain, fate, punishment, good, and evil with Hwanung as their leader, and they were also in charge of 360 tasks of mankind.
>
> During this time a bear and a tiger that lived together in a cave prayed to be transformed into mankind. Hwanung gave them one bundle of mugwort and 20 cloves of garlic and ordered them not to see sunlight for 100 days. The bear transformed into Ungnyeo 21 days after avoiding the sun, but the tiger did not turn into a man because it was not able to keep away from the sun for the duration of the banned period. Hwanung joined with the re-incarnated Ungnyeo, and Dan'gun Wanggeom was born of the union. Dan'gun decided on Pyeong'yang as the capital and named the country Joseon in the year of *gyeongin*, the 50th year after Yao ascended to the throne of China. Later he moved the capital to Asadal (阿斯達) of Mt. Baegak and ruled for 1,500 years.

When Gija was appointed to rule Joseon in the year of *gimyo* after King Wu ascended to the throne of Zhou China, Dan'gun hid from Asadal and became a hermit with supernatural powers at the age of 1,908.

The plot of the story of the Heavenly Descent (天孫降臨, Tenson-Kourin in Jap.) of Hwanin → Hwanung → Dan'gun is very similar to the succession of Amaterasu Omikami (天照大神) → Ninigino Mikoto → Emperor Jinmu (神武天皇) in the founding myth of Japan. But when Gija survived the downfall of the Yin dynasty at the hands of Zhou China and was appointed by King Wu to govern Joseon, Dan'gun abdicated the throne and became a mountain god.

In 1280 when *Residual Events of the Three Kingdoms* was completed, Goryeo submitted to Yuan (元) China after a long war that began in 1231. Under such background, looking for the root of the founding myth of Joseon in the Heavenly Descent of Dan'gun and claiming that Gija, revered by Confucius as one of three men of virtue, had succeeded Dan'gun is full of meaning.

Dan'gun is supposed to have been founded on the 50th year of the ascension of Yao to the throne, but this period is legendary even in Chinese history. Existence of Yin China was verified by deciphering inscriptions on bones and tortoise carapace, and King Wu of Zhou China destroyed King Zhou of Yin around 1046 BC. Gija Joseon was supposed to have existed in those days, and it does not seem as if Gija was a fictitious character from the perspective of Chinese history.

Confucians of the Joseon period put more weight on "the belief that Gija came east" rather than the Dan'gun myth, and claimed Joseon to be "little China" because "the ways prescribed by the ancient kings" of the three generations of idyllic peace in the history of China were already transmitted in Joseon prior to Confucius. The evidence is sought in the words of Confucius in the *Analects of Confucius*:

The viscount of Wei withdrew *from the court*. The viscount of Chî became a slave *to Châu*. Pî-kan remonstrated with him and died.

Confucius said, "The Yin dynasty possessed *these* three men of virtue."

- "Wei Zi Qi" (or Wei Tsze, 微子), *Analects of Confucius*

The "Biography of Wei Zi Qi of Song" (宋微子世家) in *Historical Records* by Sima Qian delineates the historical legend of the three men of virtue in much detail that can support the words of Confucius. According to it, Wei Zi Qi was an older half-brother of King Zhou, and Ji-zi (Gija) and Bigan (比干) were uncles of King Zhou. Wei Zi Qi left the state after the failure of his repeated urgings to King Zhou to repent his lascivious and debauched ways. Gija pretended to be crazy and became a slave; he sang his sorrow as he played the *geomungo* (a half-tubed zither with six strings) and lived in retirement among the common people. That tune is called "jizi-cao." Bigan was killed for speaking honestly. They were all benevolent people with patriotism.

After King Wu of Zhou destroyed Yin China, he visited Ji-zi and questioned about the kingly way that conforms to the Decrees of Heaven. Ji-zi told the story of how the Heavenly Ruler awarded the *Hong Fan Jiu Chou* (洪範九疇, nine great laws on how to govern a nation) to King Yu (禹王): First is *wuxing* (五行), second is *wushi* (五事), third is *bazheng* (八政), fourth is *wuji* (五紀), fifth is *huangji* (皇極), sixth is *sande* (三德), seventh is *qiyi* (稽疑), eighth is *shuzhi* (庶徵), and ninth is *wufu luji* (五福六極, Five Blessings and Six Extremes). He recommended for the emperor to cultivate *wushi* (*mao* 貌, *yan* 言, *shi* 視, *ting* 聽, *sai* 思) and search for a way to rule the people through *huangji*.

Let us briefly review *huangji*, which is an especially important element for a ruler to understand deeply. The content of *huangji* as mentioned to King Yu by Ji-zi (Gija) means for the ruler to establish the most righteous principles and all people to follow the most righteous principles and enjoy the Five Blessings (longevity, wealth, health, love of virtue, and peaceful death). Moreover, this is to defend the most righteous principles of not disdaining elderly widowers and widows, not fearing or shunning powerful people. The kingly way will be transmitted far and wide and the state peacefully governed if a ruler follows the righteous way and he is not biased or unfair in his ruling.

The principles of civilian government as advocated by Confucians were the policy during the 500 years of Joseon dynasty. An advantage in that is the lack of military leaders fighting for power; however, Confucian schools and political parties formed around positions of power, and it was difficult for a king to adhere to the righteous path as a ruler because he was dragged into party strife.

Yeongjo, the 21st king who ruled from 1724 to 1776, advocated "Tangpyeongchaek" (蕩平策, Policy of Impartiality) from "Hong-fan" in the *Book of Documents*: "The kingly way will be transmitted far and wide if unbiased and fair, and the kingly way will be peaceful if fair and unbiased." Jeongjo (r. 1776-1800) who succeeded Yeongjo also advocated this in an attempt to allay party strife (see Ch. 18).

Gija was a benevolent man who elucidated for King Wu of Zhou China (whom Confucius worshipped) the great law of administering a state. *Historical Records* states as follows:

> There King Wu appointed Ji-zi to Chaoxian, and did not consider him as a vassal of Zhou dynasty. Ji-zi thereafter entered into governance, and looked back on the ruins of Yin China. He wanted to cry out loud as sadness overwhelmed him at the sight of rice and millet growing in the ruins of the royal chambers. But he did not, because he thought it might be disrespectful to the Zhou dynasty and not manly; instead, he composed a poem and sang his sentiment.

> Ears of barley are growing well
> The leaves of rice and buckwheat are full of luster.
> The advent of that cunning child made things go awry.

Cunning child, of course, refers to King Zhou. All of the people of Yin supposedly shed tears when they heard this poem.

Gija Joseon Was a Paradise for Confucians

As mentioned previously, Gija was a factual figure who existed in Chinese history and not a figment of imagination. If he was a figment of imagination, then Emperors Zhou and Wu must of necessity be figments of imagination. But it would be impossible to prove the existence of Gija Joseon (Jizi Chaoxian in Ch.) from Joseon history.

Even then, the scenario of claiming that Gija Joseon was the result of Gija the transmitter of *Hong Fan Jiu Chou* to King Wu, the founder of the Zhou dynasty, prior to Confucius being assigned to Joseon, was ideal for the Confucians in the Joseon period who considered Joseon to have succeeded "small China" Gija. When Yi Seong-gye (李成桂), the founder of the Joseon dynasty, originally destroyed the Goryeo dynasty and chose "Joseon" for the name of his new country, this derived from Gija Joseon.

Dan'gun and Gija are part of the founding myths of Gojoseon, and from archeological research results an ancient state called Gojoseon is estimated to have been established around the 5th century BC. Yin dynasty is supposed to have fallen in the 11th century BC (around 1046 BC) in Chinese history. It does not seem probable for a dynasty called Gija Joseon to have existed in this period. But Gojoseon experienced an influx of the people of Yan from the periphery of the Liaodong region of China's northern borders when the unified dynasty of Han was established in 202 BC in continuation of Qin dynasty. Wiman (衛滿), a leader of Yan, chased King Jun (準王) of Gojoseon out of the throne in 194 BC. This is the so-called Wissi Joseon (衛氏朝鮮), the first state of ancient Korea historically verifiable. King Jun fled south after his loss of sovereignty to Wiman and became King Han after invading Mahan (馬韓).

Emperor Wu of Han China invaded Wissi Joseon in 108 BC and established and ruled four commanderies (四郡: Nangnang, Jinbeon,

Imdun, and Hyeondo).[1] Only Nangnang (Le-lang in Ch.) commandery around Pyeong'yang survived and was later merged into Goguryeo in 313. Han China was divided into Former Han and Later Han in the middle, with Wang Mang of Xin dynasty (8-23 AD) as the turning point. Emperor Guang-wu (光武帝: Liu Xiu 劉秀, r. 25-57 AD) was the one that toppled Xin and revived Han China. He also reached the apex of history with military might as one of the many local military leaders who competed for power at the end of Xin dynasty. He left behind the famous saying, "softness is stronger than hardness." Emperor Gwang Wu-di was a wise ruler in carrying out the meaning of his name, "*wu*" (武), which means "to stop fighting" (止戈) when the Chinese character is broken down to the basic elements. In continuation of Former Han, he also considered Confucianism important and attempted to revolutionize politics based on it.

Historical Records was written by Sima Qian in the Former Han period, and *History of the Han Dynasty* was the next historical document in an annalistic and biographical style and completed around early Later Han dynasty (late half of the first century AD). The majority of *History of the Han Dynasty*, which consists of 100 volumes, was completed by Ban Gu (班固, 32-92) who continued his father Banbiao's (班彪) work. Ban Gu wrote the *History of the Han Dynasty*, which is the history of Former Han, in the Later Han dynasty; in doing so, historical facts on Joseon contained therein are classified under the veil of contemporary history. The important thing is that Gija is also mentioned there.

> When the way of the Yin dynasty declined, Ji-zi went to Chaox-ian and taught the people propriety and righteousness, farming and sericulture, and weaving, and established a constitution containing eight clauses banning things to the Le-lang Chaoxian people.

---

[1] A commandery was a military outpost. Han dynasty China established four commanderies in the northeastern region of what is currently part of China. (S. Lee)

However, beautiful customs since Gija still remained and the people did not need to hide things because there was no worry about theft at the beginning of the Nangnang commandery. This changed when thieves became rampant and customs became disorderly after merchants from Han China came and went. That is why eight clauses banning things were increased to over 60, according to *History of the Han Dynasty*.

> The innate nature of the eastern savages is docile, which is different from the three other uncivilized barbarians (savages to the north, west, and south) who Chaoxian people. Thus there was a reason for Confucius lamenting about the Way not being practiced (in China) and saying that he wanted to cross the sea on a raft and live with the nine wild tribes of the east (the nine wild tribes or the region where they lived).

> • Geography, "Yan" (燕), *History of the Han Dynasty* (漢書)

A statement made by Confucius is also recorded in the *Analects of Confucius*, and the content of the statement agrees with *History of the Han Dynasty*.

> The Master was wishing to go and live among the nine wild tribes of the east. Someone said, "They are rude. How can you do such a thing?" The Master said, "If a superior man dwelt among them, what rudeness would there be?"

> • "Zi Han" (or Tsze Han, 子罕), *Analects of Confucius*

> The Master said, "My doctrines make no way. I will get upon a raft, and float about on the sea."

> • "Gongye Zhang" (or Kung-Yê Ch'ang, 公冶長),
> *Analects of Confucius*

The state in which Confucius was born was Lu and the neighboring state was Zhai, which were both near the Shandong peninsula. The

Shandong peninsula was just across the sea from the Korean peninsula, and a waterway was developed from olden days. Confucians from the Joseon dynasty understood this excerpt from the *Analects of Confucius* as the admiration of Joseon by Confucius who roamed from one state to the next and spread his words in China. In other words, Joseon became such a "state of Oriental ruler" after Gija went east that even Confucius admired it. There was no other happiness for Confucians than this.

Jang Ji-yeon (張志淵, pen name of Wiam 韋庵, 1864-1921) was a journalist as well as a Confucian who opposed Japanese invasion during the last days of the Joseon dynasty. He resigned from journalism after the "annexation" of Korea to Japan in August 1910 and wrote *The Origin of Confucianism in Joseon.* The preface of the book reads as follows:

> Gija, the Taishi (太師) of Yin China, fled from the Zhou dynasty and came in the Dan'gun period and civilized the east with the ways of the Hong Fan Jiu Chou. Heaven awarded Hong Fan Jiu Chou to King Yu of Xia dynasty; Gija learned its ways and transmitted it to King Wu of Zhou.... Gija himself came to Joseon after transmitting it to King Wu, and civilized us by teaching us the eight clauses. Portions of the eight clauses are missing, but Confucius revealed in "Zan" (贊) of the *Book of Changes*, "Ji-zi civilized the savages." *Myeongi* (明夷) means to reveal the way in the east. Therefore, it is not far-fetched to say that Joseon is the founding state of Confucianism. The meaning behind Confucius saying he "wants to cross the over on a raft," or "wants to live in the savage land to the east" in the *Analects of Confucius* originated from this.

The Origin of Confucianism in Joseon can be said to be the very first historiography of Confucianism in Korea. The author of this book wrote it while drowning his sorrow with alcohol at the loss of his nation. Thus there is some repetition and confusion, but what is emphasized is that Korea is a nation that followed the kingly way since Gija Joseon. Could it be possible that he was criticizing Japan's way of ruling by force through this statement, even if only indirectly?

Last names in Korea basically consist of one character such as Kim (金) or Yi (李), but there are some rare instances of two characters such as Hwangbo (皇甫), Namgung (南宮), or Seonu (鮮于). The people of the Seonu clan still pride themselves as being the descendents of Gija.

3

Confucianism in the Three Kingdoms Period

Goguryeo, Baekje, Silla, and Gaya

The Three Kingdoms period in the history of Korea refers to the period when Goguryeo, Baekje, and Silla were struggling for power. According to *Kojiki* or *Nihonshoki*, Japan was intimately related to this period as well, especially since the late 4th century.

The territory of Korea today is divided by Mt. Baekdu to the north, the Amnok River (Yalu River in Ch.) and the Duman River forming the boundaries from east to west, and the peninsula stretching to the south. However, Goguryeo feuded with various Chinese states in the Three Kingdoms period due to the Liaohe River in northeast China being the territorial boundary and possessing a large territory from the Liaoning peninsula to the middle of the Korean peninsula. The capital of Goguryeo was first established in Tonggao (Gungnaeseong in Korean; today's Jian region in China) north of the middle reaches of the Amnok River, but moved to Pyeong'yang in 427 AD as Goguryeo gradually expanded south.

The people of Baekje had integrated five Mahan (馬韓) clans and established Baekje along the basin of Han River from Gyeonggi Province to Chungcheong and Jeolla Provinces. Baekje deserted the Han River basin due to pressure from mighty Goguryeo and barely maintained power by gradually settling along the Geum River basin with Gongju or Buyeo as the capital.

Moreover, the 12 tribes of Jinhan (辰韓) were incorporated into Silla with Gyeongju as its center east of the Nakdong River in the

34

southeastern peninsula. Silla could not avoid being culturally backward because of a more difficult time coming in contact with advanced Chinese culture in comparison to Goguryeo or Baekje due to
the geographical condition. Likewise, the reception of Buddhism or
Confucianism did not proceed as easily as with the other two countries due to the lengthy continuation of local cultures.

The Gaya federation consisted of six Gaya nations, such as
Byeonhan of 12 tribes, Geumgwan Gaya around Gimhae region, and
Daegaya around Goryeong region, and was loosely formed around
the lower and western region of the Nakdong River. Gaya is also
called Gara (加羅), from the reading of the character "*han*" (韓) as
"*gara*," which may have originated in Japan. Independent development in Gaya could only be slow because Gaya had to fight against
Silla, Baekje, and Japan over the kingdom's rich iron resources.
According to the "Eastern Barbarians" (東夷傳, *Tungi-chuan* in Ch.)
in *The History of the Three Kingdoms*, Byeonjin "produces iron, all of
which the kingdoms of Han, Wei (濊), and Wo (倭) purchase."
Various markets use iron to buy things, and this is similar to the usage
of *qian* (錢, unit of currency) in China.

The legend of "Susanoono Minoto" is very interesting in connecting iron sand production of the Izumo region in Japan and
Byeonjin region.

> Susanoono Minoto, who was exiled from Takamagahara in Japan,
> went to Soshimori in Silla. He said he did not want to live there
> and reached Mt. Torikami, which is upstream of Hinogawa in
> Izumo. There are gold and silver in Hanhyang (韓鄉, interpreted
> as the birthplace of Korean peninsula based on the meaning of
> the Chinese characters). He planted trees at random in the Izumo
> region after saying that there must be ships in the kingdom that
> his son rules in order to have traffic with that country. It was as if
> a beard plucked and sown turned into *cryptomeria japonica*, chest
> hair turned into Korean spindle tree, hair from the buttocks
> turned into fir tree, and eyebrow turned into camphor tree.
>
> • "Kamiyo I" (神代 上, Age of the Gods), *Nihonshoki*

Shiba Ryotaro's interpretation of this legend is interesting ("The Iron Sand Road" (砂鐵), *Walking Horizontally*, Vol. 7). In a word, a great quantity of firewood is needed to produce iron sand. But the forest in this area of Korea is weak in the power to reproduce when judging by geographical features and climatic conditions. It could be that a group of iron sand producers had moved across the ocean and reached Izumo in search of new forest resources; Susanoono Minoto may have been the founder of this group.

Whatever the case may be, the kingdom of Gaya became integrated into Silla, Geumgwan Gaya in 532 and Daegaya in 562. Silla achieved rapid growth from the time it was unifying Geumgwan Gaya of the lower Nakdong River basin. It is presumed that many of the people of Gaya who lost the kingdom migrated to the Kitakyushu or Yamato region in Japan and transmitted the culture of the Korean peninsula there.

Nangnang commandery centered around Pyeong'yang was established when Emperor Wu of Han China attacked Gojoseon in 108 BC and was under the rule of Wei from 238. Wei is the country that destroyed the Later Han dynasty. Wei changed into a dual commandery system by dividing the former Nangnang commandery into Nangnang and Daebang commanderies. Ultimately, in 313, Nangnang commandery was toppled by Goguryeo and Daebang commandery was toppled by Baekje, thereby completely eradicating 400 years of Chinese force in the Korean peninsula.

As mentioned previously, Emperor Wu of Han China was the emperor who declared Confucianism as the state religion. The number of people who received Confucian education among the Korean scholar-officials, including the viceroy of Nangnang and Daebang commanderies, must naturally have been large. This cannot be ignored when considering the fact that Confucianism was transmitted early on in Goguryeo and Baekje that unified Nangnang and Daebang commanderies.

Goguryeo Cultivates Good Men through the National Confucian Academy

According to the "Goguryeo bongi" (高句麗本紀, Annals of Goguryeo) in *Historical Records of the Three Kingdoms*, King Sosurim (小獸林王, r. 371-384), the 17th king of Goguryeo, established the National Confucian Academy (太學), educated his people accordingly during the second year of his reign (372), and promulgated the constitution in the following year. Constitution refers to criminal law and administrative law that are the basis of national unity developed in ancient China. But it was necessary to cultivate good men who possessed Confucian education in order to enforce the constitution. The National Confucian Academy was the Confucian educational institution most similar to the Confucian school in the times of Emperor Wu of Han when Confucianism was the state religion.

Another important description of the same period mentions transmission of Buddhism. During the period of sixteen kingdoms of five barbarians (316-439), King Fujian (符堅) of Former Qin China sent Monk Sundo (順道, Shundao in Ch.) to Goguryeo in the second year of the reign of King Sosurim (372) to deliver images of Buddha and the scriptures; Monk Ado (阿道, Edao in Ch.) was also sent in the fourth year of the reign of King Sosurim (374). King Sosurim built Chomun Temple in the following year and established Monk Sundo there, and also built Ibullan Temple where Monk Ado was stationed. This was described as the beginning of Buddhism in Korea.

Thus the year 372 was truly a landmark for the cultural history of not only Goguryeo but all of Korea in that the National Confucian Academy was established by Confucians and Buddhism was introduced.

It cannot be maintained that Confucianism was introduced by the establishment of the National Confucian Academy. The usage of Chinese characters must be widely spread among the lowest class as a prerequisite for the best Confucian educational institution to be established. To understand this, there is a need to consult the following excerpt from "Goryeo bongi" (Record of Goryeo) in the *Old History of the Tang Dynasty*.

> The general public also loves to read. Big and small houses are built along the roadside until the house of poverty and menial job is reached. That house is called Gyeongdang, a private school, in Goguryeo. Unmarried young men read and learn archery here. There are various books such as the Five Confucian Classics, *Historical Records*, *History of the Han Dynasty*, *History of the Later Han Dynasty* by Fenye, *The History of the Three Kingdoms*, *Jinyangqiu* (晉陽秋) by Sun Cheng (孫盛), *Yu Pian* (玉篇), *Zitong* (字統), *Zilin* (字林), and *Selected Literature* (文選, *Wenxuan* in Ch.). *Selected Literature* is most loved among them.

While it is true that this description was written after Goguryeo moved the capital from Tonggao to Pyeong'yang, it does show that private schools in Goguryeo existed even in the remotest hamlet, and that the youths were educated to achieve both literary and military accomplishments through reading and archery practice. The most loved book in Goguryeo was *Selected Literature*, which is a collection of Chinese poetry and prose compiled by Crown Prince Shaoming (邵明太子) during the reign of his father, Emperor Wudi (武帝, r. 502-549) of Liang of the Southern Dynasties in China.

In addition, according to the Annals of Goguryeo in *Historical Records of the Three Kingdoms*, King Yeongyang (嬰陽王, r. 590-618) commanded the Learned of the National Confucian Academy Yi Mun-jin (李文眞) to compile five volumes of Goguryeo history called *New Compilation* (新集). The following is an account of this event.

> Yi Mun-jin (李文眞), the Learned of the National Confucian Academy, compiled an abridged version of old historical documents into five volumes entitled *New Compilation*. Written characters were used (in Goguryeo) from the beginning of the kingdom; it is said that someone recorded the history of the king in 100 volumes and called it *Yugi*. *Yugi* was rearranged and compiled at this time.

As much as Goguryeo suffered from disturbances of war, its histori-cal documents of *Yugi* (留記) and *New Compilation* were not handed down to today, but the Learned of the National Confucian Academy Yi Mun-jin was probably one of the Learned of the Five Confucian Classics. The tombstone of King Gwanggaeto was built by King Jangsu (長壽王, r. 413-491) to commemorate the achievements of his father with 1,800 free-style Chinese characters denoting the biography of King Gwanggaeto (廣開土王; alias King Hotae, 好太王).

The Self-Destruction of Emperor Yang of Sui China Who Attacked Goguryeo

There was no end to division and civil strife in the great land of China after Later Han fell in 220 AD. This was the so-called turbulent age of sixteen kingdoms of five barbarians. Yang Jian (楊堅) of Northern Zhou (北周) became Emperor Wen (文帝) in 581 follow-ing the abdication of young ruler Emperor Jing (靜帝); he rebuilt the kingdom into a powerful and unified empire of Sui (隋) and estab-lished its capital in Changan (長安). The tension between Goguryeo and Sui China heightened during this time due to Goguryeo's refusal to submit to Sui.

Goguryeo was the strongest of the Three Kingdoms in the Ko-rean peninsula. Emperor Wen of Sui China attacked Goguryeo in 599 with a large army of 300,000 to prevent Goguryeo from forming an alliance with Eastern Turks (東突厥) in the north. But this expedition failed due to flood, storm, and lack of food. Emperor Yang (煬帝, r. 604-618) succeeded Emperor Wen and was the emperor who developed a great waterway that connected the Yellow River (Huanghe), Haishu, and Yangtze River from Zhuo Jun (what is now Beijing) in the north to Yuhang (余杭, today's Hangzhou) in the south. But Emperor Yang and the fate of the Sui dynasty were doomed as a result of the failure of the ambitious Goguryeo expedi-tion.

According to a Chinese document on the Goguryeo expedition of 612, Emperor Yang himself led this conquest and gathered a great army of 1,133,800 in Beijing, which was the army outpost. It is said that it took the army 40 days to leave Beijing, and the length of the formation reached over 1,000 *li* (393 km). The great waterway made it possible to recruit so many men and supplies from the south. But when the war broke out, the defense line of Goguryeo, including Liaodong Castle of the coast of the Liaohe River, did not allow the approach of the Sui army by repelling Sui attacks. The Sui army became anxious about the protracted war waged by Goguryeo. Several commanders including Yu-wen Shu (宇文述) advanced south with a detachment of 305,000 in order to attack Pyeong'yang directly. Goguryeo's General Euljimundeok allowed the Sui army to approach Pyeong'yang, but launched a protracted war of defending the castle. The Sui army, suffering from exhaustion and shortage of supplies, finally retreated. The retreating Sui army suffered a crushing defeat at Sashui (薩水, old name of Qingchuan River, 淸川江), where it was surrounded and attacked; only 2,700 Sui soldiers escaped.

Emperor Yang tenaciously launched another expedition in 614, but the kingdom reached an uncontrollable state as the rear supply route commander Yang Xuan Gan (楊玄感) revolted and "groups of robbers" rose up in rebellion in various regions of the kingdom. Emperor Yang fled to Li Palace (離宮) in Yangzhou (楊州), but his chief minister Yuwen Huaji (宇文化及) beheaded the emperor and used his head as a sacrificial offering. Thus ended the Sui dynasty's brief period. Li Yuan (李淵), one of the generals of Sui dynasty, established the Tang dynasty in 618 and became its founder.

Emperor Yang, the second ruler of Sui, is evaluated as a tyrant, but Emperor Taizong (太宗, r. 626-649), the second ruler of Tang, is evaluated as a wise ruler. *Zhenguan zhengyao* (貞觀政要), which contains the record of questions and answers exchanged between Emperor Taizong and his vassals, was used in Korea and Japan as textbook for "the study to become a good emperor." The basic consistency of this book is the heartfelt intent toward the continua-tion of ancestor achievements on "the founding of a kingdom."

Emperor Yang became a tyrant because he failed in this, but Emperor Taizong became a wise ruler because he succeeded in this. It may be that Emperor Taizong considered Emperor Yang as a role model of what not to do.

Emperor Yang could only be denounced as a tyrant in that he harassed his people in order to build the great waterway and a second capital in Luo-yang in a short period as well as to send expeditions to Goguryeo. The great waterway, however, which was completed during the reign of Emperor Yang, greatly influenced the economic history of China. The power of a sovereign is great, and Emperor Yang could not control his desire for power.

The civil service examination system established by Emperor Wen of Sui China and the establishment of Confucianism as the state religion by Emperor Wu of Han China have decidedly influenced the political and cultural history of China and Joseon. In contrast to the previous custom of appointing good men based on status within the aristocracy, the civil service examination was a landmark system from which men were chosen according to ability.

Goguryeo was also a northern threat to Emperor Taizong. Thus in 645 Emperor Taizong led an army of 100,000 to attack Goguryeo. He was successful in seizing Liaodong Castle, but not in conquering Anshi Castle. Goguryeo was a kingdom mighty enough to defend itself against the united empires of Sui and Tang China.

Baekje People Were Skillful in Writing

Description on Confucianism in Baekje cannot be found in the *Historical Records of the Three Kingdoms*, but according to the historical records of China or *Nihonshoki* of Japan, Confucianism was introduced as early on in Baekje as in Goguryeo.

It is written in the *Nihonshoki* that King Muryeong (武寧王, r. 501-523) of Baekje sent Danyangi, one of the Learned of the Five Confucian Classics, to Japan in 513 (the 7th year of the reign of Japan's Emperor Keitai). This can be said to demark the beginning of the fundamental adoption of Confucianism in Japanese history. The

41

Learned of the Five Confucian Classics was a system established by Emperor Wu of Han China when he made Confucianism the state religion. The Five Confucian Classics refer to the classic Confucian books prior to the Cheng-Zhu School (or Cheng-Chu School): *Book of Changes*, *Official History* (尙書, *Shang-shu* in Ch.), *Book of Poetry* (*Maoshi* in Ch.), *Record of Rites*, and *Spring and Autumn Annals*.

During the reign of King Muryeong, Baekje left the place of its origin around the Han River basin (Gwangju, Gyeonggi Province region of today) and moved the capital to Gongju along the Geum River basin under the pressure of southward advancement of Goguryeo. King Muryeong approached Japan and the Liang of the Southern Dynasties in order to counter Goguryeo's threat. Emperor Wudi of Liang China, who established the system of the Learned of the Five Confucian Classics in 505, was known for being the wisest ruler in the South Dynasties at the time. The Learned of the Five Confucian Classics of Baekje was probably modeled directly after it. The following record appears in the "Muryeong wangjo" in "Baekje bongi" (百濟本紀, Annals of Baekje) of *Historical Records of the Three Kingdoms*:

> In November (of 521), an emissary was sent to Liang to pay tribute. We have been weakened after suffering a defeat at the hands of Goguryeo in the past, but we gradually became stronger because we were granted approval as friendly relations this year after a list containing several defeats over Goguryeo was presented.

Emperor Wudi of Liang was happy with King Muryeong's tribute and granted a title of "Baekje's Great General of Liaodong" to him. The Confucianism that was transmitted in the direction of Liang of Southern Dynasties → Baekje → Japan was the Chinese Classics of the Southern Dynasties; its academic tradition differs from that of the Chinese Classics of the Northern Dynasties, which developed out of Zhangan or Luo-yang.

Pronunciation of Chinese characters in Japan can be confusing in many instances due to the mixture of *go'on* and *kan'on*, and the pronunciation used in the Classics of the Southern Dynasties was *go'on.* It is estimated that the mixture of *go'on* and *kan'on* occurred when Japanese foreign students who accompanied the Japanese Emissary to Tang China later transmitted the *kan'on* of the Chinese Classics of the Northern Dynasties.

Let's go back in time. In 260 when King Goi (r. 234-286) was on the throne, Baekje had six prime ministers of first rank as part of its centralized system: Naesin Jwapyeong (of communication of royal edicts), Naedu Jwapyeong (of finance), Naebeop Jwapyeong (of rituals), Wisa Jwapyeong (of the royal guards), Jojeong Jwapyeong (judiciary), and Byeonggwan Jwapyeong (of military affairs). Based on the characteristics of the work, the six prime ministers as well as scholar-officials in each rank must have had Confucian education. There were six ranks, with Jwapyeong being the first rank, followed by Dalsol as second rank.

Add to this the fact that when the people of Baekje fled to Japan after Baekje fell at the hands of Silla in 660, Emperor Tenji acknowledged the ranks of Jwapyeong or Dalsol as is and used the high-ranking refugee scholar-officials as professionals in law, the Five Confucian Classics, and military strategy. An example of this is Emperor Tenji providing living quarters to Jwapyeong Yeo Ja-jin and Gwisiljipsa (originally Dalsol) in Gamo-gun, Omi Province.

"Baekjejeon" (Record of Baekje) in the *History of the Zhou Dynasty* (周書) contains the following description:

> The people (of Baekje) consider horseback riding and archery important, and in addition they like the classics or history. A superior man among them can write with great skill, as well as understand the yin and the yang and the five elements. The *Yuanjia* calendar of Song China is used, and January was chosen so as to include *jianyin* (建寅).[1] Also, they are skilled in medicine, fortune-telling, and divination…. There are many (Buddhist) monks, nuns, and pagodas, but no Daoists.

---

[1] *Jianyin* (建寅) is a Chinese word used to denote a specific time of the season. (S. Lee)

The "Baekjeguk jeon" (Story of the Kingdom of Baekje) in *Old History of the Tang Dynasty* contains descriptions about Baekje importing the Five Confucian Classics, Zi (子, anthology of the Hundred Schools of Thought), and historical documents (such as *Historical Records* and *History of the Han Dynasty*), as well as the Chinese method of writing a congratulatory letter or a memorial to the throne.

In compiling historical documents on Baekje, "Geunchogo wangjo" (Record of King Geunchogo) in "Annals of Baekje" of the *Historical Records of the Three Kingdoms* quoted a statement from "Old Records" as follows:

> Baekje has yet to record its history since its founding, but for the first time the Learned Ko Heung (高興) wrote *Documentary Records* (書記) at this time. But there is no way of knowing who Ko Heung is because his name does not appear in any other books.

Buyeo, the capital of Baekje, turned into ashes at the time of its downfall in 660. Thus it is not possible for *Documentary Records* or a biography of Ko Heung to have survived.

A quote mentioned above in the "Record of Baekje" of the *History of the Zhou Dynasty* contains a statement of how the "*Yuanjia* calendar of Song China is used in Baekje, and January was chosen to contain *jianyin*." As well, it is stated in the "Record of Baekje" in the *History of the Sui Dynasty* (隨書) that "Baekje adopted the *Yuanjia* calendar and made January the month of *jianyin*." Song mentioned here refers to China's Song dynasty (420-479) during the Southern and Northern Dynasties period.

It is recorded that Japan officially began to use a calendar in January of the 12th year of the reign of Emperor Suiko (推古天皇, 604). According to the *Nihonshoki*, two years prior to this event Monk Gwalleuk (觀勒) of Baekje went to Japan in the 10th year of the reign of Emperor Suiko with books on calendar-making, astrology, geography, alchemy, and necromancy. The Japanese Imperial Court chose three or four young Confucian students and attempted to make them learn from Gwalleuk, among whom Oyatama Furu (祖玉陳) of

Yakono Fubito (陽胡史) mastered calendar-making, and Otomo Suguri (大友村主) and Goso (高聰) mastered astrology. The inference is that the calendar first used in Japan is Song's Chinese *Yuanjia* calendar as transmitted by Gwalleuk.

It is stated in the same *Nihonshoki* that in April of the 32nd year of the reign of Emperor Suiko (624), a monk wielded an ax on his own grandfather. Gwalleuk submitted an appeal to the throne at this time to establish upright priesthood and the way of priesthood to control monks. It is said that Gwalleuk and Kuratsukuribe Dokushaku were appointed to the upright priesthood and the way of the priesthood, respectively, and they investigated and recorded each temple's dependent arising, monk's thought in realizing the way, and the month and year of entrance into priesthood.

National History Written during the Silla Period

Silla was spread out in the southeastern region of the Korean peninsula. It had little contact with mainland culture and maintained the old customs since Jinhan for a long time. This is demonstrated by the fact that the title of the monarch and the name of the nation were not uniform until King Jijeung (智證王, r. 500-513). For instance, various titles used to refer to the monarch were Geoseogan (居西干), Chachaung (次次雄), Isageum (尼斯今), and Maripgan (麻立干), and the nation was sometimes called Sara (斯羅), Saro (斯盧), or Silla. This means that a nation that closed itself to the outside world and foreign relations was poor.

King Jijeung followed the advice of several vassals and established the name of the nation as Silla: "'Sil' stands for the achievements of virtue and goodness which are new every day, and 'la' stands for inclusion of all directions." A posthumous title of honors was conferred for the first time after King Jijeung passed away. The title "king" was chosen to denote the ruler during the reign of the next monarch, King Beopheung (r. 514-540). Thus an internationally accepted title for the monarch and name of the kingdom were chosen.

In the 7th year of his reign, King Beopheung (520) promulgated law and enacted the rank of official dress as well as the color and style to be worn to court by all scholar-officials. Silla was 140 years late in promulgating the law; Goguryeo had already instituted law in 373. The sovereign power was so weak that it was controlled by a unified aristocracy, and thus the completion of a centralized administration in the form of a legal system probably occurred much later.

This may be a digression, but many times Koreans are thought to be part of the Chinese ethnic group because Korean last names are in the Chinese style. The Chinese style of using last names became generalized in the upper aristocracy only since the Late Silla period; just the origin (family origin) and first and middle name were used before then.

It is stated in the "Record of Silla" of *Book of Liang Dynasty* (梁書) that Silla did not use Chinese characters, and Baekje people were used as translators to communicate with Chinese people prior to the transmission of Confucianism.

> Because written characters did not exist, knife marks were made on wood as signs. When communicating (with China), a medium of Baekje (translator) must be used.

However, Silla underwent a change during the reign of King Beopheung and, as mentioned previously, law was propagated in 520 and Buddhism was officially recognized in 535. It advanced toward the lower basin of Nakdong River in 532 and unified Geumgwan Gaya that was in the Gimhae region, which opened the way for intercourse with various dynasties in China through the securing of ports on the estuary of Nakdong River.

In 545, the 6th year of the reign of King Jinheung (r. 540-576), the General of the Ministry of Military Affairs in charge of the military reported to the throne as follows:

> The history of a nation is to record the good and bad of the sovereign and his vassals, and to transmit laudable deeds and deplorable deeds to ten thousand generations to come. What founda-

tion would the future generations have with which to understand (this period) if national history is not compiled?

- "Silla bongi" (新羅本紀, Annals of Silla), Sixth Year of King Jinheung, *Historical Records of the Three Kingdoms*

The king was greatly moved by this opinion, and ordered the compilers of national history such as the Great Achan (fifth of the 17 official ranks) to gather literary men from far and wide to compile national history.

Won-gwang's Five Secular Injunctions and the Code of the Youth Corps

There was no friction between Confucianism and Buddhism in Silla at the time, and it seems as if Confucian virtues were also introduced into Buddhism as practical ethics. Won-gwang (圓光) was an eminent monk who lived during the reign of King Jinpyeong (眞平王, r. 579-632). He went to Jinling (金陵, currently Nanjing) in Chen (陳) dynasty China in 581 to learn Confucianism. But he became fascinated with the Buddhist canon; he advised the sovereign when he came back to Silla in 600 after studying the three baskets of Buddhism including the scriptures, commandments, and treatise (三藏: 經律論). Gwisan (貴山) and Chuhang (箒項), warriors of Saryang-bu (one of the 6 *bu*s of Silla), heard of his reputation and desired to attain learning that could be applied to life in a secular world. There are 10 prohibitions in the precepts of the Bodhisattva, but Won-gwang proposed Five Secular Injunctions (世俗五戒) for laymen because he did not think people living in the secular world could achieve all ten prohibitions. The following appears in "Won-gwang seohak" (圓光西學, Western Learning of Won-gwang) in Volume 4 of *Residual Events of the Three Kingdoms*:

1. Serve the king with loyalty.
2. Obey your parents.
3. Be honorable with friends.
4. Never retreat from battle.
5. Be selective about taking a life.

When the two warriors asked once again about the fifth item, Won-gwang explained that unnecessary destruction of life must be avoided and the time and the object of killing must be discriminately selected. Items 1, 2, and 3 are all on Confucian virtues, while items 4 and 5 reveal Silla's spirit of the warrior. The eminent monk Won-gwang did not exclude Confucianism; rather, he recommended it as a secular virtue.

The Code of the Youth Corps (花郎徒) was created in 576, with handsome youths of aristocratic families at its center during the reign of King Jinheung. This was a training group connected to the *maitreya* faith for young men.

> The purpose behind organizing the Code of the Youth Corps is to teach filial piety, respect, loyalty, and faithfulness to the talented among the gathered young men; this is another aspect of governing a nation.
>
> • "Mireuk seonhwa" (彌勒仙花),
> Volume 3 of the *Residual Events of the Three Kingdoms*

The virtues of filial piety, respect, loyalty, and faithfulness as put forth by the Code of the Youth Corps corresponded to Won-gwang's Five Secular Injunctions. In other words, the spirit of the Code of the Youth Corps was the union of the belief in realizing an ideal society for laymen by the *maitreya bodhisattva* and training in Confucian virtues. People of the times called Hwarang "mireuk seonhwa."

The Code of the Youth Corps later became the dynamic force behind Silla unifying the Three Kingdoms. Silla's leaders were the chosen elite through everyday group activities in the Hwarang.

In honor did they train with each other, found pleasure in music and dance, and went on excursions to mountains and seas, no matter how far. One's good and bad aspects were revealed through these activities, and good men were thus chosen and recommended to the Imperial Court. This is why Kim Dae-mun wrote in the *Hwarang segi* (Chronicles of the Youth Corps) that "wise vassals and faithful retainers as well as good commanders and brave soldiers were produced from here."

> • "Annals of Silla," King Jinheung,
> Historical Records of the Three Kingdoms

In the history of Korean Confucianism, Buddhism and Daoism were scorned as "cults" after the Learning of Master Zhu was transmitted to Korea in the late Goryeo period.

Silla overcame Baekje in 660 and Goguryeo in 668 as mentioned above. This resulted in the integration of the entire Baekje region and part of the Goguryeo territory south of the Daedong River into Silla. This book will refer to the Silla of the Three Kingdoms period as the "Former Silla period" and the end of the Three Kingdoms period to the downfall of the Silla dynasty in 935 as the "Late Silla period."

As described above, Goguryeo, Baekje, and Silla introduced Confucianism or Buddhism that transcended miscellaneous folk culture or belief in the process of nation-building to strive for spiritual solidarity; internationality was common in regions of Asian culture due to this.

Baekje's Learned of the Five Confucian Classics Goes to Japan

According to *Kojiki* of Japan, Wanikishi (Wang-in in *Nihonshoki*) presented Japan with 10 *Analects of Confucius* and one volume of *One Thousand Characters* in the 15th year of the reign of Emperor Ojin (284) and became the teacher of Crown Prince Ujino Waki Iratsuko in the following year. Emperor Ojin is supposed to have been the child of the surreal Emperor Chuai and Empress Jingo, according to the popular view on ancient Japanese history. As well, his life is

49

supposed to have spanned 110 years, which is somewhat unrealistic. *One Thousand Characters* is an elementary Chinese classic textbook compiled by Zhou Xing Si (周興嗣) in response to the command of Emperor Wudi of Liang China (r. 502-549) of the Southern Dynasties. And, of course, *Analects of Confucius* is a memoir of Confucius and his disciples, but its annotation entitled "Correct Interpretation of the Analects of Confucius (論語義疏)" was written by a scholar named Huang Kan (黃侃) of the Liang dynasty. The periods of the reign of Emperor Wudi of Liang China and King Muryeong of Baekje overlap.

Wang-in the Learned became the progenitor of the Baekje-descent Kawachinofumi clan in Japan. This story may be a family legend made up to give credence to the occupation of the Nishi fumi clan which flourished from engaging in literary works centered around Furuichi (today's Habikino City, Osaka) on the coast of Yamatogawa.

One Thousand Characters and *Analects of Confucius* were probably transmitted to Japan from Baekje when King Muryeong sent the Learned of the Five Confucian Classics Danyang to Japan in 513 (7th year of the reign of Emperor Keitai). Japan was ready to receive the Learned of the Five Confucian Classics, which meant that Chinese characters were used prior to this period; and it is a fact that the Nishi fumi clan of Kawauchi and the Hikai fumi clan of Yamato were active in literary works. It is not impossible to study *Analects of Confucius* after a thorough understanding of *One Thousand Characters*. It is said that the usage of Chinese characters in Japan generally began around the 5th century.

The Learned of the Five Confucian Classics Danyang was dispatched by King Muryeong of Baekje as mentioned above. He was the father of King Seong (also known as King Seongmyeong, r. 523-554) who transmitted Buddhism to Japan. It seems as if dispatch of the Learned of the Five Confucian Classics from Baekje was based on an alternating system. Not only was the Learned of the Five Confucian Classics Wang Yu-gwi (王柳貴) replaced by Ma Jeong-an (馬丁安) in 554 (15th year of the reign of Emperor Kinmei), but the

Learned of the Science of Divination, the Learned of Calendar-Making, the Learned of Medicine, and Gatherer of Medicinal Plants were dispatched as well.

Buddhism was transmitted to Japan by King Seong following King Muryeong's dispatch of the Learned of the Five Confucian Classics, which led to a great debate on whether the god should be considered indigenous or foreign. In other words, this could be considered a preview of the idea for Asuka culture. Parallel and simultaneous culture of Buddhism and Confucianism or aspects adopted prior to them cannot be ignored in the formation process of Asuka culture.

As mentioned before, Baekje moved its capital southward from Castle Hansan located on the Han River basin (Gwangju, Gyeonggi Province region) to Ungjin on the Geum River basin (today's Gongju), and again to Sabi (today's Buyeo) in 538 due to pressure from Goguryeo in the north.

Baekje formed an alliance with Silla, which was also feeling threatened by Goguryeo, and advanced to the Han River basin in 551 but lost the territory to Silla. King Seong lost his life in 554 during the battle fought in retaliation against Silla's betrayal. King Muryeong and King Seong approached Japan or China as a diplomatic policy to counteract Goguryeo and Silla. King Muryeong, who dispatched the Learned of the Five Chinese Classics, and King Seong, who transmitted Buddhism to Japan, are definitely people who should not be forgotten in Japanese culture and thought. The discovery of magnificent burial goods from the tomb of King Muryeong that King Seong had had made in the Songsan-li, Gongju City, South Chungcheong Province, became a great topic of conversation in Japan as well.

4

Confucianism in the Late Silla Period

Silla Unifies the Three Kingdoms

The turbulence of northeast Asia and China directly influenced generation upon generation of dynasties in the Korean peninsula. Difficult responses were required to be made by the Korean peninsula in each instance on which the destiny of the kingdom depended.

Silla, which was unevenly distributed in the southeastern region of the Korean peninsula in the late 7th century, unified the territory south of Daedong River by conquering Baekje in 660 and Goguryeo in 668. This is the so-called Late Silla period. This was in main due to Silla's success in forming an alliance with the Chinese Tang dynasty based on the diplomatic policy of "being friendly with distant kingdoms and attacking neighboring kingdoms" through adroitly utilizing the great turbulence within China.

As examined in Chapter 3, great empires such as Sui or Tang dynasties of China could not force Goguryeo to its knees. A description of the situation immediately after the failure of the Goguryeo expedition by Emperor Taizong of Tang China in 645 draws attention, however. Kim Chun-chu (金春秋), who later became King Muyeol, visited Changan in 648 and said the following during his audience with Emperor Taizong of Tang:

"Our land is far across the ocean but served the dynasty of the son of Heaven for a long time. But Baekje is strong as well as cunning and frequently raids our land. What is more, Baekje raised a big army last year (11th year of the reign of King Seondeok) and blocked the road that must be traveled to seek an audience with the son of Heaven by toppling scores of castles by invading deep into (the territory of Silla). If Your Majesty does not lend the military of the son of Heaven in order to subjugate the power of the villainous Baekje, our subjects will all be taken prisoner. Then we will not be able to send tributes, nor will we be able to report on state affairs."

Emperor Taizong strongly agreed with his opinion and authorized the dispatch of troops.

- "Annals of Silla," 2nd year of the reign of King Jindeok, *Historical Records of the Three Kingdoms*

Baekje and Silla were old foes. Silla reported to Tang that it could not send tribute because the road to Tang was blocked by Baekje, thereby scheming to make mischief between Tang and Baekje. In addition, Kim Chun-chu notified Tang of Silla's intention of changing its ritual clothes to those of China and of sending his son King Mun to "serve" Emperor Taizong. To "serve" here means a type of diplomatic hostage wherein a prince or a member of the royal family of a foreign nation is sent to guard the Son of Heaven as a close attendant; this greatly influenced Tang's foreign policy. This foreign policy, which continued thereafter, was a manifestation of Silla's continued alliance with Tang China.

Goguryeo was an old foe of Tang since Sui dynasty, and from Tang's point of view, overcoming Baekje by forming an alliance with Silla would be equivalent to Goguryeo being attacked from the north by Tang and from the south by a united Silla-Tang army. As promised, Emperor Gaozong (or Kao Tsung) of Tang China dispatched troops to Baekje in 660 after Emperor Taizong passed away. It is probable that Empress Wu Zetian (則天武后), who was a brave female fighter and the favorite of the emperor, made the ultimate decision for the sickly and weak-willed Emperor Gaozong. Silla realized the unification of the Korean peninsula by overcoming Baekje first and Goguryeo later based on Kim Chun-chu's foreign policy of being friendly with distant kingdoms and attacking neighboring kingdoms.

The commander-in-chief of Silla was a member of the Youth Corp called Kim Yu-shin (金庾信 595-673). It is recorded in "Kim Yu-shin," Volume 1 of *Residual Events of the Three Kingdoms* that he trained in the art of swordsmanship in 612 at the age of 18 and was chosen for the Youth Corp. A great combination of Kim Chun-chu in diplomacy and Kim Yu-shin in military affairs made Silla's unification possible.

But the alliance between Tang and Silla was nothing but a dream. Tang established Andong Dohobu (安東都護府) in Pyeong'yang, the capital of Goguryeo, and planned to control not only Goguryeo but Silla and Baekje as well. In response, Silla troops formed an alliance with the wanderers from Baekje and Goguryeo and was finally successful in chasing Tang out of Andong Dohobu all the way to Xin Cheng (新城, what is now Fushun 撫順) north of Pyeong'yang in 676 after many battles. Thus Late Silla's territory was restricted to south of the Daedong River.

The kingdom of Balhae was created after the Goguryeo and Malgal people joined forces in their continued struggles against Tang China around the Songhua River basin in what used to be part of Goguryeo territory north of the Daedong River, with Goguryeo's old general Dae Jo-yeong at the lead. Ultimately, the Three Kingdoms of Goguryeo, Baekje, and Silla of the olden days turned into two kingdoms of Late Silla and Balhae. Japan dispatched reinforcements to save Silla, but established diplomatic relations with Balhae in order to keep Late Silla in check from north and south after its defeat at Baek River (白江).

Bitter Baekje People Migrate to Japan after the Fall of Their Nation

Baekje, which had deep ties with Japan, fell in 660. The surviving retainers such as Boksin (福信) took siege of Juryu Castle (周留城, what is now Hansan in South Chungcheong Province) and sent a messenger to Japan to request reinforcements and the return of Prince Buyeo Pung (扶餘豊, also known as Pungjang 豊璋) who was staying in Japan at the time. Imperial Prince Nakano Oe (who later became Emperor Tenji) arrived at the Asakura Palace (朝倉宮) in Tsukushi and dispatched a troop of 27,000 in 663. An internal strife arose between Buyeo Pung and Boksin after Buyeo Pung's return to Baekje, however, which led to the death of Boksin at the hands of Buyeo Pung. The Silla troops used that time to conquer Juryu Castle. Japanese troops were decimated by the Tang navy at the mouth of Geum River called Baek River (Baekchon River, 白村江, in Japanese historical books). *Comprehensive Mirror for Aid in Government* (自治通鑑, *Zizhi tongjian* in Ch.) describes this as follows:

> Four battles were waged against the Japanese forces at the estuary of Baek River, all of which were won. Four hundred of their ships were burned; smoke filled the sky and the ocean turned red.

Why did Buyeo Pung kill Boksin at such a critical time when national existence was at stake? That is a puzzle. At the time of Pungjang's return, Japan awarded him the government post of Shochukan (織冠) and married him to the younger sister of Onoomi Komoshiki. If that is the case, even if Baekje was revived by the Japanese reinforcement and Buyeo Pung became king, there was a high possibility of Baekje becoming a dependent state of Japan. Boksin may have requested the return of Buyeo Pung and the dispatch of Japanese reinforcement, but he probably did not anticipate events to take such a turn. Was his distrust of Buyeo Pung the cause of internal strife?

Whatever the case was, King Buyeo Pung of Baekje fled to Goguryeo after the defeat at Baek River, and Princes Chungseung (忠勝) and Chungjwa (忠佐) surrendered with their servants. Many people of Baekje also defected to Japan. The following statements on this issue can be found in the *Nihonshoki*: "around 400 men and women of Baekje were allowed to live in Kanjaki-gun, Omi Province in the year 665" (February of the 4th year of the reign of Emperor Tenji) or "in the year of 669, around 700 men and women including Jwapyeong Yeo Ja-jin (餘自進) and Gwisiljipsa (鬼室集斯) migrated to Gamo-gun (蒲生郡) in Omi Province (近江國)" (8th year of the reign of Emperor Tenji). There is also a record on over 60

Jwapyeong and Dalsol such as Jwapyeong Sataek Somyeong (沙宅紹明, who held the post of Beopgwan Daebo 法官大輔), Gwisiljipsa (鬼室集斯, who held the post of Hakjikdu 學職頭), and Dalsol Heo Solmo (許率母, one of the Learned of the Five Confucian Classics) being awarded official Japanese posts in 671.

Emperor Tenji ascended to the throne in 668 at Otsu Palace in Omi Province. Attention should be paid to the fact that not only did Japan award the Baekje refugees the same official posts held in Baekje, but that they were concentrated in Omi Province near the capital of Otsu. According to the preface in *Kamifuso*, the oldest collection of Chinese classics in Japan, Emperor Tenji thought as follows:

> Putting great value on learning is the best way to cultivate customs and achieve enlightenment. Learning to practice morality and to take care of one's body from someone else would be better. Thus a school is established, talented people recruited, five rites chosen, and 100 laws enacted.

The Taika Reform as conceptualized by Emperor Tenji in the excerpt above seems to indicate civil administration based on the politics of centralized power with Baekje as its model, and not on the hitherto practiced great king administration that depends on the balance of power among the powerful families. He expected his successor Prince Otomo to realize this. Therefore, Emperor Tenji invited refugees from Baekje as honored guests to educate Prince Otomo.

> Scholars Sataek Somyeong, Taphon Chuncho (塔焜春初), Gil Tae-sang (吉太尚), Heo Solmo, and Bonso Gwija (本素貴子) were invited as honored guests. The Crown Prince has a good nature and enjoys studying ancient things throughout. When he takes up a brush, whatever he writes becomes an essay; when he talks, his words become a discussion.

The names of the honored guests mentioned above were all from Baekje; the intellectual group consisted of Sataek Somyeong who was well versed in law, Taphon Chuncho and Bonso Gwija who were knowledgeable about military strategy, Gil Tae-sang an expert healer, and Heo Solmo who was renowned for his knowledge of the Chinese classics.

Prince Otomo was killed in the Jinshin Disturbance led by Prince Oama, who was the younger brother of Emperor Tenji and who later became Emperor Temmu, in 672. But the intellectual refugees from Baekje and their descendants played such a big role in the Japanese establishment of a constitutional state that continued into the reigns Temmu and Emperor Jito that it is impossible fully to calculate it.

The title "Emperor" was first used by Emperor Temmu. The relationship with Silla improved in the 13th year of his reign. It seems as if he was critical of Emperor Tenji's anti-Silla policy. The *Nihonshoki* describes Sataek Somyeong's passing away on June 6 of 673, the same year that Emperor Temmu ascended to the throne.

> He was praised as a genius for his sagacity and intelligence. The Emperor was surprised (to hear of his death) and conferred the rank of Donoshoshi, and further conferred the highest official rank of Daejwapyeong from Baekje wherein he originated.

An envoy from Silla such as Kim Seung-won (金承元) and other messengers visited Japan in the same year to congratulate Emperor Temmu on ascending to the throne, and Emperor Temmu sent a corresponding delegation to Silla with Otomono Murajikunimaro as Ambassador. Fundamentally, however, the tension between Japan and Silla gradually increased after the defeat at Baek River, and Japan accelerated its centralization of power to tighten control. The last time Japan dispatched an envoy to Silla was in 884. In this atmosphere, some of the descendants of the Korean peninsula changed the root of family names to those that could be easily confused with family names from China by adding names such as Jin or Han.

An incident that represents the friction between Silla and Japan at the time occurred during the morning assembly at the Hanyuandian (含元殿) in Penglai Palace (蓬萊宮) which the delegations from various countries attended to pay homage to Emperor Xuanzong (玄宗) of Tang China on New Year's Day in 753. The tenth Japanese

Emissary to Tang China was Ambassador Fujiwara no Kiyokawa and Vice Ambassador Otomo Gomaro. Japan was seated second on the west side and Tibet was first. Silla, on the other hand, was seated first and Arabia second on the east side. A Japanese historical document describes how the Vice Ambassador Otomo solemnly protested this seating arrangement in front of all delegations by stating that "Silla has been a tributary state of Japan from long ago" and requested for a change in seating order.

Fujiwara no Kiyokawa had full power during the reign of Empress Koken, who ruled Japan from 759 to 762; he ordered the building of 500 warships to conquer Silla, trained solders, and planned to educate translators in the Silla language. His plans did not come to fruition, but Japanese anti-Silla sentiment can be inferred from this. Japan, burning with resistance against Silla, sent delegations back and forth between Japan and Balhae by the opening of the waterway between Tsuruga in Hokuriku and Duman River (Tumen River in Ch.). This waterway was also used as one of the paths for delegations to reach Changan in China as well as for contacting Confucian scholars.

The first time Balhae sent a delegation to Japan was in the year 727. The 24 members of the delegation landed in Ejo (today's Hokaido region), during which 16 people including Chief Envoy Ko In-ui (高仁義) and the eight survivors including Ko Jae-deok (高齊德) delivered a message to the Japanese Emperor in Nara from the Great King Muye, the second sovereign of Balhae. A Japanese historical document entitled *Chronicles of Japan II* (續日本紀) contains the following excerpt:

> Muye has humbly unified Jebeon (諸蕃), and has reclaimed the old territory of Goguryeo and preserved the old customs of Buyeo.

This shows that the Balhae people prided themselves on having descended from Goguryeo and Goguryeo also claimed itself as an old "extension of Buyeo."

Wonhyo, Seol Chong, and Seol Jung-eop

Buddhism flourished in the Late Silla period. As Seokguram and Bulguk Temple in Gyeongju represent this, there existed virtuous monks, Wonhyo (元曉, 617-686) or Uisang (義湘, 625-702). UNESCO has declared Seokguram of Toham Mountain in Gyeongju as well as the Palman Daejanggyeong (Tripitaka Koreana, which consists of 80,000 woodblocks of the most complete Buddhist texts) preserved in the Haein Temple from the Goryeo period in South Gyeongsang Province, as a world cultural heritage.

Uisang was a virtuous monk who studied under Zhiyan (智儼), the second leader of the Flower Garland (華嚴, Huayan in Ch.) sect of Buddhism, in China in 661; he became a star pupil along with Fazang (法藏, otherwise known as Xianshou, 賢首). He built Buseok Temple and transmitted the tenets of the Flower Garland in Silla after his return there. Wonhyo abandoned his studies in China in the middle, but he was a learned monk whose writings were well known in China as well as Japan. He based his fundamental thoughts in "the doctrine of all-encompassing harmony" which reconciled and unified all religious sects. Whereas the tenets of the Flower Garland were Buddhism for the elite, Wonhyo transmitted the Pure Land religion (淨土敎) widely by claiming that the ignorant commoners who cannot read the Buddhist scriptures could attain eternal bliss if they only recite "*Namah Amitabha*" ("I put my trust in the Amitabha Buddha").

Confucian scholars who represented the Late Silla period are Kang Su (强首) and Seol Chong (薛聰). King Muyeol (Kim Chun-chu), who achieved Silla's unification of the Three Kingdoms, favored the learned monk Wonhyo so much that his daughter Princess Yoseokgung's hand was given in marriage; Seol Chong was born from this marriage. Volume 46 of the "Record of Seol Chong" in the *Historical Records of the Three Kingdoms* contains the following description:

Chong realized the truth from birth, because his nature was sagacious. He interpreted the nine Confucian Classics (九經: *Book on Filial Piety* 孝經, the *Analects of Confucius* 論語, *The Works of Mencius* 孟子, *Book of Changes* 易經, *Book of Documents* 書經, *Book of Poetry* 詩經, *Record of Rites* 禮記, *Spring and Autumn Annals* 春秋, and *Dictionary* 爾雅) into various dialects to teach others.[1] He is upheld as the suzerain of Confucianism even today.

Seol Chong's son Seol Jung-eop (薛仲業) visited Japan in 779 as a Pangwan (middle-ranking official) of the Silla delegation (Chief Envoy: Kim Nan-son, 金蘭孫). The "Jinin of Japan" (日本國眞人) presented Pangwan Seol with the "Jeungsillasa seolpangwan siseo" (贈新羅使薛判官詩序) because he was impressed by the *Geumgang sammae gyeong nonso* (金剛三昧經論疏, Commentary on the Diamond Sutra) written by Wonhyo, Pangwan Seol's grandfather.[2] The document contains the following:

> I greatly regret not having met the Great Monk Wonhyo after reading *Commentary on the Diamond Sutra* written by him. I heard that Ambassador Seol (Jung-eop) from Silla is the grandson of the Great Monk. Although I am unable to meet the grandfather, I wrote this poem as an indication of happiness at meeting his grandson.

The Japanese document that corresponds to this excerpt from *Historical Records of the Three Kingdoms* is *Chronicles of Japan II* (續日本紀, New Year's Day in the 11th year of the reign of Emperor Konin); it contains a record of a Silla envoy being awarded a Japanese court position. More specifically, the rank of *jeong* 5-*pumha* and the rank of *jong* 5-*pumha* were supposedly granted to Chief Envoy Kim Nan-son and Daepangwan Seol Jung-eop (薩仲業), respectively.

---

[1] This referred to the Korean writing system devised by means of using Chinese characters for their sound and/or corresponding meaning values in Korean. (Ha Woo-bong)

[2] "Jinin" was the first rank of the eight ranks enacted in 684 by Emperor Temmu. (Ha Woo-bong)

The National Academy and the Reading of Texts in Three Gradations

Unification of the Three Kingdoms occurred from Kim Chun-chu's ascension to the throne as King Muyeol (武烈王, r. 654-661) and his successor King Munmu (文武王, r. 661-681). The National Academy (a Confucian school that was at one time called the National Confucian University, 太學監) was established in Silla in 682 when there was a lull in the struggle against Tang China after Goguryeo and Baekje fell. The Imperial University in China, which was established under the direction of Emperor Taizong of Tang China, was the model for the National Academy. Silla used military might to win the conflict among the Three Kingdoms, but Silla realized that it was imperative to use the principles of civilian government to bring harmony to the nation as well as foster government officials in great quantities to fill new roles.

According to "Jikgwanji" (職官志) in the *Historical Records of the Three Kingdoms*, the National Academy employed the Learned and their assistants under one *gyeong* (卿), and the students were divided into the following three courses for education:

A: *Piety, Analects of Confucius, Record of Rites,* and *Book of Changes*

B: *Piety, Analects of Confucius, Maoshi,* and *Commentary to the Spring and Autumn Annals by Zuo Qiuming*

C: *Piety, Analects of Confucius, Official History,* and *Selected Literature*

Attention should be paid to the fact that *Piety* and *Analects of Confucius* were taught among all three grades.

Furthermore, a civil service examination in the reading of texts in three gradations was created in 788 to employ bureaucrats, with the ranks divided into *sangpum* (highest grade), *jungpum* (middle grade), and *hapum* (lowest grade) based on the following subjects:

Sangpum: *Commentary to the Spring and Autumn Annals by Zuo Qiuming, Record of Rites,* one subject from *Selected Literature, Analects of Confucius,* and *Piety*

Jungpum: *Quli* (曲禮), *Analects of Confucius,* and *Piety*

Hapum: *Quli* and *Piety*

Among the three gradations, those who are well versed in the Five Confucian Classics (Book of Poetry, Book of Documents, Book of Changes, Spring and Autumn Annals, and Record of Rites), the Three Histories (Historical Records, History of the Han Dynasty, and History of the Later Han Dynasty), and the Hundred Schools of Thought were appointed by special order. Teukpum is of a much higher grade than sangpum, and it seems as if Confucian scholars who studied in Tang China belong to this group.

It can be seen that the contents of study at the National Academy in Silla and the subject of the civil service examination in the reading of texts in three gradations fundamentally began with *Quli* with emphasis on *Piety* and *Analects of Confucius* taught in all grades. *Quli* is a section in the *Record of Rites* and contains detailed information on how to write about rites. The National Academy also taught subjects on the study of arithmetic such as *Zhuijing* (綴經), *Sankai* (三開), *Jiuzhang* (九章), and *Luzhang* (六章) which were taught by the Learned and their assistants.

To enroll in the Academy, one must be below the rank of *daesa* (大舍, 13th of the 17 official ranks) without being assigned to an official post and between the ages of 15 to 30; the duration of the schooling was nine years.[3] Those who could not keep up with the teachings were expelled, but those who had the ability but were not able to perform up to expectation were allowed to stay at the Academy for longer than the nine years. The graduates of the Academy were given the ranks of either *daenama* (大奈麻) or *nama* (奈麻), the 10th and the 11th official ranks.

---

[3] Someone who had an official rank did not necessarily hold an official post. (S. Lee)

Confucianism in Late Silla went through a complete change by adopting the literary style of the flourishing Tang dynasty (712-756, during the reign of Emperor Xuanzong). This, however, simultaneously acted as the impetus that weakened the martial spirit of the Youth Corp that was visible immediately before and after the unification of the Three Kingdoms. Permeation of the trend for holding civil ideas in reverence among the nobles who revered the flourishing Tang dynasty culture came to the point where Silla called itself the "land of virtuous men." Emperor Xuanzong of Tang China wrote a parting poem to Zuozanshandaifu (左贊善大夫) Xingdao (邢璹) as follows when Xingdao was sent to Silla as an envoy:

> "Silla (calls itself) the land of virtuous men. [They are] very familiar with composition and (the usage of idiomatic phrases from the Chinese classics and scholarship), and are almost on a par with China. You were chosen as the envoy to Silla, because your scholarly attainments are many and you are well-versed in discussions. Once you reach your destination, give commentaries on the (Confucian) Classics in order for them to fully understand, and put your effort into transmitting the Classics widely. (Thereby let the people of Silla) become aware of how much Confucianism is flourishing in China."
>
> In addition, there are supposedly many Silla people who are good at the game of *go* (also known as *weiqi*), and thus Yang Ji-ying (楊季鷹), a superior player of the game of *go*, was chosen as the vice envoy.

- "Record of Silla" Old History of the Tang Dynasty

Another popular event other than the game of *go* in the aristocratic society of Gyeongju was entertaining beside a meandering stream. There is a historical spot called Poseokjeong in Gyeongju where entertainment was provided beside a curved stream. In other words, this is a game of an aristocratic bent where nobles would sit beside a curved stream with flowing water and create poems on the spot after imbibing the alcohol contained in a cup when the cup stopped in front of them. This entertainment was originated in China by the

63

master calligrapher Wang Xi-zhi (王羲之) of Nanjing in 353 in the period of Eastern Jin (317-420) after the fall of Later Han and the period of the three kingdoms (of Wei 魏, Shu 蜀, and Wu 吴). Wang Xi-zhi invited prominent people of the times and entertained them in the way of *liushang qushui* (流觴曲水), wherein people would sit beside a curved stream, drink out of a cup delivered to them via the current of the stream, and spontaneously create new poems. *"Shang"* (觴) refers to the cup floating on the water. The preface written by Wang Xi-zhi in the cursive style for the collection of these poems is the famous "Lan Ting" Prologue (蘭亭序).

Silla had a "bone-rank" system (骨品制度) that locked in the "rank" (品, status) based on "bone" (骨, bloodline). The kings and high-ranking scholar-officials of the central government in Silla and Late Silla were mostly "hallowed-bone" (聖骨, those whose parents were both of royal blood) or "true-bone" (眞骨, royal nobility wherein one of whose parents was of royal blood). The kings since the reign of King Muyeol were of true-bone, but his successors were of hallowed-bone lineage. The ranks of "head-rank 6," "head-rank 5," and "head-rank 4," which are lower than the ranks held by true-bone lineage, were filled by regular nobility. But Silla, which unified the entire territory of Baekje and part of Goguryeo, could not govern with just the scholar-officials of hallowed-bone and true-bone lineages. Thus the National Academy and the civil service examination in the reading of texts in three gradations were established to expand the source of scholar-officials for ranks below head-rank 6 to regular nobility. As mentioned above, one of the criteria for enrolling in the National Academy was that the candidate must have the rank of *daesa* or lower without being assigned to an official post, which means that these were probably the sons of regular nobility of head-rank 6 or lower.

This limited regular nobility to an assisting role in the aristocratic politics centered around hallowed-bone and true-bone lineage when the bone-rank system was maintained, although the civil service examination in the reading of texts in three gradations was the door through which regular nobility were able to be elevated. Dissatisfaction of regular nobility toward the traditional bone-rank system of Silla increased continuously and became the internal cause that accelerated the political decline in Late Silla.

Changan in Tang China Is the City for Confucian Scholars

With the placidity of a great empire after it succeeded in destroying the greatest threat in the east in the form of Goguryeo, Tang dynasty was generous in sharing its culture with Silla, which periodically sent tributes and political hostages to Tang. Tang also acknowledged Silla's widespread right to self-govern over "Xinluo Fang" (新羅坊), where many Silla people lived scattered in Chishanpu (赤山浦) and along the Shidao Bay in Shandong. Tang was generous to Japan as well despite the battle of the Baek River. Abeno Nakamaro (later renamed as Zhao Heng in Chinese) symbolizes Tang's magnanimity in that he went to Tang China in 717 during the reign of Emperor Xuanzong to learn Confucianism and advanced to the position of Emperor's Secretariat. Emperor Taizong of Tang became the supreme ruler of the Silk Road, the heart of the trade route that directly connected people and commodities of the West with Changan. General Go Seon-ji (高仙芝) led the troops in protecting the front line of the Silk Road in the reign of Emperor Xuanzong. Ko Seon-ji was born in Tang China, but his father, Ko Sa-gye (高舍雞), was a man from Goguryeo. As seen above, Tang China was an international state that accepted diverse ethnic groups and was not afraid to employ the able among them; Changan (today's Xian, 西安) as Tang's capital was an international city.

Many of Silla's Confucian scholars and Buddhist monks went to Tang to study. Silla established its National Academy much later than Goguryeo or Baekje, but sent requests to Tang from early on to permit Confucian students from Silla to study there.

In May of the 9th year of the reign of King Seondeok (640), the king requested Tang China for permission to dispatch some of the young royalty to Tang to study Confucianism there. At the time, Emperor Taizong of Tang dynasty gathered renowned Confucians from all over the globe to serve as educators, and he himself would visit the Imperial University from time to time to assign them to give lectures and hold discussions. Students who were knowledgeable about one or more of the Great Confucian Classics (*Record of Rites*, *Spring and Autumn Annals*, and *Commentary to the Spring and Autumn Annals by Zuo Qiuming*) were employed as educators. The student residence was enlarged by 1,200 units and the number of students was increased to 3,260. Thus scholars from the four corners of the earth came to the capital [of Tang] in droves. The young from Goguryeo, Baekje, Gaochang (高昌, in the Dunhwang region), and Tufan (土蕃, in Tibet) were also dispatched to Tang to study there.

- 9th year of the reign of King Seondeok, "Annals of Silla,"
  Historical Records of the Three Kingdoms

The Imperial University of Tang was truly an international school during the reign of Emperor Taizong in Changan. The Imperial University was in charge of the *Taixue guan* (太學館), *Simen guan* (四門館), *Shu guan* (書館), *Lu guan* (律館), and *Suan guan* (算館) in connection with Confucianism, and as such, the Learn and the assistants of each guan were called *Xue guan* (學館), while the chancellor (祭酒), *Siye* (司業), and *Chengbu* (丞簿) of the university were referred to as *Jian guan* (監官). The duration of the schooling was nine years except for the study of law, which lasted six years.

There is no way to know everything about the Confucian students enrolled at the Imperial University, but there are many sketchy reports about them in the historical materials of Tang and Silla. For example, the following report can be found in the "Record of Silla" in the *Old History of the Tang Dynasty*:

In May of the 5th year of Gaeseong (840), a total of 105 people including the envoy to report on the death of the king, prisoners, and students from Silla were authorized to return based on the report from Honglu Temple (鴻臚寺). (The same information is in the 2nd year of the reign of King Munseong of the "Annals of Silla," *Historical Records of the Three Kingdoms*.)

Moreover, civil service examination for foreigners called "Guest and Tributary Examination" (賓貢科) was enforced in Tang. Some of those who passed this exam returned home, but others stayed in Tang to take up government posts. Some instances of students from Silla are below:

> Among the students who were sent to Tang by Silla, not a few passed the civil service examination during their studies at the national university, and stayed in Tang to take up government posts (instead of returning home). Since Kim Un-gyeong (金雲卿) from Silla first passed the Guest and Tributary Examination in the 820s, 58 Silla students including Kim Ga-gi (金可紀), Bak In-beom (朴仁範), Choe Seung-wu (崔承佑), and Choe Chi-won (崔致遠) passed the civil examination in the 80-some years until the late Tang dynasty. Choe Chi-won is the most famous among them.

> • Piao Zhen-shi (朴眞奭), *Zongchao qingshan sanqiannian* (中朝 親善 三千年) Yanbian People Publisher, 1984

The Confucian students who returned to Silla from Tang China, including those who passed the Guest and Tributary Examination, were not that active as compared to the Buddhist monks who studied in China. Confucian scholars with the status of head-rank 6 and below could not hold an important role in the central political world under the bone-rank system. Representative of this is Choe Chi-won.

Choe Chi-won and Choe Eon-wi Win Literary Fame in China

Choe Chi-won (857-?) returned to Silla from China in 885. He is said to have left many literary works in records, but the only ones existing today are 20 volumes of *Gyewon pilgyeong* (桂苑筆耕, Plowing the Cassia Grove with a Writing Brush), and only a few of his epigraphs and poems have been transmitted. His additional name is Go-un (孤雲), and he went to Tang in 868 at the age of 12. His father was supposed to have sent him off after saying, "you are not my son if you cannot pass the civil service examination within 10 years." Choe Chi-won became a literary licentiate after he passed the Guest and Tributary Examination in 874, six years after he went to Tang China. Emperor Xizong (僖宗) of Tang China heard of his fame and appointed him to the post of Zhenyu (眞尉) in Lishui (溧水), Jiangsu (江蘇省).

Choe Chi-won gained literary fame in China in 879 during the Riot of Huangchao (黃巢), when he presented the "Xihuang-chaoshu" (檄黃巢書) while working as lieutenant of Gaopian, Bingmadoutong (高騈 兵馬都統). He was appointed to the post of Shiyushi Neigongfang (侍御史 內供奉, a type of Royal Household Attendant) for his meritorious service, and was awarded the *zijinyudai* (紫金魚袋, belt in the shape of a golden fish worn by the government officials of and above rank 3).

Choe Chi-won was appointed to the post of lecturer as well as a mid-level scholar-official at the Academy of Letters (翰林學士) upon his return to Silla at the age of 29 in 885. Politics in Silla at the time were very disordered to the point where they were difficult to control. He submitted a plan containing 10 stratagems on important issues of the times to be resolved in an attempt to save the fate of the declining country, but none of his recommendations was executed. He left the government posts and wrote his feelings in poems whenever the mood struck him as he wandered from the mountains to the ocean and used books as pillows. He retired to Haein Temple to avoid the world in his old age, and that is where he met his death.

It is said that he foretold the fall of Silla and the rise of Goryeo by leaving the following verse behind him: "Silla is a leaf turned brown, while Goryeo is a green pine tree" (鷄林黃葉 鵠嶺靑松). Choe Chi-won, who was head-rank 6, must have despaired under the bone-rank system of Silla. The only option left for him was to leave the secular world and follow "the way of a rambling, aesthetic enjoyment of nature."

Guyun (顧雲) wrote a parting poem entitled "Zengruxiange"

(贈儒仙歌) upon Choe Chi-won's return to Silla. It contains the following verses.

> He came across the ocean on a boat at the age of 12;
> 十二乘船渡海來
> His writings shook the kingdom of China;
> 文章撼動中華國
> He wrote his heart's dictate during the civil service examination;
> 十八橫行戰詞苑
> His arrow found its mark.
> 一箭射破金門策

Choe Chi-won had association with the poet Zhangqiao (張喬) and others of Tang dynasty, but his relationship with Guyun seems to have been especially close. Choe Chi-won wrote the poem "Muchunjishihuo guyunyoushi" (暮春卽事和顧雲友使) to express his sentiments about his impending departure as the day drew nearer. This is included in *Dongmunseon* (東文選, Anthology of Korean Literature), Volume 2, which is a book of poems compiled during the Joseon dynasty.

Choe Chi-won lived a life of "Pungyudo" (風流道) that combines the teachings of Confucius, Lao-zi, and Buddha rather than that of a Confucianist, and he was a literary giant who was equal to the literati of Tang China. "Pungyudo" is defined in Choe Chi-won's work, "Nannangbi seomun" (鸞郞碑序文) and is printed below.

> There is an abstruse way in this land called *pungryu*. The foundation of teaching resides within prehistory, the content of which includes the three religions of Confucianism, Buddhism, and Daoism. It directly enlightens people.

> • King Jinheung, "Annals of Silla,"
> Historical Records of the Three Kingdoms

According to his explanation, the way of a rambling, aesthetic enjoyment of nature combines the teachings of the three religions:

"Be filial at home and be loyal to the king" of Confucius, "Do not be idle, and carry out the unspoken teachings" of Lao-zi, and "Do not carry out any evilness but carry out all goodness" of Buddha.

Choe Chi-won had a younger cousin on the paternal side by the name of Choe Eon-wi (崔彦撝, 868-944). He also went to Tang China to study in 891 and passed the Guest and Tributary Examination in 906. In the next year, however, the chaotic period of civil war of the five dynasties at the end of Tang began as the dynasty of Tang China fell and changed to the Later Liang dynasty. This was very similar to the conditions of late Silla. Choe Eon-wi returned to Silla during the reign of Emperor Zhenming (貞明, 915-921) of Later Liang. He returned to Silla during the divided "Later Three Kingdoms" period. Wang Geon (王建) from a local gentry of Gaeseong seceded from the central government and established a new nation and called it "Goryeo." The weakened Silla dynasty was incorporated into Goryeo in 935.

Choe Eon-wi played an important role in the sphere of "civil administration" while holding the posts of Great Scholar (大學士) and Pyeongjangsa (平章事) at the Academy of Letters by actively assisting Wang Geon during the founding period of the new Goryeo dynasty.[4] His thoughts are deduced to be the same as or similar to those of Choe Chi-won. The lives of Choe Chi-won and Choe Eon-wi represent the despair and hope of head-rank 6 under Silla's bone-rank system.

Wang Geon was from a nameless family of local gentry in a peripheral region in aristocratic Silla. He gained the world from on top of a horse's saddle and, as a founder of a dynasty, knew the secret of scholarship and military might must go hand-in-hand in order to govern all under Heaven. Thus he embraced and gave preferential treatment to the civil ministers of Silla in order to continue the political and cultural know-how of the Silla dynasty. Choe Eon-wi is an example of this. Choe Seung-no, who will be mentioned later, also was a defector from Silla.

---

[4] Pyeongjangsa (平章事) was a government post.

5

Goryeo, the Land of Buddhism

Goryeo Dynasty and Turbulent East Asia

The sovereignty of Silla was maintained by the true-bone aristocrats instead of the hitherto hallowed-bone aristocrats. Opposition and rebellion within the aristocracy against absolute sovereign power continued to occur as of the 8th century. Confusion within the central political world began with the assassination of King Hyegong (惠恭王, r. 765-780).

In particular, Kim Heon-chang (金憲昌), the governor of Ungju, became independent of Silla during the Rebellion that bears his name (金憲昌), established the Kingdom of Jangan (長安國), and proclaimed the year as Gyeongun (慶雲). Chungcheong and Jeolla Provinces as well as parts of Gyeongsang Province cooperated with him for a time, but he was subjugated three years later. Strife among local barons in various locations occurred due to the central political world. A series of people appeared who, having left Gyeongju, the capital of Silla, established themselves elsewhere and called themselves "lord of the castle" or "general"; the order of the central government did not reach the local magnates. As well, many farmers migrated, created rebellions, or relied on local gentry for protection in order to avoid severe taxation and corvée duty.

The shifting anti-government forces gradually gathered power to form independent kingdoms, which later became three kingdoms — the so-called "Later Three Kingdoms" period. Gyeon Hwon (甄萱), one of the newly emerged powers, established himself in Mujinju (武珍州, today's Gwangju in Jeolla Province) and named his kingdom "Later Baekje." Later Baekje was the greatest threat to Silla, enough to attack Gyeongju and kill King Gyeong-ae (景哀王). Another newly emerging power was Gung Ye (弓裔) who was a prince of Silla; he formed a military consisting of farmers from Gangwon, Gyeonggi, and Hwanghae Provinces and called it "Later Goguryeo." The name of the kingdom was changed later to "Majin" (摩震) and then to "Taebong" (泰封). But Gung Ye lost the hearts of the people by calling himself a Maitreya Buddha and changing into a tyrant. He was assassinated by Wang Geon, his second-in-command; the capital was moved to Gaeseong; and the kingdom renamed "Goryeo." Wang Geon is the founder of Goryeo, and this occurred in 918.

Attention should be paid to the eruption of desire in the people from old Baekje and Goguryeo to reinstate their kingdoms as soon as the centralized authoritarian rule of the Silla dynasty relaxed, despite Silla's unification of the Three Kingdoms. A case in point is the kingdoms being named "Later Baekje" and "Later Goguryeo." Wang Geon's "Goryeo" also implies inheriting old Goguryeo.

Wang Geon schemed for the unification of Later Three Kingdoms by merging with Silla and by eliminating Later Baekje. As stated previously, the purpose of a merger with Silla was to absorb the administrative experience and culture in establishing a new dynasty. Ultimately, King Gyeongsun (敬順王), the last king of Silla, took his vassals with him and surrendered to Wang Geon in 935. Wang Geon welcomed the sovereign of Silla and his vassals. Gyeon Hwon of Later Baekje also capitulated to Goryeo when disagreement arose between him and his son Sin-geom (神劍). Wang Geon oppressed Sin-geom by military might and achieved unification of the Later Three Kingdoms in 936.

The evolving processes of Silla and Tang seemed as if the two nations were linked together: The division of Silla → Later Three Kingdoms → reunification (936) by Goryeo is very similar to that of Tang China's ruin (907) → struggles among the Five Dynasties → unification by Song dynasty (宋, 960). Sugawara Michijane, the appointed Japanese envoy to Tang China, recommended in 894 to stop sending envoys to Tang. The reason for this recommendation is rumored to have been that Japan's culture reached a level where there was nothing more to learn from Tang; but Tang's culture was the best in the world despite the deterioration of the dynasty. It appears that the recommendation to stop sending envoys to Tang was made because of symptoms that appeared due to the disturbances in the last days of Tang.

The Rebellion of Huangchao (875-884), which occurred at the end of Tang dynasty, was the decisive blow for the aristocratic society. Although Huangchao dealt in smuggled salt, he was intellectual enough to take the civil service examination even though he failed. His salt-smuggling operation had a national network in which the poor participated. The government's monopoly over salt in those days brought it a great portion of profit. The greater the profit in salt-smuggling, the greater the damage to the government. Zhu Quanzhong (朱全忠) came to the fore during the Rebellion of Huangchao which lasted for close to ten years, destroyed the Tang dynasty in 907, and founded the Later Liang dynasty. A chaotic period of Five Dynasties competing for supremacy in the region followed thereafter, which is referred to as the chaotic period of Civil War of the Five Dynasties.

Emperor Shizong of Later Zhou (後周), which was one of the Five Dynasties at the end of Tang dynasty, was a brilliant military man. Zhao Kuang-yin (趙匡胤) enjoyed the full confidence of Emperor Shizong and simultaneously held the posts of Commander-in-Chief of the Army and Commandant of the Royal Guards. The seven-year-old Emperor Gongdi (恭帝) succeeded to the throne after Emperor Shizong died without realizing his dream of uniting China. With Zhao Pu (趙普) at the head, those who served Zhao Kuang-yin in an advisory capacity started to scheme for a way to put Zhao Kuang-yin on the throne. Loyalty between the lord and his vassals dropped to a low level during this period of struggle for power.

Zhao Kuang-yin was crowned as emperor in 960 by his vassals while camping at Chen Qiao (陳橋驛) on his way to invade Liao (遼) to the north. He named the kingdom Song. This was the so-called

"Chen Qiao Incident." "Founding of Song China" (宋太祖) in *Summary of the Eighteen Histories* (十八史略, *Shibashilue* in Ch.), Volume 6, describes the scene as follows:

> The soldiers waited for morning after having reached an agreement to "enthrone Dianjian (點檢, Zhao Kuang-yin) as the emperor and then conquer the northern region." Dianjian did not know anything, for he went to sleep dead drunk. The soldiers knocked on Dianjian's bedroom door at dawn in their armor with white swords in hand and said, "We the generals do not have a ruler; it is our desire to serve the Commandant of the Royal Guards as the emperor." Dianjian was startled and attempted to get into his clothes, but his soldiers dragged him out, put the emperor's golden robe on him, stood in formation, and cheered. The soldiers suggested they parade southward (the capital of Bianjing 汴京, today's Kaifeng 開封) with Dianjian on horseback, but Dianjian refused. He entered the capital through the gates after he organized the soldiers with the sworn vows of several generals not to violate [the city] at all. Emperor Gongdi finally abdicated the throne.

Zhao Kuang-yin must have been generous and popular with his vassals because he became an emperor while he was still not fully conscious due to drinking. The founder of Song and his successor Taizong unified the Five Dynasties at the end of Tang and achieved what Emperor Shizong of Later Zhou (後周) could not.

Wang Geon's Goryeo unified the Later Three Kingdoms in 936. Big incidents that shook the constitutional system continuously arose in Japan as well in the early half of the 10th century in the form of the Shohei and Tenkei rebellions. In the Gwandong district, Taira no Masakado banished central-government-appointed Kokushi and called himself "the new emperor," as he ruled most of the Gwandong region. But the Rebellion of Taira no Masakado ended due to betrayal from within. Also in the same era, Fujiwara no Sumitomo led the pirates from Setonaikai into a riot and raided Dazaifu, but this riot was suppressed by government troops. These rebellions that occurred in concert in the east and west obviously shocked the aristocrats of the central government who were immersed in elegant dancing and singing.

The Goryeo dynasty attempted to form an alliance with Japan by sending envoys there on two occasions, but Japan turned down the suggestion each time. Japan's hypersensitivity toward Silla continued on ever since the failure at Baek River despite the change in dynasty from Silla to Goryeo. But an incident occurred to resolve such stubborn feelings of the Japanese. In 1019, 3,000 privates of unknown nationalities raided Tsushima and Ikinoshima, looted 1,300 men and women and 400 head of cattle and horses at Hakata Bay, and escaped north through the East Sea by way of the Korean peninsula. In 1018 to 1019, Goryeo was on full alert to defend itself because Khitans launched their third invasion. Rumor spread not only in the Bakufu of Kyoto but Dazaifu in Kyushu as well of the suspicion that these privates were from Goryeo. This shows there was no passage or communication between Goryeo and Japan. But the Goryeo navy recaptured 600 Japanese people from these pirates and returned them to Japan on two occasions. This is the so-called "Invasion of Toi." The meaning of "Toi" is not clear, but the Korean word for it is "doe," which is a "name" for northern raiders. In other words, "Toi" refers to the Jurchen clan. This ultimately meant that the Jurchen clan from the region of the Hamgyeong Province raided Japan by way of the East Sea.

Private traders went back and forth between Goryeo and Japan after the "Invasion of Toi," but there was still no diplomatic route between the two kingdoms. Thus the Goryeo period was one of severed diplomatic relations with Japan. "Yuan pirates" (a terminology used in Japanese history to refer to the attempted invasions of Japan by the Mongol forces of Yuan dynasty) and "Japanese marauders" occurred in this period.

Goryeosa (History of Goryeo) of 1350 states that "the Japanese marauders invaded Goseong, Junglim, and Geoje. The invasion of the Japanese marauders began in this way." Thereafter the Japanese marauders advanced to the southern part as well as the west coast of the Korean peninsula and went on rampages inland. The Goryeo government sent an envoy to General Ashikaga in Kyoto, Tandai

Imagawa, and Ryoshun of Kyushu to request that the Japanese marauders be restrained and for peaceful relationship between the two kingdoms. However, Ashikaga Bakufu's orders did not reach western Japan; besides, it was not the right time for Japan to open diplomatic relations, because it was undergoing civil war due to the division of the Southern and Northern Dynasties.

Wang Geon's Ten Articles of Instruction That Advocated the Adoption of Buddhism

Goryeo established Buddhism as the founding ideology. The founder of Goryeo, Wang Geon, wrote the Ten Articles of Instruction (訓要十條) for his descendants later in life. Clause 1 is as follows:

> The founding of our kingdom was clearly due to the divine protection of many Buddhas. Thus temples for Zen Buddhism and the Textual School of Buddhism must be built, head monks dispatched to burn incense, and each temple administered by them. A traitor may gain control and struggles over Buddhist temples may occur with the request of the monks; this must of course be prohibited.

> • April in the 26th year of the reign of Taejo,
> *History of Goryeo*

As seen above, Taejo advocated reverence for Buddhism in Clause 1.[1] Buddhism in the Goryeo period was also state-protected, as was the case in the Silla period. That did not mean that Confucian was excluded. Silla scholars such as Choe Eon-wi who returned to Silla after studying in Tang China and became mid-ranking officials at the Office of Special Advisors at the end of the Silla dynasty acted as advisors to Taejo in the founding process of Goryeo. That is the reason for Clause 10 encouraging Confucianism to be practiced at the same time as Buddhism.

---

[1] Taejo is the posthumous name for Wang Geon. (S. Lee)

When the kingdom and the family are at peace, should Chinese classics on ethics, politics, and history be widely read to use what happened in the past as a mirror for making the mind humble and cautious today? Duke of Zhou [of China] was a great sage. He recommended "Non-Idleness" (無逸, one of the sections in the *Book of Documents*) to King Cheng and admonished him. Our descendants must also draw it and hang it on the wall in order for them to reflect upon it whenever they leave or enter [the door].

Clause 10 contains a warning about the difficulty of continuing with the work of the ancestors, which is as difficult as founding a kingdom. This means that the Chinese Classics and historical documents must be read in order to continue governing the kingdom. Zhou Gonggan, the younger brother of King Wu of Zhou, taught "Non-Idleness" to young King Cheng as part of the study to become a good emperor. Wang Geon used this ancient history as an example and cautioned [others] to adopt "Non-Idleness" (do not feel pleasure comfortably) in *Book of Documents* in particular among the Chinese Classics and the Four Books as the motto.

On the other hand, Wang Geon criticized Silla's policy of overly revering Han dynasty China and emphasized its adoption in Clause 4 while taking into consideration the differences in the clime and human nature of Goryeo even if the culture on propriety and music came from China.

We the Orient have respected the style of Tang from old and followed all of its culture on propriety and music. But it cannot be carried out in the same way because of the change in region and clime as well as different human nature. It is only that the Khitans are from the land of birds and beasts. Their customs and language are different, and thus their system of attire must not be followed.

The basic doctrines of the Ten Articles of Instruction established Buddhism and Confucianism by practicing Buddhism primarily and Confucianism secondarily based on fundamental doctrines of Unified Silla. But geomancy as advocated by Do Seon (道詵, 827-898) toward the end of the Silla period is deeply ingrained in the Ten

Articles of Instruction. According to geomancy, each location contains weakness vs. strength as well as obedience vs. disobedience. A propitious site is both "strong" and "obedient," and descendants will flourish if dwellings and graves are built on such a spot. It is said, however, that a site of both weakness and disobedience brings ill luck, and as such, a temple must be built to block improvidence.

It goes without saying that Gaeseong, the capital of Goryeo, was situated on a propitious site with Mount Song'ak (松嶽) in the background, but Pyeong'yang, the capital of old Goguryeo, was considered important and its status was raised to that of western capital as stated below in Clause 5:[2]

> I accomplished a great deed with the unseen assistance of the mountains and streams of the Three Kingdoms. There are many water sources in the western capital, and thus, the western capital is the basis of the veins of our land, a land from wherein great tasks can be achieved for all times. Maintain peace by touring the region for 100 days in February, May, August, and November.

Wang Geon was fervent about the policy on the northern regions, as can be seen in the revival of Pyeong'yang (the western capital), the old capital of Goguryeo that fell into ruin during the Unified Silla period. The western capital became a stronghold for the effort to recover lost territory of old Goguryeo in the form of the policy on the northern regions. Balhae fell under the Khitan ruler Yehlu Apaochi (耶律阿保機) in 926, and the Heir Apparent Daegwanghyeon (大光顯) of the last ruler of Balhae brought tens of thousands of Balhae drifters and submitted to Goryeo in those days. Wang Geon's policy on the northern regions could only conflict with the Khitans. This is the reason for Clause 4 of the Ten Articles of Instruction being antagonistic toward the Khitans as "the land of birds and beasts."

The main purpose of the Khitans was to advance to the Hwabei region [in China]. This was the time of the civil war period of the

---

[2] Song'ak is the name of a mountain in Pyeong'yang, North Korea. (S. Lee)

Five Dynasties. The Khitans finally took over 16 of the prefectures (including Yunzhou and Yanzhou in those days but Beijing and Datong today) of Yanyun (燕雲) in the Hwabei region from the Later Jin dynasty in 936. The Khitan cavalry was the greatest northern threat to Goryeo and Song China. Therefore Goryeo agreed to send tributes to Song China and accepted Song's calendrical method early in 936, because its relationship with Song China was considered of the utmost importance.

This geomancy, however, absurdly left behind the root cause of discrimination against regions due to Clause 6 of the Ten Articles of Instruction as stated below:

> The shape of the mountains and the appearances of the land south of Chahyeon (車峴, the Charyeong Mountain Range) outside the Gongju River gives the feeling of going contrary [to nature], and the people are also contrary. There is the possibility of leading a rebellion or perpetrating offenses against the royal family with bitterness united if the people from this region manage to participate in state affairs through marriage to the maternal relatives of the queen or the royal family. Moreover, they were slaves of government offices or temples, the poor (underprivileged people like the slaves) of Jin (津) and Yeok (驛), and they will bring calamity by preying on the powerful and by bringing chaos to politics with artful words. Do not give them work by assigning positions to them even if they are law-abiding people.

The region south of Chahyeon refers to North Jeolla Province south of the Charyeong Mountain Range, i.e., the territory of Later Baekje. I was able to get a bird's-eye view of this region as I flew over this territory several times from Yeosu, the southern-most part of South Jeolla Province, to Gimpo Airport in Seoul; the river currents of this region are the slowest in the Korean peninsula, the plains wide, and it is the best source of food because the mountains and the ocean provide food in abundance. Wang Geon's intense abhorrence of and suspicion of Later Baekje may stem from the fact that the Silla dynasty of the Gyeongsang Province surrendered to him, but Later Baekje of the Jeolla Province fought until it was overpowered by

Goryeo. The sentence that includes "with bitterness united" is an indicator of this. Paradoxically, it also tells of the fact that there was a whirlpool of bone-deep bitterness against "betrayal" in this region that had to be controlled with military power even after Wang Geon defeated the Later Baekje.

Appointing Men of Merit Extensively through the Civil Service Examination

Wang Geon, who founded the Goryeo dynasty, was not of the aristocracy from the end of the Silla dynasty. It is difficult to know the truth because the backgrounds of dynastic founders are usually embellished. He seems to have come from a provincial magnate family in Gaeseong that had managed to accumulate money and military power by being involved in maritime trade from Hyeolgujin (穴口鎭, today's Ganghwa) at the mouth of the Imjin River. In this sense the Goryeo dynasty was established by denying the bone-rank system of Silla dynasty as the Song dynasty in China denied the aristocracy of the Tang dynasty. Toward the end of Silla, local gentry independent of the centralized government defended regional authority in the regions of Ju and Jin of the Later Three Kingdoms period. The Goryeo dynasty was very unstable in the beginning because it was founded amidst the balance of power among these local gentry. This instability is revealed clearly in the dispute surrounding the succession of Hyejong (惠宗) and Jeongjong (定宗) to the throne after Taejo's reign.

It was necessary to strengthen the sovereignty through centralization of power in order to stabilize the dynasty. To do so, confrontations with meritorious vassals who were indispensable in founding the dynasty were unavoidable. Fierce opposition was naturally expected. These meritorious vassals were past comrades-in-arms to the fourth king, Gwangjong (光宗, r. 949-975), who spent much time on the battlefields with his father, Taejo, to achieve unification of the Later Three Kingdoms.

80

Gwangjong enjoyed reading *Zhenguan zhengyao* by Emperor Taizong of Tang China as part of his study to become a sovereign. Taizong (Li Shi-min 李世民, r. 626-649) of Tang China not only helped his father Gaozu (高祖, Li Yuan 李淵) found the Tang dynasty, but he continued with his father's work and effected great accomplishments as the second emperor. [3] *Zhenguan zhengyao* is a collection of questions and answers he had had with his vassals; it was compiled by a historian by the name of Wu Jing (吳兢) as a textbook for studying to become a good sovereign. Gwangjong preferred to read *Zhenguan zhengyao*, probably because he inherited his father Taejo's goal and was conscious of his role in achieving the tasks his father set out to accomplish.

The first item enacted by Gwangjong was the Slave Review Act of 956. During the chaotic period of the Later Three Kingdoms, local gentry created small semi-autonomous fiefs and wielded great power independent of the central government; the basis for their economic and military power was in making slaves out of prisoners of war and drifters. The Slave Review Act investigated the status of the slaves and recovered the status of those who were originally drifters.

Moreover, the civil service examination system started in 958, which has had a great meaning in the history of Korean Confucianism. This national test, through which men of scholarly attainment were appointed to government office with the concept of selection based on topics, continued for almost 940 years until its discontinuance during the time of the Gabo Reform Movement of 1894.

Implementation of the civil service examination system was an important measure for promoting the descendants of landed vassals who rendered meritorious service at the time of founding the kingdom by absorbing them as well as for establishing a new relationship between sovereign and vassals based on Confucian ethics.

---

[3] Li Shi-min (李世民) was the birth name of Emperor Taizong, and Li Yuan was the birth name of Emperor Gaozu of Tang dynasty. (S. Lee)

This was a period before the founding of Song dynasty, China. The Goryeo dynasty sent and received envoys with the Five Dynasties and with the Later Tang dynasty in particular. Shuangji (雙冀) came with the envoy from Later Tang but became a Goryeo subject upon his inability to return to his homeland due to an illness. Gwangjong appointed Shuangji to the post of a mid-level bureaucrat at the Academy of Letters in the capacity of an examiner, and began a national examination that appointed scholar-officials through the Composition Examination course (製述科, another name for Literary Licentiate Examination) based on rhetoric (詞章), such as poetry (詩), odes in the form of a Chinese poetic genre (賦), eulogy (頌), and planning (策), as well as the Classics Examination course (明經科) based on the Five Classics containing *Book of Changes*, *Official History*, *Book of Poetry*, *Record of Rites*, and *Spring and Autumn Annals*. The Composition Examination course was considered important especially in the Goryeo period, because it took after the civil service examination system of Tang China which emphasized rhetoric. In other words, the civil service examination begun by Emperor Wen who founded the Sui dynasty included three courses: the Licentiate, Classics examination, and Literary Licentiate. There were two courses, Classics examination and Literary Licentiate, in the days of the Tang dynasty, and more emphasis was put on the Literary Licentiate centered around rhetoric than the Classics Examination course centered around the Five Classics – as desired by Empress Wu Zetian (則天武后), wife of Emperor Gaozong of Tang China.

Be that as it may, this was the birth of the *sadaebu* class that is comprised of bureaucrats limited to one generation of status as an alternative to customary aristocracy. [4] A protected appointment system (蔭敍制), however, was created as a compromise for the vassals who rendered meritorious service during the founding of the kingdom, wherein one of the offspring of bureaucrats holding the rank of 5-*pum* or above was appointed to a government post without having to pass the civil service examination.

---

[4] A *sadaebu* was a high-ranking scholar-official. (S. Lee)

Choe Seung-no (崔承老, 927-989) from Gyeongju in Silla of old was a veteran retainer who advised many generations of kings from Taejo, the founder of Goryeo, to the sixth king, Seongjong. He presented "Current Affairs (時務) Clause 28" at the request of King Seongjong in 982 when the king ascended to the throne. In the introduction, Choe Seung-no frankly commented on the administrative achievements of past generations of kings in order to aid Seongjong's morality.

According to Choe Seung-no's comment on Gwangjong, the latter was a wise ruler whose policies were clear and fair and whose punishment and rewards were not confused for the first eight years. But he believed in Buddhism in a misguided manner and turned into a tyrant who wasted the kingdom's finances and sentenced "old retainers and veteran generals" and their entire families to death during his last 16 years of reign.

In short, Gwangjong's policy of centralization of power resulted in taking away the vested rights of old retainers and veteran generals, i.e., vassals who rendered meritorious service during the founding of the kingdom, which created furious resistance on their part. Gwangjong in turn oppressed them with cruelty. He believed in Buddhism erroneously because he had to rely on the power of the Buddhist temples in order to fight against the old retainers and veteran generals.

The civil service examination system ultimately was characterized as excluding old retainers and veteran generals who were of rebel troops or mercenaries and instead absorbed the 6-*dupum* aristocrats of the end of the Silla period who were restricted from entering the political world due to the bone-rank system. Gwangjong, who was opposed by the old retainers and veteran generals, appointed the Buddhist monk Hyegeo (惠居) to the post of the Most Reverend Priest and Danmun as the king's teacher. Gwangjong was also the one who established the state examination for Buddhist monks (僧科) as a civil service examination that regulated the qualifications of Buddhist monks. The best ranks for Buddhist monks based on the state examination were the Great Seon Mentor (大禪師) among Zen Buddhists and the Patriarch (僧統) among non-Zen Buddhists. This is because the greatest honor of the Most Reverend Priest and the king's teacher were chosen from these two ranks.

The Trend of Disdaining Military Officials Blooms

On top of the Composition Examination and the Classics Examination courses as part of Erudite Examination, there were Miscellaneous Examinations on practical as well as professional matters, such as Legal Examination course (明法業), Mathematics course (明算業), Medical course (醫業), Fortunetelling course (卜業, astrological astronomy), and Geography course (地理業), among the civil service examinations of the Goryeo period; the status of the applicants was lower in comparison to that of the applicants for the Composition Examination and Classics Examination courses. Moreover, most of the bureaucrats were made up of those who passed the Composition Examination course (or Literary Licentiate Examination), of which the rhetoric was a part of its test subject because this course was emphasized rather than the Classics Examination course, of which the Confucian Classics was part of its test subject. In other words, the civil service examination in Goryeo and Joseon differed in that the rhetoric was superior to the Confucian Classics in the civil service examination of the Goryeo period, whereas the civil service examination in the Joseon period emphasized the Confucian Classics rather than the rhetoric. In this sense, the civil service examination of Goryeo was similar to that of Tang dynasty China, and the civil service examination of Joseon was similar to that of Song dynasty China.

Qualification for the civil service examination was open to all freemen except for those originating from the residential district for the outcast or the lowborn, which included the disobedient of the five elements, the five low-born groups, the traitors, and the unfilial. Due to practical issues, however, it was realistically impossible for those not of the small and mid-sized landowner class or higher to study for the civil service examination.

There were Erudite Examination and Miscellaneous Examinations to rise in status as a government official and even a state examination for Buddhist monks to become a Buddhist monk, but Military Examination was missing. The system of the two orders of scholar-official and military-official of the *yangban* began in Korean history during the Goryeo period. The dual order system containing the scholar-official order and the military-official order were divided and solidified in 976 when the Stipend Land Law (田柴科) of paying government officials based on rank with the revenue from the land was implemented. Encouragement of scholarship and disdain of military arts within the civil service examination resulted in the elimination of military arts. This is presumed to have been a movement thought out carefully against old retainers and veteran generals who had private armies at the founding of the kingdom.

Therefore, posts of the military official order were probably a way through which government offices were appointed by customarily protected appointments or soldiers who rendered distinguished military service. This was the cause of the scholar-official order's arrogance and disdain toward the military official order. To Goryeo and Song China, the cavalry of the Khitans was a great threat from the northern region. Emperor Shengzong (聖宗, r. 982-1031) of Liao invaded Goryeo on three occasions — in 993, 1010, and 1018 — concerning the territorial rights to the land west of the Amnok River. During the second invasion of 1010 especially, the invaders only retreated after Gaegyeong was burned down completely by the king of Goryeo in fleeing to the southern region of Naju.[5]

Goryeo ultimately regained peace in 1021 by deciding to come under the investiture of Liao. The Jurchens who were under the control of Liao, however, declared independence, called their kingdom Jin (金), destroyed Liao in 1125, and emerged as a new threat in the north. Confronting such a northern threat with the principles of civilian government was of course impossible. To protect the safety of Goryeo from the turbulence of the dynastic transition from Liao

---

[5] Gaegyeong was another name for Gaeseong, the capital of Goryeo. (S. Lee)

to Jin, the Military Arts Program (武學齋) was established as an educational institute to foster military officials, and the Military Examination (武科) was implemented as part of the civil service examination during the reign of King Yejong (睿宗, r. 1106-1122) when a debate arose on the issue of whether "the combination of scholarship and military arts is the root of national enlightenment" or not. But the Military Arts Program was discontinued in 1133 because of fear that quarrels might arise between the military officials and the scholar-officials due to the emergence of the former.

It was natural for the discontent of the military officials to grow, and there was no way for their morale to improve under the disdain of the talented literary scholar-officials. From the start of the founding of a nation, there are rebellions led by military officials resulting in the emergence of regimes of military officials. The principles of civilian government wherein scholarship was encouraged and military arts scorned continued in Goryeo to the end of the Joseon dynasty. Thus the disastrous habit of depending on external powers due to neglect in building autonomous military power has lasted until today, along with submissive diplomacy toward the Chinese dynasties to maintain the safety of the kingdom.

Gwangjong enacted the civil service examination system in order to correct the "weak ruler, strong vassals" sovereignty established at the early stages of founding the kingdom on the one hand, but on the other hand the system also acted as a prescription of poison that eliminated the old retainers and veteran generals who were comrades-in-arms of the founder Taejo. This could not be done within one generation, of course, and the foundation of the dynasty finally stabilized in the reign of the sixth king, Seongjong, after repeated advances and lapses.

While Taejo was the founder of a dynasty through "military arts," Gwangjong could only follow the achievements of his father through "scholarship." There are many instances of dynasties lasting for only a short period due to failing to uphold the achievements of the predecessors. A typical example of failure is Emperor Yang of Sui dynasty in China, and Taizong of Tang China is an example of its success. Gwangjong, who was evaluated by Choe Seung-no to enjoy reading Taizong's *Zhenguan zhengyao*, symbolizes the difficulty in continuing with the achievements of the predecessors whereby he could be considered a wise ruler or a despotic ruler.

There was a similar problem when Zhao Kuang-yin became the founder of Song dynasty China in 960. There were many upper-classmen and brothers who were his blood brothers during the five dynasties at the end of Tang dynasty when the local rulers fought for power. They were all ambitious. In an advisory capacity, Zhao Pu counseled Zhao Kuang-yin that taking possession of their military power was of priority. Zhao Kuang-yin welcomed the military groups when he became the new emperor, fed them alcohol, and humored and pacified them with cunning words — all the while dismembering the groups' military power and posting them to remote regions. This is the famous legend of the unparalleled hard-drinker Zhao Kuang-yin's "laying down of military power for alcohol" (杯酒釋兵權).

But it was in the second generation that Taizong (r. 976-997) was able to realize his predecessor's ambition after dismantling the commanders-in-chief of provincial armies. He created a new frame-work for the dynasty by selecting bureaucrats who were subservient to the emperor through greatly expanding the civil service examina-tion to mass-produce Confucian vassals to replace commanders-in-chief of provincial armies. Moreover, he mobilized learned men from the five fallen kingdoms at the end of Tang dynasty to participate in great compilation projects, such as the 1,000-volume *Imperial Readings of the Taiping Xingguo Era* (太平御覽), in order to absorb them into the new system by diffusing their discontent. Emperors in Chinese History who have achieved their predecessors' dreams carried out extensive cultural projects, such as the *Interpretation of the Five Confu-cian Classics* commissioned by Emperor Taizong of Tang dynasty and the *Yongle Encyclopedia* (永樂大典) commissioned by Emperor Yongle of Ming dynasty. Goryeo's Gwangjong ruled from 949 to 975, before the reign of Taizong of Song. But the commonality in both rulers opting for the civil service examination as a means to carry out their predecessors' dreams is unexplainable.

6

Seongjong Elevates Confucianism

History of Goryeo and Essential History of Goryeo

Before discussing the main subject, it is best to briefly examine *Goryeosa* (高麗史, History of Goryeo) and *Goryeosa jeolyo* (高麗史節要, Essential History of Goryeo), which were compiled by the Joseon government to chronicle Goryeo history after its fall.

Just as the Goryeo government compiled *Historical Records of the Three Kingdoms* to chronicle the history of the preceding dynasty, Joseon also commenced the compilation of the history of Goryeo in the beginning of its own dynasty. When a new dynasty compiles the history of the previous dynasty, however, it is only natural that various evaluations are made about the preceding dynasty in order to leave a record of justification for the new dynasty.

Goryeoguksa (高麗國史, National History of Goryeo) was compiled in the 4th year of the reign of the founder of the Joseon dynasty (1395), with Jeong Do-jeon (鄭道傳) and Jeong Chong (鄭摠) leading the effort. There was a debate on impartiality being compromised because Jeong Do-jeon participated deeply in the political history at the end of Goryeo, despite the fact that he was a Confucian scholar who was also the premier vassal of merit through his act of declaring the military leader Yi Seong-gye as king. Jeong Do-jeon was later killed by Taejong Yi Bang-won (李芳遠), the third king and political opponent.

This will be discussed later when dealing with the problems of the transitional period from the Goryeo dynasty to the Joseon dynasty. Whatever the case may be, Taejong ordered Ha Ryun (河崙) and others to revise *National History of Goryeo*. What exists today as *History of Goryeo* is the annalistic and biographical style of chronicle that was revised in 1451 after going through many complications with Kim Jong-seo (金宗瑞) and Jeong In-ji (鄭麟趾) leading the task. The content of the narrative of the annalistic and biographical style emphasizes man.

A historical document focusing on the chronological style entitled *Essential History of Goryeo* was completed in 1454 with Kim Jong-seo and Jeong In-ji leading the task as well. The annalistic and biographical style and the chronological style both have advantages and disadvantages, but these two books supplemented the advantages and disadvantages of each other.

Whereas the historical facts of previous kings were dealt within the "Bongi" ("Benji" in Ch.) in *Historical Records of the Three Kingdoms*, they were dealt within the "Sega" ("Shijia" in Ch.) in *History of Goryeo*. "Benji" has contained the history of sovereigns while "Shijia" has contained the history of feudal lords (kings) in authentic history of China since Sima Qian's *Historical Records*. According to *Jin goryeosa jeon* (進高麗史箋, Progressive History of Goryeo) by Jeong In-ji, "Usage of 'Bongi' was avoided and 'Sega' was used instead to show the importance of justification." In other words, "Sega" was used to lower the status of "kings" of Goryeo in contrast to that of "emperors" of China.

When the tones of the two historical documents are examined, *History of Goryeo* reflects the relative effort to objectively record the historical facts of the times, whereas *Progressive History of Goryeo* reflects the deep reverence for Confucianism upheld by the history officials who participated in the compilation. In other words, comments of "the history official said" are inserted in many places in *Progressive History of Goryeo*. And severe criticism against Buddhism and Daoism as cults is then given.

There are not a few compiled records of posthumous chronicles of the reign of generations of kings in the Goryeo period. But as long as *Goryeo wangjo sillok* (高麗王朝實錄, Veritable Records of the

Goryeo Dynasty) compiled with those records is not extant, these two historical documents are in fact the basic historical materials for research on Goryeo history. Parts missing from these two historical documents should be supplemented through private collections and/or epigraphs.

Choe Seung-no Criticizes Buddhism

If the Ten Articles of Instruction by Wang Geon is the basic principle of the founding period of Goryeo, then the Twenty-Eight Items on Current Issues (時務二十八條) left behind by veteran civilian official Choe Seung-no is important in providing great principles during the period of continuing with the unfinished work of predecessors. Seongjong, the sixth king (r. 982-997), realized the greatness of his predecessors by appointing Choe Seung-no as the Munhwasijung (門下侍中).[1]

Choe Seung-no was a 6-*dupum* aristocrat born in Gyeongju, the capital of Silla. He moved to Gaegyeong when King Gyeongsun as the last king of Silla defected to Goryeo as mentioned before. At the age of 12 when he read *Analects of Confucius* in front of Goryeo's Taejo, Choe Seung-no was praised and chosen as a student of Wonbongseong (元鳳省, a government office in charge of education). To Choe Seung-no who personally experienced the periods from Taejo to the reign of the sixth king of the Goryeo dynasty, establishing and continuing on with the works of predecessors made up contemporary history itself.

At the time of ascending to the throne, King Seongjong required government officials of 5-*pum* or higher at the capital and various strategic locations to submit sealed opinions. Choe Seung-no's Twenty-Eight Items on Current Issues was submitted in response to this request. There is a rather long foreword to the Twenty-Eight Items on Current Issues in Choe Seung-no's appeal to the king in

---

[1] Munhwasijung was the highest post in Goryeo government and early Joseon government. (S. Lee)

which he reminisces of Taejo's founding a kingdom and comments on successive administrations of Hyejong, Jeongjong, Gwangjong, and Gyeongjong thereafter ("Choe Seung-no," Yeoljeon, *History of Goryeo*).

In the beginning of the foreword, Choe Seung-no points out the fact that Wu Jing compiled a political question-and-answer collection with Emperor Taizong of Tang China called *Zhenguan zhengyao*, and recommended Hyeonjong to follow "the politics of Taizong." He expected Seongjong to complete the task of stabilizing the Goryeo dynasty as set out by his predecessors through continuation of the great task, as did Taizong. His review of the four reigns (Hyejong, Jeongjong, Gwangjong, and Gyeongjong) following Taejo was to "warn Seongjong about today by using the past as a mirror." Then what was the ultimate image of a ruler Choe Seung-no expected from Seongjong?

> Your Majesty's adoption and execution of the goodness of (preceding kings) and caution over their badness, as well as excluding work that is not urgent and stopping efforts that are not profitable, should make Your Majesty on high comfortable and His people on low rejoice by Your Majesty's actions. Think of the beauty of perfection with the mind that desires to do the beginning well, and reverently should not rest even if every single day is to be rested. Your Majesty should not think highly [of Yourself] even if [Your Majesty] did become a ruler due to being held in high esteem. Fortune will come by itself without pursuing it and misfortune will disappear by itself without having to wish it away if only affection for humbling the self is strengthened and the mind that worries over the people not discontinued. How can [Your Majesty's] lifespan not last for 10,000 years and [Your Majesty's] reign not continue for 100 generations?

The phrase "misfortune will disappear by itself without having to wish it away" from the excerpt above is an admonition for the king not to become immersed in Buddhism. Only 22 of the Twenty-Eight Items on Current Issues presented to the king by Choe Seung-no remain as a record. The other six Items were dispersed and lost during the Gyeongsul Invasion (庚戌兵亂, Invasion of Gaegyeong by the Khitans in 1010).

The basic contents of the existing 22 Items are on how to strengthen the sovereignty in order to realize centralization to even the lowest officials in the provinces. The two obstacles to realizing this are the powers held by the temples and local gentry.

The most emphasis among the 22 Items was on criticizing Buddhism. Moreover, the criticisms were not about Buddhism itself but the tyranny of the monks or waste of state finance on Buddhist events. As mentioned previously, the first of the Ten Articles of Instruction emphasizes "Buddhist nation" as the founding ideology of the Goryeo dynasty, and at the same time warns of the bad influence of Namseol Temple in the second Article.

> Several temples were all built after Doseon (道詵) performed divination on the mountains' and streams' obedience or disobedience to nature. Doseon said, "If you build a temple at a random location not selected and blessed by me, the reign of a king will not be everlasting because the auspicious effect of the site will be destroyed." I am concerned that in the future the kings, barons, queens, and courtiers will each build more temples by claiming that they are places of prayer. Silla fell because Buddhist temples were built left and right at the end of Silla, and the auspicious effect of the sites was damaged. Thus precaution must be taken.

> - 26th year of the reign of Taejo, "Sega," *History of Goryeo*

The result, however, was not the same as cautioned by Taejo. Let us look at two examples pointed out by Choe Seung-no on Buddhist abuse. Instances of the tyranny of monks (Item 10) are as follows:

> Your humble servant has heard that monks staying at inns and stations when traveling back and forth between districts and counties have whipped and scolded government officials and the populace [of the regions] for not greeting or receiving them properly. The abuse is great, because the government officials and the populace question that this is their duty but are afraid to

92

speak out. This abuse must be eliminated by prohibiting groups of monks from lodging at inns and stations from now on.

The case of the Namseol Temple (Item 16) is as follows:

Many build temples as each individual pleases under the justification of performing good according to the custom of the secular world. Moreover, the monks of the capital and the provinces requisitioned the populace from powerful government officials of the provinces and districts and forced them to construct temples because of the necessity for private residences. That took precedence over public service; the people suffered greatly due to this. I implore you to strictly forbid this, and further, to severely punish [participating] government officials and eliminate forced labor of the populace by instructing Annam (安南, military administrative organ to control Later Baekje of old) and Andong (安東, military administrative organ to control Silla of old) to investigate [the situation] in faraway places and instructing Eosadoseong (御事都省) to examine nearby places.[2]

Moreover, the important issue is that the king, who should be instructing the direction of affairs of state, was confusing Buddhist affairs and government affairs, and was wasting government funds while not paying attention to government affairs due to immersion in Buddhist affairs. These were pointed out in the foreword that evaluated past kings. In short, the purpose of Choe Seung-no's criticism of Buddhism is to support the first and carry out the second of Taejo's Ten Articles of Instruction. The only difference is that Choe Seung-no commented on current issues, i.e., the greatest issues confronting political life, while Taejo linked the temple of Namseol with geomancy and [used it to] caution [his subjects].

Another obstacle to centralization of power was the local gentry. As mentioned before, powerful magistrates of provinces and districts conspired with the monks to force people to construct temples. In order to prevent that, magistrates appointed by the king must be stationed in the provinces and orders from the central government

---

[2] Eosadoseong was a high-ranking post. (S. Lee)

must be made to penetrate to the regional government. Item 7 points out the following:

> The task of administering to His people by the one who is king is not the same as performing ordinary tasks at individual houses. Thus magistrates must be divided and dispatched to look out for the interest of the people. Your Majesty's ancestor (Taejo) attempted to establish regional offices (provincial offices) after the unification of the Later Three Kingdoms but did not have the time to do so due to the confusion inherent in the beginning [of the kingdom]. Reflecting quietly on this now, the provincial magnates infringe on the people and commit atrocities under the false pretext of public duty; the people are in a state where they cannot survive. I implore Your Majesty to establish regional offices. Although officials cannot be dispatched to all regions at once, first assign one government official for a combination of ten or so provinces and counties; then assign two to three government officials for each regional official and entrust them to look after the people.

The fact that Gwangjong instigated the civil service examination was mentioned in the previous chapter. Not another word is needed to clarify that this was a measure to recruit new government officials with merit who will replace the "*hyangho*" (鄕豪, local gentry). But that number was very limited because an organized education system had to be established then to provide the necessary government officials to be dispatched to the central government as well as the provincial government. The civil service examination and education are like two wheels of a cart. An organized education system that could train talented people in mass quantity to be dispatched to various regional offices in each province was not established at that time. This was one of the important tasks to be realized from this point forward.

Buddhism for Moral Training, Confucianism for Statecraft

Original Confucianism is a system of thought that integrates ethics and politics. Thus "self-cultivation" in the private sphere of moral

94

training is a prerequisite for "governing others" in the public sphere of politics. But Buddhism does not contain political thought. Taejo already pushed forward with his ideology of a Buddhist nation in the first of the Ten Articles of Instruction. At the same time, he urged the simultaneous learning of Chinese Classics and historical documents in Article 10. In other words, the pillar of founding ideology was Buddhism, but the political thought that supplemented it was Confucianism. Choe Seung-no desired to separate Buddhist affairs of faith in the private sphere from government affairs in the public sphere to prevent confusion in the public and private spheres based on division of the role of each. He states as below in the 20th of the Twenty-Eight Items on Current Issues:

> Honoring and believing in the Buddhist canons cannot be said to be not good. But even if the sovereign, *sadaebu* (scholar-officials), and the common people are said to be for public morality, it is not the same. The sufferings of the common people are strengths and what tools they use are personal possessions. Therefore abuse does not extend to others. But the people must toil and the possessions of the people are used in the case of a sovereign. Emperor Wudi of Liang dynasty China in the old days gained the goodwill of his common people through his nobility as son of Heaven, but all people considered this to be incorrect. The evils did not reach the subjects and the people, because the sovereign cogitated deeply on this and referred to the *Doctrine of the Mean* (中庸). According to what Your Majesty's servant has heard, a person's happiness and misery as well as fortune and poverty are all assigned at the time of birth. This should truly be accepted in purity. Revering Buddhism is to plant the karma for afterlife, but the returned gain from that is little, to say the least. Thus, the key to governing the kingdom is not there.
>
> Moreover, the three religions (Confucianism, Buddhism, and Daoism) each have professed deeds, but they should not be confused as being one. Practicing Buddhism is the foundation of moral training, and practicing Confucianism is the foundation of statecraft. Moral training is for the afterlife, and statecraft is the work of today. Today is near and the afterlife far; is it not wrong to throw away that which is near and pursue that which is far?

What he advocates, in other words, is to prevent confusion between the two by clarifying the division of role between Buddhism for moral training and Confucianism for statecraft, and between Buddhism for the afterlife and Confucianism for the present. In comparison to Buddhism being the main and Confucianism the follower in Taejo's Ten Articles of Instruction, Confucianism for the present is the main and Buddhism for the afterlife is the follower here.

As the Goryeo dynasty neared its final days, there was no help for the decadence of Buddhism that received hearty protection from the state. This ultimately turned into Confucians proscribing Buddhism and the emergence of the Joseon dynasty, but the indications were already developing. But Choe Seung-no was a scholar as well as a politician who practiced both Confucianism and Buddhism in affirming Buddhism for moral training as well as Confucianism for statecraft. Unlike the School of Master Zhu at the end of the Goryeo dynasty that rejected Buddhism itself as a cult, he merely excluded the cohesion between Buddhism and politics while considering the realization of the Confucian political ideal.

The State Considers the People Its Foundation

Seongjong ascended to the throne in 982, 46 years after unification of the Later Three Kingdoms by Taejo in 936. King Gwangjong was not able to complete the founder's task; thus Choe Seung-no presented the Twenty-Eight Items on Current Issues to King Seongjong in his expectation that the new king would continue the task. Choe Seung-no criticized the monks as well as local gentry out of his desire to strengthen and look after the welfare of the people who form the foundation for the dynasty.

Taejo emphasized "Non-Idleness" contained in *Book of Documents,* in particular in Article 10 of the Ten Articles of Instruction. He advocated agriculturalism, meaning that the monarch must know of and personally experience the sufferings of the peasants. "Non-Idleness" in *Book of Documents* begins with the following words:

Duke of Zhou said, "Ahhh. A man of virtue must consider as his foundation the lack of pursuing pleasure. He must know the difficulties of farming and turn from pleasure as well as understand how much suffering the common people are going through. When the common people are examined, the parents are hard at farming but their sons do not know the difficulties of farming and instead seek pleasure; moreover, they say preposterous things while pursuing pleasure. They say scornful things about their parents — that the older people do not know how to seek pleasure."

"Non-Idleness" is, in short, a caution to "have concern first for the worries of the world and find joy in pleasure last." Throughout all ages and kingdoms, failure to continue with the predecessors' great works was due to forgetting the tension and difficulties experienced during the founding of dynasties and instead comfortably enjoying pleasures as those in a privileged position. Admonitions contained in "Non-Idleness" that Taejo wrote for his descendants also apply today.

In the spring of his second year as king, Seongjong "personally tilled the royal field and prayed to Shennong (神農) and worshiped Houji (后稷).[3] (The king) praying for bountiful harvest and tilling the royal field began from this (second year of the reign of Seongjong, *Essential History of Goryeo*)." "Shennong" is China's legendary sovereign who taught the people to farm. "Houji" is also a legendary figure who was the minister of agriculture during the period of Shun [of Yin dynasty China]. In other words, the purpose of "tilling the royal field" is for the king to personally experience the sufferings of the farmers and pray for a bountiful harvest by offering grains from there to Shennong and Houji, the gods of farming.

Furthermore, not only did Seongjong appoint Choe Seung-no to the post of Munhasirang Pyeongjangsa (門下侍郎平章事), he delivered the following message in his fifth year:

People are to be considered the foundation of the government, and the people will consider food to be the Heaven. To gain the

---

[3] Houji was a government post given to Ji Qi (姬棄) for assisting Shun of Yin dynasty China by teaching the people to farm. (S. Lee)

hearts of all people, three farming days (farming in spring, summer, and autumn) should not be taken away. The 12 prefects and the divisional commanders of all provinces should stop all sundry tasks and attend only to the task of encouraging farming from now until autumn. I will in truth dispatch my royal ministers to examine the diligence and idleness of the governors based on the conditions of the plains, and rewards or punishments will be doled out accordingly.

> • 5th year of the reign of Seongjong,
> *Essential History of Goryeo*

But promotion of agriculture and encouragement of scholarship constitute the two nuclei of Confucian politics. As can be seen in the royal message, it was necessary to reorganize the education system for training large numbers of government officials who would serve the king in local governments in order to realize the intentions of the king. Seongjong was greatly resolute on this issue.

Schools Must Be Established

Seongjong considered it imperative to spread Confucian virtue for centralization of power, which is the apex of sovereignty. Thus he commanded as follows in the ninth year of his reign: "...the foundation for statecraft is nothing more than filial piety. Send the royal ministers to the six provinces to find filial sons, filial grandsons, considerate husbands, and virtuous women." He commended those who fit into the four categories, appointed them to official ranks and handed out awards thereafter. The king issued the following message about these commendations:

> The king and the queen are the head of the people, and people are the heart of the lord. Fortunate are we if they perform good deeds, and worrisome are we if they conduct evil deeds. Highlighting filial piety is to reveal the mind of beautiful customs. Even the foolish people of the fields strive to be filial; how can government officials and gentlemen of virtue be lazy in serving

their ancestors? A filial son of a family invariably becomes a loyal vassal of the state. It is my hope that many scholars will repeat my words and think about them.

> • 9th year of the reign of Seongjong,
> *Essential History of Goryeo*

According to this message, the intention of the king was to make loyal vassals by commending the filial among the common people. In other words, the principle of national unity is to "make a harmonious home and serve the state," and the key was the relationship between ruler and vassal joined by Confucian virtue.

Seongjong established 12 prefects throughout the kingdom and demoted the hitherto local gentry to local functionaries. The sons of local functionaries from all provinces, districts, and counties were called to the capital to be educated in the second year of the reign of Seongjong (983). In addition, an attempt was made to establish schools to train capable people and recruit officials of merit from among them through the civil service examination in order to promote "the custom of the Duke of Zhou."

However, students in the capital who wanted to go back to their hometowns appeared in succession in the fifth year of the reign of Seongjong. Therefore, 1,400 rolls of cloth were awarded to 207 students who returned home, whereas 106 mourner's hats and 265 bags of rice were awarded to the 53 students who decided to stay in the capital. Worried that those who returned home would not continue studies without teachers, people who were knowledgeable in Confucian Classics and medicine were recruited as the Learned of the Chinese Classics and the Learned of Medicine, respectively, and each dispatched to the 12 prefects in the next year. Moreover, they were to recommend those talented in the Confucian Classics or medicine to the central government while they stay in the localities ("Schools," Seon'geoji 選舉志, *History of Goryeo*). This shows that an organized education system for recommending capable people from the provinces to the central government had not yet been established.

Establishment of the National University as the best academic center was finally determined in the 11th year of the reign of Seongjong (992), and applicable government officials were ordered to scout for an appropriate location to build libraries and educational facilities. The following message was delivered upon issuing farmsteads as the financial wherewithal for this effort:

> The one who is king must put priority on school to obtain the world. How can the standard be set if writing down the customs of Yao and Shun, practicing the doctrines of the Duke of Zhou and Confucius, and revealing the vertical relationship between the ruler and his vassals by establishing the constitution and system of a kingdom are not entrusted to wise Confucians? …There is yet no equipment for learning and no detailed research on training capable people. The secretary will be commanded to issue farmsteads for appropriate sites to erect educational facilities throughout; make vessels by polishing gold and jade. All Confucians in general should know what I am attempting to accomplish.

The preparations for building the National University seem to have been under way prior to this. There is a record of the Learned Yim No-seong (任老成) returning from Song China and submitting manuals on "Daemyodangdo" (大廟堂圖, A Diagram of Great Shrines), "Sajikdangdo" (社稷堂圖, A Diagram of Altars for the Land and Grain Gods), "Munseonwang myodo" (文宣王廟圖, A Diagram of the Shrine for King Wenxuan), "Jegido" (祭器圖, A Diagram of Utensils for Rituals), as well as one volume of "Chilsibi hyeondo" (七十二賢圖, A Diagram of 72 Benevolences) in the second year of the reign of Seongjong. Thus, it is suspected that the model for the National University was the "Great Learning" (大學) of Song China.

Seongjong departed this world at the young age of 38 in 997 on his 16th year of reign, but it is likely that the site of the National University was not completed during his lifetime, because issues with the Khitans in the north were tense.

In 993, one year after the establishment of the National University was determined, the Khitans invaded by crossing the Amnok River; they demanded tributes. However, Seo Hui (徐熙) led the negotiations and cunningly claimed that the reason for not being able to give tributes to the Khitans was that the roads were blocked by the Jurchens east of the Amnok River. The Khitans withdrew after promising dominium. As a result, the glibness of Seo Hui's tongue expanded the northwestern boundary of Goryeo to north of the Amnok River.

The king of the Khitans at the time was Shengzong (r. 982-1031). The Liao cavalry personally led by Shengzong ravaged all cities in Hebei, China, in 1004 and reached Chanzhou (today's Shanyuan 澶淵) on the coast of the Yellow River. Across the Yellow River is Kaifeng (開封), the capital of Song China. But Shengzong was not confident of the outcome of a decisive battle due to an overly distant supply route and entered into a peace treaty with Emperor Huizong of Song China. The treaty specified that Song China would send 200,000 rolls of silk and 100,000 *nyang* of silver to Liao annually as tributary payment, instead of the past obligation of Liao as the younger brother and Song the older brother.[4] This was a significant revision to the Sino-centrism ever since the Qin and Han Empires. This is the so-called "Treaty of Shanyuan" (澶淵之盟).

The Liao forces concentrated their efforts on attacking Goryeo now that they had made peace with Song China, and the second invasion in 1010-1011 was followed by the third invasion in 1018-1019, when they reached Gaegyeong, the capital of Goryeo. But they could not invade further into Goryeo territory because the king had fled south. The 100,000 cavalry troops led by Xiao Pai-ya (蕭排押) arrived near Gaegyeong in the third invasion, but they began to pull back due to the fear that the rear supply route would be cut off. Commander Kang Gam-chan (姜邯贊) struck a fatal blow to the retreating Liao forces at Guju (龜州) and only a few thousand

---

[4] *Nyang* is an old monetary unit in Korea and is a unit of measure; 1 *nyang* is equivalent to 37.5 g. (S. Lee)

escaped. This is the background for which peace between the two kingdoms was recovered in 1021 after Liao abandoned attempts to conquer Goryeo with force.

Commander Kang was also one of the civilian officials. Military power over the state had been in the hands of civilian officials. Military Examination was not available as part of the civil service examination then. Kang Gam-chan was a Pyeongjangsa (平章事) before he became a commander. It is said that the *yangban* system was established in the Goryeo period, but that was only for the scholar-official order to a certain extent.

The decision to establish the National University may have been made in 992, but the struggles and tension against the Liao troops continued from the first invasion in 993 to the return of peace in 1021. In particular, Gaegyeong was turned into a mound of ashes in 1011. Seongjong passed away in 997. In the end, preparations for the National University had to wait until the reign of Yejong (睿宗, r. 1106-1122) and King Injong (仁宗, r. 1122-1146).

Interchange between Goryeo and Song Dynasty China

Liao dynasty, which threatened Goryeo and Song from the northern regions, was destroyed by the Jin dynasty founded by the Jurchens. Goryeo and Song China were still on the defensive over their northern territories. Moreover, the route that served as the land path of Hwabei and Dongbei regions between Goryeo and Song became the territories of Liao and Jin. Thus trade and cultural interchange between Goryeo and Song had to be conducted through the sea route.

The period of Song dynasty (including Northern Song and Southern Song) from the founding in 960 to its fall at the hands of Yuan dynasty China in 1279 coincides with the first half of the Goryeo dynasty. The major sea route between the two kingdoms until the 1030s was the Dengzhou (登州) peninsula in Shandong, China, and Yeseong Port (禮成港, the entrance to the Yeseong River), an outer port of Gaegyeong. Ships from China left Dengzhou to cross the Yellow River, arrived at Cho Island (椒島) at the estuary of the Daedong River, and advanced south toward Yeseong Port. This was the northern route.

But the northern route to the Shandong peninsula could not be used when the power of Liao extended to the Hwabei region and confronted Song China, so a southern route was used instead. The major southern course was from Zhejiang (浙江) Castle in Mingzhou (明州, today's Ningbo 寧波) to Quanzhou (泉州) in Fujian (福建) Castle. There was a Goryeo legation in Mingzhou that received delegates and traders. Chinese ships that left from Mingzhou or Quanzhou put to port at Heuksan Island on the southwestern tip of the coast of the Korean peninsula, sailed north through the Yellow Sea, and arrived at Yeseong Port.

Envoys went back and forth through the northern route of Gaegyeong → Yeseong Port → Dengzhou → Kaifeng and southern route of Gaegyeong → Yeseong Port → Mingzhou (or Quanzhou) → Kaifeng between Gaegyeong in Goryeo and Kaifeng in Song China. Not only did these routes become pipelines for diplomatic relations, they also served for human and material interchange.

An envoy from Song China by the name of Xu Jing (徐兢) wrote a book entitled *Xuanhuo fengshi gaoli tujing* (宣和奉使高麗圖經, *Seonhwa bongsa goryeo dogyeong* in Kr. and hereinafter referred to as *Gaoli tujing*). He joined the delegation of Chief Envoy Lu Yun-di (路允迪) and Vice Ambassador Fu Mo-qing (傅墨卿) to Gaegyeong in 1123; the book describes what he saw and heard as well as what people talked about while he was in Gaegyeong for over a month. According to this book, Ubyeong Nanjeong (右碧瀾亭) and Jwabyeong Nanjeong (左碧瀾亭) were the inns where the Chinese envoy stayed in Yeseong Port, and they stayed in Suncheon-gwan (順天館) within the city of Gaegyeong. Aside from inns for the Chinese envoy, there were Cheongju-gwan (淸州館), Chungju-gwan (忠州館), Sajeom-gwan (四店館), and Ibin-gwan (利賓館) on the outside of the south gate where the Chinese traders gathered. Gaegyeong and Yeseong Port as an outer port were locales where Chinese products and culture came in, and the coast of the Yeseong River that connects Gaegyeong and the outer port is presumed to be the foothold for distribution overflowing with international atmosphere, because merchants from as far away as Arabia came.

7

The National University
and Twelve Private Schools

Private Schools Surpass the National University

The embodiment of National University could not come to fruition in the first half of the 11th century due to two invasions by Liao in 1010-1011 and 1018-1019 as examined in previous chapters. There was no room to substantially organize the education system even after the war due to restoration and reconstruction issues. Such a void in government schools was filled by the sudden rise of private schools.

Choe Chung (崔冲, 984-1068) was a senior civilian official who advised several kings until he resigned from his post as Munhwasijung, since he passed the civil service examination at the top in 1005. But his fame was in his educational activities in the sudden rise in private schools, which earned him the honorific title of "Teacher of Nine Halls" (九齋先生) or "Teacher East of the Sea" (海東夫子) instead of as a politician.

He was from Haeju in Hwanghae Province near Gaegyeong, according to the "Choe Chung," Yeoljeon, *History of Goryeo*. Choe Seung-no recommended emphasizing Confucianism to Seongjong as described in the previous chapter. Although he had the same surname as Choe Chung, Choe Seung-no was from Gyeongju at the end of the Silla dynasty. In other words, unlike Choe Seung-no, who was of the head-rank 6 at the end of Silla, Choe Chung was a civilian official and Confucian scholar who was recruited through his merit via the civil service examination that was instituted in 958.

Choe Chung, who also held the past position of examiner of the civil service examination, established nine academic institutions in Ja'un-dong at the foothill of Mount Song'ak in Gaegyeong because of many students wanting to take the civil service examination under him. The names of the nine academic institutes are the Nine Halls of Nakseong (樂聖), Daejung (大中), Seongmyeong (誠明), Gyeong-eop (敬業), Jodo (造道), Solseong (率性), Jindeok (進德), Daehwa (大和), and Daebing (待聘). These names are all from Confucian classics.

Those who passed the civil service examination but were not assigned to a government office were in charge of teaching the nine Confucian Classics (*Book of Changes*, *Book of Poetry*, *Book of Documents*, *Book of Rites*, *Etiquette and Rites*, *Record of Rites*, *Commentary to the Spring and Autumn Annals by Zuo Qiuming* 春秋左氏傳, and *Commentary to the Spring and Autumn Annals by Gu Liang* 春秋穀梁傳) and the Three Histories (*Historical Records*, *History of the Han Dynasty*, and *History of the Later Han Dynasty*). Moreover, the large Gwibeop Temple (歸法寺) was rented in the summer for intensive summer classes. Students who studied at the Nine Halls were later referred to as the "Disciples of Master Munheon" (文憲公徒, Master Munheon is the posthumous title for Choe Chung), among whom the rate of passing the civil service examination was the highest. An exclusive academic sectarianism naturally formed between master and disciple of the Nine Halls under such circumstances.

The Nine Halls of Choe Chung stimulated the growth of private schools, which led to the formation of 12 private cliques of disciples including the "Disciples of Master Munheon." The other 11 cliques of disciples and founders are shown in the table on the next page.

It is not that the National University did not exist as a government school before the rapid expansion of private schools. The applicants for the civil service examination were concentrated in private schools because the educational level of the private schools surpassed that of the National University.

Name of Clique	Founder	Past Position
Disciples of Hongmun (弘文公徒)	Jeong Bae-geol (鄭倍傑)	chief minister (侍中)
Disciples of Gwangheon (匡憲公徒)	No Dan (盧旦)	councilor initiate (參政)
Disciples of Namsan (南山徒)	Kim Sang-bin (金尙賓)	chancellor (祭酒)
Disciples of Seowon (西園徒)	Kim Mu-che (金無滯)	*bongya* (僕射)[1]
Disciples of Master Munchung (文忠公徒)	Eun Jeong (殷鼎)	chief minister
Disciples of Master Yangsin (良愼公徒)	Kim Ui-jin (金義珍)	*pyeongjang* (平章) *nangjung* (郞中)[2]
Disciples of Master Jeonggyeong (貞敬公徒)	Bak Myeong-bo (朴明保)	*pyeongjang* (平章)
Disciples of Master Chungpyeong (忠平公徒)	Hwang Yeong (黃塋)	*bulsang* (不詳)
Disciples of Master Jeongheon (貞憲公徒)	Yu Gam (柳監)	chief minister
Disciples of Seo Si-rang (徐侍郎徒)	Mun Jeong (文正) Seo Seok (徐碩)	*sirang*
Disciples of Gusan (龜山徒)	Bul Sang (不詳)	*bulsang*

---

[1] *Bongya* corresponds to the rank of *jeong 2-pum*. (S. Lee)
[2] *Nangjung* was an official of the 5th rank. (S. Lee)

King Munjong encouraged the growth of the National University while pinpointing the cause of its stagnation as follows: "The responsibility for many students of the National University giving up studies recently is in the academies." Confucian students and law students who had studied in the National University for nine years and for six years, respectively, and did not have good grades were ordered to be dispelled (17th year of the reign of King Munjong, *Essential History of Goryeo*). Desirable government officials to the dynasty must be trained at a government school as expected, and the formation of academic cliques between masters and disciples in private schools is an obstacle to the centralization of power in the king. These private schools were abolished in 1392 in the late Goryeo period following a reorganization of the National University (otherwise known as Sungkyunkwan).

Additionally, Munjong was a king who upheld Buddhism, and his fourth son was Uicheon (義天, 1055-1101), the State Preceptor Daegak (大覺國師). Uicheon was a scholarly monk representing Buddhist culture of the Goryeo period; he was the founder of Cheontae School (Tiantai School in Ch.) in Korea after learning the recondite principles of the Flower Garland sect in Song China while simultaneously training in the Tiantai sect at the Tianzhu Temple (天竺寺). He established the Directorate of Buddhist Scriptures (教藏都監) in Heungwang Temple (興王寺) after his return from Song China, wherein he published *Sinpyeon jejonggyojang chongnok* (新編 諸宗教藏總錄, New Catalogue of Buddhist Sectarian Writings) that consists of 1,010 sections, 4,740 volumes, by collecting Buddhist scriptures and annotations from Liao and Song China as well as from Japan and adding ancient books of Korea. Uicheon was a Buddhist scholar in Buddhist history of Goryeo comparable to Wonhyo and Uisang who represented Silla Buddhism.

Around 200 Students at the National University

The National University was reorganized in the first half of the 12th century as a government academy, and it surpassed the private schools in the reigns of the 16th and 17th kings, Yejong and Injong. Yejong issued the following edict in 1106, the year he ascended to the throne:

> Those who hold the posts above justices, governors, and district magistrates of the three cities (Gaegyeong, Seogyeong, and Donggyeong) and eight prefectures must pass the Erudite Examination and must have jurisdiction over school affairs as well.

- "School," Seon'geoji, *History of Goryeo*

Seven special courses at the National University were established in 1109 when the organization process of the National University is examined through "School," Seon'geoji (選舉志) in *History of Goryeo*, of which *Book of Changes* was taught in Yeotaekjae (麗澤齋), *Official History* was taught in Daebingjae (待聘齋), *Book of Poetry* (*Maoshi* in Ch.) was taught in Gyeongdeokjae (經德齋), *Book of Rites* was taught in Guinjae (求人齋), *Daili* (戴禮) was taught in Bogeungjae (服膺齋), and *Spring and Autumn Annals* in Yangjeongjae (養正齋) for the 70 Confucian students recruited by merit. Art Lecture Hall (講藝齋) for teaching military arts was built for the first time, and eight students were enrolled. Furthermore, an educational endowment called the Fund for Nurturing Worthies was created to financially assist students to study.

The purpose of Yejong enforcing the training of military arts at the Art Lecture Hall and establishing the Military Examination to recruit military officials by merit is as follows:

> The two studies of scholarship and military arts are the foundation of the national enlightenment. The reason for instructing to build both schools early on is to train many students in preparation for the recruitment of future generals and premiers by merit.

- "School," Seon'geoji, *History of Goryeo*

In the background was the pressure from the changing situation of the Jurchens' Jin dynasty that emerged as the new supreme ruler in the stead of Liao China in the northern region. Thus it was not possible to casually wait for good generals to emerge from among civilian officials in an emergency.

In the 11th year of the reign of Injong (1133), however, the National University discontinued Art Lecture Hall and the Military Examination as part of the civil service examination due to the fear that a dispute between civilian officials and military officials might arise from the emergence of the latter. Thus the *yangban* system of the times emphasized civilian officials, and military officials were nothing more than assistants. When he ascended to the throne, Injong ordered the government official in charge of protocols on important ceremonies and legislation to execute an education system in the National University in honor of the wishes of his father. In other words, six colleges of the capital within the National University were established in Gaegyeong, while local schools were established in the provinces, districts, and counties of the countryside. The six colleges of the capital refers to the National College (國子學), National Confucian College (太學), Four Portals College (四門學), Law College (律學), Calligraphy College (書學), and Accounting College (算學); enrollment criteria and teaching information for each school were specifically prescribed. The six colleges can be roughly classified into Confucian courses of National College, National Confucian College, and Four Portals College as well as practical learning courses of Law College, Calligraphy College, and Accounting College. The teaching contents of National College, National Confucian College, and Four Portals College have as common subjects *Book on Filial Piety* and *Analects of Confucius* while the students are expected to specialize in one of the following: *Book of Changes, Book of Poetry, Book of Documents, Book of Rites, Etiquette and Rites, Record of Rites, Commentary to the Spring and Autumn Annals by Zuo Qiuming, Commentary to the Spring and Autumn Annals by Gong Yang,* or *Commentary to the Spring and Autumn Annals by Gu Liang.*

The qualifications for enrollment in National College, National Confucian College, and Four Portals College differed according to

110

status although the subjects taught were the same. Applicants must be the offspring of civilian and military officials of 3-*pum* or above to qualify for enrollment in the National College, the offspring of 5-*pum* or lower rank for National Confucian College, and the offspring of 7-*pum* or above for Four Portals College. The number of students in each college was limited to 300. Moreover, students of the Law College, Calligraphy College, and Accounting College, as well as colleges in the province, counties, and local schools were restricted to civilian and military officials of 8-*pum* or above and commoners. In other words, practical courses became established as scholarships for those of lower status in comparison to that of Confucianism.

Aside from the six colleges of the capital, Medical Office (太醫監) and Astronomy Office (司天臺) were in charge of technical management by being in charge of training in medicine as well as in astronomy, geography, and the *yin-yang* principle, and the qualification for enrollment in these are inferred to be the same as the status for Law College, Calligraphy College, and Accounting College of the six colleges of the capital.

The social status of the enrolled students in the six colleges of the capital and local schools can be classified as follows. Those with the status of 7-*pum* and above had monopoly on the Confucian courses (National College, National Confucian College, and Four Portals College), and those with the status of 8-*pum* and below as well as commoners could enroll in the practical courses (Law College, Calligraphy College, and Accounting College) and the local schools in the provinces. Moreover, people of low birth and criminals were not qualified to enroll.

Thus the civil service examination system of the times was constructed in such a way that civilian and military *yangban* of 7-*pum* or above monopolized the qualifiers for the Composition Examination course and the Classics Examination course to become the backbone of bureaucrats, and the 8-*pum* and below as well as the commoners assisted the civilian and military *yangban* through practical and technical management after qualifying for Legal Examination (明法科), Mathematics Examination course (明算科), Calligraphy Examination course (明書科), Medicine Examination course, Geography Examination course, or Fortunetelling course (卜科). The differential structure of putting importance on Confucianism and negligence of practical learning in the national education and the civil examination system is a bad habit that consistently existed from the Goryeo dynasty to the Joseon dynasty.

The policy of encouraging scholarship by Yejong and Injong does not seem to have been achieved smoothly due to resistance from the conservative bureaucrats. Yejong pointed out the following in the second year of his reign (1107) prior to the establishment of the seven special courses at the National University:

> Cultivating wise men through establishing schools is the foundation of politics since the three generations (of Xia, Yin, and Zhou). But the discussion on the post of secretary has not been concluded. This must be put into effect at the earliest possible moment.

Additionally, students of the National University gathered at the royal palace, protested against the passive government measures on education, and petitioned the king as follows in the eighth year of the reign of Yejong. According to the passage above, the number of students at the National University seems to have been limited by financial restrictions to around 200:

> Your subjects have quietly heard of the Censorate (御史臺) reporting that a few with good deportment and grades should remain and others given leave to go due to the exorbitant cost of training so many students at the national colleges. Your subjects are distressed on behalf of the kingdom. Respecting scholarship and fostering talented people are the foundation of statecraft. That is why the sages and wise men of old emphasized this. Although Confucius wandered here and there without holding an official rank, he cultivated 3,000 disciples. Han Wengong (韓文公, Han Yu 韓愈) of Tang China was demoted to the post of Chaozhou (潮州), which was considered a poor province. But saying that it was a disgrace of the province for not being able to recommend able people to the imperial court because provincial

112

schools had been closed for a long time, able scholar Zhao De (趙德) was commanded to manage the provincial school and gather students. Moreover, he used his salary to pay for the food (of the students). Our kingdom is bountiful because it has done no less than unifying the Three Kingdoms, and customs and civilization are taught to match three generations. However, he who calls himself the secretary desires to reduce the number of national students from the already low 200 to even less because this is considered a waste of funds. How can this be the will of our king who elevates the way and reveres Confucianism?

The National University as Seen through the Eyes of the Envoy from Song China

Xu Jing from Song China who was visiting Gaegyeong in the year of Won during the reign of Injong (1123) described the National University in his collection of observations [in Goryeo] entitled *Gaoli tujing*:

> The National University is located south of Hoebin-gwan (會賓館), and on its front gate hangs a signboard that says "National University." In the midst of it is the Seonseongjeon (宣聖殿: a royal palace dedicated to Confucius), and the dormitory was open on either side in which all students resided. The previous location was too small and it was moved to the current location of Yehyeonbang (禮賢坊). The institute was enlarged to accommodate the increased number of students.
>
> • "National University," Vol. 16, *Gaoli tujing*

In 1123, the year when Injong ascended to the throne, his father Yejong established the seven special courses at the National University. Thereafter Injong built the National University into six colleges in the capital, and thus it must have grown larger in scale.

Xu Jing also commented on the Confucian customs in Goryeo:

The eastern barbarians are gentle in nature, and it is the land where virtuous men did not die out. Further, Ji-zi was assigned to rule the territory of Joseon, and customs that have become convention follow the 8 Articles of old. The men are very proper and the women follow faithfulness correctly. Vessels with feet are used for eating and drinking, and people give way to others when on the road. They are different from the uncouth northern savages who press their hair flat against the head, whose hands and feet are rough, whose pigtails are wrapped in a large hood, where father and son sleep together, and relatives use the same coffin.

- "Confucianism," Vol. 40, *Gaoli tujing*

An additional description is as follows:

It was recently learned after a messenger reached that land that there are tens of thousands of collections of books in Imcheon-gak (臨川閣), and Cheongyeon-gak (清燕閣) is full of four sections of Gyeongsajajip (經史子集 4部). These are maintained by establishing the National University and recruiting Confucian officials by merit. The institution is new and large, and surprisingly upholds the system of Yueshujikao (月書季考) of the National Confucian Academy. All students will eventually take up posts as government officials of the royal court, carry themselves with dignified manner, speak well, and possess a pleasing appearance. As well, two or three Confucian schools and bookstores face each other on the streets of each village. Offspring of commoners or bachelors live together and learn the Confucian Classics from a teacher. When older, groups are formed and studies continue at a rented temple or Daoist temple. Even the lower class groups and children learn by following the provincial teachers. Ahhh, how very deep indeed [is the learning].

He saw that Confucianism in Goryeo was tilted toward the rhetoric and immature in Chinese Confucian Classics, however, and pointed this out as follows:

114

In general, rules of the four tones in Chinese Classics (聲律, poetry) are revered and learning of the Chinese Confucian Classics is not mature yet. The writings are similar to those of the Tang dynasty.

Confucianism of Goryeo emphasized commentaries and rhetorical Han and Tang Schools, and the point made above comprehends well the characteristics of Goryeo Confucianism that put more importance on the rhetoric than the Five Classics due to Tang China's influence.

As the title indicates, however, *Gaoli tujing* is a collection of writings of experience on the "diagrams" and "the Classics" of Gaegyeong, which he wrote during his stay of one month so that Gaegyeong could be introduced in China. A great social upheaval called the Rebellion of Jingkang of 1126-1127 (靖康之變) occurred in China as soon as Xu Jing returned there. Portions of the "diagrams" were lost during the Rebellion, and not until the reign of Emperor Qianlong of Qing China were the sections on "the Classics" revised and published in 1793.

The Rebellion of Jingkang refers to the civil war that occurred in 1125, during which Emperor Huizong (徽宗) relegated his throne to his son Qinzong (欽宗) and fled south when Jin China's cavalry approached near Kaifeng from the directions of Yanjing (today's Beijing) and Shanxi. The Jin cavalry had destroyed the Liao dynasty. But both Emperor Huizong and his son surrendered at the end and were taken to Wuguocheng (五國城: near today's Heilong River in Yilan). With this event as the turning point, the Song period before this rebellion is called the Northern Song dynasty, and the period after this rebellion is called the Southern Song dynasty.

How Beautiful Is the Blue of the Goryeo Celadon

Emperor Huizong of Song China collected pictures and calligraphic works using his power and wealth as a first-rate artist. It is important to digress for a moment to show the association with the *Gaoli tujing*.

115

There seems to have been quite a number of artists in the Goryeo period according to records, but the most existing works are Buddhist paintings. More, a majority of these Buddhist paintings are in Japan because the monks dispatched to Joseon during the Muromachi Era took them back to Japan with them.

The artist Yi Yeong (李寧) of Jeonju in Jeolla Province was known to Emperor Huizong and the artist circles in Song China. He went to Kaifeng in 1124 immediately before the outbreak of the "Rebellion of Jingkang" as an entourage of Yi Ja-deok (李資德), messenger to Song China. He drew the Scene of Yeseong River (禮成江圖) at that time at the request of Emperor Huizong. The waterfront view of Yeseong River from Yeseong Port to Gaegyeong was perhaps the talk within the envoy dispatched to Goryeo. Emperor Huizong, who was also a first-rate artist, was very impressed with Scene of Yeseong River by Yi Yeong; not only were Hanlin Daizhao (翰林待詔), Wang Ke-xun (王可訓), Chen De-zhi (陳德之), Tian Zong-zhi (田宗之), and Zhao Shou-zong (趙守宗) ordered to learn the art of painting from Yi Yeong, but Yi Yeong was awarded the food and wine as well as bolts of beautiful satin and silk ("Yi Yeong," Yeoljeon, *History of Goryeo*). Emperor Huizong built a painting gallery directly under his control and personally instructed the artists; he also collected paintings and curios. The scene of Yeseong River was probably destroyed during the confusion of the "Rebellion of Jingkang." What a lamentable turn of events.

While on the subject of paintings, let us investigate Goryeo celadon and the custom of drinking tea as described in the book entitled *Gaoli tujing*. Xu Jing describes the pottery and trays used in Goryeo in detail in *Gaoli tujing*. There would have originally been "paintings" in this book, but they must have been lost due to the reason mentioned above. The custom of drinking tea in Goryeo is described as follows:

Local tea is bitter and acidic in taste. Only tea made of young tea leaves and *longfengcituan* are valued, and thus merchants sell quality tea. Drinking tea was liked from the olden days, and more and more utensils for drinking tea were required. Golden teacups with glowers and birds, small vases of blue, silver braziers, and pots

116

for boiling water all follow the system of China.... Tea is drunk three times a day, followed by water that has been brewed twice. Goryeo people consider the second brewing to be medicinal. [The server of tea] becomes happy when the messengers [from China] drink all [of the tea]; [he/she] goes away with a reproachful glance when the tea is not fully drunk. Thus effort is expended to drink it all.

- "Utensils," Vol. 32, *Gaoli tujing*

The following is written about Goryeo celadon:

Goryeo people call the blue color of pottery "color *fei*" (翡色). The color and hue are most beautiful, because the way of making this color has become very elaborate in recent years. The pot for holding alcoholic beverages is shaped like a cucumber, with a small lid on top. There is also one that is in the shape of a duck with an upside-down lotus flower.

Powder tea was in fashion even among the commoners, and tearooms spread during the Song dynasty period because people had enough to eat. Thus bitter and acidic local tea of Goryeo may not have suited the taste buds of the Song messenger who was used to powder tea.

Celadon of course originated from Song China. The origin of china from Jingdezhen (景德鎮) that flourished in the Southern Song period is Cizhou (磁州) in Northern Song. It seems that coal instead of charcoal was fairly widely used as fuel in Northern Song in those days. Chinaware created through the heat from coal is called "*ciqi*" (磁器, or *jagi* in K.), named after the place of production. Xu Jing was a good judge of porcelain. He was so struck with admiration for the blue hue used in Goryeo celadon that he introduced the color as "*fei*." Color *fei* refers to the bluish hue of the beautiful wings of a kingfisher.

Myocheong's Insurrection

The Jurchens were under the domination of Liao, but Liao was destroyed by the Jurchens under the leadership of Aguda (阿骨打) in 1115, wherein he declared himself first emperor of the newly named kingdom of Great Jin (大金). Song dynasty cooperated with Jin to destroy its old enemy Liao, but Jin attacked Kaifeng in 1127, took Huizong and Qinzong as prisoners, and forcefully took thousands of members of the imperial family, aristocrats, and experts to the north. Jin dynasty used Song to destroy Liao, and then destroyed Northern Song in the end. This is the "Rebellion of Jingkang" as mentioned above. The rapid growth of Jin China became the source of turbulence once again in East Asia.

Summary of the Eighteen Histories describes the pillaging of Kaifeng, the capital of Northern Song, by the invading Jin troops as follows:

> Approximately 3,000 people, including the Empress, Crown Prince, Emperor's brothers, women of the royal family, and the imperial family, went forward to stand before the Jin troops. Everything in the castle was searched, including offspring, gold and satin, treasures, carts and clothes, utensils, and books; the castle became empty of government officials as well as commoners. Thereafter the king of Jin dynasty promulgated an edict that proclaimed a different surname, from which the former Grand Preceptor Zhang Bang-chang (張邦昌) was invested with the throne as Emperor Chu (楚帝).[3] The two emperors of Song China were taken north.

> - "Qinzong of Song," Vol. 7,
> Summary of the Eighteen Histories

Jin China planned to become civilized through this plunder. Huizong was a lover of antique paintings and calligraphic works and a first-

---

[3] Grand Preceptor was the highest government post of advisor to the emperor. (S. Lee)

118

rate artist, but it seems that he was a failure as a politician. He used granite to artificially create the Mountain of Ten Thousand Years (萬歲山) and transported precious flowers and extraordinary rocks from the south of China to Kaifeng. Depending on the item, sometimes as much as several thousand coins for one flower and tens of thousands of coins for one rock were wasted. Frequent riots by the commoners were a matter of course.

Domestic troubles and external threats continued in Goryeo during the first half of the 12th century when the Jin dynasty, formed by the Jurchens, toppled Liao and Northern Song and spread throughout the northeastern territory to the central territory of China.

The biggest source of external threat was, of course, the relationship with the Jurchens. Various disputes arose due to the fact that the present-day Hamgyeong Province had been the residential area of the Jurchens before the unification of Jin dynasty. Therefore Goryeo troops with Yun Gwan (尹瓘) as general subjugated this territory in 1107 and proceeded with fortification, thus establishing a vague boundary. In 1126, Jin demanded King Injong of Goryeo become a subject of Jin. Of course there were discussions objecting to that, but peace was maintained through adopting the protocol of serving Jin China as a kingdom of big brother at the assertion of the powerful vassal Yi Ja-gyeom (李資謙).

The greatest source of internal strife was "Myocheong's Insurrection" of 1135. Along with Baek Su-han (白壽翰), Monk Myocheong used geomancy to claim that the capital must be moved to the western capital (Pyeong'yang) where the auspicious effect of a site was full of vigor because Gaegyeong was already enfeebled. Bureaucrats at the capital who were from the western capital such as Jeong Ji-sang (鄭知常) agreed as expected. The purpose of moving the capital to the western capital was independence from the Great Jin policy. This was a protest of the bureaucrats at the capital against adopting the protocol of submission to Jin. Moreover, they advocated the building of Daehwa Palace in Pyeong'yang as well as creating an appellation for the year and raising the title of king to emperor so that Goryeo would be on an equal footing with Jin and Song China.

One of the representative bureaucrats at the capital who opposed the move of the capital to the western capital was Kim Bu-sik, who later compiled *Historical Records of the Three Kingdoms.* The bureaucrats at the capital ultimately divided into Gaegyeong faction and Seogyeong (western capital) faction, whereby friction arose. Jeong Ji-sang and Kim Bu-sik were both civilian officials, but Kim Bu-sik represented the Chinese Classics school, whereas Jeong Ji-sang represented the school of the rhetoric. In other words, this confrontation was between the Gaegyeong faction that recommended serving the Jin dynasty and the Seogyeong faction that advocated independence.

Myocheong finally raised troops and called the new kingdom "Daewi" (大爲, Great Accomplishment), the appellation of the year as "Cheon-gae" (天開, Heavenly Commencement), and his troops "the Heaven-Sent Force of Loyalty and Righteousness" (天遣忠義軍). Words such as "great" (大) or "heaven" (天) were avoided per the protocol of serving China. Their spirit can be seen in "naming the year and proclaiming the king emperor." As a general, Kim Bu-sik seized command of military power over internal strife, but it took him one year to behead the bureaucrats of the Seogyeong faction such as Jeong Ji-sang, Kim An, Baek Su-han, and others, and to suppress Myocheong's force of Seogyeong faction who stubbornly resisted. "Yeoljeon" of History of Goryeo condemned Myocheong in the article on treason, and Jeong Ji-sang was only briefly mentioned at the end.

Zhu Xi Perfects the Confucian System of Thought

The system of thought of the Song School (Cheng-Zhu School) as new Confucianism to replace the Han and Tang Schools of the past was perfected in the Song (Northern and Southern Song) dynasty period. It is sometimes simply called the Learning of Master Zhu, because the person who integrated it is Zhu Xi (name is Hui 熹, and pen name is Huian 晦庵, 1130-1200) of Southern Song dynasty.[4] The Learning of Master Zhu was transmitted to Goryeo during its declining years and penetrated the history of Confucianism in Joseon as the systematic doctrinal studies for over 500 years during the Joseon dynasty after it succeeded the Goryeo dynasty. Now is the time to briefly examine the historical background in which the formation of the Song School occurred.

Northern Song dynasty was destroyed due to "the Rebellion of Jingkang" of the Jin dynasty as mentioned above, and the imperial family, including the last two emperors Huizong and Qinzong, were taken north. But Qinzong's younger brother Prince of Kang (康王) survived. The surviving retainers declared Prince of Kang as Emperor Gaozong and the capital as Linan (臨安, today's Hangzhou). This is the beginning of the Southern Song period in 1127.

The pro-peace faction and the resistance faction were in conflict within the Southern Song dynasty. The leader of the resistance faction was the infamous Yuefei (岳飛). He was imprisoned and later executed by Qinhui (秦檜), the minister of the pro-peace faction. Peace was obtained by signing a peace treaty with Jin dynasty in 1141. The content of the peace treaty was humiliating and without historical precedence in China in that the new boundary with Jin China was to be the Huaihe River (淮河), which granted the Northern Song territory to Jin; furthermore, the emperor of Southern Song must pay obeisance to the emperor of Jin, who until now was held in disdain.

Accordingly, Qinhui is denounced even today as the agent of Jin China and a traitor. But it was not a simple problem to determine whether to continue to maintain the existence of the Song dynasty, albeit only Southern Song, through peace or to fight against Jin China with the possibility of total annihilation. It is presumed that the existence of Song dynasty including Southern Song would have become extinct if resistance continued.

---

[4] The Learning of Master Zhu is also called Neo-Confucianism. The Learning of Master Zhu will be called Neo-Confucianism from here on. (S. Lee)

Justification for "reverence for China and exclusionism of all foreigners" that considers Song as the center and Jin as foreign is strongly embedded in the Learning of Master Zhu perfected during the Southern Song period as clear exclusionism against Jin. There were some scholars of the Learning of Master Zhu in Joseon who succeeded to this concept without change, and the thought of "valuing Ming and devaluing Qing" became prevalent in the world of Confucianism in the mid-17th century when the Qing dynasty toppled the Ming dynasty in China.

Ironically, however, the Southern dynasty that discarded the Northern Song dynasty flourished more than ever before. The high-ranking government officials who escaped from Northern Song to Southern Song longed for Changan, Luo-yang, and Kaifeng, the capitals of the unified dynasties of old and felt such great anger that they advocated justification for exclusionism in the loss to Jin. But the glory of these cities was achieved through the absorption of the riches from south of the Huaihe River. The main artery was the great waterway built by Emperor Yang, the despot of Sui dynasty. Southern Song dynasty no longer had the burden of China despite sending 250,000 *nyang* in silver and 250,000 rolls of satin as tribute to Jin, and thus the economy and culture flourished.

Hangzhou as the capital of Southern Song dynasty is located in the southernmost region of the great waterway that connects the Yellow River, Huaihe River, and Yangtze River from south to north. It developed into a world-class city with the convenience of water and land transportation, and it also had great plains as well as scenic spots due to large rivers and many lakes running through it. It is said in *The Book of Marco Polo* (東方見聞録) that Marco Polo could not hide his surprise at the unprecedented sight of Hangzhou's prosperity. The following is an introduction of a passage:

> The following is the environment of this city. On one side is a beautiful and clear lake, and on the other side is a large river. Numerous canals connect the river that flows through the city and washes away filth. These flow into lakes and ultimately to the ocean. Thus the air is clean. One can go anywhere in the heart of the city through the streets or the canals. Both the streets and ca-

nals are wide enough for carts, and boats can easily pass. Necessities for the citizens are also transported. There are 12,000 bridges, most of which are made of stone, but there are a few wooden bridges. Bridges over major canals and commercial centers are cleverly built in the shape of an arch so that even the large ships do not have to hoist down the mast to pass under the bridges. The carts or horses can pass on the roads without discomfort due to their levelness despite the height of the bridges. Small boats can pass under any bridge. There is no need to be surprised at the large number of bridges, because, as mentioned before, countless waterways surround and flow through this city just as if it is a city on water. Many bridges are needed to make the comings and goings of the citizens unrestricted.

Japan was outside the sphere of East Asia that was formed by northern tribes in the first half of the 12th century during which northern Jin dynasty emerged as a threat to Song dynasty China and Goryeo. Thus it was not directly affected by the vicissitudes of mainland China as was Goryeo. Japan had a buffer zone between it and the kingdoms of northeast Asia in the form of the Korean peninsula as well as the geographic advantage of being an island with an ocean in between.

The first half of the 12th century was a turbulent period in Japan in that the regent politics of the Fujiwara family crumbled and made a transition to a shogunate. Kamakura Bakufu by Minamoto no Yoritomo was established in 1192. The Fujiwara family completely excluded other families from power and monopolized the Setsho and Kanpaku in the first half of the 11th century, but warrior clans called "the warriors of archery and horsemanship," who were independent from the aristocrats in the capital, emerged in various regions. These warrior clans were divided into two *samurai* groups that supported either Kanmu Taira or Seiwa Minamoto. This is the premise under which the warrior society was formed through the power struggles between Taira and Minamoto clans.

The relationship between the imperial court of Kyoto and the shogunate under the regent politics is very similar to the relationship between Wang Geon at the capital and the local gentry in the early years of Goryeo. If that is the case, how was it possible for Goryeo to evolve into a dynastic society based on centralized power while excluding or absorbing old retainers and veteran generals who had regional power? It may be that the civil service examination was utilized and new kinds of bureaucrats who were educated with Confucianism were employed to create the framework for national government. As mentioned in Chapter 5, the civil service examination commenced in 958 during the reign of Goryeo's Gwangjong, and the principles of civilian government were established thereafter. In other words, the principle of dynastic integration was attributed to Confucianism, and the relationship between the king and his vassals was linked with that principle.

But the warrior class who served the aristocrats of the imperial court became independent and began a distinctive history of the shogunate during the second half of the 12th century in Japan. In the world of *shoguns* where ability is everything, the relationship between ruler and subjects as well as the hierarchical relationship were influenced by capability, and Confucian justification did not work.

8

Is the Period of Military Regime the Dark Age?

We Will Govern the Kingdom from Now on

The private mercenaries of the magnates at the capital as well as in the provinces were gradually absorbed into the government troops. The military troops at the capital were composed of two armies and six commanderies; the commander was the general and the assistant general was the lieutenant general. Furthermore, military troops were stationed in the provinces and counties.

But as mentioned previously, Kang Gam-chan, who struck a great blow to the invading Jurchen forces, and Kim Bu-sik, who suppressed Myocheong's Insurrection, were both civilian officials. In other words, civilian officials had authority over the military forces during national emergencies. Uijong (毅宗, r. 1146-1170) was so lost to Buddhism and Daoism that monks and Daoists frequented the royal palace, and much of the national funds were wasted on Buddhist and Daoist events during his reign. Moreover, he ordered the construction of a detached palace, a palace for the Crown Prince, and gardens at scenic spots to indulge in "poetry composition competition" with close civilian officials, because he liked poetry and prose. Generals and/or lieutenant generals had to escort the procession.

An example is when the head monk Gagye (覺倪) of Beopcheon Temple (法泉寺) prepared alcoholic drinks and side dishes at Dallyeong-won (獺嶺院) in preparation for the royal procession.

The monarch did not know when to stop creating rhyming catchwords with many of the scholars. Lieutenant General Jeong Jung-

125

Jung-bu and other commanders were angry due to fatigue and tiredness; they began to have second thoughts.

- 18th year of the reign of Uijong, *Essential History of Goryeo*

People like Kim Don-jung (金敦中), the son of Kim Bu-sik, ridiculed the military officials by lighting fire to Lieutenant General Jeong Jung-bu's beard. The civilian officials who became tired after entertainment commanded the military officials to wrestle, and the monarch as well as the civilian officials clapped in merriment when a civilian official Han Roe (韓賴) slapped the cheek of Lieutenant General Yi So-eung (李紹膺), who lost a wrestling match during the monarch's entertainment at Bohyeon-won (普賢院).

On the very same day of the entertainment at Bohyeon-won (普賢院), generals Jeong Jung-bu (鄭仲夫), Yi Ui-bang (李義方), Yi Go (李高), and military officials in charge of the royal escort started a rebellion with the cry, "kill all civilian officials," to which the troops responded. The military officials dethroned Uijong and put his brother Myeongjong (明宗, r. 1170-1197) on the throne. The rebellion of military officials did not stop as a one-time resistance against the indignities caused by civilian officials, for in the background was the anti-structural wrath against the Goryeo dynasty's encouragement of scholarship and disdain of military arts.

The Council of Generals (中房), a consulting organization for generals and lieutenant-generals in those days, took over the real power in government. This is similar to the Bakufu that appears in Japanese history. Power struggles among the military officials did not stop, however, and the reign kept changing hands in a dizzying whirl from Yi Go → Yi Ui-bang → Jeong Jung-bu → Gyeong Dae-seung (慶大升) → Yi Ui-min (李義旼). Military reign finally took root in 1196 after Choe Chung-heon (崔忠獻) murdered and took over power. The military reign of the Choes continued for 62 years (1196-1258) through four generations from Choe Chung-heon → Choe Yi (崔怡: later renamed as Wu, 瑀) → Choe Hang (崔沆) → Choe Ui (崔竩). The significance of the Choe regime ensuring political

126

stability by controlling the abuse of power by military officials is great.

The monarchy did exist in Goryeo during the 62 years of military control, but the Choe clan freely decided who should be put on the throne. There was a 30-year war with the Mongols (元) during the Choe regime, but Goryeo dynasty surely would not have survived if the regime of the scholar-officials had continued.

Kamakura Bakufu was established by Minamoto no Yoritomo in 1180 in Japan, but the emperor was preserved in the period before and after the establishment of the military regime of the Choe clan. This is similar to the preservation of the monarchy in the Goryeo dynasty under the military regime of the Choe clan. In comparison to the destruction of the military regime of Goryeo during the war with the Mongols, however, Japan's shogunate achieved an autonomous development that continued for around 700 years until the fall of the Edo Bakufu in 1868.

The Choe Regime Gives Preferential Treatment to the Literati and Confucian Scholars

After the rebellion of military officials of 1170, there was a scheme to reinstate Uijong to the throne. For example, Military Commander of the Northeast Side Kim Bo-dang (金甫當) raised an army against the Choe clan in 1173 but failed in his purpose. The families of the civilian officials were massacred in retribution. Lieutenant General Jin Jun (陳俊) and military officer Kim Bu (金富) among the military officials were against indiscriminate killings. Kim Bu urged Jeong Jung-bu and Yi Ui-bang to take care as below:

> Kim Bu said, "It is difficult to know the will of Heaven and the minds of people. How can the world be said to contain only a few people like Kim Bo-dang when all those attired in full dress (civilian officials) are murdered while wielding power but without a differentiating principle? The way to achieve permanence is to stabilize the minds of the civilian officials by forming marriage alliances with them through our offspring."

127

The catastrophe stopped when all followed this advice. The grandsons of Jin Jun, Sik (湜), Hwa (澕), and On (溫), all passed the civil service examination; the official post of Jin Sik was that of Royal Secretary, and Hwa and On became famous for their writings. Kim Bu's son Chwi-ryeo (就礪) and grandson Jeon (佺) served as prime ministers for two generations; their descendants are upheld as wise even today.

> • Yi Je-hyeon, *Scribblings of Old Man Oak*,
> Vol. 2 of the First Collection

As such, the hitherto established prestige of the clique of civilian officials hit bottom after the rebellion of military officials, and the position of the civilian officials and military officials reversed so that "the civilians" served "the military." As can be seen in the cases of Kim Jun or Kim Bu in the above excerpt, attention should be paid to the fact that a new *sadaebu* class was formed during the military regime by the descendants of the self-same military officials who were disdained by the civilian officials aggressively applying for the civil service examination. This new *sadaebu* class was the driving force behind the dynastic shift from Goryeo to Joseon later.

Moreover, the period of military regime was full of uprisings of farmers or base-born people as a period during which inferiors overthrew superiors. This was a type of class liberation movement from which "residential districts for outcasts" were promoted to counties. In other words, this was a period when a great social change arose in a fixed society that gave privilege to civilian officials through the eruption of energy by the oppressed military officials and commoners at the bottom of the social status.

Yi Je-hyeon (李薺賢, 1287-1376), the author of *Yeogong paeseol* (Scribblings of Old Man Oak), was one of the literati and a politician who represented Goryeo in the declining days. His question-and-answer session with King Chungseon (忠宣王, r. 1308-1313) relays the situation of the Confucian scholars during the period of military regime.

King Chungseon asked, "Culture of this land in the past was second only to Chinese culture. Scholars of today all follow the monks in memorizing the passages [of the Classics]. There are many who labor with each character and phrase to write sentences without practical use and few who are familiar with the Confucian Classics and practice virtuous conduct. What is the reason for this?"

The subject (Yi Je-hyeon) answered.

"…Unfortunately, (the civilian officials) were all suddenly murdered without discrimination between good and bad when the rebellion of military officials occurred at the end of Uijong's reign. Those who escaped from the clutches of death fled deep into the mountains, threw off the full dress [of the royal court], and lived the rest of their lives in monks' robes. Shin Jun (神駿) and Oh Saeng (悟生) are such. Later the state recovered reason to elevate scholarship, but the sons of scholars with the will to learn had to go deep into the mountains in search of those wearing monks' robes because there was no one to teach them…. Thus this subject believes that the cause began here with following the monks in memorizing the passages [of the Classics]. Who will turn their backs on faithful Confucians and follow Buddhist monks and discard practical learning and memorize the passages [of the Classics] if Your Majesty clarifies the ways of the wise monarchs of old by expanding schools, putting effort in education as well as literary arts, and throwing light on Five Schools of Buddhism?"

The period of military regime can be said to be a period of synthesis between Confucianism and Buddhism, in which the rhetoric that does not conflict with the two creeds was popularized wherein "Confucians wearing monks' robes" appeared by overcoming the boundary of "Confucianism" and "Buddhism." Schools similar to the Japanese *terakoya* (propagated in the Edo period) were provided in Goryeo for educational purposes.[1]

---

[1] *Terakoya* (temple schools) in the Edo period were private elementary schools for children of commoners. (S. Lee)

However, the Choe regime adopted a policy of giving preferential treatment to the literati and Confucians. Representative of the literati was Yi Gyu-bo (李奎報, 1168-1241) who was employed by Choe Chung-heon. He is the author of *Dongguk isanggukjip* (東國李相國集, Collected Works of Minister Yi of Korea). Choe Wu, the second leader of the Choe clan, also had as his resident guests the literati and Confucians. Choe Ja (崔滋, 1188-1260) was a representative of the literati whose collected works is titled *Bohanjip* (補閑集, Supplementary Jottings in Idleness). Yi Gyu-bo and Choe Ja are literati who excelled in the rhetoric but can hardly be called Confucians. The general trend of the times was to revere the rhetoric rather than the Confucian Classics.

Struggles against the Mongols for 30 Years

Jin China founded by the Jurchens toppled the Liao dynasty founded by the Khitans, and the Mongols who established the greatest empire in history across the Eurasian continent emerged as a new threat in the northern region after they destroyed Jin China. Kubilai Khan of the Mongols founded the kingdom of the Great Yuan (大元) dynasty in 1271 and named its capital "Grand Capital" (大都: today's Beijing). Goryeo fought a war with the previous Mongols from 1231 for 30 years. This was a national crisis on which the survival of the Goryeo dynasty depended. But unlike the Jin or Southern Song dynasties of China, the Goryeo dynasty miraculously was able to survive; this war was fought under the command of the military regime of the Choe clan.

Genghis Khan was elected emperor in 1206 at the Council of Chieftains of various Mongolian tribes. The main targets for invasion for the Mongols in East Asia were the Jin and Southern Song dynasties in the northern region of China. The Mongols destroyed Jin China in 1234 and Southern Song China in 1279. The Northern Song dynasty was brought down by Jin China when Northern Song allied itself with Jin China to destroy its old and visible enemy Liao.

130

Southern Song was also destroyed by the Mongols when it cooperated with the Mongols to fell Jin China.

The Mongols began an invasion of Goryeo in 1231 before the destruction of Jin and Southern Song. Goryeo first came in contact with the Mongol troops in 1218. Some of the Khitans under the control of Jin China invaded the northern area of Goryeo when the Mongols attacked Jin China and held sway over the territory through using Gangdong Castle (江東城: Pyeong'an Province) as the base of operation. The Goryeo troops got rid of the enemy in concert with the Mongol forces led by Ha Zhen (哈眞), and this became Goryeo's first contact with the Mongols.

Thereafter the Mongol envoy asked for tributes that were impossible to meet and behaved outrageously. The Mongol envoy Zhuo Guyu (著古與) was assassinated near the Amnok River in 1225 on his way back to his homeland after collecting the tribute from Goryeo. The Mongols held the Goryeo regime responsible for this and broke off all domestic relations. Using the assassination of the Mongol envoy as an excuse, the Mongol cavalry led by Ogedei (撒禮搭) conquered several castles in Pyeong'an and Hwanghae Provinces, surrounded Gaegyeong, and some detachments went as far south as Chungju in Chungcheong Province. This is the first of the so-called Mongol invasions and the beginning of the 30-year war. The Goryeo administration finally gave 70 pounds of yellow gold, 1,300 pounds of white gold, 1,000 pieces of clothing, 170 horses, as well as massive quantities of goods to several of the generals. In response, the Mongol forces withdrew, leaving behind 72 *darugachi* (one of the official positions of the Mongols dispatched to Goryeo).

Choe Wu of the military regime assassinated the 72 *darugachi* and moved the capital to Ganghwa Island at the estuary of the Han River after deciding to terminate diplomatic relations with the Mongols. The peasants on the mainland were ordered to resist the Mongols by building strongholds on islands or mountain fortresses. The Mongols sent troops in waves to lay waste to the mainland and put pressure on the monarch on Ganghwa Island to come back to shore to attend the Royal Court. There were some Goryeo people such as Hong Bok-won (洪福源) and his son Hong Da-gu (洪茶丘) who surrendered to the Mongol forces and went under Mongol domination by creating a colony for Goryeo people near today's Seonyang. Hong Da-gu in particular was remarkably active when the Mongols attacked Goryeo in leading Goryeo troops composed of deserters from campaigns against Japan.

Goryeo peasants could not receive support from the central forces, and thus they had no choice but to fight off the Mongols by creating autonomous defense mechanisms. Mountain fortresses or islands scattered throughout each region were utilized as strongholds for resistance. Attacking mountain fortresses and islands was the most difficult role for the Mongol cavalry, whose forte was mobile warfare on great plains.

The Mongol forces retreated when Gojong agreed in the fifth invasion (from July of 1253 to January of the following year) to go to Gaegyeong and send Prince Chang to attend the Royal Court of the Mongol emperor. But the Mongol forces invaded later for the sixth time to hold Goryeo accountable because they said Goryeo had not truly surrendered if all of the ministers of the military regime of the Choe clan, including Choe Hang, a third-generation general, did not come ashore with the Goryeo monarch and the prince. The commander-in-chief was Jalairtai. *History of Goryeo* contains the following record on the ghastliness of the battle:

> As many as 206,800 men and women became prisoners of the Mongol troops this year (1254), and the number of people massacred cannot be accounted for. The provinces and districts we pass have all been reduced to ashes. At no other time has it been this bad since the riot of the Mongol troops.
>
> • 41st year of the reign of Gojong, "Biography,"
> *History of Goryeo*

In the end, the monarch as well as civilian official Yu Gyeong (柳璥) schemed to eliminate the resistance faction in order to make peace with the Mongols, and had Choe Ui, the fourth general of the Choe regime, murdered in 1258 with the help of military official Kim In-jun (金仁俊). Crown Prince Jeon (倎: later became Wonjong 元宗) attended the Royal Court of the Mongols, promised peace, and vowed to tear down Ganghwa Castle. But Yim Yeon (林衍), a military civilian of the resistance faction, killed Kim In-jun and contradicted Wonjong by advocating complete resistance after gaining power. It was not until Yim Yu-mu (林惟茂), the son of Yim Yeon, was assassinated with support from the Mongols in 1270 after inheriting the position of power from his father that the military regime ended. The relatively stable Choe regime continued for 100 years since the rebellion of military officials in 1170, but it ended 62 years later in its fourth generation.

The great Mongol war that began in 1231 ended with the pro-peace faction coming out ahead of the dizzying assassinations between the resistance faction and the pro-peace faction with the support of the Mongol forces. The Troops of the Three Elite Patrols (三別抄軍) of the resistance faction, which opposed the monarch going ashore and the attendance of the Crown Prince at the Mongol Royal Court, continued the fight by leading the navy while moving the strongholds from Ganghwa Island to Jin Island and again to Jeju Island. This is the so-called insurrection of the Three Elite Patrols.

Invasion of Japan

After subjugating the Goryeo dynasty, Yuan China invaded Japan twice. The first invasion occurred in 1274 with strongholds in the Korean peninsula, and the second invasion occurred in 1281 with strongholds in the Korean peninsula and Southern Song China. These are called in Japanese history Bun-ei Battle and Koan Battle, respectively; the two combined are called "the Yuan expeditionary force" to denote invasion of the Yuan. Japan attributed "*kamikaze*" to be the source of defeating the Yuan-Goryeo allied troops on both occasions; some debate that "Japanese piracy" in the late Goryeo period was revenge against Goryeo's attack against Japan ahead of Yuan. *Yuan Expeditionary Force* by Hatada Takashi is a masterpiece that provides a verifiable counterargument to such crude statements. Takashi argues as follows:

> From Japan's perspective, Japan is safe as long as Goryeo resists the Mongols. Japan will face a crisis when that resistance weakens or no longer exists. That is why the Mongol invasion of Goryeo and Goryeo's struggles against it must be taken into consideration when "the Yuan expeditionary force" is reviewed.

As mentioned previously, the Mongols destroyed Jin China in 1234 and Southern Song in 1279, but the 30-year war between Goryeo and the Mongols began even before the two in 1231. This leads to the question of why the Mongols persisted in invading Goryeo from such an early stage.

The Mongols thought to use Goryeo as an outpost for attacking Southern Song or Japan in the beginning. The greatest weakness of the Mongol Calvary was that it lacked experience in sea battles. Therefore the Mongols had to depend on the naval battleships of Goryeo in order to attack Southern Song and Japan. The matchless Mongol forces on the Eurasian continent probably never expected Goryeo to resist for over 30 years.

However, the Mongols gradually considered Goryeo as an outpost for the invasion of Japan because not only were the five *choyusa* dispatched to Japan at different times ignored, but Japan did not even bother to respond.[2] "To ignore a dispatch" like this was to challenge the sender. But the plan for dispatching expeditionary forces to Japan became greatly complicated due to the insurrection of the Three Elite Patrols following return of the monarch to Gaegyeong.

The origin of the Three Elite Patrols is the Night Patrol (夜別抄), which was created by the administration of the Choe clan to maintain security. This was expanded to the two corps of the Left Elite Patrol (左別抄) and the Right Elite Patrol (右別抄), while the Army of Transcendent Righteousness (神義軍), made up of escaped

---

[2] *Choyusa* was a temporary government post for counseling and activated to give warning to the populace during wartime. (S. Lee)

soldiers from Mongol imprisonment, was added to the two to become the Three Elite Patrols. The leadership of Bae Jung-son (裴仲孫) and Noh Yeong-hui (盧永禧) opposed the return of the monarch to Gaegyeong and put On (溫) of the royal blood on the throne to confront the Wonjong administration in Gaegyeong. The troops of the Three Elite Patrols took control of 1,000 ships moored in Ganghwa Island and moved the stronghold to Jin Island in the southwestern region of the Korean peninsula.

A prior task of Commanding General Xin Dou (忻都) as the appointed commander of the expeditionary force to Japan and Lieutenant Commanding General Hong Da-gu was to subjugate the Troops of the Three Elite Patrols after merging with the Goryeo troops led by Kim Bang-gyeong (金方慶) prior to invading Japan. The Troops of the Three Elite Patrols continued to resist after moving the stronghold to Jeju Island and elected Kim Tong-jeong (金通精) when the Goryeo-Mongol allied forces occupied Jin Island. The battles fought between the Goryeo-Mongol allied forces and the Three Elite Patrols acted as amphibious allied tactical rehearsals for the invasion of Japan. The naval troops of the Three Elite Patrols at one time expanded power to the coasts of Jeolla and Gyeongsang Provinces and formed an alliance with the anti-Yuan insurgents to attack shipyards or threaten base camps for the invasion of Japan.

The Goryeo-Mongol allied forces barely managed to suppress the troops of the Three Elite Patrols in Jeju Island in 1273. Thus strictly speaking, the anti-Yuan war which began in 1231 ended in 1273. The first invasion of Japan by the Goryeo-Mongol allied forces started the following year in 1274.

The main force of the first invasion of Japan, or the so-called Bun-ei Battle in Japanese history, consisted of 15,000 Mongol troops (Mongols, Han China, and the Jurchens) led by Commanding General Xin Dou (忻都) and Lieutenant Commanding General Hong Da-gu, and the Goryeo troops consisting of 900 battleships and 5,600 soldiers, including enlisted soldiers, oarsmen, and sailors led by Governor Kim Bang-gyeong. This was a heavy burden to bear for devastated Goryeo that had recently experienced 30 years of war. But

Shikken Hojo Tokimune of the Kamakura Bakufu who defeated the first invasion became overly confident and beheaded Du Shizhong (杜世忠), a temporary official with the mission to exhort the people during wartime, sent by Yuan in Kamakura in 1275. Zhou Fu (周福), an old vassal of Southern Song with whom Japan had friendly relations, and others were also sent as an envoy in 1279 but were beheaded in Hakata as well. Goryeo could not avoid participating in the second invasion of Japan in 1281. But the fortuitous typhoons that miraculously occurred at the times of both invasions saved Japan and became the background from which the doctrine of the land of god was born.

Kubilai gave a princess in marriage to Prince Sim (諶), son of Wonjong, who was residing in the Great Capital as hostage prior to the invasion of Japan. Thus Goryeo became the kingdom of Yuan's son-in-law. As Yuan emperor's son-in-law, the Goryeo monarch received royal envoys or generals from Yuan from an upper seat in a southward direction (the direction of a king's seat) after Crown Prince Sim ascended to the throne and became King Chungnyeol (忠烈王, r. 1274-1308). This was the traditional east-west seating arrangement for meetings. The only negative thing was that the title of the monarch was changed from "*jong*" (宗) to "king," which was a step back.

Commanding General Xin Dou (忻都) and Lieutenant Commanding General Hong Da-gu were granted audience with Goryeo's King Chungnyeol in March of 1281, a year before they headed for Happo (合浦, today's Masan), where the stronghold of the Goryeo-Mongol allied forces was located to launch the second invasion of Japan.

> The king discussed duties with Xin Dou and Da-gu. The king sat southward, and Xin Dou and others sat eastward. The king and the envoy faced each other in an east-west direction since Goryeo's subjugation. The people rejoiced in the fact that now Xin Dou does not dare stand on equal footing. Xin Dou went to Happo.

The protocol of the royal family of Goryeo, by forming a marriage tie with the Yuan royal family, enabled the royal family of Goryeo to sit in a southward direction and not as equals when meeting with the royal envoys and generals of ·the Yuan emperor. In other words, the Goryeo royal family was able to maintain dignity by granting audience to Yuan vassals from a superior position. This marriage tie is generally described as a disgraceful symbol of subordination in historical documents of Korea. Through this tie, however, not only was Goryeo guaranteed relative autonomy in a subordinate relationship with Yuan, but it was able to import the culture of Song China with Yuan as the medium.

Culture Blossoms under the Sword of Military Officials

The compilers of *History of Goryeo* listed the names of Choe Chung-heon as well as all of the rulers of the Choe clan and Bae Jung-son, leader of the insurrection of the Three Elite Patrols, in the category of traitors in "Yeoljeon." The compilers were Confucian scholars of the early Joseon dynasty, and such a way of compiling can be seen as a reflection of the thought on encouraging scholarship and disdaining military arts. Many of the historical documents of Korea today classify the period of military regime as "the Dark Age of Confucianism" or "the Dark Age of culture." This too is probably a reflection of the thought on encouraging scholarship and disdaining military arts which does not consider the coexistence of military officials and culture possible.

It would be good to recall the degeneration of Uijong and the civilian officials around him prior to the rebellion of military officials. Just as Emperor Huizong, the last emperor of Northern Song dynasty in China, was a first-rate artist but a failure as a sovereign, Uijong was "a king who liked poetry and prose" but a failure as a monarch. In their indolent life, the king and the civilian officials who counseled him forgot the advice contained in "Non-Idleness" of the Ten Articles of Instruction which the founder of Goryeo left for his descendants. Flowery phrases or Confucian theories of a debauched king and his civilian officials were overshadowed by the national crisis in the form of struggle for survival under the invasion of the Mongols who had conquered the Eurasian continent. The degree of reversal of order would be excessive on this matter if one were to say, "Confucianism exists even after the nation fell."

The period of military regime was definitely "the Dark Age of Confucianism" to the civilian officials who encouraged scholarship and disdained military arts. But the military regime appointed offspring of military officials or local functionaries who were excluded by the clique of civilian officials to central government through the civil service examination. In a word, the original merit system of the past was employed rather than the clique of civilian officials. The appointees were of the small- and mid-sized landowning class, and they formed a new bureaucratic class that was in charge of actual work under the military regime. This signifies the emergence of a new *sadaebu* class that replaced the aristocratic *sadaebu* class.

Instances that indicate that the period of the military regime may have been the "Dark Age of Confucianism" but by no means the "Dark Age of culture" are given below.

The greatest source of pride as a world cultural heritage among Goryeo culture would probably be the first usage of metal type printing and *Jaejo goryeo daejanggyeong* (再彫高麗大藏經, Reprinted Tripitaka Koreana). These are both from the military regime period and created during the fight against the Yuan invasion. Goryeo printed 50 copies of *Gogeum sangjeong yemun* (古今詳定禮文, Texts on Prescribed Rituals of the Past and Present) using copper type in 1234 and distributed them to each government office. This is the very first record of metal type printing in the world. The oldest extant printed material in movable type from the Goryeo period is *Jikji simgyeong* (直指心經, Direct Pointing to Mind Sutra, 1377), held in reserve in the national museum in Paris. According to Chinese documents, an unknown expert did create tin types, but they were not distributed because the ink did not spread evenly. Instead, wooden types seemed to have been invented by a scientist named Wang Zhen (王禎) for publishing personal agricultural notes.

Buddhism in the Goryeo period was state-protected Buddhism as was the case in the Silla period. After discussing the issues with many of his vassals, Hyeonjong prayed to overcome the national crisis based on the divine protection of Buddha in 1011 when the second Khitan invasion occurred. In addition, the typesetting of the Tripitaka Koreana commenced in 1019 and the task completed in 1087. The first version of the Tripitaka Koreana that had been preserved in Buin Temple (符仁寺) in northern Daegu was burned during the Mongol invasion. The nine-story stupa of Hwangnyong Temple in Gyeongju was destroyed then as well.

The military regime of the Choe clan also commenced the re-printing effort of Tripitaka Koreana in 1236 to overcome the national crisis based on the divine protection of Buddha by establishing a typesetting center in Ganghwa Island and a division in Jinju district. The Choe clan owned much of the land in and around Jinju as *sigeup*.[3] This was the financial resource for reprinting Tripitaka Koreana. The xylographic book completed in 1251 contains 80,125 pieces and 162,516 pages. This is generally called "Goryeo palman daejang-gyeong" (Tripitaka Koreana), which is preserved in Haein Temple in Hapcheon-gun of South Gyeongsang Province. In other words, the Tripitaka Koreana lost in fire at Buin Temple was the first publication and the extant version in Haein Temple is the reprinted version. The UNESCO World Heritage Committee has registered this Tripitaka Koreana along with Bulguk Temple and Seokguram in Gyeongju as world cultural heritage. This reprinting task that took 15 years during the period of struggles against the Yuan invasion was a splendid undertaking that could not have been imagined without the strong faith of the Choe clan administration and the mobilized people.

The *shogun* or *daimyo* (Japanese feudal lord) dispatched envoys on 80-some occasions to request the Tripitaka Koreana in the Muro-machi Era. Tripitaka Koreana from Korea exists in various parts of Japan today. The first record of an envoy dispatched to request the scriptures is Myoha, the Most Reverend Priest of Japan, dispatched by Tandai Imagawa and Ryoshun of Kyushu in the 14th year of the

---

[3] *Sigeup* was village land awarded to government officials as salary. (S. Lee)

reign of King Wu (1388) at the end of Goryeo, wherein fancy goods and 250 prisoners kidnapped by Japanese pirates were offered in exchange for the request of Tripitaka Koreana (14th year of the reign of King Wu, *History of Goryeo*, Vol. 50). Shunoku Myoha was a votary and the teacher of Ashikaga Yoshimitsu who was responsible for forming an alliance with Korea.

Likewise, the fact is that the representative culture of the Goryeo period is the Buddhist culture that selected "Buddhist nation" as the founding ideology is the same as the Silla culture of the preceding dynasty. Buddhism definitely received overprotection for reasons of being a Buddhist nation, and it is true that adherence between sovereignty and Buddhism brought about decay. However, Confucians who greatly influenced the spiritual world of the Goryeo populace included Uicheon (1055-1101), State Preceptor Daegak who established the Cheontae School in Goryeo, and Jinul, National Preceptor Bojo.

More important is the fact that the Goryeo dynasty was able to maintain an autonomous kingdom, albeit imperfect, through the 30 years of military regime struggles. This can only be called a miracle, in that great kingdoms such as the Jin and Southern Song dynasties disappeared under the trampling hooves of the Mongol cavalry.

Not only Goryeo but all of East Asia were swept away in a great whirlwind of change due to the thundering advances of the Mongols. Goryeo was greatly influenced by Song China in cultural ways, among which Confucianism is representative. Both the Goryeo and Song dynasties were joined in solidarity against the threat from the northern tribes. But Northern Song, which was originally established in 960 by Zhao Kuang-yin, was destroyed by a northern tribe that later became Jin China in 1127, and Southern Song struggled desperately for survival against outside forces but was destroyed by the Mongols of the northern tribe in 1279.

The Mongol forces overcame Jin China in 1234 and shared a border with Southern Song. Kubilai Khan finally gained surrender of Southern Song after launching a six-year-long offensive and defensive battle while staying in Xiangyang Castle (襄陽城), which was built by Southern Song with concerted effort as a defensive stronghold. The power of the Mohammedan cannon brought from Arabia by the Mongol forces decided this long battle. Premier Bai Yan was in command of the Mongol forces that advanced south from Xiangyang. Wen Tian-xiang (文天祥) was appointed prime minister of Southern Song during its struggle for survival. In spite of continued resistance against the Mongol forces from Yashan (厓山島) in Guangdong (廣東) until 1279 after Linan (Hangzhou) fell into the hands of the Mongols in 1276, the history of Southern Song ultimately ended 320 years after the founding date. Kubilai Khan asked Wen Tian-xiang to submit, but then ordered his beheading in the Grand Capital (capital of Yuan China and today's Beijing) at his refusal to submit. Wen Tian-xiang died for the great cause of "reverence for China and exclusionism of all foreigners" as a model of Song Chinese *sadaebu*.

Japan was able to achieve autonomous development during the turbulent period in East Asia caused by the vicissitudes of the northern race because it was outside the realm of the northern race with Genkainada in between. The two Mongol invasions were the first experience of war since reinforcement was dispatched to Baekje in 663. The Kamakura Bakufu may have won the war against the "Yuan pirates," but not one additional piece of territory was gained. There was naturally no money for the king to award the Gokenin (samurais who have a lord and vassal relationship with their lords), who are the foundation of the existence of the Bakufu. Thus, Gokenin's distrust and the penury of the Bakufu ultimately became the deathblow for the Kamakura Bakufu; it was followed by internal strife owing to division of south and north. In this sense, Japan could not but be affected by the turbulence in East Asia, even if only indirectly.

9

The Learning of Master Zhu Comes to Korea from Yuan China

The Study of the Principle of Human Nature Based on the Doctrine of Innate Goodness of Mencius

Song China became divided into the Northern period in which the capital was in Kaifeng and the Southern period in which the capital was moved southward to Linan after losing its territory north of the Huaihe River to Jin China. The political consciousness of the *sadaebu* class was raised during the Song period due to the confrontation between the New Doctrine Faction and the Old Doctrine Faction in the Northern Song period and the confrontation between the pro-peace faction and the resistance faction toward Jin China in the Southern Song period. Unlike the aristocratic clique of civilian officials, the *sadaebu* studied to pass the civil service examination on their merit; the *sadaebu* were bureaucrats of the ruling class who were engaged in politics but restricted to one generation of service. The scholarship is, of course, the Confucianism of "governing others after self-cultivation."

Interpretation of the Five Confucian Classics, a collection of commentaries on the Five Confucian Classics written during the Han period, became the Confucian textbook for the civil service examination during the reign of Emperor Taizong of Tang China. Thus commentaries of the Han period and the rhetoric of the Tang period could not answer questions on the way to "statecraft and tranquility for all under Heaven" that arose within the political consciousness of the *sadaebu* in the Song period, nor resist the heretical Buddhist philosophy. This is the background from which the Song School emerged as Neo-Confucianism during the Song period. This Song

Neo-Confucianism during the Song period. This Song School is called the Cheng-Zhu School or the Learning of Master Zhu.

The Diagram of the Great Ultimate (太極圖說) that developed cosmology by Zhou Dun-yi (周敦頤) became the foundation for building the system of thought of the Song School; Zhou Dun-yi provided the key to a grand philosophical scheme that united the mandate from Heaven and human nature. In addition to Zhou Dun-yi, Zhang Heng-qu (張橫渠), Cheng Ming-dao (程明道), and Cheng Yi-chuan (程伊川) emerged to extend the system of thought comprised of theories from cosmology to humanism, education, self-cultivation, and policy. These four Confucian scholars from the Northern Song period are called "Zhou, Zhang, and the Two Chengs" (周張二程: these four are collectively called the Four Teachers of Ethics).

In contrast, Zhu Xi (1130-1200) was a scholar who was active in the Southern Song period. His name is Hui and pen names are Ziyang (紫陽) and Huian (晦庵). He wrote 14 volumes of *Reflections of Things at Hand* with his friend Lu Zu-qian (呂祖謙), the content of which is organized into 14 areas on the most important theories of Zhou, Zhang, and the Two Chengs. This is the primer as well as the basis for the Cheng-Zhu School. In other words, Zhu Xi organized and compiled each field of Neo-Confucianism developed from the Northern Song period, summarized them, and completed a consistent system of thought. Especially central to the Learning of Master Zhu is the doctrine of "nature is the principle" developed from humanism as put forth by Cheng Yi-chuan. Thus the Learning of Master Zhu is also called the study of the principle of human nature.

"Dao-ti" (道體) 37 of *Reflections of Things at Hand* contains the following statement of Cheng Yi-chuan:

> Human nature is the principle. If light shines forth from where the principle emanates, that which is not good does not exist. How can things be not good when the conditions for joy, anger, sorrow, and pleasure do not radiate forth?

143

The passage below is contained in "Dao-ti" 39:

> Human nature comes from Heaven and its ability comes from material force (氣, *qi* in Ch.). The ability will be pure if the material force is pure, and the ability will be impure if the material force is impure. Contained within the ability are those which are good and not good, but there is nothing which is not good in nature.

In other words, Cheng Yi-chuan clearly distinguishes between "the principle" (理, the metaphysical) and "the material force" (氣, the physical), and states that that which is not good does not exist in "nature = principle" before the feelings of joy, anger, sorrow, and pleasure radiate forth. His doctrine of "nature is the principle" imbues the doctrine of innate goodness put forth by Mencius with metaphysical and philosophical grounds. Moreover, that which is good and that which is not good coexist in the talents of men, which materialize as purity or impurity in the physical material force. Xun-zi and the doctrine of his school, which criticized Mencius by advocating "the doctrine of innate evilness," were finally rejected as being "heresy."

Liu Xiang-shan (陸象山, 1139-1192) among the scholars of Song also challenged the Learning of Master Zhu with "the mind is the principle" (心卽理). He opposed Zhu Xi's claim of "nature is the principle" by distinguishing "mind" (心), "nature" (性), and "compassion" (情); he advocated that the "mind is the principle" in stating "the mind and the principle cannot be two different things" by comprehending the mind to be in perfect harmony of nature and compassion. Wang Yang-ming (王陽明, 1472-1528) developed the doctrine of Liu Xiang-shan in the Ming China period, leading to fierce debates between the Learning of Master Zhu and the Wang Yang-ming School and to the division of the world of Confucianism into two trends. Both started by pursuing the teachings of the sages, but the Wang Yang-ming School emphasized "honoring virtuous nature," whereas the Learning of Master Zhu emphasized "maintaining constant inquiry and study" (道問學). The divergence occurred when different things were emphasized.

Chapter 27 of the *Doctrine of the Mean* contains the following passage:

> Therefore the superior man honors his virtuous nature and maintains constant inquiry and study, seeking to carry it out to its breadth and greatness so as to omit none of the more exquisite and minute points which it embraces; and to raise it to its greatest height and brilliance so as to pursue the course of the Mean. He cherishes his old knowledge, and is continually acquiring new. He exerts an honest, generous earnestness in the esteem and practice of all propriety.

Honoring virtuous nature and maintaining constant inquiry and study are originally one in the *Doctrine of the Mean* and not separate. Zhu Xi also understood them in this way, but long debates between the Cheng-Zhu School faction and Liu-Wang School over which of the two should be emphasized finally led to this division: On the one hand, nature is the principle as the maintenance of constant inquiry and study; on the other, the mind is the principle as the honoring of virtuous nature.

The Learning of Master Zhu, which eliminated "sympathy" from the unity of "nature," "sympathy," and "mind," considers the goal to be the self-cultivation of that which pursues the doctrine that nature is the principle and approaches it. It is difficult to deny that this is but an expression of one aspect of the ascetic rigorism of the Learning of Master Zhu.

Furthermore, the Learning of Master Zhu fundamentally revised the Five Confucian Classics which, until then, had acted as the basic scriptures of Confucianism. In short, importance was put on the chronicle of the sayings and doings of Confucius in the form of *Analects of Confucius* and *The Works of Mencius* by Mencius in the Han and Tang Schools until then and *Great Learning* and the *Doctrine of the Mean* that are independent sections of *Record of Rites* were combined into "Four Books." *Analects of Confucius* is not included in the Five

Confucian Classics, and Mencius was no more than just one of the Hundred Schools of Thought. The Four Books are considered more important than the Five Confucian Classics, thus referring to them as "the Four Books and Five Confucian Classics" (四書五經).

In addition, the Learning of Master Zhu recommended that Confucianism should be introduced in the following order: The *Great Learning* be mastered first, after which the *Analects of Confucius* or *The Works of Mencius* should be read, and then they should be finished off by the *Doctrine of the Mean*. *Commentaries on the Four Books* (四書集注) is the commentaries on the Four Books by Zhu Xi. Another aspect of Zhu Xi is that he was a superior bibliographical scholar of Chinese Classics. Commentaries made by the scholars of the Han and Tang dynasties are called "old commentaries," whereas commentaries made by Zhu Xi are called "new commentaries."

The School of Master Zhu excluded all other Liu-Wang Schools (also known as the Wang Yang-ming School) from the Song and Ming periods, and the Cheng-Zhu School consolidated a position as the only successor to the orthodox teachings of Confucius and Mencius. Thus only the flow connected to this orthodoxy is the "learning of the Way" (道學). This is the reason for including "Daoxue zhuan" (道學傳) in *History of Song* (宋史) as separate from "Rulin zhuan" (儒林傳).

Huang Gan (黃幹), who happened to be the best pupil and son-in-law of Zhu Xi, discusses the succession of orthodox teachings as follows in "Daotong" of *Doings of Zhu Xi* (朱子行狀):

> Zengzi and Zisi succeeded the declining tradition of the Way after Confucius; and light was shed on the tradition only since the times of Mencius. Zhu Xi, Cheng-zi, and Zhangzi succeeded the discontinued tradition of the Way, and it was revealed for the first time in the times of the Master (Zhu Xi).

146

Yuan China Revives the Learning of Master Zhu Persecuted in the Southern Song Period

Politics in the Goryeo period were handled by the *sadaebu* class with Confucian education following the employment of the civil service examination instead of the aristocratic lineage of civilian officials. However, Confucianism of the Han and Tang Schools focused on the Five Confucian Classics, whereas the rhetoric of the Tang period is emphasized more than the exegetics of the Han period. The Learning of Master Zhu that attained greatness in the Northern Song and Southern Song periods was transmitted to Goryeo through Yuan, destroyer of Southern Song. It is a historical irony for Goryeo scholars of the Learning of Master Zhu that the Learning of Master Zhu, which was strict about distinguishing between things Chinese and things non-Chinese, was transmitted to Goryeo by a dynasty of northern barbarians that destroyed Southern Song in China.

Zhu Xi died peacefully in 1200, but things went awry with his censure of powerful courtiers such as Han Tuo-zhou (韓侂冑) of an opposing faction, which led to the Learning of Master Zhu suffering for four years prior to his death in 1196. The Learning of Master Zhu, however, was adopted as the official scholarship of the Yuan period, and the study of the Learning of Master Zhu was essential in order to apply for the civil service examination in the Ming and Qing periods. The Learning of Master Zhu, which was persecuted in Southern Song in China, was revived by Yuan of the northern barbarians, and furthermore, settled in as the official scholarship. This may be something that neither Cheng-zi nor Zhu Xi could have imagined in a lifetime.

The civilian officials fostered increased communication between Goryeo and Beijing after the extended war against Yuan came to a close and marital ties between Yuan and Goryeo royal families were established. Emperor Renzong reinstated the civil service examination in 1315 that had been abolished for a long time in the Yuan period. Attention is to be paid to the fact that the examination focused around the passages and annotations of Zhu Xi in the Four Books. Emperor Wu of Han China arguably could have made

Confucianism into systemic teaching by making it the state religion, but the Learning of Master Zhu became systemic teaching in the Yuan period by uniting with the civil service examination.

Yuan was a militaristic dynasty made up of horse-riding people that put more importance on military officials than civilian officials. They expected those bureaucrats who passed the civil service examination to administer by mastering the original meaning of the Confucian Classics and not to have exegetical knowledge and rhetorical refinement. With the systematization of doctrinal studies of the Learning of Master Zhu, the meaning of the Classics naturally became more important than commentaries or rhetoric.

Yao Shu (姚樞, 1203-1280) was an important personage in transmitting the Learning of Master Zhu from the Song period to the Yuan period. He held various high offices of the Yuan dynasty consecutively, and as such he established the Hall of Supreme Ultimate and put a Southern Song prisoner and Confucian scholar by the name of Zhao Fu (趙復) in charge of training junior members. Two great Confucian scholars representing the Yuan period are Xu Heng (許衡, pen name is Luzhai 魯齋) and Wu Deng (吳澄, pen name is Caolu 草廬). Xu Heng was immersed completely in the Learning of Master Zhu, but Wu Deng was an eclectic of Zhu-Liu in that he revised parts of the Learning of Master Zhu through integrating it with the good points of Liu Xiang-shan.

Scholars mentioned above all lived during the turbulent times during which Jin and Southern Song fell. They contributed to the continuation of the Learning of Master Zhu as completed in the Song period without interruption. Moreover, Zhu Xi's doctrines of "false learning of Jin" were adopted as the civil service examination, a turn of events which even Zhu Xi himself would not have thought possible in his lifetime. Later Zhu Xi scholars who were more particular about the distinction between Chinese and non-Chinese were very critical of Xu Heng and Wu Deng for serving two dynasties by entering the Yuan government service.

The civilian officials of Goryeo who had association with Beijing naturally became focused on the Learning of Master Zhu as

Neo-Confucianism. King Chungseon (忠宣王, r. 1308-1313), who liked scholarship, abdicated the throne to King Chungsuk (忠肅王, r. 1314-1330) early on and built the Hall of Ten Thousand Volumes (萬卷堂) on his private property in Beijing. He collected books, and the hall acted as a medium through which civilian officials of Goryeo had association with scholars of Yuan China. In short, Yuan China played the role of connecting the scholarship of Song and Korean Confucianism.

Yi Je-hyeon had association with eminent scholars such as Yao Sui (姚燧), Yan Fu (閻復), Yuan Ming-shan (元明善), Yu Ji (虞集), and Zhao Meng-fu (趙孟頫) when he went to Beijing at the request of King Chungseon, among whom Yao Sui was the Xu Heng's disciple and Yao Shu was Xu Heng's uncle. As well, Yu Ji was the disciple of Wu Deng. Zhao Meng-fu was a master painter and calligrapher, and his "pine-snow calligraphy style" (松雪體) became very popular in late Goryeo and early Joseon periods. Prince An-pyeong, who was famous as a noted calligrapher of the early Joseon dynasty, was a master at this pine-snow calligraphy style. The calligraphy style of Ou Yang-xun (歐陽詢, 557-641) of early Tang China was fashionable prior to the transmission of the pine-snow calligraphy style to Korea. In a word, King Chungseon's Hall of Ten Thousand Volumes mediated cultural exchange between the foremost literati in the Yuan period and Goryeo literati.

Yuan received the Learning of Master Zhu from the Southern Song dynasty and adopted commentaries of Zhu Xi as the textbook for the civil service examination. Nor were other aspects of Chinese culture debased; Yuan China possessed a worldly view and was liberal not only with Song scholarship but with all cultures and religions.

The militaristic kingdom of Mongolia held fast to the position of the dominant ethnic group over the Han ethnic group. Rather than hiring Han ethnic groups, Yuan China utilized "people with colored eyes" (色目人, Islamic Turks and Iranians), i.e., people from neighboring nations bordering western China who had a knack for commerce, as the think-tank of the Mongol empire by appointing them as economic bureaucrats. Class structure based on ethnicity dominated Yuan; the Han ethnic group called "the Han people" (漢人) during the Jin rule were placed below the economic bureaucrats, and the Han ethnic group called the "Southerners" (南人) or "the barbarians" (蠻子) of the Southern Song were below them.

The Mongol tribes did not consider Chinese civilization to be the best because they already knew about western civilizations bordering China through the expeditions of the west before their domination of China. Rather, they were cautious about the weakening of the Mongol civilization due to becoming Han-like. Considering such Mongol tribes as savages is the result of the self-righteousness of Chinese and Goryeo intellectuals.

The "Shoushi calendar" (授時曆) was invented by Guo Shoujing (郭守敬) in the Yuan period through stimulation from the Islamic calendar, which is a great calendar-making method in that it was created 300 years earlier than the western Gregorian calendar but similarly computes one year as 365.2425 days. This calendar-making method greatly influenced not only China but Korea and Japan as well. The great Mohammedan cannon from Arabia that was used to penetrate the impregnable Xiangyang Castle when Kubilai besieged Southern Song for six years was new weaponry invented by a Persian expert.

The symbol of Mongol nationalism is the unique invention of the Paspa script by a Tibetan monk so that the new characters could be used in official documents. The Mongol tribes first used Uighur characters to write the Mongolian language but were not satisfied with that and ordered the invention of unique characters.

King Chungseon was introduced above as having built the Hall of Ten Thousand Volumes (萬卷堂) on private property in Beijing as a salon for exchange between Yuan and Goryeo civilian officials. He seems to have possessed quite a bit of influence as a royal son-in-law even after his abdication of the throne. Yi Je-hyeon introduces the following anecdote in *Ikjenango* (益齋亂藁):

Monks from the Xianbei tribe petitioned Emperor Renzong in the early period of Yeonu (延祐, the name of the reign of Emperor Renzong of Yuan, r. 1314-1320).

"Paspa (八思巴), the emperor's teacher, benefited the kingdom by inventing the [Mongol] script. If it pleases Your Majesty, a command must be made throughout the kingdom to build a shrine for him as was done for Confucius."

The emperor issued a royal edict to the court nobles and elders to hold a council. Guogong Yang An-pu (揚安普) emphasized this. King Chungseon said to An-pu:

"Master Paspa has performed a meritorious deed by inventing the script. Commemorating him must befit the protocol of old; how can he be equated to Confucius? Confucius was teacher to all kings, and as such, is commemorated for his virtue and not for services rendered. I am concerned that future generations may have two different perspectives [on this issue]."

The shrine for Master Pasta was executed as planned, but those who heard the speech (of King Chungseon) agreed. The emperor authorized establishing the civil service examination when Yao Sui's opinion was presented to the emperor by the king (Chungseon). Li Meng (李孟) reported to the emperor and executed [his duties] when he was appointed to the post of Chief Administrator (平章政事, Pingzhang Zhengshi in Ch.), but the essence was mostly the king.

- "Biography," Vol. 9, *Ikjenango*

The Xianbei monks put importance on the "meritorious service" rendered by Paspa, whereas King Chungseon emphasized the "virtue" (德) of Confucius. This is indeed a perspective worthy of a Confucian. The civil service examination was revived in the 4th year of the reign of Emperor Renzong of Yuan (1315), but it was realized through the combined efforts of Yao Sui → King Chungseon → Li Meng. Renzong decided to implement the civil service examination in order to internally systematize the abilities of the Southern Song Confucians and absorb their discontent.

Attention should be paid to the fact that the Four Books were added to the hitherto examination subjects of the Five Confucian Classics, as well as making Four Books and Five Confucian Classics by Zhu Xi the standard. This is probably in consideration of Southern Song Confucians having been trained in the Learning of Master Zhu. Another point is that the three-level system of the civil service examination containing *xieshi* (解試, first-level examination conducted in the provinces), *xingshi* (省試, second-level examination conducted by the central government), and *dianshi* (殿試, third-level examination conducted in the palace) from the Song period was adopted. The founder of Song China adopted *dianshi* with the foresight of recruiting new bureaucrats by merit directly under him to personally bestow favor and grace onto future vassals.

Joseon dynasty's 500 years of the civil service examination system accepted the Learning of Master Zhu as the standard scholarship of the meaning of Confucian Classics and adopted the three-stage system of the civil examination system by following in the footsteps of the examination system of the Yuan period. The Joseon period called the different stages *hyangsi* (鄕試, first-level test conducted in the provinces), *boksi* (覆試, second-level test conducted by the central government), and *jeonsi* (殿試, final test conducted under the personal attendance of the sovereign).

Yuan China, however, put a damper on the policy of overly revering Han dynasty China by putting the Tibetan monk who invented the symbol of Yuan nationalism in the form of Paspa script on a par with Confucius. This invention prevented the identity of the nomadic tribes from disappearing. This is the big difference between the Mongol tribes of Yuan from the Khitans of Liao and Jurchens of Jin who were also conquering dynasties of the northern tribes, but were buried under reverence for China.

Ahn Hyang Shouts for Confucian Reform

The sovereign and civilian officials of Goryeo first came into contact with the Learning of Master Zhu in the Yuan period. Ahn Hyang

152

(安珦, pen name is Hoeheon 晦軒, 1243-1306) shouted for reform of Goryeo Confucianism based on the Learning of Master Zhu at this time. Ahn Hyang went to Beijing among the retinue of the prince who later became King Chungseon in the 16th year of King Chungnyeol's reign (1290). He came into contact with Zhu Xi's letters that were distributed in Beijing then and learned that they inherited the "orthodox spirit of the instruction of Confucius." He brought back with him Zhu Xi's letters as well as drawn images of Confucius and Zhu Xi ("Hoeheon seonsang yeonbo," 晦軒先生年譜, Chronology of Master Hoeheon).

At the time, even the National University as headquarters of Confucian education was in ruins in Goryeo, which probably meant that Buddhism or shamanism was prevalent among the populace. Ahn Hyang wrote a famous poem to lament this deplorable situation:

Incense burns everywhere, all pray to Buddha;
　　香燈處處皆祈佛
the sound of cylindrical oboe in each household, all serve the spirits; 簫管家家盡祀神
in two or three rooms alone stands the shrine of Confucius;
　　獨有數間夫子廟
only full of spring grass, there is no human shadow;
　　滿庭春草寂無人

He proposed to the government to improve the education system and to collect Scholarship Funds to support the students at the National University as its chief secretary in 1304:

"The duty of the prime minister is to put education first. The Fund for Nurturing Worthies is running dry and cannot foster scholars. If it pleases Your Majesty, ranks 6-*pum* and above as well as ranks 7-*pum* and below should be differentiated and made to pay one *geun* [600 g]) for the former and cloth to replenish the Fund for Nurturing Worthies. Principal funds should be preserved and the Scholarship Fund should be replenished by interest." The prime minister followed his advice. The sovereign (King

Chungnyeol) also ordered money and grains be paid from the royal warehouse.

- "Ahn Hyang," Yeoljeon, *History of Goryeo*

Let us examine a somewhat long excerpt from "Yugukja jesaengmun" (Literature to Open the Eyes of the Students at the National University) to understand his educational thought:

> The way of the sages is nothing more than ordinary ethics. It would be enough for offspring to be filial, vassals be loyal, homes be ruled with propriety, friends keep faith, and each cultivates himself with piety. The Buddhists desert their parents and move out of the house, which is equivalent to barbarian groups in their betrayal of ethics and obligations. The schools are closed, scholars do not have scholarly attainments, Buddhist documents are preferred in learning, and the meaning of nihilistic quiescence (虛無空寂) is elevated and believed as aftereffects of the recent wars. I consider these with deep regret. Long ago I obtained the writings of Zhu Huian (朱晦庵, Zhu Xi) in China; his meritorious service of revealing the way of the sages and excluding Zen (禪) and Buddhism (佛) is on a par with that of Zhongni (Confucius). It is best to learn about Huian first in order to learn about Zhongni. Students should not be inattentive to the pursuit of knowledge in reality after reading new books.

Ahn Hyang became fascinated with the Learning of Master Zhu because he highly valued Zhu Xi's "meritorious deeds of vindicating the way of the sage (Confucius) and of excluding Daoism and Buddhism." He always hung a portrait of Zhu Xi in his room in reverence in later life and created his pen name of "Hoeheon" by using the character from Zhu Xi's pen name of Huian. He transmitted the Learning of Master Zhu to Goryeo in 1290, the 90th year of the death of Zhu Xi. Following Ahn Hyang, Baek Yi-jeong (白頤正, 1260-1340) studied and collected books on the doctrine of the study of the principle of human nature of Cheng and Zhu (程朱) for 10 years while staying in Beijing as part of King Chungseon's retinue; he brought the books back with him when he returned to Korea.

From National University to Sungkyunkwan, a Professional School

The name of Goryeo's national college was changed from National University to Sungkyunkwan in the 34th year of the reign of King Chungnyeol (1308). Moreover, Sungkyunkwan was turned into an independent professional Confucian university by putting the Law College, Calligraphy College, and Accounting College of the National University under the management of specialized government offices.

As mentioned before, the Cheng-Zhu School was completed in the Northern Song and Southern Song periods in the form of Neo-Confucianism and adopted into the civil service examination in the Yuan period, and not a few Goryeo Confucians took the civil service examination of Yuan. Yi Saek also took the examination in Yuan China and passed it with first place in the *kuaishi* (會試, second examination) and second place in *dianshi*. Thus the Cheng-Zhu School was transmitted to Goryeo by the civilian officials who went back and forth from the Grand Capital (Beijing) of Yuan China.

In the 16th year of the reign of King Gongmin (1367), Yi Saek (李穡, pen name Mog-eun 牧隱, 1328-1396), who later became the chancellor (大司成) of Sungkyunkwan, studied at the Imperial University in Beijing for three years from 1348 before he passed the civil service examination. He submitted Eight Clauses on Administration (時政八條) to King Gongmin in 1352 after he came back to Goryeo. He assumed in "Nonsunghak" (論崇學) that of the eight clauses, "the study of national literature, the foundation of cultivating customs, and able men are the foundation of politics and education," and gave important suggestions for making Sungkyunkwan active. Among these was his statement that "those holding government posts must pass the civil service examination, and those applying to take the civil service examination must have studied at Sungkyunk-wan. This signifies rejection of exclusive sectarianism, i.e., "disciples," between teachers and students in private schools.

Folk uprisings of the "Red Turban Bandits" (紅巾賊) led by believers of the White Lotus Teachings (白蓮教) occurred in various parts of Chin toward the end of the Yuan period; Zhu Yuan-zhang (朱元璋), the founder of Ming dynasty in 1368, was also part of this. The Red Turban Bandits also trespassed into Goryeo in 1359 and 1361 to pillage. Especially in 1361, King Gongmin was forced to flee to Andong in Gyeongsang Province, because the 100,000-some pillagers closed in toward Gaegyeong.

King Gongmin appointed Yi Saek jointly as Pangaeseong (判開城) and as Chancellor of Sungkyunkwan after rebuilding Sungkyunkwan due to the destruction from the raid of the Red Turban Bandits. He was in charge of the capital of Gaeseong and education. A program on Four Books and Five Confucian Classics was instituted in the rebuilt Sungkyunkwan. The Five Confucian Classics is, of course, the scripture of the studies of Han and Tang dynasties, whereas the Four Books and Five Confucian Classics is the scripture of the Cheng-Zhu School. The students of Sungkyunkwan came to systematically study the Four Books and Five Confucian Classics in the following order: Great Learning Program → Analects of Confucius Program → Works of Mencius Program → Doctrine of the Mean Program → Record of Rites Program → Spring and Autumn Annals Program → Book of Poetry Program → Book of Documents Program → Book of Documents Program → Book of Changes Program.

From this time on, Sungkyunkwan changed into a sanctuary for learning that fostered a new bureaucratic class of the Cheng-Zhu School, different from the old bureaucratic class of the studies of Han and Tang dynasties. Gwon Geun (權近), a pupil of Yi Saek, wrote as follows in "Chronology" for his teacher:

> After the military disturbance of the year of Sinchuk (1361), the sovereign (King Gongmin) rebuilt Sungkyunkwan on the old site

of the Sungmun Hall in order to revive the school, because the school had been devastated. Because there were only a few students, only Kim Gu-yong (金九容) from Yeongga, Jeong Mong-ju (鄭夢周) from Ocheon, Bak Sang-chun (朴尙衷) from Banyang, Bak Ui-jung (朴宜中) from Milyang, and Yi Sung-in (李崇仁) from Gyeongsan were chosen as scholars of the study of the Confucian scriptures at one time. They held other official posts while studying. The Master (Yi Saek) was in charge of them, and he was the first to hold a joint position as chancellor.

Scholars gathered from all over in the spring of the following year of Gapsul, and the master divided the Confucian Classics and taught. Questions were discussed and investigated at the end of the lectures each day. The master calmly selected the Doctrine of the Mean while distinguishing his revelations and compromises, but he made an effort to fit them into the doctrines of Cheng and Zhu; he did not tire even when the sun went down. Thus the study of the principle of human nature became great in Korea, and scholars turned away from the habit of writing and memorizing the rhetoric while pursuing the principle of the body, mind, nature, and mandate of Heaven (身心性命); people did not become captivated by heterodoxy because they considered Confucianism the foundation. They also made loyalty upright while not pursuing doctrinism so that aspects of old customs and scholarship were improved greatly. These were the results of the master's teachings and persuasion.

Yi Saek played the role of changing the educational content of the rebuilt Sungkyunkwan to promote the Learning of Master Zhu as transmitted by Ahn Hyang, as well as bridging the Learning of Master Zhu to the Joseon dynasty. But he was a loyal subject of the Goryeo dynasty. He opposed Yi Seong-gye's seizing of power and died soon after from being implicated in treasonous activities with his two sons. He left behind 55 volumes of the *Mogeunjip* (牧隱集, Collected Works of Mog-eun). Yi Saek was the very man who advanced the School of the Study of the Principle of Human Nature in Joseon, but *History of Goryeo*, which was compiled in the early Joseon period, was cold toward him. It severely criticized his scholarship for "not being pure because he did not exclude Buddhism as a scholar of the Learning of Master Zhu."

Confucians of Silla or Goryeo broadly practiced not only Confucianism but Buddhism or Daoism as well. As Choe Seung-no stated in the Twenty-Eight Items on Current Issues, "practicing Buddhism is the foundation of moral training, and practicing Confucianism is the foundation of statecraft." This was the general perspective on Confucianism and Buddhism (儒佛觀) of Goryeo's *sadaebu* class. Scholars of the Learning of Master Zhu in the Joseon period considered this to be impure and deleted it from Confucian history or spoke ill of it. It would be difficult to evaluate this rigid doctrinism in favor of the Learning of Master Zhu as being objective.

Opposing of Buddhism, and Transition in Dynasty

The Goryeo dynasty founded by Wang Geon in 918 was replaced by the Joseon dynasty of Yi Seong-gye in 1392. This was a revolution in surname change — from the Goryeo Wang clan to the Joseon Yi clan.

As can be seen in his "Literature to Open the Eyes of the Students at the National University," since the transmission of the Learning of Master Zhu by Ahn Hyang the harmony between Confucianism and Buddhism gradually degenerated into a confrontation between the two. This is because the Han and Tang Schools focused on commentaries and rhetoric while "lacking philosophy," whereas the Learning of Master Zhu contained a consistent system of thought. Thus a collision between the two could not be avoided.

How did the School of Master Zhu in late Goryeo period react when the ideology of a "Buddhist nation" was falling with a bang during the turbulence of the end of Goryeo and the beginning of Joseon? To discuss this, attention is paid to Jeong Mong-ju (鄭夢周, pen name is Po-eun 圃隱, 1337-1392) and Jeong Do-jeon (鄭道傳, pen name is Sambong 三峰, 1342-1398) at this time. These two people both met a tragic end by being assassinated at the end of Goryeo and beginning of Joseon, but the perspective of these two on the dynastic transition from Goryeo to Joseon was totally opposite.

Jeong Mong-ju met his demise while opposing the founding of the Joseon dynasty through his view of loyalty in "not serving two dynasties" (不事二朝). Jeong Do-jeon, on the other hand, became a first-class meritorious vassal from the perspective of transition in dynasty by serving Yi Seong-gye as the sovereign. This naturally turned his teacher Yi Saek and his upperclassman Jeong Mong-ju into political adversaries. Jeong Mong-ju and Jeong Do-jeon were both killed by Yi Bang-won (李芳遠, later becomes Taejong, the third sovereign of Joseon dynasty), son of Yi Seong-gye. This complicated turn of events will be discussed later. Jeong Mong-ju and Jeong Do-jeon passed the civil service examination in 1360 and 1362, respectively. Jeong Do-jeon was the recorder of travel logs when Jeong Mong-ju was dispatched to China as ambassador in honor of the birthday of the Chinese emperor (聖節使) in 1384.

The continent of China also experienced turbulence at the end of Goryeo and beginning of Joseon. The uprising of the White Lotus Teachings spread profusely through a chain reaction in late Yuan period. The White Lotus Teachings was a secret society of the *Maitreya* faith that was somewhat anti-establishment and believed in the *Maitreya Bodhisattva* descending to earth and giving salvation to mankind. They were called the "Red Turban Bandits" because the rebels wore red turbans around their heads. In 1368, Zhu Yuan-zhang, a son of a sharecropper, rose in stature during this peasant uprising and dominated the entire territory of China; he decided on Great Ming (大明) and *Hongwu* (洪武) for the name of the kingdom and the appellation of the year, respectively. The history of Yuan China which had lasted for approximately 100 years came to an end as Shundi (順帝), the last emperor of Yuan China, abandoned the Grand Capital and fled to the great plains in the northern regions.

As mentioned above, the Goryeo royal family had marital ties with the Yuan imperial family. And influential pro-Yuan politicians became great landowners by wielding real political power and combining land and slaves. Therefore expansion of large farmsteads enriched the private purses of the pro-Yuan faction while oppressing the national finance. But Yuan, the root of this, fell. The School of Master Zhu formed an alliance with the newly emerged power of Ming China and pursued a restructuring of the kingdom through reforms such as the land system. Jeong Mong-ju and Jeong Do-jeon as part of the School of Master Zhu were pro-Ming reformists.

It would be appropriate to say that "decline is brought about by the union of religion and national power" is an ironclad rule throughout all times and places. Such was what happened with Christianity in Medieval Europe and national followers in modern Japan. The Buddhism of Goryeo period was not exempt from this. There was disturbance in Goryeo period that centered on whether generations of kings emphasized Buddhism or Confucianism. Buddhism is the founding ideology of the Goryeo dynasty. Thus past criticisms of Buddhism made by civilian officials were criticisms about the decadence of Buddhism arising from the union with sovereignty as well as the waste of national finances due to the building of temples or holding Buddhist services rather than criticism of Buddhism itself.

There are two anti-Buddhist camps among the School of Master Zhu; Jeong Mong-ju and Jeong Do-jeon each represent one camp. Known as the "founder of the study of the principle of human nature in the East," Jeong Mong-ju of course excluded Buddhism. He recommended the following as the chancellor of Sungkyunkwan during a royal lecture when the sovereign desired to appoint Monk Chanyeong (粲英) as the royal preceptor in the third year of the reign of King Gongyang (1391):

> The way of a Confucian is that which is practiced in everyday life. Food and the relationship between man and woman are common to mankind, but therein contain the principle. The way of Yao and Shun did not stray from it. Movement and stillness, talking and quietness, when properness is achieved, are the way of Yao and Shun; these standards are not very high or difficult to discharge from the start. But the teachings of Buddha are different. One must part with relatives, denounce the relationship between man and woman, sit alone inside a cave, wear clothing made of

grass, eat roots, and revere the search for emptiness and Nirvana. How can this be called the way of everyday life?

- "Jeong Mong-ju," Yeoljeon, *History of Goryeo*

His admonition did not change King Gongyang's determination in the end, but he put loyalty first as a loyal vassal of the Goryeo dynasty that was already faced with the symptoms of the end; he considered reviving the dynasty by reforming Buddhism.

Jeong Do-jeon, however, intrinsically criticized Buddhism as the national policy of Goryeo and fundamentally denied the Buddhist tenets and advocated the superiority of Confucianism. Indeed, he initiated "appreciation of Confucianism and depreciation of Buddhism" of the Joseon dynasty based on transition in dynasty. He wrote *Simmun cheondap* (心問天答, Heaven's Answers to Questions of the Mind, 1375), *Simgiri pyeon* (心氣理篇, On the Mind, Material Force, and Principle, 1394), and the most specific and orthodox book written in 1398 called *Bulssi japbyeon* (佛氏雜辨, Array of Critiques on Buddhism) to criticize Buddhism.

Heaven's Answers to Questions of the Mind was written before the establishment of the Joseon dynasty; it is a simple book in an essay style that has "Heaven" answering the questions of "the mind." In the same year he was exiled for denouncing a pro-Yuan and anti-Ming book by the faction of the powerful vassal Yi In-im (李仁任). Jeong Do-jeon continued a life of ostracism, exile, and wandering; his theory of transition in dynasty was criticized not only by pro-Yuan faction but also by the School of Master Zhu such as Yi Saek and Jeong Mong-ju, who believed in not serving two lords (不事二君). He probably found the time to write *On the Mind, Material Force, and Principle* and *Array of Critiques on Buddhism* when the Joseon dynasty was founded after he did his utmost for the transition in dynasty with his close friends such as Jo Jun (趙浚).

An explanation of each book will be omitted, and the gist of *On the Mind, Material Force, and Principle* is as follows:

The book is composed of three sections: "Simnangi" (心難氣, The Mind's Criticism of the Material Force), "Gi'nansim" (氣難心, Material Force's Criticism of the Mind), and "Iyusimgi" (理諭心氣, The Principle of Confucian Enlightenment of the Mind and Material Force). "The mind" as mentioned here refers to the self-cultivating mind of Buddhism, "material force" refers to the cultivated material force of Daoism, and "the principle" refers to loyalty in Confucianism. In short, the main content is the admonition to follow the Buddha-mind and Daoist material force through "righteousness of loyalty." Therefore he concludes that "[it is] beautiful and shines forth. It came into existence prior to Heaven and Earth, and thus the material force was born of the principle and the mind also came from the principle."

Below is a list of the table of contents of *Array of Critiques on Buddhism* for the reader to make a general conjecture on the contents, because another book will have to be written to fully explain the contents.

1) "Bulssi yunhoejibyeon" (弗氏輪廻之辨, Buddha's Argument on Rebirth), 2) "Bulssi ingwajibyeon" (佛氏因果之辨, Buddha's Argument on Karma), 3) "Bulssi simseongjibyeon" (佛氏心性之辨, Buddhist Concept of the Mind and Nature), 4) "Bulssi jagyong siseongjibyeon" (佛氏作用是性之辨, Argument on the Buddhist Assertion That the Physical and Mental Functions Are Absolute and Transcending in Themselves), 5) "Bulssi simjeokjibyeon" (佛氏心跡之辨, Argument on the Buddhist Discrimination between Function and Nature of the Mind), 6) "Bulssi mae-eo-dogijibyeon" (佛氏昧於道器之辨, Buddhist Argument on Ignoring of the Difference between Phenomenon and Substance), 7) "Bulssi hwegi illyunjibyeon" (佛氏毀棄人倫之辨, Critique of Buddhism's Irresponsibility of Cardinal Human Relations), 8) "Bulssi jabijibyeon" (佛氏慈悲之辨, Criticism of the Buddhist Mercy), 9) "Bulssi jingajibyeon" (佛氏眞假之辨, Criticism of Buddha's Discernment between What Is Genuine and What Is False), 10) "Bulssi jingajibyeon" (佛氏地獄之辨, Buddha's Critique of Hell), 11) "Bulssi hwabokjibyeon" (佛氏禍福之辨,

Criticism of Practical Results of Buddhist Devotion), 12) "Bulssi geolsikjibyeon" (佛氏乞食之辨, Criticism of Buddhist Mendicancy), and 13) "Yubul dongijibyeon" (儒佛同異之辨, Argument on the Differences between Confucianism and Buddhism).

As Jeong Do-jeon's close friend, Gwon Geun wrote a critique as follows in the preface of *Array of Critiques on Buddhism* as an advocate of the effort to transition from one dynasty to the next when he heard of Jeong Do-jeon's purpose in writing the book:

> The bad influence of Buddha destroys ethics so that near destruction of mankind will definitely be reached someday by beasts. Those who advocate wise teachings must truly consider this [Buddhism] as the enemy and attack with concerted effort. I considered ousting this without hesitation when I had my mind bent on it early on. But now that His Majesty (Taejo) understands my words and accepts stratagem, I cannot oust it despite my inclination. It will not be ousted (in my lifetime). (But Jeong Do-jeon) wrote this book so that the future generations can realize at some point in time due to his inability to suppress his indignation. Perhaps to make anyone easily understand, there are many vulgar and troublesome analogies as well as the usage of violent language so that the readers cannot do as they wish. But the right and wrong between Confucianism and Buddhism can be clearly distinguished through this book, and I can die in peace knowing that this book will be passed on, although it is not widely used today.

> - "Bulssi japbyeon seolseo" (佛氏雜辨說序,
>   Preface to Array of Critiques on Buddhism), *Yangchonjip*
>   (陽村集, Collected Works of Yangchon), Vol. 17

Jeong Do-jeon's intensity of spirit of anti-Buddhism doctrine is clear. But the later scholars of the study of the principle of human nature in Joseon, and specifically the Sarim Faction who seized political power by opposing the Hungu Faction in early Joseon period, praised the integrity of "do not serve two lords" as advocated by Jeong Mong-ju but branded Jeong Do-jeon as "an apostate." Another irony of history is that the scholars of the Learning of Master Zhu who considered Buddhism as the visible enemy treated the most meritorious vassal who led the founding of "the Confucian nation" as "an apostate." It does not matter whether the [royal family] is of a Wang clan or a Yi clan for the promotion of the national interests and provision for the welfare of the people from a populist understanding of the statement made by Mencius on "The people are the most important element *in a nation*; the spirits of the land and grain are the next; the sovereign is the lightest" ("Jin Xin, Part II," 盡心章句 下, *The Works of Mencius*). However, justification for the Learning of Master Zhu relies on the proposition of "not serving two dynasties."

Jeong Do-jeon and Gwon Geun were close friends during the transition of dynasties, but their personalities differed greatly. As can be inferred from the critique of his teacher Yi Saek as mentioned previously, Gwon Geun is of a moderate personality. But Jeong Do-jeon is of an extreme personality, enough to turn a meritorious vassal of the Goryeo dynasty (Yi Saek) and his upperclassman Jeong Mong-ju into political adversaries. It can be said that the two made a good team, one soft and the other firm. Gwon Geun praised Jeong Do-jeon in the preface of *Array of Critiques on Buddhism*: "Just as Mencius succeeded the orthodox teachings of the three sages (Yu, Duke of Zhou, and Confucius), Jeong Do-jeon succeeded the orthodoxy of Mencius." This critique provides a very important key word to understanding the thought and behavior of Jeong Do-jeon, who emphasized Mencius's government based on the people more than the justification of the Learning of Master Zhu.

10

Transition in Dynasty, from Goryeo to Joseon

King Gongmin's Anti-Yuan Policy

The reign of King Gongmin, the 31st sovereign of Goryeo, was a turbulent period in East Asia. The Chinese dynasty changed from Yuan to Ming in the north, and Japan suffered from internal strife between southern and northern territories as well as invaders in the south. As mentioned in the previous chapter, Zhu Yuan-zhang, one of the rebel leaders of the Red Turban Bandits (centered on the White Lotus Teachings) settled in Nanjing as the capital in 1368 and named the kingdom the Great Ming. Zhu Yuan-zhang as the founder of the Ming dynasty immediately marched north to the Great Capital to threaten Yuan China. The last emperor of Yuan, Shundi, commanded the Mongol military clans to come to his aid but fled northward to Shangdu (上都: Kaipingfu 開平府) when no one responded; the Great Capital fell into the hands of the Ming troops. Thus the supreme ruler of China changed from Yuan to Ming. Yuan after this period is referred to as Northern Yuan (北元).

Shundi passed away in 1370, and the mother of the Crown Prince was of the Goryeo Gi clan (奇氏) and one of the two wives of the emperor. The Crown Prince, the progeny of the Gi clan, who succeeded to the throne of Northern Yuan was Zhaozong (昭宗). He decided on Karakorum (capital of the old Mongol empire) as the base of operations and looked for a chance to return to China while working in concert with pro-Yuan faction in Goryeo as well. But after the founder of Ming China, Taizu, conquered Manchuria in

165

1387 and delivered a crushing blow to the remaining powers near what is now the Nomonhan region in 1388, the Mongol tribes became divided into smaller tribes without possibility of recovery.

Goryeo was an independent kingdom but Yuan interfered in many issues. For example, Eastern Expedition Field Headquarters (征東行省) was originally established for the purpose of invading Japan, but it still remained after the failed second invasion of 1281 to be used for interference in the domestic affairs of Goryeo. Moreover, Yuan dispatched government officials for direct supervision of the Dongning Commandery (東寧府) near the western capital (Pyeong'yang): Governor-General of Ssangseong District (雙城摠管府) centered around Hwaju (和州, Yeongheung) and Governor-General of Tamna District in charge of the horse-raising farms in Jeju Island. The Dongning Commandery and Governor-General of Tamna District were immediately discontinued, but the Governor-General of Ssangseong District remained the same.

Not only did the influential pro-Yuan families as represented by the Gi clan with marital connections to the Yuan imperial family have control over real political power, they became owners of great farms with much land and slaves by taking over government-owned land as well as land owned by peasants and turning the peasants into slaves. Among this pro-Yuan group were those who submitted a request to the Yuan emperor to nullify the royal family of Goryeo in favor of direct dominance under Yuan as a district.

King Gongmin executed a daring anti-Yuan policy at the end of the Yuan period by joining forces with anti-Yuan uprisings of local military leaders south of the Yangtze River. Goryeo formed an alliance with Zhang Shi-cheng (張士誠), one of the local military leaders stationed out of Suzhou; Zhang was a rival of Zhu Yuan-zhang who later founded the Ming dynasty.

Not only did King Gongmin purge the pro-Yuan faction including Gi Cheol (奇徹) and close down the Imunso of the Eastern Expedition Field Headquarters in 1356, he also made a clean sweep of anything that resembled the Mongols among the systems or customs. Thus it would be appropriate to view the transition in dynasty from Goryeo to Joseon that became complete in 1392 to have begun in 1356. He also recovered the Governor-General of Ssangseong District with force of arms and cleansed the Mongol influence within Goryeo. Yi Seong-gye's father Yi Ja-chun (李子春) was appointed to the post of Military Commander of the Northeast Side at this time for his meritorious deed in convincing Governor-General of Ssangseong District to act in concert with King Gongmin from within. Monk Pyeonjo (遍照, secular name is Shin Don, 辛旽) was appointed as the Most Reverend Priest in 1365, whereby he was given great authority to be in charge of the affairs of state.

Pyeonjo submitted a request to King Gongmin to establish the Directorate for Reclassification of Farmland and Farming Population and to investigate the land and slaves jointly possessed by influential pro-Yuan families in order to return the farmland to the original owners and to free the slaves. This was a big blow to the large pro-Yuan farm owners. But Shin Don was ultimately killed in 1371 because the resistance of the pro-Yuan powers in Goryeo was tenacious, despite the fact that Yuan had already been chased back home to the northern region.

King Gongmin, however, was beset with foreign troubles in the form of continuous invasions by Japanese raiders, which kept him from concentrating on the recovery of national sovereignty and reform activities. With Japan suffering from a civil war of the south and north, Japanese raiders invaded the southern coastline of Korea in 1350 and gradually broadened the raids close to the capital, and their numbers also increased. Thus warehouses in the coastal regions for storage of rice collected as tax had to be moved inland in 1360. Invasions of the Red Turban Bandits from the northern regions occurred in 1359 and 1361 as well. Yi Seong-gye, who distinguished himself during the 1361 engagement with the Red Turban Bandits to recover the capital, also stood out during punitive expeditions against Japanese raiders. In September of 1380, troops led by Yi Seong-gye surrounded a troop of Japanese raiders who made inroads deep into Jeolla Province to a ridge in Namwon. Expert archer Yi Seong-gye killed Akibatsu, the leader of the Japanese raiders, and annihilated the Japanese raiders who became flustered after their leader was lost.

There are various legends about Akibatsu, but he remains an unknown figure.

The troops of Yi Seong-gye, the strongest military troops at the end of the Goryeo period, were formed by the local powers of Hamgyeong Province where Goryeo and Jurchen tribes coexisted in harmony since his father Yi Ja-chun meritoriously recovered the Governor-General of Ssangseong District. There was a hidden hero who shone on the side of Namwon by the name of Yi Ji-ran (李芝蘭). He was a Jurchen, and his original name was Turan Timur. Yi Seong-gye awarded the family name of Yi and considered him a meritorious vassal in founding Joseon. The troops led by Yi Seong-gye were greatly empowered by the Jurchen cavalry led by Yi Ji-ran. Regardless, Yi Seong-gye inherited the unfinished work of King Gongmin and completed the recovery of anti-Yuan sovereignty through a dynastic transition.

Yi Seong-gye Steers His Horse Away from Wihwa Island

Taizu of Ming China announced his intention to establish Cheol-lyeong Commandery (鐵嶺衛) where Yuan maintained the Gover-nor-General of Ssangseong District. Upon the advice of a prominent leader of a pro-Yuan faction by the name of Choe Yeong (崔瑩), King Wu (禑王) decided to attack Liaoning in response. Choe Yeong was put in charge of the entire 50,000 mobilized troops in 1388 as Regional Military Commander of Eight Provinces (八道都統使), and Jo Min-su (曺敏修) and Yi Seong-gye were appointed to the posts of Regional Military Commander of the Left Flank and Regional Military Commander of the Right Flank, respectively, as the Frontline Commanders (戰線司令官).

But when they reached Wihwa Island downstream of the Am-nok River, the river could not be crossed due to overflowing because of much rain. Yi Seong-gye sent a missive to the king indicating the impossibility of the Liaoning expedition. The content of this so-called "Four Impossibilities" is as follows.

First, it is not profitable for a small kingdom to attack a bigger kingdom.

Second, it is not appropriate to mobilize large troops in summer.

Third, there is the possibility of Japanese pirates invading the southern parts if large troops are concentrated in the northern parts.

Fourth, bows cannot be used due to the melting of the bowstrings in summer when it is rainy and sweltering much, and soldiers suffer from many diseases.

Yi Seong-gye ignored the decision of the central government and turned the troops toward Gaegyeong; he incarcerated King Wu in Ganghwa Island and banished Choe Yeong to a distant region. Jo Min-su supported Crown Prince Chang as successor to King Wu, but Yi Seong-gye opposed this. Ultimately, King Chang (昌王) was also dethroned and banished in 1389, and a seventh-generation descendant of Sinjong, the 20th sovereign of Goryeo, was chosen. He was King Gongyang (恭讓王, r. 1389-1392), the last king of Goryeo.

According to the claim of Yi Seong-gye, false sovereigns of the Shin clan were dethroned and the true Wang clan was put on the throne because kings Wu and Chang were both illegitimate offspring of Shin Don. It is recorded in *History of Goryeo* that King Gongmin was without issue by his queen, and King Wu was the progeny of Shin Don's slave concubine Banya (般若) and, as such, an illegitimate son of Shin Don; there is no way to know the truth because the history was compiled from the viewpoint of the Joseon dynasty. There is a high likelihood that this was a plot of the faction in favor of a dynastic transition to debase the birth of King Wu because he ascended to the throne with the support of Yi In-im, a prominent figure of the pro-Yuan faction.

At any rate, sovereign power may just as well not have existed in the period of King Wu → King Chang → King Gongyang period at the end of Goryeo, and the existence of the Goryeo dynasty was in a precarious position. The troop withdrawal from Wihwa Island and the execution of land system reform at the advice of Jo Jun spurred on the decline of Goryeo.

Yi Seong-gye seized actual power over the government with military might after the military retreat from Wihwa Island. He burned deeds of public and private land and declared Rank-Land Law (科田法) in 1391. The main gist of this is to restrict rank-land, which gave bureaucrats the right to collect rent from state-owned land (收租權), to Gyeonggi Province, while all other land in the kingdom was turned into public land wherein the right to collect rent reverted to the government. This land taxation (田制) reform not only struck a crushing blow to the economic foundation of the pro-Yuan faction that had become great landowners through joint possession of land and slaves, but shook the very foundation of the Goryeo dynasty which relied on the economic support of the great landowners. This is why King Gongyang lamented, "The law on private land which has been passed down since the days of the royal ancestors is changed suddenly in my reign."

The final obstacle in the process of the transition in dynasty from the Goryeo dynasty of the Wang clan to the new dynasty of the Yi clan was the loyal faction who followed the dictum of "do not serve two dynasties" — representative of which was Jeong Mong-ju. He was ultimately murdered by Yi Bang-won, Yi Seong-gye's fifth son, in April of 1392.

In July of the same year, Yi Seong-gye ascended to the throne at the request of the Privy Council (都評議使司), and the Confucians who supported him were Jeong Do-jeon, Jo Jun, and Nam Eun, with Yi Bang-won at the lead. Yi Bang-won was a Confucian scholar who had already passed the Erudite Examination of the civil service examination in 1383, and the examiner at the time was Yi Sung-in.

A chapter closed on the history of Goryeo dynasty that had lasted for 34 generations and 474 years since its founding in 918 by Wang Geon. Goryeo was able to maintain an existence as an independent kingdom by overcoming major national crises such as invasions from Liao and Yuan. Goryeo experienced dynastic changes in China from Song → Yuan → Ming, each time facing difficult diplomatic issues.

The process of Yi Seong-gye retreating from Wihwa Island in 1388 to become Taejo of the Joseon dynasty in 1392 in fact parallels the scenario of military commander Zhao Kuang-yin of Later Zhou becoming the founder of the Song dynasty in China through the "Chen Qiao Incident." His younger brother Zhao Kuang-yi (趙匡義), who led the effort to put Zhao Kuang-yin on the throne, later became Taizong of Song and achieved the monumental task of continuing with the achievements of his predecessors. Yi Bang-won, the fifth son of Yi Seong-gye, also became the third Taejong later and continued with his father's achievements with his son Sejong for two generations. The history of the 500 years of the Joseon dynasty is grounded on such a foundation.

It is possible to seize a kingdom through "force," but it is not possible to govern the kingdom through it. This was an ironclad rule of oriental studies since the time of Emperor Wu of Han China on how to become a good emperor.

To survive after his parents and older brother died, Zhu Yuan-zhang became a mendicant monk at a temple at the age of 17; he thereafter joined the Red Turban rebel forces. Liu-bang of Han and Zhu Yuan-zhang of Ming are the only two rulers among the generations of Chinese dynasties to have come from poor peasant stock and rise in the world to become sovereigns. Chen You-liang (陳友諒) and Zhang Shi-cheng were the two greatest rivals to Zhu Yuan-zhang until the last when Zhu Yuan-zhang declared the founding of Great Ming. "Scholarship" turned Zhu, a leader of the rebel forces, into a sovereign who recovered "China." Excellent literati such as Song Ryeom (宋濂, Song Lian in Ch.), under whose directive 210 volumes of *History of Yuan* (元史) were later compiled, and Yu Gi (劉基) worked together with Zhu. The slogan shouted by Zhu during his march to the Great Capital of Yuan was, "Let's drive the savages away and recover China." In other words, he resigned his role as the leader of the rebel forces and advocated nationalism to the Han people.

The "military might" of Yi Seong-gye also relied on the Confucianism of Jeong Do-jeon or Jo Jun to achieve a new dynasty. In short, the Joseon dynasty was established by a union of the "military might" and the "Confucianism" of Yi Seong-gye as advocated by his advisors. This applies to Gwon Geun, who later joined the task of founding the Joseon dynasty as a "Confucian." Gwon Geun earned the enmity of pro-Yuan Yi In-im with his attempt to interfere against welcoming the envoy from Northern Yuan who were chased away from central China to the northern plains. Gwon Geun was living a secluded life in Chungju, Chungcheong Province at the time of the transition in dynasty when his banishment for being involved in continuous incidents was revoked. The fact that the founding of the Joseon dynasty started from the outset by depending on these Confucians is very important in comprehending the characteristics of the new dynasty. In other words, this is not the case of "winner take all" among the many local military leaders who competed with each other for power, but the establishment of a new dynasty as an extension of anti-Yuan and pro-Ming as well as anti-Buddhism doctrine as put forth by the School of Master Zhu.

Taejo's Letter of Instruction on Ascending to the Throne

Yi Seong-gye established a new dynasty and became Taejo (r. 1392-1398) in July of 1392. The government body that chose him to be king was the Privy Council that determined the greatest policies of the nation through a parliamentary system. According to the content of the request made by the Privy Council to Yi Seong-gye for ascension to the throne, King Wu, who ascended to the throne with the support of the pro-Yuan faction, was deemed an illegitimate offspring of Shin Don, and thus King Wu and his son King Chang were not of the blood of King Gongmin. They were demoted to plain Shin Wu (辛禑) and Shin Chang (辛昌), respectively.

> The Wang clan (the lineage of Goryeo kings) was discontinued after the death of King Gongmin without a successor. Shin Don took advantage of this situation and stole the throne but left be-

cause he sinned, and the spirit of the nation was again discontinued when his son Chang inherited the throne. Fortunately, Jeong-
chang Buwongun (定昌府院君: King Gongyang) was able to
take control of state affairs with the help of a general, but he
could not carry out his duties because he had lost the support of
the public and close friends due to his confused state of mind.
Who can rectify one that has been deposed by Heaven? Government posts will always be appointed to the virtuous, and the post
of the ruler cannot be left empty for long. Based on the sentiment of the entire nation (outside of China), title and rank must
be corrected and the minds of the people stabilized with honor
and virtue.

- July of the first year of the reign of Taejo, *Taejo sillok*
  (太祖實錄, Veritable Records of King Taejo)

Yi Seong-gye presented the Letter of Instruction on Ascending to
the Throne that contains 17 items after receiving the above request
from the Privy Council. With the focus on a plan to stabilize the lives
of the people of each government sphere, it outlined the punishment
for those opposed to the transition in dynasty and treatment of
descendants of the Wang clan.

The Joseon dynasty, of course, carried out *yangban* politics composed of both scholar-official order and military-official order. Thus
the education system that trained able men and the civil service
examination system through which able men were recruited by merit
were emphasized. The Letter of Instruction states as follows on this
issue:

> Neither scholar-official nor military-official orders must destroy
> the other by one having more power than the other. Able men
> must be trained through reinforcement of national schools in the
> capital and local schools with students performing scholarly ac-
> tivities. The law of the civil service examination originally was to
> recruit able men by merit for the nation, but the public civil ser-
> vice examination was run by private relations who referred to
> each other as *jwaju* or student. This is counter to the original in-
> tention.

The relationship between *jwaju* and the student mentioned here refers to the corrupt practice of forming "personal ties" between the *jwaju* as an examiner who oversaw the examination and students who passed the civil service examination under his supervision. Therefore emphasis was put on creating a system that promoted national schools (Sungkyunkwan and four other schools) and local schools as well as a sovereign-vassal relationship that directly connected the sovereign to the new officials.

The civil service examination was executed in three separate stages of beginning, middle, and final examinations, wherein the names of the 33 final qualifiers were turned over to the Ministry of Personnel (吏曹) to be appointed as bureaucrats (of the scholar-official order). Attention should be drawn to the fact that although temporarily put into practice in the Goryeo period, the excluded Military Examination ultimately was emphasized.

> The law of training in martial arts is to be supervised by Military Training Command (訓練監). The Seven Military Classics (武經七書) and archery skills should be instructed, and the extent of mastery over the Classics and degree of mastery of skills should be tested. Distribute identification to the final 33 qualifiers equal to the Erudite Examination and send their names to the Ministry of Military Affairs (兵曹) to wait for appointment.

A separate chapter will be devoted to examining the educational system for training able men and the civil service examination for recruiting able men by merit in the Joseon dynasty because of the importance in understanding the political characteristics of the dynasty.

The interesting point here is the treatment of the Wang clan who were the descendants of past generations of Goryeo sovereigns.

> Assign Majeon District in Gyeonggi Province to Wu, descendant of the Wang clan, and appoint him as Gwiui-gun (歸義君);[1] have

---

ㄱ Gwiui-gun (歸義君) was a government post. (S. Lee)

him officiate the sacrificial rites of the Wang clan. Allow the remaining descendants to go wherever in the provinces they will, and allow their wives and male servants to live together as before. The government officials of application regions should assist so that the Wang descendants do not lose their living.

The Letter of Instruction also defines the punishment for each of the 56 politicians and scholars who opposed the transition in dynasty.

> The secretary (government official in charge of this) said, "The 56 people including Wu Mun-bo (禹文寶), Yi Saek, and Seol Jang-su (偰長壽) created a faction during the previous dynasty to foment a rebellion and stirred up trouble at the forefront. They must be punished according to law as a warning to later generations." But I plan to allow them their lives out of pity.

Moreover, bloodshed due to political revenge was prevented by ordering government officials to be stripped of their posts and made into commoners, and by floggings, banishment, and house arrest. There was, of course, some bloodshed due to unforeseen events, but an effort was made to reduce it to the minimum when compared to the horrendous purge executed by Taizu at the start of the Ming dynasty. In addition, the transition in dynasty made by Yi Seong-gye took on the form of a last royal abdication by King Gongyang of Goryeo instead of a coup d'état.

Members of the Wang clan are hard to find in Korea today except for immigrants from China. It is said that the descendants of the Wang clan changed the family name to Jeon (全), Jeon (田), or Ok (玉) in fear of persecution and discrimination. All of the new family names contain the Chinese character "*wang*" (王), which shows the lingering attachment to the Wang family name.

The founding ideology of the Joseon dynasty is "appreciation of Confucianism and depreciation of Buddhism." Taejo's Letter of Instruction at the Time of Ascension to the Throne that outlines the fundamental principles of national affairs does not mention a word on "depreciation of Buddhism." He was a military official, but he appointed Confucian scholars close to him as Royal Lecturers

(經筵官) after he ascended to the throne, commanded them to give lectures on *Extended Meaning of the Great Learning* (大學衍義) by Zhen De-xiu (眞德秀), a Southern Song scholar of the Learning of Master Zhu, and considered learning to become a good emperor a fundamental guideline. He drew a distinct line on the doctrine of depreciation of Buddhism with his advisors but did not hide his belief in Buddhism. This is natural for a military man who often came near death.

Before he ascended to the throne, Taejo respected the Great Monk Muhak (無學大師) Jacho (自招) as his lifelong spiritual guide. The two were always together. After he abdicated the throne, Taejo devoted his life to reciting the Buddha to achieve a perfect state of spiritual concentration. The attitude of "appreciation of Confucianism and depreciation of Buddhism" was not clearly put forth nor was the framework of "a Confucian state" completed until the reigns of the third king Taejong and the fourth king Sejong.

The Name Joseon Is Beautiful and Its History Old

Relations with China were considered important by past dynasties of Korea. To make the relationship with the greater kingdom of China harmonious, Korea adopted the diplomacy of a smaller nation built on the thought of the kingly way for serving a greater nation.

The new dynasty, with Yi Seong-gye as the founder, continued to dispatch envoys to Ming China in order to receive its acknowledgement. But the new founder (Emperor Hongwu, 洪武帝) of Ming China did not acknowledge the investiture of the sovereign of the new dynasty. Emperor Hongwu desired centralization of internal politics and refused to become involved in the transition of the Joseon dynasty. The official reason given was that Joseon was "an independent nation with its own unique culture." But the real reason seems to have been fear of communication with his old rival Zhang Shi-cheng.

The founder of Joseon dispatched Jo Ban (趙胖) as envoy to Ming to deliver the agreement of the Privy Council the day after his ascension to the throne. Taizu of the Ming dynasty did not acknowledge the new investiture, but fortunately did ask for the name of the new dynasty. In response, Yi Seong-gye sent back the two names of "Joseon" (朝鮮) and "Hwaryeong" (和寧), on which he deliberated with the civilian officials, and requested that the son of Heaven choose one. Joseon's envoy Han Sang-jil (韓尙質) returned in February of 1393 with the response from the Ming founder. Below is the content of the response:

> Only the name Joseon is beautiful, and its origin of old. The nation will prosper in generations to come if this name is taken as the foundation and a model and if Heaven is considered as its body and its people governed thusly.

Yi Seong-gye issued a royal edict to proclaim the change of the name of the new dynasty to "Joseon" and issued amnesty to all political criminals who opposed the transition in dynasty. The statement by Taizu about "only the name 'Joseon' is beautiful and its history old" naturally refers to "Gija Joseon" (refer to Ch. 2). Jeong Do-jeon states as follows:

> There was more than one name for the nation in the east. There were three nations called Joseon: Dan'gun Joseon, Gija Joseon, and Wiman Joseon.... Only Gija was appointed by King Wu of Zhou dynasty China to govern Joseonhu. Today the emperor (of Ming China) commands "Only the name Joseon is beautiful, and its origin of old. The nation will prosper in generations to come if this name is taken as the foundation and a model and if Heaven is considered as its body and its people governed thusly." What Emperor Wu of Zhou commanded of Gija is commanded of His Majesty (Taejo of Joseon), giving justification to the deed and appropriateness to the words. Politics and enlightenment flourished and manners became proper, because Gija told Emperor Wu of the constitution, expanded on the meaning, and created eight clauses of teachings for execution in Joseon. Because of this, the name of Joseon will become known throughout the world in the future.

177

- "Administrative Code of Joseon" (朝鮮經國典),
  Sambongjip (鄭道傳集, Collection of
  Works by Sambong), Vol. 7

In other words, it is judged that there were Dan'gun Joseon, Gija Joseon, and Wiman Joseon in ancient times with the name of the founder in front, but the name of "Gija Joseon" is the most beautiful and has the longest history.

The catch phrase "Chosŏn — the Land of the Morning Calm — a Sketch of Korea" used today as a slogan for tourism in Korea is a subtitle from the 1885 book translated by the American astronomer Percival Lowell.

Is Serving a Greater Nation Dependence?

Of the six ministries of the Joseon government, the Ministry of Rites was in charge of diplomatic relations with neighboring nations. The Ministry of Rites was also in charge of education. This came from the way of thinking of stabilization depending on "propriety" with neighboring nations. Diplomatic relations with China were based on "propriety of serving a greater nation," and relations with Japan were based on "propriety of equal nations." Does this mean that "serving a greater nation" — China — is being "dependent"?

Mencius responded that there were two methods of "a small nation serving a greater nation" and "a greater nation serving a smaller nation" when King Xuan (宣王) of Zhai China asked, "Is there a way in dealing with neighboring nations?"

> There is. But it requires a perfectly virtuous *prince* to be able, with a great *country*, to serve a small one, — as, for instance, T'ang served Ko, and king Wǎn served the Kwǎn barbarians. And it requires a wise *prince* to be able, with a small *country*, to serve a large one, — as the king T'âi served the Hsün-yü, and Kâu-ch'ien served Wû. He who with a great *State* serves a small one, delights in Heaven. He who with a small *State* serves a large one, stands in awe of Heaven. He who delights in Heaven will affect with his

love and protection the whole kingdom. He who stands in awe of Heaven will affect with his love and protection his own kingdom.

- "King Hui of Liang," Part II, *The Works of Mencius*

This is the kingly way of Mencius on dealing with neighboring nations. The Joseon sovereign was able to preserve the safety of a small nation from the threat of a bigger nation by adopting the propriety of "a smaller nation serving a greater nation" toward the Chinese emperor. In other words, he avoided a haughty attitude and took on the propriety of a smaller nation toward a bigger nation.

There are many instances of Japanese historical documents or even textbooks being written as if "independent" history did not exist for Joseon, because the diplomacy of Joseon toward China of serving a greater nation is regarded as that of "a dependent nation." However, Joseon was "an independent nation with a unique culture" even in the Ming and Qing periods. Viewing "serving a greater nation" simply as "dependence" does not attempt to understand the thought of the kingly way of Confucianism, because of being tainted by the western doctrine of rule of might that considers a stronger nation making a weaker nation dependent the principle of competition for survival.

Tribute is acknowledged only after the sovereign of a smaller nation receives a letter of appointment from the Chinese emperor. Reciprocating a tribute usually exceeded the tribute itself, which was a profitable government trade to the small nation but a big burden for China. Therefore, China requested for Joseon to send tribute only "once every three years," but in contrast, Joseon requested to send a tribute "thrice each year" or "four times per year" instead and achieved it.

The relationship of Joseon with China connected by land was important enough to affect national existence. The Amnok River, which is a boundary between the two sides, becomes passable when frozen during winter. This is the reason Yi Seong-gye in the past advocated that "it is not appropriate to mobilize large troops in summer." "The propriety of serving a big nation" was a prudent choice for a stable and continuous diplomatic, commercial, and cultural exchange with the greater nation of China.

Seoul, the Capital for 500 Years

Seoul, the capital of Korea, was called Hanyang (漢陽) in the Goryeo period. This turned into Hanseong (漢城) when it became the capital of the Joseon dynasty. Seoul originally was a common noun meaning "the capital." Thus, the *Seoul* of Silla is Gyeongju and the *Seoul* of Goryeo is Gaeseong (originally Gaegyeong). Hanseong had been called Seoul to generally mean the capital during the 500 years of the Joseon dynasty and has now become the proper noun for the Korean capital.

After he ascended the throne, Yi Seong-gye attempted to build a new capital in order to renew public sentiment. The first site with potential was inside the new city at the foot of the Gyeryong Mountain in Chungcheong Province. But objection to Gyeryong Mountain as being inappropriate from the viewpoint of geomancy was prevalent. So Hanyang was finally decided on, and the capital was renamed as Prefecture of the Capital (漢城府).

In September of 1394, a government office for creating a royal palace in the new capital was established and the basic plan for building the new capital was created. The basic concept was to build the king's palace facing south on a location north of Seoul at the foot of Bugak Mountain because the sovereign had to rule while facing south. Jeong Do-jeon was commanded to create a name for the king's palace.

Jeong named it Gyeongbok Palace (景福宮) after a verse from *Book of Poetry*, "a man of virtue will bring you good fortune for ten thousand years." With Gyeongbok Palace facing south, an ancestral temple of the royal family enshrined the ancestral tablets of the past sovereigns and queens including the past four ancestors of Taejo on the left (in the east) according to the principle of "the ancestor shrine on the left and the shrine for the gods on the right." On the right (in the west) was the national altar for worshipping the gods of land and five grains. "Filial piety" and "farming" were the two mainstays of the new dynasty.

The main gate to the Gyeongbok Palace was Gwanhwa Gate, which guarded the road south (known now as Sejongno or Sejong Street), and to the left and right of it a district containing central organs of national administration such as the State Council was constructed. Jongno (or Jong Street) passed this government district and continued all the way to the shops in the Great East Gate (Dongdaemun) to the left. There was a belfry that tolled the opening and closing hours of the three great gates (Great South Gate, Great East Gate, and Great West Gate) that guarded the royal road to the capital city. Thus original Chinese characters representing Jongno were "鐘路" and not "鍾路" as it is today.

Taejo Yi Seong-gye moved the capital from Gaeseong to Seoul in October 1394 and entered Gyeongbok Palace on the 28th of the same month; the history of Seoul as the capital began from this point on. The urban district of old comprised the valley surrounded by Bugak Mountain to the north, Nam Mountain (or Namsan) to the south, Inwang Mountain to the west, and Nak Mountain (or Naksan) to the east; flowing water from surrounding mountains met at Cheonggye Stream and flowed through the urban district to the east. Cheonggye Stream joined Jungnang Stream outside the Great East Gate and flowed into the Han River by way of a southward detour around Nam Mountain. This Cheonggye Stream was covered over and only the street name of Cheonggye remains now.[2]

According to the theory of geomancy, Bugak Mountain was the guardian mountain of the capital of Seoul, and Bukhan Mountain was the protective mountain. Inwang Mountain to the west of Bugak Mountain is right of the guardian mountain, Nak Mountain to the east is left of the guardian mountain, and Nam Mountain to the south faces the guardian mountain.

The castle surrounding the capital was "a place that guards against riots and protects the people." Temporary Office of Con-

---

[2] Chonggye Stream is currently being restored; the restoration should be finished by the end of 2005. (S. Lee)

struction (都城造築都監) was established in September of 1396, and over 18,000 people from all over were mobilized to build a castle that connected the ridges of Bugak Mountain, Nak Mountain, Nam Mountain, Inwang Mountain, and Bugak Mountain with a length of 18 km. The off-season for farmers from January to February of 1397 was used to complete most of the basics except for a few parts. The Great East Gate, Great South Gate, and Great West Gate were built, and Sukjeong Gate (肅靖門) was built due north. But Sukjeong Gate was not called the Great North Gate. Sukjeong Gate had been barred since its building, and it was used only when the sovereign held sacrificial rituals for clear days during floods or sacrificial rituals for rain and bountiful harvest during droughts. With an expedited job, the outline was completed within approximately two years (1394 to 1396) after the Joseon dynasty decided to move the capital to Hanyang.

As mentioned above, the official name of the new dynasty was "Joseon." But there were Dan'gun Joseon, Gija Joseon, and Wiman Joseon in ancient times. These were collectively called "Gojoseon," and the Joseon dynasty was called "Yissi Joseon" (李氏朝鮮) or the abbreviated "Yijo" (李朝) to distinguish it from the other Joseon. Thus the term Yijo period will be intermingled with Joseon in this book, depending on the need.

11

Jeong Do-jeon and Gwon Geun as the Two Greatest Masters of the Confucian Nation

Jeong Do-jeon Draws Up a Plan for a Confucian Nation

Yi Seong-gye was a military official of the pro-Ming faction who responded to the struggles of newly emerging Ming against Yuan in China and uprooted the pro-Yuan power in Goryeo to contrive for complete recovery of national sovereignty. Therefore he did not have a prospect for a Confucian nation; rather, he was a devout Buddhist throughout his life. His fifth son Yi Bang-won who passed the civil service examination and Confucians Jo Jun and Jeong Do-jeon were the ones who busied themselves to realize the transition in dynasty of appreciating Confucianism and depreciating Buddhism based on the military might of Yi Seong-gye.

Jeong Do-jeon first met Yi Seong-gye in Hamju (咸州, Hamheung) in 1383. Since Yi In-im of the pro-Yuan faction put King Wu on the throne in 1375, Jeong Do-jeon continued his life of banishment and wandering for 10 years. He visited Yi Seong-gye who was then the Dojihwisa (都指揮使) of the northeast side and famous for militarism; there Jeong gained a new prospect on transition in dynasty after his contact with the military troops. After Yi Seong-gye retreated at Wihwa Island in 1388, those who were in favor of the transition in dynasty executed the reform of despotism and military system at the same time. The five-army system of the past was changed to the three army system, and Yi Seong-gye had control over military power in his hand by becoming Chief Regional Commander of the Three Army System (三軍都摠制使); Jo Jun became Commander of the Left Army, and Jeong Do-jeon became Commander of the Right Army. Military power concentrated on Jo Jun and Jeong Do-jeon with Yi Seong-gye as the focal point was a great threat to the royal family, as were the meritorious vassals who commanded private armies following the laxity of centralized power toward the end of Goryeo. Thus the opposition was strong.

It is not an exaggeration to say that the prospect for the Confucian nation of Yi Seong-gye was laid out by Jeong Do-jeon for the most part. Whenever drunk, he would say, "Liu-bang, the founder of Han China, did not take advantage of Zhang Liang (張良); rather, Zhang Liang took advantage of the founder of Han China." China was swept up in an upheaval in the years before the birth of Christ after the death of the founding emperor of Qin China. The two forces that became conspicuous were Xiang Yu of Chu and Liu-bang of Han dynasties. Liu-bang, who was ten at first, finally drove Xiang Yu into a corner without allies and founded the Han dynasty after gaining the world in 202 BC. The secret to his gaining the world was that he was good at handling able staff such as Zhang Liang, Xiao He (蕭何), and Han Xin (韓信). Zhang Liang among the three acted as Liu-bang's advisor. The statement of Jeong Do-jeon can be understood if Yi Seong-gye is placed in the position of Liu-bang and Jeong Do-jeon in the position of Zhang Liang.

Jeong Do-jeon passed the Erudite Examination of the civil service examination in 1362; he taught the Learning of Master Zhu as an educator at Sungkyunkwan after its establishment in 1370 along with Jeong Mong-ju and Yi Sung-in under Chancellor Yi Saek and sharply criticized Buddhism and Daoism as heterodoxy. He spent a life of vicissitude since 1375 when King Wu ascended to the throne. He wrote a Confucian book entitled *Hakja jinamdo* (學者指南圖) during his wanderings toward the end of the Goryeo period, *Joseon gyeonggukjeon* (朝鮮經國典, Administrative Code of Joseon) in 1395, *Gyeongje mungam* (經濟文鑑, Mirror of Governance) in 1396, *Gyeongje mungam byeoljip* (經濟文鑑別集, Supplement to Mirror of Governance) and *Array of Critiques on Buddhism* in 1398 as representative works after the founding of the new dynasty. He was killed by Yi

Bang-won in 1398 during what was later referred to as "the riot of princes." Jeong Do-jeon also compiled 37 volumes of *National History of Goryeo* with Jeong Chong in 1396, but Taejong Yi Bang-won, the third king, ordered a revision. There is no way he would have written from an objective viewpoint because Jeong Do-jeon was deeply involved in the political history of late Goryeo.

Looking at his works, it is seen that he put all his efforts into drawing up a basic framework and prospect for the new dynasty for six years from 1392 at the founding of the dynasty to his death in 1398. Appreciation of Confucianism and depreciation of Buddhism is often talked about as a theory, but remains only that and carries no weight in academic circles without a factual basis for the idea.

In *Administrative Code of Joseon*, the duties of each organ were defined in the Six Codes of Law (六典制: Governance 治典, Taxation 賻典, Rites 禮典, Administration 政典, Law 憲典, and Manufacturing 工典) of the centralized administrative organization according to what could be referred to as the oldest administrative code of law in China in the form of *Book of Rites*. Jeong Do-jeon urged to "make the throne righteous" on the first page of *Administrative Code of Joseon* and cited the following excerpt from the beginning of the *Book of Changes*:

> The great asset of a sage is position, and the great virtue of Heaven and earth refers to the creation and fostering of life. How can this position be maintained? Only through virtue.

According to that book, virtue (仁) for maintaining the position of a ruler refers to governance based on the people.

> The position of a ruler can be called high and noble. But the world is large and there are many people in it. If their heart is not given, there will be great worries. The people are weak but cannot be threatened with might, and they are foolish but cannot be fooled by cleverness. If their heart is given, they will obey; if their heart is not given, they will leave. There is not the slightest room between their goings and comings. But to gain their heart is not

to temporarily contrive through private will and not to lead to an incorrect road for fame. There is only virtue. If the ruler takes the creation and fostering of life on Heaven and earth as his mind and governs in a way that does not bring harm unto others, people throughout will rejoice and look up to him as to a parent.

Virtuous government as advocated by Mencius is to "govern in a way that does not bring harm unto others" as refers to "the mind that does not bring harm unto others" (不忍人之心), i.e., governing with the heart that cannot stand to see the unhappiness or sufferings of the people.

Jeong Do-jeon clearly explains the reason for why "the people are the Heaven" as below:

> On the whole, the ruler relies on the nation, and the nation on its people. The people are the foundation of the nation and the Heaven of the ruler. Thus the king would show respect and accept the house registers of his people in *Book of Rites*.
>
> • "Panjeok" (版籍), Condolences (賻典),
> *Administrative Code of Joseon*

Jeong Do-jeon also wrote *Mirror of Governance*, in which he provides direction on the duties and mental attitude to be held by government officials from the prime minister of the central government to officials of the Office of Inspector General (臺諫), each provincial governor, and magistrates of each district and county.

The item to note here is that the importance of the Office of Inspector General system was emphasized in order to prevent conspiracy politics based on monarchic authoritarianism. The Office of Inspector General system was originally developed in China. The Inspector (臺官, *daegwan* in Kr.) is also called Remonstrator (言官, *eon-gwan* in Kr.) and was in charge of investigating and impeaching corrupt officials, and the Advisor (諫官) was an official in charge of admonishing the king; these offices were distinguished from general administration. This system was of course executed in the Goryeo

186

period as well, but the functions were not systematically carried out to the full. Jeong Do-jeon told the following anecdote as an example of China and Goryeo:

> There lived an official of the Office of Inspector General in the previous dynasty. When the king said, "I do not desire for the officials of the Office of Inspector General to act in accordance with the will of the prime minister," the official responded by saying, "Your Majesty's servant will not only not act in accordance with the will of the prime minister, your will will not be carried out, either."
>
> How admirable! It is possible to wield fundamental principles if only all officials of the Office of Inspector General follow this.

- "Inspector and Advisor," *Mirror of Governance*

Which Is Rational, Monarchism or the Prime Minister System?

Jeong Do-jeon also wrote *Supplement to Mirror of Governance* in which is mentioned the responsibility and mental attitude of the one who is king by way of citing historical facts from China and the Goryeo period. He completed the blueprint for systematization to suit the ideology of a Confucian nation in *Administrative Code of Joseon, Mirror of Governance*, and *Supplement to Mirror of Governance*. It is true that these are his personal opinions. But, as will be discussed later, they can be fundamentally considered to have been all reflected as is in the regime of the Joseon dynasty, such as Six Codes of Law and the Office of Inspector General system.

Particular attention is paid to the point that monarchic authoritarianism is rejected and actual power of administration is allocated to the prime minister. Thus the natural disposition of the ruler in terms of being confused, clear-minded, strong, or weak does not become an issue.

The system of the Six Codes is carried out effectively and all official duties are regulated when a proper person is the prime minister. Therefore it is said that "the responsibility of a ruler lies in his dealings with one prime minister." The authority of a prime minister is great, because he must serve the ruler above him and govern all of the people by commanding the vassals under him.

Moreover, vagueness or clearness and the strength or weakness of a ruler is not the same. A state of fairness must be achieved by taking after what is beautiful, righting what is wrong, aiding what is righteous, and correcting what is incorrect. The minister is to assist [the ruler] and correct [what is incorrect].

- "Introduction," Administrative Code of Joseon, Politics

The Sarim Faction, which considered the Learning of Master Zhu as the greatest scholarship, entered the world of central politics and promoted "moral politics" in the latter half of the 16th century. Members of this faction claimed that the political upheaval in the nation all depended "solely on the mind of the ruler" and tenaciously coerced the king to cultivate a perfect personality, which led to various disputes with the king; this is one of the causes of the "literati purge" (士禍). It is unrealistic to browbeat all monarchs to become saints, because they are human. Jeong Do-jeon acknowledged that there may be individual differences between monarchs in vagueness or clearness of mind and in strength or weakness of character; the prime minister must therefore "take after what is beautiful, right what is wrong, aid in what is righteous, and correct what is incorrect." Thus, the position of the prime minister must be alternated to minimize political disputes because political disputes are part of the responsibility of the prime minister who must assist the king.

Let us look at the case of the Ming dynasty in China.

Emperor Hongwu of the Ming dynasty took the case of high treason by Hu Wei-yong (胡惟庸) as a rare opportunity to execute a massive purging in 1380 and abolished the Chancellery for Internal Affairs, the highest general administration office, and directly administered the Six Boards (六部: Personnel 吏部, Taxation 戶部, Rites 禮部, War 兵部, Punishment 刑部, and Manufacturing 工部) under it. Such monarchic authoritarianism was fairly well maintained during the reigns of great men such as Emperor Hongwu or Emperor Yongle in the early Ming period, but later emperors distanced themselves from bothersome remonstrators and refused to grant interviews to ministers due to their aversion of politics. Emperors became more removed from politics as generations passed, and the eunuchs were put in charge of political decisions (called "response in red" because ratification is made with a red brush); this became the biggest deep-seated disease in the politics of Ming China.

The prime minister system was ultimately chosen in forming the Joseon government, and the State Council with three state councilors of Chief State Councilor, Second State Councilor, and Third State Councilor controlled the vassals and became the greatest administrative office. Under this directive is the Six Ministries — Personnel, Taxation, Rites, War, Punishment, and Manufacturing — modeled after the Six Codes of Law from *Book of Rites*. The head of each ministry was called Minister (判書). These three state councilors and six ministers were the "*samgong yukgyeong*" (三公六卿).

Moreover, Office of Censor General (司諫院) and Office of Inspector General (司憲府) were established in which the former was in charge of remonstrating and refuting the king and the latter for discussing statecraft of the times and maintaining law and order among the vassals. Head of the Office of Censor General is called Censor General, and head of the Office of Inspector General is called Inspector General. Attention should be paid to the Sarim Faction using this official post of the Office of Inspector General as a foothold for emerging into the central political world in defiance of the Hungu Faction later.

Taejo Yi Seong-gye established a place for royal lectures to be given by Confucians from the outset of his reign; this is mentioned in *Administrative Code of Joseon* as follows:

His Majesty employed Royal Lecturers for the first time and had them act as advisors. (His Majesty) always said, "The Great Learning is for the ruler to establish a standard for all ages. Zhen Xi-shan (眞西山) enlarged on the meaning of the *Great Learning* and created *Extended Meaning of the Great Learning*. There is nothing better than this for the order of governing and the foundation of scholarship for the sovereign."

- "Royal Lectures," Administrative Code of Joseon, Vol. 13

Zhen Xi-shan referred to Zhen De-xiu, a scholar of the Learning of Master Zhu (pen name is Xi-shan, 1178-1235) of the Southern Song dynasty. He was a scholar who preserved the Cheng-Zhu School even after it was forbidden due to "the false learning of Jin" and a politician who attempted to recover the honor of Zhu Xi when at the imperial court. Song Ryeom recommended *Extended Meaning of the Great Learning* to Zhu Yuan-zhang, founder of Ming China, as the textbook for "studying to become a good emperor." The efforts of Zhen De-xiu and Wei Liao-weng (魏了翁) were great in lifting the ban in 1211 against the Learning of Master Zhu as "the false learning of Jin," which had been proclaimed in 1196. Zhen De-xiu also wrote one volume of *Heart Meridian* (心經) in addition to 43 volumes of *Extended Meaning of the Great Learning*; *Heart Meridian* greatly influenced Yi Hwang (李滉), the highest authority on the study of the principle of human nature in Joseon. The scholarship of Zhen De-xiu was the Learning of Master Zhu based on extermination of human desire and shedding of light on the law of nature, but he lacked originality as a scholar in that he put value on "reverence" as the law of the mind which all sages have transmitted rather than investigation of the law of nature.

Jeong Do-jeon was probably the person who recommended *Extended Meaning of the Great Learning* as the textbook for "studying to become a good emperor" to Yi Seong-gye. Jeong did not enforce appreciation of Confucianism and depreciation of Buddhism to Taejo Yi Seong-gye, nor was it or expected of him, because that is the duty to be performed by the prime minister.

190

Gwon Geun Is in Charge of the Educational Policy of the New Dynasty

If Jo Jun and Jeong Do-jeon were the two great Confucians of the transition in dynasty, Jeong Do-jeon and Gwon Geun can be called the twin stars of the Confucian nation at the end of Goryeo and the beginning of Joseon.

The pen name of Gwon Geun (權近, 1352-1409) is Yangchon (陽村); he wrote an anthology titled *Collected Works of Yangchon.* He entered the bureaucratic road by passing the Erudite Examination of the civil service examination in 1368 and, as with Jeong Do-jeon, he lived a life of exile during the reigns of King Wu → King Chang → King Gongyang toward the end of Goryeo due to being thrust aside by the pro-Yuan faction. The new dynasty was founded while he was living in seclusion in Chungju in Chungcheong Province after his banishment to Ikju (益州, Iksan) was removed. As a radical in the transitioning of the dynasty, Jeong Do-jeon turned from his teacher Yi Saek and upperclassman Jeong Mong-ju by considering them political rivals. But Gwon Geun did not lose his respect for the two. He reminisced as below in the preface of the anthology of Jeong Do-jeon:

> Our *jwaju*, Master Mog-eun (Yi Saek), entered Piyong (辟雍: National Confucian Academy in Yuan China) from early on by following the family precepts and studied a scholarship that is large, correct, delicate, and detailed. After returning to Goryeo, Confucian scholars studying overseas considered him their master. Scholars such as Po-eun Jeong (Jeong Mong-ju), Do-eun Yi (Yi Sung-in), Sambong Jeong (Jeong Do-jeon), Banyang Bak (Bak Sang-chun), and Yun So-jong (尹紹宗, pen name is Musong 茂松) all understood his scholarship deeply. Sambong was especially close to Po-eun and Do-eun, and gained more by discussing and studying with each other. And he considered it his responsibility to exclude heterodoxy at all times when teaching his underclassmen.

- "Jeongsambong munjipseo" (鄭三峰文集序), *Collected Works of Yangchon*, Vol. 16

Yi Saek was the master of the School of Master Zhu that was active during the end of Goryeo and the beginning of Joseon as Gwon Geun states. Among the school's adherents, Mog-eun Yi Saek, Po-eun Jeong Mong-ju, and Do-eun Yi Sung-in were called "the three Eun" of the end of Goryeo; they all opposed the transition of the dynasty. Gwon Geun transcended differences in political positions and evaluated them with ample regard.

Gwon Geun was mainly in charge of the educational policy in the founding period of the new dynasty as the Academician of the Office of Royal Decrees as well as the Chancellor of Sungkyunkwan. In other words, he provided the fundamental direction and secured the foundation for nurturing able men to administer the dynastic system conceptualized by Jeong Do-jeon.

Representative works written by Gwon Geun are *Ip'hak doseol* (入學圖說, Diagrammatic Treatise for Entering upon Learning), which is the very first serious writing on the principle of human nature in Korean Confucian thought, and *Ogyeong cheon'gyeonnok* (五經淺見錄), which is a historical research of the Five Confucian Classics. Confucians at the end of Goryeo and the beginning of Joseon knew that the study of the principle of human nature supported the anti-Buddhism doctrine, but this *Diagrammatic Treatise for Entering upon Learning* shows for the first time how the study of the principle of human nature as the core of the Learning of Master Zhu was understood by them. He put the most effort into writing 26 volumes of *Yegi cheon'gyeonnok* along with *Diagrammatic Treatise for Entering upon Learning* and *Ogyeong cheon'gyeonnok*; he devoted 14 long years to writing *Yegi cheon'gyeonnok* at the behest of his teacher Yi Saek.

In his later years, Gwon Geun submitted a request to the third king Taejong (r. 1400-1418) of his desire to leave all his government posts and finish verifying the procedures in *Record of Rites* ("Cheong-hae myeonbonjik jonggo yegi jeolcha jeon" 請解免本職終考禮記

節次箋, *Collected Works of Yangchon*, Vol. 26). Taejong did not grant his request and issued the following answer:

> Since ascending to the throne I have thought to reveal the foundation of governing the nation by gathering Confucian scholars to the left and right of me to give royal lectures on Chinese classics. You are a model for the younger generations, because your natural disposition is pure, discerning, magnanimous, and subtle so that your scholarship is well versed in Six Confucian Classics and your research is not shallow and issues forth profound knowledge of the sages of the past. And *Cheon'gyeonnok* and *Diagrammatic Treatise for Entering upon Learning* you wrote are used as guidelines for all scholars. Thus (I have) appointed (you) to hold the joint offices of Prime Minister and Royal Lecturer and chancellor of Office for Annals Compilation and Sungkyunkwan so that the study of the principle of human nature can be heard. How can the depth of discussion on scholarship be said to be less than that of the wise Yi Yin (伊尹) and Fu Yue (傅說) of Yin dynasty? Methods on recording and deleting can already be learned from *Spring and Autumn Annals*, and the teachings of knowledge and courtesy were admired by Ya Sheng (亞聖: Yanzi 顔子). Truly, your duty is to open my mind morning and night and to tell me the key to the Great Way with the "scholarship of reverence for all things" (毋不敬) and the teachings of "not thinking in an evil way" (思無邪).

- "Bulyun bidap" (不允批答: written by Nangsa Yu Sa-nul, 郎舍 柳思訥), *Collected Works of Yangchon*, Vol. 16

Taejong talked about Shenzong commanding Liu Shu (劉恕) and Fan Zu-yu (范祖禹) to assist Si Maguang of Northern Song China to write *Comprehensive Mirror for Aid in Government*, after which he said he would take the same action. Moreover, he convinced Gwon Geun to remain in office to complete the task of ascertaining the truth of the differences and similarities in *Record of Rites* as a deathbed request by his teacher. This is a scene that vividly describes a Confucian aspect of the king. Pupils of Gwon Geun — Gwon Wu (權遇), Byeon Gye-ryang (卞季良), Maeng Sa-seong (孟思誠), Heo Jo (許稠), Kim Ban (金泮), and Kim Jong-li (金從理) — were vassals from Goryeo who participated in establishing a nation in the reigns of King Taejong and Sejong.

It Is Difficult for Two Heroes to Coexist

The issue of who should succeed to the throne after Taejo led to a family feud. Yi Seong-gye had six sons and two daughters from his first wife of the Han (韓) clan and two sons and a daughter from his second wife of the Kang (康) clan. His first wife passed away in 1391, a year before Yi Seong-gye ascended to the throne; of the six sons, the first son Yi Bang-wu (李芳雨) and sixth son Bang-yeon (李芳衍) died early, and second son Bang-gwa (李芳果), third son Bang-ui (李芳毅), fourth son Bang-gan (李芳幹), and fifth son Bang-won were left, among whom Prince Yi Bang-won had ambition, was popular, and had literary and military abilities. More, Bang-won was a Confucian scholar, good enough to pass the civil service examination in the late Goryeo period. The second wife of Yi Seong-gye from the Kang clan passed away in 1396, leaving behind Bang-beon (李芳蕃) and Bang-seok (李芳碩). In other words, Yi Seong-gye had four legitimate sons by his first wife and two by his second wife.

What Yi Bang-won could not stand was the fact that Yi Seong-gye passed over four of his legitimate sons by his first wife to declare the still young Bang-seok as Crown Prince. This may be the result of Yi Seong-gye's devoted love for his second wife. Yi Seong-gye solicited Jeong Do-jeon and Nam Eun to educate and guide the Crown Prince. Jo Jun opposed the appointment of Bang-seok as the Crown Prince and supported Yi Bang-won as the successor. The appointment by Yi Seong-gye of the youngest prince by the second wife is clearly a deviation from the ordinary way of succession to the throne.

It seemed as if the issue of succession to the throne was close at hand in 1398 when Yi Seong-gye took to bed due to illness. In

August of the same year, Yi Bang-won ordered the murder of the two sons by Yi Seong-gye's second wife of the Kang clan, Bang-beon and Bang-seok, as well as those who supported them, such as Jeong Do-jeon and Nam Eun, and declared Bang-gwa, the second legitimate son of Yi Seong-gye, as the Crown Prince by carrying out a coup d'état through collusion with Jo Jun and making Ha Ryun (河崙) be on his side. This was the first riot of princes. In September, Taejo Yi Seong-gye handed over the throne to Bang-gwa and retired to Hamju (Hamheung). The successor was the second king Jeongjong (r. 1398-1400).

Jeongjong planned on passing on the throne to Yi Bang-won in the near future in order to survive. But Bang-gan, the fourth son of Yi Seong-gye, became jealous of the power of his younger brother Bang-won and carried out a coup d'état with the urgings of Jijung-chuwonsa (知中樞院事) Bak Po (朴苞) in February 1400. This was the second riot of princes. The private military troops of Yi Bang-won and Ha Ryun engaged in battle with and succeeded in suppressing the supporters of Bang-gan. Jeongjong retired thereafter, and Yi Bang-won ascended to the throne as the third king Taejong.

The first riot of princes was a battle between half-brothers, but the second riot of princes was between brothers born of the same mother. Not only did Yi Bang-won kill Jeong Mong-ju and Jeong Do-jeon in late Goryeo to early Joseon periods, he ascended to the throne only after he murdered his half-brothers Bang-beon and Bang-seok and drove out his older brother Bang-gan to To Mountain (兎山) in Hwanghae Province.

After he ascended to the throne, Taejong repeatedly sent messengers to Hamheung to request Yi Seong-gye to return to the capital, but Taejo did not agree. Yi Seong-gye finally returned to Seoul in 1405 with the persuasion of the Grand Master Muhak Jacho, but his life was devoted to chanting the Buddha to achieve mental concentration until his death in Changdeok Palace in 1408.

The eight years from 1392 when Yi Seong-gye founded the Joseon dynasty to 1400 when Taejong ascended to the throne was a laborious period wherein the old regime fell and a new regime was created. Gwon Geun was the greatest reformer who assisted in searching for a new order within the downfall of the old system and creating a new society in the reign of Taejong (1400-1418).

Distinction between legitimate children and children by second wives was severe in the Joseon period. At the time, there was a "law preventing children born of concubines and *yangban* and descendants from holding high office" that prevented them from holding the position of *hyeonjik* (顯職: a high government post that is equivalent to or higher than 5-*pum*), no matter how great the family or how talented the individuals. This is said to have originated from the first riot of princes. In other words, the feud between relations occurred due to Yi Seong-gye appointing Bang-seok, the son of his second wife, as Crown Prince and eliminating the princes from his first wife.

Whatever the case may be, Yi Bang-won and Jeong Do-jeon were avowed friends and two mainstays of the transition in dynasty from Goryeo to Joseon. The riot of princes shows well that it is difficult for two heroes to coexist.

Serving Ming China as a Great Nation

In 1399, one year after the riot of princes, "the Purge of Jingnuo" (靖難之變) began in Ming China. "The Purge of Jingnuo" was a blood feud between Emperor Jianwen (建文帝) and King of Yan (燕王) over the throne after Emperor Hongwu of Ming dynasty died in 1398. In comparison to the four-year-long internal strife called "the Purge of Jingnuo," the riot of princes in Joseon was merely a tempest in a teapot.

Zhu Yuan-zhang ascended to the throne in 1368 as Emperor Hongwu, the founder of Ming dynasty in China. Coming from a poor family, he conspired with regional landholders and executed a massive purge by discovering corruptions carried out by the provincial bureaucrats who had threatened the lives of farmers. Further, he purged meritorious vassals with whom he went through hardships and veteran generals as well so that he could only rely on blood relations. Emperor Hongwu had a total of 26 sons with his first wife and concubines, among whom he had five sons by his Empress of the Ma (馬) clan who was known to be wise. Emperor Hongwu gave military power to his five sons and granted fiefdoms to them so that they could defend the nation close to the borders.

Zhu Dui (朱棣), the fourth son, was the best in literary and military accomplishments and popular among Emperor Hongwu's five sons. He was appointed as King of Yan at the front lines of Beiping (北平: Beijing, capital of Yuan) to fight against the surviving power of Northern Yuan.

Zhu Biao (朱標), the first son of Zhu Yuan-zhang, was the Crown Prince, but he died early when Emperor Hongwu was alive; his grandson became the Crown Prince instead. Emperor Jianwen ascended to the throne in 1398 after Emperor Hongwu passed away.

Tacticians such as Huang Zi-deng (黃子澄, or Tzu-ch'eng) and Zhai Tai (齊泰) surrounded the weak and scholarly type that was Emperor Jianwen; they pursued a scheme to uproot the powers of various kings who might be a threat to the throne. Of course, the final goal was the King of Yan. A resourceful monk named Dao Yan (道衍) assisted the King of Yan. Psychological and informational spying continued for a long time between Nanjing, where Emperor Jianwen had a stronghold, and Beiping, where King of Yan had a stronghold. Among the eunuchs surrounding Emperor Jianwen was a spy for King of Yan. King of Yan ultimately challenged Emperor Jianwen with the great justification of subduing military disturbance or crisis by "purging treacherous vassals surrounding the ruler." There were fluctuations in battle, but ultimately the troops of King Yan conquered Nanjing Castle in 1402 and King of Yan ascended to the throne as the Great Emperor Yongle (永樂帝, r. 1402-1424). He ascended to the throne in Nanjing but began constructing the massive Zijin Castle (紫禁城) in Beiping and declared it the capital after renaming it Beijing in 1421; Nanjing became the second capital.

The existence of the second emperor, Jianwen, was erased in Chinese history, but Emperor Qianlong of Qing China revived it later. One of the Confucians who shared the fate of Emperor

Jianwen and died to preserve his integrity was Fang Xiaoru (方孝孺). He was an outstanding disciple of Song Lian, the best Confucian scholar of the early Ming dynasty, and as such King of Yan ordered him to write a record on the ascension of the former to the throne. But the latter wrote that "the Yan enemy usurped the throne." Not only was he executed for his act but his family and scholars also died.

As mentioned previously, the founder of Ming China, Emperor Hongwu, had a tendency to focus on internal affairs and did not do much about foreign relations because he emphasized the recovery of "China," which was about to become obsolete due to the rule of the Mongols. He did not send a letter of appointment to Yi Seong-gye who ascended to the throne by successfully leading a transition in dynasty with the excuse that Joseon is "a free nation with its own unique culture." In spite of this, the Joseon government did the best to be submissive to Ming China in good faith by unilaterally dispatching envoys to China on the New Year, on the birthday of the emperor, and on the birthday of the imperial crown prince. Emperor Hongwu requested that "tributes be sent once every three years" by saying "propriety of the past feudal lords must definitely be observed by sending tributes every three years."

It was not only essential for the Joseon dynasty to receive the approval of the Chinese emperor for the stability of the dynasty, but a great profit could be made through tributary trade. Chinese policy on tributary trade was "to dispense large presents for small tributes received," i.e., reward much in return for a small amount of valuable tributes. Joseon Confucians fervently desired to increase intercourse with Chinese culture by traveling back and forth from Beijing, the center of politics and culture in China, because Joseon was also a Confucian nation. Thus, they were not satisfied with sending tributes only once every three years but desired to send tributes thrice a year instead.

Taejong was ruling as the third king of Joseon when Emperor Yongle ascended to the throne. Ha Ryun was dispatched to China in 1402 to congratulate the ascension of Emperor Yongle to the throne, and the longstanding diplomatic issue for Ming China on serving a greater nation was resolved in a single stroke in October of 1402 when the Chinese envoy who accompanied Ha Ryun back to Joseon brought with him the letter of appointment and golden seal of Emperor Yongle.

In comparison to Ming China's founder Emperor Hongwu focusing on internal affairs, Emperor Yongle can be said to be the type of an emperor who was bold in foreign expansion. He was the first emperor of China to lead an expedition force past the Gobi Desert five times in order to prevent the return of the Mongols, who were the greatest threat from the northern regions. A Muslim eunuch called Zheng He (鄭和) from Yunnan (雲南) served to navigate seven expeditions into the eastern coast of Africa by way of South Asia and Calcutta in southern India for 28 years from 1405 on. This occurred 60-some years before Vasco da Gama sailed from Lisbon in Portugal and reached Calcutta on the western shore of India in May of 1498 by going around the southern tip of Africa. Tributary envoys from diverse kingdoms traveled back and forth to Beijing from the regions conquered by Zheng He, and Beijing prospered into an international city with gatherings of valuable products from around the world.

The monumental task of continuing with the achievements of his predecessors was begun by Emperor Hongwu and succeeded by Emperor Yongle. The civil service examination was given based on the Learning of Master Zhu since the Yuan period, but the Learning of Master Zhu cemented its unassailable position as a systematic doctrinal study. It is very well known that 12,000 books and 22,800 volumes of a type of encyclopedia entitled *Yongle Encyclopedia* were compiled under the reign of Emperor Yongle. Moreover, as the three fundamental documents of the Cheng-Zhu School based on new annotations replacing old annotations of the studies of Han and Tang dynasties, three books entitled *Grand Code of the Five Confucian Classics* (五經大典), *Grand Code of the Four Books* (四書大典) based on the new annotations by the Cheng-Zhu School, and *Grand Code of the Principle of Human Nature* (性理大典), which combined together was a collection of the doctrine of the study of the principle of human nature, became necessary books to be kept near at hand for

Confucians during the Ming and Qing periods in China as well as in Joseon.

Coexisting with Japan as a Neighbor

A "neighborly" relationship began between Joseon and Japan after the Japanese "piracy" issue was resolved.

Internal war continued over legitimacy after the Kamakura Bakufu fell in Japan in 1333 when the imperial family was divided into Southern and Northern dynasties. With this internal rebellion as background, the local gentry of Kitakyushu organized the common people and invaded Goryeo as the primary target. Japanese piracy from the Southern and Northern Dynasties period to early Muromachi period is called the first period of Japanese piracy.

A channel for diplomatic relations between Goryeo and Japan was discontinued since Wang Geon founded the Goryeo dynasty in 918. Goryeo dispatched Kim Yong (金龍) and Kim Il (金逸) to the second general Ashikaga Yoshiakira of Muromachi Bakufu in 1367 to request supervision over the pirates. Monks Bonto (梵盪) and Bonryu (梵鏐) from Tenryu-ji Temple (天龍寺) were sent to Goryeo in return as Japanese envoy along with the returning Goryeo envoy. This was the first traffic of envoys between the two nations. Foreign relations in the Muromachi period were handled by the greatest intellectuals of Japan of the times in the form of Zen Buddhist monks of Kyoto Gozan (five great Zen temples of Kyoto).

Na Heung-yu (羅興儒) of Goryeo visited Tokyo in 1375 as ambassador to Japan and requested the prohibition of Japanese piracy. Monk Ryoju accompanied Na Heung-yu on the return journey to Goryeo and delivered a document from the Japanese government written by Monk Shuza of Tenryu Temple to the Goryeo government.

> We have not been able to collect tributes for nearly 20 years since the rebelling vassals hold sway in Kyushu in the western sea. (The piracy) is an invasion of (your nation) by evil Japanese people of

the western sea amidst this confusion and not ordered by us. Generals have gone deep into this territory, and both camps are fighting each other fiercely. We promise to Heaven and Sun that the piracy will be forbidden when Kyushu is recovered.

- "Sinu" (辛禑), Yeoljeon, *History of Goryeo*

Orders from Muromachi Bakufu did not reach Kyushu in those days because the Southern Dynasty continued the resistance under the direction of the Kanenagashinno power. Thus, Imagawa Ryoshun led the effort to suppress the pirates after becoming the Kyushu Tandai. It can be seen that the Goryeo administration and Muromachi Bakufu stood on an equal footing on controlling Japanese piracy.

Following this, Jeong Mong-ju visited Kyushu Tandai Imagawa Ryoshun in 1377 and Han Guk-ju (韓國柱) visited Ouchi Yoshihiro of Suo no kuni requesting control over Japanese pirates. Imagawa Ryoshun repatriated hundreds of prisoners kidnapped by the pirates, and Ouchi Yoshihiro dispatched some 180 soldiers led by Bak Geo-sa to Goryeo to participate in a punitive expedition to suppress Japanese pirates. This was a prerequisite for Muromachi Bakufu to form diplomatic relations with Goryeo.

Extraordinarily, however, Japan realized unification of the Southern and Northern Dynasties when Emperor Gokameyama of the Southern Dynasty abdicated the crown in favor of Emperor Gokomatsu of the Northern Dynasty in response to the calling by the third general Ashikaga Yoshimitsu in 1392 when the Joseon dynasty was founded. Ashikaga Yoshimitsu simultaneously ordered Kyushu Tandai to control the pirates and dispatched Monk Soa (祖阿) to Ming China to request a diplomatic alliance in 1401. He provided the emperor of Ming China with the name of the Japanese monarch as Minamoto Mitsuyoshi and began trading with Great Ming.

Eight Provinces and Three Ports of Joseon

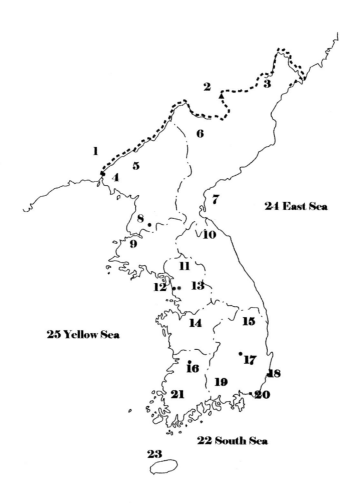

24 East Sea

25 Yellow Sea

22 South Sea

1. Amnok River (aka Yalu River in Ch.)
2. Baekdu Mountain
3. Duman River (aka Tumen River in Ch.)
4. Uiju
5. Pyeong'an Province
6. Hamgil Province
7. Yeongheung Port
8. Pyeong'yang
9. Hwanghae Province
10. Gangweon Province
11. Hanseong
12. Jemul Port (Incheon)
13. Gyeonggi Province
14. Chungcheong Province
15. Gyeongsang Province
16. Jeonju
17. Daegu
18. Yeom Port
19. Naei Port
20. Busan Port
21. Jeolla Port
22. South Sea
23. Jeju Island
24. East Sea
25. Yellow Sea (West Sea)

Ashikaga Yoshimitsu dispatched Monk Shuto to the Joseon court in 1404 under the name of the Japanese monarch Minamoto Mitsuyoshi. With the emperor of Ming as a fixed point, Joseon and Japanese monarchs began to have interchange of "alliance" with propriety on the same level.

Joseon opened Busan Port and Naei Port for residence and trade in the sixth year of the reign of Taejong (1406) in an effort to transform the "pirates" into "trade merchants." Yeom Port (Ulsan) was opened later to make three opened ports. The pirates raided China or Southeast Asia thereafter, and this is the later period of Japanese piracy.

"Serving a greater kingdom" of China and "alliance" with Japan were traditionally the two mainstays of Korean foreign relations, but the diplomacy of serving the greater kingdom of China had priority. Relationship with China was the most important for preserving the security of Joseon. The role played by Taejong was great in cementing the foundation and stabilizing relations with neighboring nations. Thanks to his efforts, internal troubles and fears of foreign invasions disappeared, which made it possible for Sejong as the next king to completely focus on internal stability and cultural enterprise.

12

Bureaucrats Armed with
the Learning of Master Zhu

Even the Village Schools Teach Only the Learning of Master Zhu

O n the subject of civil service examination for appointing able men, Taejo Yi Seong-gye stated in the Letter of Instruction at the Time of Ascension to the Throne, "Neither erudite nor military examinations can be discontinued." Military examination was omitted from the Goryeo period except for a very short period. Yi Seong-gye, a military official, attempted to rectify that. But the force of habit of revering scholarship and neglecting the military still could not be changed. Taejo Yi Seong-gye, who ascended to the throne in Suchang Palace (壽昌宮) within Gaeseong in July of 1392, ordered the building of Sungkyunkwan in eastern Sunggyobang (崇敎坊) and the move of the capital to Hanseong at the same time. Sungkyunkwan was the best educational institute since the Goryeo period. But the capital was moved to Gaeseong, albeit temporarily, during the beginning of the dynasty starting with the riot of princes that occurred twice; this task was completed in the seventh year of the reign of Taejong (1407).

There may have been transformation in educational contents and system, but the total number of students was 200 according to the regulation in *Gyeongguk daejeon* (National Code) and had the characteristics of being a school for applying for "the big class" (a popular name for the civil service examination) of the Erudite

Examination. According to the "Code of Rites" in *National Code*, enrollment criterion was age 15 or over as follows:

> First, enrollment criterion in principle is for those who are classics and literary licentiates. Classics licentiate and literary licentiate refer to those who have passed the Classics Licentiate Examination and Literary Licentiate Examination.
>
> Second, the following people will supplement the ranks if there is a lack of enough classics and literary licentiates:
>
> ① students of the four government schools who are knowledgeable about *Elementary Learning* as well as one of the Four Books;
>
> ② those who hold government posts due to the merits of their ancestors (descendants of meritorious vassals or high-ranking official) and are knowledgeable about *Elementary Learning*;
>
> ③ those who in the past had passed the Erudite Examination, the first-level test conducted in the provinces for the Classics Licentiate and Literary Licentiate Examination, or the test conducted by the Prefecture of the Capital (漢城試).

The civil service examination of the Joseon period put more importance on the Erudite Examination as opposed to the Military Examination. But only the Erudite Examination existed in the Goryeo period except for a very brief period as mentioned above, and Composition Examination course based on the rhetoric was valued more than the meaning of the Confucian Classics of the Classics Examination course. The meaning of the Confucian Classics was valued rather than the rhetoric in the Joseon period. The small class for the Erudite Examination conducted in the provinces was divided into the Literary Licentiate Examination of the rhetoric and the Classics Licentiate Examination of the meaning of the Confucian Classics, but the big class of the Erudite Examination in the capital combined the Composition Examination course and Classics Examination course of the Goryeo period and put value on the meaning of the Confucian Classics.

As well, four schools (四部學堂: there were five schools originally) in addition to Sungkyunkwan were established in Seoul as institutes for secondary education: East Village School, West Village School, South Village School, and Central Village School. One hundred students were enrolled in each school, for a total of 400. Status distinction between *yangban* and commoners was not given for learning in the four schools. There was the Office of the Royal Family Education (宗學) for the offspring of royal clansmen. This is equivalent to "Gakushuin" (Peers School) in Japan prior to World War II.

Institutes for secondary education in the form of local schools were established in the centers of *bu*, grand prefectures, *mok*, prefectures, counties, and districts.[1] The number of enrolled students was 90 for each institute in the *bu*, grand prefectures, and *mok*, and 70 in prefectures, 50 in the counties, and 30 in the districts. Students 16 and under were not included in the total number of students, because village schools were for Classics Licentiate Examination and Literary Licentiate Examination of the civil service examination held in the provinces.

Sungkyunkwan, four schools, and village schools were government schools, and as such, the government actively strove for expansion by providing land allocated for scholarship, slaves, and textbooks. Moreover, seven standards for job evaluation of provincial magistrates were defined in "Gogwa" (考課, Evaluation of Merits) of *National Code*, Ijeon (吏典) as ① agriculture and sericulture must thrive, ② schools must flourish, ③ civil suits must be brief, ④ wiliness and slyness must not exist, ⑤ be governed by military government, ⑥ increase in the number of houses and families, and ⑦ corvée must be made equal. It can be seen that the first and second most important items among these were promotion of agriculture and doctrinal studies.

But there were various financial troubles in promoting schools, and maintenance and operation of the student dormitory in particular was a headache. The four schools in Seoul and village schools in the provinces were equally institutes for secondary education, but the

---

[1] *Bu* was an administrative district smaller than *mok* but bigger than a county; *mok* was an administrative district bigger than *bu*. (S. Lee)

four schools were like subsidiaries of Sungkyunkwan and received special privileges in comparison to village schools. For example, students of the four schools who had not passed the Classics Licentiate Examination and Literary Licentiate Examination could directly enroll in Sungkyunkwan by passing the examination to become a Classics licentiate.

There were private schools in the form of village schools for elementary education and private academies for secondary education to supplement government schools. Of course, institutional regulations did not apply, and the instructional contents varied because these were private schools. But the village schools played a big role in elementary education and the crusade against illiteracy among the low-born and common class. This was exactly the same as Japan's Terakoya.

There were instances of private village schools opening through the creation of an "affiliation for private village schools" by the smallest unit of community in country villages and *li* (hamlets), where a schoolmaster would be invited to teach in them; or a schoolmaster might open a school by gathering students instead. Moreover, a landowner might invite a renowned Confucian scholar to educate his children. Contents of education in village schools were very important as educational institutes for commoners without restriction as to enrollment criteria. The curriculum might vary, depending on the schoolmaster in charge, but it would be appropriate to assume the following:

First, fundamental reading and writing of Chinese characters would be learned through *One Thousand Characters*, followed by *Dongmong seonseup* (童蒙先習, Children's First Learning), *Myeongsim bogam* (明心寶鑑, Exemplar of Pure Mind), and *Elementary Learning*. *Elementary Learning* was supposedly compiled by Zhu Xi, but in actuality it was a primer for the Learning of Master Zhu that was edited by his friend Liu Zi-deng (劉子澄) at the request of Zhu Xi. The curriculum leading up to *Elementary Learning* was the preparatory curriculum for learning the Four Books and Five Confucian Classics. Village schools were the preparatory stage for entering the four schools and local schools that were the institutes for secondary education, but village schools could teach classes comparable to secondary education so that the students could apply for the Classics or Literary Licentiate Examination.

Textbooks used in the Four Books and Five Confucian Classics after completion of *Elementary Learning* were all commentaries made by Zhu Xi, and the learning process was in the order of the *Great Learning* → *Analects of Confucius* → *The Works of Mencius* → *Doctrine of the Mean* as prescribed by Zhu Xi. A particular issue was that the contents of education taught in village schools were limited to a portion of Confucian civilization that was distant from everyday lives; the village schools functioned as institutes of education for commoners and formed a wide network within the provincial country villages. In comparison to "reading, writing, and abacus calculation" that were taught in Japan's Terakoya in addition to writing letters, abacus sum, and bookkeeping that were deemed essential in real life, the educational contents in Joseon from the introductory stage were dominated by Confucianism, or rather, the Learning of Master Zhu. Village schools of Joseon were popular educational facilities rooted definitively in the *minjung* (people), but the majority of students dropped out in the middle in each stage of the curriculum, thereby creating many illiterate people.

Private academies were private schools that were almost on a par with local schools. The prototype of a private academy was the White Cloud Academy (白雲洞書院), which was erected by Ju Se-bung, Magistrate of Public Morality, in Gyeongsang Province in 1543 to commemorate Ahn Hyang, who was the first to transmit the Learning of Master Zhu in the late Goryeo period. In 1550, Yi Hwang, another magistrate of public morality, submitted an appeal to the king and was awarded a plaque personally written by the king naming the place as the Academy of Received Learning (紹修書院) as well as land, slaves, and books. This was the start of a royally endowed private academy.

The original goal of private academies was to commemorate sages of old and educate younger generations with their scholarship and virtue. In the beginning, the contents of education in reality surpassed that of the village schools, which were government schools in the provinces, and the rate of passing the first-level test conducted in the provinces was rather high. Private academies became common since the latter half of the 16th century, and they turned into hotbeds of factions as party strife intensified within the Sarim Faction, advancing into the political world of the central government. Factions gave rise to abuses. The number of private academies increased in direct proportion to the severity of party strife. In other words, parties that were ousted from the political world of the central government used private academies in the provinces as their base of operation to preserve power and as the hotbed for a chance to launch a counterattack.

According to what has been examined above, military arts were not included in the curriculum of private academies → local schools, the four colleges, and private academies → Sungkyunkwan. *Yangban* politics of Joseon was controlled by high-level bureaucrats who studied in Sungkyunkwan and passed the Erudite Examination of "the big class." Therefore *yangban* politics meant scholar-official order, and the civilian government's encouraging of learning and disdaining of military arts were continued, despite the Military Examination being part of the civil service examination. The period of civilian government in the Joseon dynasty overlapped the shogunate governments of Muromachi, Sengoku, and Edo periods in Japan. But the frailty of the Joseon civilian government was revealed when Toyotomi Hideyoshi attacked Joseon as an extension of the period of the warring states.

Was the Civil Service Examination Conducted Fairly?

The social status system of Joseon can broadly be divided into *yangban*, free-born commoners, and the lowborn. All Koreans wanted to be *yangban*, and many professed themselves to be "*yangban*." But *yangban* politics were established by a very small minority because the majority of the people were lowborn and especially commoners.

There is no other word as ambiguous as the word "*yangban*." There was no lawful regulation (this is the cause of ambiguity), but until the end of the Joseon period in general, one could not call himself a *yangban* unless "a family member was a Hyeon'gwan (顯官: high rank of 5-*pum* or above) within the last three generations." Last three generations refers to the current generation through the great-grandfather.

A record of lineage is called *jokbo* in Korea, and just because an ancestor of seven to ten or more generations in the past was a Hyeon'gwan did not make all descendants *yangban*. For the sake of convenience, *yangban* is defined here as the scholar-official order who passed the Erudite Examination and the military-official order who passed the Military Examination. Thus people could not hereditarily be of the scholar-official or military-official order. People who were of the *yangban* class but who did not pass the civil service examination were called "*baekdu*" (白頭) or "*baeksu*" (白首: this refers to the fact that they did not wear a headpiece), which was not only an embarrassment for the individuals but was also "unfilial" to ancestors and clansmen. The psychological pressure in actuality was great.

The civil service examination was very strict according to the *National Code*. The Erudite Examination was regulated as follows in the *National Code*:

> The examination is given once every three years. Preliminary examination is given in the fall of the previous year; the second-level test and final test conducted under the personal attendance of the sovereign conducted by the central government are conducted in the following spring. Those of the ranks equal to or below that of Tonghun Daebu (通訓大夫: lower-level officials of Jeong 3-*pum*) can apply for the Erudite Examination, and those of ranks equal to or below that of Tongdeongnang (通德郎: rank of Jeong 5-*pum* or below) can apply for the Classics Licentiate Examination and/or Literary Licentiate Examination (magistrates cannot apply for the Classics Licentiate Examination or Literary Licentiate Examination).

> • "Rites," National Code

The following is an expansion on the excerpt above:

The Erudite Examination was conducted once every three years and called the triennial examination. Application for the big class of the Erudite Examination was restricted to those who had already passed the Classics Licentiate and Literary Licentiate Examinations (small class). This small class was an examination for the students of the four schools or the local schools that contained Classics Licentiate and Literary Licentiate Examinations; as such, those who passed the Classics Licentiate Examination were called classics licentiates, and those who passed the Literary Licentiate Examinations were called literary licentiates. Many gave up on applying for the big class in the late Joseon dynasty period because most of the qualifiers of the big class of the Erudite Examination became fixed according to the lineage of civilian officials. Classics licentiates and literary licentiates who passed the small class were of "the local *yangban*" (鄕班), i.e., influential *yangban* in the provinces.

The Erudite Examination was given in three stages: the preliminary examination, second-level test conducted by the central government, and a final test conducted under the personal attendance of the sovereign. As a rule, a total of 330 people were selected in the preliminary examination from a pool of those who had passed the first-level test conducted in the provinces (240 selected), a test conducted by the Prefecture of the Capital (40 selected), or *gwansi* (館試, preliminary examination open to only Sungkyunkwan students: 50 selected). Of course, there may have been various changes in the distribution of those selected depending on the number of applicants of the first-level test conducted in the provinces; the number taking the test conducted by the Prefecture of the Capital; and the number for the preliminary examination open to only Sungkyunkwan students.

Those who passed the preliminary examination (classics licentiates and literary licentiates) applied for the second-level test conducted by the central government under the Ministry of Rites (禮曹) after the completion of a prescribed course in Sungkyunkwan in Seoul. Thirty-three people were then selected from the applicants. Examination scores of the thirty-three applicants were ranked during the final test conducted under the personal attendance of the sovereign. Those who passed the civil service examination were divided into three groups based on their score: 3 people for *gapgwa* (first ranking), 7 people for *eulgwa* (second ranking), and 23 for *byeonggwa* (third ranking). The person who passed the civil service examination with the highest score within the first ranking group was called "Jangwon Geupje" (壯元及第). It was very difficult in principle to pass the examination at the top of the group, because the 33 who competed from all over the nation were selected during the triennial examination.

People in Seoul had more chances of applying for the civil service examination in the latter half of the Joseon period because of irregular examinations, such as the augmented examination (增廣試), examination given after the king visited the National Confucian Shrine (謁聖試), examination given in the presence of the king in Chundangdae of Changgyeong Palace (春塘臺試), examination given on the day of a festival (節日製), and *hwanggam* examination (黃柑製).[2] Thus emergence of a greater number of those who passed the Erudite Examination than the number of available government posts brought about a monopoly over government posts based on academic cliques, civilian official cliques, and regional cliques; moreover, it became a major factor in intensifying party strife.

Taken into account in the civil service examination was the ability of the applicant as well as his family background. This was because the applicant not only had to submit his name, clan seat (本貫), and place of residence at the time of registering at the Nongmyeongso, but also had to submit a list of personal information on the last four generations of the linear family members, such as names, birthdays, posts held, and a character reference from a bureaucrat of 6-*pum* rank or above. In particular, it was impossible for a non-*yangban* to apply for the examination in reality, because information as to whether the father, grandfather, and great-

---

[2] Tangerines were distributed to the test-takers during the *hwanggam* examination. (S. Lee)

grandfather of the applicant had held the post of Hyeon'gwan was clearly stated in the list submitted. As party strife escalated, it was unthinkable to gain character references from a 6-*pum* or above for children of opposing factions, regardless of the character or ability of the individual.

The Military Examination was also a triennial examination. It did not have distinctions of small class or big class as in the Erudite Examination, but it did have the three stages of preliminary examination, second-level test conducted by the central government, and a final test conducted under the personal attendance of the sovereign. According to the *National Code*, preliminary examination included the examination held by the Bureau of Military Training (訓鍊院) and first-level test given by Byeongma Jeoldosa in each province. Those who passed the preliminary examination (120 total) were gathered in Seoul, where the second-level test was conducted under the Ministry of Military Affairs as well as the Bureau of Military Training, 28 people being selected on the basis of the score from the final test conducted under the personal attendance of the sovereign: 3 first ranking, 5 second ranking, and 20 third ranking. One who passed the Military Examination but was not appointed to an official post was referred to as *seondal* (先達).

Examination subjects were composed of practical subject examinations on Chinese Confucian classics (經書) and military tactics, archery and horseback archery, and *gyeokgu* (擊毬, the martial art of hitting a ball from horseback). As with the Erudite Examination, the Military Examination was very difficult to pass, as nationwide only 28 people were selected every three years. But what was stated in the National Code was in principle only; many irregular examinations occurred even in the case of the Military Examination. Military officials were hired in a dizzying rush in groups of several hundred or sometimes even over a thousand, especially during the periods of the Imjin War and Jeong'yu War led by Toyotomi Hideyoshi. The deterioration of the quality of military officials spurred the trend of "encouraging scholarship and disdaining military arts"; this made the offspring of *yangban* avoid the Military Examination, and not only commoners but even the lowborn could advance themselves as military officials depending on martial arts skills. This was the reason for the Military Examination being called "the Examination for Selecting Many Officials" (萬科).

Korean history refers to the Japanese invasion of Korea led by Toyotomi Hideyoshi in 1592 as the Imjin War. The Joseon dynasty was divided into two periods (first half and second half), with this event as the demarcation. One of the great social changes in the second half of the Joseon period was the loss of prestige of the *yangban* class that had been the pillar of dynastic politics and the active social advancement of the common class in its stead. The general loss of power within the *yangban* class can be inferred to have begun with the military official class. Likewise, in order to replenish the continuous penury of national finances after the Imjin War, "selling of government posts and the peerage" (賣官賣爵) became common, leading to mass production of *yangban* in name only.

As noted above, the final test conducted under the personal attendance of the sovereign for Erudite Examination and Military Examination was the last phase of the civil service examination in the Joseon period. This system was begun by the Taizu of Song China, a rite for forming a "bond between water and fish," between the king and the *yangban* who made up the bureaucratic group that existed in Joseon. In his Letter of Instruction at the Time of Ascension to the Throne, Taejo Yi Seong-gye warned of the formation of private debts of gratitude between examiner (lecturer) and one who passed the examination, as was the case in the Goryeo period.

Seong Hyeon (成俔, 1439-1504) was a civilian official who was active in the reigns of the seventh king, Sejo, and the ninth king, Seongjong. The following paragraph is in his collected writings, *Yongjae chonghwa* (慵齋叢話, Assorted Writings of Yongjae):

There were only two examiners, Jigonggeo (知貢擧) and Dong-jigonggeo (同知貢擧), at the civil service examination of the last dynasty, and they were appointed for their fame as civilian officials. The way an *eunmun* (恩門, an examiner) viewed the applicants was as if they were his children, and the applicants viewed

215

the *eunmun* as a parent.[3] ...Although the Jigonggeo system no longer exists in the present dynasty, the names of the applicants and the lecturers exist... Now they stare at each other as if at strange creatures, and they push each other away and strike out against the other. Changing phases in social conditions can be seen from this.

In other words, it can be seen that the relationship of "debt of gratitude one owes to one's teacher" between the Jwaju and applicant gradually became weak, and that the two groups "stare at each other as if at strange creatures, and they push each other away and strike out against the other." The reign of Seongjong (r. 1470-1494) during which Seong Hyeon was active was also a period when discord between different generations of the Hungu Faction and the Sarim Faction began.

There were Interpretation Examination (譯科), Medical Examination (醫科), Bar Examination (律科), and Astrology Examination (陰陽科) as part of Miscellaneous Examination, i.e., examination on miscellaneous studies, in addition to Erudite Examination and Military Examination in the civil service examination of the Joseon period.

The social status in this era was divided into *yangban*, commoners, and the lowborn as mentioned before; there was also a class referred to as the "middle class" between the *yangban* and the commoner class.[4] This middle class hereditarily studied and applied for the Miscellaneous Examination. The Interpretation Examination was an employment examination for interpreters in foreign negotiations, and as such, foreign literature such as Chinese literature (漢學), Mongolian literature (蒙學), Manchurian literature (女眞學), and Japanese literature (倭學) were taught at the Bureau of Interpreters of Foreign Languages (司譯院). Medical education for the Medical Examination

---

[3] *Eunmun* denoted the examiner who oversaw the very examination he had passed. (S. Lee)

[4] The "middle class" was composed of technical officials and local government clerks. (S. Lee)

was handled by the Bureau of Medicine (典醫院) and Public Dispensary (惠民署), and legal education for the Bar Examination was handled by the Ministry of Punishments (刑曹). The Astrology Examination was divided into three divisions of astronomy, geography, and fortunetelling, which were taught by the Office for Observance of Natural Phenomena (觀象監).

In short, the Miscellaneous Examination acted as employment examinations for government officials who gave practical and technical support to the politics of the *yangban* class. Miscellaneous Examination consisted of just the preliminary examination and the second-level test without the final test conducted under the personal attendance of the sovereign, as was the case of the Erudite Examination and Military Examination. As mentioned above, the final test conducted under the personal attendance of the sovereign was originally a rite to create a bond between the king and the bureaucratic group of *yangban* like "the bond between water and fish." Those who passed the Miscellaneous Examination were not *yangban*, and thus were not treated as well. Arithmetic was taught by the Ministry of Taxation (戶曹), painting was taught by the Office of Paintings (圖畫署), and learning of the Way was taught by the National Daoist Temple (昭格署); each professional was employed based on "the law of employing *yangban* as civilian and military officials."

Studies for Miscellaneous Examination, i.e., practical studies such as foreign literature, astronomy, geography, medicine, law, arithmetic, and painting, were considered "miscellaneous studies" and thus disdained. Moreover, such studies were considered only for the middle class and became almost exclusively hereditary. This way of thinking that respected the Chinese Confucian Classics and disdained practical studies (miscellaneous studies) was one of the major causes of stagnation in scientific technology.

Veritable Records of the Joseon Dynasty, a Great Cultural Heritage

Let us change the subject for a moment to the *Veritable Records of the Joseon Dynasty*. This text is fundamentally historical material that covered over 500 years of the Joseon period. "Veritable record" refers to the record of the king's lifetime, and as such, began with the founding of the Joseon dynasty in 1392 in *Veritable Records of King Taejo* and to the 27th and the last king of the dynasty in *Sunjong sillok* (Veritable Records of King Sunjong). Taejo Yi Seong-gye ascended to the throne in July of 1392 but abdicated the throne to Jeongjong in September of 1398; he passed away in 1408 at the age of 74. Taejong issued an order for compiling *Veritable Records of King Taejo*, which contained the history from July 1392 to December 1398; the document was completed in 1416. The compilation of *Veritable Records of King Taejo* under the command of Taejong became a precedent, and compilation of veritable records continued until the end of the dynasty.

Joseon was annexed by Japan on August 22, 1910, during the reign of Sunjong (純種, r. 1907-1910), the last king of the Joseon dynasty. The reign of Gojong (高宗, r. 1863-1907), the king preceding Sunjong, was a period of Joseon's invasion during Japan's Meiji period. Compilation of *Gojong sillok* (Veritable Records of King Gojong) and *Veritable Records of King Sunjong* were started by the Office of the Yi Royal Family, which was established under the direction of the Government-General of Japan in Joseon, and completed in 1935. The format was supposed to have been copied from the record of the 25th king, *Cheoljong sillok* (Veritable Records of King Cheoljong), but just the fact that the *Veritable Records of King Gojong* and *Veritable Records of King Sunjong* were compiled during the colonial period under the supervision of Japan went against the basic principle of the compilation of veritable records as well as leaving big problems content-wise.

Veritable Records of the Joseon Dynasty was a work of extensive historical material that was unparalleled in the world, with a total of 1,894 volumes and 888 books from the first generation of *Veritable*

Records of King Taejo to the 25th *Veritable Records of King Cheoljong*, even without including 48 volumes of text and four volumes of table of contents of *Veritable Records of King Gojong* and four volumes of text, one volume of table of contents, and 17 volumes of supplements of *Veritable Records of King Sunjong*.

The general rule was to establish the Office for Compilation of the Veritable Records to compile the records of a preceding king after his death. Objective depiction was not possible if a powerful royal biography was written during the king's lifetime. That this general principle had been observed during the 500 years of the Joseon dynasty raises the value of the *Veritable Records of the Joseon Dynasty* as historical material.

Following is a table of the *Veritable Records of the Joseon Dynasty*.

	Name of Veritable Records	No. of Years	No. of Vol.	Compilation Year	Remarks
1	*Taejo sillok* (Veritable Records of King Taejo)	7	15	1416	
2	*Jeongjong sillok* (Veritable Records of King Jeongjong)	2	6	1426	
3	*Taejong sillok* (Veritable Records of King Taejong)	18	36	1431	
4	*Sejong sillok* (Veritable Records of King Sejong)	32	163	1454	Volumes below Vol. 128 are on five rites, music scores, Jiriji, the Seven Emotions; Vol. 11 is missing.
5	*Munjong sillok* (Veritable Records of King Munjong)	2	12	1455	
6	*Danjong sillok* (Veritable Records of King Danjong)	3	15	1466	

7	*Sejo sillok* (Veritable Records of King Sejo)	13	49	1471	Volumes 48 and 49 are music scores.
8	*Yejong sillok* (Veritable Records of King Yejong)	1	8	1472	
9	*Seongjong sillok* (Veritable Records of King Seong-jong)	25	297	1499	
10	*Yeonsangun ilgi* (Life of Yeonsan-gun)	12	63	1509	
11	*Jungjong sillok* (Veritable Records of King Jungjong)	39	105	1550	
12	*Injong sillok* (Veritable Records of King Injong)	1	2	1550	
13	*Myeongjong sillok* (Veritable Records of King Myeong-jong)	22	34	1571	
14	*Seonjo sillok* (Veritable Records of King Seonjo)	41	221	1616	
15	*Seonjo sujeong sillok* (Revised Veritable Records of King Seonjo)	41	42	1657	
16	*Jeongjok sanbon gwanghaegun ilgi* (Jeongjok Mountain Version of the Life of Gwanghae-gun)	15	187	1634	A portion is printed but most are manuscripts.
17	*Taebaek sanbon gwanghaegun ilgi* (Taebaek Mountain Version, Life of Gwanghae-gun)	15	187	1634	Revised version.

18	*Injo sillok* (Veritable Records of King Injo)	27	50	1653	
19	*Hyojong sillok* (Veritable Records of King Hyojong)	10	21	1661	There is one supplemental book.
20	*Hyeonjong sillok* (Veritable Records of King Hyeonjong)	15	22	1677	There is one supplemental book.
21	*Hyeonjong gaesu sillok* (Updated Veritable Records of King Hyeonjong)	15	28	1683	There is one supplemental book.
22	*Sukjong sillok* (Veritable Records of King Sukjong)	46	65	1728	All volumes except Vol. 4 have corrections and revisions.
23	*Gyeongjong sillok* (Veritable Records of King Gyeongjong)	4	15	1732	
24	*Gyeongjong sujeong sillok* (Revised Veritable Records of King Gyeongjong)	4	5	1781	
25	*Yeongjo sillok* (Veritable Records of King Yeongjo)	52	127	1781	
26	*Jeongjo sillok* (Veritable Records of King Jeongjo)	24	54	1805	One supplemental and one duplicate of supplements.
27	*Sunjo sillok* (Veritable Records of King Sunjo)	34	34	1838	One supplemental and one duplicate of supplements.
28	*Hyeonjong sillok* (Veritable Records of King Hyeonjong)	15	16	1851	There is one supplemental book.

29	*Cheoljong sillok* (Veritable Records of King Cheol-jong)	14	15	1865	There is one supplemental book.
30	*Gojong sillok* (Veritable Records of King Gojong)	44	48	1935	There is one supplemental book.
31	*Sunjong sillok* (Veritable Records of King Sunjong)	4	4	1935	There are one table of contents and one supplemental book.

For instance, the deceased Kim Il Sung of North Korea mobilized government-sponsored scholars to write many of his autobiographies and biographies during his lifetime; these were published in Japan as well. This is probably the first time in Korean history that so many biographical manuscripts had to be written during the lifetime of the highest absolute authoritarian. But there is no way that the contents of these materials were objective. As was the case with Stalin's *The Russian Social-Democratic Party and Its Immediate Tasks,* which was compiled under Stalin's order during his lifetime, it is clear that the manuscripts compiled under the direction Kim Il Sung will become scrap paper when his devout followers also die.

Ordinarily, an Office for Compilation of the Veritable Records was established when a king passed away, and a high-level government official was appointed to be in charge. Compilers of history who focused on events (記事官: chronicler) in the Office for Annals Compilation within the Office for Compilation of the Veritable Records would take into consideration records on politics or administration of the times, daily records written by the royal chronicler who served the king closely, and other documents when writing the veritable records. Bonggyo (奉敎: Jeong 7-*pum*), Daegyo (待敎: Jeong 8-*pum*), and Geom-yeol (檢閱: Jeong 9-*pum*) belonging to the Office of Royal Decrees also worked as compilers of history focusing on events for the Office for Annals Compilation. The status of these individuals was low, but all were able men who passed the Erudite Examination; the king was strictly prohibited from looking at the daily records written about him by the royal chronicler.

It is natural for generations of kings to have the utmost interest in what records would be left for future generations. Thus compilation of the veritable records required the existence of the Office of Censor General that managed admonishments and refutations against the king and played the role of strictly restraining the king from abusing sovereign power. But there was one instance of a purging of royal chroniclers called the Literati Purge of the Year of Muo (1498), the fourth year of the reign of Yeonsan-gun, the most infamous despot among generations of kings. The incident originated with the leakage of daily records written by royal chronicler Kim Il-son (金馹孫).

The Office for Compilation of the Veritable Records completed an officially certified set of the veritable records by going through three stages, using records on politics or administration of the times and daily records written by the royal chronicler as basic materials. A first draft was drawn up, and that was revised to create a second draft, which was completed through a second revision to create the final draft. But basic materials such as records on politics or administration of the times, daily records written by the royal chronicler, first draft, or second draft were more valuable than the final draft of the veritable records. Regrettably, however, basic materials for the veritable records were destroyed once the final draft was completed, and the papers were recycled by the Paper Manufactory (造紙署). This was to prevent secrets from leaking out to future generations.

The preservation of completed veritable records was an especially serious matter because of the possibility of destruction during wartime and other disasters. Four sets of each of the veritable records of Taejo, Jeongjong, and Taejong were transcribed in the beginning, from which one set was kept in the Office for Annals Compilation, and the others distributed to Chungju in Chungcheong Province, Jeonju in Jeolla Province, and Seongju in Gyeongsang Province, where archives for the safekeeping of historical materials were built. Starting with the *Veritable Records of King Sejong*, four sets were printed by metal type as soon as the compilation was completed.

But the veritable records kept in Seongju, Chungju, and the Office for Annals Compilation were destroyed in 1592 when Toyotomi

Hideyoshi invaded Joseon. Only the sets in the custody of the archive for the safekeeping of historical materials in Jeonju survived with the efforts of Confucians Ahn Ui (安義) and Son Hong-nok (孫弘祿), who used personal funds to transport the documents first to Naejang Mountain in Jeongeup-gun, a second time to Haeju in Hwanghae Province via the ocean, and finally to Myohyang Mountain in Pyeong'an Province; they barely managed to preserve the documents when the fighting became fiercer. They should be awarded commendations in history for rendering the greatest cultural service in the 500-year history of the Joseon dynasty.

Despite financial difficulties after the Japanese troops retreated, three sets of veritable records from Taejo to Injong were printed in sequence from 1603 to 1606. Thus there were a total of five sets of the *Veritable Records of the Joseon Dynasty*: three of newly printed sets, one of the original sets from the archive for the safekeeping of historical materials in Jeonju, and one revised set. Only a portion of the five sets of the veritable records was kept in the Office for Annals Compilation in Seoul; the rest were distributed among the new archives for the safekeeping of historical materials that were built in Mani Mountain in Ganghwa Island, Taebaek Mountain in Bonghwa-gun of Gyeongsang Province, Myohyang Mountain in Yeongbyeon-gun of Pyeong'an Province (later moved to Jeoksang Mountain in Jeolla Province), and Odae Mountain in Pyeongchang-gun of Gangwon Province.

The set preserved in the Office for Annals Compilation was still lost even after all this care due to various ups and downs, but the four sets preserved in Mani Mountain, Taebaek Mountain, Jeoksang Mountain, and Odae Mountain were in good condition at the time of the annexation of Korea to Japan in 1910. The set preserved in Odae Mountain was given to Tokyo Imperial University, but destroyed in the great earthquake of Gwandong in 1923. Moreover, the set preserved in Jeoksang Mountain was lost during the confusion of the Korean War (it is presumed that the set was moved to North Korea) following Korea's liberation; thus the only original sets of the *Veritable Records of the Joseon Dynasty* existing in Korea are those preserved in Mani Mountain and Taebaek Mountain.

In hindsight, the veritable records were tossed around as was the fate of the Joseon dynasty, but this massive quantity of basic historical materials survived due to many sets being made and maintained in separate places. This is the circuitous path traveled by the *Veritable Records of the Joseon Dynasty*.

When Did the Veritable Records of the Joseon Dynasty Disappear?

Compilation of the veritable records of generations of kings was already in place in the Goryeo period. The following is found in the "Hwangjuryangjeon" (黃周亮傳, Biography of Hwang Ju-ryang), Yeoljeon, *History of Goryeo*:

> When the Khitan troops first conquered Gyeongseong (Gaeseong) and burned the palace and the books into ashes, Ju-ryang visited various regions to collect materials under the royal edict of the king (Hyeonjong) and offered to the king a total of 36 volumes containing records of seven generations from Taejo to Mokjong.

In other words, the Khitan troops that invaded Gaeseong burned the palace in the second year of the reign of Hyeonjong (1011), and the books kept there turned into ashes. Burned were veritable records from Taejo Wang Geon, the founder of Goryeo, to the 7th king, Mokjong (穆宗). Hyeonjong commanded Hwang Ju-ryang to restore 36 volumes of veritable records on seven generations of previous kings.

There is a record of Kim Bu-sik receiving a royal command to compile the veritable records from Uijong to the 17th king Injong as the official in charge of the task.

> (Kim Bu-sik) created and submitted the history of Silla, Goguryeo, and Baekje (this refers to *Historical Records of the Three Kingdoms*) in the 23rd year of the reign of Injong (1145). The king sent eunuch Choe San-bo (崔山甫) to (Kim Bu-sik's) private

residence to deliver a royal communiqué as well as flower wine from a king to a vassal…. [Kim Bu-sik] was commanded to compile the veritable records of King Injong and appointed to the post of Nangnang-gun Gaegukhu (樂浪郡開國侯), awarded village land with 1,000 houses, and the authority to collect tax from villages of 400 families for private use after Uijong ascended to the throne.

- "Gimbusikjeon" (Biography of Kim Bu-sik), Yeoljeon,
  History of Goryeo

Another instance was Yi Je-hyeon's participation in compiling the veritable records of three reigns of the 25th to 27th kings, King Chungnyeol, King Chungseon, and King Chungsuk ("Yijehyeonjeon" [Biography of Yi Je-hyeon], Yeoljeon, *History of Goryeo*). It can be seen that the veritable records of generations of kings from the veritable records of the first Taejo to the last King Gongyang were compiled even in the Goryeo period.

King Chungnyeol (r. 1275-1308) commanded Min Ji (閔漬) and Gwon Bo (權溥) to compile a comprehensive history of Goryeo entitled *Sedae pyeonnyeon jeolyo* (世代編年節要).

A long time ago King Chungnyeol commanded Min Ji to revise and expand *Cheonchu geumgyeongnok* (千秋金鏡錄, Reflections from the Mirror of This Age) by Zheng Ke-chen (鄭可臣). But it did not happen because the nation suffered from numerous events and difficulties. Proofreading and editing were done by Gwon Bo and others later, and [the finished work] is called *Sedae pyeonnyeon jeolyo*. [The completed work] was submitted to the king in 7 volumes, from King Hogyeong the Great (虎景大王, a legendary ancestor of Taejo Wang Geon) to Wonjong (元宗), with an attachment of the world map. *Bonguk pyeonnyeon gangmok* (本國編年綱目) was also written.

- "Minjijeon" (Biography of Min Ji),
  Yeoljeon, *History of Goryeo*

It is now a known fact that the achievements of generations of kings of the Goryeo period were recorded in a chronological style in the *Sedae pyeonnyeon jeolyo* and *Bonguk pyeonnyeon gangmok*, but, unfortunately, these two books have not been passed on to today. It would not be possible to compose such a historical book in the chronological style without basic historical materials such as the *Veritable Records of the Goryeo Dynasty*.

There is a record of the veritable records being moved around due to the Mongol invasion (Yuan) from the north followed by the Japanese invasion from the south coming all the way inland in the second half of the Goryeo period. The records were in the custody of the archive in Chungju at the end of the Goryeo period. *History of Goryeo* and *Essential History of Goryeo* probably used the veritable records as a reference. But a document that tells of the circumstances of the disappearance of this massive *Veritable Records of the Goryeo Dynasty* has not been discovered. The archive in Chungju was destroyed during the Imjin War; there was no record of this archive being destroyed, but the possibility of the *Veritable Records of the Joseon Dynasty* being destroyed along with this archive cannot be ruled out altogether. At any rate, this is a lamentable matter.

13

Sejong and Sejo, Kings of Achievements

Erecting a Demarcation Epitaph on Baekdu Mountain

No other king in 500 years of Joseon dynasty receives as much unreserved praise as the fourth king, Sejong (r. 1418-1450). The street in front of Gyeongbok Palace is named Sejong Street, and there is King Sejong the Great Memorial Hall in Seoul; moreover, various events commemorating his achievements are celebrated annually. Sejong has been idealized as a "sage king," but his second son Prince Suyang (首陽大君), who later became the seventh king Sejo (r. 1455-1468), is described as "a tyrant." Was he so?

Sejong was born as the third son of Taejong, the third king of Joseon. Taejong, who had twice experienced "the riot of princes" for the ascension to the throne at the beginning of the founding of the kingdom, was cautious in selecting the Crown Prince from the four sons by his first wife. Taejong opted for his third son Prince Chungnyeong (忠寧大君) rather than his first son Prince Yangnyeong (讓寧大君) as the Crown Prince due to the repeated aberrant behavior of Prince Yangnyeong. Taejong took on the role of assistant to the king until his death in 1422 after he abdicated the throne to Sejong in 1418.

Great cultural activities undertaken during the 32 years of reign of King Sejong were made possible with the stability of internal affairs of state and foreign policy nurtured by Taejong. The Hall of Worthies (集賢殿) was an academy established by Sejong for planning or realizing cultural activities. Outstanding civilian officials were gathered there, and Sejong directly led the cultural activities. Sejong laid down the organization and the number of full-time scholar-officials at the Hall of Worthies in 1420. The duties of the 20 scholar-officials of the Hall of Worthies were originally the study of ancient statutes (old institution of China and Joseon); official announcements of appointment by the king; and compilation of history books. In addition, 10 of the scholar-officials were appointed to the post of Royal Lecturer to give lectures on the Chinese Confucian Classics to the king, and the other 10 scholar-officials were appointed to the post of Royal Lecturer to the Crown Prince.

Sejong commanded Academician Byeon Gye-ryang (卞季良) to select promising young scholars and have them temporarily released from all tasks so that they could read books in a mountain temple. This is the so-called selecting talented civilian officials and giving them a break from duties to study. Moreover, the range of books to be read was not restricted only to Confucianism, but was open to diverse subjects from the classics and history to the Hundred Schools of Thought, astronomy and geography or medicine, and even fortunetelling. This is the reason for the cultural activities of the reign of King Sejong not stopping at the study of Confucian Classics, but being diverse in each field including history, astronomy, geography, agriculture, medicine, music, the art of war, and even Buddhism, which evoked a protest from the scholars of the Hall of Worthies. Truly, this was not a wholehearted support of the study of the principle of human nature but a scholarship for "the practical application of statecraft" that was necessary for "a ruler." Dokseo-dang (讀書堂) was institutionalized later, in which talented civilian officials were selected and given a break from their duties to study in a mountain temple. Sejo, the seventh king and infamous "despot," inherited these cultural activities from his father.

Particularly important is the creation of the Paper Manufactory for wide distribution of various books to scholars; moreover, the paper manufacturing method was improved by encouraging the planting of paper mulberry trees in suitable lands throughout the kingdom, as well as printing activities thriving due to repeated reforms in the printing type.

As the pioneer of movable type printing in the world, Korea began to use metal types as early as 1234 during the Goryeo period with the printing of *Texts on Prescribed Rituals of the Past and Present*. But printing by using metal types was not carried out in an organized manner until "metal movable types minted in the year of *gyemi*" (1403) began to be used for printing by the government-run Type Foundary in 1403. "Metal movable types minted in the year of *gyeongja*" (1420), "metal movable types minted in the year of *gabin*" (甲寅字, 1434), and "metal movable types minted in the year of *byeongjin*" (丙辰字, 1436) were created in the reign of Sejong alone as revisions on printing types. Most of the documents that have survived to today have been printed with the copper metal movable type minted in the year of *gabin*. To make an additional remark, Gutenberg, called the inventor of the movable type printing, opened a printing factory in Mainz, Germany, in 1450.

Another of the achievements made during the reign of Sejong was expanding the northern boundary of the kingdom to what is known today as the Duman River and the Amnok River. Sejong actively pursued developing this region where the boundary was not clearly defined because the Jurchens and Joseon people lived together in this region. The two ethnic groups co-existed in this region after the Daedong River was established as the northern boundary after Silla unified the Three Kingdoms in the 660s. Sejong commanded Kim Jong-seo to build the six garrison forts of Jongseong (鐘城), Onseong (穩城), Hoeryeong (會寧), Gyeongwon (慶源), Gyeongheung (慶興), and Buryeong (富寧) in the basin of the Duman River in the northeastern province of Hamgyeong. Invasion by the Jurchens was prevented by ordering Choe Yun-deok (崔潤德) to build four commanderies in the northwestern region (Yeoyeon 閭延, Jaseong 慈城, Muchang 茂昌, and Uye 虞芮) near the middle reaches of the Amnok River on the one hand, while pursuing an assimilation policy. On the one hand, a regularly scheduled market was held in Gyeongseong and Gyeongwon so that Jurchen horses and fur could be traded for Joseon clothing, rice, and farming equipment.

These boundaries were of course not settled upon agreement between kingdoms, for these boundaries were formed prior to the Jurchens, who were dwelling together in the region, establishing Later Jin dynasty or Qing dynasty that followed Jin. Emperor Kangxi (康熙帝) of the Qing dynasty dispatched Wula Congguan (烏喇總管) and Mu Ke-deng (穆克登) in 1711 to investigate the boundary and reach an agreement with Joseon's Bak Gwon (朴權), a temporary envoy for greeting foreign envoys, to erect a demarcation epitaph on the dividing ridge of the Amnok River and Duman River in order to protect the sacred ground of the birthplace of his ancestors. The three ports of Yeom Port, Busan Port, and Naei Port were opened to allow for the residence of Japanese and for peaceful trade as a preventive measure against recurrence of Japanese invasions in the south.

Proper Characters Will Be Made for the People

The most valuable legacy among the cultural activities of Sejong was the enactment of the *hunmin jeong'eum* (Korean alphabet). The Korean people were thereby able to freely express unique words, ideas, and sentiments. This is in reality the greatest landmark in the history of the Korean people. The promulgation of the Korean alphabet on October 9 in the 28th year of the reign of King Sejong (1446) is celebrated today in Korea by various events, and this day is called "Han'geul Day" (Korean Alphabet Day). This day is a conversion of September 10 of the 28th year of the reign of King Sejong that is mentioned in Jeong In-ji's "Epilogue" of the *Hunmin jeong'eum* (訓民正音, Proper Sounds to Instruct the People) into the solar calendar.

The Korean alphabet was already completed in 1443 according to the record in December of the same year in *Veritable Records of King Sejong*, which is the 25th year of the reign of Sejong.

The king personally made 28 characters of the Korean script. The characters are based on the ancient graphic style; each character contains initial sound, vowel, and final syllable sound. These three items must be added to create a character. In general, Chinese characters or colloquialisms of our nation can be written using the new script, and the ideographic style is simple and to the point without difficulty in switching. This is called the Korean alphabet.

According to the "Epilogue" by Jeong In-ji, he along with Choe Hang (崔恒), Bak Paeng-nyeon (朴彭年), Shin Suk-ju (申叔舟), Seong Sam-mun (成三問), Kang Hui-an (姜希顏), Yi Gae (李塏), and Yi Seon-no (李善老) made interpretations and examples of the new Korean script under the command of Sejong after the Korean alphabet had been completed. In other words, Sejong showed prudence by ordering the scholars to study the new characters for practical application after their creation in 1443 and then officially distributing them in 1446.

King Sejong's thoughts on politics are briefly but clearly reflected in "Eoje seomun" (御製序文, Royal Foreword) in the front of *Proper Sounds to Instruct the People*:

> The language and sounds of our kingdom cannot be communicated in Chinese characters because they are different from Chinese language and sounds. Thus there are many instances of unlearned people desiring to say something but not being able to do so. With compassion for this plight of the people, I have enacted 28 new characters. The purpose of this is to make learning and usage in everyday life easy.

There was a unique Korean language passed down from ancient times in those days, but Chinese characters were used to denote the words. Thus the words and the letters did not match. Seol Chong in the Silla period invented a writing system unique to Silla by means of uniting the sound and meaning of Chinese characters to denote the language of Silla. Jeong In-ji used this Korean writing system, which is devised by means of using Chinese characters to denote the Korean sounds and/or corresponding meaning; but this system could not express even one out of ten thousand Korean words.

"Royal Foreword" reflects the independent spirit of enacting a script appropriate for the unique national language. The script used in Korea was Chinese, but with different characters and sound as compared to its use in China. The Korean alphabet attempted to overcome this discord between the sound and the alphabet. Moreover, the enactment of easy-to-learn script for the people who did not have the time or energy to learn difficult Chinese characters in order to express themselves was clearly a populist position. In the relationship of the ruler (君) — vassals (臣) — people (民), communication between the ruler and his vassals were done through Chinese characters. But Sejong attempted to destroy the barrier of written communication among the three groups by enacting an alphabet that could be used by the people.

The spirit of independence refers to the harmony between "independence" and "serving the greater" and not the denial of the latter by the former. A symbolic example would be the debate on whether Dan'gun or Gija should be valued more as the progenitor of Korea. Dan'gun was enshrined within the tomb of Gija in Pyeong'yang until the reign of Sejong, but the tomb of Dan'gun was separately built in 1425 and a decision was made to hold ancestor worship of King Dongmyeong (Jumong 朱蒙), the founder of Goguryeo, with the other two. In other words, this reflected the historical awareness of Goguryeo as a continuation of Dan'gun Joseon.

The Korean alphabet of today is composed of 14 consonants (initial sounds) and 10 vowels, totaling 24 phonetic characters, but the original Korean alphabet at the time of enactment contained 17 consonants and 11 vowels totaling 28 characters. "Epilogue" by Jeong In-ji described the expressive capability using the Korean alphabet as follows:

> There is no difficulty converting to the 28 characters; the script is brief and yet to the point, precise and thorough. Thus a smart man will understand all by the end of the morning, and even those who are not smart will be able to learn within 10 days. The meaning of Chinese literature can be understood when inter-

preted with this [the new Korean script], and the circumstances can be grasped when lawsuits are heard through this. The tune and pitch of the alphabet are harmonious because the alphabet's rhyme can distinguish well between clear and dull sounds; there is no inadequacy in the alphabet's usage; and everything can be expressed [with the new alphabet]. The sound of the wind, crying sounds of cranes and roosters, even the barking of dogs can be expressed.

The Korean Script Interferes with Scholarship

Those who were proponents of serving the greater nation of China could have definitely opposed the enactment of the Korean alphabet by Sejong as a unique alphabet that differs from the Chinese characters. A representative opinion opposing the propagation of the Korean alphabet was the appeal submitted by First Counselor (副提學) Choe Mal-li (崔萬理) of the Hall of the Worthies and his faction in February of the 26th year of the reign of Sejong (1444), a year after the completion of the Korean alphabet. The appeal contained six items, of which the first three items were representative of a model for admiring Chinese culture and thought. Below is a summary of the three items:

First, our court has pursued the policy of respecting the bigger state with utmost sincerity and has respected the Chinese system since the founding of the dynasty, but (this) is an embarrassing turn of events for serving and admiring the culture and thought of the great nation.

Second, although winds and soils vary from region to region, there has been no separate writing system for local dialects in the nine provinces (ancient China was divided into nine provinces) from ancient times. Only such as the Mongolians, Tanguts, Jurchens, Japanese, and Tibetans have their own writings. But they are barbarians and unworthy of our concern. It has been said that the barbarians are transformed only by means of adopting the Chinese ways; I have never heard of the Chinese ways being transformed by the barbarians. Creating a separate script is like Joseon deserting China and allying itself with the savages.

Third, the writing system invented by Seol Chong in the Silla period may be a vulgar countrified language devised by means of using Chinese characters to denote the sounds and/or corresponding meaning of Joseon, but it does use Chinese characters commonly used in China. If the new script is propagated, petty clerks will neglect the more difficult Chinese literature and only learn the new script. To distance oneself from the old and find pleasure in the new brings about trouble throughout all ages, and this new script is nothing more than a novel technology. [It] will bring harm to learning and is not helpful in politics.

- February of the 26th year of the reign of King Sejong,
  Yeoljeon, *Veritable Records of King Sejong*

Creating new characters and propagating them is a great cultural revolution. As with transition in dynasties, the occurrence of such an opposition is very natural. Sejong held an audience with them in the palace to answer questions. Part of the question-and-answer session is below. Sejong told Choe Mal-li and others as follows:

You say that the use of letters for phonetic value violates old practices. Is not Seol Chong's writing system devised by means of using Chinese characters to denote the sounds and/or corresponding meaning the same? Likewise, is not the main objective of a writing system devised by means of using Chinese characters to denote the sounds and/or corresponding meaning to make it useful to the people? Why do you and your associates believe the work of Seol Chong to be good, yet you reject the work of your sovereign? Do you have knowledge of the rhyming book? Do you know how many consonants and vowels there are in the four tones and seven sounds? If I do not correct the rhyming book now, who will?

Sejong was an authority on phonology. Choe Mal-li and his faction could not answer the questions of the king at all.

Prior to the enactment of The Korean alphabet, Sejong issued an order in 1432 to First Counselor Seol Sun (偰循) of the Hall of Worthies to compile *Samgang haengsildo* (三綱行實圖, Illustrated Conduct of the Three Bonds) in order to enlighten the populace with Confucian ethics. Cases of filial sons, loyal vassals, and virtuous women described in historical documents were mentioned here and distributed in the capital as well as the provinces; illustrated interpretations were attached for those who did not know Chinese characters. Confucianizing the customs of the people required overcoming a big obstacle of written words.

Sejong did not stop at having illustrated interpretations after The Korean alphabet was completed, but had *Illustrated Conduct of the Three Bonds* translated into the Korean script and distributed. The criticism of Jeong Chang-son (鄭昌孫), a Compiler of the Hall of Worthies, on this subject was reprimanded severely by Sejong as follows:

> Jeong Chang-son says, "I have not yet seen any emergence of loyal vassals, filial sons, and virtuous women since the distribution of the *Illustrated Conduct of the Three Bonds*. Conduct of a person depends solely on his/her disposition; how can people learn [to be virtuous] only after the Korean alphabet is used?" How can these words come from a Confucian who can distinguish reason? [He is] a useless and vulgar scholar.

Sejong commanded the Correctional Tribunal to arrest Choe Mal-li and his faction for one night and released them the following morning.

The distribution and development of the Korean alphabet, however, was deterred under the *yangban* class who thought as the Choe Mal-li faction did, and as such, disdained and oppressed the alphabet as a script for women or Buddhist nuns. As a result, a small number consisting of the *yangban* class enjoyed a privileged position over the majority of the populace of the illiterate classes who did not know the difficult Chinese characters.

The Korean alphabet was not given its due until the late Joseon period. After returning from the U.S. in 1896, Seo Jae-pil (徐載弼)

established the Korean alphabet as the "national alphabet" when he founded the *Dongnip sinmun* (Independence News) using only the Korean alphabet, and began journalistic activities to propagate the concept of civil rights to men and women of the populace. Ju Si-gyeong, a journalist, became a pioneer in propagating the Korean alphabet after systematically studying it.

Today, exclusive usage of the Korean alphabet in South and North Korea has become a sizeable obstacle to interchange with nations using Chinese characters that have had historically long relationships with Korea. It is difficult to understand the meaning of Chinese words when written in the Korean alphabet, even when the Korean alphabet is understandable. For example, Gwangju (廣州) in Gyeonggi Province and Gwangju (光州) in Jeolla Province are the same in the Korean alphabet. The two Korean family names of Kang (姜) and Kang (康) are pronounced the same, and thus it is unknown as to which clan the family name belongs if written only in the Korean alphabet. It is said that 70 percent of the Korean words used today are supposed to be Chinese words written in the Korean alphabet. As Sejong had said, Korean characters became more difficult to understand rather than easier to understand when Chinese words were written in the Korean alphabet. Thus there is a problem when the voice of the "ultra-nationalists for the Korean alphabet" is too loud. It may not be the perfect solution, but should the usage of a mixture of the Korean alphabet and Chinese characters be taken into consideration?

The Six Martyred Ministers and the Six Loyal Subjects

Sejo (r. 1455-1468), the second son of Sejong and seventh king of Joseon, participated in his sire's cultural activities as Prince Suyang. He achieved much by continuing with the activities of his sire, but his reputation was not very good despite this. This was because he usurped the throne from his nephew Danjong (端宗, r. 1452-1455). The circumstances surrounding this event are as follows:

The Crown Prince, an older brother of Sejo, ascended to the throne as King Munjong (文宗, r. 1450-1452) when Sejong passed away. During the last years of Sejong, Munjong managed national affairs for his sire, but he himself died two years and three months after ascending to the throne. The new king was 12-year-old Danjong. Chief State Councilor Hwang Bo-in (黃甫仁) and Second State Councilor Kim Jong-seo (金宗瑞) were in charge of advising Danjong at the death-bed request of Munjong. Sovereign power was in name only, and political power was in the hands of these two vassals.

Prince Suyang and Prince Anpyeong, second and third sons of Sejong from his first wife, respectively, were both capable princes and rivals. Prince Anpyeong was a man of refinement with literary talent as a master of calligraphy, whereas Prince Suyang had great desire for power and had much interest in military affairs — enough to compile *Yeokdae byeongyo* (歷代兵要, Generations of Military Essentials) with Gwon Nam (權覽), who was a literary writer with the Hall of Worthies. Prince Suyang was the oldest among the living sons of Sejong after his older brother Munjong died, and he could not sit by and watch the sovereign power that continued to weaken from the reigns of Munjong to Danjong become even weaker under the control of the two prime ministers.

One of the important debates since the beginning of Joseon in the division of power was whether dynastic politics should center on the king or the prime ministers. In other words, the issue was on how much authority should be allotted to the three state councilors of the State Council in the relationship of the King → State Council → Six Ministries. As mentioned previously, meritorious vassal Jeong Do-jeon during the founding of the dynasty conceptualized a system where the prime ministers would be the focal point. But a king-centered system was implemented from the reigns of Taejong to the fourth king Sejong, since Yi Bang-won, the fifth son of dynastic founder Yi Seong-gye, killed Jeong Do-jeon during the "riot of princes" and ascended to the throne as the third king Taejong in 1400. In the reigns of Munjong and Danjong, however, this changed to "weak ruler, strong vassals." It is likely that Prince Suyang usurped the throne through a coup d'état in 1453 to remedy the crisis faced by the king-centered system and revert back to it. The process of the coup d'état was as follows.

Hwang Bo-in and Kim Jong-seo approached Prince Anpyeong to counter the power of Prince Suyang. Prince Suyang achieved a coup d'état and killed Kim Jong-seo and Hwang Bo-in when Munjong passed away. Prince Anpyeong followed a royal command to drink poison after being exiled to Ganghwa Island under the pretext of attempting to usurp the throne of Danjong at the invitation of the two state councilors. This coup d'état is called "the Purge of the Year of Gyeyu" (癸酉靖難). The two who played the role of advisors in this purge were Gwon Nam and Han Myeong-hoe (韓明澮), direct descendants of Gwon Geun; they were the most meritorious vassals of this purge. Confidants of Prince Suyang urged Danjong to abdicate after gaining power through the coup d'état, and Prince Suyang ascended to the throne as the seventh king Sejo in 1455 after declaring young Danjong as having abdicated.

The scenario of Sejo's usurpation of the throne was similar to that of the Emperor Jianwen's throne being usurped by his uncle, King of Yan (Emperor Yongle), as mentioned in a previous chapter. They are both referred to as "purging," which means eliminating villainous vassals close to the ruler. Emperor Yongle usurped his nephew's throne, but his political record shows that he was the greatest emperor in the history of Ming in achieving the monumental task of building waterways.

However, there was a group within the scholars of the Hall of Worthies who considered Prince Suyang's lapse of virtue against Danjong as unjust and schemed for a counter-coup d'état to restore Danjong to the throne. This group consisted of five civilian officials — Seong Sam-mun (成三問), Bak Paeng-nyeon (朴彭年), Yi Gae (李塏), Ha Wi-ji (河緯地), Yu Seong-won (柳誠源) — and one military official by the name of Yu Eung-bu (兪應孚); it was later referred to as "the Six Martyred Ministers" (死六臣). The plan for a coup d'état was discovered beforehand, and the ministers were executed. In addition, Sejo first reduced Danjong to a lower rank of

Nosan-gun (魯山君) and then exiled him to a remote place called Yeongwol in Gangwon Province in 1457 to prevent a return. Sejo then killed Danjong by commanding him to take poison. Actually, the plan for a coup d'état can be said to have driven Danjong to his death. The Sarim Faction put on a pedestal the Six Martyred Ministers' loyal doctrine of "not serving two lords," along with Jeong Mong-ju, who died for his country at the end of the Goryeo period by "not serving two dynasties" after the Sarim Faction advanced into the central government in the latter half of the 16th century.

Sejo discontinued the Hall of the Worthies after the counter-coup to restore Danjong; neither did he listen to the admonitions of the officials of the Office of Inspector General. This does not mean that he was despotic about government administration as generally thought. He publicly discussed statecraft and scholarship by arranging for occasions during which all vassals took turns telling their opinion to the king instead of the hitherto closed competition. He evaluated the vassals through the discussions. All vassals in these stances refer to the civilian and military bureaucrats who were invited to the palace to answer the inquiries of the king. The contents of the discussions did not stop at the Cheng-Zhu School, but included such topics as Confucius or Mencius, studies of Han and Tang dynasties of China, history, military science, astronomy, geography, and medicine. Sejo's knowledge was great from having participated in the cultural activities of his father, Sejong.

In addition to the Six Martyred Ministers, there were also the Six Loyal Subjects who lived the rest of their lives secluded from the world after despairing of politics. One of them was Kim Si-seup (金時習, pen name is Maewoldang 梅月堂, 1435-1493). He was a genius, enough to be called a prodigy when he learned Confucianism, but he converted to Buddhism from the shock of the usurpation of the throne by Sejo. His Buddhist name is Seoljam (雪岑). He did not devote himself to Buddhism, but lived a life of a convert as a half-Confucian and half-Buddhist while traversing the world; he appeased his pent-up feelings with poetry. *Maewoldangjib* (Collection of Works of Maewoldang) is an anthology of his works.

With strong leadership, Sejo reestablished the sovereign power that had been reduced to mere appearance during the reigns of Munjong and Danjong. Distinguished scholar-officials who were in charge of cultural activities in the Sejong period, such as Jeong In-ji, Choe Hang, Shin Suk-ju, Kang Hui-an, and Seo Geo-jeong (徐居正), participated in this. These are called the Hungu Faction (勳舊派).

Shin Suk-ju (pen name is Bohanjae 保閑齋, 1417-1475) in particular was the foremost member of the Jiil Faction (知日派) in the entire period of Joseon as a politician who combined both literary and military accomplishments. He was a scholar of the Hall of the Worthies and successively held key posts during the reigns of Sejong, Munjong, Danjong, Sejo, Yejong, and Seongjong. He mostly served Sejong and Sejo among the six monarchs when the short-lived reigns of Munjong, Danjong, and Yejong are excluded.

He visited Muromachi Bakufu in Kyoto as recorder of travel logs for the envoy to Japan (對日通信社: chief envoy was Byeon Hyo-mun, 卞孝文) in the 25th year of the reign of Sejong (1443); he also visited Beijing as recorder of travel logs for the Ambassador of Gratitude Prince Suyang in the second year of the reign of Munjong (1452). The regulation regarding Joseon-Japan diplomatic relations was completed in the reigns of Sejong and Sejo. The one who played a leading role in this was none other than Shin Suk-ju, and the regulation is presented in detail in "Jobing eungjeopgi" (朝聘應接記) in *Haedong jegukgi* (海東帝國記), which he completed writing in the second year of Seongjong (1471). The story of his will to Seongjong stating "It is my greatest wish to not lose the peacefulness with Japan" is famous. The Sarim Faction later loathed Shin Suk-ju as a traitor. Being a loyal subject to one king does not always mean being a loyal subject to the nation; there is a possibility of the opposite.

Prince Suyang and Prince Anpyeong

Sejo "appreciated Confucianism" according to the national policy of the Joseon dynasty, but did not "depreciate Buddhism"; rather, he chose Buddhism as the target religion. His father, King Sejong, also leaned toward the Buddhist faith in his last years and commanded Prince Suyang to write *Seokbo sangjeol* (釋譜詳節, Auspicious Details of the Buddha's Genealogy), a biography of Sakyamuni, to pray for the peaceful repose of the deceased Queen who was the first wife of Sejong and the mother of Prince Suyang. *Worin cheon'gang jigok* (月印千江之曲, Songs of the Moon's Imprint on a Thousand Rivers) is the song written by Sejong in the Korean alphabet to praise the piety of Sakyamuni after reading *Auspicious Details of the Buddha's Genealogy*. Sejo combined the two books into one and published it as *Worin seokbo* (月印釋譜, Buddha's Genealogy) in 1459 (5th year of the reign of Sejo).

Especially important among the Buddhist policies of Sejo was the fact that he established the Superintendency for the Sutra Publication (刊經都監) in 1460 to pursue annotations (in Korean) of Buddhist scriptures as a national project. This was in consideration of enlightening the common class through Buddhism in contrast to Confucianism for the learned. The Korean alphabet was put into practical use through these annotations. Examples are 10 volumes of *Neung'eomgyeong eonhae* (楞嚴經諺解), seven volumes of *Myobeop yeonhwagyeong eonhae* (妙法蓮華經諺解), one volume of *Geumganggyeong eonhae* (金剛經諺解), one volume of *Geumganggyeong eonhae* (金剛經諺解, Commentaries on the Diamond Sutra), one volume of *Banya simgyeong eonhae* (般若心經諺解, Commentaries on the Sutra of the Heart of Prajna), and 12 volumes of *Wongakgyeong eonhae* (圓覺經諺解). In other words, the Korean alphabet as enacted by Sejong became popular among commoners and womenfolk and distant from the elite scholarship of Confucianism by forming a connection with the Buddhist religion through Sejo's project of annotating Buddhist scriptures.

As mentioned before, Sejong was the third son of Taejong and was called Prince Chungnyeong prior to becoming king. Prince Yangnyeong, first son of Sejong, lived a liberal life and enjoyed refinement and hunting. The second son, Prince Hyoryeong, entered the priesthood and became a devout Buddhist. Taejong and Sejong cemented the foundation of a Confucian nation by adopting a policy of suppressing Buddhism, but Sejong leaned toward the Buddhist faith in his later years and Sejo became a protective ruler of Buddhism due to the influence of Prince Hyoryeong.

Most Confucians of the Hungu Faction who participated in the cultural activities during the reigns of Sejong and Sejo as represented by Kim Su-on (金守溫) actively participated in this project of annotating Buddhist scriptures. Tapgol Park on Jongno in Seoul is famous for being the originating point of the March 1 Movement in 1919. This is a temple site where Sejo built Daewon'gak Temple (大圓覺寺); only the 13-story stupa remains to remind citizens of the glory of bygone days. The Controller-General (都提調) of the blueprint for the Daewon'gak Temple was Prince Hyoryeong, and Kim Su-on praised the policy of Sejo in supporting Buddhism in his writing, "Daewongaksa bimyeong" (大圓覺寺碑銘, Epitaph of Daewon'gak Temple).

The life of Kim Si-seup, one of the Six Loyal Subjects, was previously described as that of a convert. He assisted in the project on annotating Buddhist scriptures, albeit indirectly, because of his friendship with Prince Hyoryeong.

> In the fall of the year *gyemi* (8th year of the reign of Sejo, 1462), His Majesty (Sejo) was translating *Yeonhwagyeong* when I went to Seoul to purchase a book. Prince Hyoryeong received authorization from His Majesty to allow me to engage in making revisions for 10 days in the Buddhist Hall (內佛堂) by telling of my writing capability.[1] I am creating the dependent arising for the Buddhist Hall because of that tie.
>
> - "Naebuldang seo-on" (Foreword to the Buddhist Hall),
>   Vol. 2, *Collection of Works of Maewoldang*

---

[1] The Buddhist Hall was constructed within the Palace during the reign of King Sejong. (S. Lee)

Kin Si-seup also attended the inauguration ceremony of Won'gak Temple and presented "Wongaksa chansi" (圓覺寺讚詩, Poetry Praising Won'gak Temple) that he composed, but he did not participate any further than that. He pleaded illness to decline the summons of Sejo and fled to the mountain temple where he had resided in the past. The poetry and prose of Kim Si-seup, as well as the way he lived, are characterized by liberalism and not restricted by loyalty as was the case with inflexible scholars of the Way. Furthermore, he did not hide his Buddhist faith which Confucians considered heretical, but rather left writings containing this faith.

Even the extremely devout scholars of the Way who disdained Buddhism stepped back and paid homage to Kim Si-seup's poetry and prose, and no one considered his belief in Buddhism heretical. Yi Yi (李珥), who wrote *Gimsiseupjeon* (Collected Works of Kim Si-seup) in 1582 under the command of Seonjo, the 14th king, summarized Kim Si-seup's life as "having a Confucian mind but leaving behind Buddhist works." His heart may have belonged to Confucianism, but his lifetime achievements were in Buddhism. The Confucian history of Korea may have been more interesting if there had been more remarkably talented people or geniuses like Kim Si-seup who were talented in various fields, rather than able students who concentrated on studying for the sake of civil service examination.

It is noteworthy to digress for a moment and discuss several issues now that Prince Anpyeong has been mentioned.

A painting called "Dream of Strolling in a Peach Garden" (夢遊桃源圖) by Ahn Gyeon (安堅), in the possession of the library at Tenri University (天理大學) in the city of Nara (奈良), Japan, has been declared an important cultural asset of Japan. This painting is a representation of a dream Prince Anpyeong had had of playing in utopia on the night of the 20th of April, 1447; it was painted before there was a rift between the brothers caused by the usurpation of the throne by Prince Suyang. Letters written by Prince Anpyeong as well as poetry of famous men of letters from the reign of Sejong, such as Jeong In-ji, Kim Jong-seo, Seong Sam-mun, and Shin Suk-ju, are contained in the painting.

As mentioned previously, Prince Anpyeong was a man of refinement and a master of the "pine-snow calligraphy style" used by noted calligrapher Zhao Meng-fu of the Yuan period. A few years later than Prince Anpyeong lived Seong Hyeon (成倪, 1439-1504), a scholar who held an important position during the reign of Seongjong. He organized ceremonial court music, music from Tang China, and the Korean music which comprised various genres of music of his times into three categories and complied *Akhak gwebeom* (樂學軌範, Guide to the Study of Music). He also wrote a collection of essays titled *Yongjae chonghwa* (Assorted Writings of Yongjae), in which he described Prince Anpyeong as follows:

> Bihaedang (匪懈堂, one of the pen names of Prince Anpyeong) is a prince who likes to learn and is especially refined. His calligraphy is the best. He is also talented in painting, *geomungo*, and the lute (琵琶); his personality is restless and moody. He likes things of old and scenic places. (He had) [a replica of] the house where Zhu Xi read and completed the Learning of Master Zhu in his later years built outside of the North Gate (in Seoul), and Damdamjeong (淡淡亭) was built south of the lake. Ten thousand books are in his possession, and literati were called to create "Sibi gyeongsi" (十二景詩) and "Sapalyeong" (四八詠).

Ink paintings of "Picture of a Lofty Scholar Watching Water" (高士觀水圖) and "Picture of a Lofty Scholar Crossing a Bridge" (高士渡橋圖) by Kang Hui-an are some of the oldest paintings from the early Joseon period that exist today. While Ahn Gyeon was a professional painter as a government painter with the Office of Paintings, the paintings by Kang Hui-an were those painted by a literati painter as a hobby. According to Seong Hyeon's view of Prince Anpyeong, he was a refined man who liked scholarship and had knowledge of paintings and calligraphy, but had a fickle personality. He did not seem to have political aspirations. He was probably dragged into the whirlpool of political strife surrounding the throne by civilian officials who felt threatened by Prince Suyang, who had an eye on restoring sovereign power and ultimately defeated the rule of Danjong under the policy of "weak ruler, strong vassals."

National Code as the Law of Force and Comprehensive Mirror of the Eastern Kingdom as Chronological History of Korea

Compilation of the *National Code* was a great task that is comparable to establishing a monument on managing and legalizing the continuation of the achievements of the founding of Taejo Yi Seong-gye, followed by Taejong, Sejong, and Sejo. Improvements were made continuously until the final version was completed in the reign of Seongjong, but the basic skeletons were built during the reign of Sejo as described below. Completed during the reign of Seongjong along with the *National Code* was *Comprehensive Mirror of the Eastern Kingdom*, the first complete history of Korea for which Sejo devoted considerable effort. As was the case of Sima Qian of Northern Song China compiling *Comprehensive Mirror for Aid in Government* that summarized the strengths and weaknesses of the complicated history of each period, there was great significance in the fact that both used the term "comprehensive mirror."

There were historical documents compiled by the government offices for each period of history in Korea in the form of *Historical Records of the Three Kingdoms*, *History of Goryeo*, and *Essential History of Goryeo*; historical documents compiled without government intervention were *Residual Events of the Three Kingdoms* by Iryeon and *Dongguk saryak* (東國史略, Abridgement of the History of Korea) by Gwon Geun. It is difficult, however, to comprehend the entire aspect of Korean history based on the annalistic and biographical style or chronological style of historical documents classified by dynasty. Sejo clearly attempted to devote himself completely to revising Confucian dynastic politics. This was directly connected to a criticism of the excessive worship of a powerful China by Korean Confucian scholars. That was the intension of Sejo in ordering the compilation of *Comprehensive Mirror of the Eastern Kingdom*. He did not deny worshipping a greater power, but the issue was how the independence of the people could be realized in accord with it.

Sejo commanded civilian officials to compile *Comprehensive Mirror of the Eastern Kingdom* in 1458, the fourth year of his reign.

> The historical records of our nation are not entirely complete, because there are omissions. It is [Our] wish to write historical documents in the compilation style by combining the history of the Three Kingdoms period and the Goryeo period. Extract from all related documents and incorporate them into the dynasty each year.

> - September, 4th year of the reign of Sejo,
>   *Veritable Records of King Sejo*

The king assigned Yang Seong-ji to be in charge of this project. Yang Seong-ji was a civil official who had already compiled the section on "Jiriji" in *History of Goryeo*. He requested the establishment of the Office of Special Advisors to manage the historical materials collected and received permission to do so. The Office of Special Advisors was to an extent a replacement for the Hall of Worthies that Sejo dissolved. There is no way to know whether the content of *Comprehensive Mirror of the Eastern Kingdom* as completed by Seo Geo-jeong and others in the reign of Seongjong realized the intention of Sejo. The completed *Comprehensive Mirror of the Eastern Kingdom* is a historical document in the chronological style containing "Woegi" (外紀, Biography of Others, from Dan'gun to the Three Hans), "Samgukgi" (三國紀, Biography of the Three Kingdoms, of the Three Kingdoms period prior to the Unified Three Kingdoms), "Sillagi" (新羅紀, Biography of Silla, on Unified Silla), and "Goryeogi" (高麗紀, Biography of Goryeo).

Compilation of *Gukjo bogam* (國朝寶鑑, Precious Mirror for Succeeding Reigns) began during the reign of Sejo and continued for generations. It was compiled for the purpose of recording the good words or benevolent rule by past generations of kings from Taejo to Munjong to be used as models for future generations of kings.

Although not completed during the reign of Sejo, the most important compilation project was *National Code*, the fundamental body of law of the Joseon dynasty. It was an objective statement of great national tasks that organized the foundation of the nation started by Taejo and continued by Taejong and Sejong. *Administrative Code of Joseon* and *Mirror of Governance* reflected the private concept of the Confucian nation held by Jeong Do-jeon as mentioned above. In this way, the Joseon dynasty excluded the will of individual governance of the king or powerful vassal from the beginning and leaned toward legalism.

Geomsang Joryesa (檢詳條例司, Office of Regulations) was established even after Jeong Do-jeon under the leadership of Jo Jun, and the compilation of *Gyeongje yukjeon* (經濟六典, Six Codes of Governance) was continued; yet there was a lack of consistency between the two books on codes. Sogyukjeon Suchanso (續六典修撰所) was established under the leadership of Ha Ryun in the seventh year of the reign of Taejong (1407) and commenced the task of revising the old Six Codes.[2] Sejo was the one who commanded the compilation of the *National Code* as an integrated code of law through the process of organizing and referring to the codes since the founding of the dynasty.

According to *Gyeongguk daejeon*seo (Foreword to the National Code) written by Seo Geo-jeong, who held the joint positions of Minister of Taxation as well as Academician of the Office of Royal Decrees in the first year of the reign of Seongjong (1470), Sejo commanded Yeongseong Buwon-gun (寧城府院君) Choe Hang, Third State Councilor Kim Guk-gwang (金國光), Seopyeong-gun (西平君) Han Gye-hui (韓繼禧), Uchanseong (右贊成) Noh Sa-sin (盧思愼), Minister of Justice Kang Hui-maeng (姜希孟), Left Assistant Secretary of the Supreme Council Yim Won-jun (任元濬), Right Assistant Secretary of the Supreme Council Hong Eung (洪應), Dong Jijungchubusa (同知中樞府事) Seong Im (成任), and Seo Geo-jeong as follows:

---

[2] Sogyukjeon Suchanso was an office established to revise *Six Codes of Governance*. (S. Lee)

The deep and wide kindness and beneficence of the ancestors as well as extensive regulations are distributed within the codes of law, such as the so-called original codes of law and the revised codes of law or record of precedents and writ of appointment (敎旨) of the Six Codes. [These are all] lawful and of good content, but management is so confusing and nonsensical that it may lead to bewilderment in obeying. This is because the subjects and clauses of the law are too broad, and many are not unified on a larger scale, so that they contradict each other. It is desired that the laws for all will be revised to correspond, taking into consideration profit and loss now.

Although the Code on Taxation (戶典) was completed in 1460 and the Code on Punishment (刑典) was completed in 1461 during the reign of Sejo, the Code on Personnel (吏典), Code on Rites (禮典), Code on War (兵典), and Manufacturing Code (工典) were completed in 1469 after the death of Sejo. Seo Geo-jeong wrote the foreword as a representative of the compilation office. Thus the compilation of the integrated code of law in the form of the *National Code* not only began under the command of King Sejo, but the draft was completed during his reign.

Under the initiative of Sejo, the Six Ministries system (Personnel, Taxation, Rites, War, Punishment, and Manufacturing) of the Joseon dynasty was a continuation of the revolutionary ideas contained in *Administrative Code of Joseon* by Jeong Do-jeon, and was organized by including diverse political experiences. If the past is retraced further, the source for this will be found in the system of the Six Codes in *Book of Rites.*

Seo Geo-jeong stated the following in "Foreword to the National Code":

The so-called Six Codes is exactly the Six Ministries of the nation of Zhou. The good law and fine meaning are well harmonized and brilliant through incorporating the good and bad points of written words and quality in "Guanzhou" (關雎) and "Linzhi" (麟趾) of Zhou (these are all volume names of poetry in "South of Zhou" of *Book of Poetry* to praise the virtue of the queen of

Zhou dynasty's King Wu). Who would dare to say that the creation of the National Code of this nation does not correspond to the government and rites of Zhou?

Of course, distribution of a fundamental code of law by a nation cannot proceed without caution. The contents of the draft of the National Code were finally completed in the 15th year of the reign of Seongjong (1484) after repeated revisions were made by reviewing it from various angles, and it was mandated to be enforced in January of the following year. But the ruling system of the dynasty also had to be revised to fit social changes. *Daejeon songnok* (大典續錄, 1492), *Daejeon husongnok* (大典後續錄, 1543), *Sokdaejeon* (續大典, 1745), *Daejeon tongpyeon* (大典通編, Comprehensive Edition of the National Code, 1784), and *Daejeon hoetong* (大典會通, Comprehensive Collection of the National Code, 1865) were compiled continuously. But it goes without saying that these were all revisions and supplements based on the *National Code*.

Whatever the case might be, the founding of the Joseon dynasty and the continuation of the tasks begun by the predecessors did not remain simply as a concept of "the Confucian nation," but became systematically documented in the *National Code* in 1484. The Hungu Faction is a faction that actually participated in politics during the founding and development of the nation.

Jeong Do-jeon and Sejo, author of *Administrative Code of Joseon* and initiator of the compilation of the *National Code*, respectively, were figures that the later Sarim Faction disliked in the extreme. Sejo in particular was the king who protected Buddhism, which was regarded by the Sarim Faction as heterodox learning. The historians of future generations reflected this feeling of the Sarim Faction, so that the achievements of Jeong Do-jeon and Sejo were distorted or underestimated.

It is the way of the world for the faction that actually participated in politics to be maligned, regardless of whether that occurs in the East or West. The Sarim Faction which emerged later as a counterforce against the Hungu Faction that actually avoided participation in politics sneered at the Hungu faction of this period. It is easy to criticize the mistakes of the faction that actually participated in politics from the position of a spectator. However, the political world of Joseon sank into a quagmire of factional struggles as soon as the Sarim Faction took over the reins of power. Many personal documents attacking political opponents were produced by the Sarim Faction, but most of the national projects representing the Joseon dynasty were carried out by the Hungu Faction. The Sarim Faction not only did not continue and develop further on the scholarship of "practical statecraft" of the Hungu Faction in the reigns of Sejong and Sejo, they wholeheartedly twisted things toward the study of the principle of human nature.

Is Serving Two Dynasties Impossible?

The Sarim Faction dominated the ideological world of Joseon from the late 16th century on. It considered the acts of Jeong Do-jeon, Gwon Geun, and the Hungu Faction as "acts of betrayal" because Jeong Do-jeon and Gwon Geun participated in overthrowing the Goryeo dynasty and establishing the Joseon dynasty, whereas the Hungu Faction supported the usurpation of the throne by Sejo. But these were evaluations based on the concept of justification from the Learning of Master Zhu and not according to the concept of Confucius. A plain example was the evaluation of Guan Zhong (or Kwan Chung, 管仲) by Confucius. Now it is time to review a dialogue between Confucius and Zi Gong (or Tsze-kung, 子貢).

> Tsze-kung said, "Kwan Chung, I apprehend, was wanting in virtue. When the duke Hwan caused his brother Chiû to be killed, Kwan Chung was not able to die with him. Moreover, he became prime minister to Hwan."
>
> The Master said, "Kwan Chung acted as prime minister to the duke Hwan, made him leader of all the princes, and united and rectified the whole kingdom. Down to the present day, the people enjoy the gifts which he conferred. But for Kwan Chung, we should now be wearing our hair unbound, and the lappets of our coats buttoning on the left side.

"Will you require from him the small fidelity of common men and common women, who would commit suicide in a stream or ditch, no one knowing anything about them?"

- "Hsien Wăn" (憲問), Analects of Confucius

Zi Gong raised a question to Confucius about the issue of Guan Zhong lacking virtue for serving two sovereigns by holding a government post through becoming a prime minister to Duke Huan (or Hwan, 桓公) despite Prince Jiu (or Chiû, 公子糾) being killed by Duke Huan. Confucius responded by saying that Guan Zhong preserved the weakened Zhou dynasty of the times and prevented it from becoming barbaric by making Duke Huan of Zhai a leader of feudal lords through enriching and strengthening the country. Unbound hair and buttoning coats on the left side were the custom of the northern nomadic ethnic group that the Han ethnic group considered barbarians. Confucius praised the fact that he was able to inherit the propriety of Zhou due to Guan Zhong.

Guan Zhong was a politician of the 7th century BC. Along with his friend Bao Shu-ya (鮑叔牙), he served Duke Xiang (襄公) of Zhai. But Duke Xiang lost his throne to and was killed by his cousin Gongsun Mozhi (公孫無知). Guan Zhong took Prince Jiu and fled to the state of Lu, and Bao Shu-ya took Prince Xiao Bo (公子 小白) and fled to the state of Ju (莒). Gongsun Mozhi was also killed by someone with a grudge, which left the throne of Zhai without a ruler. Jiu and Xiaobai headed for Linzi (臨淄), which was the capital of Zhai, to ascend to the throne. Guan Zhong attempted to put Jiu on the throne by killing Xiaobai, rival of Jiu, but Jiu was killed and Xiaobai became the sovereign instead. Xiaobai was Duke Huan. Of course Duke Huan tried to kill Guan Zhong and appoint Bao Shu-ya as the prime minister. But Bao Shu-ya advised him of the uncommon ability of his friend Guan Zhong and got appointed as the prime minister, which led to the establishment of the golden age in Zhai. This is what is referred to as "the friendship of Guan and Bao."

Confucius did not deny the fact that Guan Zhong served two sovereigns to protect the way of China and used enriching and strengthening the country to make Duke Huan a leader of all the princes. There is an equal number of those who criticize and sympathize with Guan Zhong among many Confucians, including Mencius. Ruling with military might is one reason for criticism, but the greatest reason is that he served two sovereigns. In a dialogue with Shao Hu (召忽: Prince Jiu's teacher) who desired to die for one sovereign (Prince Jiu), Guan Zhong stated, "The time to die is when the judicial authority of the state of Zhai has collapsed, the ancestor shrine of the royal family is destroyed, and ancestor worship is discontinued; you cannot die for one sovereign. Live for the interest of Zhai" ("Daikuang" 大匡, *Guanzi* 管子).

The following apt statement made by Guan Zhong concisely expresses his political idea:

Propriety is known when the storeroom for rice is full; glory and disgrace is known when there is sufficient food and clothing.

- "Mumin" (牧民, Governing the People), *Guanzi*

The period in which Guan Zhong lived was a time when the power of the Zhou dynasty that reigned over China was almost non-existent, so that internally the rivalry of local barons among the feudal lords was prevalent and externally the dynasty was exposed to the threat of barbarians. Guan Zhong assisted Duke Huan of Zhai to become a leader among princes and protected the Zhou dynasty from the external threat of savages by securing the state internally through the suppression of the rivalry among local barons. His thought is "the theory of pursuing riches before educating," which puts priority on a rich nation and profitable people to resolve the livelihood of the people; only thereafter will people be educated to know propriety as well as glory and disgrace. Confucius disregarded the fact that Guan Zhong served two sovereigns and said, "Down to the present day, the people enjoy the gifts which he conferred," because he agreed with the achievements of Guan Zhong.

Zi Gong asked Confucius, "What is government?" Confucius concisely responded by stating, "...there be sufficiency of food, sufficiency of military equipment, and the confidence of the people in their ruler" ("Yen Yuan," *Analects of Confucius*). The faith of the people will be lost if food is not considered more important than the military, and "...if the people have no faith [*in their rulers*], there is no standing (*for the State*)."

The Joseon dynasty executed a Confucian government. The fundamental duty of the Confucian in charge of the government must overcome loyalty to one dynasty and one ruler in order to put priority on "sustaining the nation and providing for the people." The military must protect the nation (sustaining the nation), and the people must be provided with food (providing for the people). The point of Guan Zhong's statement to Shao Hu, "for the interest of Zhai, you cannot die for one sovereign," refers exactly to this.

14

The Sarim Faction Emerges and Literati Purges Continue

The Emergence of the Sarim Faction

The Hungu Faction was not that concerned about being a political party; it was christened thus by historians at a later period. Therefore, the characteristics of the Hungu Faction were fundamentally different from the formation of the Four Factions (四色黨派) of the Sarim Faction that formed by first dividing into the Dong'in Faction (Eastern Faction) and the Seoin Faction (Western Faction) with a definite sense of partisanship, of which the Eastern Faction was later divided once again into the Namin Faction (Southern Faction) and the Bugin Faction (Northern Faction), and the Western Faction was divided again into the Noron Faction (Old Doctrine Faction) and the Soron Faction (Young Doctrine Faction). If it is necessary to distinguish between the Hungu Faction and the Sarim Faction, the former was a Confucian group that actually participated in real politics during the founding and growth of the Joseon dynasty based on the transition in dynasty, whereas the latter was a Confucian group that opposed the transition in dynasty and avoided actual participation in real politics by turning its back on the Joseon dynasty and returning to a provincial country village life. The period prior to the emergence of the Sarim Faction can be referred to as a period without political parties, where the Confucian group that actually participated in politics jointly concentrated on the "practical" scholarship for founding and developing a dynasty.

The members of the Hungu Faction became meritorious vassals for participating in the founding of the dynasty by Taejo Yi Seong-gye, ascension to the throne by Taejong, and usurpation of the throne by Sejo. And each time they became owners of great farms and formed a privileged class by being awarded slaves and/or land bestowed on meritorious subjects (功臣田) on top of stipend land (科田) distributed to the bureaucrats.[1] Opposition to this was made by the Sarim Faction. Yejong succeeded to the throne after Sejo passed away, but he also passed away only 14 months after his ascension to the throne; Seongjong succeeded Yejong and sat on the throne at the young age of 12. Supervision of politics by the queen of Sejo from the Yun family was implemented for seven years until Seongjong became an adult. The status of the Hungu Faction seemed rock solid as it gained power by becoming related to the king; an example is Han Myeong-hoe, the foremost meritorious vassal during the usurpation of the throne by Sejo, who married off his eldest daughter to Yejong and his second daughter to Seongjong. As of the seventh year of the reign of Seongjong (1476) when Seongjong began to personally govern, however, a leader of the Sarim Faction by the name of Kim Jong-jik (金宗直, pen name is Jeompiljae 佔畢齋, 1431-1492) was appointed to restrain the Hungu Faction with marriage ties to the king, and the policy to oppress Buddhism was pursued to revive Confucian politics. The Buddhist way of cremation was forbidden, places for reciting the *Namah Amitabha* within the castle town of Seoul were abolished, and the monks were forbidden to enter the castle town.

As discussed previously, the Hungu Faction was in charge of compiling not only the *National Code* and *Comprehensive Mirror of the Eastern Kingdom*, which were completed during the reign of Seong-jong but also *Dongguk yeoji seungnam* (東國與地勝覽, Augmented Survey of the Geography of Korea), which is a geography book that was begun in the reign of Sejo and completed in the 12th year of the reign of Seongjong (1481). In addition, 130 volumes of *Anthology of*

---

[1] Stipend land was land awarded to government officials of certain ranks. (S. Lee)

Korean Literature were completed in 1478. This was a compilation of poetry and prose written by Confucians from the Silla period to that time, and works of renowned Buddhist monks were not excluded. The names of civilian officials such as Noh Sa-sin, Kang Hui-maeng, Seo Geo-jeong, and Yang Seong-ji representing the Office of Compilation were enumerated in "Jin dongmunseon jeon" (進東文選箋); they all belonged to the Hungu Faction. It was possible to interpolate the writings of generations of literati in each famous sight and historic site to suit the inclination of the literati in *Augmented Survey of the Geography of Korea* because *Anthology of Korean Literature* was available.

Projects on document compilation during the reign of Seongjong were a continuation of the projects from the reign of Sejo, as detailed above. Kim Jong-jik of the Sarim Faction did play an active role in the compilation projects, but the old scholars of the Hungu Faction were principally in charge, and the scholarship did not wholeheartedly support Confucianism. Historians who disliked Sejo altered facts so that the projects seemed to be the result of the policy of Seongjong in appreciating Confucianism.

Kim Jong-jik passed the Erudite Examination in the fifth year of the reign of Sejo (1459), and the Sarim Faction began to enter the political world of central government around the 15th year of the reign of Seongjong (1484). Kim Gweng-pil (金宏弼), Jeong Yeo-chang (鄭汝昌), and Kim Il-son (金馹孫) became active in central politics as a continuation of Kim Jong-jik. They were all from Yeongnam, but their genealogy of thought belongs to the school of Jeong Mong-ju, who opposed the transition in dynasty at the end of the Goryeo period and persisted in "not serving two dynasties."[2] Jang Ji-yeon describes this in his book entitled *The Origin of Confucianism in Joseon* as follows:

Po-eun (Jeong Mong-ju) is the religious leader of our Eastern Learning of the Principle, and as such, the scholarship of Song

---

[2] Yeongnam region refers to Gyeongsang Province, which is the southeastern part of the Korean peninsula. (S. Lee)

China's Confucian scholars belonging to the School of Cheng-Zhu began from here in actuality. Po-eun transmitted this to Gil Jae (吉再, pen name of Ya-eun 冶隱), Ya-eun in turn transmitted this to Kim Suk-ja (金叔滋, pen name of Gangho 江湖), and Gangho to his son Kim Jong-jik; Jeompiljae transmitted this to Kim Gweng-pil (pen name of Hanhwondang 寒暄堂), Hanhwondang in turn transmitted this to Jo Gwang-jo (趙光祖, pen name of Jeong-am 靜庵). This is an orthodox genealogy of the Learning of the Principle continued after Po-eun.

"Orthodox faction" of the study of the principle of human nature was synonymous with leading faction; at the late Joseon period, Jang Ji-yeon evaluated the genealogy of thought that was continued on by the Sarim Faction in the Confucian history of Korea since the reign of the 14th king, Seonjo (宣祖, r. 1567-1608), based on the "scholastic mantle" of the Sarim Faction that linked the following people in succession: Jeong Mong-ju → Gil Jae → Kim Jong-jik → Kim Gweng-pil → Jo Gwang-jo. Yi Saek as well as Jeong Do-jeon and Gwon Geun of the end of Goryeo and the beginning of Joseon are excluded from this. Today's researchers of Korea understand the mainstream of Korean Confucian history in this way.

The scholastic position of Jeong Mong-ju took root in the Yeongnam region, because Gil Jae (1353-1419) sequestered himself in Gyeongsang Province's Seonsan (善山) at the end of Goryeo and the beginning of Joseon in persisting with his principle of "not serving two dynasties" in opposition to the transition of dynasty. Thus he became popular among scholars without a government post who held antipathy toward the Hungu Faction. Gil Jae was invited to be the Learned of Bongsang (奉常博士) when the third king Taejong was still the Crown Prince because they had studied together at the end of the Goryeo period. He firmly refused the appointment by claiming his adherence to the principle of "not serving two families" (不事二姓), i.e., the Wang family of Goryeo and the Yi family of Joseon cannot both be served.

Important keywords for understanding the ideological characteristics of the Sarim Faction are that of highly respected Jeong Mong-ju "not serving two dynasties," Gil Jae "not serving two families," and the Six Martyred Ministers "not serving two rulers." It is important to be linked to this genealogy of thought when considering the nature of the thought of the Sarim Faction that confronted the Hungu Faction concerning the transition in dynasty. This spirit of "loyalty" was revealed by the Sarim Faction later.

While the Hungu Faction participated in national projects for administration as a faction that actually participated in politics, the Sarim Faction practiced the scholarship of self-cultivation based on the Cheng-Zhu study of the principle of human nature and established a firm basis centered around the Yeongnam region. They led a stable life as small and mid-size landowners and were able to cement their status as regional leaders through the shrines of the four schools or Confucian folk reform based on village code.

The Sarim Faction gradually entered the political world of central government as mostly officials of the Office of Inspector General (bureaucrats of the Office of Censor General and the Office of Inspector General), since Seongjong personally governed and denounced the Hungu Faction with marriage ties to the king by revealing their misdeeds during the royal lectures or discussions. By the latter half of the reign of Seongjong, it became difficult for the Hungu Faction to confront the insurgence of the Sarim Faction because the majority of the Hungu Faction who led the founding and growth of the dynasty were not of this world or were too advanced in years. The scholarship of the Sarim Faction grounded on the "principle of human nature" was not only remote from reality but was very inflexible and thus had the characteristics of making practical scholarship reduced in size and regressing. A great scholar of the study of the principle of human nature and a sharp critique did not necessarily make a great politician. A great politician must be realistic enough to be able to drink water without being choosy about its purity and impurity.

In fact, Kim Jong-jik attended a session where vassals gave opinions to Sejo when he became an inspector of the Office of Inspector General after passing the Erudite Examination in the fifth year of the reign of Sejo. The vassals that took turns telling opinions to the king during the reign of Sejo have been mentioned in a previous chapter. Sejo had an idea of assigning promising young civilian officials to the seven fields of astrology, geography, astronomy, pitch, medicine, fortunetelling, and history of poetry, and promoting professionals in each field. This is a resurrection of the system from the Sejong period of selecting talented young scholars of the Hall of Worthies and giving them a break from their duties to study. But Sejo abolished the Hall of Worthies after the incident with the Six Martyred Ministers. Sejo asked Kim Jong-jik for an opinion with the thought of assigning him to the field of the history of poetry during a session of vassals giving their opinions to the king. Kim Jong-jik submitted his response as below:

> Only Poetry, prose, and history should be handled by Confucians. The rest, however, are miscellaneous learning; how can they be called things which Confucians must expand effort to learn?

> - August of the 10th year of the reign of Sejo,
>   *Veritable Records of King Sejo*

According to Kim Jong-jik, "history of poetry" was the only scholarship to be studied by Confucians, and the rest, such as astronomy, geography, pitch, and medicine, were "miscellaneous learning" and not fit for Confucians to learn. At this, Sejo commanded him not to study history, had the Ministry of Personnel release him from his post as inspector, and stated as follows:

> Jong-jik is a frivolous person. How can Jong-jik say so when I have inclinations toward miscellaneous learning?

The difference between the Hungu Faction's scholastic perspective of putting importance on practical learning (*silhak*) from the reign of Sejong to Sejo and the Sarim Faction's scholastic perspective of disdaining practical learning as miscellaneous learning is vividly apparent here. The scholastic perspective of the Sarim Faction is exactly what the later Silhak School (School of Practical Learning) pointed out as "impractical learning." The fact that Sejo was attentive to miscellaneous learning as referred to by the Sarim Faction can be inferred from the following dialogue shared with Shin Suk-ju:

> King Sejo said, "All scholarship must be accurate. Even miscellaneous learning such as the study of medicine or arithmetic must be precise."
>
> Shin Suk-ju responded to the king, "All of the people who study today do not attempt to be precise in their work (professional knowledge), but only prepare for the test to become government officials. This is not very desirable. It may be impossible for all who study many fields to have expertise in their works, but it should be sufficient to have two or three among them to have thorough knowledge of it."
>
> Sejo said, "That is so."

> • May of the 9th year of the reign of Sejo,
> *Veritable Records of King Sejo*

When the Sarim Faction dominated the academic world later, the after-effect of Confucianism in Joseon devoting itself completely to the study of the principle of human nature and degrading practical learning as miscellaneous learning so that the content of the scholarship became reduced was immeasurably great. How "Joui jemun" (弔義帝文, Lament for the Righteous Emperor) which Kim Jong-jik wrote to criticize the usurpation of the throne by Sejo in a roundabout way became the start of "Literati Purge of the Year of Muo" will be described later.

Yeonsan-gun and the Literati Purges

There were only two kings without the posthumous epithet of "jo" (祖) or "jong" (宗) in the 500 years of the Joseon dynasty: Yeonsan-gun and Gwanghae-gun. This is because they were both deposed by vassals to restore order. For example, Yi Seong-gye was a posthumous name, and Taejo was the posthumously conferred epithet. Another example is that Yi Bang-won was a posthumous name, and

Taejong was the posthumously conferred epithet. There was a law that prevented the recording of posthumous names in the Joseon dynasty period; this also applied to individuals. For instance, Yi Hwang was the posthumous name of a great Confucian of the 16th century, and Toegye was his pen name. Depending on the discussant, some only refer to him as Toegye to avoid the usage of his posthumous name. There is no objective standard for referring to someone with the pen name or posthumous name. Establishing a "sacred area" for names of kings and individuals to prevent trespassing is an obstacle for attaining objectivity in the research of history.

The case of Gwanghae-gun will be discussed later in detail. He coped well as king during the whirlwind amidst the transition of Ming to Qing dynasty, but was dethroned by a coup d'état led by the Seoin Faction, which revered and served Ming.

Let us go back to the main discourse. Literati purge refers to the incident of the Sarim Faction challenging the Hungu Faction and getting suppressed as a result. There were four big instances of literati purges until the Sarim Faction penetrated into the political world of central government in the reign of the 14th king Seonjo. These were the so-called Four Great Literati Purges, which began with the Literati Purge of the Year of Muo in 1498, followed by the Literati Purge of the Year of Gabja in 1504, the Literati Purge of the Year of Gimyo in 1519, and the Literati Purge of the Year of Eulsa in 1545. Yeonsan-gun (r. 1495-1506) was dethroned by a coup d'état and called a despot perhaps because the Literati Purge of the Year of Muo and the Literati Purge of the Year of Gabja occurred during his reign. But the characteristics of the two literati purges differ.

Yeonsan-gun was the first-born son of Seongjong. He was a very motivated king in that he dispatched secret royal commissioners to understand popular sentiment at the beginning of his ascension to the throne, ordered the compilation of *Precious Mirror for Succeeding Reigns* for the first time since Sejo, and executed a conciliatory policy toward the Jurchens in order to stabilize the defense of the outlying regions in the north. He kept the Sarim Faction that had its base of operation in the Office of Censor General or the Office of Special Advisors at a distance, because he disliked to be coerced into listening to their admonitions or royal lectures. Thus he incurred the antipathy of the Sarim Faction.

The Office for Compilation of the Veritable Records was established and compilation of *Veritable Records of King Seongjong* began after Seongjong passed away. Dangsang-gwan Yi Geuk-don (李克敦) of the Office for Compilation of the Veritable Records discovered Kim Jong-jik's "Lament for the Righteous Emperor" among the daily records drafted by the royal chronicler Kim Il-son.[3] Kim Il-son was Kim Jong-jik's pupil. Yi Geuk-don understood the meaning of "Lament for the Righteous Emperor" as a criticism of Sejo's usurpation of the throne from Danjong and his ultimately killing him by comparing Sejo to the ancient history of Xiang Yu's killing of King Huai (懷王) of Chu China. Yi Geuk-don, who belonged to the Hungu Faction, discussed this with Sejo's favorite vassals Noh Sa-sin and Yu Ja-gwang (柳子光), after which this was used as a pretext to oppress the Sarim Faction; Yeonsan-gun put Yu Ja-gwang in charge of interrogating Kim Il-son. Many members of the Sarim Faction such as Kim Il-son were either executed or exiled due to this Literati Purge of the Year of Muo. The grave of the already dead Kim Jong-jik was dug up and his corpse subjected to "the capital punishment for the dead" (剖棺斬屍).[4]

Six years later, not only the Sarim Faction but the Hungu Faction also became the objects of oppression in the Literati Purge of the Year of Gabja. Han Myeong-hoe, who was the premier vassal of Sejo as well as the leader of the Hungu Faction, also was subjected to the capital punishment for the dead.

Yeonsan-gun grew up under the care of a nanny, because his biological mother, Queen Yun, was deposed when he was four. Lack of a mother's warm love during the development process could have had a great influence on his personality. His father, Seongjong, was a

---

[3] Dangsang-gwan was a higher-level official of or above 3A-Upper rank. (S. Lee)

[4] "The capital punishment for the dead" (剖棺斬屍) involved the corpse being hacked or the neck of the corpse being beheaded and the remains displayed in the streets after the coffin was dug from the grave.

ruler who had a love of learning as well as a love of women. Queen Yun scratched the face of lascivious Seongjong with her fingernails and left scratch marks. Dowager Queen Insu (仁粹大妃), the mother of Seongjong, became angry and sent poison to Queen Yun as a death penalty after sending Queen Yun back to her family. Court vassals close to the king and the Crown Prince were given strict instructions not to let this go into the ears of Yeonsan-gun, who was chosen as the next king. But Yeonsan-gun found out about this fact through the informant Im Sa-hong (任士洪) in the 10th year after he ascended to the throne (1504). He became angry to the point of seeming to be crazed and meted out punishment to the Sarim and Hungu Factions randomly after ordering an investigation of those who participated in punishing his mother. Thus this cannot be called a "literati purge" in the strict sense of the word.

Yeonsan-gun became debauched after he found out about the tragic death of his mother and committed violence by transforming into a demon of revenge. A coup d'état with Former Ijo Champan (吏曹參判) Seong Hui-an (成希顔) and Ji Jungchubusa (知中樞府事) Bak Won-jong (朴元宗) as leaders was finally raised in 1506. [5] They exiled Yeonsan-gun to Ganghwa Island, and Prince Jinseong (晉成大君), second son of Seongjong, was put on the throne as Jungjong. This was "King Jungjong's Restoration of Rectitude."

Confrontation between the Sarim Faction and the Hungu Faction

Jungjong (中宗, r. 1506-1544) attempted to cleanse the nightmare from the reign of Yeonsan-gun as quickly as possible and pursued a policy of revering Confucianism as a continuation of the period of his father, Seongjong, after he ascended to the throne at the request

---

[5] Ijo Champan was a Jong 2-*pum* rank of the Ministry of Personnel, and Ji Jungchubusa was a Jeong 2-*pum* rank of the military officials belonging to the Privy Council (中樞府) in the Joseon period. (S. Lee)

of the vassals who dethroned the previous king to restore order. Jungjong planned to pursue reform by appointing the Sarim Faction, which had suffered greatly from the two literati purges, to government posts in order to curb the power of the vassals who dethroned the previous king. He appointed Jo Gwang-jo (1482-1519) the leader of the Sarim Faction.

Jo Gwang-jo was born in Seoul but moved to Eocheon (魚川) in Pyeong'an Province at the age of 17 when his father was appointed as overseer of horse station (察訪) there. Kim Gweng-pil lived in exile in a nearby area of Huicheon (熙川) as an aftermath of being associated with the Literati Purge of the Year of Muo. He became interested in the Learning of Zhu Xi by feeling sympathetic toward the thought of Kim Gweng-pil after becoming acquainted with him. This became the impetus for expanding the Sarim Faction from the Yeongnam region to Seoul.

Jo Gwang-jo passed an examination given after the king visited the National Confucian Shrine in the 10th year of the reign of Jungjong (1515). After undergoing an elite course of Sungkyunkwan, Office of Inspector General, and Office of Censor General, he rapidly advanced in ranks without precedence to jointly hold the highest post in the Office of Inspector General in 1518 as Inspector General as well as Royal Instructor to the Crown Prince. This shows how much trust Jungjong had in Jo Gwang-jo. In the same year, Jo Gwang-jo pointed out the flaw in disproportionate emphasis on the subjects of the civil service examinations until now and advocated the establishment of an examination overseen by the king called the Examination for the Learned and Virtuous (賢良科), wherein civilian scholars who were learned and virtuous but did not hold government posts were selected based on recommendations. The king accepted this recommendation and executed it, appointing 28 out of the 120 recommended.

In addition, Jo Gwang-jo was responsible for distributing a village code that classified encouraging goodness in each other (德業相勸), regulating each other to restrict evil acts (過失相規), maintaining propriety in interaction with each other (禮俗相交), and

265

assisting each other during hardships (患難相恤) as virtues to make Confucian morals pervasive among the populace. What was executed then was the "Village Code of the Lu Clan" (呂氏鄉約) as created by Lu Dai-jun (呂大鈞) of the Song period in China. The central figures of the regional community based on the village code were the Confucians living in country villages, and they became the political foundation of the Sarim Faction in the provinces. Therein contains the secret to the Sarim Faction's ability to recover as if invulnerable after repeated literati purges.

The village code was provided to various regions even after the downfall of Jo Gwang-jo, but the Examination for the Learned and Virtuous stopped after just one time. Debates on the Examination for the Learned and Virtuous not being fair as well as being an attempt of Jo Gwang-jo to create a private political party were raised by the meritorious vassals of the Hungu Faction who participated during the founding of the nation. It is true that objective evaluation on the subjects was possible, but evaluation on virtuous acts could only be subjective.

Originally, Jungjong ascended to the throne with the support of the vassals of the Hungu Faction who dethroned the previous king to restore order. In spite of this, however, the newly rising members of the Sarim Faction, including Jo-Gwang-jo, intensified confrontations with the veteran Hungu Faction by defaming the latter. Calling oneself a man of virtue and the other narrow-minded was a logic used by Ou Yang-xiu (歐陽修) of the Northern Song period to create a "theory on factionalism" (朋黨論). But Xun-zi stated, "Ability, nature, and intellect of men of virtue and small men are all the same" ("Glory and Shame," 榮辱, *Xun-zi*). In other words, he concluded that there was no difference in temperament between the two.

Many outstanding scholars of rhetoric such as Nam Gon (南袞) were of the Hungu Faction. But Jo Gwang-jo stated that the rhetoric was shallow; he was wholeheartedly devoted to the study of the Confucian Classics to the point that he persuaded even the king to write poetry or dedicate poems. In that sense, it is possible to perceive the confrontation between the Hungu Faction and the Sarim Faction as the confrontation between two factions of the rhetoric and the study of the Confucian Classics within Confucianism. Members of the Hungu Faction such as Nam Gon refuted this by stating that "the rhetoric is indispensable in diplomatic relations with Japan and in serving a greater nation of China." Jungjong, who attempted to put Jo Gwang-jo in an important post to curb the Hungu Faction, seemed to have become rather overwhelmed with Jo Gwang-jo's constant persistence in preaching about studying and cultivation of virtue and in slandering the Hungu Faction during the royal lectures.

The crisis felt by the Hungu Faction against Jo Gwang-jo for expanding the power of the Sarim Faction by executing the Examination for the Learned and Virtuous deepened daily. Jo Gwang-jo at this time claimed that there were false meritorious vassals among the 103 of the Jeongguk Gongsin (靖國功臣) who participated in King Jungjong's Restoration of Rectitude, and requested the king to take away the status of meritorious vassal from 76 of them.[6] The counterattack of Nam Gon, Sim Jeong (沈貞), and Hong Gyeong-ju (洪景舟) of the Hungu Faction began with the consent of Jungjong at this point. This is the Literati Purge of the Year of Gimyo in 1519. Jo Gwang-jo was exiled to Neungju (綾州) in Jeolla Province and awarded poison along with Kim Jeong (金淨), Kim Sik (金湜), and Kim Gu (金絿). Those of the Sarim Faction who were divested of government positions through Jo Gwang-jo were completely banished from the political world of central government.

As can be seen from the obstinate exclusion of the rhetoric by Jo Gwang-jo, the Sarim Faction was a Confucian group that wholeheartedly emphasized the Learning of the Master Zhu. The great sixteenth-century Confucian Yulgok Yi Yi evaluated Jo Gwang-jo as below:

---

[6] Jeongguk Gongsin was a title awarded to vassals who performed meritorious service for the nation. (S. Lee)

The Learning of the Principle has not been transmitted in our nation. Jeong Mong-ju of the previous dynasty provided a clue, but he was not accurate in its measurement. Kim Gweng-pil of our dynasty approached its key but lacked much. The existence of the study of the principle of human nature today is due to his efforts, because those who revere it gathered so that Jo Gwang-jo could advocate the learning of the Way.

- October of the 22nd year of the reign of Myeongjong,
  Seokdam ilgi (石潭日記, Diary of Seokdam)

The Learning of Master Zhu is Neo-Confucianism established in the Song dynasty period in China. Unlike the general "Rulin zhuan," *History of Song* contains a biography entitled "Daoxue zhuan," which records the biography of the faction of Cheng-Zhu School. This is why the Sarim Faction upheld Jo Gwang-jo as the originator of the learning of the Way in Joseon and revered him and those who were purged with him as "wise men of *gimyo*."[7]

The aim of the faction for transition in dynasty or the Hungu Faction until now was a matter of Confucian politics from the top that comprehensively embraced Confucianism. Confucianism is an ideology of statecraft, and practical learning spanning each field cannot be absent in order to realize that ideology. Thus they could be Confucians as well as managers of cultural activities of all fields for practical application of statecraft.

But the goal of the Sarim Faction was moral politics based solely on the Learning of Master Zhu. The ideal of Jo Gwang-jo was the realization of the learning of the Way in thought and politics; enriching and strengthening a country was second to that. He stated the following:

From old, the merit of the rule of might was appreciated by many rulers, and carrying out the kingly way was rare. It is rather

---

[7] "Wise men of *gimyo*" referred to the members of the Sarim Faction who were awarded poison for participating in the Literati Purge of the Year of Gimyo. (S. Lee)

268

easier to achieve results from enriching and strengthening a country with rule of might, but how can the way of benevolence and
righteousness exist? Governing in the kingly way does not show
results in a short period of time, but achieves great things in the
far future.

- "Wonja boyanggwan sigye" (元子輔養官時啓),
  Jeong-am jip (靜庵集, Collection of Works
  by Jeong-am), Vol. 1

Joseon suffered from "Japanese invasions" in the 1590s and "Manchu
invasions" in the 1620s to the 1630s. Could the nation be protected
and the *minjung* saved through the way of benevolence and righteousness with hegemonic tribes bordering to the south and north? The
forte of the scholars of the Way was talking about the Way of
benevolence and righteousness rather than discussing the policy on
statecraft and providing for the people as the main responsibility of
politicians. In reality, however, it was much more difficult to enrich
and strengthen a country than to preach about benevolence and
righteousness. Moreover, prevarication with abstract words did not
work, because its success or failure can be visible to the eyes.

The confrontational attitude of Jo Gwang-jo toward the Hungu
Faction might have been based on extremist and ideological obses-
sion with the Learning of Master Zhu being the only scholarship, and
not on personal feelings. He said the following during his imprisonment:

This servant is only 38 years of age. Having been born into this
world, I can only rely on the trust of the heart of the king. I
thought avarice to be the root of indiscriminate vices within the
nation, and thus considered it important to renew the pulse of
the nation.

- "Okjung gongsa" (獄中供辭), *Jeong-am jip*, Vol. 1

Jungjong's "mind of the ruler" became further and further distant
from the Sarim Faction and had to rely on the Hungu Faction again

by finally banishing the Sarim Faction from the political world of central government. The perspective of Jo Gwang-jo about how a ruler should act was very firm, but it overwhelmed Jungjong. Below is the response Jo Gwang-jo submitted during an examination after the king visited the National Confucian Shrine on the subject of his perspective of a ruler:

> Therefore well-versed kings of old knew that innumerable changes are grounded in the mind of the rulers. All things come from the Way, because the mind is made to be upright in order to bring out the Way as virtue is gained through government and righteousness through coping with things. And the movement of heaven and earth is smooth because ethics between father and son, and the role of the ruler and vassal contain the principle. This is the way of correctness of Yao, Shun, and Yu.

> - "Alseong byeolsichaek," *Jeong-am jip*, Vol. 2

"Innumerable changes are grounded in the mind of the ruler" was Jo Gwang-jo's perspective on a ruler. The king was a human being as well and thus there could be differences of being wise or foolish and liking or disliking politics and scholarship. It was far from reality to pressure a ruler to be nothing less than a wise ruler. This was the reason for having all vassals assist the deficiency in a ruler. If the reality of dynastic politics were examined, a king was not elected based on natural disposition but on inherited bloodlines. Why did the mind of Jungjong become distant from the Sarim Faction, including Jo Gwang-jo? That was due to the excessive expectation about the role of king and to persistent preaching to make the king a saintly ruler.

> At the time, the gentlemen (the Sarim Faction) took up position in court with the favorite of the king; there is nothing they did not say and there is nothing they did not carry out among what they said. The young rising members were brave in reform but did not consider whether the reform was opportune under the circumstances; people all turned their faces away when discussions became sterner. Opinions would continuously come out at

the royal lectures, because the meaning of a sentence would be discussed in all directions so that lectures given in front of the king or Crown Prince that began in the morning would last until sunset. The king would yawn or stretch from great weariness, or be impatient and complain that he was growing bored while sitting; but they did not realize.

- "Yeonbo," Appendix, *Jeong-am jip*

As a result, only ideology preceded them but they did not have the scope to consider whether appropriate under the circumstances. Such a perspective of Jo Gwang-jo on a ruler contrasted with Jeong Do-jeon's perspective of the early Joseon dynasty (refer to Ch. 11). He revealed the perspective on a ruler after explaining the importance of the role of prime minister.

Also, dimness and brightness or strength and weakness of the natural disposition of a ruler are not equivalent. A state of great impartiality can be achieved by following what is beautiful [good], correcting what is evil, aiding what is right, and correcting what is not right. Thus, "aspect" (相, *sang* in Kr.) means "to aid in correcting."

- "Chongseo" (Introduction), Governance,
Administrative Code of Joseon

According to Jeong Do-jeon, a ruler could be dim, bright, strong, or weak because he was an ordinary human being. Prime ministers gave advice to the throne. In other words, this was a theory of the division of roles wherein the king reigned and the prime ministers governed. There was a world of difference between the two perspectives on a ruler.

Grand Master Bo-u Revives Buddhism

Injong ascended to the throne when Jungjong passed away after 39 years of reign, but Injong met an untimely death within eight months.

271

Therefore, Myeongjong (明宗, r. 1545-1567) ascended to the throne as the 13th king. Queen Janggyeong, Jungjong's second wife, gave birth to Injong, and Queen Munjong (文定王后), his third wife, gave birth to Myeongjong; the two queens were both of the Papyeong Yun clan. The lawful wife of Jungjong was deposed after King Jungjong's Restoration of Rectitude.

An internal power struggle between the Yun clan began, consisting of a family feud between the followers of the maternal uncle of Injong, Yun Im (尹任), and the maternal uncle of Myeongjong, Yun Won-hyeong (尹元衡). Yun Im was referred to as "the Big Yun," due to his being the maternal relative of Jungjong's second wife; Yun Won-hyeong was referred to as "the Little Yun" due to his being the maternal relative of Jungjong's third wife. Queen Munjong governed as a regent for eight years when Myeongjong ascended to the throne at the young age of 12. The followers of her younger brother Yun Won-hyeong gained power and carried out sweepingly suppressive acts, such as awarding poison, massacre, and banishment to the followers of Yun Im who had power during the period of Injong. The Sarim Faction also suffered from this suppression, because the followers of Yun Im promoted the Sarim Faction, albeit for only a short time, during the reign of Injong. This was the Literati Purge of the Year of Eulsa in 1545.

The reign of Myeongjong began with the Literati Purge of the Year of Eulsa, which was a bloody persecution led by the Little Yun Faction against the followers of the Big Yun Faction, but it was also the period of revival of Buddhism following the reign of Sejo's protective rule of Buddhism. Monks changed into ragtag monks without distinction from shamans of the laypeople as a result of continuous persecution of Buddhism after Sejo passed away, and the dignity of Buddhism sank further. Queen Munjeong, who was of the Buddhist faith, became saddened by this decline and kept Grand Master Bo-u (普雨大師) near her after he was introduced to her by Jeong Man-jong (鄭萬鍾), a monk in charge of the property of Buddhist temples of Gangwon Province. Grand Master Bo-u was the head monk of Baekdam Temple (百潭寺) and became very active in reviving the dignity of Buddhism.

Various religious sects of the Goryeo period were reorganized and unified as either Zen or the Textual School of Buddhism in the early Joseon period, but Grand Master Bo-u revived these various sects and assigned Tongnyeong (統領) to control each of them.[8] A more important measure was the revival of the state examination for Buddhist monks and monk certificate (度牒制: a certificate of qualification given to a monk) that were abolished by Yeonsan-gun. Two prominent monks, Hyujeong (休靜) the Grand Master Seosan (1520-1604) and Yujeong (惟政) the Grand Master Samyeong, were very active in leading monk troops to battle during the Imjin War, as both had passed the Monk Certificate Examination (禪科) as part of the state examination to become a Buddhist monk.

When Queen Munjeong passed away in 1565, the 20th year after Myeongjong ascended to the throne, Confucians concentrated on denouncing Grand Master Bo-u; Grand Master Bo-u was finally beaten to death after being banished to Jeju Island. The state examination for Buddhist monks was subsequently abolished. The Sarim Faction, which was extreme in rejecting Buddhism, slandered Bo-u as "a wicked priest" and claimed "there was a romantic alliance with Queen Munjeong"; there are still some who believe these statements. Fortunately, *Heo-eungdangjip* (虛應堂集, Collected Works of Heo-eungdang) compiled by Taegyun (太均), a disciple of Grand Master Bo-u who revered his teacher, circulated the document in secret. Moreover, Yujeong (惟政) the Grand Master Samyeong participated in revising it and adding an epilogue to it. Through this book we can see the bountiful knowledge and lofty character of Bo-u, who was well versed in the ways of both Confucianism and Buddhism. Bo-u, Hyujeong, and Yujeong provided distinguished service in reviving Buddhism in Joseon.

---

43 Tongnyeong (統領) was a person in charge of everything within the sect. (S. Lee)

Yujeong, who was active in the Imjin War, met with Tokugawa Ieyatsu at Fushimi Castle in Kyoto a year after the latter became the Seiidai Shogun in 1604. Visiting Japan as an envoy to find out the circumstances there, Yujeong confirmed the intention of Tokugawa Ieyatsu to recover diplomatic relations at this meeting, and 1,390 prisoners of war taken to Japan were returned. This became the first step in diplomacy that lasted for approximately 260 years with the Tokugawa Bakufu.

Was there a civilian official who had enough courage to throw himself into the center of the invading nation under the panic-stricken circumstances immediately after the war? The revival of the state examination for Buddhist monks by the efforts of Bo-u achieved a great result just by producing two able men in Hyujeong (休靜) the Grand Master Seosan and Yujeong (惟政) the Grand Master Samyeong. Hyujeong wrote *Cheongheojip* (清虛集) and Yujeong wrote *Samyeongjip* (四溟集, Collected Works of the Grand Master Samyeong). These two books as well as the *Collected Works of Heo-eungdang* are valuable contributions that stand out from the collection of single-minded Confucian works of the Joseon period.

The Sarim Faction Divides into Dong'in and Seoin

The Sarim Faction politics were realized in the reign of Seonjo after experiencing four literati purges. Prominent leaders of the Sarim Faction such as Yi Hwang (李滉, pen name is Toegye 退溪, 1501-1570) and Gi Dae-seung (奇大升, pen name is Gobong 高峰, 1527-1572) held key government posts even after the Literati Purge of the Year of Eulsa. Yi Hwang put a distance between the power politics of Yun Won-hyeong and himself and repeated the cycle of going into government service and returning to his hometown. Seonjo appointed Yi Hwang to the post of Minister of Rites at the same time as his ascension to the throne, but Yi Hwang used illness as an excuse to return to his hometown immediately. He could have been afraid of a new literati purge following a change in the king. He went back to Seoul in 1568 because he could no longer refuse the callings of the king and attended several of the royal lectures, but returned to his hometown at age 68 after recommending Gi Dae-seung for the position of Minister of Rites.

Gi Dae-seung was from Gwangju in Jeolla Province and was strongly influenced by Yi Hwang. His uncle Gi Jun (奇遵) suffered in the Literati Purge of the Year of Gimyo along with Jo Gwang-jo and was executed after banishment. Gi Dae-seung was an official of the Office of Inspector General at the time and gave a lecture on *Great Learning* at the first royal lecture with Seonjo on October of 1567 when Seonjo ascended to the throne. The content of the long lecture is quoted below, as it is significant in persuading Seonjo to carry out the politics of the Sarim Faction. He stated the following after first presupposing that judgment of the right and wrong of the past political incidents (literati purges) must not be passed in vagueness:

> Our nation is partial and the customs are not perfect. Thus there is none with even a modicum of knowledge who has not met with misfortune. Jeong Mong-ju remained faithful to loyalty and piety, and became the founder of the Eastern Learning of the Principle by learning the scholarship of Cheng and Zhu. Unfortunately, however, he sacrificed himself to realize virtue when Goryeo fell. The person who followed Jeong Mong-ju in our dynasty is Kim Jong-jik. His scholarship has an origin, his behavior also decorous, and he is sincere in his teaching of his juniors. Seongjong appointed him to the post of Minister because of his wisdom, and [Kim Jong-jik] did not conform to the world.
>
> People met with the misfortune of literati purges in the period of Yeonsan-gun, but Jong-jik was also affected because his pupil provided the cause, i.e., because Kim Gweng-pil was the disciple of Kim Jong-jik. Jong-jik respected writing and Gweng-pil did his best to put that into practice. That is why Seongjong also appreciated Gweng-pil and appointed him to the post of Jwarang.[9] But he was exiled and punished for a great crime in the Literati Purge of the Year of Gabja during the reign of Yeonsan-gun because he was a follower of Jong-jik. When he ascended to the throne, Jungjong took pity on Gweng-pil's wise talent and

---

[9] Jwarang was a rank of Jeong 6-*pum* of the Six Ministries. (S. Lee)

posthumously honored him by conferring the post of the Third State Councilor.

Jo Gwang-jo is the disciple of Kim Gweng-pil. Jo Gwang-jo also was well versed in scholarship and attempted to recover the way and block the source of avarice in the world, but died without achieving his goal. And to this day what is right and what is wrong are not clearly defined. Popular sentiment will rejoice and follow only when a right thing is called right and a wrong thing is called wrong. Yi Eon-jeok received a pardon already, but he not only is not guilty, he is recently without knowledge or virtue as well.... I sincerely hope that Jo Gwang-jo and Yi Eon-jeok will be honored and that popular sentiment will flourish. Good men were punished when Yi Gi (李芑) and Yun Won-hyeong controlled the government, and those who achieved their desire are agents of the group. Thus the tendency to covet is prevalent, and the customs of the world all became such. Those who are called honest and upright today will not be able to avoid being considered dishonest and crooked in comparison to the past. Provincial magistrates are equally dishonest and crooked.

- October of the year of ascension to the throne,
Veritable Records of King Seonjo

Yi Eon-jeok (李彦迪, pen name is Hoejae 晦齋, 1491-1553) who, along with Jo Gwang-jo, was praised by Gi Dae-seung, actually participated in the Literati Purge of the Year of Eulsa on the side of the oppressor, but finished out the rest of his life in exile in the northern region of Ganggye (江界) after he became the target of machinations by the Yun Won-hyeong faction. He left many works on the Learning of Master Zhu, including *Guinnok* (求仁錄); Yi Hwang and Gi Dae-seung followed in his footsteps.

The lecture presented by Gi Dae-seung in front of the king and Crown Prince coincided with the evaluation of Jang Ji-yeon as previously mentioned, i.e., the orthodoxy of Joseon Confucianism revered by the Sarim Faction was the genealogy linking Jeong Ju-mong → Kim Jong-jik → Kim Gweng-pil → Jo Gwang-jo. Gi Dae-seung advocated the restoration of the reputation of people such as

Jo Gwang-jo and Yi Eon-jeok who were implicated in the literati purges and antagonized the followers of Kim Gae (金鎧) who criticized Jo Gwang-jo and supported Nam Gon, a political rival of Jo Gwang-jo. Gi Dae-seung, who held the post of Censor General as the highest position, returned to his hometown and concentrated on the study of the principle of human nature in the third year of the reign of Seonjo (1570). The questions and answers exchanged with Yi Hwang, which will be examined in the next chapter, became the start of the dispute over the study of the principle of human nature.

Seonjo intended to actualize moral politics and to restore the good name of the Sarim Faction that suffered from literati purges. However, internal factional disputes within the Sarim Faction began on a different level than that of the conflict between the Hungu Faction and the Sarim Faction. This was the division of and confrontation between the Dong'in Faction and the Seoin Faction.

The Ministry of Personnel was the department that had jurisdiction over personnel among the Six Ministries at the central government. The posts of Hiring Secretaries (銓郎: Senior Secretary 正郎 and Junior Secretary 佐郎) were of low rank but important insofar as having the power to recommend officials for high positions in the three offices (Office of Inspector General, Office of Censor General, and Office of Special Advisors). As mentioned previously, the Sarim Faction had denounced the Hungu Faction whose marriage ties to the king helped obtain high positions in these three offices. To the Sarim Faction, speech rather than actual politics was the greatest weapon.

A conflict arose between Sim Ui-gyeom (沈義謙) and Kim Hyo-won (金孝元) over the post of Hiring Secretaries; the former was a younger brother of the Lady of the Sim clan (one of Myeongjong's wives) and the latter was a disciple of Yi Hwang. Politicians became involved in this conflict, and partisanship formed. There were many older people among the followers of Sim Ui-gyeom, but the young and the vigorous formed the core of the followers of Kim Hyo-won. There is no question that Kim Hyo-won was a member of the Sarim Faction, but Sim Ui-gyeom, a maternal uncle of the royal family, also

277

exerted effort to recover the tainted reputation of the Sarim Faction after the literati purges with Gi Dae-seung immediately after Seonjo ascended to the throne. This conflict within the party came to the fore as of the eighth year of the reign of Seonjo (1575).

The reason for the nickname of the two parties, Dong'in and Seoin, was that the house of Sim Ui-gyeom was west of Seoul in Jeongdong, and the house of Kim Hyo-won was east of Seoul at the base of Nak Mountain.

After Yi Hwang and Gi Dae-seung retired to their hometowns, Yi Yi (李珥, pen name is Yulgok 栗谷, 1536-1584) became Inspector General and received the wholehearted trust of Seonjo. He was a central figure in the Sarim Faction and busy attempting to prevent internal fission. He also transferred Kim Hyo-won as Buryeong Busa (富寧府使) in Hamgyeong Province and Sim Ui-gyeom as Gaeseongbu Yusu in Gaeseong temporarily to allow the heat between the two factions to cool.[10] But the Dong'in Faction criticized Yi Yi for supposedly supporting the Seoin side by pointing out that Kim Hyo-won was assigned to a northern frontier further away from Seoul than Sim Ui-gyeom. They found issue with the distance between the new post and Seoul. Thereafter Yi Yi was attacked by the Dong'in Faction for sympathizing with the Seoin Faction by "assisting the Seoin and oppressing the Dong'in."

Gi Dae-seung and Yi Yi expected a political reform in the period of reign of Seonjo through the Sarim Faction's criticism of the Hungu Faction from the perspective of not holding government posts. But the conflict and hostility within the Sarim Faction that began with the division of the faction into Dong and Seo developed in an unexpected direction. This feud could not be arbitrated by the authority of the king.

This was an example of how petty the party strife of both factions was. Two years prior to the invasion of Joseon in 1592 by

---

[10] Buryeong Busa was a government officer in charge of prefectures and grand prefectures in Buryeong, Hamgyeong Province; Gaeseongbu Yusu (開城府留守) was a Jeong 2-*pum* government official in charge of Gaeseong. (S. Lee)

Toyotomi Hideyoshi, the envoy to Japan visited Japan at its request to congratulate Japan's unification. Chief Ambassador was Hwang Yun-gil (黃允吉) of the Seoin Faction and Vice Ambassador was Kim Seong-il (金誠一) of the Dong'in Faction. After meeting with Toyotomi Hideyoshi face to face and delving into the circumstances of the enemy, Hwang Yun-gil reported Toyotomi Hideyoshi as having an ambition to invade, and Joseon must not be caught unprepared. But Kim Seong-il presented an opposing view suggesting that Hwang Yun-gil's opinion could confuse the public mind unreasonably and that Toyotomi Hideyoshi was not that great a man. Third State Councilor Yu Seong-nyong (柳成龍) also studied under Yi Hwang with Kim Seong-il; he of course supported the opinion of a fellow student. There was no room for another discussion over the division of judgment over Toyotomi Hideyoshi within the government, ultimately leading to the success of the surprise attack by the Japanese troops in 1592.

The point in time when politics led by the Sarim Faction started in the late half of the 16th century was almost 200 years after the founding of the Joseon dynasty. The vigor of founding a nation and continuing with the monumental task gradually became stagnant and a reform in Confucian politics based on change in generation was required. The Sarim Faction pursued this reform in the form of "moral politics" of the Learning of Master Zhu. Thus Jo Gwang-jo became the originator of the Sarim Faction. But the Sarim Faction that should have been in charge of the reform did not live up to the demand of the times. Not only that, utterly disruptive party struggles that began with the division of the faction into Dong'in and Seoin became the origin that brought about political and ideological confusion and decline that far outweighed the end of the Hungu Faction.

15

Dispute on the Study of the Principle of Human Nature Shakes the Political and Scholastic World

Yi Hwang and the Yeongnam School

The study of the principle of human nature in Joseon Confucianism was in its zenith prior to the intensification of the party strife within the Sarim Faction. This is because a portion of the Sarim Faction retired from world politics in the first half of the 16th century due to the Literati Purge of the Year of Gimyo in 1519 and the Literati Purge of the Year of Eulsa in 1545. That portion of the faction heightened the philosophical contents of Confucianism through self-actualizing scholarship in remote regions by pursuing the teachings of men of letters. This is why these people are referred to as rustic literati (山林).

Seo Gyeong-deok (徐敬德, pen name is Hwadam 花譚, 1489-1546) was a scholar who represented the study of the principle of human nature in the 16th century by consistently studying scholarship that transcended the secular world. He introduced the doctrine of material force as the principal (氣一元論) in a manuscript called "Igiran mu-eosin-ga?" (What Are the Principle and Material Force?) ("Won-igi" 原理氣, Origin of the Principle and Material Force, in *Hwadamjip*, Collected Works of Hwadam, Vol. 2). A heated debate followed on whether "the theory of the principle and material force of the Four Beginnings and the Seven Emotions" (四端七情理氣論) should be understood in terms of the doctrine of the principle as the principal or the doctrine of material force as the principal developed between Yi Hwang and Gi Dae-seung and between Yi Yi and Seong Hon (成渾, pen name is Ugye 牛溪, 1535-1598). There was no exclusion of doctrinal differences in connection with the party prior to the division of the Sarim Faction into Dong'in and Seoin.

The world of Confucianism in the latter half of Joseon divided into the Yeongnam School (嶺南學派) with the founder as Yi Hwang, and the Giho School (畿湖學派) with the founder as Yi Yi, through this debate on the study of the principle of human nature. The formation process of the Yeongnam School will be examined first.

Yi Hwang was born in Ongye-li (溫溪里), Yean-hyeon (禮安縣), Gyeongsang Province (what is now Dosan-myeon, Andong-si in North Gyeongsang Province). As an outstanding scholar and virtuous man, he became a politician in the period of Myeongjong. This was also a period of suffering for the Sarim Faction second only to the Literati Purge of the Year of Eulsa in 1545 due to the followers of Yun Won-hyeong being in power. Yi Hwang entered government service after passing "the big class" of the Erudite Examination in 1534 but lost the passion for politics ever since the Literati Purge of the Year of Eulsa. He repeated the cycle of entering government service, resigning his post, and returning to his hometown whenever Myeongjong summoned him. There were many learned men who respected his academic achievements. In 1560, the year he turned 60, he planned on building Dosan Village School (陶山書堂: later to become Dosan Academy) and on concentrating on educating younger generations in his hometown. But he returned to his hometown only in 1568 due to unceasing summons from Myeongjong and Seonjo; he passed away two years later at the age of 70. He left extensive writings behind, which were also transmitted to Japan and reprinted in the Edo period. In particular, *Jaseongnok* (自省錄) and *Jujaseo jeolyo* (朱子書節要, Synopsis of Zhu Xi's Letters) were valued highly to the point where these two books were displayed in the dens of Japanese scholars of the Learning of Master Zhu.

Yi Hwang was a scholar of the study of the principle of human nature who most faithfully delineated and elucidated on the doctrines of Zhu Xi; the study of the principle of human nature by Gi Dae-seung and Yi Yi derived from criticism of, and admiration for, Yi Hwang. The study of the principle of human nature by Yi Hwang was forged and refined through his debates with Gi Dae-seung on the subject. The disputes of the two scholars were called "Sachil iginonbyeon" (四七理氣論辨, Argument on the Principle and Material Force of the Four-Seven). "Four-Seven" mentioned here referred to Four Beginnings in *The Works of Mencius* and seven feelings in *Records of Rites*. The Four Beginnings had "the feeling of commiseration" as the origin of virtue, "the feeling of shame and dislike" as the origin of righteousness, "the feeling of reverence and respect" as the origin of propriety, and "the feeling of approving and disapproving" as the origin of knowledge. In other words, the Four Beginnings were the starting point of virtue, righteousness, propriety, and knowledge. Seven Emotions referred to happiness, anger, sadness, fear, love, hate, and greed (喜怒哀懼愛惡欲).

Gi Dae-seung visited Yi Hwang in Seoul in 1558, the same year he passed the Erudite Examination. He asked Yi Hwang for an opinion on *Cheonmyeong doseol* (天命圖說, Diagram of Heaven's Mandate) by Jeong Ji-un (鄭之雲, pen name is Chuman 秋巒, 1509-1561). Jeong Ji-un was from Goyang in Gyeonggi Province and studied under Kim Jeong-guk (金正國, pen name is Sajae 思齋, 1485-1541), a disciple of Kim Gweng-pil. Jeong Ji-un was a scholar of the study of the principle of human nature who concentrated solely on self-actualizing scholarship. The debate arose because Yi Hwang revised the content on "the Four Beginnings emanated from the principle, and the Seven Emotions emanated from material force" (四端發於理 七情發於氣) in *Diagram of Heaven's Mandate* to "the Four Beginnings are emanated by the principle, and the Seven Emotions are emanated by material force" (四端理之發 七情氣之發). In other words, he correlated the Four Beginnings with the principle and the Seven Emotions with material force from the perspective of dualism of the principle and material force

282

(理氣二元論) as proposed by Zhu Xi [*Toegye jeonseo* (Collected Works of Toegye) Part I, "Nonsadan chiljeongseo" (論四端七情書, Discussions on the Writing of Four Beginnings and Seven Emotions)].

The gist of the counterargument by Gi Dae-seung wondered whether the substance of the Four Beginnings and Seven Emotions were the same but the names different. The Four Beginnings and Seven Emotions could not be dualistically divided and applied to the principle or material force, but instead the Four Beginnings might refer to a part within the Seven Emotions (pure goodness is the Four Beginnings) and the Seven Emotions might refer to the entirety (including good and bad). This debate continued for almost eight years.

In order to simplify a disputed point of argument and to facilitate comprehension, in contrast to Yi Hwang having understood the Four Beginnings and Seven Emotions as dualism of the principle and material force, Gi Dae-seung understood the Four Beginnings to be included within the Seven Emotions from a perspective of dualism of the Four Beginnings and Seven Emotions. Yi Hwang adopted the proposition of "the Four Beginnings are emanated by the principle, and the Seven Emotions are emanated by material force" (四端是理之發 七情是氣之發) stated in *Classified Conversations of Master Zhu* (朱子語類) as his doctrine as a teacher without room for concession, with the intention of elucidating a way to approach pure goodness of the four beginning from the impure Seven Emotions containing a mixture of goodness and badness, by grounding the foundation for preserving the principle of Heaven and eliminating human greed in "the Four Beginnings are emanated by the principle." This also approached the doctrine of innate goodness advocated by Mencius.

The critique of Gi Dae-seung clearly saw through the weakness in the dualism of the principle and material force that divides and applied the Four Beginnings as emanating from the principle and the Seven Emotions as emanating from material force. Thus Yi Hwang had to revise his doctrine somewhat, and he came up with the theory of mutual issuance of the principle and material force: "The Four

Beginnings are emanated by the principle but material force obeys it, and the Seven Emotions are emanated by material force but the principle rides on it." He discussed this in *Seonghak sipdo* (聖學十圖, Ten Diagrams of the Learning of the Sages), which he wrote two years before his death for Seonjo, who had just ascended to the throne.

> Regarding the emotions of the Four Beginnings, they are purely good and without evil if the principle issues and material force follows in accord. But the principle is hidden by material force and is lost and degenerates into what is not good if the principle's issuance does not occur. If the Seven Emotions are issued by material force and mounted by the principle, there is nothing which is not good; but the material force will get out of control and become evil by obliterating the principle if the issuance of material force is not accurate. Master Cheng said, "If one discusses the nature but does not consider material force, it is incomplete; if one discusses material force without considering nature, there is a lack of clarity. If one treats them as two, it is incorrect."

> • "Diagram of the Saying 'The Mind Combines and Governs Nature and the Feelings'" (心統性情圖說), *Ten Diagrams of the Learning of the Sages*

It is important to be cautious about the point that the Four Beginnings issued by the principle and the Seven Emotions issued by the material force as mentioned by Yi Hwang are not equivalent at all. The mind controls both human nature and emotions; the substance of the mind is the "silent and unmoving" nature while the function of the mind is the emotion of "interacting after feeling." Thus scholars must first know and achieve "the cultivation of the mind by preserving the substance and responding to its function" that cultivates nature and reduces the emotions. Therefore, "the theory of mutual issuance of the principle and material force" is a perspective thoroughly drawn from the doctrine of the principle as the principal. The students of Yi Hwang who followed this doctrine formed the Yeongnam School which divided the Confucian world in Joseon.

The Wang Yang-ming School Is Also a Scholarship

A little before Yi Hwang's time, the scholarship of Wang Yang-ming (name is Shou Ren 守仁, 1472-1528) and his academic nemesis were active in Ming China. Wang Yang-ming advocated that "the mind is the principle," but Luo Zheng-an (羅整庵, name is Qin Shun 欽順, 1465-1547, also known as Lo Ch'in-shun) criticized this viewpoint from the perspective of the advocates of the Learning of Master Zhu.

The Learning of Master Zhu became systematic doctrinal studies for the civil service examination in the Ming period as was the case in the Yuan period. Moreover, *Grand Code of the Four Books*, *Grand Code of the Five Confucian Classics*, and *Grand Code of the Principle of Human Nature* were compiled as nationally authorized textbooks under the royal command of Emperor Yongle in the early Ming period. Thus room for original works on the Learning of Master Zhu gradually decreased, and the general tone of the advocates of the Learning of Master Zhu became "the way of Confucians was fully investigated and studied by Zhu Xi; the only thing left is for it to be practiced in life."

The Wang Yang-ming School emerged to stir up the stagnated Learning of Master Zhu faction. Wang Yang-ming, born to an illustrious family, studied the Learning of Master Zhu and even passed the civil service examination. But he continuously questioned the theory of the Learning of Master Zhu that claimed the existence of a principle in all things, and "suddenly penetrated" the internal and external principles after investigating the internal principle of the mind and the external principle of things. This is because the principle of things that is external and the principle of the mind that is internal do not coincide. He became ill from excessively thinking about this issue. Therefore, he shifted the focus from the principle of things that exist externally to the principle of the mind existing internally in order to overcome the inconsistency, which is "the mind is the principle" proclaimed through "all principles are within my mind."

This doctrine was also known as the "Liu-Wang School" in honor of Liu Xiang-shan and Wang Yang-ming, because Liu Xiang-shan, a rival of Zhu Xi, had already advocated that the mind is the principle in the Song China period. Wang Yang-ming arrived at this doctrine from questioning the Learning of Zhu Xi. The doctrine of Wang Yang-ming arose from his criticism of the commentaries on *Great Learning* by Zhu Xi. Zhu Xi considered *Great Learning* as the foremost Chinese Confucian Classic among the Four Books. Zhu Xi, however, interpreted the part from *Great Learning* on "*gyeongmul chiji*" (格物致知, *gewu zhizhi* in Ch.) intellectually as "investigation and study of the principle of all things" and created *Daixue zhangju* (大學章句, Great Learning Divided by Chapters and Sentences). Based on "Daixue guben" (大學古本, Old Text of the Great Learning), an original writing among the *Records of Rites* whose very existence became a dim memory due to being overshadowed by *Great Learning Divided by Chapters and Sentences*, Wang Yang-ming criticized Zhu Xi's interpretation. Wang interpreted investigation of things and cultivation of knowledge as "guiding the existence of things in the right way and recovering the original innate knowledge of man." In other words, Zhu Xi's fragmented investigation of things and cultivation of knowledge were transformed into simple and clear realization of innate knowledge.

As explained in "Jin Xin" of *The Works of Mencius*, "realization without having to think deeply is innate knowledge." In other words, innate knowledge is wisdom that man has from birth and not Zhu Xi's "first realize the principle by studying widely, and then put the principle in action"; Wang Yang-ming advocated unity of knowledge and action based on innate knowledge. For example, filial piety is within the mind of man from birth, and it is not something that cannot be practiced because the principle is unknown.

As such, in the Wang Yang-ming School, the teachings of the sage and wise were not the exclusive property of the *sadaebu* through reading and research, but rather that all common people who could not afford the luxury of reading and research had the innate knowledge to achieve the state of a sage. Also, this innate knowledge inherent in man is claimed to be the decree of Heaven in preserving the decree of Heaven and eliminating the greed of man.

Luo Zheng-an was a scholar of the Learning of Master Zhu, and as such, launched a counterargument against Wang Yang-ming's criticism of Zhu Xi's theory on investigation of things and cultivation of knowledge. But he advocated that the principle exists only within material force (理氣一體論) in *Knowledge Painfully Acquired* (困知記, *Kunzhiji* in Ch.), which revised Zhu Xi's dualism of the principle and material force. This book greatly influenced Yi Hwang and Yi Yi's study of the principle of human nature.

Yi Hwang not only criticized Luo Zheng-an's theory that advocates that the principle exists only within material force but also wrote "Jeonseupnok nonbyeon" (傳習錄論辨, Arguments against Record of Instructions, in Vol. 41 of *Collected Works of Toegye*) especially to criticize Wang Yang-ming. *Record of Instructions* (傳習錄) contains analects between Wang Yang-ming and his followers and was the introductory book for the Wang Yang-ming School as was Zhu Xi's *Reflections of Things at Hand*. Yi Hwang passed strict judgment by stating that the doctrine of "the mind is the principle" and "unity of knowledge and action" as advanced by the Liu-Wang School was as heterodox as the School of Zen [Buddhism].

> The difference between Zhu Xi and Liu Xiang-shan are as follows. If the former is Confucian, then the latter is Zen; if the former is orthodox, then the latter is unorthodox; the former is just, but the latter is private and chaotic.

But Yi Hwang did not discuss the doctrine on realization of innate knowledge that Wang Yang-ming advocated in his later years. It is presumed that the *Record of Instructions* read by Yi Hwang was the first print (volume one of the completed *Record of Instructions*) prior to Wang Yang-ming's advocacy of the realization of innate knowledge as the fundamental principle of scholarship.

The Wang Yang-ming School, which formed another version of Neo-Confucianism along with the Learning of Master Zhu, was rejected by the overwhelming arguments advanced by Yi Hwang and the Yeongnam School faction that followed from the beginning of its introduction to Joseon. The Wang Yang-ming School was transmitted by Jeong Je-du (鄭齊斗, pen name is Hagok 霞谷) who did not kneel down to the criticism of the scholars of the Learning of Master Zhu; he lived in seclusion in a remote village called Hagok on Ganghwa Island and passed down the teachings of Wang Yang-ming there, and the Ganghwa School (江華學派) somehow managed to continue its existence.

There was no change in the fact that the Learning of Master Zhu that represented Confucianism in the Song and Yuan periods in China also served as the systematic doctrinal studies of the Ming and Qing periods, but there was also the Wang Yang-ming School in the Ming period and philologico-bibliographical study in the Qing period. But in Joseon one could not challenge the Learning of Master Zhu as the only scholarship without having the courage to withstand the critique of Yi Hwang and other Confucians who followed him.

Diversity rather than uniformity in thought or scholarship is advisable. Uniform authoritativeness of specific thought or learning is an obstacle to liberal development and invites stagnation within the world of thought.

Yi Yi and the Giho School

Yi Yi and Yi Hwang formed the twin peaks of the Joseon study of the principle of human nature. The Giho School, which was formed by the followers of Yi Yi, divided the Joseon Confucian world into two with the Yeongnam School. When the party strife began after the Sarim Faction divided into the Dong'in Faction and the Seoin Faction in the Seonjo period, Yi Yi attempted to bring reconciliation between the two factions, but instead was criticized for assisting the Seoin and oppressing the Dong'in by the Dong'in Faction and accused of being a member of the Seoin Faction.

Yi Yi was born in the 21st year of the reign of Jungjong (1536) in Gangneung, Gangwon Province, where the family of his mother, Madam Shin Saimdang, lived. Madam Shin Saimdang was a female artist who decorated a page in the history of Korean painting. He went into Mount Geumgang and became absorbed in Buddhism for one year after the three-year mourning period for his mother who passed away when he was 16, because he could not overcome his sadness and spiritual confusion. This provided a pretext for a personal attack from the Dong'in Faction later on. Members of the Dong'in Faction like Censor General Song Eung-gae (宋應漑) used the excuse that people like Yi Yi should not be allowed to participate in politics. They criticized Yi Yi's act of living on a mountain and learning Buddhism after having quarreled with his father's concubine when his mother passed away. This vilification of Yi Yi was continued by the Dong'in Faction even when the issue of burying the corpse of Yi Yi in the National Confucian Shrine arose. The rigidity of thought on the Learning of Master Zhu as the only scholarship had already entered a stage that was almost beyond help.

Luo Zheng-an, who was mentioned earlier, was a scholar who passed the Literary Licentiate Examination and rose to the government post of Libu Shangshu (吏部尙書: equivalent to the Minister of Personnel of Joseon) as a scholar of the Learning of Master Zhu, but he was deeply infatuated with Buddhism until he was 40. But no one in China spoke ill of him after hearing about his past. Luo Zheng-an changed his previous way of thinking for some reason and leaned toward the Cheng-Zhu School, supported the Cheng-Zhu School while excluding Buddhism, and criticized the Wang Yang-ming School most sharply. This was possible because he was well versed in the core of Buddhism.

There are those among Chinese scholars who conclude that the "with all of one's mind know nature" as advocated by Cheng-zi and Zhu Xi is a way of thinking that originated from the Buddhist "with clear mind realize one's nature," and that the theory of the Cheng-Zhu School on the nature of the mind is externally Confucian but internally metaphysical, or Buddhist. The Learning of Master Zhu and Buddhism are fundamentally not as different as the scholars of the study of the principle of human nature who have not studied Buddhism intrinsically think. There does not seem to have been another Confucian of Joseon who understood Buddhism well and who sharply criticized Buddhism intrinsically based on his knowledge other than Jeong Do-jeon, the author of *Array of Critiques on Buddhism* of the early Joseon period.

Yi Yi entered the world of bureaucracy as a Junior Secretary of the Ministry of Taxation in 1564 at the age of 29, since he joined the world at the age of 20 and decided to follow Confucianism after coming down from Mount Geumgang. People called him "the Master of the Top Score Nine Times" because he applied for the civil service examination nine times up to that point and received the highest score each time. He met Yi Hwang for the first time in 1558 at the age of 23. Yi Hwang was an eminent senior scholar of 58 at the time. The attitude of Yi Yi was to "hold a government post in the world and study in retirement"; he passed away at the age of 49 in 1584. In comparison, Yi Hwang was a scholar who strongly leaned toward "study in retirement."

The basic characters of Yi Yi's scholarship reflected his thoughts on politics through incorporation of his thought on good governance there. Even in the study of the principle of human nature, however, he criticized Yi Hwang's doctrine through the six-year debate on "the Debate on the Principle and Material Force of the Four-Seven" with Seong Hon. The difference between Yi Yi and Yi Hwang was that Yi Yi was also a scholar of the Learning of Master Zhu but not an absolutist about Zhu Xi as was Yi Hwang, and Yi Yi presented his own unique opinions by putting Zhu Xi's doctrines in relativistic terms.

As mentioned previously, Yi Hwang advocated "the theory of mutual issuance of the principle and material force" wherein the Four Beginnings and Seven Emotions are divided and included in the principle and material force, of which the Four Beginnings are issued forth by the principle and followed by material force, and the Seven Emotions are issued by material force and the principle "gets a free lift." Seong Hon held firmly to the position of the doctrine of material force as the principal in that "the principle controls material force and material force gives the principle a ride," which is very similar to Yi Hwang's theory. Yi Yi, however, was critical of the theory of mutual issuance of the principle and material force. For example, he discussed his answer to a question from Seong Hon as follows:

> The original meaning when Zhu Xi said "(the Four Beginnings) issue forth from the principle and (the Seven Emotions) issue forth from material force"… is nothing more than that "the Four Beginnings refer to the principle only and the Seven Emotions include material force as well," and it is not thought that he meant to say "the Four Beginnings issue forth first from the principle and the Seven Emotions issue forth first from material force." Toegye argues based on this (doctrine of Zhu Xi) by stating that "the Four Beginnings issue forth from the principle and material force follows it, and the Seven Emotions issue forth from material force and the principle rides on it." It is correct to say that "the Seven Emotions issue forth from material force and the principle rides on it." This is not limited to the Seven Emotions in particular, but rather, the Four Beginnings also issue forth from material force and the principle rides on it.
>
> - "Dapseong howon imsin" (答成浩原 壬申),
>   *Yulgok jeonseo* (Collected Works of Yulgok)

Attention should be put on the opinion that "not limited to the Seven Emotions in particular, but rather, the Four Beginnings also issue forth from material force and the principle rides on it" in the above excerpt. According to Yi Yi, sympathetic emotion emanates from material force, but the reason for emanation of material force as the basis of sympathetic emotion is humanity before material force is aroused. He expanded on this answer:

> In general, what emanates is material force, and the reason for the emanation is the principle. Without material principle, emanation cannot occur; without the principle, there is no reason for material force to emanate. This cannot change even if a sage is resurrected. How can (the principle and material force) be said to be able to emanate each other when the relationship between the two is not of the beginning and end, nor is it of division and union?

Thus material force is "active" because it emanates, but the principle, which is the reason for the emanation, is "inactive." The former has the means and an end as well as a beginning and an end because it has a form, but the latter has none of those because it does not have a form. In other words, the principle is a general thing that transcends time and space because it is emanated by material force, but in comparison, material force is limited in time and space. Yi Yi called this *"itong giguk"* (unrestricted principle and restricted material force), and further, he considered that among the Seven Emotions wherein material force emanates and the principle rides on it, the Four Beginnings were an aspect of goodness and the Seven Emotions an overseer that included the Four Beginnings.

The opinion of Yi Yi on the relationship between the Four Beginnings and Seven Emotions corresponds to the claim of Gi Daeseung on "the principle and material force cannot be divided with the Four Beginnings and Seven Emotions" when criticizing Yi Hwang. This is Yi Yi's "doctrine of material force emanating forth and the principle riding it" based on material force as the principal in opposition to Yi Hwang's "theory of mutual issuance of the principle and material force" based on the doctrine of the principle as the principal.

100,000-Strong Troops Must Be Built in Preparation for Uprisings

Yi Yi also considered realization of moral politics to be ideal. However, he did not stop at the study of the principle of human nature that is far removed from reality; he did not retreat even after the mudslinging and criticism by the Dong'in Faction, but fought singly to combine academics with practice. Representative works on political philosophy include *Dongho mundap* (東湖問答, Catechism at Eastern Lake), which was written at the age of 34, and *Seonghak jibyo* (聖學輯要, The Essentials of the Studies of the Sages), which was written at the age of 40.

Just as with *Ten Diagrams of the Learning of the Sages* by Yi Hwang, *The Essentials of the Studies of the Sages* was written for Seonjo as a

292

study to become a good emperor; the difference in scholastic perspectives of the two is revealed well in that *The Essentials of the Studies of the Sages* is a book on political philosophy that combines self-cultivation and governing others while *Ten Diagrams of the Learning of the Sages* can be said to put emphasis on self-cultivation. *Catechism at Eastern Lake* is a book that discusses his political philosophy and practical issues in the form of question-and-answer sessions between a guest and the master of the house. The content of this is as follows:

1) "Non-gundo" (論君道), 2) "Non-sindo" (論臣道), 3) "Non-gunsin sangdeukjinan" (論君臣相得之難), 4) "Non-dongbang dohak bulhaeng" (論東方道學不行), 5) "Non-ajo godo bulbok" (論我朝古道不復), 6) "Non-danggeumjisise" (論當今之時勢), 7) "Non-musilwi sugijiyo" (論務實爲修己之要), 8) "Non-byeongan wiyonghyeonjiyo" (論辨姦爲用賢之要), 9) "Non-anminjisul" (論安民之術), 10) "Non-gyoinjisul" (論敎人之術), and 11) "Non-jeongmyeong wi chidojibon" (論正名爲治道之本).

The content of the political philosophy of Yi Yi is linked to practical issues. For example, he describes his perspective on scholarship in "Non-gunsin sangdeukjinan" as follows:

Guest: There was no lack of people who read even after the period of Han China. What type of learning is the so-called learning of the Way?

Master of the House: You seem to have little knowledge now that I've heard your words. Learning of the Way means to reveal goodness through investigation of things and cultivation of knowledge, and to cultivate the body through sincerity and correct mind; accumulation of these will become the virtue of Heaven, and these will become the way of the kings if they are practiced. Reading is just one of the ways of the investigation of things and the cultivation of knowledge. What difference is there with a parrot that repeats words well if what was gleaned from reading books is not practiced? Emperor Wudi of Liang China read 10,000 books but became a prisoner of Wei in the end. How can this be referred to as the learning of the Way?

There was a period of Southern and Northern Dynasties (420-589) in the history of China wherein the Northern Dynasties (Northern Wei and Eastern Wei) of the Xianbei tribe were in conflict with the Southern Dynasties (Song, Zhai, Liang, and Chen). Emperor Wudi of Liang China named the kingdom of Liang and selected Jiankang (建康: today's Nanjing) as the capital after overthrowing Zhai China. Emperor Wudi's name was Xiao Yan (蕭衍). He had a talent for civil and military arts, for he had read 10,000 books and employed literati aristocrats to develop a golden period for the culture of the Southern Dynasties. But in his later days, he became fascinated with Buddhism and wasted finances, dying of anger during his confinement after the rebellion of General Hou Jing (侯景) of Northern Wei.

Yi Yi emphasized that reading 10,000 books as Emperor Wudi of Liang China did cannot be called learning of the Way if it does not help to enrich and strengthen the nation and the nation falls. Jo Gwang-jo said that enriching and strengthening the nation is by the rule of might, but to Yi Yi the learning of the Way was the means to realize the enrichment and strengthening of the nation.

The Sarim Faction since Jo Gwang-jo considered the village code as the fundamental enlightenment of the people to infiltrate the benevolent and good customs of Confucianism. Seonjo also commanded the enforcement of the village code in response to the request of various vassals. Yi Yi objected at the royal lecture as follows:

> The time is not ripe in my humble opinion. Providing for the people must be first and teaching them must be after that. The poverty of the people has never been this extreme before. Thus [the people] must be saved from this evil rapidly, and the village code must be applied after the needy circumstance of the commoners is resolved.

> • February of the 7th year of the present king,
> *Gyeong'yeon ilgi* (經筵日記, Diary of the Royal Lectures)

This was the "doctrine of wealth first and learning later" that was supposed to provide the subsistence of the people before civilizing them.

Japan's invasion of Joseon under Toyotomi Hideyoshi began in 1592, exactly 200 years after the founding of the Joseon dynasty in 1392. Yi Yi lived during the period immediately before this invasion. The period of founding and continuing the task of establishing the dynasty ended and the Hungu Faction who participated in them has already disappeared from history. Contradictions between "the laws of the past kings" and reality were experienced in the period during which Yi Yi lived, and these contradictions were becoming obstacles to new development. Yi Yi considered the period in which he lived to be a period of reform based on changing laws. Reform meant revolution in that it denoted the tightening of laxity. In "Memorial in Ten Thousand Words" (萬言封事) that was submitted to Seonjo at the age of 39, Yi Yi claims as follows:

> The laws were scrupulously careful when the preceding kings of our kingdom first established them. But they must be adapted because times and work have changed and some evil practices exist. Wrong codes [executed] afterwards must be reformed with haste and without hesitation. Is it not said in documents that change must occur when one is confronted with a difficult situation, and one will be adaptable toward change? I humbly beg Your Highness on my knees to keep this in mind and think of the disposition of adaptability.

What were the reasons for the king and his vassals to indecisively hesitate on being flexible in order to develop a new stage of dynastic politics?

> Luckily, Your holy and luminous Majesty will (now) be able to govern widely for a generation when laws are created to suit the times, because [Your Majesty] is concerned with scholarship and

is considerate of the lives of the people. But [Your Majesty] seems to have little resolution to be flexible, being afraid of losing whatever advances are made due to stopping in the midst of a reform. Those who are [Your Majesty's] servants do not dare to discuss flexibility because they are afraid of being criticized as worriers of Wang An-shi (王安石) and are circumspect in their fear that they may become a repeat of what happened in the year of *gimyo* (what happened to the followers of Jo Gwang-jo during the Literati Purge of the Year of Gimyo).[1]

Seonjo was the king who organized the politics of the Sarim Faction but could only watch in indecision when factional disputes began within the Sarim Faction after it became divided into the Dong'in and Seoin Factions. The Sarim Faction had to recommend specific solutions for changing the law and not stop at criticizing the Hungu Faction just for the sake of criticism. The recommendations are Yi Yi's *Catechism at Eastern Lake* and *The Essentials of the Studies of the Sages* presented at the royal lecture. But not one of Yi Yi's proposals for reforming the law could be realized even with the king's trust due to the attack of factional criticism of the Dong'in Faction after Yi Yi was stigmatized as a member of the Seoin Faction. His thought on changing the laws became the forerunner of the practical learning of later times.

It is noteworthy that Yi Yi made a statement on the doctrine of training 100,000 troops at a royal lecture in front of the king in 1583 when he was appointed as the Minister of Military Affairs. This was nine years before Toyotomi Hideyoshi began the Imjin War.

The Master (Yi Yi) delivered a speech at a royal lecture:
"The spirit of the kingdom has hit rock bottom. There will be great calamity in less than 10 years. I implore Your Majesty to train military troops consisting of 100,000 men in advance; station 20,000 in the capital and a troop of 10,000 in each province,

---

[1] Wang An-shi was a poet, writer, and politician of Song China and held the post of prime minister during the reign of Emperor Shenzong. He attempted various reforms, including abolition of tax immunities of big landowners, but was opposed by other politicians. (S. Lee)

but exempt them from household tax and train them in military arts. They should also be replaced every six months to protect the capital as well as to prepare all 100,000 to protect the capital. We will otherwise incur disaster in the event that a war occurs because the townspeople must be gathered in a hurry to fight."

Yu Seong-nyong said, "That is not right. Training military troops when there is no trouble is to incur disaster."

The Master's words were not carried out, because all of the vassals attending the royal lecture agreed that the Master's statement was overly apprehensive. The Master said the following to Yu Seong-nyong after the royal lecture:

"A worldly Confucian is originally unfamiliar with circumstances; do you say words to that effect as well?"

- *Yulgok jeonseo* (栗谷全書, Collected Works of Yulgok), Vol. 34, Appendix 2

Yi Yi passed away the following year, but his doctrine of training 100,000 troops was ignored as being "overly apprehensive." Yu Seong-nyong lamented as below when the Imjin War started at last:

Now that I look back, Yimun Seonggong (李文成公, Yi Yi) was a true sage. The kingdom would not be in this situation if his statement had been accepted at the time.

Yu Seong-nyong was a prominent disciple of Yi Hwang and politically one of the central figures of the Dong'in Faction. He was engaged in commanding the war effort and the foreign relations with Ming China as the Third State Councilor during the Imjin War. *Jingbirok* (懲毖錄, Record of Regret and Restraint) is a diary of his experiences. This book, whose title is from the passage on "I restrain future troubles by disciplining myself" in the *Book of Poetry*, is a record of self-reflection on the Imjin War.

The Dong'in Faction Is the Yeongnam School and the Seoin Faction Is the Giho School

Joseon Confucianism excluded the Wang Yang-ming School, which was prevalent in the Ming period in China, and solely studied the Learning of Master Zhu as of the 16th century. This was the big difference between Joseon and other Confucian cultural regions such as China or Japan.

The debate on the study of the principle of human nature, however, did not stop at the philosophical dimension within the advocates of the Learning of Master Zhu; rather, it showed an aspect wherein disciples would pass on the teacher's doctrines, and school ties as well as regionalism intermingled to become connected with various schools and factions. As a result, differences in doctrines became the cause of confrontation between factions, or they were used as factional doctrines to attack the other faction. The union between doctrines and opinions of the factions naturally resulted in severely obstructing the freedom to study the Learning of Master Zhu, since that was wrapped in the study of the principle of human nature itself. In fact, the Learning of Master Zhu in Joseon as of the 17th century fundamentally did not exceed the level of 16th-century Yi Hwang and Yi Yi.

The Dong'in Faction contained many disciples of Yi Hwang and Jo Sik (曺植, pen name is Nammyeong 南冥, 1501-1572) and regionally belonged to the Yeongnam School. When this Dong'in Faction became divided into Namin Faction and Bugin Faction, the disciples of Yi Hwang and Jo Sik divided into the Namin Faction (南人派: centered around North Gyeongsang Province) and the Bugin Faction (北人派: centered around South Gyeongsang Province), respectively.

Moreover, the Seoin Faction included many of the disciples of Yi Yi and Seong Hon and regionally belonged to the Giho School. This Giho School became divided into Nangnon (洛論: centered around Gyeonggi Province) and Horon (湖論: centered around Chungcheong Province) through a "debate on whether the nature of man and things are the same or not" (人物性同異論). Regional confrontation in the political culture of Korea firmly took root in this time.

The debate on whether the nature of man and things were the same in the first half of the 18th century was expanded after the disciples of Gwon Sang-ha (權尙夏), top disciple of Song Si-yeol (宋詩烈), the head of the Noron Faction, became divided into Horon and Nangnon following the branching off of the Seoin Faction into the Noron and the Soron Faction. The debate centered on the study of the principle of human nature in Korean Confucian thought following the 16th-century debate on the theory of the principle and material force of the Four Beginnings and the Seven Emotions.

From this debate which swept through the world of Confucianism in Joseon and consumed tens of thousands of words, proponents of the doctrine that the nature of man and things are the same referred to the sentence on "What Heaven has conferred is called THE NATURE" (天命之謂性) in Zhu Xi's *Zhongyong zhangju* (中庸章句, The Doctrine of the Mean Divided by Chapters and Sentences) to support their claim, while the proponents of the doctrine of the difference in the nature of man and things, on the other hand, referred to the sentence on "Life is what we call nature" (生之謂性) in "Gao Zi, Part I" of *The Works of Mencius* to support their claim. Proponents of the two contrasting doctrines ultimately became divided into different factions.

The group of Confucian scholars who supported Han Won-jin (韓元震, pen name is Namdang 南塘, 1682-1751), a representative of the doctrine of the difference in the nature of man and things and one of the disciples of Gwon Sang-ha (權尙夏, pen name is Su-am 遂菴, 1641-1721), was called Horon, because Horon resided in Hoseo (湖西, Chungcheong Province). The Confucian group that agreed with Yi Gan (李柬, pen name is We-am 巍巖, 1677-1727), a representative of the doctrine that the nature of man and of things are the same, was called Nangnon because most of them were from

Gyeonggi Province, although Yi Gan resided in Chungcheong Province.

The Yeongnam School considered Yi Hwang to be its founder, and the Giho Schools considered Yi Yi to be its founder. And as such, these two were the twin peaks that divided the Joseon Confucian world, because the Horon and Nangnon Factions are internal off-shoots of the Giho School. But Yi Hwang and Yi Yi, who represented the twin peaks of Joseon Confucianism, did not create factions. Secession of the Sarim Faction into Dong'in and Seoin occurred after Yi Hwang passed away; Yi Yi attempted to prevent the secession of the Dong'in and Seoin Factions and bring about reconciliation between the two.

Despite this, each school formed a faction in order to gain political power, and mutual gains and losses turned into power struggles for limited government posts. The metaphysical debate over the study of the principle of human nature, whether on the doctrine of the principle as the principal, the doctrine of material force as the principal, the doctrine on the nature of man and things as the same, or the doctrine of the difference in the nature of man and things, was not directly connected to any political issues. The problem was that differences in academic opinions were associated with antagonism between factions or regions, and that promoted political confusion and destroyed the very freedom of academic debates.

Another point that cannot be overlooked was the debate over categorizing scholars of practical learning as "the miscellaneous class" and distinguishing them from "the scholarly class" by dividing the study of Confucian Classics and practical learning and referring to the latter as "miscellaneous learning" in the reign of Seongjong (r. 1469-1494) at the advent of the Sarim Faction in the political world of central government. The Hungu Faction that led the "fine-tuning" of the Joseon dynasty studied Confucian Classics and practical learning as part of the scholarship for practical statecraft. They were able to leave great cultural assets behind, because both Confucianism and Buddhism were practiced during the period of Sejo. Miscellaneous learning firmly took root as secular learning for the multitude mostly in the period of Injo (r. 1623-1649); Injo became king with the support of the Seoin Faction. The Sarim Faction only revered the study of the principle of human nature even among the Learning of Master Zhu and went through segregation and confrontation due to differences in opinion about it. This left a negative legacy of emphasizing the study of Confucian Classics and disdaining practical learning in the academic history of Korea.

As factional disputes escalated, the civil service examination with the original purpose of appointing scholars based on ability gradually turned into a gateway to cliquishness (distinguished family, school, or regions). Government posts could not be attained even after passing the civil service examination without marital ties to the clique in power, playing a decisive role in destroying the opposite faction, or bribery if nothing else worked. If the *yangban* of the first half of the Joseon period was called "*yangban* of the civil service examination," then the *yangban* of the second half could be referred to as "*yangban* cliquishness." The following is a quote from "Li Yun" (禮運) in *Record of Rites*: "When the Grand course was pursued, a public and common spirit ruled all under the sky.... Now that the Grand course has fallen into disuse and obscurity, the kingdom is a family inheritance." A bit of cliquishness that attempts to change everything in the kingdom to private property is "*yangban* cliquishness."

The majority of the Confucians in the provinces abandoned hopes of entering the political world of central government and had to settle for being provincial *yangban* with the honorific title of Classics Licentiate or Literary Licentiate after applying for the first-level test conducted in the provinces in order to maintain the family standing. There was only a small advantage in that the names were not mentioned, such as Classics Licentiate Kim or Literary Licentiate Kang.

Confucius roamed the world with his disciples for 14 years in later years to obtain a government post. The following statement he made then in his failure to obtain a post was repeated by the [provincial] Confucians, half in pride and half in resignation:

> With coarse rice to eat, with water to drink, and my bended arm for a pillow — I still have joy in the midst of these things. Riches

and honors acquired by unrighteousness are to me as a floating cloud.

- "Shu Er," Analects of Confucius

Affability but Not Adulation Is the Way of the Virtuous Man

Why did the thought of the learning of the Way of the Sarim Faction give rise to endless factional disputes? What has been examined thus far can be summarized as follows.

Joseon dynasty was consistent in carrying out Confucian politics since the founding of the dynasty. Of course, the [political] leaders were Confucians. But there was a fundamental difference between the Confucian perspective of the Hungu Faction and the Sarim Faction; the demarcation point for this is the Sarim Faction taking over control [of the government] in the latter half of the 16th century. In essence, the Confucian perspective of the Hungu Faction was comprehensive, but the perspective of the Sarim Faction was confrontational.

The Confucian scholars of the Hungu Faction who were in charge of founding and building the Joseon dynasty focused on "statecraft" and comprehensively developed the "practical" scholarship necessary for it. Translation and publication of Buddhist classics into the Korean alphabet was executed in the reign of Sejo. Moreover, academics for the sake of verifying personal claims were suppressed and scholars participated in group compilation projects under the royal edict so that historic contributions were faithfully made that would not otherwise have been possible individually. Specific examples of collaborative results of the Hungu Faction that are commemorations of their efforts are the enactment of the Korean alphabet, compilation of the fundamental statutes of the Joseon dynasty in the form of the *National Code,* the first comprehensive history of Korea entitled *Comprehensive Mirror of the Eastern Kingdom*, a geographic document named *Augmented Survey of the Geography of Korea*, a collection of poetry and prose since the Silla period entitled *Anthology of Korean Literature,* and a history of war from Emperor Wu of Han China to the end of Goryeo in periodic sequence called *Dongguk byeonggam* (東國兵鑑, Mirror of Wars of Korea). This contrasts with the period of the Sarim Faction during which collections written by individuals to support personal claims abounded.

The Hungu Faction was made up of scholars of the Learning of Master Zhu, but mostly did not show interest in the study of the principle of human nature other than *Diagrammatic Treatise for Entering upon Learning* as a pioneering work written by Gwon Geun at the end of Goryeo and the beginning of Joseon. Thus the period wherein the Hungu Faction was in charge of politics may be said to have been a period devoid of the study of the principle of human nature

The Sarim Faction was also comprised of scholars of the Learning of Master Zhu. But in contrast to the Hungu Faction, the Sarim Faction carved out the aspect of the study of statecraft or philologico-bibliography included in the Learning of Master Zhu in contrast to the Hungu Faction; the Sarim Faction was mostly concerned with the study of the principle of human nature. To the Sarim Faction, the Learning of Master Zhu became almost synonymous with the study of the principle of human nature.

The emergence of a revolutionary Confucian group in a new age was an indubitable demand of the times as the Hungu Faction, which led the founding and establishing of the dynasty, gradually became weak and corrupt after 100 years. This was in the 16th century. But the Sarim Faction as the new political leader was inclined toward the politics of the Learning of Master Zhu as the only scholarship by focusing on "the principle of human nature" instead of realistic politics. Moreover, decline in development was incurred through demoting "practical" learning as miscellaneous learning and "enriching and strengthening a country" as the rule of might.

Originally, the doctrine of the Learning of Master Zhu as the only scholarship considered Cheng-Zhu School as the only orthodoxy among Confucianism and strictly excluded other thoughts or value systems. It established an academic faction by strongly pushing for "singleness" rather than "harmony" and then formed a faction by gathering its followers. Thus "support those of the same clique and exclude others" was maintained. Confucius said that the way of the virtuous man is indeed "affability but not adulation," i.e., being in harmony with different people. This is perceived to be the root cause of political history becoming factional history since the emergence of the Sarim Faction.

Rustic Literature Blooms in the Honam District

The Yeongnam and Giho Schools existed, but why didn't the Honam School exist? Distinguished scholars such as Gi Dae-seung, Kim In-hu (金麟厚, pen name is Haseo 河西), and Yi Hang (李恒, pen name is Iljae 一齋) from the Honam district were on par with Yi Hwang and Yi Yi academically in the 16th century. But the interconnectedness of the school was severed following the stigmatization of Jeolla Province as the "hometown of treason" after the treasonous incident involving Jeong Yeo-rip (鄭汝立) in 1589 and attendant discrimination against Honam people in being appointed to government posts.

Jeong Yeo-rip studied under Yi Yi and entered the political world after having passed the Erudite Examination due to his proficiency in the Classics and history as well as the Hundred Schools of Thought. He belonged to the Seoin Faction but became the target of Seoin Faction's hatred after he attached himself to the Dong'in Faction which had power in those days. His action was a betrayal from the perspective of the Seoin Faction. He formed a secret association called the Association for Great Unity (大同契) when he gained popularity among Confucians in Jeonju, Jeolla Province, after moving there. He also gathered discontented monks, descendants of good families without government posts, and the middle class in Jeolla and Hwanghae Provinces. According to stories passed down, Jeong Yeo-rip created a prophecy about "the downfall of Yi and the rise of Jeong" and spread it; the truth of the story cannot be verified.

To capture the capital, Jeong Yeo-rip and his followers schemed to attack Seoul from the north and south and take over by stirring up revolts in Jeolla Province and Hwanghae Province during the winter of 1589. But Yi Chuk (李軸), Magistrate of Anak in Hwanghae

Province, found out about this and reported it. Thus started the oppression of the Dong'in Faction by the Seoin Faction. Jeong Yeo-rip fled to Juk Island (竹島) in Jinan-gun of Jeolla Province and committed suicide there. This oppression is referred to as the Major Criminal Case of the Year of Gichuk (己丑獄事). The person in charge of this criminal case was Jeong Cheol, who was living in exile in Damyang in Jeolla Province after losing the political struggle against the Dong'in Faction.

Jeong Cheol (鄭澈, pen name is Song Gang 松江, 1536-1593) was about the same age as Yi Yi; they studied together at the Dok-seodang after being selected to take a break from personal duties to do so. It was during this time that Yi Yi wrote *Catechism at Eastern Lake*. Jeong Cheol was born in Seoul and was an old friend of Myeongjong who later became king. Jeong Cheol was able to befriend the Myeongjong because his two sisters married into the royal family, but his eldest brother was calamitously affected by the Literati Purge of the Year of Eulsa in 1545. Jeong Cheol followed his father, Jeong Yu-chim (鄭惟沈), who wandered from one place of exile to another. They were able to settle down at the foothill of Seong Mountain (星山) in Changpyeong, Damyang-gun in Jeolla Province upon the determination of his father to settle there after receiving a pardon in 1551.

Jeong Cheol studied under Gi Dae-seung, patterned himself after Kim In-hu along with Yi Hwang at Sungkyunkwan, and passed the special course of the Erudite Examination at the top of his class in the 17th year of the reign of Myeongjong (1562). He was appointed to the post of Jipyeong (持平) of the Office of Inspector General and was close to Yi Yi and Seong Hon of the Seoin Faction. He was violent, liked alcohol, and had vehement confrontations with the Dong'in Faction to the point that he received advice from Seonjo and Yi Yi to stop drinking.

Gwandong byeolgok (關東別曲, Song of Gwandong), an ode to the scenery of Gwandong, is one of the masterpieces representing Jeong Cheol's *gasa* literature which he wrote after being appointed to the post of Governor of Gangwon Province in 1580.[2] He was appointed as Inspector General in 1584 but went to his hometown after being oppressed by the Dong'in Faction. Thereafter he wrote "Seongsan byeolgok" (星山別曲, Little Odes on Mount Star) such as "Samiingok" (思美人曲, Song of Thoughts on Beauty) and "Sok samiingok" (續思美人曲, Song of Thoughts on Beauty Again) to laud the scenery of Seong Mountain in the four years during his seclusion.

Jeong Cheol returned to the capital and became the leader of investigating the treasonous incident involving Jeong Yeo-rip of the Dong'in Faction in 1589; he was merciless in oppressing the Dong'in Faction. He was promoted to the post of Second State Councilor after handling this incident. The other two of the three state councilors were both of the Dong'in Faction, with Yi San-hae (李山海) as the Chief State Councilor and Yu Seong-nyong as the Third State Councilor.

But conversely, Jeong Cheol was put in a position where he was the target of immediate retaliation from the Dong'in Faction. The three state councilors agreed to support Gwanghae-gun (光海君) as the Crown Prince in 1591 due to the fact that Seonjo did not have a legitimate son by his queen.

While Yi San-hae and Yu Seong-nyong kept silent because they knew Seonjo favored Sinseong-gun (信城君), another son born of a concubine, only Jeong Cheol dared to speak frankly to the king about the necessity of selecting Gwanghae-gun as the Crown Prince. This incident was rumored to have been planned by Yi San-hae; Jeong Cheol incurred the wrath of Seonjo and was exiled again.

Because of the discord about an appropriate punishment for Jeong Cheol, the Dong'in Faction became divided into two factions: the Namin Faction centered around Wu Seong-jeon (禹性傳) and Yu Seong-nyong, and the Bugin Faction centered around Yi Bal (李潑). In comparison to the recommendation of the Namin Faction for

---

[2] *Gasa* literature was a form of vernacular narrative verse, usually without stanzaic division. (S. Lee)

banishment only, the Bugin Faction strongly pushed for execution. This was clearly indicative of the vicissitudes of the period of Gwanghae-gun, who ascended to the throne after Seonjo.

Jeong Cheol was pardoned at the outbreak of the Imjin War in 1592, and he passed away on Ganghwa Island in December of 1593 after completing his responsibility as ambassador of gratitude dispatched to Ming China. *Songgang gasa* (松江歌辭, Anthology of *Gasa* by Songgang) is a monumental collection of works of Korean literature written by Jeong Cheol that contains four *gasa* literature and 800 *sijo*.[3]

Miraculously, Yun Seon-do (尹善道, pen name is Gosan 孤山, 1587-1671), a second great *sijo* writer on a par with Jeong Cheol in the history of Korean literature, lived in the Honam district at the time, but there was no direct teacher-student relationship between the two. One was born 50 years before the other, and Yun Seon-do was a member of the Namin Faction that separated from the Dong'in Faction but was a political rival of Jeong Cheol of the Seoin Faction.

Yun Seon-do was on his way to Jeju Island to find serenity after being hurt by the party strife against the Seoin Faction, but instead settled on Bogil Island in Haenam-gun, Jeolla Province, because of the clement climate. There he wrote great representative works of *sijo* literature such as "Eobu sasisa" (漁父四時詞, Fishermen's Song of the Four Seasons), while soothing his heart that suffered from political strife.

Jeong Cheol and Yun Seon-do were literati who rusticated in the country after being defeated in political strife. They spent their exile in the Honam district, and thus Honam district became the birthplace for "literature written during rustication." It is fundamentally difficult for heart-tugging literature to emerge from the extremely anti-rhetoric custom of the learning of the Way as part of the study of Confucian Classics. There are many works that preach about the study of the principle of human nature or the learning of the Way by borrowing the form of Chinese poetry or *sijo* in the literary history

---

[3] *Sijo* is the most popular and mnemonic poetic form for vernacular verse, commonly consisting of three lines. (S. Lee)

of the Joseon period, but these by-products cannot touch the hearts of man.

It is said that "what is soft will take over what is strong." This is the wise saying of Emperor Gwang Wu-di who revived Later Han China after overthrowing Wang Mang of the state of Xin who overthrew Former Han. This is an abuse of the philosophy of principle which banished emotions.

Was there a spiritual climate in the Honam district that cultivated the *gasa* literature of Jeong Cheol or the *sijo* culture of Yun Seon-do which escaped the stiff ambience of the learning of the Way? *Chunhyangjeon* (The Story of Chunhyang) of which every Korean is aware, was also created in Namwon, Jeolla province. The love of Yi Mong-nyong and Seong Chun-hyang, *yangban* son of the Busa of Namwon and daughter of a *gisaeng*, that transcended the formidable wall was an immoral act in the eyes of the learning of the Way.[4] But it is certain that there was a spiritual climate that welcomed such a soft world of "emotions" in the Honam district.

---

[4] *Gisaeng* is a female entertainer and belongs to one of the lowest classes; as such, Chunhyang was at the mercy of the *yangban* class. (S. Lee)

16

Situation in East Asia Becomes Chaotic Again

Japan Attacks Joseon

As mentioned in Chapter 11, the Joseon dynasty sent envoys to Japan and began trading after signing an alliance with the third general of Ashikaga Yoshimitsu of the Muromachi Bakufu in 1404. Joseon stopped dispatching envoys to Japan during the frequent bouts of civil war and the period of disturbed public peace after the Onin Uprising in Japan in 1467. The last ambassador was sent to Japan in the 25th year of the reign of Sejong (1443). Japan, on the other hand, sent over 60 envoys and continued to send envoys until 1573 when Ashikaga Yoshimitsu, 15th and last general of Muromachi Bakufu, was banished by Oda Nobunaka.

Fighting without justification continued in Japan for another 100 years after the Onin Uprising. This period, which is known as the Sengoku period, saw shifting alliances among the Sengoku Japanese feudal lords. Joseon at this time had been immersed in a peaceful atmosphere for 200 years under the civilian government since the founding of the Joseon dynasty, despite the purges within the leading class and factional disputes between Dong'in and Seoin Factions.

Unification of the entirety of Japan by Toyotomi Hideyoshi in 1590 led to a one-sided dispatch of envoys to Joseon, which was a great opportunity to recover the normal alliance with a neighboring nation. The following sentence is contained in the sovereign's communiqué to Toyotomi Hideyoshi sent with a group of envoys with Hwang Yun-gil as Chief Envoy; Kim Seong-il as Vice Ambassador was dispatched to Japan in the same year.

I would hope for friendship between neighboring nations through giving speedy consideration to trust.

Toyotomi Hideyoshi, however, did not seem to know what "an alliance" between Joseon and Japan from the Muromachi period was. He misunderstood the group of Joseon envoys as an envoy of surrender to him, and in a corresponding communiqué he requested Joseon to guide his troops that were headed to invade Ming China. This gave the appearance that he mistook the Joseon kingdom as part of Japan's Sengoku.

After the envoy to Japan returned to Joseon, opinions between the Dong'in and Seoin Factions were in conflict on the possibility of invasion by Toyotomi Hideyoshi. In the meantime, Toyotomi began construction of Nagoya Castle as a supply base in the northern tip of Kyushu in September of 1591, and manpower and supplies for this were mobilized from all over Japan. Why did the literati of Joseon only focus on an armchair theory and not bother to gather information about Japan from Kitakyushu, which is just across the sea from the southern part of the Joseon peninsula? How preposterous!

The 1st Army of 18,000 men led by Gonishi Yukinaga landed in Busan on April 12, 1592 and was a completely unexpected attack from Joseon's perspective. This was followed by other landings, including a troop of 15,000 men led by Kato Kiyomasa. This is what was referred to as "the Imjin War" in Joseon and "Bunroku no eki."

What did Toyotomi Hideyoshi hope to gain by invading Joseon? He openly professed his desire "to conquer Tang China as well as the southern kingdoms." He suffered from great delusions of grandeur in that he requested Joseon to guide the invading Japanese troops headed for Ming China. It can be seen that the ultimate goal of his invasion was China, but his delusions of grandeur first suffered a setback in Joseon. On the 20th day after landing in Busan, Japanese troops entered Seoul on May 2. The 1st Army led by Gonishi Yukinaga marched north toward Pyeong'yang and reached it on June 16. Meanwhile, the 2nd Army of Kato Kiyomasa advanced into Hamgyeong Province in order to find the two princes (Imhae-gun and

Sunhwa-gun) who went there to gather loyal soldiers to fight for the king.

The king and his followers of literati deserted the public and fled, going all the way to Uiju, which is close to the border with Ming China, to request the assistance of Ming. The Secretary of the Board of Military Affairs of the Ming regime at the time was Shi Xing (石星). He authorized a rescue force despite the internal opposition within the Ming government.

The northward march of the Japanese troops stopped in Pyeong'yang before the Ming troops became seriously involved. One of the reasons was that supplies to the front line became difficult due to the anti-Japanese activities of righteous troops in various regions at the home front, and a second was that the maritime supplies from the coast of the Yellow Sea became unusable due to the naval activities led by General Yi Sun-shin (李舜臣) on the southern seashores.

Forty thousand Ming troops led by Commander-in-Chief Li Ru-song (李如松) recaptured Pyeong'yang with the cooperation of Joseon troops and launched a counteroffensive land warfare against Japanese forces. Li Ru-song was the son of Chief Commander Li Cheng-liang (李成梁) of Ming China who was stationed to suppress the Jurchens of Manchuria; father and son were both fierce generals of Joseon descent. Japanese troops were able to take a breather by succeeding in defending the office of official interpreter in Byeokje, but they were not able to turn the tide of defeat. In April of 1593, Japanese troops retreated from Seoul to the southeastern region of the peninsula one year after landing in Busan; there they built a bridgehead and began peace negotiations with Ming. Joseon of course opposed the peace negotiations.

As a result of long negotiations, Ming dispatched messengers, including Chief Ambassador Yang Fang-heng (楊方亨) and Vice Ambassador Shen Wei-jing (沈惟敬), to convey Ming Emperor's letter of appointment granting investiture that strictly stated, "Thou wilst be appointed as the king of Japan" in Osaka in January of 1596, but did not authorize tributary trade by separating "investiture" and "tribute." The Joseon envoy accompanied the Ming messengers, but Toyotomi Hideyoshi did not authorize an audience because he was angry over the Joseon king not sending a prince as prisoner.

Peace negotiations broke down, and Toyotomi Hideyoshi resent upwards of 147,000 troops in June 1597. The troops advanced into the rich grain districts of Jeolla and Chungcheong Provinces which were not targets of the first invasion. The dream of "Tang and southern kingdoms" was destroyed, and the single goal was to occupy four southern areas of Joseon — Gyeongsang Province, Jeolla Province, Chungcheong Province, and Gyeonggi Province. This is the Jeong'yu War (1597), which is called "Keicho no eki" in Japan.

Japanese troops occupied Namwon, Jeolla Province, on August 15, 1597, and advanced into Jiksan in Chungcheon Province on September 8, but they retreated into a castle they had built around the southern seashore. A stalemate ensued. Relics of Japanese castles between Ulsan in Gyeongsang Province to Suncheon in Jeolla Province still remain today. The five great families including Tokugawa Ieyasu and Maeda Toshiie hid the death of Toyotomi Hideyoshi and ordered the retreat of the Japanese troops from the Korean peninsula. In this way, Toyotomi Hideyoshi's delusions of grandeur were not realized in Asia and disappeared after leaving behind a great source of trouble for generations to come.

In 1600, Tokugawa Ieyasu defeated "the Army of the West" that had supported the Toyotomi clan in the Battle of Sekigahara. He made efforts to restore severed diplomatic relations with Joseon and Ming China. Some Joseon prisoners of war were returned at Tsushima in exchange for reestablishing diplomatic relations. With Yu Jeong (惟政) at the lead, a group of messengers sent to investigate Japan (探賊使) went to Fushimi Castle in Kyoto and held an audience with Tokugawa Ieyasu with the assistance of So Yoshitomo, lord of Tsushima. At the time, Tokugawa Ieyasu stated as below to Yu Jeong:

I was in Gwandong in the year of Imjin and did not have anything to do with this war. Joseon and I do not have any ill feelings
toward each other. I look for peaceful relations.

- Matsuura Masatada, "Mansongwongong," *Chronicles of
  Diplomatic Relations with Joseon* (朝鮮通交大紀), Vol. 4

From this perspective, Tokugawa Ieyasu did not send any troops to
the front lines in Joseon. This meeting became a turning point in
reestablishing diplomatic relations between the two parties in that
Tokugawa Ieyasu had supreme power in Japan, and his will to resume
diplomatic relations was confirmed. There were some ups and downs,
but Joseon dispatched an envoy in 1607 to Japan for the first time
since the war under the guise of responding to the courtesy of the
Japanese envoy and to return with the prisoners of war. The response
was to send a return communiqué to the first communiqué sent from
the Japanese government as well as to return with the Joseon prisoners of war who were taken to Japan during the war. This delegation
was dispatched three times to Japan in the transitional period of
resuming diplomatic relations immediately after the war. The name
of the delegation was changed to ambassador to Japan in 1636.

According to the Treaty of the Year of Giyu (己酉約條) in
1609, Japanese residences in Joseon were established in Busan, and
trade with Tsushima in Japan began. Japanese residences in Joseon
were first built in Port Dumo, but later moved to a better office that
was 110,000 *pyeong*, which is ten times the original size.[1] This was due
to the increase in volume of trade and travels to and from the two
nations because the Japanese residences in Joseon became central to
the diplomatic relations and commerce of the Tokugawa Bakufu.
Tsushima was put in charge of the Japanese residences in Joseon.

Joseon maintained a political relationship throughout the entire
period of Muromachi and Edo Bakufu except for approximately 30
years of Azuchi and Momoyama periods, including the seven years
of invasion by Toyotomi Hideyoshi.

---

[1] *Pyeong* is a unit of measure for land: 1 *pyeong* = 3.954 sq. yards. (S. Lee)

Joseon's diplomatic relationship with Japan in the first period continued until Ashikaga Yoshiakira, the last general of the Muromachi Bakufu, was banished by Oda Nobunaka in 1573 (see Ch. 11). But Joseon could not send an envoy to Japan because of the weak power base of Muromachi Bakufu after the Onin Uprising in 1467, and the abnormal relationship of Japanese envoys unilaterally visiting Joseon continued.

Even in the late Joseon period, diplomatic relations with the Edo Bakufu continued for around 260 years until the last Bakufu general Tokugawa Yoshinobu returned the sovereignty to the Meiji emperor in 1867. The reason is that Tokugawa Ieyasu, who became the Seii Daishogun in 1603, constructed the Bakuhan system that was like a rock based on achievements since the establishment of the Edo Bakufu to the second and third shoguns, Hidetada and Iemitsu. The relationship of "colleague" was changed to that of "ruler and vassal" under the Bakuhan system by executing ruthless territorial shifts and changes against the Sengoku warlords for three generations from the founding of Edo Bakufu in 1603 to when the third shogun Iemitsu passed away in 1651, which made it possible to sever revolts against superiors that resembled militarism of the Warring States period in Japan.

An envoy of Joseon were sent for the last time in 1811 to Tsushima bearing gifts when internal and external contradictions in the Edo Bakufu intensified as it entered the 19th century; but this did not mean that diplomatic relations between Japan and Joseon were severed until Tokugawa Yoshinobu returned the sovereignty in 1867. Dongnae-bu in Joseon and Tsushima in Japan continued to send messengers back and forth and to allow Japanese residents in Joseon to trade. From the perspective of the history of Joseon-Japan relations, Ashikaga Yoshimitsu and Tokugawa Ieyasu are memorable politicians in that the former cultivated diplomatic relations with Joseon in the stead of "Japanese invaders," and the latter revived diplomatic relations with Joseon which had been severed due to "Japan invasions."

Kang Hang Is the Loyal Su Wu of Today

It is not that Confucianism did not exist in Japan prior to the Edo period (1603-1867, also known as the Tokugawa period). Confucianism was transmitted from generation to generation among the learned families of the imperial court as a transformation of the *daigakuryo* (an institute for training officials of the central government) in the Heian period (794-1185). Moreover, Zen Buddhist monks who studied in Song China learned about the Cheng-Zhu School to protect Buddhism. And they were all exclusive — "learning handed down within the family" — and not open to the public.

Zen Buddhist monks who took off their monk's robe became Confucian scholars who emerged after studying Confucianism as a doctrine to spread Buddhism. Fujiwara Seika and Hayashi Razan were both Zen Buddhist monks who became Confucians.

Fujiwara Seika (1561-1619) established Confucianism in the Edo period; he was originally a Zen Buddhist monk of the Shokoku Temple in Myojuin, Kyoto. His name as a monk was Sunsujwa. Sujwa was the second highest rank next to the head priest of a Buddhist temple, followed by Seojang (secretary), Jangju (administrator of books), Jigaek (guide), Godu (treasurer), and Yokju (bathing assistant).[2] Tokugawa Ieyasu went straight to Kyoto after winning the Battle of Sekigahara in October of 1600 and commanded Fujiwara Seika to give a lecture on *Great Learning*. From then on, he wore clothes worn by Confucians instead of the clothes of a monk. That denoted his renunciation of the post of Sujwa. His disciple Hayashi Razan extolled this as "the origin of Confucianism in our kingdom."

The person who provided a strong motive to Fujiwara Seika to become independent as a Confucian was Kang Hang (姜沆, pen name is Su-eun 睡隱, 1567-1618). Kang Hang studied under Seong Hon, the famous Confucian of the 16th century, and passed the Erudite Examination in 1593. As a lieutenant of the Ministry of

---

[2] Seojang was in charge of writing letters, Jangju was in charge of maintaining books, Jigaek was in charge of guiding visitors, Godu was in charge of finance, and Yokju was in charge of assisting with bathing. (S. Lee)

Taxation during the Jeong'yu War, he was in charge of supplying military provisions for the troops of Joseon and Ming China protecting Namwon Castle. When he attempted to escape from Yeonggwang-gun with his family to Jeolla Province after losing the August 1597 battle of Namwon Castle, he was captured and became a prisoner of the navy led by Todo Takatora. He was first taken to Iye in Otsu Castle (today's Otsu City in Ehime Prefecture) and then to Fushimi in Kyoto, where he later met Fujiwara Seika.

Kang Hang returned to Joseon in May of 1600 with the cooperation of Fujiwara Seika and his students; he left behind a detailed record of the circumstances and experiences of Japan which he saw and heard in the form of *Ganyangnok* (看羊錄). In it he describes his meeting with Fujiwara Seika as follows:

> I have come in contact with Japanese monks from time to time in order to learn about the circumstances of the Japanese kingdom since I have come to the capital of Japan (Kyoto). There were some among them who understood characters (Chinese literature) and knew reason. Among them were Ian (given name is Yoshida Sojun, Sumino Kuraryoi's younger brother and medical officer of the Bakufu) and Lian (disciple of Yoshida Sojun) who visited sometimes to meet with me in my confinement. There was also Sunsujwa of Myojuin. He is a descendent of Fujiwara no Teika and teacher to Akamatsu Hiromichi, the Lord of Tajima. He is very bright, and there is not a classical document he has not read and mastered. There is not a place in Japan that will accept him due to his firm and stern personality. Tokugawa Ieyasu built a house in the Japanese capital and attempted to give 2,000 *seok* of rice annually after hearing of his outstanding talent.[3] Sunsujwa did not live there, nor did he accept the rice. He only associated with Kinoshita Katsutoshi (Lord of the Obama Castle) and Akamatsu Hiromichi.

> • "Jeokjung gyeonmunnok," *Ganyangnok*

---

[3] *Seok* is a unit of measure for grain. 1 *seok* is equivalent to approximately 5.12 bushels in the U.S. system. (S. Lee)

"Shun of the Myojuin" as mentioned in the excerpt above is of course Fujiwara Seiki's name as a monk. He was a strong scholar who lived in honorable poverty and refused the warm hospitality of Tokugawa Ieyasu. The financial sponsor who supported his Confucian studies was Akamatsu Hiromichi, lord of Taketa Castle in Tajima. Before becoming the lord of Taketa Castle, Akamatsu was the lord of Tatsuno Castle in Banshu. He was ordered by Tokugawa Ieyasu to commit *hara-kiri* after fighting on the side of "the Army of the West" in the Battle of Sekigahara.

Fujiwara Seika and Akamatsu performed the greatest deed in pioneering Confucianism in the Edo period. Fujiwara Seika was able to commission many Confucians including Kang Hang to copy the Four Books and Five Confucian Classics with the financial support of Akamatsu, and Seika added Japanese reading marks based on the new annotations by Zhu Xi to create *Bunsho tattokuroku* (四書五經倭訓). This could be considered the very first textbook of the Cheng-Zhu School in Japan.

Hayashi Razan (1583-1657) was a disciple of Fujiwara Seika and as such, was one of the "Four Heavenly Kings of Fujiwara." He was also a Zen Buddhist monk at Kenninji Temple, one of the five great Zen temples of Kyoto, before he became independent as a Confucian. He evaluated the significance of *Bunsho tattokuroku* with the reading marks as follows:

> The Learned in Confucianism in this kingdom have only read the interpretations of Han and Tang China and put Japanese reading marks on Chinese Confucian Classics from old. But they know less than one-tenth of the Cheng-Zhu texts. Thus there are few who know the study of the principle of human nature. Whereupon the master (Fujiwara Seika) recommended to Akamatsu [to take on this project], and Kang Hang and a number of others were commissioned to copy the Four Books and Five Confucian Classics. The master followed the interpretations of Cheng-Zhu, which is the version with Japanese reading marks. His service [to Japanese Confucianism] is considered great.

317

- "The Deeds of Master Seika,"
Collected Works of Hayashi Razan

Hayashi Razan was lecturer to four successive generations of Tokugawa generals from the second general Tokugawa Hidetada, third general Tokugawa Iemitsu, and fourth general Tokugawa Ietsuna since becoming a lecturer for Tokugawa Ieyasu at the recommendation of Fujiwara Seika in 1607. His uncle Ueno Shinobugaoka later became the head of Shoheiko to lead Confucianism in the Edo period. Japanese Confucianism had consisted of studying commentaries of Han and Tang China, but Fujiwara Seika was the starting point of new Cheng-Zhu School in the world of Confucianism in the Edo period.

A detailed report of what he had seen and heard was submitted to Seonjo by Kang Hang upon his return to Joseon in 1600, after which he concentrated on the education of the younger generation and writing while living in seclusion in Bulgap-myeon, Yeonggwang-gun in Jeolla Province. He was enshrined in Yonggyesa (龍溪祠), wherein hangs a tablet that the 19th king Sukjong personally inscribed with the words, "present-day Su Wu." Su Wu was a person from Han China who continued with Confucianism during his captivity with the Huns for 19 years before returning to China. The title of *Ganyangnok* also originated from this ancient history. In addition to *Ganyangnok*, manuscripts he had left were published as *Su-eunjip* (睡隱集) by a disciple named Yun Sun-geo.

Indecision of Gwanghae-gun

Disturbances in East Asia did not stop with the end of the Japanese invasion led by Toyotomi Hideyoshi. The disturbances continued with Ming China fighting against Later Jin and Qing in the northeastern region of China until Ming was destroyed in 1644.

Joseon was able to alleviate the threat from the southern region by recovering diplomatic relations with Japan in 1607, but it could not avoid being concerned about the confrontation between Ming and Qing. This influenced the history of thought in Joseon, the circumstances of which will be briefly reviewed below.

Seonjo fled to Uiju bordering Ming China in 1592 during the Imjin War and established not only a royal court in the temporary residence for the king in Uiju but also made a division of the royal court after appointing Gwanghae-gun as the Crown Prince. Actual sovereignty was handed over to the Crown Prince. Gwanghae-gun ascended to the throne in 1608 with the death of Seonjo. Gwanghae-gun did not have a posthumous epithet because he was dethroned by the coup d'état led by the Seoin Faction (King Injo's Restoration of Rectitude) who supported Injo in 1623. Only two kings, Yeonsan-gun and Gwanghae-gun, were dethroned in the 500 years of the history of the Joseon dynasty as mentioned before.

The reign of Gwanghae-gun (r. 1608-1623) was full of several difficult tasks, including the reorganization of the disorderly national system, reconstruction of the destroyed palace, revival of the economy, and the collection of scattered documents for publication. Anti-Ming nationalist power arose among the Jurchens to shake off the dominance of Ming while the Ming troops were concentrated in the northeastern regions during the seven-year war with Japan. The mainstay of this effort was Nuerhachi (or Nurhachi, 1559-1626) who later became the first founder of Qing China.

Joseon owed a debt of gratitude to Ming dynasty China for lending assistance during the Imjin War. In that sense, Joseon was being forced to make a difficult choice between Ming and the newly rising power of Qing. In fact, the new threat from the northern region was one of the causes of Joseon suppressing extreme anti-Japanese sentiments within the kingdom to facilitate the recovery of diplomatic relations with Tokugawa Bakufu.

Before the unification, the Jurchen tribes in Manchuria were divided into three great tribal groups: Jianzhou tribe from the upper reaches of Mudan River to the area of Baekdu Mountain shared a border with Joseon; Haixi tribe near Songhua River; and Yeren tribe from the lower reaches of Heilong River to the area of Yanhaizhou. Nuerhachi was the chieftain of the Jianzhou tribe.

Ming China had established a Nuergan Command Post from the period of Emperor Yongle to divide and rule the Jurchens indirectly. Tributary trade with Beijing was permitted by inspecting the royal letter issued by the emperor to each chieftain of the Nuergan Command Post at checkpoints along the border. The Jurchens exchanged expensive ginseng or marten pelts for daily necessities from China such as cloth or salt. This conciliatory policy was successful, because the exchange was very profitable for the chieftains.

The family name of Nuerhachi was Aixinjueluo (愛新覺羅 in Chinese characters). He began to emerge ahead of the many chieftains due to Ming general Li Cheng-liang, who was in charge of guarding Manchuria. Li Cheng-liang was of Joseon blood from Liaoning, and his son, Commander-in-Chief Li Ru-song of the Ming troops, was dispatched to Joseon during the Imjin War.

Manchuria had been Ming territory since the reign of Emperor Hongwu, but the real ruler of the Liaoning region outside the palisade (fence that denotes the border in the remote areas) from the Liaoning Plains to the Liaodong peninsula was Li Cheng-liang. Li Cheng-liang came to know Nuerhachi when Ming attacked Jianzhou and killed Nuerhachi's father and grandfather; they should not have been killed, because they were considered to be allies. Nuerhachi was given 30 royal letters and 30 heads of horses as compensation. Thereafter, Nuerhachi was in collusion with Li Cheng-liang and increased his private army with the profits gained from tributary trade. In other words, Li Cheng-liang nurtured Nuerhachi.

Ming's net around Nuerhachi intensified when Li Cheng-liang was dismissed from office in 1608. In resistance, Nuerhachi determined to become independent of Ming China and proclaimed the founding of Later Jin in 1616 in Xingjing to signify the continuation of Jin which had destroyed Northern Song of old. He ascended to the position of Khan. Thus, Nuerhachi as Taizu of Qing is like the reincarnation of Aguda of Jin China. He is extraordinary in that he advocated nationalism of the Jurchens, and his most representative deeds were the enactment of the Manchu script by writing down the Manchu language with Mongol script represented by phonetic signs, and the compilation of a historical document of the Jurchen tribes with the new Manchu script entitled *Old Chronicle of the Manchu* (滿文老檔, *Manwen laodang* in Ch.).

Manzhou (滿州) originated from Mañjuśrī (文殊師利, also known as Bodhisattva of Wisdom and Intellect, 文殊菩薩) of Tibetan Buddhism that was introduced from Mongolia. Huangtaiji (皇太极), second emperor of the Qing dynasty, changed the name of his tribe from Jurchen to Manzhou. The Jurchens considered Nuerhachi to be the reincarnation of the Bodhisattva of Wisdom and Intellect. Manzhou was historically a distasteful name to the Han people in China, but to the Manchurians it was a proud name that represented their ethnic identity.

Of course, Ming China could not neglect the emergence of Later Jin. Yang Hao (楊鎬), who fought in the Imjin War in March of 1619 as Military Commissioner of Ming troops consisting of 100,000 men, unfolded a siege plan to destroy Xingjing in one fell swoop.

Nuerhachi broke through the siege laid by Ming troops at Sarhu, east of Fushun, took over Shenyang and Liaoyang Castles with violent force, and advanced to the western region of Liaohe. The Battle of Sarhu was a skirmish that warned of the alternation of Ming and Qing.

Prior to attacking Xingjing, Shenzong (神宗, Emperor Wanli 萬歷, r. 1572-1620) sent a request to Gwanghae-gun for the dispatch of Joseon troops. Gwanghae-gun was hesitant to participate in a war which would turn the Later Jin into an enemy even before the postwar reconstruction over the "Japanese invasion" was completed. But Joseon owed a debt of gratitude to Ming China for sending reinforcements during the Imjin War. Gwanghae-gun stood in front of a forked road in that he was forced to choose between Qing or Ming, the former to justify protecting the national interest and the latter to repay the debt of gratitude.

Minister of Justice Kang Hong-nip (姜弘立) and Byeongsa of Pyeong'an Kim Gyeong-seo (金景瑞) were appointed as Commanding General and Lieutenant Commanding General, respectively; they were dispatched with a force of 13,000 men. Gwanghae-gun gave a secret instruction to Kang Hong-nip to observe the situation carefully before committing his troops to a particular course of action.

The Joseon forces which joined the Right Wing South Route Force of Ming forces led by Regional Commander Liu Ting (劉綎) surrendered to the Later Jin troops in the Battle of Sarhu, and Kang Hong-nip became a prisoner. Those [in Joseon] who were pro-Ming and anti-Qing viciously attacked Gwanghae-gun and Kang Hong-nip.

The Seoin Faction that proclaimed the great justification of pro-Ming and anti-Qing provoked a coup d'état supporting Injo in 1623 and ultimately gained power by banishing Gwanghae-gun. This was King Injo's Restoration of Rectitude. Dowager Queen Inmok (仁穆大妃, Seonjo's queen consort of the Kim clan) stated as follows in a message to denounce the sin of Gwanghae-gun for being an ingrate:

> Our kingdom has submitted to the Heavenly Court (Ming China) for close to 200 years; this relationship is that of ruler and vassal in terms of loyalty, and father and son in terms of grace. We cannot forget the debt owed in the year of Imjin for eternity. The preceding king (Seonjo) wholeheartedly served [Ming] during his reign of 40 years, and he never sat with his back against the west while alive. Gwanghae-gun forgot the grace [of Ming] and acted contrary to morality and arrived at peace with the savages by having two conflicting minds without fear of the decree of Heaven. By giving secret instruction to Kang Hong-nip to observe the situation carefully before committing his troops to a particular course of action in the year of *gimi* (1619), the entire [Joseon] force surrendered immediately.

The advent of the regime of the Seoin Faction that banished Gwanghae-gun by advocating pro-Ming and anti-Qing naturally gave rise to conflict with Later Jin (Qing).

King Injo's Restoration of Rectitude and the Manchu Invasion of 1627

Injo, who ascended to the throne through the coup d'état of the Seoin Faction, was the grandson of Seonjo. From the onset of his ascension to the throne in 1608, Gwanghae-gun was involved in factional disputes between the Daebuk Faction (大北派, Large Northern Faction) and the Sobuk Faction (小北派, Little Northern Faction) that branched out of the Bugin Faction. He was later banished by King Injo's Restoration of Rectitude. As a result, his unethical act derived from "killing of a sibling and incarceration of the mother" provided the Seoin Faction with the perfect excuse for denouncing him. The high-handed method used to establish militaristic power was similar to that used by the third king Taejong and seventh king Sejo.

Let us broadly reason out the process. There was no legitimate son to succeed Seonjo, and Gwanghae-gun was the second oldest son of a royal consort. There was an opinion that Imhae-gun, eldest son of a royal consort, was not suitable to succeed to the throne because he was a prisoner of Kato Kiyomasa's troops in the Imjin War, but he tenaciously held onto the hope of ascending to the throne. But Queen Inmok, another royal consort of Seonjo, gave birth to Prince Yeongchang (永昌大君) in 1606. Some of the members of the Bugin Faction (Sobuk Faction) requested that young Prince Yeongchang be the successor and that Queen Inmok act as regent.

In comparison to Prince Yeongchang who was only a child of three, Gwanghae-gun was a full-grown man of 33. Gwanghae-gun not only fought against the Japanese invasion in the Imjin War by leading the division of the royal court, but also had experience ruling the dynasty when Seonjo passed away in 1608. Naturally, the Daebuk Faction that supported Gwanghae-gun and the Sobuk Faction that supported Prince Yeongchang were sharply divided.

Genealogy of the Four Factions

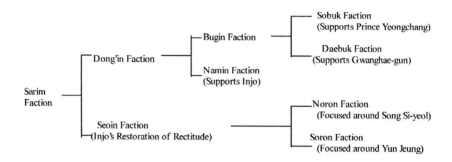

The Daebuk Faction including Jeong In-hong (鄭仁弘) and Yi I-cheom (李爾瞻) put Gwanghae-gun on the throne and simultaneously forced Imhae-gun to commit suicide, killed Prince Yeongchang, and incarcerated his mother the Dowager Queen Inmok in Gyeong'un Palace (慶運宮). This was the so-called "killing of a sibling and incarceration of the mother."

Jeong In-hong spearheaded the effort to eliminate the political rivals of Gwanghae-gun in order to put Gwanghae-gun on the throne. Jeong In-hong was a leader of the Daebuk Faction and eminent student of Jo Sik; he led troops [against the Japanese invaders] in the Imjin War in Hapcheon, Gyeongsang Province, by following the example of his schoolmate Gwak Jae-wu (郭再祐), who began the righteous struggle in Uiryeong, Gyeongsang Province. Jo Sik and Yi Hwang originally were the twin peaks of the Yeongnam School, but the Namin Faction which was directly under Yi Hwang and the Bugin Faction which was directly under Jo Sik came to a serious confrontation because Jeong In-hong criticized Yi Eon-jeok, who was admired by both Yi Hwang and Jo Sik ("Hoetoe byeoncheokso," 晦退辨斥疏). The Bugin Faction divided into the Daebuk Faction and Sobuk Faction based on the issue of whether to support Gwanghae-gun or not.

A clean sweep was to be made of rivals who challenged the sovereignty of a king in order to strengthen this sovereignty. Killing a sibling and incarcerating the mother was one way to solidify sovereignty. But Kim Ryu (金鎏) and Yi Gwi (李貴) of the Seoin Faction who vigilantly watched for a chance for the throne justified a coup d'état with the pro-Ming and anti-Qing doctrine by calling Gwang-hae-gun to account for killing a sibling and incarcerating the mother.

The Daebuk Faction went through a purge due to King Injo's Restoration of Rectitude by the Seoin Faction, and the Sobuk Faction that supported Prince Yeongchang experienced a purge by the Daebuk Faction before that. Thus both the Sobuk and the Daebuk Factions which branched out from the Bugin Faction suffered a downfall. Political power now lay in the hands of the Seoin Faction who instigated the restoration of rectitude, and Namin Faction joined this political structure.

Gwanghae-gun was first banished to Ganghwa Island after King Injo's Restoration of Rectitude, but he was moved to Jeju Island in 1636 to prevent any contact with Qing China during the Manchu invasion of Korea in 1636. His life of vicissitudes ended there in 1641 at the age of 67. The Bugin Faction was completely destroyed, since the Sarim Faction divided into Dong'in Faction and Seoin Faction during the reign of Seonjo, and the Namin Faction united with the Seoin Faction to support Injo.

Nuerhachi did not have any reason originally to be antagonistic toward Joseon. His main goal was to unite the Manchu tribes and become independent of Ming China. However, the Seoin Faction ended up provoking the Manchus by loudly advocating "value Ming and devalue Qing." Not only that, the Seoin Faction administration continued to provide supplies and support to Mao Wenlong (毛文龍), a Ming general in charge of the Liaodong region, when he established a military command post of Ming China called Donggangjin on Ga Island (椵島) in Cheolsan (鐵山), Pyeong'an Province. He executed harassing tactics from the rear toward the Liaoning region in 1621 after the Later Jin forces took over Shenyang and Liaoyang Castles; he was considered "the general from the dynasty of the son of Heaven."

Thus Later Jin forces could not leave the Seoin Faction administration of Joseon nor Ming General Mao Wenlong alone in order to put its strategy about mainland China into action. The two "Manchu invasions" in 1627 and 1636 can only be said to have been incurred by the Seoin Faction administration.

Taizong Huangtaiji (r. 1626-1643) became the Khan after Taizu Nuerhachi died in 1626. He gave a force of 30,000 men to Amin (阿敏) to attack Joseon in January of 1627. This is the Manchu invasion of 1627. The Jin cavalry crossed the Amnok River when it was frozen, destroyed the forces of Joseon and Mao Wenlong in Pyeong'an Province, and reached Pyeong Mountain of Hwanghae Province. Mao Wenlong was able to avoid any calamity by hiding on an island, but his troops were decimated in Cheolsan, Seoncheon, and like places in Pyeong'an Province.

Injo had fled to Ganghwa Island and now sent a request for peace to Amin, and the Later Jin force retreated only after a pact of brotherhood between the two kingdoms was signed. The role of Kang Hong-nip was instrumental in achieving reconciliation under such a magnanimous condition by returning to Joseon with the Later Jin forces and becoming active in arbitrating the relationship with the Joseon government. But a debate raged within Joseon as to whether he was a loyal vassal or a traitorous vassal; he was imprisoned after being stripped of all offices and titles because he was charged for being a traitor by those who loudly advocated reverence toward Ming and exclusion of Qing. He was an important personage in maintaining brotherly relations with Later Jin.

The reaction of the Seoin Faction toward Later Jin was not amicable after the Manchu invasion of 1627. Taizong Huangtaiji changed the name of Later Jin to Great Qing (大淸) and became emperor with the support of the representatives from the Manchu, Mongol, and Han tribes in Shenyang (Mukden in Manchu) in 1636. This was a proclamation by Qing China that it was a dynasty of peaceful harmony among the three tribes with the Manchu tribe as their leader.

Injo of Joseon did not dispatch a congratulatory messenger to the brother kingdom of Qing when Taizong became emperor. In response, Taizong of Qing China sent the Dragon Bone Brigade and the Horse Brigade to request Joseon to behave with the protocol of a vassal state. Injo ignored this request and did not even meet with the

Qing envoy. No matter what internal conditions were like [in Joseon], this was a clear challenge to Qing China.

The Manchu invasion of Korea started in 1636 when Taizong of Qing personally commanded a force of 100,000 men with the Horse Brigade of 4,000 men leading in front and invaded [Joseon] for the second time. The royal family and the families of vassals fled to Ganghwa Island in the midst of this great confusion, but the king and his vassals were besieged in Namhan Mountain Fortress when they fled there because the road to Ganghwa Island was blocked. There were 120,000 people defending the castle with enough rations to last for 50 days only, and loyal soldiers did not rally to fight on behalf of the king. The Qing force camped next to a stream below the castle and did not even attempt to initiate a decisive battle. They waited for the ripe persimmon to drop from the tree, and they would go only so far as to shake the tree sometimes, i.e., the Qing force had only to wait for food to be depleted. On top of this, Ganghwa Island fell [into the hands of Qing troops], and the royal family and the families of vassals who fled there became prisoners.

The anti-reconciliation group continued to overpower the pro-reconciliation group within the Namhan Mountain Fortress even amidst the hopeless siege; representative of the anti-reconciliation group was Minister of Rites Kim Sang-heon (金尚憲, pen name is Cheong-eum 清陰, 1570-1652). But the anti-reconciliation group only voiced their justification of revering Ming and denouncing Qing; it did not have any specific counterplan to resist the invasion for the 10 years since the first Manchu invasion. This may be called a lackadaisical mentality.

According to *Byeongjarok* (丙子錄, Record of the Year of Byeongja) by Na Man-gap (羅萬甲), the ambience [within Namhan Mountain Fortress] was such that only those with a great deal of courage could advocate reconciliation during the siege.

> In general, people could not voice other opinions, because discussions in these times viewed anti-reconciliation as a noble sentiment, but appeasing barbarians as part of a reconciliation plan as a disgraceful idea.

Minister of Personnel Choe Myeong-gil (崔鳴吉, pen name is Jicheon 遲川, 1586-1647), one of the meritorious vassals of King Injo's Restoration of Rectitude, was one of the advocates of reconciliation despite it being abusively called a "disgraceful idea." After 45 days of being under a siege, Injo ran out of schemes and ultimately had to show proper protocol of a vassal by kneeling thrice and bowing nine times in front of Taizong of Qing China according to the advocates of reconciliation. This occurred in January of 1637 in Samjeondo on the outskirts of Seoul. He suffered this indignity due to being caught up in useless justification.

The conditions set by the Qing dynasty for peace negotiations with Joseon were Joseon's severance of relations with Ming, Joseon observing the protocol of a vassal state to Qing, sending two Joseon princes as hostages, dispatching Joseon troops as reinforcement in the war against Ming, and sending annual tributes. Crown Prince Sohyeon (昭顯世子) and Prince Bongnim (鳳林大君) were taken to Shenyang as a result of the peace negotiation, but Injo was fortunately exempted from being taken. The spirit of the kingdom was maintained due to the resolute efforts of the advocates of reconciliation. In this sense, Choe Myeong-gil must be considered the foremost meritorious vassal because he led those who advocated reconciliation. The intention of Qing was to enforce Joseon to serve Qing with proper protocol of a smaller nation toward a greater nation, not to dominate Joseon.

Confucianists of Joseon traditionally felt righteous indignation due to sorrow and mortification because they had to serve the barbaric Qing; they lauded the anti-reconciliation group that advocated reverence of Ming and exclusion of Qing without any prospects for victory. When the core of the matter is examined, the anti-reconciliation group was not opposed to serving Qing itself; it was nothing more than racial prejudice that called serving Ming of the Han tribe noble, but serving Qing of the Manchu tribe disgraceful.

Exemplar of Korean Medicine, a Classic in Oriental Medicine

Exemplar of Korean Medicine was completed by Heo Jun (許浚, 1539-1615), one who had passed Miscellaneous Examination and was not involved in the party disputes; this provided a ray of sunshine during the dark period when civilian officials of the Joseon dynasty were preoccupied with party disputes. The lives of the people were wretched, with rampant spreading of disease throughout the kingdom during the seven years of the Imjin War. Seonjo commanded the court physician Yang Ye-su (楊禮壽, 1530-1600) to compile medical documents; one of the compilation committee members was Heo Jun, a court medical officer. But the compilation project was stopped and the committee members dispersed during the Jeong'yu War. Heo Jun, however, privately continued the compilation task, and completed the compilation of all 25 volumes of *Exemplar of Korean Medicine* in the second year of the reign of Gwanghae-gun (1610). Gwanghae-gun was greatly pleased and commanded immediate printing of this book; it was published three years later.

Heo Jun systematized the book according to the climes of Joseon and the constitution of the people by consulting massive Chinese medical documents. He organized the contents of medical documents such as *Hyangyak jibseongbang* (鄕藥集成方, Compilation of Native Korean Prescriptions) and *Uibang yuchwi* (醫方類聚, classified Collection of Medical Prescriptions), which were completed in the reign of Sejong in early Joseon dynasty as well as other medical documents. This book was considered an encyclopedia for oriental and herbal medicine, and it is still valued as a classic in oriental medicine. *Exemplar of Korean Medicine* was reprinted and distributed in China in 1763 and 1890 as well as in Japan in 1724 and 1799.

The structure of the book consists of six volumes on internal medicine, four volumes on external medicine, 11 volumes on gynecology, pediatrics, and miscellaneous illnesses, three volumes on liquid medicine, and one volume on acupuncture and *moxa* (the application of heat to certain points of the body).

Moreover, Heo Jun wrote other medical books, including *Eonhae gugeupbang* (諺解救急方, Emergency Prescriptions in Vernacular Korean) and *Eonhae taesan jibyo* (諺解胎産集要, Collection of Essentials of Childbirth in Vernacular Korean), in vernacular Korean to make the art of healing more widespread among the people.

Heo Jun followed as court physician to the king when Seonjo fled to Uiju. Seonjo conferred upon him the title of Yangpyeong-gun (陽平君) and the rank of Sungnok Daebu (崇祿大夫, Jong 1-*pum*) as compensation for his meritorious services rendered in the days of refugee life. But that was canceled because the officials of the Offices of Inspector General and Censor General of the Sarim Faction raised a commotion about the title and rank not being suitable for one from a class of middle people who had passed Miscellaneous Examination. Gwanghae-gun reinstated it after Seonjo had passed away.

As explained above, the Hungu Faction combined the study of Confucian Classics and practical learning as learning of practical statecraft before the emergence of the Sarim Faction in the political world of central government. The Sarim Faction which emerged to confront the Hungu Faction distinguished between the study of Confucian Classics and practical learning, however, and cemented the study of Confucian Classics as the learning for high-ranking "scholarly class" and practical learning as the learning for low-ranking "miscellaneous class." Emphasis on the study of Confucian Classics by the Sarim Faction that participated in the decision-making of national policies was a great misdeed in the academic history of Korea.

The Silhak School formed in the 18th century through criticism of the Sarim Faction's put-down of "impractical learning" that was far from reality. One of those was Bak Ji-won (朴趾源, pen name is Yeonam 燕巖, 1737-1805) who criticized the learning of the scholarly class because they only honored rhetorical flourishes without paying attention to the [national] economy and debated over nature and the Heavenly mandate without any political policy.

330

A scholar's studies in practice include the principles of agriculture, manufacturing, and trade. The three occupations must await the research of scholars before they should be realized. There must be professionals who investigate and are familiar with and can quickly act in agriculture, commerce, and manufacturing. Who should they be if not scholars? It is my humble thinking that the error of [the scholar] not participating in agriculture, manufacturing, and commerce in later generations was due to the error of not studying practical learning.

> • "Gwanong socho," (課農小抄,
> Selections of Advice for Agriculture),
> *Yeonamjip* (燕巖集, Collected Works of Yeonam)

As mentioned before, the Sarim Faction advocated the Learning of Master Zhu as the only scholarship. The Learning of Master Zhu was originally a scholarship that included ontology (the doctrine of the principle and material force), the doctrine on ethics (nature is the principle), bibliographical study (annotations of the Four Books and Five Confucian Classics), and theory on social policy. The Joseon Confucians who belonged to the Sarim Faction diminished the Learning of Master Zhu as if Confucianism were the study of the principle of human nature and created a trend of "supporting those of the same clique and excluding others" from one side of the debate on the study of the principle of human nature. Schools and factions divided according to whether the scholar took the position of the principle as the principal or material force as the principal in the debate on the study of the principle of human nature.

As Bak Ji-won appropriately pointed out, the fundamental cause that made Joseon society so poor was the tide of disdaining the practical learning that was the scholarship needed for vitalizing the profession of the farmers, artisans, and merchants. Wasting a million breaths in debating the study of the principle of human nature could not save the common people from poverty. Scholars wasting breath in useless debates constituted abandonment of social responsibility. Thus the Silhak School criticized such study as impractical learning. Miscellaneous learning to become medical official, translation official, judicial official, astronomy official, painting official, or official in charge of expenses and foodstuff for the Japanese residents ultimately became extremely exclusive hereditary learning for the middle class, which in turn obstructed the development of the middle class.

Compilation of past generations of veritable records on Joseon kings was described in Chapter 12. Veritable records were records of the life of the king compiled after his death. Veritable records on Yeonsan-gun and Gwanghae-gun, who were dethroned due to restoration of rectitude, however, were recorded as *Life of Yeonsan-gun* and *Life of Gwanghae-gun* in the 500-year history of the Joseon dynasty. Neither could be impartial, because both were compiled from an opposing factional viewpoint of the vassals who initiated the restoration of rectitude.

Three drafts were typically made in veritable records: first, second, and final. The general rule was to erase the rice paper used in creating the first and second drafts of veritable records for recycling when the final version was completed, so that they were not passed onto future generations. But in addition to the final draft of *Life of Gwanghae-gun* preserved by the Archive of Jeongjok Mountain Castle on Ganghwa Island and Archive on Jeongjok Mountain in Muju, Jeolla Province, a second draft was preserved by the Archive on Taebaek Mountain in Gyeongsang Province. Moreover, the quantity of the second draft is twice that of the final draft, which speaks to the revision process the second draft went through. In short, the final draft seems to be a condensed version of the second draft.

Those who instigated King Injo's Restoration of Rectitude that had dethroned Gwanghae-gun were of the Seoin Faction. The immoral and traitorous acts of Gwanghae-gun, such as killing his kin in the process of ascending to the throne and his betrayal of Ming China, were especially emphasized in *Life of Gwanghae-gun,* a reflection of the position of the Seoin Faction.

Compilation of veritable records of the reign of Gwanghae-gun from February 1608 to March 1623 began in 1624 and was completed 10 years later with some confusion in the process. The king had to flee to Gongju immediately after the restoration of rectitude because Yi Gwal (李适), one of the meritorious military officials of

King Injo's Restoration of Rectitude, initiated an uprising; he again fled to Ganghwa Island in 1627 due to the Manchu invasion. Therefore many of the daily records written by the royal chronicler of the king on Gwanghae-gun were lost.

Whatever the case may be, the fact that the second draft remains is an anomaly in compiling veritable records, but fortunate in that some of the processes of changes and corrections between the second and final drafts can be seen. The happenstance of the surviving two drafts provides important material in knowing another aspect of the compilation process.

From Ming to Qing

The Manchu tribe rose to power rapidly in the northeastern region of China while Ming sent reinforcement forces to Joseon during the invasion of Joseon in 1592 by Toyotomi Hideyoshi and the struggle between Ming and Qing of China continued until 1644. This was the so-called period of chaos in East Asia.

Emperor Wanli, Shenzong, of Ming China ascended to the throne at the age of nine and ruled for 48 years. A hint of restoration appeared in the Ming dynasty where the ambience of decline prevailed through political and financial reform in the first 10 years with the assistance of Premier Great Scholar Zhang Ju-zheng (張居正, 1525-1582). Zhang Ju-zheng, who was sometimes called the prime minister with an iron arm, oppressed irresponsible public opinions that criticized the reform of the central government and closed academies from whence these opinions originated. His death invoked the continuation of anarchy and endless factional disputes due to the resurrection of oppressed public opinions. He in his lifetime created *Diagram of Emperors* (帝鑑圖說) for the young emperor in order to teach the ways of sages, but Emperor Wanli became less wise and was moved by public censure to divest his teacher of office and title as well as confiscate his assets.

Xizong (憙宗, r. 1620-1627, Emperor Tianqi 天啓) who followed Emperor Wanli was the most foolish ruler of the Ming dynasty.

He left all political decisions up to a great scoundrel of a eunuch by the name of Wei Zhongxian (魏忠賢) during the seven years of his rule and he himself focused on being a carpenter. He suffered from a dislike of politics because he was tired of factional disputes. Wei Zhongxian committed suicide when the voices denouncing him grew stronger, and his own partisans were eradicated after Yizong (毅宗, r. 1627-1644), last emperor Chongzhen (崇禎帝) of Ming, ascended to the throne in 1627.

General Mao Wenlong of Ming China settled in Gado of Pyeong'an Province in Joseon; he was a faithful vassal of Wei Zhongxian. He accumulated wealth through smuggling between Joseon and China while using bribery to maintain his position. He defended Ningyuan Castle outside Shanhai with all his might after he lost his supporter, but was beheaded by the courageous general Yuan Chonghuan (袁崇煥), who had prevented Later Jin forces from invading China.

Nuerhachi passed away in 1626, and Huangtaiji, who replaced him, died in 1643. The six-year-old Emperor Shunzhi (順治帝, r. 1643-1661) ascended to the throne; his uncle Dorgon (多爾袞) was regent to the young ruler.

The Ming dynasty collapsed from within in the end. Bandits ran rampant everywhere in the late Ming period, of which a group led by Li Zi-cheng (李自成) became prominent. Li Zi-cheng used to work at a stable, but he was different from other bandits in that he advocated revolutionary slogans by inducing literati to join him. Eunuchs in collusion with the forces of Li opened the outer gates of the imperial palace in Beijing when the forces of Li Zi-cheng laid siege in March 1644, and Li Zi-cheng marched to Tiananmen at once. Civilian and military officials of Ming China knelt in front of him. Emperor Chongzhen hung himself on Prospect Hill (also known as Longevity Mountain) north of the Forbidden City. The only other person who followed the emperor in death was eunuch Wang Cheng-en (王承恩).

Wu San-gui (吳三桂) deterred the Eight Banners of Manchu by protecting impregnable Shanhai with the special forces of Ming at the time of Li Zi-cheng's march into Beijing. Wu sent a request for reinforcements to Dorgon after hearing of Li Zi-cheng's advance into Beijing and retreated to Beijing. The Qing forces not only entered Shanhai without a fight, but the troops with Wu San-gui in the lead entered Beijing after destroying the forces of Li Zi-cheng.

Dorgon commanded the populace of Beijing to observe a three-day mourning period for Emperor Chongzhen, who met his solitary death after being chased by the Li followers, and built an imperial tomb for the burial of the emperor with full propriety. This was an impudent attempt to garner popular sentiment, but the relationship between the Manchu tribe and the Han Chinese was that of the conqueror and the conquered. Representative of this was the ordinance to shave the traditionally braided and tied hair of Han Chinese men to look like men of the traditional Manchu tribe. Submission or resistance to the Qing dynasty was discerned through how the hair was worn; resisters were ruthlessly oppressed. This was a nationalistic enforcement enacted by the conqueror against the conquered.

In September of 1644, Emperor Shunzhi moved from Shenyang to Beijing, where Dorgon welcomed him. Crown Prince Sohyeon also moved to Beijing from Shenyang at this time, whereupon he became acquainted for a short time with a Jesuit missionary by the name of Adam Schall von Bell.

Thus the Ming dynasty which had existed for 280 years came to an end, and the Qing period began. The protagonist of the great drama from the march of Li Zi-cheng into Beijing in March to the fall of Ming in September of 1644 was Dorgon. The continuation of Nuerhachi → Huangtaiji → Dorgon provided great leadership. The scheme of "eliminating barbarians with barbarians" was a conventional method utilized by past Chinese dynasties. Dorgon turned this around to conquer China by using "Han Chinese to control Han Chinese," achieving the miracle of the minority Manchu tribe dominating the majority population of Han Chinese.

The Yuan dynasty founded by the Mongols in the past had dominated Han Chinese with the assistance of Islamic Turks and Iranians as financial officials. In comparison, the Qing dynasty founded by the Manchus overthrew the Ming Chinese through the collaboration of the Han Chinese and was able to maintain dominance over the Han Chinese. This was the big difference between Yuan and Qing and therein contained the secret of Qing with a Manchu population of 500,000-600,000 (of which grown men numbered 150,000) ruling two hundred million Han Chinese.

Dorgon played an important role in ruling Qing China before passing away at the young age of 39 in 1650, but he was surrounded by a whirlpool of dark and shady jealousy. Suksaha, who held a grudge against Dorgon, falsely told Emperor Shunzhi of Dorgon's scheme to take over the throne. Dorgon would not have welcomed Emperor Shunzhi into Beijing if he had had such aspirations. But Emperor Shunzhi believed this false accusation, and assets belonging to Dorgon were confiscated and his vassals were banished from the royal court. It was very similar to Shenzong's behavior toward Zhang Ju-zheng, the teacher who was like a parent.

What was to happen to Manchuria after the capital of Qing was moved from Shenyang to Beijing? How was the cradle of this civilization with the natural resources of forests and hunting grounds in Manchuria to be preserved? The forest was a great source of income for the Manchus since Taizu Nuerhachi. It was a treasure-house of both high-quality fur like marten and valuable ginseng. This issue remained a big problem for over a hundred years for four generations of rulers from Emperor Shunzhi to Emperor Yongzheng (雍正帝) to Emperor Qianlong (乾隆帝).

The three eastern provinces of Shenyang, Jilin, and Heilong River were established in Manchuria to function separately from mainland China, and a general was appointed to each province to directly administer it as a military zone. Manchuria was designated as "off-limits" in the reign of Emperor Qianlong to prevent the migration of agricultural people of Han China and Joseon. The greatest threat to the Manchus was the invasion of farming people who used spades and hoes to drastically alter land from forests and hunting grounds to farmsteads.

The Han Chinese were agricultural people who built the Great Wall of China and thought of the Mongol and Tungus tribes as savages. Joseon Confucians also followed this thinking, although Chinese considered Joseon people to be "eastern barbarians." But these agricultural people were fearful destroyers of nature who could destroy the foundation of the Manchu life from the roots by transforming great forests into agricultural land. Indeed, the three eastern provinces where the Manchu tribe originated were destroyed piecemeal by migrant farmers from Hebei and Shandong of China and the Korean peninsula in the 19th century so that the Manchus had nowhere to go to in 1912 when the Qing dynasty fell. This was a big contrast to the Mongols who returned to the northern plains when the Yuan dynasty fell.

17

Is Sino-Centrism Truly Justified?

Crown Prince Sohyeon and Adam Schall

Crown Prince Sohyeon (1612-1645) was taken as hostage to Shenyang in December of 1636. Accompanying him were his wife of the Kang family, his younger brother Prince Bong-nim, and 300-some people. New living quarters were erected for them. Qing China did not think of Crown Prince Sohyeon as just a hostage but as the successor to the throne. There were 13 conditions for peace in the Manchu invasion of 1636, and Crown Prince Sohyeon was a guarantee for those conditions being met. Qing China used him as a window through which all demands to the Joseon government were made.

The regime of Injo and the Seoin Faction in Joseon swore fealty to Qing and observed the protocol of a subject but adhered firmly to the basic view of pro-Ming and anti-Qing while internally resisting the disgrace of being under Qing. Thus, conditions for peace with Qing were not faithfully carried out. Crown Prince Sohyeon was called to account for this. He was under much anxiety day and night in order to prevent the relationship between the two kingdoms from worsening.

Demands for military supplies were great because strong young Manchu men were all mobilized for war, but the demand for Joseon forces to be mobilized to participate in a war to conquer Ming was truly a difficult issue due to the fact that the Joseon government, which revered Ming, would not carry out the demand faithfully.

Crown Prince Sohyeon and Crown Princess Kang went hunting, used bribery, and held banquets for high-level officials or commanders of the Qing dynasty in order to avoid conflict between the two kingdoms. A great deal of money that could be used freely was needed for the upkeep of living quarters. To support this need, Joseon prisoners of war taken to Qing by the Qing forces were gathered, and they grew food from cultivated land as well as traded with merchants from Qing and Joseon to the extent that a market formed in front of the living quarters.

Injo installed a eunuch attendant in the living quarters of the Crown Prince and his wife so that every move could be closely watched for secret reporting. Injo and the Seoin Faction regime bitterly slandered the behavior of the Crown Prince by stating that the successor to the throne could not express his submissiveness to Qing nor hunt with the barbarians or go into trade. But another viewpoint, the Crown Prince did what he did to prevent a dispute with Qing because he was the Crown Prince.

Crown Prince Sohyeon accompanied Emperor Shunzhi from Shenyang to Beijing in September 1644 due to the dynastic transition from Ming to Qing. For 70 days thereafter while living in Wenyuan Pavilion within the compounds of the Forbidden City, he came to know Adam Schall (Johann Adam Schall von Bell with a Chinese name of Tang Ruo-wang 湯若望, 1591-1666) who lived within the gates of Xuanwu.

Adam Schall was a German-born Jesuit missionary who was knowledgeable about technologically advanced western science. He came to China in 1622 and was instrumental in compiling *Eternal Calendar of Emperor Chongzhen* (崇禎曆書, *Chongzhen lishu* in Ch.) containing western astronomy and mathematics carried out under the supervision of Xu Guang-qi (徐光啓) toward the end of Ming from 1632 to 1634. The Current Standard Calendar which was used in the Qing dynasty as of 1645 and in Joseon as well as of 1653 was created by Adam Schall at the request of Dorgon.

Compilation of *Eternal Calendar of Emperor Chongzhen*, which was the foundation for the Current Standard Calendar, was a huge project realized through the proposal and supervision of Xu Guang-qi at the end of the Ming dynasty, but the fact that the project was continued into the Qing dynasty was solely due to the resoluteness of Dorgon. Dorgon entrusted Schall with the seal of the new Imperial Observatory in Beijing which combined the former Imperial Observatory in Beijing and the Western Calendar Office established by Xu Guang-qi; moreover, Adam Schall was appointed head of the Imperial Astronomy Bureau.

According to *Book of Documents*, the first responsibility of a sovereign since the days of Yao and Shun was to "demand labor of [the people] only at the proper season." The office that was in charge of demanding labor of the people was the Imperial Observatory in Beijing in China and the Office for Observance of Natural Phenomena in Joseon. The very act of entrusting the seal of the Imperial Observatory in Beijing to Adam Schall, a westerner and a Jesuit missionary at that, was in itself unthinkable to apologists of Sinocentrism; the extreme rational thinking of Dorgon can be seen from this. The significance of Crown Prince Sohyeon having contact with Adam Schall and forging a link with westerners was immeasurable.

Adam Schall gave not only an icon of God but also many documents on astronomy translated into Chinese along with astronomical instruments. Below is a letter written by Crown Prince Sohyeon as a token of his appreciation for the gifts:

I am deeply touched and appreciative of the gifts of an icon of God, astronomical instruments, and documents on astronomy you presented to me previously; they were not expected. I skimmed over two or three books to learn that they contain lofty doctrines on spiritual cultivation and cultivation of moral characters. These can shed light of knowledge, as they are unknown enough to almost be called darkness in my native kingdom. I felt a chill go through me because not only will the icon of God bring peace to the minds of those who see it hanging on the wall, but also cleanse the dirt from the secular world. I was not aware of the existence of the astronomical instruments and documents; thus I am elated and at the same time wondering if I am dreaming that they are in my possession. It's not that similar items do not exist in my kingdom; but [the ones in my kingdom] do not seem to be accurate in calculating the movements of celestial bodies for several hundred years, and false calculations are not viewed with suspicion. I am so elated to receive such valuable items. I will not only use them in the royal court when I return home, but will make the knowledge into books and disperse them among learned people. Our desert land will be graced with transformation into a sanctuary of learning in the near future, and our people will thank the European science.

- *History of Christianity in Joseon* (朝鮮西教史) by Yamaguchi Masayuki, pp. 41-43 (original text in Latin)

Crown Prince Sohyeon, however, returned the icon of God with respectfulness by stating that the sanctity of the item might be considered profane, as the Joseon public might consider Christianity a "heretic religion." Attention here should be paid to the sentence on the successor to the throne asserting his desire to make the astronomical instruments and documents into books at court and dispersing them to learned people when he returned home. The contents of western documents translated into Chinese that were transmitted by Crown Prince Sohyeon, however, were not recorded in the historical documents in Joseon. Why is that?

Injo did not attempt to hide his open loathing of Crown Prince Sohyeon when the latter returned to Joseon in 1645 after eight years of living as a hostage. Previously, the Crown Prince attempted to return with Crown Princess Kang so she could mourn the death of her father, Third State Councilor Kang Seok-gi (姜碩期). But Injo refused to authorize the return of Crown Princess Kang to attend the memorial for her father. Injo feared that the Crown Prince was attempting to steal the throne with the support of Qing, and the Seoin Faction was afraid of revenge from its enemies because they led King Injo's Restoration of Rectitude.

The Crown Prince returned to Joseon in January 1645 but died of a mysterious illness two months afterwards. This event is recorded as follows in *Veritable Records of King Injo*:

The Crown Prince fell ill a short period after he moved east and passed away a few days later. His entire body turned black and his lifeblood seeped out of seven places in his body.

> • June in the 23rd year of the reign of Injo,
> *Veritable Records of King Injo*

All vassals requested to try Yi Hyeong-ik (李馨益), the medical official in charge of Crown Prince Sohyeon, to find out the cause of death, but Injo firmly refused. This was clearly poisoning when viewed through the symptoms of illness. Moreover, the rite of placing the corpse of the Crown Prince in a coffin and the burial ritual were all rushed summarily with only a few close followers authorized to participate. Prince Bongnim was appointed Crown Prince immediately thereafter. Many vassals opposed this because the oldest legitimate son must succeed to the throne, and next in line was the oldest legitimate grandson according to the regulation on ascension to the throne.

Prince Bongnim became Hyojong (孝宗, r. 1649-1659) after ascending to the throne, thanks to the determination of Injo. He also lived as hostage in Shenyang along with Crown Prince Sohyeon, but he returned to Joseon with hostile feelings toward Qing. The ascension of Hyojong to the throne went against the regulation of ascension, and it later became the cause of party strife on propriety debates that became a prelude to the loss of legitimacy of the bloodline of the eldest legitimate son.

The evil influence of Injo did not stop at the poisoning of the Crown Prince. Injo commanded the Crown Princess to drink poison a year after and persecuted her siblings and several vassals who protested his command. He also lashed out at his three grandsons fathered by Crown Prince Sohyeon. He killed two of them after banishing the three young children to Jeju Island where it would have been difficult for them to survive without parents regardless of the circumstances. Crown Prince Sohyeon's eldest son Seokcheol (石鐵) was 12, second son Seonglin (石麟) was eight, and third son Seokgyeon (石堅) was four at the time. Hyojong later called Seokgyeon to

342

the capital and invested the child with the title of Gyeong'an-gun (慶安君). Could this have been to compensate for the little pang of consciousness he felt for severing the bloodline of his older brother, Crown Prince Sohyeon?

The posthumous epithet of Injo includes the character "*in*" (仁, benevolence), but he was a brutal king and can only be described as being far removed from the meaning of his epithet. Of course, his immoral behavior could not have been carried out without the agreement of the Seoin Faction; his posthumous epithet was also created by the Seoin Faction. Does this then give the Seoin Faction the right to censure Gwanghae-gun for "killing his siblings and incarcerating the mother" as well as justify King Injo's Restoration of Rectitude?

The administration of the Seoin Faction was forced to take on the outward attitude of subservience to the Qing dynasty because Gwanghae-gun was dethroned and Crown Prince Sohyeon was poisoned, but expansion to the north [Qing] was discussed internally with daring confidence; this is not the attitude of a kingdom of virtuous men. The history of thought in Joseon was greatly distorted by these two duplicitous extremes of serving Ming and excluding Qing. Furthermore, the human communication path to Adam Schall, who was a central figure in research of western learning in China as well as the head of the Imperial Astronomy Bureau of the Imperial Observatory in Beijing, was gone with the strange death of Crown Prince Sohyeon.

A determination was made in the fourth year of the reign of Hyojong (1653) to use the western calendar-making method of "Current Standard Calendar" as of 1654 as mentioned before. Controller Kim Yuk (金堉, pen name is Jamgok 潛谷, 1580-1658) of the Office for Observance of Natural Phenomena submitted an appeal to the court in December of 1645 to adopt the Current Standard Calendar when he learned of its use in China. The Shoushi calendar from the Yuan period was used almost in the original form of the Ming calendar until then, but several differences between the movements of celestial bodies and the calendar had occurred.

Joseon was a tributary state of Qing China. Therefore the king of Joseon must accept the first day of the new year assigned by Qing China, use attendant appellation for the year, and distribute the calendar throughout the kingdom. Joseon thus had to adopt the new Current Standard Calendar of Qing in the stead of the Ming calendar. Joseon adopted the Current Standard Calendar not because of the conceptual superiority of western science, but because it had to as a symbol of respect for Qing.

The Qing forces received a striking blow from the western cannons (or cannons of the red-haired barbarian) built under the direction of Adam Schall before they advanced into Beijing. The Qing forces overpowered the Ming forces due to superior archery and horse-riding skills, but they could not break into Ningwen Castle outside of Shanhai despite the superior fighting technique of the western cannons. Nuerhachi was soundly defeated in 1626 when he attacked Ningwen Castle because the Ming commander Yuan Chonghuan used these cannons; Nuerhachi died due to injuries from this battle.

Kong Youde (孔有德) and Geng Zhongming (耿仲明), who had served under Mao Wenlong in the past, led a mutiny in 1633 and went across the ocean to surrender to Huangtaiji of the Later Jin dynasty. They had with them a western cannon used by the Ming troops. Huangtaiji was so elated by this that he named those who surrendered "troops sent by Providence" and the cannon "cannon of the red-haired barbarian general."

In other words, Adam Schall seemed to the Qing troops to be a sort of war criminal for assisting the Ming troops. When the Manchus entered Beijing in 1644, Dorgon ordered the Han Chinese to vacate the inner castle (north castle) and move to the outer castle (south castle) within three days so that the Manchus as new rulers could live in the inner castle. But the chapel of the Jesuits was in the inner castle.

Adam Schall along with fellow Jesuit missionary Nicolas Longobardi (Chinese name is Long Hua-min, 龍華民) petitioned Dorgon that it would be difficult to move documents or engraved plates necessary to improve the calendar and appealed to be permitted to remain in the chapel of the inner castle. Dorgon accepted this request and allowed them to live in the inner castle.

Dorgon was broad-minded enough to objectively evaluate the scientific knowledge the Jesuit missionaries had and to appoint one of them to the head of the Imperial Astronomy Bureau of the Imperial Observatory in Beijing. The Jesuit missionaries were to utilize science and technology for the new Qing dynasty despite the fact that they assisted the Ming troops against Qing.

Injo and Dorgon were the antithesis of each other in that Injo severed the relationship with Adam Schall by killing Crown Prince Sohyeon, while Dorgon befriended Adam Schall and assigned him to the important position of head of the Imperial Observatory in Beijing — despite Schall having been part of the Ming defense troops. The magnanimity of Dorgon toward the Jesuit missionaries brought cultural prosperity to the reigns of Emperors Shunzhi and Kangxi. The Jesuit missionaries realized the big expectations of Emperor Kangxi.

Is Justification Important Despite the Downfall of the Kingdom?

Korean thought traditionally experienced turbulence whenever China underwent dynastic changes due to the issue of whether the new dynasty was "Chinese" or "barbarian." China underwent a dynastic transition from barbarian Yuan to Chinese Ming at the end of Goryeo and beginning of Joseon. Consensus among the advocates of the Learning of Master Zhu at the end of Goryeo dynasty was anti-Yuan and pro-Ming. The only fissure occurred as to whether to support or protest the transition in dynasty from the Goryeo dynasty of the Wang family to the Joseon dynasty of the Yi family.

Confrontation between the Chinese Ming and barbarian Qing turned into war, and transition in dynasty occurred in China in 1644 because of the dethroning of Gwanghae-gun due to King Injo's Restoration of Rectitude in 1623. The justification of serving Ming and excluding Qing was prevalent in the world of thinking in Joseon.

Loyalty to Ming in the form of a debt of gratitude for dispatching reinforcements during the Imjin War was particularly strong.

The thought of excluding Qing developed into "the northern expansion policy" and settled into the world of thought in Joseon in the reign of Hyojong (r. 1649-1659). The ruling power of this period was the Seoin Faction, and the central figure in the world of thought and politics was Song Si-yeol (宋詩烈, pen name is U-am 尤庵, 1607-1689). He belonged to the direct line of Yi Yi's Giho School and was a master of the study of rites. The title of his collection is *Songja daejeon* (宋子大全, Encyclopedia of Master Song); he was the only person among Joseon Confucian scholars to be referred to as Master Song (宋子) on a par with Confucius, Mencius, Cheng-zi, and Zhu Xi. But opinions praising and critiquing him strongly disagree. He was revered by the Seoin Faction as "Master Song," and then later by the Noron Faction when the Seoin Faction divided into Noron and Soron Factions. There was a military official by the name of Song Jun-gil (宋浚吉, pen name is Dongchundang 同春堂, 1606-1672) who was appointed to a high position by Hyojong. He also inherited the orthodoxy of the Giho School and was of the Seoin Faction and later of the Noron Faction, as was Song Si-yeol; Song Si-yeol and he were two great masters.

Song Si-yeol was from Hoedeok in Chungcheong Province; he became teacher to Prince Bongnim after passing the Classics Licentiate Examination of the civil service examination at the top in 1633. The experience of the Manchu invasion of Korea in 1636 and resistance to Prince Bongnim being taken to Shenyang as hostage greatly influenced the formation of his thoughts.

He claimed that the only person who inherited the orthodox teachings of Confucius was Zhu Xi, and as such, believed firmly in the Learning of Master Zhu as the only scholarship, almost as if to declare that "his words are all correct and his behavior all proper." Song Si-yeol's basis of the logical structure for the northern expansion policy is clearly shown in Clause 13 of "Gichuk bongsa" (己丑封事), which contains the words "defeat barbarian enemies through improvement in politics." He submitted it to Hyojong in

1649, the same year that the latter ascended to the throne. "Gichuk bongsa" is a great document that contains a total of 13 clauses describing the fundamental principles of politics — from self-cultivation of a king to becoming a statesman. A big supposition of the northern expansion policy as mentioned in Clause 13 is "right-eous justification."

> Confucius wrote *Spring and Autumn Annals* to reveal the justice in great integration to all under Heaven and to the future genera-tions. Thus most know that China must be respected and enemies must be hated. Zhu Xi also vindicated humiliation by paying re-spect to the heavenly principles through drawing inferences from moral principles. "Human way cannot be achieved if virtue and righteousness are discarded. But there is nothing greater in virtue than the relationship between father and son, and nothing greater in righteousness than the relationship between ruler and vassal. This is the secret of three bonds (三綱) and the root of five rela-tions (五倫). Moral principles and moral laws are extreme; there is nowhere to hide from them on earth." …whenever this para-graph is read, I think to neglect even one word or a phrase from it is to allow etiquette and music to fall to the ground, and hu-manity becomes impossible to save because it becomes beastly.

Righteous justification is a concept of revering China and excluding all foreigners, and this is concretely embodied in the doctrine of valuing Ming and devaluing Qing. Song Si-yeol regarded the relation-ship between the emperor of Ming and the king of Joseon as that of father-son from the viewpoint of virtue and as that of ruler-vassal from the viewpoint of loyalty. He stated as follows about Shenzong Emperor Wanli in particular for dispatching reinforcements during the Imjin War:

> In addition, ancestral temples and sovereignty of our kingdom that were in ruins in the upheaval of the Imjin War revived and people who were driven out to death have regained life under the grace of Shenzong Emperor Wanli. There is not one tree, one plant, or a strand of hair of the people in this kingdom that is not influenced by the emperor's grace.

347

Thus Song Si-yeol could not forgive Commanding General Kang Hong-nip and Lieutenant Commanding General Kim Gyeong-seo of the Joseon forces dispatched to the Battle of Sarhu under the request of Ming in 1619 for surrendering to the Qing troops without a fight due to the secret communiqué from Gwanghae-gun.

> Moreover, Gwanghae (Gwanghae-gun) outrageously let the prestige of the country fall and turned it barbaric by instructing Hong-nip and Gyeong-seo to surrender the entire army to the barbarians. Our great king (Injo) recovered correctness, cleansed ignominy, and made it as clean as the sun and the moon by advocating righteousness so that this can be passed on by all vassals and the people to the world and future generations.

He stated that the way to justify oneself and be loyal to Shenzong of Ming was to prepare to expand to the north; and further, that success or failure and gains or loss must not be taken into consideration in order to carry this out, even if the kingdom fell.

> I prostrate myself in front of Your Majesty to firmly avow that these barbarians (Qing) are the great enemy of our ruler and parent and as such should not live under the same sky. Hatred must be built upon one another, pain must be endured and resentment held, anger must be accrued among humble words (diplomatic documents to Qing), the pain of determination and perseverance must be sustained even more sincerely among the gold pieces (tributary things to Qing). More, even the spirits should not be privy to important secrets of the nation, and the firmness of will must be pledged for five to seven years and not slacken in 10 or 20 years so that even Meng Bi (孟賁) and Xia Yu (夏育) (two legendary strong men of ancient China) cannot take it away.

The above paragraph is full of spirit and righteousness, but its reasoning is in reality on a par with "justification must survive although the country may fall." This was an extremely dangerous way of thinking for a great politician who was responsible for the state. The greatest crisis faced by the Qing dynasty after dominating China was definitely the Revolt of the Three Feudatories (三藩之亂) from

1673 led by Wu San-gui and others. But Song Si-yeol's northern expansion policy was not linked to these uprisings; it was proposed many years earlier in 1649.

Reckless Northern Expansion Policy Which Ignores Reality

Song Si-yeol's northern expansion policy can be viewed as an extremely dangerous statement. The dangerousness should be revealed through a cool-headed examination of the bias for conquering the barbarians of the north.

The reign of Hyojong (1649-1659) overlapped the reign of Emperor Shunzhi of Qing (1643-1661). Dorgon, who dealt a striking blow to the Ming dynasty, passed away in 1650. Emperor Shunzhi ascended to the throne at the age of six, triumphantly entered Beijing in 1644, and personally governed for 10 years from 1651 to 1661 under the supervision of regent Jirugaran, or King Zhengqing, after Dorgon passed away. Emperor Shunzhi died at the early age of 24, but the dynasty continued to flourish for three generations under his son Emperor Kangxi, grandson Emperor Yongzheng, and great-grandson Emperor Qianlong.

Emperor Kangxi ascended to the throne in 1661 at the age of eight; four prime ministers assisted in governing at first, but Emperor Kangxi personally began to rule as of 1669. The last 20 years of the life of Song Si-yeol who advocated for northern expansion overlapped with the period wherein Emperor Kangxi reigned. Emperor Kangxi was an emperor who firmly built the foundation for the Qing dynasty during the 61 years of his reign. He was a strict scholar of the Learning of Master Zhu in his creed toward learning and life; *Collected Works of Zhu Xi* and *Grand Code of the Principle of Human Nature* were compiled under his command. Not only that, he was well enough versed in western astronomy and mathematics to be on par with Xu Guang-qi of the late Ming dynasty. He became known throughout Europe after the French Jesuit missionary Bouvet published a book titled *Emperor Kangxi* (康熙帝傳) in Paris in 1697. But Song Si-yeol could not view Qing China with objectivity because he was a prisoner of ethnic prejudice against the Manchus.

Song Si-yeol personally wrote "love others as one loves oneself" and "rebuke others as one rebukes oneself," hung these admonitions on the left and right side of the audience wall, and made them his motto. This shows the strictness with which he controlled himself as a scholar of the Learning of Master Zhu, yet he was very interested and generous in adopting western learning. The height of Chinese culture, along with the Ming period, is 134 years of Qing culture from 1661 when Emperor Kangxi ascended to the throne to 1795 — extending through Kangxi, Yongzheng, and Qianlong.

The grandeur of the early Qing period can be seen by great compilation projects, such as *Dictionary of Kangxi* (康熙字典), *Collection of Past and Present Books* (古今圖書集成), and *Collected Works of Four Branches of Books* (四庫全書). For example, *Collected Works of Four Branches of Books,* completed in the reign of Emperor Qianlong, was not only the greatest compilation project of Chinese cultural thought along with *Annotative List of the Complete Library of the Four Branches of Books* (四庫全書總目提要), it remains supreme as the essence of a bibliographic explanation of Chinese literature. There was, of course, some trouble brought on by a slip of the pen in the three generations of the compilation process. But most of the troubling contents brought on by this slip of the pen were criticism of the barbaric Qing dynasty. The Qing dynasty was not lenient enough to leave ethnic prejudice alone. Emperor Yongzheng wrote, "I know moral justice; I do not know there is a difference between the Manchus and Han Chinese," in his *Great Righteousness Resolving Confusion* (大義覺迷錄). This was a manifestation of Qing China being a melting pot of the Manchus and Han Chinese.

Mentioned above are great compilation projects on traditional culture in China, but 100 volumes of *Luli yuanyuan* (律曆淵源), compiled under the command of Emperor Kangxi and printed during the reign of Emperor Yongzheng, was a great commemorative project that included a mixture of eastern and western culture, including the fields of calendar-making, mathematics, and music. This book also influenced practical learning in Joseon. Emperors Kangxi, Yongzheng, and Qianlong were strict scholars of the Learning of Master Zhu, but ruled with an inclusive and pluralistic sense of the value of religions and cultures of diverse peoples.

Emperor Kangxi was not only an emperor of civil administration, but was valorous as well. The greatest crisis of the early Qing period was the Revolt of the Three Feudatories led by a combination of Wu San-gui (吳三桂) of Yunnan, Geng Jing-zhong (耿精忠) of Fujian, and Shang Zhixin (尚之信) of Guangdong against the Qing dynasty in 1673. The justification for this revolt was "restoration of Ming." The battlefront stretched for over 2,000 kilometers from the Fujian Castle to the east and Gansu Castle to the west. Emperor Kangxi as a young man spurned the wavering officials of the central government and completely suppressed the uprising with unswerving determination in 1681 after nine long years of war. Furthermore, the main forces of his military had already become Han forces' Green Battalion and not the fallen Eight Flags of Manchu. Taiwan, the last foothold for the restoration of Ming, came under Qing control in 1683 after the Revolt of the Three Feudatories.

A problem also arose in the Dongbei area from which the Qing dynasty originated. Cossacks from Russia built castles and fortifications in the Heilong River basin such as Nerchinsk and Albazin, and fur and natural resources popular among western aristocrats were plundered. Emperor Kangxi attacked and destroyed these castles and fortifications. At the request of Qing, Joseon troops also participated in this war between Qing and Russia. The Treaty of Nerchinsk was agreed upon in 1689 to block Russia's eastward advancement.

Emperor Kangxi did not pay attention to annexation of the Korean peninsula. Injo was called before Taizong of Qing China and forced to vow to observe the propriety of serving Qing at the time of the Manchu invasion of 1636. Advocates against reconciliation with Qing claimed this to be an indignity, but Joseon was able to preserve itself autonomously due to this vow of Injo. If Joseon, whose kingdom was smaller than any Chinese province, did carry out a reckless invasion of Qing, the end would have far surpassed the indignity suffered in the Manchu invasion of 1636. Moreover, the three eastern Chinese provinces that bordered northern Joseon were a "holy land" to the Qing because they were the birthplace of the Qing dynasty.

Then how did Song Si-yeol evaluate Joseon's military power for invasion of Qing China? This is also included in Clause 13 of "Gichuk bongsa."

> All say in today's discussion that [invading the north] is impossible due to weak military force. But Goguryeo defeated Sui and Tang dynasties' great forces of one million with one-third the force of our country (Joseon dynasty), and a hero like Taizong of Tang fought a hard battle at Anshi Castle. These barbarians are cunning beasts. The sharpshooters of our kingdom are crack shots who were not available then. The only urgent task of today is to train troops, appoint commanders, store military rations, and make military law more rigorous.

A claim opposing Song Si-yeol by stating that invasion of the north was dangerous due to weak military power would be more correct. Goguryeo was able to defeat the invasions by Sui and Tang China because the border with China was limited to the northern region of Liaohe and did not take up 1/3 of the territory as was the case with Joseon. Goguryeo was the largest and strongest dynasty in the history of Korea with territory extending from the Liaoning region to the Han River in the middle of the Korean peninsula. The cannons (used by the best artillery sharpshooters at that time) in which Song Si-yeol entrusted his confidence were a weapon used by the Japanese troops in the Imjin War. But the Qing forces were already mass-producing western cannons called red(-haired) barbarian cannon in the mid-17th century which the Jesuit missionary Ferbist (Chinese name is Nan Huai-ren 南懷仁) created; Qing was able to suppress the Revolt of the Three Feudatories with these cannons.

It is a notion that is suspect, but Joseon at the time probably could not have gathered and trained a force of 100,000 men, which is the number of men led by King of Pingxi (平西王) Wu San-gui in the uprising. "You will not have a problem winning if the enemy is known" as written in *Military Strategy of Sun-zi* is a wise saying that transcends all time. The northern expansion policy sounds courageous but can only be said to be a reckless claim that does not know the enemy at all.

The onset of the problem began in King Injo's Restoration of Rectitude in 1623. The point of dispute was whether the coup d'état that dethroned Gwanghae-gun and put Injo on the throne was "preserving the kingdom comes first" or "maintaining justification."

Gwanghae-gun opted for preserving the kingdom by staying neutral in the internal war between Ming and Qing China. This correct choice arose from his experience of leading a division of the royal court against Japan during the Imjin War. He was dethroned by the Seoin Faction that was pro-Ming and anti-Qing, however, for neglecting to repay the debt of gratitude to Ming.

Joseon politics seemed to have had two choices toward Qing during the transition phase from Ming to Qing in China:

Course A: Gwanghae-gun → pro-reconciliation and serving China → Crown Prince Sohyeon (mysterious death)

Course B: Injo → anti-reconciliation and advocacy of invading the north → Crown Prince Bongnim (ascended to the throne as Hyojong)

If the first (Course A) had been taken, not only diplomatic relations of serving Qing China would have been established, but commercial and cultural exchange would have proceeded smoothly in addition to an adoption of western learning through the interchange between Crown Prince Sohyeon and Adam Schall. The Seoin Faction denied the first course by claiming righteous justification and selected the second (Course B) as the orthodoxy in the history of Korea. In short, the Seoin Faction (Noron Faction) used this historical viewpoint to justify King Injo's Restoration of Rectitude in 1636. This viewpoint is still followed to this day.

Originally, "restoration of rectitude" meant to "suppress an uprising to restore order." But restoration of rectitude could stir up an uprising instead of suppressing it. It is doubtful that King Injo's

Restoration of Rectitude continued to be faithful to its original meaning.

The unrealistic scheme to invade the north disappeared like a shadow, but the northern expansion policy that developed from anti-reconciliation toward Qing became conceptualized and independently dispersed and excessively distorted the history of thought in the Joseon period. The world of Joseon Confucianism disdained the Qing dynasty because the tradition of Chinese civilization had supposedly become barbaric since Qing took over China; moreover, Qing people were called "barbarians" or "dogs and sheep" (a defamatory expression used to refer to the nomadic people) to make fun of them. The vainglorious idea that Joseon was "little China" by being the only nation to inherit the orthodoxy of Chinese culture permeated Joseon thereafter.

Joseon politically served Qing China with propriety but ideologically considered it to be barbaric, and such a distorted perspective on China blinded Joseon to an objective view of Qing. This was the historical background from which Joseon Confucians considered the world, including the Qing dynasty, as barbaric until modern times. The greatest ideological obstacle in Joseon was the task of overcoming this closed worldview when Westerners (or "Western barbarians") and Japan (or "Japanese barbarians") pressured Joseon to open its ports in the latter half of the 19th century. The fight against this obstacle cost Joseon the chance to humbly learn the advanced culture of "the barbarians" and to build a foundation to strengthen itself.

Is Contradicting Zhu Xi Disturbing and Behaving Contrary to the Confucian Tenets?

The Seoin Faction later divided into the Noron Faction and the Soron Faction, with Song Si-yeol at the center of the former in opposition to the latter. The factions were originally referred to as "Four Factions," but in reality it shrank to three factions — the Noron Faction, Namin Faction, and Soron Faction — due to the destruction of the Bugin Faction (including Daebuk and Sobuk) at the time of King Injo's Restoration of Rectitude.

Yun Hyu (尹鑴, pen name is Baekho 白湖, 1617-1680) was stigmatized by Song Si-yeol as "one who disturbs and behaves contrary to the Confucian tenets" because he revised Zhu Xi's *The Doctrine of the Mean Divided by Chapters and Sentences.*

There was an anonymous book titled *Dongguk bungdang wonryu* (東國朋黨原流, The Origin of Korean Factionalism) by a Noron scholar in the late 19th century. According to this book, Yun Seon-geo (尹宣擧, 1610-1669), a friend of Song Si-yeol and a member of the Seoin Faction, was also close to Yun Hyu and understood Yun Hyu's doctrine. But Song Si-yeol could not stand such an indecisive attitude on the part of Yun Seon-geo. Thus Yun Seon-geo was urged to see things in black and white and cut all ties with Yun Hyu.

> The teachings of Zhu Xi are like the sun at the center of the sky; those who dare to claim other opinions disturb and behave con-trary to the Confucian tenets. The scholarship is suspect if an at-tempt is made to shelter rather than ignore this [preposterous] claim as a scholar. Moreover, Seon-geo is the maternal grandson of Ugye (Seong Hon), and Seon-geo was reproached in good faith with the statement that there is no telling how much harm will be caused if somehow he becomes a member of Yun Hyu's faction. Seon-geo finally said, "I will immediately break off all connections because Hyu is the *yin* and black in terms of *yin* or *yang* and black or white." U-am (Song Si-yeol) responded to this by saying, "all will be relieved if you followed this."

However, Song Si-yeol's distrust of Yun Seon-geo did not disappear. The two belonged to the Seoin Faction, but Song Si-yeol was directly linked to Yi Yi and Yun Seon-geo to Seong Hon. Song Si-yeol openly expressed his distrust of Yun Seon-geo in an epitaph erected for the latter, which led to a rebellion against Song Si-yeol by Yun Jeung (尹拯), son of Yun Seon-geo. Thus the Seoin Faction finally con-fronted each other after dividing into the Noron Faction with Song Si-yeol at the center and the Soron Faction with Yun Jeung at the center. This is the so-called "Hoe-Ni debate" because the home of Song Si-yeol was in Hoedeok in Chungcheong Province and the home of Yun Jeung was in Niseong in Chungcheong Province.

At the age of 22, Yun Hyu added a personal bibliography and commentaries mainly on the Confucian Classics while writing a document on the principle of human nature called *Sadan chiljeong insim dosimseol* (四端七情人心道心說, Theory of People's Mind on the Four Beginnings and the Seven Emotions). His representative work was *Dokseo-gi* (讀書記, A Record of Readings), which is a compilation of bibliographical study on *The Doctrine of the Mean*, *Great Learning*, *Book on Filial Piety*, *Book of Poetry*, *Official History*, *Book of Rites*, *Records of Rites*, and *Spring and Autumn Annals*, among which the focus was particularly on *The Doctrine of the Mean* and *Great Learning*. Zhu Xi created *Commentaries on the Four Books* by separating *The Doctrine of the Mean* and *Great Learning* from *Record of Rites* and incorporating these two with the *Analects* and *The Works of Mencius* as well as adding new annotations.

Yun Hyu's attitude toward the Confucian Classics was not limited to presenting the views of Zhu Xi, but also to present his own unique opinions by incorporating various views. Below is a brief examination of "Foreword to The Doctrine of the Mean" in *Dokseo-gi* as an example:

> Originally, Huiweng (晦翁, Zhu Xi) created his own doctrine by gathering and blending many views when annotating various Confucian Classics. But he still trained with the literati and personally experienced them; moreover, he always discussed, redefined, and continuously revised what was not manifested in doctrines or not achieved through conduct or in proper place until immediately prior to his death. Moreover, he always said, "I finally realized the inappropriateness of previous doctrines by so-and-so on more than a few occasions through discussions and questions from friends." Such is also his willingness to adopt the goodness and to search for correctness without hesitating about repetition. I should follow his example and act accordingly.

Jungyong jujajanggu borok (中庸朱子章句補錄, Supplement to The Doctrine of the Mean Divided by Chapters and Sentences) by Yun Hyu supposedly supplemented Zhu Xi's *The Doctrine of the Mean Divided by Chapters and Sentences*, but in reality it corrected the division

356

of chapters and incorporated his own annotations. Additional attention should be paid to *Daehak gobon byeollok* (大學古本別錄, Separate Record on the Old Text of the Great Learning). This *Old Text of the Great Learning* was actually criticized by Wang Yang-ming as "Zhu Xi's Great Learning Divided by Chapters and Sentences has distorted the mind of the sage by dividing Record of Rites within the ancient writings of 'great learning' into one chapter of Classics and 10 sentences of annotations."

In contrast to Song Si-yeol, Yun Hyu did not view the Learning of Master Zhu as a complete system as seen in the "Foreword to The Doctrine of the Mean." Rather, he stated his desire to learn Zhu Xi's passion and method in the assiduous search to select goodness from various views and seek correctness without satisfaction until completion of his doctrines.

Song Si-yeol severely criticized Yun Hyu in *Ganseo japnok* (看書雜錄) for not considering Zhu Xi as absolute.

> Hyu frontally excludes Zhu Xi, and how can it be said that his evil influence is not more than 100 times that of the doctrine of acting in self-interest or loving all equally of Yang and Mo (楊墨)? If this is left alone, it will lead beasts to not stop at devouring people but people will indeed reach a point of devouring one another.

"The doctrine of acting in self-interest or loving all equally" mentioned here is an excerpt from *The Works of Mencius*. Mencius criticized Yang and Mo as follows: [1]

> *If you listen to* people's discourses throughout it, *you will find that* they have adopted the views either of Yang or of Mo. *Now,* Yang's principle is—"each one for himself," which does not acknowledge the *claims* of the sovereign. Mo's principle is—"to love all equally," which does not acknowledge *the peculiar affection due to*

---

[1] Yang refers to a Daoist philosopher Yang Zhu (楊朱) who lived at the beginning of the period of the Warring States in China, and Mo refers to Mozi, a Confucian philosopher. (S. Lee)

a father. But to acknowledge neither king nor father is to be in the state of a beast.

- "Teng Wen Gong, Part II" (滕文公章句 下, or Tăng Wăn Kung), *The Works of Mencius*

The world will fall into a beastly state because ruler and father are not acknowledged by Yang Zhu and Mozi, the former an individualist full of self-interest who denies loyalty between ruler and vassal, and the latter a philanthropist who advocates "loving all equally" and thus denying filial piety between father and son.

The latter part of the excerpt by Song Si-yeol is from "Zheng-shi" (正始) in *Records of Things Knowledgeable in a Day* (日知錄, *Rizhilu* in Ch.) by Gu Yan-wu (顧炎武, pen name is Ting-lin 亭林, 1613-1683) who lived in the period at the end of Ming and beginning of Qing and began the philologico-bibliographical study by advocating investigation of the truth based on fact in the Qing period.

There is the state of the fall of a nation and of the fall of the world [into disorder]. How can a distinction between the fall of the nation and the world [into disorder] be made? I say this. "The change in the family name and appellation of the kingdom is the fall of a nation. The state of leading beasts, feeding man, and men eating each other through the breakdown of humanity and righteousness is the fall of the world."

According to Song Si-yeol's reasoning, Yun Hyu not only deviated from Zhu Xi but became a beast "without father or king" and an enemy of mankind "that lets the world fall [into disorder]." This is a condemnation that crosses the boundary of scholarly Confucian debate.

Yun Hyu did not oppose Zhu Xi, but rather he could be said to be a bibliographical scholar of Chinese Classics who departed from Zhu Xi's doctrines. But the source of stigmatizing such a great Confucian scholar as "one who disturbs and behaves contrary to the Confucian tenets" was Song Si-yeol. Thereafter, this radical stigma was abused as a deadly weapon by the Seoin Faction and the Noron

Faction that later branched off from it to which Song Si-yeol belonged. The Noron Faction in particular had the most power among the various factions and held the reins of power for the longest period. The Confucian scholars of Joseon could not escape from the Learning of Master Zhu as the only scholarship due to their fear of the power and oppression of the Noron Faction, and that has continued until the modern period.

Ideology is a sharp weapon like a razor blade not only in the Learning of Master Zhu. A razor blade is easy to use in shaving a beard, but it is more efficient to use a blunt weapon such as an axe to cut down a big tree.

The first Joseon envoy to Japan with Kim Gi-su as the ambassador visited there in April of 1876 immediately after the signing of the Treaty of Ganghwa Island between Joseon and Japan in February 1876. Kim Gi-su met with Minister of Culture Guki Ryuichi and exchanged the following questions and answers on the scholarship of Joseon:

> Guki Ryuichi: Does your country only revere the scholarship of Zhu Xi? Or are there other scholars who are revered as well?
>
> Kim Gi-su: The scholarship of my country has recognized only Zhu Xi for the past 500 years. Those who turn their backs against Zhu Xi are immediately treated as rebels and severely punished, and those who write about Buddhism or the words of Lao-zi during the civil service examination are banished to faraway regions. Only Zhu Xi exists for those in high and low positions as well as classes because the national law is very strict.

> • "Mundap" (問答九則),
> Record of a Journey to Japan, Vol. 2

The trend of "civilization" dominated Japan after the Meiji Restoration in the year of 1876 when Kim Gi-su visited. But Joseon lived as "little China" and could not take even a step away from the ideological exclusivity that revered only the Learning of Master Zhu.

What Mourning Clothes to Wear Turns into Party Strife

There was a genre called "study of rites" in Joseon Confucianism. The *Five National Rites* (國朝五禮儀) completed in 1474 was a national ritual system. Five rites refer to funeral rites (凶禮), military rites (軍禮), protocol for guests (賓禮), and auspicious court ceremony (嘉禮). But the method of observing family rites in the homes of the common *sadaebu* became a big issue by accompanying the intensification of the study of the Learning of Master Zhu.

Rite was defined in "Tangong" Part II (檀弓下) of *Record of Rites* by Ziyou (子游), one of the disciples of Confucius:

> Feelings can be suppressed to express rites, or feelings can be shown more through the usage of things (clothing or utensils). To show feelings immediately and express them quickly is the way of the barbarians…. To control expression of feelings suitably is indeed what is called rite.

For example, family rites could be viewed as the expression of feelings adjusting according to certain forms of various rites of passage; this alternately involved joy and sorrow within a family. Scholars of the Learning of Master Zhu in Joseon claimed that not only learning but family rites must also be executed according to the "Family Rites of Zhu Xi" (朱子家禮, also referred to as Family Rites of Wengong 文公家禮), but the contents were too general to be applied in Joseon. There existed, however, a compilation of the doctrines of Zhu Xi on family rites by Qiu Jun (丘濬, 1420-1495), a prominent scholar of the Learning of Zhu Xi of early Ming period entitled *Propriety of Family Rites* (家禮儀節).

A pioneer of the study on family rites based on the doctrines of Zhu Xi in Joseon was Kim Jang-saeng (金長生, pen name is Sagye 沙溪, 1548-1631), who wrote *Garye jimnam* (家禮輯覽, Exposition of Family Rites) and belonged to the Giho School. Song Si-yeol became a great scholar of rites by learning from Kim Jang-saeng. Almost at the same period as Kim Jang-saeng, the doctrine of propriety as advocated by Jeong Gu (鄭逑, pen name is Han-gang 寒岡, 1543-1620) became mainstream in the Yeongnam School.

The main goal of the study of rites for the advocates of the Learning of Master Zhu was to sweep away extant shamanistic and Buddhistic systems that were passed down in family rites since the Goryeo period of the *sadaebu* and to make people appreciate Confucianism and depreciate Buddhism completely. It was not possible, however, to eliminate shamanistic faith and the Buddhistic system from the homes of the common class because shamanistic and Buddhistic powers were that strong.

Family rites consisted of four categories: coming-of-age ceremony, wedding ceremony, mourning rites, and memorial rituals. Of the four, mourning rites were considered especially important. A dispute surrounding this arose between the Giho School (the Seoin Faction) and the Yeongnam School (the Namin Faction). Each school put its reputation on the line to practice and polish the doctrine of propriety, and the debate gradually became sharper.

Disputes over propriety refer to debates over the doctrine of propriety. The dispute between Song Si-yeol and Yun Hyu grew into factional disputes between the Seoin Faction and the Namin Faction, and changes in political power were accompanied by repeated purges of opposite factions. The origin of this issue was the loss of legitimacy of the bloodline of the eldest legitimate son due to what Injo did. In short, the problem arose when Injo did not follow the regulation of the royal family by naming his successor the second son Prince Bongnim as the Crown Prince instead of the traditional succession of the oldest son (Crown Prince) → oldest grandson (oldest son of the Crown Prince).

Hyojong passed away in 1659, and Hyeonjong (顯宗, r. 1659-1674) ascended to the throne. The mourning period to be observed by King Injo's second queen on the occasion of the death of Hyojong became an issue at this time. Song Si-yeol claimed that the mourning period in which the second queen of Injo (of the Jo clan) had to wear mourning clothes was one year because Hyojong was Injo's second son despite succeeding Injo to the throne. The party strife over propriety began with Heo Mok (許穆) of the Namin Faction objecting to Song Si-yeol of the Seoin Faction. Yun Hyu who joined the Namin Faction criticized Song Si-yeol's claim as being injurious to the dignity of the ruler. He further claimed that despite Hyojong being a second son, Hyojong must be accorded the dignity of a first-born son because he was a king; and thus the full respect of mourning clothes made of hemp cloth (for three-year mourning) must be worn. This was the start of the dispute over propriety.

The one-year mourning period advocated by the Seoin Faction was observed as a result of the first dispute over propriety; the Namin Faction which lost the dispute over propriety was exiled from the coalition government with the Seoin Faction that had continued since King Injo's Restoration of Rectitude. This dispute over propriety repeatedly occurred whenever mourning rites had to be observed in the royal family, thereby continuing the transfer of political power and revenge between the two factions. "Study of rites" in Joseon Confucianism was equivalent to training in the doctrine of propriety to obtain submission of the opposite faction by putting the authority of the faction on the line.

According to the "Quli" of *Records of Rites*, debate or factional dispute over the doctrine of propriety was another world to the commoners because propriety did not extend to the commoners. This was nothing more than a contemptible fight for self-gain and a life-and-death fight within the *yangban* class. Family rites differed between different factions, and marriage ties could not be achieved within the *yangban* class of different factions.

Originally, Song Si-yeol and Yun Hyu had scholarly interchange and respected each other in their youth. Yun Hyu was born into a family of the Sobuk Faction, but the Sobuk Faction was annihilated after being defeated in a political strife against the Daebuk Faction, in which the Sobuk Faction supported Prince Yeongchang after the death of Seonjo and the Daebuk Faction supported the ascension of Gwanghae-gun to the throne. Thus Yun Hyu could maintain his friendly relationship with members of various factions because he did not belong to any faction and thus was not burdened with factional loyalty. But both Song Si-yeol and Yun Hyu were swept into party strife by this debate: Yun Hyu was compelled to take poison in 1680 under the regime of the Seoin Faction, and Song Si-yeol was forced to drink poison in 1689 under the regime of the Namin Faction.

Song Si-yeol was banished to Jeju Island, and he was given poison in Jeong-eup, Jeolla Province, while being transported from Jeju Island to Seoul. At that time Song Si-yeol asked his star pupil Gwon Sang-ha to take care of things after his death and wrote one Chinese character "*jik*" (直) as a guideline for learning and behaving. His factionalism was truly strong in thought and politics. This was comparable to Islamic and Christian monotheistic religions confronting each other by calling each other heretical. The chilling and dismal trend of monotheistic thought in which the Learning of Master Zhu was the only scholarship and regarded anyone who deviated from its thought as "one who disturbs and behaves contrary to the Confucian tenets" began from Song Si-yeol.

The Cheng-Zhu School and the Liu-Wang School are of course part of Song period Neo-Confucianism. The Learning of Master Zhu as the only scholarship had already begun with Yi Hwang's slander of the Liu-Wang School in Joseon, but it was not utilized in power struggles to purge opposing factions.

The Seoin Faction that belonged to the genealogy of Yi Yi and Seong Hon divided into the Noron Faction of Song Si-yeol and the Soron Faction of Yun Jeung. Yi Geon-chang (李建昌, pen name is Yeongjae 寧齋, 1852-1898) of the Soron Faction wrote a book on critical analysis of the history of party strife entitled *Dangui tongnyak* (黨議通略) in the latter half of the 19th century. According to this book, Chief State Councilor Yi Jun-gyeong (李浚慶, pen name is Donggo 東皐, 1499-1572) already predicted the division of the Sarim Faction into Dong'in and Seoin in the fourth year of the reign of Seonjo (1571) prior to the actual occurrence. Yi Jun-gyeong stated as follows in the jointly signed appeal presented to the king:

> People are talking grandiosely and attempting to create cliques. This will become a great trouble to the nation.

Many people were gathered around Yi Yi at the time. He presented a counterargument as below in an appeal to the king:

> How can there be cliques when the royal court is clean and pure?
> It is said that a person becomes kind when he nears death, but the words are misleading in the case of Jun-gyeong.

It seems that Yi Yi himself did not predict the Dong'in and Seoin split to lead to party strife that destroyed each other. Remonstrators of the Sarim Faction who held the rein over the government added their voices to Yi Yi's and advocated for the removal of all offices and titles held by Yi Jun-gyeong. But Yu Seong-nyong opposed this by stating as follows:

> If it is unwarranted for a minister to give advice at his deathbed, his words can be ignored. But to punish him is extreme.

The Sarim Faction divided into Dong'in and Seoin three years after Yi Jun-gyeong passed away in 1575, and an endless history of party strife began thence. The prediction of Yi Jun-gyeong had come true. One hundred years later, a terrible calamity in the form of party strife developed in the 1680s as the Seoin Faction killed Yun Hyu and the Namin Faction killed Song Si-yeol over mere mourning rites of the royal family which did not have any relation to the original duty of Confucian politics in the form of statecraft and providing for the people. The spirit of "propriety" had already disappeared in the dispute over propriety and only the formality of the study of rites existed. But it is stated in *Analects of Confucius* that "In practising the rules of propriety, a natural ease is to be prized."

This chapter has wholly criticized Song Si-yeol's northern expansion policy and his thought on considering any Confucian scholar who broke away from Zhu Xi as one who disturbs and behaves contrary to the Confucian tenets. However, *U-am sasang yeongu nonchong* (Collection of Research on U-am's Thoughts, 1992) published by the Association of Confucians (斯文學會) of Korea not only fully affirms the thoughts of Song Si-yeol as an authority on the subject, but the association seems to use the book as "an impetus to revive independent and nationalistic spirit as well as national and historical views of U-am." The tenor of the argument was to defend the party opinions of the Seoin or Noron Faction of premodern times.

I happened to briefly glimpse at a book entitled *Joseon hugi joseon junghwasasang yeongu* (Chinese Thought in Joseon in the Late Joseon Period) by Prof. Jeong Ok-ja of Seoul National University while writing this chapter. This book seems to further exaggerate and give high marks to King Injo's Restoration of Rectitude, Song Si-yeol, and above-mentioned issues.

> King Injo's Restoration of Rectitude is a change in government which occurred through the joint efforts of the Seoin and Namin political factions comprised of the true followers of the study of the principle of human nature in particular among the Sarim Faction. As such, it is the turning point wherein a new development begins in late Joseon society (p. 11).
>
> The latter half of the Joseon period promoted culture unique to Joseon and established the spirit of the times for revering Chinese thought in Joseon which claims to possess the best culture in the world (p. 12).

This attitude is high-spirited indeed, but the reader should be able to comprehend that this attitude is in direct contrast to a fundamental opinion after reading this chapter.

18

Practical Learning Blooms during the Reigns of Enlightened Rulers Yeongjo and Jeongjo

What Is a Faction?

After the Sarim Faction divided into the Dong'in and Seoin Factions in the eighth year of the reign of King Seonjo (1575), each faction repeatedly divided into smaller cliques instead of merging under "great unity" because "petty differences" were magnified out of proportion. This was aggravated to a point where arguments would deteriorate into murder.

Yi Ik (李瀷, pen name is Seongho 星湖, 1681-1763) was a leader of the Silhak School (School of Practical Learning) and consistent in not holding any government post throughout his lifetime. He commented as follows on his own experience of the abuses of factional disputes:

> Since King Seonjo, one divided into two, two became four, and again four became eight to kill and be killed like enemies. This is passed down from one generation to another. They hold government posts under the same royal court and live in the same land but do not have any intercourse with each other until they become old and die.

> * "Bungdangnon" (朋黨論, On Factions),
> *Gwagurok* (藿憂錄, Records of Concerns for the Underprivileged)

Factional disputes began in earnest when Hyojong passed away in 1659, and the controversy over the length of the mourning period for the second wife of Injo (of the Jo clan) escalated between Song Si-yeol and Yun Hyu. This dispute between the two officials grew into a factional dispute between the Seoin and Namin Factions. Factional disputes continued for the next 65 years during the reigns of King Hyeonjong (r. 1659-1674), King Sukjong (r. 1674-1720), and King Gyeongjong (r. 1720-1724). In particular, there was never a period without factional disputes during the 46 years of the reign of King Sukjong, the longest single reign in a 65-year period.

There are those who view these factional disputes within the Sarim Faction positively as pioneering "political parties" by curbing the absolute power of one particular faction. However, that argument is confused about the difference between political parties versus factions. Instead, it would be closer to the truth to view factional disputes as a vicious cycle of revenge and annihilation through total denial of each other.

Changes in political power (*hwan'guk*: 換局) and the various stages in factional disputes are periodically organized as follows:

First year of the reign of Hyeonjong (1660): The first dispute over propriety after the death of King Hyojong. The Seoin Faction was victorious over the Namin Faction.

Fifteenth year of the reign of King Hyeonjong (1674): The second dispute over propriety. The Namin Faction took revenge against the Seoin Faction (Reversal of the Political Situation in the Year of Gabin).

Sixth year of the reign of King Sukjong (1680): The Seoin Faction came into power and took revenge against Heo Jeok and Yun Hyu of the Namin Faction (Reversal of the Political Situation in the Year of Gyeongsin).

Ninth year of the reign of King Sukjong (1683): The Seoin Faction divided into the Noron and Soron Factions (Hoe-Ni debate).

Fifteenth year of the reign of King Sukjong (1689): *Namin* Faction came into power and took revenge against Song Si-yeol and Kim Su-hang of the Noron Faction (Reversal of the Political Situation in the Year of Gisa).

Twentieth year of the reign of King Sukjong (1694): The Noron Faction came into power and took revenge against the Namin Faction (Reversal of the Political Situation in the Year of Gapsul).

First and second years of the reign of King Gyeongjong (1721-1722): The Soron Faction came into power and oppressed the Noron Faction.

Not only were people not able to execute political reform due to fear of consequences in the face of such rapid turnover in political power of various factions and repeated revenges carried out as mentioned above, but it was obvious that politicians with practical abilities and faithfully accumulated administrative know-how could not be groomed. The main point of contention among the Noron, Namin, and Soron that lasted for 65 years was factional dispute over propriety, however, and not about political issues on state affairs or reform of personal livelihood. The controversy between Song Si-yeol and Yun Hyu was about the proper mourning period for the queen. In short, it would be best to delete these 65 years of ignominious history full of slander, abuse, intrigues and executions, confusion in politics, and factional disputes one by one from the Confucian history of Korea, if possible.

Only the scholar-official order and the military-official order among the *yangban* class had power, and internal power struggles of these official orders appeared in the form of factional disputes. The scholar officials and military officials claimed that the party they belonged to was "the party of the virtuous"; each tenaciously adhered to the belief that the opposing factions were the "factions of men of little caliber," and thus must be removed from nearness to the king.

Such reasoning followed that of Ou Yang-xiu (also known as Ou Yang Hsiu, 歐陽修, 1007-1072) of Northern Song dynasty China. Fierce party strife between Wang An-shi (王安石) of the New Doctrine Faction and Sima Guang (司馬光) of the Old Doctrine Faction also existed during the Northern Song dynasty, and it was generally said that Northern Song fell because of this. Ou Yang-xiu, who belonged to the Old Doctrine Faction, disagreed with this opinion that factions abused their powers; he expounded on his theory on the validity of factions in "On Factions" in 1044.

> It is the natural order of things for virtuous men to create a faction with other virtuous men because they share the same way, and for narrow-minded men to create factions with other narrow-minded men because of gain. But it is my humble opinion that a faction exists only for the virtuous men and not for the narrow-minded men.

The reason was that narrow-minded men could easily disband when united for gain; this was called a "pseudo-faction." There was no change in virtuous men from start to finish, however, because they congregated based on reason. This was indeed "true faction." He added further:

> Thus he who becomes a ruler must spurn the pseudo-factions of narrow-minded men and only appoint the true faction of virtuous men. Then will the world be governed.

True faction and pseudo-faction mentioned here referred to the Old Doctrine Faction and the New Doctrine Faction respectively. This could only be called a self-centered logic of "sheltering ours and striking out at others." Why was this so?

The reign of Shenzong as the sixth emperor of Song during which period Wang An-shi was prime minister was the height of prosperity in Song dynasty, and at the same time monetary economy was well developed. But two of the greatest abuses that accompanied monetary economy were the impoverishment of farmers and small shop owners through the practice of usury and the drain on national finance due to this. One of the new doctrines espoused by Wang An-shi was the Green Sprouts Law with the intent to rescue farmers from the hell of usury.[1] This, of course, incurred the opposition of

---

[1] Green Sprouts Law was a low-interest loan of money and grains to

the landowners and loan sharks. He also established the City Trade Center Law to protect small merchants from the exploitation of large merchants, but this brought him to the point of downfall due to the resistance of eunuchs and the unprincipled coalition of lobbying merchants.[2]

As the name implies, the Old Doctrine Faction opposed the new doctrines and adhered to the laws of the kings of old. There were many supporters of the Old Doctrine Faction among the advocates of the Learning of Master Zhu because the brothers Cheng Mingdao and Cheng Yi-chuan were of the Old Doctrine Faction. Justification for the Cheng-Zhu School was a thought that was not familiar with reform politics, because reform of politics accompanies change and/or destruction of the old justified order to a certain degree.

Wang An-shi was broad-minded enough to appoint Sima Guang, who opposed the new doctrines in a nominal sinecure post, thanks to which Sima Guang was able to complete the renowned *Comprehensive Mirror for Aid in Government* in 19 years. The relationship between Wang An-shi and Sima Guang was that of virtuous men in spite of the opinions of the followers of both factions.

In an excerpt mentioned above in "On Factions," Yi Ik very accurately proclaimed that all factions are formed based on gain.

Factions arise from fights, and fights arise from profit and loss. It is natural for the root of a faction to become deeply implanted as profitability is more urgently needed and for the solidarity of the faction to cement as profitability becomes prolonged.... Why do factions exist? The number of those who pass the civil service examination has grown by leaps and bounds due to the frequency with which the civil service examination was held, and one's attitude has not become stable due to partialities.

---

farmers in spring and fall to tide them over until harvest. (S. Lee)

[2] City Trade Center Law was the establishment of trade centers in major cities so that items which small merchants could not sell were purchased or accepted as collateral for a loan. (S. Lee)

Civilian officials and followers of the faction in power were appointed to the post of government officials in the late Joseon period through frequent holding of special examinations which were irregular examinations in addition to the triennial examinations. Thus attaining a government position without collusion with powerful factions of civilian officials was not possible even after passing the civil service examination because the number of available posts was limited.

Party disputes were not the confrontation of virtuous men and narrow-minded men; rather, they were no different than excluding opposing parties from the king by disparaging them as of narrow-minded men and watching out for an opportunity to monopolize power. Party disputes were power struggles that protected people of the same mentality and attacked people who were different in the form of "shelter ours and strike out at others."

Yi Ik argued for the reform of the civil service examination as a countermeasure for uprooting party strife, and further, advocated for the union of scholar and farming by claiming that the basic cause of factional struggles arose from separation between scholars and farming.

> Would not the world be governable if people were not treacherous and greedy? Treacherousness and greed arise from lack of goods, and goods are lacking because efforts are not put into farming.... People will consider farming their duty and become used to it and be comfortable in what they do if scholars and farming become one, so that the capable and the virtuous are chosen from the remote regions as fish play in the water and birds go back to the forest instead of having them wait for self-recommendation.

> • "Yukdu" (六蠹), Foreword in
> Insignificant Explanations of Seongho (星湖僿說)

Establishment of Coalition Government through the Policy of Impartiality

The period of Yeongjo and Jeongjo mentioned here refers to the 76-year reign of Yeongjo (英祖, r. 1724-1776) and Jeongjo (正祖, r. 1776-1800) who ruled after Gyeongjong.

Yeongjo put forth the Policy of Impartiality throughout his 52-year reign to put a stop to the political confusion caused by party strife, and Jeongjo also upheld that. The Policy of Impartiality was a phrase taken from a sentence in "The Great Plan" (洪範), *Book of Documents*: "Nonpartisan and impartial, the Kingly Way is widely transmitted; fair and impartial, the Kingly Way is level." In short, this policy aimed to induce a change in the relationship between each faction from opposition to coalition by realizing the goal of governing in the kingly way.

Yeongjo succeeded Gyeongjong as king and was Gyeongjong's younger half-brother; he was called Yeoning-gun (延礽君) prior to his ascension to the throne. The Soron Faction put Gyeongjong on the throne, but because Gyeongjong did not have any sons to succeed him, the Noron Faction supported the appointment of his half-brother as the Crown Prince. The Soron Faction oppressed the Noron Faction fiercely, and Yeoning-gun himself rendered his resignation as Crown Prince on several occasions without success.

After Gyeongjong passed away, confrontation between the Soron and Noron Factions reached an extreme degree of tension because the Soron Faction spread a rumor that the Noron Faction poisoned Gyeongjong. Yeongjo ascended to the throne under these circumstances and executed the Policy of Impartiality to end the vicious circle of endless revenge and attempted to establish a coalition government based on moderate members of both factions who supported the policy. The logic in furthering this theory was the "theory of both parties being correct and both parties being incorrect." A member in one party was imbued with absoluteness and thus "correct," while the opposing parties were frontally negated and regarded as "incorrect" in party strife. This was the so-called black-

and-white logic. Both parties contained correctness and incorrectness, however, and thus reconciliation and coalition between the two parties were induced through the logic of adopting what was correct and throwing away what was incorrect.

The Policy of Impartiality advocated by Yeongjo put the Noron Faction that supported him to the throne as the mainstream and had the Soron and Namin Factions participate on the side. Kim Han-gu (金漢耉), father to Yeongjo's second queen (of the Kim clan), and Hong Bong-han (洪鳳漢), father to the wife of Crown Prince Jangheon (莊獻世子, 1735-1762) who was in line to succeed Yeongjo, were both leaders of the Noron Faction. The Noron Faction was the maternal relation of the royal family during the reign of Yeongjo.

In 1762 and under the manipulation of Kim Han-gu and others, someone by the name of Na Gyeong-eon (羅景彦) submitted to Yeongjo a repeal containing 10 misdeeds of Crown Prince Jangheon. Yeongjo became angry and rescinded the title of Crown Prince from Jangheon without first checking into the facts, and the unprecedented tragedy occurred of Jangheon starving to death after being locked in an empty rice bin for seven days. The Noron divided into the Byeok Faction (辟派, Faction of Principle) and the Si Faction (時派, Faction of Expediency), the former faction claiming justification of this incident by mentioning the strange behaviors of the Crown Prince and the latter faction sympathizing with the stand of the Crown Prince. The Byeok Faction of the Noron Faction falsely charged the Crown Prince because it was afraid of the eventuality of the Crown Prince, who opposed the tyranny of the Noron Faction, from ascending to the throne.

Yeongjo later repented the death of the Crown Prince by starvation and atoned for his death by awarding him the posthumous title of "Crown Prince Sado" (思悼世子). The son of Crown Prince Jangheon (the eldest grandson of Yeongjo) ascended to the throne in March of 1776 as Jeongjo. The son of Crown Prince Jangheon who committed a great crime against nation and society could not succeed to the throne, of course. Thus Yeongjo registered his eldest grandson by Crown Prince Jangheon as the successor to the deceased Crown

Prince Hyojang (孝章世子, 1719-1728) in 1728 to make way for him to succeed to the throne.

Jeongjo ascended to the throne at the age of 25 and during an audience with all of his vassals proclaimed:

> Ahh! I am the son of Crown Prince Sado. The preceding king (Yeongjo) made me the successor to Crown Prince Hyojang because he considered orthodoxy of the royal family important.

Jeongjo announced that he was not the son of Crown Prince Hyojang but the son of Crown Prince Sado who died due to the Noron Faction's scheming. This was an overt challenge to the Noron Byeok Faction. Jeongjo punished main members of the Byeok Faction such as Kim Han-gu and Hong Bong-han who covertly and openly obstructed his ascension to the throne. The second queen of Yeongjo (of the Kim clan) was the daughter of Kim Han-gu, leader of the Byeok Faction. The Noron Byeok Faction managed to preserve power under the protection of the second queen even during the reign of Jeongjo and waited for an opportunity to launch a counterattack. In 1801, a year after Jeongjo passed away, the second queen led a plot of revenge against the Namin Faction in the form of the "Sinyu Persecution of 1801" (辛酉敎難), which will be discussed later.

Below is a representation of the general shift in academic cliques and factional cliques since the division of the Sarim Faction into the Dong'in and Seoin Factions in 1575:

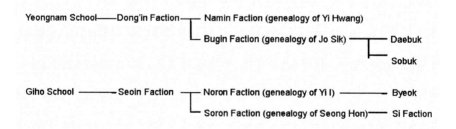

Jeongjo Gathers Talented Men to Gyujanggak Archives

Jeongjo created Gyujanggak Archives (奎章閣) within Changdeok Palace in 1776 and called it the Cabinet. Civilian officials who became divided through the factional disputes were called together and domestic and foreign documents were gathered to carry out not only royal lectures where political affairs were discussed with the king but also the pivotal functions of various cultural activities. The Gyujanggak Archives were indeed the intellectual center of the reign of Jeongjo. It performed the same role as that of the Hall of Worthies established by Sejong in the early Joseon period.

Jeongjo appointed Chae Je-gong (蔡濟恭, pen name is Beonam 樊巖, 1720-1799) of the Namin Faction to the post of Academician of Gyujanggak Archives, after which he was promoted to Third State Councilor, then Second State Councilor, and finally Chief State Councilor. Namin Faction was the archenemy of the Noron Faction. There were a total of six officials at Gyujanggak Archives in addition to four Geomseo-gwan (檢書官): two Jehak (提學), two Jikjehak (直提學), one Jikgak (直閣), and one Daegyo (待敎).[3] These were all very close to Jeongjo. Those appointed to the post of Geomseo-gwan included Bak Je-ga (朴齊家, pen name is Chojeong 楚亭, 1750-?), Yi Deong-mu (李德懋), and Yu Deuk-gong (柳得恭) who could not prove their abilities until then. This delay was due to the fact that they were discriminated against because although they were sired by members of renowned *yangban* families of the Noron Faction, their mothers were concubines. They had interchange with bibliographical scholars of Chinese Classics in the Qing dynasty while traveling back and forth from Beijing to purchase books. Jeongjo indiscriminately appointed members of the Namin genealogy

---

[3] Jehak was Academician of Gyujanggak with the rank of Jong 1-*pum* or Jeong 2-*pum*; Jikjehak was Assistant Academician of Gyujanggak with the rank of Jong 2-*pum* or Jeong 3-*pum*; Jikgak was an official of Gyujanggak with rank of Jeong 3-*pum* to Jong 6-*pum*; Daegyo was an official of Gyujanggak with rank of Jeong 7-*pum* to Jeong 8-*pum*; and Geumseo-gwan was editor-compiler of Gyujanggak. (S. Lee)

and the Noron genealogy who until then were arch-enemies as officials of Gyujanggak Archives and Geomseo-gwan.

Yu Hyeong-won (柳馨遠, pen name is Ban-gye 磻溪) pioneered the Silhak School that bloomed in the periods of Yeongjo and Jeongjo, but the figure that inherited and developed the thought into a school was Yi Ik. Yu Hyeong-won and Yi Ik both belonged to the Namin Faction and were scholars who did not hold government posts. Teacher-student relations as well as marriage ties were not formed if factions differed in those days, and thus scholars of the Namin genealogy who were excluded from the political world gathered around Yi Ik. This was the Seongho School. Not only did Jeongjo select Chae Je-gong of the Namin Faction as prime minister; he also appointed Yi Ga-hwan and Jeong Yag-yong, who were eminent men of the Seongho School, to important posts in the latter half of his reign.

A group of scholars of the Noron genealogy was among the Silhak School; this group was the Bukhak School (北學派, Northern Learning School) of the late 18th century centered around Hong Dae-yong (洪大容, pen name is Damheon 湛軒, 1731-1783), Bak Ji-won, and Bak Je-ga. Unlike the Seongho School of the Namin genealogy, the Bukhak School of the Noron genealogy passed on observation records of visits to Beijing during an opportunity to accompany the Joseon envoy to Yenching (old name for Beijing). Representative records were *Damheon yeon-gi* (湛軒燕記, Damheon's Account of Travels to Yenching) by Hong Dae-yong based on his accompaniment of the envoy in 1765, *Yeolha ilgi* (熱河日記, Jehol Diary) by Bak Ji-won based on his accompaniment of the envoy in 1780, and *Bukhagui* (北學議, Discourse on Northern Learning) by Bak Je-ga based on his visit to Beijing in 1778 with Yi Deong-mu in the capacity of Geomseo-gwan to purchase books for Gyujanggak Archives.

Bak Ji-won was able to travel from Yenching to Rehe (old name for Chengde) because Emperor Qianlong was at the summer villa in the mountains when Bak Ji-won arrived in Yenching. *Jehol Diary* is highly rated as one of the foremost works of Korean literature on travels because it contains works of various genres in addition to observations of Beijing or Rehe. These members of the Bukhak School visited Beijing during the reign of Emperor Qianlong, a ruler who liked scholarship.

Philologico-bibliographical study in Qing China reached a climax focusing on the study of Confucian Classics and history during the 60 years of rule of Emperor Qianlong. Previous emperors Kangxi and Yongzheng were strict scholars of the Learning of Master Zhu, but Emperor Qianlong preferred the philologico-bibliographical study that was the mainstream of the academic world at the time, symbolized by *The Complete Library of the Four Treasures* (四庫全書). The archive for The Complete Library of the Four Treasures was built in 1772 under the command of Emperor Qianlong, and the total number of works of classical literature collected in 10 years reached 79,224 volumes and 3,458 categories of rare and precious manuscripts throughout the world. Seven sets, including the original and copies, were created so that the original was stored in Wenyuan Pavilion within the Forbidden City and the rest stored in various locations around the kingdom. This was an ambitious compilation project that exceeded the works his grandfather, Emperor Kangxi, had commanded for the compilation of 10,000 volumes of *Collection of Past and Present Books*. Bak Je-ga became well acquainted with Ji Yun (紀昀, 1724-1805), who was old enough to be his father, and maintained communication with the latter whenever he visited Beijing; Ji Yun was in charge of compiling *The Complete Library of the Four Treasures*. The cultural growth in the reign of Emperor Qianlong, during which members of the Bukhak School visited, was backed by financial prosperity. The members of the Bukhak School advocated the learning of Qing China as "beneficial use of things and enriching of life," and the practice of "northern learning" to enrich production and lives of people and to eliminate poverty. Three tasks recommended by Yu the Great were written in "The Counsels of Yu the Great" (大禹謨) in *Book of Documents*.[4]

---

[4] "Northern Learning" refers to scholarship from Qing China in this instance. (S. Lee)

Create harmony through correctness of virtue, beneficial use of things, and improvement in the lives of the people.

Bak Ji-won, however, switched the order of correctness of virtue, beneficial use of things, and improvement in the lives of the people and stated, "improvement in the lives of the people can be achieved through beneficial use of things, and correctness of virtue can be achieved through improvement in the lives of the people ("Dogangnok" 渡江錄, Record of the Do River, in *Jehol Diary*). In short, beneficial usage and improvement in the lives of the people must be pursued to achieve correct virtue in "the theory of pursuing riches before educating." This doctrine of Northern Learning toward Qing China was a 180-degree turnaround in logic and was the antithesis of the northern expansion policy advanced since Song Si-yeol.

In comparison, the Seongho School's academic interests lay in research of the study of Confucian Classics and reform of the system to promote the doctrine advocating that any study must contribute to society. The goal of both the Seongho School and the Bukhak School — the former's advocating that any study must contribute to society or the latter's thinking that beneficial use of things and enriching of life go together — was similar to the Hungu Faction in its practical application of statecraft in planning and founding the Joseon dynasty. The main interests are not the impractical learning of the study of the principle of human nature or the study of rites, but practical learning that looks directly at real problems and attempts to resolve them.

Yu Hyeong-won, Pioneer of Practical Learning, Broadens the Scope of Scholarship

Yu Hyeong-won was born in Seoul and was a scholar of the Namin Faction. He moved to a remote village in Uban-dong, Buan-gun in Jeolla Province in 1653 to escape from the whirlpool of party strife and died there. He completed *Ban-gye surok* (磻溪隨錄, Ban-gye's Treatises) while living in seclusion for 20 years. A contemptible fight for self-gain between the Seoin Faction and the Namin Faction developed out of the debate between Song Si-yeol and Yun Hyu on the doctrine of propriety. Transfer of political power and revenge repeatedly occurred during the period in which he lived. This period was ruled by the Seoin Faction's tyranny in thought in that Yun Hyu and Bak Se-dang (朴世堂, 1629-1703) were stigmatized as disturbing and behaving contrary to the Confucian tenets just because they ignored or criticized Zhu Xi.

Jeong Je-du (1649-1736) was barely able to preserve the doctrine of Wang Yang-ming by moving from Seoul to a remote place on Ganghwa Island. The latter half of the 17th century to the first half of the 18th century in which Yun Hyu, Bak Se-dang, and Jeong Je-du were active was a period of attempting resistance against the trend in Joseon Confucianism of wholehearted support of the Learning of Master Zhu and of desperate attempts to explore freedom in studying comprehensive and diverse Confucian Classics. But the efforts ultimately failed in front of the Seoin Faction—the tyrant of thought of the Noron Faction. This was the very period when Yu Hyeong-won left Seoul to live in a remote village.

Yu Hyeong-won was a pioneer of the Silhak School because of his main work titled *Ban-gye's Treatises*. This book was written after several different fields of learning were researched, but these research documents do not exist today. Oh Gwang-un (吳光運) commented about Yu Hyeong-won as follows in "Haengjang" (行狀, Biography) of *Ban-gye's Treatises*:

> I have learned that the foundation of *Ban-gye's Treatises* is not about the virtue of Heaven and the kingly way only after reading the Master's outline of the doctrine of the principle and material force, treatise and study of the principle of things, and interpretation of the Confucian Classics. Moreover, he can discuss about astrology (astronomy), pitch (music), strategy of warfare, selecting a teacher, trajectory of the planets, and condition of the mountains and streams with great familiarity because of his many writings on Jeong-eum Jinam, Mugyeong Saseo, Yeojiji, and the system of localized administration. The master can indeed be

called a Confucian master who combines the essence and utilization of things as well as much learning and propriety at all times.

He was called "a Confucian master" in reference to the fact that his studies were wide-ranging and far-reaching and not limited to the Learning of Master Zhu alone. *Ban-gye's Treatises* is comprised of 26 volumes in 14 books, with 10 sections as described below; it was begun in 1653 and completed in 1672.

①　Land taxation; ② supplement to land taxation; ③ educational system; ④ employment of bureaucrats; ⑤ government organizations; ⑥ stipend land system; ⑦ military duty system; ⑧ supplement to military duty system; ⑨ sequel; and ⑩ addendum to the system of localized administration.

Historical justification for his claims is provided in the "Examination" of each section by referring to documents of China or Joseon. As can be seen from the structural content of the book, the core focus is on reform of the land system, and with this as the foundation it expands to reform of the educational system, civil service examination system, and military system as well. Why did he put emphasis on land taxation reform? This was because land was the foundation of everything under Heaven.

A ruler may attempt to rule the world, but the property of the people will not be stable if the land system is not good, corvée is not equitable, number of houses and families are not clear, military ranks are not organized, lawsuits will not stop, punishments are not fair, accepting bribery will not disappear, and customs will not be pure. Although attempts will be made to conduct politics well and to encourage enlightenment, neither will be done well. What is the reason for this? Land is the great foundation of the world. If the great foundation is not questioned, nothing will attain its due.

- "Jeonje," (田制, Land Taxation), Part I, *Ban-gye's Treatises*

In short, the land taxation reform advocated public ownership of land because unlimited private ownership of land was the source of all evil. Based on this, his thought was of corresponding military and agriculture reform in which a system of equitable distribution of land under the principle of "possession of the land in the hands of those who farm the land" was followed by a corresponding military reform. Below is the core of this thought:

> In general, 100 *bo* should be counted as one *mu*, 100 *mu* as one *gyeong*, and four *gyeong* as one *jeon*.[5] One man should receive and occupy one *gyeong* (he should receive 1 *jeon* if there are four men), pay tax according to the law, and one soldier should be sent per four *gyeong*.

- "Jeonje," (田制, Land Taxation), Part I, *Ban-gye's Treatises*

Each farmhouse should be given 100 *mu* and taxed according to the law on the harvest (1/15). Military duty should be such that one man out of four families must be chosen to serve, and the other three families must help the family whose man was serving his term. Ultimately, this was an idea about abolishing all burdens other than paying tax of 1/15 on the harvest and sending one man from four families to serve in the military.

In the system of cultivating and employing able men, schools should be established in three stages nationally in the form of town schools (in each district and county) → province schools (in each province) → National Confucian Academy (at the capital), and appropriate able men should be selected from them at the capital and dispatched to appropriate positions in the provinces. The aim was to abolish the civil service examination based on poetry and prose or the study of Confucian Classics and instead enforce the tributary system based on virtuous acts and discernment.

---

[5] *Bo* and *mu* are units of area; 1 *bo* = 3.954 sq. yds.; 1 *mu* = 99.174 m^2. (S. Lee)

Namin scholars of practical learning examined whether the system of equitable distribution of land mentioned in *Ban-gye's Treatises* could be put into practice in reality. For example, reform measures such as Yi Ik's system of limiting land possession and Jeong Yag-yong's land distribution system were proposed. As can be glimpsed from *Ban-gye's Treatises*, Yu Hyeong-won's scholarship was about the reform of military, educational, and civil service examination systems based on stability of agricultural life from land reform; this was in direct contrast to the academic traditions centered on the study of the principle of human nature. Even more, his research not only included the study of Confucian Classics but various fields which were disdained by the scholars of the study of the principle of human nature as miscellaneous studies. In other words, he destroyed the wall between the study of Confucian Classics and miscellaneous studies, according to "Biography" by Oh Gwang-un. This was the reason for his being evaluated as a "Confucian master."

The only work by Yu Hyeong-won that exists to date is *Ban-gye's Treatises*. Yeongjo commanded Chancellor Hong Gye-hui (洪啓禧) to write a biography when *Ban-gye's Treatises* became the talk of the town among some scholars in the mid-18th century. The king ordered the book to be published in the 45th year of the reign of Yeongjo (1769); it was issued the following year.

According to the biography written by Hong Gye-hui, the scholarship of Yu Hyeong-won adopted the method of approaching the core of various issues by viewing things as immobile or mobile. If immobility were understood as land and mobility as able men in *Ban-gye's Treatises*, then the issues of reconsolidation of education, selection of able men for government office, and conscription for military service should be based on the foundation of the land system. Unlike its humble title, *Ban-gye's Treatises* is not a collection of simple opinions on reform, but a systematically organized book on statecraft from beginning to end.

Seongho Yi Ik Writes an Encyclopedia while Living in Seclusion

Yi Ik was born in Unsan, Pyeong'an Province, in the seventh year of the reign of Sukjong (1681) where his father, Yi Ha-jin (李夏鎭), was exiled. Yi Ha-jin was the Inspector General of Namin Faction but was banished by the Seoin Faction after the latter gained power through the Reversal of the Political Situation in the Year of Gyeongsin in 1680. Yi Ik moved to Cheomseong-li, Ansan-gun in Gyeonggi Province one year after he was born because his father passed away in 1682. Yi Ik's second eldest brother Yi Jam (李潛) who taught Yi Ik was flogged to death in 1706 for submitting an appeal to the king in defense of their father. Yi Ik abandoned studies for the purpose of passing the civil service examination and lived in seclusion after having directly witnessed the woes of party strife.

Fortunately, however, Yi Ha-jin had in his possession many thousands of books he had purchased during his travel to Beijing in the fourth year of the reign of Sukjong (1678). The scholarship of Yi Ik did not stop at Confucianism but was encyclopedic in scope, including western Catholicism and sciences, thanks to the books his father left behind.

Yi Ik belonged to the Namin Faction, and as such concentrated on the Cheng-Zhu School and Yi Hwang's scholarship in the beginning, but gradually distanced himself from the study of the principle of human nature which was unrelated to real life; he later concentrated his interests on current affairs, i.e., immediate issues faced in real life. He expanded the thoughts of Yi Yi and Yu Hyeong-won on statecraft; he stated that the two most knowledgeable scholars on "current affairs" since the founding of the Joseon dynasty were Yi Yi and Yu Hyeong-won (Foreword in "Changes in Law," *Insignificant Explanations of Seongho*).

Insignificant Explanations of Seongho is a collection of "insignificant stories" as the title states, but the contents are encyclopedic in scope. Reform plans covering the entire national administration he had advanced are contained in 20 volumes of *Japjeo* (雜著, Miscellaneous

Stories) and 19 volumes of *Records of Concerns for the Underprivileged*; the two books are mostly the same. The table of contents of *Miscellaneous Stories* is as follows:

1. Gonggeo saui (貢擧私議, Private Evaluation of Recommended Men); 2. Seon-geo saui (選擧私議, Private Evaluation of Selected Men); 3. Non-gongsa (論貢士, Discussion on Those Who Passed the First-Level Test Conducted in the Provinces); 4. Non-hakje (論學制, Discussion on the Educational System); 5. Non-yong'in (論用人, Discussion on Employing Men); 6. Bungdangnon (朋黨論, Theory on Factionalism); 7. Non-gan'gwan (論諫官, Discussions on Advisors); 8. Non-eosa (論御史, Discussion of Royal Emissary); 9. Non-ryeyu (論賂遺, On Bribery); 10. Gyunjeon-non (均田論, Theory of Equitable Distribution of Land); 11. Non-gwaljeon (論括田, Discussion on Land Management); 12. Non-buse (論賦稅, Discussion on Tax Levy); 13. Non-hogu (論戶口, Discussion on Household); 14. Non-gyeongbi (論經費, Discussion on Expenditure); 15. Non-jojeok (論糶糴, Discussion on Exchange of Grain); 16. Non-jinhyul (論賑恤, Discussion on Relief Aid); 17. Non-byeongje (論兵制, Discussion on Military Duty); 18. Non-nobi (論奴婢, Discussion on Slaves); 19. Non-jeonhwa (論錢貨, Discussion about Money); and 20. Non-gyeongjang (論更張, Discussion on Reformation of Old Systems).

Yi Ik insisted that old systems must be reformed if evil influences were created in "Discussion on Reformation of Old Systems." Many, however, considered it best to adhere to the old systems because of fear of revenge from political enemies in case the reformation of the old systems failed. The reform ideas of Yi Ik and Yu Hyeong-won were not executed in those times because of this fear.

In general, many of his (Yu Hyeong-won's) words overlap with Yulgok's words. A few examples are that unnecessary posts should be abolished but appointed posts must be made to work for a long period; virtuous act must be given priority when employing people; small troops should be combined; children of slaves should not be made into slaves. Yulgok has stated the same as well. But these issues are not reformed because [people] are afraid of what might happen when the reform fails.

Yi Ik sharply criticized the idea that people keenly felt the necessity for such reforms but hesitated to act upon them because of private understandings.

There is fear that abolishing unnecessary posts and combining small troops would lead to obstacles in promotion due to a lesser number of people, and advancement will be blocked if one stays at one post for long; if people are employed based on their virtuous acts, those whose only talent lies in poetry and prose will not be employed. Also, the master will lose slaves if the children of slaves do not become slaves. How can big reforms be expected when these smaller things cannot be reformed?

The 1801 Persecution of Catholics in Joseon Crushes Budding Western Learning

The fact that Yi Ik cultivated thought that was receptive to Western Learning and that the Seongho School inherited and developed this thought was a more landmark event in the history of Korean thought than the ideas of Yi Ik on good governance. The Jesuit missionaries in Beijing played the role of a medium in the acceptance of Western Learning by Joseon.

Matteo Ricci (Chinese name is Li Matou, 利馬竇), a Jesuit missionary, entered Beijing in 1601. Other Jesuit missionaries who followed in his footsteps translated western science books on astronomy, mathematics, calendar-making, and geography into Chinese characters. The distribution of these works was used as a means to propagate missionary activities. The envoy to Yenching brought much of this information back to Joseon.

Despite the fact that Yi Ik did not hold any government posts, he read an unparalleled number of documents on Western Learning which were translated into Chinese and learned about western instruments. This was the reason for his ability to overcome the traditional Confucian doctrinarism. Among the documents on Western Learning transmitted to Joseon, he commented on Matteo Ricci's *The True Meaning of the Lord of Heaven* (天主實義), Giulio Aleni's (Chinese name is Ai Rulue, 艾儒略) book on world geography titled *Complete Map of All Nations*, interpretation of Ptolemy's astronomy by Emmanuel Diaz (or Manuel Dias, Chinese name is Yang Ma-no, 陽瑪諾) in a book titled *Epitome of Questions on the Heavens* (天文略), by addition of a postscript.

Not only did Yi Ik realize that the earth was round in contrast to the Confucian theory that heaven was round and the earth was square after reading *Epitome of Questions on the Heavens*, but was convinced of it through *Complete Map of All Nations*, a book on world geography that contained the results of the discovery of the new continents and circumnavigation of the earth. By overcoming the theory that heaven was round and the earth was square, wherein China was at the center and barbarians at the four corners of the earth, he was able to objectively view western religion and sciences that were different from those of China.

Yi Ik's attitude toward western Catholicism and science was clearly revealed in "Bal cheonju silui" (跋天主實義, Epilogue to the True Meaning of the Lord of Heaven). He criticized Catholicism which talked about "heaven and hell" in the life after death just as in Buddhism, and was contradictory to the concerns of Confucianism over how life should be lived in this world as being only an illusion. But he rated the astronomy, geography, mathematics, and calendar-making of the West highly as being marvelous methods that did not exist in the East. In other words, this was an acknowledgement of the doctrine of "eastern ways and western machines" in which Confucianism was considered superior to Catholicism but western science superior to eastern science. There was a big difference between his thought and that of those inflexible scholars who were so concerned about the orthodox teachings of Confucius → Mencius → Cheng-zi → Zhu Xi because they considered the Learning of Master Zhu as the only scholarship.

Yi Ik's best students Ahn Jeong-bok (安鼎福, pen name is Sun-am 順庵, 1712-1791) and Gwon Cheol-sin (權哲身, pen name is Nog-am 鹿菴, 1736-1801) were in line to carry on the Seongho School after Yi Ik passed away in 1763. Some of the younger pupils under the tutelage of Gwon Cheol-sin began to gradually proceed from academic interest in Western Learning to the Catholic faith. Yi Byeok was the central figure of this transition.

Ahn Jeong-bok, the eldest of the Seongho School, gathered Yi Ik's manuscripts and compiled them into *Insignificant Explanations of Seongho.* In his concern for the possible attack from opposition under the manipulation of the Noron Byeok Faction, he expounded on the issue of Catholicism as "heresy" in *Cheonhakgo* (天學考, Cogitation on the Teachings of Catholicism) and *Cheonhak mundap* (天學問答, Confucian Answers to the Teachings of Catholicism) and warned the younger pupils of the Seongho School of the dangers in admiring Catholicism.

Yi Seung-hun (李承薰, 1756-1801), one of the pupils of Gwon Cheol-sin, accompanied his father Yi Dong-uk (李東郁) when the latter was appointed recorder of travel logs in the envoy to Beijing. Yi Seung-hun listened to the advice of Yi Byeok and sought out a Jesuit missionary in Beijing by the name of Jean Joseph de Grammont (Chinese name is Liang Dong-cai, 梁棟材) to be baptized before returning to Joseon. This occurred in March of 1784. With this as an impetus, the Korean Catholic Church was created in the following year of 1785 with Yi Seung-hun, Yi Byeok, and Gwon Il-sin (權日身, the younger brother of Gwon Cheol-sin and son-in-law of Ahn Jeong-bok) as the focal point.

As feared by Ahn Jeong-bok, however, "purging of heterodoxy" that criticized not only the Catholic faith of the Seongho Faction but also the study of Western Learning ultimately drove the Namin Faction into a corner. Not even Jeongjo and Prime Minister Chae Je-gong could protect Catholicism. Someone came up with the following idea to prevent the oppression of Catholics from spreading further: "even a Catholic believer must be treated as a human being and only the Catholic documents must be burned."

However, Chae Je-gong passed away in 1799 at the old age of 80, and Jeongjo followed suit in 1800 at the age of 49. Sunjo (純祖, r. 1800-1834), son of Jeongjo, ascended to the throne at the young age of 11. Queen Jeongsun started to play a big role in politics as the second wife of Yeongjo. She was the younger sister of Kim Gu-ju (金龜柱), a leader of the Noron Byeok Faction. She became the Dowager Queen as the oldest of the royal family and acted as regent for the young ruler Sunjo. She appointed members of the Noron Byeok Faction to important government posts, such as Kim Gwan-ju (金觀柱) and Sim Hwan-ji (沈煥之), who had been excluded from politics during the reign of Jeongjo. The newly appointed officials formulated the plan for the 1801 Persecution of Catholics in Joseon as an excuse to oppress the Namin Faction.

Central figures of the Seongho School such as Gwon Cheol-sin and Yi Ga-hwan were imprisoned, Jeong Yak-jong (丁若鐘, pen name is Seongjo, 選菴), Yi Seung-hun, and Hong Nang-min (洪樂敏) were executed, and Jeong Yak-jeon (丁若銓) and Jeong Yag-yong were exiled in the 1801 Persecution of Catholics in Joseon. Among those punished were three Jeong brothers, Jeong Yak-jong, Yak-jeon, and Yag-yong.

After this incident the ambience of Joseon thought became such that people dared not approach Catholicism or Western Learning without being prepared to ruin one's entire family. The first half of the 19th century was a period in which East Asia gradually began to feel the shock of the west in earnest. Knowledge about the west was imperative in order to cope with it, but unfortunately, the study of Western Learning that began to bud within the Seongho School was ruthlessly crushed at the start. It is not an exaggeration to say that Korean movement towards modern thought took a different course than Japan or Qing China because of this 1801 incident.

Qing Is an Advanced Nation, the Bukhak School Shouts

As mentioned before, Yi Ik was able to overcome the traditional theory that assumed heaven was round and the earth was square with

China at the center of the earth and the ethnic groups at the four corners of the earth as barbaric through reading *Epitome of Questions on the Heavens,* which explained Ptolemy's astronomy, and *Complete Map of All Nations,* a geography book that reflected the geographic discovery of maritime navigation. Hong Dae-yong of the Bukhak School took this one step further and altered the worldview of China vs. barbarians by shouting that "China and the barbarians are the same." "The doctrine of Northern Learning," which was the antithesis to "the northern expansion policy," was founded on such a worldview. Important leaders of the Bukhak School were Hong Dae-yong, Bak Ji-won, and Bak Je-ga of the Noron Faction who were active mainly in the latter half of the 18th century.

Hong Dae-yong wrote what could be called a type of philosophy book titled *Uisan mundap* (毉山問答). This book is a discussion between "Master Heo" (Daoist) and "Sil-ong" (scholar of practical learning), where the latter refutes the stereotypes of the former. "Sil-ong" makes the following objections in discussing "the distinction between China and non-China" and "the distinction between internal and external" as referred to in Confucianism:

> China is 180 degrees different if viewed from the west. Chinese people consider China to be the righteous world and the west to be the backward world. Western people consider the west as the righteous world and China as a backward world. They are indeed both the same world in that they both have the heaven up high and the earth below. Thus there does not exist a vertical or a reversed world; they are both righteous worlds.

There was little distinction between China and the four barbarians from the perspective of the doctrine of a round earth. East Asia and the western nations could both be the righteous world or the backward world; in this thought, they were "all righteous worlds." The basis for discrimination such as superior and inferior positions, internal and external, valuable and common, and high and low between China and non-China disappeared. Conversely, this worldview that the world was round was a landmark thought in that it could overthrow the worldview of the westerners who considered it a duty to Christianize uncivilized nations because Christian nations were thought to be civilized and non-Christian nations to be barbaric.

Bak Ji-won wrote the foreword in *Discourse on Northern Learning*, a book written by Bak Je-ga who studied under him; in it he criticized the tendency of the Joseon Confucian world to consider it "embarrassing to learn from China now that the owner of China is a barbarian."

> They shave their heads and the lappets of their coats are buttoned on the left side, but the land on which they live is China of Han, Tang, Song, and Ming since the three generations (of Xia, Yin, and Zhou). Those who live on this land are indeed the descendants of Han, Tang, Song, and Ming. If the law is good and the system beautiful, it is only right to go in front of the barbarians to learn from them — to say nothing of the vastness of its scope, precision of its mind, creativity of its creations, and brilliance of its sentences that preserve the original aspects of Han, Tang, Song, and Ming since the three generations.

In other words, Bak Ji-won distinguished the ruling Manchus from the non-ruling Han people and said that the Chinese civilization since the three generations still permeated Qing China. This argument was rhetorical in that it raised an objection to the worldly Confucians who disdained Qing China as "having become barbaric"; his real intention was to say that one should take barbarians as teachers if they have something worth learning. Thus this should be comprehended in the same line as not only learning "Northern Learning" from Qing China but also "Western Learning" from the western barbarians.

This is very similar to the thought of Wei Yuan (魏源) as expressed in the foreword of his book, *Illustrated Treatise on Nations across the Sea* (海國圖志): "We must learn the special skills of the barbarians and use them to control them." Wei Yuan lived in the first half of the 19th century toward the end of the Qing dynasty before its downfall due to losing the Opium War. "Cut hair and left lappet" referred to cutting of hair and Chinese garments that symbolized the nationalism of the Manchus.

There were many in Korea who viewed the northern expansion policy as "independence" or "resistance" toward Qing China, but it was no different than worship of the powerful Ming. This was nostalgia for the lost spirit of Ming China by admiring Chinese culture and thought that had already been deserted by the Chinese people. If that were the case, then was the doctrine of Northern Learning worshipping the powerful Qing? This could be called an independent position for subjectively receiving foreign culture based on a scientific worldview that denied both China and non-China.

Yi Ga-hwan and Jeong Yag-yong of the Seongho School (the Namin Faction) and Bak Je-ga, Yi Deong-mu, Yu Deuk-gong, and Seo Ri-su of the Bukhak School (the Noron Faction) were employed as close advisors to the king in the reign of the enlightened ruler Jeongjo in the latter half of the 18th century, but the Silhak School could no longer exist as a faction after the death of Jeongjo due to the machinations and oppression of the opposing faction.

Bak Je-ga Emphasizes the Importance of Commerce

The Noron Byeok Faction had control over actual power even during the Jeongjo period. And because of this, Yi Ga-hwan and Jeong Yag-yong were greatly restricted in activities and were exposed to the censure of those advocating the purge of heterodoxy. Bak Je-ga, one of the four Geomseo employed by Jeongjo, was of the Noron Faction but was a close acquaintance of Jeong Yag-yong of a different faction. His thought on reform was the most progressive among the Silhak School. That was why Bak Ji-won remonstrated with Bak Je-ga in the capacity of teacher for the latter's excessiveness.

Three items will be examined from "Byeong-o sohoe" (丙午所懷) which Bak Je-ga submitted to the king on January 22 of the 10th year of the reign of Jeongjo (1786) in his capacity as Jeonseolseo Byeolje (典設署 別提).[6]

---

[6] Jeonseolseo Byeolje was a Jeong 6-*pum* or Jong 5-*pum* rank of the Ceremonial Tent Office. (S. Lee)

The first is development of sea routes for foreign trade. He stated the following at the beginning of "Byeong-o sohoe":

> The greatest vice in our nation is poverty. What would relieve poverty? The only way is to trade with China. A messenger from this court should be sent to the Dept. of Rites in China with the following diplomatic communication: "It is a common principle of the world to trade what one has for what one does not have. Nations such as Japan, Ryukyu Islands, Annam, and the west are trading with Minzhong, Zhejiang, Jiaozhou, and Guangdong (in China). If Your Majesty permits, trade must occur with various foreign nations via the sea." The Dept. of Rites in China will give its consent in the evening of the same day if such a request is made in the morning.

There was of course some trade with China at the borders, and government trade was conducted by merchants who accompanied the envoy to Yenching. What Bak Je-ga especially emphasized was commerce through water routes. Moreover, trade with China via waterways was like trading with many foreign nations, because merchant ships from Japan, Thailand, Annam, and the west came and went from various ports in China. In addition, economic gain was not the only advantage of trading with various nations. Books of the world and manuals on ships, cars, the royal chambers, and household goods could be purchased. Biases of narrow-minded worldly Confucians were expected to be naturally broken down without the necessity for denunciation if trade with China began. In other words, Bak Je-ga was already unfolding a theory on the unilateral opening of the port in 1786.

Second, he advocated inviting a western Jesuit missionary from Beijing to teach the children of the nation "a way to make beneficial use of things and enrich life."

> I have heard that the westerners who make books on the calendar at the Imperial Observatory in Beijing are all familiar with geometry and well versed in the method of making beneficial use of things and enriching life. Capable men who are good administrators will grow abundant like grass within a few years if these men

are invited and treated well with the budget from the Office for Observance of Natural Phenomena and our children are made to learn astronomy and astrophysics in our nation.

Bak Je-ga visited Beijing as Geomseo-gwan in 1778, 1790, and 1801 to purchase books. Those in charge of astronomical observations and calendar-making in Beijing at the time were western missionaries. As mentioned previously, transmission of Catholicism and Western Learning into Joseon until then was indirectly done through western books translated into Chinese by Jesuit missionaries. He advocated inviting Jesuit missionaries to teach Western Learning directly to the children of Joseon. He was merely desirous of differentiating between Catholicism and Western Learning; this strategy was to prevent the Jesuit missionaries from spreading religion but hallow them to teach scientific technologies (method of making beneficial use of things and enriching life). He was concerned that the Jesuit missionaries would not comply with his plan if they were not treated well.

This was not an unrealistic proposal at all. The missionaries each provided a service with scientific knowledge in Qing China under the strict policy of Emperor Qianlong prohibiting religious proselytizing. For example, Augustin von Hallerstein (Chinese name is Liu Songling, 劉松齡) and Anton Gogeisl (Chinese name is Bao Youguan, 鮑友管), with whom Hong Dae-yong communicated in writing at the Southern Church of Beijing in early 1766, were working on astronomical observations or calendar-making at the Imperial Observatory in Beijing.

Michel Benoit (or Benoist, Chinese name is Jiang Youren, 蔣友仁), author of *Whole Map of the World* (坤與全圖), was in charge of creating and printing 104 pieces of copperplate maps by adding Xingjang and Siberian regions to the *Whole Map of China* (皇與全覽圖, *Huangyu quanlantu* in Ch.) under the command of Emperor Qianlong. *Whole Map of the World* was also introduced in Joseon. *Whole Map of China*, which was completed in 1717 by Jesuit missionaries under the command of Emperor Qianlong, was a survey map of China and outlying regions.

393

Inviting Jesuit missionaries to teach "the method of making beneficial use of things and enriching life" went beyond the reform of production and of ending interpersonal problems; it was directly connected to strengthening of the national defense. Bak Je-ga stated the following:

> Military troops should be prepared after being combined with the daily necessities of the people to eliminate waste. Carts are not weapons but they can be used naturally to transport military supplies. Bricks are not weapons but they can be used to build castle walls for all of the people. One hundred techniques and cattle breeding are not for the military, but horses for the three armies as well as offensive and defensive machines cannot be used as weapons if they are not prepared or in shape. Therefore the upper story of a castle gate, lookout tower, spears and shields, and hitting and spearing movements are the end of the military troops; talented scholars and usable machines are the foundation of military troops.

- Introduction in "Byeongnon" (兵論, Military Theory),
Discourse on Northern Learning

The Russo-Japanese hegemonic struggles over Joseon could not be eliminated because Joseon did not have the ability to defend itself. There was no thought of taking a westerner as teacher for 100 years since "Byeong-o sohoe" by Bak Je-ga. Indeed, Bak Je-ga was farsighted beyond his time.

Third was to have descendants of good families without government posts take up suitable professions to prevent idleness.

> People who are idle are parasites on the kingdom. The number of idle people increases because the number of descendants of good families without government posts increases. There are many people in the kingdom who belong to this group, and it is impossible to stop their number from increasing with just one government post.

Bak Je-ga surprisingly suggested that this unused labor be channeled to become water transporters or merchants. He also claimed that they should be assisted with funds or shops so they could "be glad of heart in their work." The civilian officials and families had supported the policy for suppressing the development of commerce, because they considered commerce "the worst profession" among the four professions: scholarship, farming, manufacturing, and commerce. Bak Je-ga, however, thought of scholars, farmers, artisans, and merchants as equal, and viewed merchants as one of the four classes in charge of distribution.

The single goal of the literati class was to become bureaucrats by passing the civil service examination through the performance of mental work; going into the professions of farming, handicraft, and commerce was considered degenerating into commoners. But there were not enough government positions to go around to all of the scholars of good families who passed the civil service examination. Naturally, cliques based on blood, school, and territorial connections formed, and a contemptible scramble for self-gain surrounding the limited number of government posts occurred. *Yangban* who were excluded from gaining government posts became idle and maintained their power and lifestyle by exploiting the commoners.

Yi Ik, a leader of the Seongho School, earlier advocated the thought of identifying scholars with farming so that good families without government posts could become involved in agriculture, and of the central government selecting able men from farming villages. This was part of an attempt to eliminate cliquishness among descendants of good families without government posts. Yi Ik's alternative idea put weight on farming. But Bak Je-ga proposed national assistance in order to induce idle descendants of good families without government posts to participate in transportation or commercial industry. His thinking put emphasis on commerce.

As mentioned above, the problem of eliminating the *yangban* class that had become idle was of common concern to both the Seongho School and the Bukhak School. Jeong Yag-yong, one of Bak Je-ga's firm friends, pointed out some items from the postscript in "Theory on Classics Licentiate" (生員論) authored by Gu Yan-wu, a

Chinese statesman who was active at the end of the Ming dynasty and beginning of the Qing dynasty.

> Lecture Similar to the existence of classics licentiate in China, there are *yangban* in our kingdom. Ting-lin (Gu Yan-wu's pen name) was concerned that the world will be full of classics licentiate, and I also am concerned that the kingdom will be full of *yangban*. But the evil influence of the *yangban* is worse. Classics licentiate is a title earned by passing the civil service examination, but *yangban* is a false title given to civilian and military officials, and there is a restriction on the number of classics licentiate but not on the number of *yangban*. There is change in the world of classics licentiate, but the status of *yangban* does not change even after 100 years once the status is obtained. Thus *yangban* produce more abuse than classics licentiate's evil influence.

> - "Balgojeongnim saengwonnon" (跋顧亭林生員論, Introduction to Ting-lin's Theory on Classics Licentiate), *Yeoyudang jeonseo* (與猶堂全書, Full Collection of Yeoyudang's Works), Vol. 1

Yangban society could subsist only if a very few "workers of the mind" (scholars) existed and the absolute majority were "workers of the body" (commoners). But the exploits and tyranny against the class of "workers of the body" became more focused as more *yangban* with empty titles were reproduced and became idle. This threatened the very existence of the *yangban* society itself. The 19th-century Joseon society was a "period of public uprising" that shook the foundation of *yangban* politics.

Increased reproduction of *yangban* of good families in the latter half of the Joseon dynasty was qualitatively different from the civilian and military officials who passed the civil service examination of the past period as stated in Chapter 15. As Jeong Yag-yong pointed out, these *yangban* of good families were *yangban* of a group that "never cast away their status even after 100 years once the status is obtained." Civil service examination was a system that originally emerged to prevent corruption of monopoly or power due to aristocrats of good families. But the function of the civil service examination itself changed due to the formation of cliques.

In addition, the scholarship of Gu Yan-wu, who wrote *Records of Things Knowledgeable in a Day*, excluded useless theories or debates of "the learning of the principle" (the mind is the principle by the Learning of Master Zhu and the doctrine of the mind is the principle by Wang Yang-ming) which was remote from the reality of the Ming period and pronounced learning of the principle as the study of Confucian Classics. Further, Gu Yan-wu was a pioneer of philologico-bibliographical study in Qing China who used strict historical research to open the way for practical learning that contributed to society in analytical study of the classics. He indicated that "learning of the principle" strayed from the scholarship of Confucius that was his starting point.

> Virtuous men of today gather many honored guests and followers to deliberate only on the mind or nature. They forsake learning and knowing of diverse things in favor of pursuing "consistent things" only and insist on "strict adherence to detail and being familiar with one thing" rather than carrying on a discussion about the sufferings in the world. Do they think by acting so that their way will surely be greater than that of Confucius, their disciples wiser than Zi Gong, and transcend the learning of Confucius to connect directly to the hearts of the two emperors (Yao and Shun)? I do not desire to be acquainted with people like these.
>
> - "Yeo-u innonhakseo" (與友人論學書),
>   *Jeongnimmunjip*, Vol. 3

Jeong Yag-yong Advocates Learning That Is Useful to People

Jeong Yag-yong (丁若鏞, pen name is Dasan 茶山, 1762-1836) was born in Ma-hyeon in Yangju-gun, Gyeonggi Province, and he belonged to the mainstream Seongho School. He left behind approximately 500 comprehensive volumes on *silhak* thought. He reminisced as below on his encounter with the Seongho School:

I was married in the same year I turned 15 (1776). I lived in Seoul when my late father (Jeong Jae-won, 丁載遠) entered government service again as Junior Secretary of the Ministry of Taxation. Master Yi Ga-hwan took the generation by storm with his learning, and all propagated Master Yi's teachings including my brother-in-law, Yi Seung-hun, who applied himself to learning at the time. I had an opportunity to obtain Master Yi's posthumous works, after which I decided to learn Master Yi's teachings.

- "Jachan myojimyeong jipjungbon" (自撰墓誌銘 集中本),
  Full Collection of Yeoyudang's Works

Jeong Yag-yong passed the Erudite Examination in the 13th year of the reign of Jeongjo (1789) and was employed in an important post with Yi Ga-hwan, who also belonged to the Seongho School through gaining the trust of Jeongjo and Prime Minister Chae Je-gong. But Jeong Yag-yong and Yi Ga-hwan were under suspicion of being related to the Catholic faith on several occasions and became the object of censure of those who advocated purging of heterodoxy because they both studied books on Western Learning. But Jeongjo and Chae Je-gong continued to protect these two.

Under the command of Jeongjo, Jeong Yag-yong wrote "Seongseol" (城說, On Castles) to build Suwon Castle and "Gijung gadoseol" (起衆架圖說, A Schematic for a Pulley) to save on construction expense and to reduce labor. This was the result of studying *Descriptions of Ingenious Devices* (奇器圖說), which was a western science book translated into Chinese by Jesuit missionary Johann Terrenz Schreck (Chinese name is Deng Yuhan, 鄧玉函). Jeongjo moved the tomb of his father, Crown Prince Sado who met a calamitous end, to a place near Suwon; perhaps he was thinking of moving the capital to Suwon as well.

Jeong Yag-yong had three older brothers, of which Jeong Yak-jeon and Jeong Yak-jong were second and third older brothers. Jeong Yak-jeon and Jeong Yag-yong were banished to Heuksan Island and Gangjin in Jeolla Province, respectively, while Jeong Yak-jong was executed because they were all implicated in the 1801 Persecution of

Catholics in Joseon. Jeong Yag-yong's relationship to Catholicism will be briefly discussed here. Jeong Yag-yong became deeply immersed in western science, such as astronomy, physics, agriculture, water irrigation, land surveying, and calculus. However, he adopted a critical attitude toward "discarding memorial rites for ancestors" by Catholics after the Jinsan Incident of 1791 in which Yun Ji-chung (尹持忠) and Gwon Sang-yeon (權尙然) of the Catholic faith discarded memorial rites for ancestors.

Fortunately, Jeong Yag-yong's maternal family (the Yun clan) lived in Haenam-gun, which was very close to the place of his banishment. Thus he lived in a mountain villa owned by his maternal relative, Yun Bak (尹博), from 1808; he was able to study the Confucian Classics and concentrate on his writings with the free usage of around 3,000 books maintained in the Yun family library until his banishment was repealed in 1818. His thought on good governance was represented in "the one *pyo* and two *seo*" in the form of *Gyeongse yupyo* (經世遺表, Design for Good Governance), *Mongmin simseo* (牧民心書, Admonitions on Governing the People), and *Heumheum sinseo* (欽欽新書, Toward a New Jurisprudence). *Admonitions on Governing the People* contained plans for improving governance of the people by the local government officials in the provinces; *Toward a New Jurisprudence* discussed revolutionizing the judicial area; and *Design for Good Governance* with a subtitle of "Bang-lae chobon" (邦禮草本) was a concept for an overall reform of the government. The foundation for his thought on good governance that is uniformly reflected in all three books mentioned above was governance based on the people.

An ongoing debate existed on whether the actions of King Tang (湯王) as a vassal of King Jie (桀王) in ancient Xia dynasty China was righteous in overthrowing and killing the tyrant King Jie. Jeong Yag-yong also participated in this debate, and revealed his opinion as below:

In general, how did the Son of Heaven come about? Did he descend from Heaven, or did he emerge from the earth? A leader is chosen to be the head of the neighborhood when five houses become neighbors. A leader is chosen to be the head of the village when five neighborhoods become neighbors. A leader is chosen to be the head of the county when five villages become neighbors. Several heads of counties choose a feudal lord, and several feudal lords choose the Son of Heaven. Thus the Son of Heaven is chosen by the people.

- "Tangnon" (湯論, Discussion of King Tang),
    Full Collection of Yeoyudang's Works, Vol. 1

But the process mentioned above was reversed as times changed.

Since the Han dynasty, the Son of Heaven appointed feudal lords, the feudal lords appointed heads of counties, heads of counties appointed heads of villages, and heads of villages appointed heads of neighborhoods. Thence those who are not servile to their superiors are called contrary. What is contrariness? In the olden days, people were chosen from bottom up, which was orderly, but now people are appointed from top to bottom, which is contrary.

- "Tangnon" (湯論, Discussion of King Tang),
    Full Collection of Yeoyudang's Works, Vol. 1

The tyrant King Jie lost the heart of his people because he behaved "contrarily" despite being chosen by his people as the Son of Heaven. Therefore, Jeong Yag-yong justified King Tang's overthrowing of King Jie as being "orderly" and natural. In addition to *Discussion of King Tang*, Jeong Yag-yong also wrote "Wonmok" (原牧) to advocate governance based on the people. The tone of these two writings bore close resemblance to "On the Prince" (原君, *Yuanjun* in Ch.), "On Ministership" (原臣, *Yuanchen* in Ch.), and "On Law" (原法, *Yuanfa* in Ch.) in *Waiting for the Dawn: A Plan for the Prince* (明夷待訪錄) by Huang Zongxi (黃宗羲, 1610-1695) who lived at the end of Ming and beginning of Qing. Jeong Yag-yong was greatly influenced by the philologico-bibliographical study of Gu Yan-wu and his disciple Yan

Ruoju (閻若璩), as well as Huang Zongxi's governance based on the people in his study of Confucian Classics and his thoughts on good governance.

Whatever the case may be, *Design for Good Governance* was literally a book on good governance which "the traitorous vassal" Jeong Yag-yong wrote for future generations during his banishment. Therefore there is room for improvement and supplementation by future scholars who agree with his thoughts. But there were several items that he proclaimed could not be changed. One of them was "Iyong-gam" (利用監), a concept to enrich and strengthen a country through Northern Learning.

He described it as follows in the clause on "Iyonggam" of Donggwan Gongjo (冬官工曹, East Hall Board Manufacturing), *Design for Good Governance*, Vol. 2.

> I keenly felt the need to learn the system of employing men with suitable skills as stated in Jesuit missionary Terrenz's *Descriptions of Ingenious Devices* which is mentioned in *Collection of Past and Present Books*, Bak Ji-won's *Jehol Diary*, and Bak Je-ga's *Discourse on Northern Learning*. And according to military official Yi Gyeong-mu (李敬懋), the weaponry and firearms are all new; Japanese swords and flintlocks used by Toyotomi Hideyoshi's Japanese troops in the Imjin War are already old. Flintlocks, whips, or clubs probably cannot be used in future invasions from the south or north. To say that the urgent task of today is to study Northern Learning is a statement that reveals the speaker's knowledge of current issues.

Thus he proposed building a separate government office called Iyonggam so that only Northern Learning would be handled there. Leading members of the Iyonggam should include one controller (提調), two Cheomjeong (僉正), two Byeolje (別提), and four educators; it would be imperative to employ talented men who were well versed in the principles of mathematics and their application.[7] What was the reason for this?

> Production of grain will be great with less effort if farming equipment is handy, and hemp cloth and silk will be plentiful with less effort if spinning and weaving machines are handy. There will not be a shortage of products from far away with less effort if systems for ships and carts are handy; multi-story buildings, arbors, and embankments become durable with less effort if pulling or lifting methods are handy. This is the so-called "useful things are plentiful because there are 100 techniques."
>
> But the source of ingenuity for these 100 techniques is all in the principle of mathematics. The basic principle of each side and degree of a triangle must be revealed before its method can be utilized correctly.

Jeong Yag-yong stated that "the source of ingenuity for these 100 techniques is all in the principle of mathematics"; in other words, the person in charge of Iyonggam must be well versed in the principle of mathematics because the basis of modern science or technology was mathematics. This is a truly landmark way of thinking because Joseon Confucians limited the development of "devices" by putting "the way" as the metaphysical on a superior position and "devices" as the physical dependent on the metaphysical. Mathematics and techniques of various artisans were held in contempt as "miscellaneous studies" and "miscellaneous techniques," respectively. Jeong Yag-yong's way of thinking was unique in that he considered the principle of mathematics to be the foundation for separating "devices" from "the way," and developing the former independent of the latter.

His thoughts on good governance as the basis for "the one *pyo* and two *seo*" was built on top of the foundation of the study of Confucian Classics of "Six Confucian Classics and Four Books." Thus his writings as a Confucianist considered the study of Confu-

---

[7] Cheomjeong and Byeolje were government posts with ranks of Jong 4-*pum* and of Jeong 6-*pum* to Jong 6-*pum*, respectively. (S. Lee)

cian Classics as the means and the study of good governance as the end. The contents combined the means and the end.

His writings, however, did not receive a warm welcome from the Confucian world of his time. He describes his vexation and grim feelings in an almost biting way:

> Six Confucian Classics and Four Books cultivate the self with this, and the one *pyo* and two *seo* achieve the world and the nation with this, which is the reason for possessing the means and the end. But those who recognize this are few, and those who are irritated are many. I won't mind burning them if the mandate of Heaven does not permit the possession of the means and the end.

The core of his thought on good governance was "enriching and strengthening the country" as seen in the concept of Iyonggam. But those who advocated the Learning of Master Zhu as the only scholarship claimed this to be rule of might by emphasizing learning of the Way only. Jeongjo said the following while alive:

> People all say that enriching and strengthening the country is rule of might.... How can discussions be held on whether making the people prosper by producing goods in plenty and preventing riots by training the troops is the kingly way or rule of might?

> - July in the 15th year of the reign of Jeongjo,
>   *Veritable Records of King Jeongjo*

Jeong Yag-yong earned the criticism of advocates of the Learning of Master Zhu as the only scholarship because he was consistent in his impartial attitude toward Zhu Xi's annotations of the study of Confucian Classics in "Six Confucian Classics and Four Books." But his *Design for Good Governance* based on the first half of the 19th century was good enough to be included as one of the three books on good governance in the 500-year history of the Joseon dynasty. The other two to be included were Jeong Do-jeon's *Administrative Code of Joseon*, written during the founding period of Joseon, and Yu

Hyeong-won's *Ban-gye's Treatises*, written during the latter half of the 17th century.

Human Nature Is Similar but Changes Based on Habit

The first paragraph of *The Doctrine of the Mean* is as below:

> What Heaven has conferred is called THE NATURE; in accordance with this nature is called The Path of Duty.

The Cheng-Zhu School divided the nature conferred by Heaven into original nature and physical disposition. The original nature of all things was considered to be the same, but that men and things could be distinguished based on the properness or inclination of the physical disposition. The same could be said for the sage or common man based on the purity or impurity of the disposition within each person.

But Jeong Yag-yong saw the doctrine of "nature is the principle" itself as having been influenced by Buddhism, and as incompatible with the relation of "nature conferred by Heaven" in Confucianism as that of fire and ice. Song period scholars of the study of the principle of human nature were severely criticized for this view.

> In general, many scholars of Song Confucianism were immersed in Zen Buddhism in the beginning and were still led by the doctrine of the principle of human nature after coming back (to Confucianism).

> - "Jin-gisimja jigiseongpyeon" (盡其心者知其性章),
>   *Maengja youi* (孟子要義, Essence of Mencius),
>   Jin Xin, Part I

Jeong Yag-yong claimed that a sage and a common man were not differentiated according to the physical disposition because they both like goodness and are embarrassed by evil. "Yang Ho" in *Analects of Confucius* stated as follows:

By nature, men are nearly alike; by practice, they get to be wide apart.

There are only the wise of the highest class and the stupid of the lowest class who cannot be changed.

In a commentary on these sentences, Jeong Yag-yong claimed the so-called great sovereigns Yao and Shun had a like inherent nature as did the so-called evil sovereign King Jie, but they had drifted apart into goodness and evil due to learned "habits."

But Confucian scholar Han Yu (韓愈, 768-824) of the Tang dynasty cemented the theory of the three classes of human nature by advocating that the wise of the highest class were good at birth and the stupid of the lowest class were evil at birth.[8] Moreover, the statement from the excerpt above that "by nature, men are nearly alike" applied only to the "middle class" that was between the wise of the highest class and the stupid of the lowest class and did not apply to the latter two. Jeong Yag-yong sharply criticized the theory of three classes of human nature by pointing out the error.

Han Yu and others limit the statement that men's nature is nearly alike to the middle class, and used the wise of the highest class and the stupid of the lowest class as nicknames for sovereign Yao and King Jie. Zuo Qiuming's unsteady and exaggerated doctrine is quoted to prove the meaning to say as follows:

"The wise of the highest class are good at birth, and the stupid of the lowest class are evil at birth."

This doctrine is merciless to the world and brings misfortune throughout all ages like flood or savage beasts. A sagacious man from birth is not afraid to fall into sin due to pride, and a thickheaded person from birth does not think to change with effort due to despair.

---

[8] The theory of three classes of human nature posits that there were three classes in human nature: goodness without learning belongs to the highest level, goodness or evil based on learning is the middle class, and evil without learning is the lowest level. (S. Lee)

- "Gongdojawal gojawal seongmuseonmu bulseonjang"
(公都子曰 告子曰 性無善無不善章),
Essence of Mencius, Gao Zi, Part I

Jeong Yag-yong claimed that the inherent nature was the same even for the wise of the highest class and the stupid of the lowest class, and goodness and evil as well as sageness and commonness of all men changed according to learned "habits" (social environment or education). The ground for the study of Confucian Classics within the foundation of his reform thought was that all men realized the humanism of "men's nature is nearly alike" through social environment or education.

The reign of Yeongjo and Jeongjo ended with the death of Jeongjo in 1800; and with the 1801 Persecution of Catholics in Joseon as a turning point, the reign of the Andong Kim clan continued until 1863. The Silhak School could not continue under such conditions. Jeong Yag-yong led a life of exile from 1801 to 1818 and passed away in 1836.

A scholar without a government post by the name of Choe Han-gi (崔漢綺, pen name is 惠崗, 1803-1879) broke the stalemate between eastern and western scholarship by proposing a union of the East and the West through "a medium for increasing knowledge." He criticized the policy of "purging heterodoxy and expulsion of things foreign" which prevented and oppressed the study of western religion and science.

> Instead of worrying about Catholicism spreading throughout the world, worry should be on all of the practical being adopted and not being usable. All of the practical being adopted and not being usable is somewhat better; the actual worry should be on using up all of the talented men and not being usable.
>
> - "Dongseo chwisa" (東西取捨), *Chucheuknok* (推測錄)

These words were truly appropriate. In "Tongsaegui" (通塞議), Jeong Yag-yong sharply criticized the closed-door politics that

406

blocked able men from going into government service because the selection process was based on origin by stating that "eight or nine out of 10 elites are cast away despite there not being enough elites to choose from."

Kim Jeong-hui Leaves His Heart on Sehan Island

Kim Jeong-hui (金正喜, pen names are Chusa 秋史 and Wandang 阮堂, 1786-1856), a disciple of Bak Je-ga, came to know masters of Qing philologico-bibliographical study such as Ruan Yuan (阮元) and Weng Fanggang (翁方綱) after visiting Beijing in 1809 by accompanying his father Kim No-gyeong (金魯敬), who was the vice ambassador of the envoy to Yenching in the first half of the 19th century when the Silhak School was disbanded. Kim Jeong-hui was greatly influenced by these two great scholars; he became a great epigrapher and is famous as a calligrapher who developed a new way of calligraphy called the "Chusa-style" by realizing the exquisite principle of ornamental seal characters used in Han dynasty stone monuments. Following the example of his teacher Bak Je-ga, Kim Jeong-hui's communication with Qing scholars was very active.

He concentrated his later years on research of epigraphy, paintings, and writings instead of developing the thoughts of the Bukhak School on good governance from 1840 because he was intermittently banished during this period. He spent nine years on Jeju Island and two years in Bukcheong, Hamgyeong Province. He was not only a master of epigraphy but also a master of the study of Confucian Classics, attested to by his position as Chancellor of Sungkyunkwan. His thought on the study of Confucian Classics did not build a wall between the Learning of Master Zhu (Song School) and philologico-bibliographical study (Han School), but rather considered the investigation of truth based on fact as the only way to the cardinal point of learning. His black watercolor paintings contained Zen beauty due to his familiarity with the School of Zen.

Kim Jeong-hui painted a black watercolor titled "Winter Scene, Cold Time of the Year," which is a masterpiece that seems to see through the mental state of the twilight years through transcendence of worldly fame and fortune.

One of Kim Jeong-hui's pupils was Yi Sang-jeok (李尙迪, pen name is Useon 藕船, 1804-1865) from a family that hereditarily held the post of translation official in Chinese for generations. Yi Sang-jeok became acquainted with many Qing literati at the dynasty's end during his travels as envoy to Yenching, and as such sent rare books purchased in Beijing to his teacher who was in exile on Jeju Island to ease the latter's tedium. The book collection included 120 volumes, such as *Wanxueji* (晚學集) written by Gui Fu (桂馥, pen name is Weiyu 未谷), *Dayunshan fangji* (大雲山房集) written by Yun Jing, and *Huangchao jingshi wenbian* (皇朝經世文編, Essays on Statecraft from the Qing Dynasty) compiled by He Chang-ling. Kim Jeong-hui painted "Winter Scene, Cold Time of the Year" in appreciation of his disciple's consideration and signed it as "Useonsisang Wandang" (藕船是賞 阮堂) in its foreword. He describes his mental state while painting "Winter Scene, Cold Time of the Year" in "the foreword" by praising literati for having transcended the secular power and gains in a world where Confucians focused only on party strife and the means to an end.

> Taishigong (太史公, Sima Qian, the author of *Historical Records*) said a long time ago that one who builds relationships on power and profits becomes estranged when one's power and profits are gone. I am like an old tree, tired of the lonesome island and detached from all these, and yet [you] were concerned about me and expended effort for many days and months from afar for me. Could the words of Taishigong be wrong?
>
> Confucius said people notice conifers are the last to lose their leaves only after the weather turns cold. Pine trees and cypress trees are conifers before and after the weather turns cold because they do not lose their leaves throughout the four seasons. That is why the sage praised the conifers especially after the cold weather sets in.

Kim Jeong-hui praised disciple Yi Sang-jeok's "faithfulness and steadfastness" by taking a sentence from "Zi Han," *Analects of Confucius,* as motif: "When the year becomes cold, then we know how the pine and the cypress are the last to lose their leaves."

Kang Wi (姜瑋, pen name is Chugeum 秋琴, 1820-1884) followed Kim Jeong-hui to places of exile in Jeju Island as well as Bukcheong, Hamgyeong Province, to learn from Kim Jeong-hui. Kang Wi was one of the representatives negotiating a treaty to avoid a military confrontation with Japan on Ganghwa Island after the Ganghwa Island Incident (also known as Unyo Incident) of September 1875. He was one of the scholars with foresight to connect the thoughts of the Bukhak School from Bak Je-ga to Kim Jeong-hui to the Modernization Faction after the Silhak School was disbanded.

I mentioned early on of fresh beauty contained within Kim Jeong-hui's ink paintings. Zen Master Cho-ui Uisun (草衣禪師 意恂, 1786-1866) of Daeheung Temple in Haenam-gun, South Jeolla Province, lived during the first half of the 19th century when "appreciation of Confucianism and depreciation of Buddhism" was still strictly adhered to. He was thoroughly familiar with not only Zen teachings but also had much knowledge about Confucianism because he learned from Jeong Yag-yong when the latter was exiled in Gangjin. He wrote *Dongdasong* (東茶頌) and *Dasinjeon* (茶神傳) after thoroughly investigating tea ceremonies.

Kim Jeong-hui was a lover of tea who, through Zen Buddhism and tea, became a close acquaintance of Zen Master Cho-ui. Moreover, Jeong Yag-yong also loved tea enough to name the mountain villa in Gangjin where he spent his days of exile Thatched Cottage on a Tea Mountain (茶山草堂) and used Dasan (茶山, Tea Mountain) as his pen name. The academic friendship between the two distinguished scholars Jeong Yag-yong and Kim Jeong-hui and Zen Master Cho-ui was rare during a period when Confucians who did not study Buddhism excluded it under "appreciation of Confucianism and depreciation of Buddhism." Kim Jeong-hui wrote the following poem:

*The aroma of tea arises as I sit silently and pour the tea halfway into the cup.
Water will flow and flowers will bloom if this is used skillfully.*

The common element among Jeong Yag-yong, Kim Jeong-hui, and
Choe Han-gi who lived immediately prior to the opening of the port
in the 19th century was that they all threw away the ideological
exclusivity of the Learning of Master Zhu as the only scholarship
and pioneered a pluralistic world of thought. But they were excluded
from policy-making positions. This overlapped the *sedo* politics of the
Andong Kim clan that lasted for 60-some years in the first half of
the 19th century.[9] The later years of Jeong Yag-yong and Kim Jeong-
hui who spent this period in exile symbolized the ideological situation
of this era.

---

[9] Sedo politics referred to a political situation where the king's in-laws (the
queen's family) wielded actual power. (S. Lee)

19

The World Is Changing

Was Qing China a Paper Tiger?

The three kingdoms of East Asia were shaken by the impact of western influence as they entered the 19th century. Their response to this shock was an important issue in determining the continued existence or demise of each kingdom. Of course the impact of western influence in East Asia did not occur for the first time in the 19th century. The unique characteristics of the 19th century were represented by missionary activities and trade through gunboat diplomacy in that the Industrial Revolution in Europe challenged the Asian system of isolation.

After losing the Opium War (1840-1842) to the British, China opened five ports including Shanghai and ceded Hong Kong under pressure to Britain according to the Treaty of Nanjing of 1842. Following this, China could not avoid signing unequal treaties with France and the U.S., including those that were extraterritorial. The East India Company's exporting of opium to China did not stop at slowly destroying the bodies and minds of the Chinese people. Guangdong was the only port for trade with the west prior to the Opium War; the East India Company had a near monopoly over trade at this port.

The aristocratic custom of drinking tea became popular in Britain in the 1820s, and a great quantity of Chinese tea was imported into Britain. Britain faced a trade deficit because it did not have export products great enough to counter the imported tea. The East India Company devised a way for opium from India to be smuggled into China. As a result, a great amount of silver flowed out of China.

411

Rise in the cost of silver due to its great outflow greatly affected the Chinese economy because the value of the coins used in the daily lives of the Chinese people went down, but the tax had to be paid with silver as a rule. The increase in the cost of silver meant a reciprocal increase in taxes.

A prohibition of opium by Imperial Commissioner Lin Zexu (林則徐, 1785-1850) can be called exercising of the right to defend China, but such justification was not effective in facing the British military force. In fact, this Opium War was the prelude to the destruction of the Qing dynasty, but the Beijing Privy Council's awareness of this crisis was very lax. In short, this crisis was understood as equivalent to a dispute with border barbarians in the distant south. There were scholars such as Lin Zexu and his close friend Wei Yuan, author of *Illustrated Treatise on Nations across the Sea*, who rang the alarm bell, but this reaction was limited to a few scholars.

The Arrow Incident that occurred in Guangzhou in 1856 was the first direct hit against the Privy Council of the Qing dynasty. Britain allied itself with the French troops and went north from Guangzhou to Tianjin. Emperor Xian Feng (咸豊帝, r. 1850-1861) entrusted the Prince Gong (恭親王, 1832-1898) whose birth name was Yixin (奕訢) with future affairs and fled to Rehe when the Anglo-French forces advanced into Beijing. This was the so-called Second Opium War.

The Treaties of Tianjin and Beijing officially opened the way for opium trade, and autonomy over tariffs was lost in lieu of paying heavy compensation. Treaties similar to that of the Treaties of Tianjin and Beijing were signed with the U.S., Russia, and Germany as well. Russia in particular gained Yanhaizhou east of the Ussuri River for mediating the treaty between Qing China and the Anglo-French, whereby naval ports were constructed in Khabarovsk where the Amur and the Ussuri Rivers met, as well as Vladivostok south of Yanhaizhou as a stronghold for advancing into East Asia.

The original defense set up by Emperor Kangxi in 1689 when he checked invading Russian military forces and prevented Russians from advancing into the east according to the Nerchinsk Treaty was

412

destroyed. The Great Powers scrambled for plundering rights in China after the Treaties of Tianjin and Beijing.

A strong ruler like Emperor Kangxi (r. 1661-1722), Emperor Yongzheng (r. 1723-1735), or Emperor Qianlong (r. 1735-1795) did not exist in China in this period, and a succession of young and weak emperors were on the throne while the First and Second Opium Wars raged in 19th-century China. Joseon also had young and ineffective kings on the throne during the same period.

Empress Dowager Cixi (or Tzu His) began ruling China as regent when her six-year-old son ascended to the throne in 1861 as Emperor Tongzhi (同治帝, r. 1861-1874). China was in the midst of the Taiping Rebellion (1851-1864) led by Hong Xiuquan (洪秀全) when Emperor Tongzhi ascended to the throne. Scholar-generals of the Han ethnic group such as Zeng Guofan (曾國藩, 1811-1872), leader of the Hunan Province Native Army (Xiang Jun in Ch.), and Li Hongzhang (李鴻章, 1823-1901), leader of the Anhui Army, became prominent in the process of suppressing this rebellion.

Qing China, which had lapsed into Sino-centric thought, began to emphasize dealings with the West as "westernization" shortly after losing the two Opium Wars instead of using the derogatory term "becoming barbaric." Thus the Self-Strengthening Movement (or Westernization Movement, *Yangwu yundong*) began in order to modernize the Chinese troops through diplomacy and the introduction of technology from the west. An organization called the Office for the General Management of Affairs with all Foreign Nations was established in 1861 to lead this effort. Those who led this Self-Strengthening Movement were bureaucrats of the Han ethnic group in favor of westernization (such as Zeng Guofan and Li Hongzhang); they rallied around Prince Gong Yixin, who wielded real power in the stead of Emperor Tongzhi. Two systems, "westernization" and "tribute," existed in the foreign relations of Qing China because the traditional tributary relationship with Joseon and Ryukyu Island was controlled by the Ministry of Rites separately from the "westernization" relationship with the west.

Progressive reformists such as Kang Yu-wei (康有爲) initiated the Hundred Days Reform with the support of Emperor Guangxu in order to break down the limitation of the Self-Strengthening Movement, which attempted to incorporate Chinese traditions as "the body" and western technology as "the tools." Empress Dowager Cixi made the reform activities difficult with the aid of the imperial staff, led by the imperial eunuch Li Lianyang (李漣英), and took political power away from Emperor Guangxu. She exiled Emperor Guangxu to the Water Terrace Pavilion (Yingtai) in the midst of the lake of the Western Gardens (Xiyuan) for 10 years. Thus the Hundred Days' Reform failed three months after it began.

The power of Empress Dowager Cixi (1835-1908) continued for 48 years, from 1861 when Emperor Tongzhi ascended to the throne to the end of the reign of Emperor Guangxu (r. 1874-1908). She passed away after appointing three-year-old Puyi (溥儀: later became Emperor Xuantong, 宣統帝) as the next emperor. Only four years later the Qing dynasty fell in 1912; in fact, the Qing dynasty died with the Empress Dowager Cixi.

Japan opened its ports in 1854 after the signing of the U.S.-Japan Treaty of Peace and Amity (or Kanagawa Treaty), approximately 10 years after China. This was due to the silent threat of four American warships led by Commodore Matthew C. Perry that landed in Uraga Port on the Miura peninsula to deliver a letter of request from President Millard Fillmore for access to Japan. But it was not until four years later in 1858 that a commercial treaty was signed, and treaties with the same conditions were signed with the Netherlands, Britain, Russia, and France in the same year. This is the so-called Ansei Treaties with five nations. These were indeed unequal treaties that included extraterritoriality, but the difference lies in that the treaty with Japan was not established after losing an armed conflict, as was the case with China. Thus Japan was able to study the west and accumulate diplomatic experience with westerners who were the objects of negotiations while extending the commercial treaties for four years, which was fortunate for Japan.

Another thing that was fortunate for Japan was that some citizens studied Dutch Learning (*Rangaku*) through trade with the Dutch

414

merchants in Dejima, Nagasaki, and kept abreast of trends in the west as well as the Opium Wars in China by reading *Dutch World News Service*, which was given by a Dutch merchant prior to the opening of the port.

As described above, Qing China had to sign the Treaty of Nanjing in 1842 as a result of losing a war with Britain, and Japan also had to agree to the Kanagawa Treaty in 1854 in deference to the armed pressure of the U.S. Each began to plan countermeasures against such external threats.

Japan was more responsive to the external threats than China, which was drowning in an inflexible frame of Sino-centrism. In general, people commonly referred to the supporters of the late Bakufu period in Japanese history as advocates of excluding foreign things. But what would have been the result if exclusion of foreign things had been enforced? The Satsu-Ei War of 1863 (war between Britain and Satsuma Port, called Kagoshima today) and the bombing of Shimonoseki in 1864 by the allied naval forces of Britain, France, the U.S., and Holland confirmed the fact that Japan invited its own self-destruction. Roju Abe Masahiro was a true "patriot" because he responded appropriately to the external threat. Korea also needed such patriots.

Since becoming a Roju (Head Councilor, the highest government post in Japan) in 1843, Abe Masahiro supervised foreign relations and national defense for 14 years until his death. He built Gaio Gakari in 1844 and built on western education by creating the Naval Training Institute (Kaigun Denshujo) in Nagasaki in 1855 and Bansho Shirabesho (institution for the translation and study of western books, later Tokyo University) in 1856. The naval officers and the naval ships used for training at the Naval Training Institute were Dutch. The professors and teaching assistants at Bansho Shirabesho were all Japanese western scholars. The thought of loyalty to king and exclusion of foreigners at the end of Bakufu became the driving force behind the overthrowing of the Bakufu and restoration of the monarchy, but the fact that the civilization course succeeded after the Meiji Restoration as a continuation of western studies at the end of the Bakufu period should not be overlooked.

Elements of International Law Is a Textbook for International Law

Illustrated Treatise on Nations across the Sea and *Elements of International Law* (萬國公法, *Wanguo gongfa* in Ch.) were two books published in China toward the end of the Qing dynasty in order to study the state of affairs and international law of the West; these two books were transmitted to Joseon and Japan as well. The response of each nation became the standard for understanding the awareness of external crisis and response of the three East Asian nations toward western impact.

Wei Yuan was spurred on by the humiliating experience of Qing China in the Opium Wars to write *Illustrated Treatise on Nations across the Sea*. This book contained 50 volumes and was published in 1844; two different versions containing 60 volumes and 100 volumes with additional supplements were published in 1847 and 1852, respectively. He was a close friend of Lin Zexu who led the prohibition on opium in Guangzhou. When Lin Zexu was relegated to the remote region of Xingjang for his role in the Opium Wars, he gave to Wei Yuan *Account of the Four Continents* (四洲志, *Sizhouzhi* in Ch.), a publication of a collection of materials on the west gathered in Guangzhou and translated into Chinese.

Wei Yuan used *Account of the Four Continents* as the basic material for compiling the world geography book titled *Illustrated Treatise on Nations across the Sea*. "Chouhai" (籌海), the first chapter of the book, discussed three countermeasure plans against the west — self-defense, combat, and diplomacy — of which the famous strategic thought of diplomacy against the west in the form of "suppress the barbarians by considering the forte of the barbarians as teachers" greatly shook Sino-centrism. Learning "the forte of the barbarians" by considering the forte as teacher was a way of thinking that did not exist in Sino-centrism.

The purpose of the Self-Strengthening Movement of Qing China was to learn "the forte of the barbarians." *Illustrated Treatise on Nations across the Sea* was transmitted to Joseon and Japan, and their

416

response provided an interesting preview to understanding the disparity in sensing external crisis in the two nations. Japan imported the 60-volume text in 1854 for the first time. It created explosive interest, leading to 23 reproductions until the end of the Bakufu period. The year of 1854 was also the year of the signing of the Kanagawa Treaty with the U.S.

In Joseon, Kim Jeong-hui focused on this during his exile on isolated Jeju Island in the South Sea. It's probable that his pupil and translation official Yi Sang-jeok sent the book to him. Kim Jeong-hui read this book in 1845, which indicates that he had the 50-volume version published in 1844. This book was not prohibited because it was written by a Chinese and so was not a Christian book. In his letter to his close friend Gwon Don-in (權敦仁), he stated, "the least to be done is to copy the ship system in *Illustrated Treatise on Nations across the Sea*" and lamented the lack of interest of statesmen. Furthermore, he evaluated Wei Yuan, the author of this book, to be critical of "attaching annotations to empty words" found in philologico-bibliographical study and to focus mainly on the study of "seeking the Truth from facts."

> *Illustrated Treatise on Nations across the Sea* is a necessary book for me, comparable to several precious things in other houses. It is important to lock the door and repulse the ships of western barbarians when they invade the border, but one who investigates in detail the state of affairs of that nation can imitate their actions. I lament that I cannot see the particulars due to my mind lacking concentration, but I think even one technology of making the sail must be learned even if all of the ship's system cannot be fully understood. Why are there not people who are interested [in this]? In general, the scholarship of Wei Moshen (魏默深, Moshen is Wei Yuan's pen name) opened another school division from the recent Chinese literature (philologico-bibliographical study); it does not adhere to commentaries on empty discussions but solely investigates the truth based on fact. His interpretation of the Confucian Classics differs greatly from those of Hui Dong (惠棟) and Dai Zhen (戴震), two leading figures of philologico-bibliographical study of the Qing dynasty; he also enjoys discussions on military affairs.

Yu Gil-jun (兪吉濬, 1856-1914), the first Korean to study abroad in Japan and the U.S., reminisced about receiving *Illustrated Treatise on Nations across the Sea* from his teacher Bak Gyu-su (朴珪壽) and how it became the catalyst for his studies overseas. Bak Gyu-su was a scholar and politician who inherited the genealogy of the Bukhak School, as was Kim Jeong-hui. This book received attention from and was privately kept by a very small number of men with foresight such as Kim Jeong-hui and Bak Gyu-su in Joseon, but was not printed and distributed as was the case in Japan. There was a huge difference in the amount of information on the unknown world of the west obtained by Joseon and Japan at the time.

To open diplomatic relations with the west, international law that is common in that world must be adhered to. *Elements of International Law*, translated and published in China in 1864, was just such a book. The Tongwen School was established in 1862 to train able men who had command of foreign languages during the Self-Strengthening Movement in China. W. A. P. Martin (Chinese name Ding Weiliang, 丁違良), president of the school, translated a book written by an American scholar of international law entitled *Elements of International Law* into Chinese in response to the demands of "self-strengthening" diplomacy in Chinese foreign relations.

This book was reproduced by Kaiseisho (successor of Bansho Shirabesho) in Japan in 1865 after Japanese reading marks were added, and additional copies were printed up to the Meiji Restoration. The first record mentioning this book in Joseon is after the Treaty of Ganghwa Island in February 1876. The following excerpt is included in *Record of a Journey to Japan*, which can be said to be the record of his report on returning to Joseon after visiting Japan as part of the first entourage of Kim Gi-su, Ambassador to Japan, in April of the same year:

> Signing of a pact by all nations based on the elements of international law is similar to the law of diplomatic pact among Qin and six nations east of Qin (of the Ages of Spring and Autumn as well as the Warring States). If one nation is in difficulty, the other nations will come to its aid; if a nation errs, the other nations will

attack it. The law of the westerners is to not be swayed by partial-
ity and not be inclined toward attacking; an erroneous act cannot
occur because actions are carried out according to regulations.

- "Jeongbeop" (政法), Record of a Journey to Japan, Vol. 2

But diplomatic issues with western nations were not included in the
agenda yet when the entourage of Kim Hong-jip as Ambassador to
Japan visited there in July of 1880. At this time, Kim Hong-jip visited
Diplomat He Ru-zhang (何如璋) of the Qing legation in Japan to
discuss balance of power mentioned in *Elements of International Law* as
follows:

He Ru-zhang: Each western nation has the law of balance of
power these days. If a nation neighbors a strong nation and there
is the possibility of troubles, each nation forms an alliance to balance the other. This is a necessary method used in the past also.

Kim Hong-jip: I saw the three words "balance of power"
recently in international law (*Elements of International Law*). But old
standards are adhered to in our kingdom, and we are afraid of the
foreign as much as flood or fierce beasts. The recent elimination
of heterodox religion was for that reason. I will report that the
great teachings are thus.

- "Daecheong heumsa pildam" (大清欽使筆談), Susinsa
girok (修信使記錄, Records of Ambassador to Japan)

Joseon only barely came to know *Elements of International Law* through
diplomatic relations with Japan as described above, but that does not
mean that interest in this book exploded as was the case in Japan.

Brought back to Joseon at this time by Kim Hong-jip was *A Policy for Joseon* (朝鮮策略) written by Huang Zunxian (黃遵憲), Counselor and Secretary to the first Imperial Chinese Legation to Tokyo.
The book was an organization of the conversation between He Ru-
zhang and Kim Hong-jip to be delivered to the Joseon king; it
contained recommendations for foreign negotiations with interna-

tional law in mind in this new international environment. The advocates of defending orthodoxy and rejecting heterodoxy in Joseon destroyed *A Policy for Joseon* as being an evil book and continuously appealed to the king to punish Kim Hong-jip who brought it into Joseon. The advocates raised an issue about this book being evil as follows: The main external threat to Joseon was from Russia to the north; "close ties with China, distance from Japan, and alliance with the U.S." was recommended as a foreign policy to counter the threat from the north. Christianity should not be excluded became the basic meaning if it encouraged people to do good deeds as did Confucianism. King Gojong accepted the high-level government officials' recommendation of *A Policy for Joseon* and pursued negotiations for opening the kingdom to the U.S. despite the vehement appeals of the advocates of defending orthodoxy and rejecting heterodoxy.

"Sedo" Politics of the Andong Kim Clan Makes the King Powerless

During the reigns of Yeongjo and Jeongjo which lasted for 76 years from 1724 to 1800, party strife was controlled through the Policy of Impartiality, and excellent achievements in politics and cultural activities were passed on to succeeding generations as mentioned above. In particular, new reforms were expected with the advancement of the Silhak School into a section of the central political world in the time of Jeongjo. But after Jeongjo passed away in 1800, there followed a succession of young kings ascending to the throne: Sunjo at the age of 11, Heonjong (憲宗, r. 1834-1849) at the age of seven, and Cheoljong (哲宗, r. 1849-1863) of a remote village on Ganghwa Island at the age of 19.

The queens of all three of the above-named kings were selected from the Andong Kim clan who belonged to the Noron Si Faction. The queen of Sunjo was the daughter of Kim Jo-sun (金祖淳), the queen of Heonjong was the daughter of Kim Jo-geun (金祖根), and the queen of Cheoljong was the daughter of Kim Mun-geun (金汶根). These three Andong Kims carried out "sedo" politics for

60-some years while disdaining sovereign power as the in-laws of a young and weak king.[1] *Sedo* in this case meant influential vassals who had the trust of the king would have real political power on behalf of the king.

The person who started the "sedo" politics of the Andong Kim clan was a renowned member of the Noron Faction by the name of Kim Jo-sun (1765-1831). He remained with the Si Faction after the Noron Faction divided into Byeok and Si. Thus he became the Daegyo of Gyujanggak Archives, and his daughter was selected as the Crown Princess during the reign of Jeongjo due to being the recipient of the trust of Jeongjo. Queen Jeongsun, second wife of Yeongjo (of the Gyeongju Kim clan), acted as regent as the Dowager Queen Mother and brought about "the 1801 Persecution of Catholics in Joseon" by reviving the Noron Faction. Kim Jo-sun of the Noron Si Faction held important government posts such as Minister of Justice in this period as well. The marriage of his daughter and Sunjo occurred in 1802, the same year that the bloody Catholic persecution concluded.

Kim Jo-sun eliminated the Noron Byeok Faction while advising the young King Sunjo in the capacity of father-in-law when Dowager Queen Mother Jeongsun passed away in 1805. The Noron Byeok Faction was the political enemy of Jeongjo, father of Sunjo. He employed the members of the Andong Kim clan in key government posts and appointed some of his associates in supporting positions in order to build the political power of the clan. The despotic system of the Noron Si Faction was achieved with the Andong Kim clan at the axis.

King Sunjo also had in-laws from the Pung'yang Jo clan, a rival of the Andong Kim clan. In the background of this rivalry was the heir-apparent to Sunjo, Crown Prince Hyomyeong (孝明世子), who passed away before ascending to the throne. The Crown Princess was the daughter of Jo Man-yeong (趙萬永) of the Pung'yang Jo clan

---

[1] "Sedo" politics referred to a situation where the queen's family members wielded real political power in the stead of the king. The king was a puppet king in such a case. (S. Lee)

and the mother of Heonjong. She later played a key role in putting Gojong on the throne after Cheoljong passed away. Queen Sunwon (純元王后), the queen of Sunjo in the Kim clan and the eldest in the palace, selected Yi Won-beom (李元範) to succeed. He was of a down-and-out royal family living an agrarian life in a remote village on Ganghwa Island, and she put him on the throne as Cheoljong when Heonjong passed away without issue. Cheoljong's wife was the daughter of Kim Mun-geun, another Andong Kim. Below is a chart of the royal family and its in-law relation with the Andong Kim clan in the 60-some years during the 19th century.

	(23rd)	(early death)	(24th)	(25th)	(26th)
King	Sunjo	Crown Prince Hyomyeong	Heonjong	Cheoljong	Gojong
Queen	Sunweon (Kim Jo-sun's daughter)	Sinjeong (Jo Man-myeong's daughter)	Hyohyeon (Kim Jo-geun's daughter)	Cheol-in (Kim Mun-geun's daughter)	Myeongseong (Min Chi-rok's daughter)

The history of the growth of Cheoljong into adulthood was a model of the growth of a member of the down-and-out royal family under *sedo* politics of "weak ruler, strong vassals." His grandfather, Euneon-gun (恩彦君), was the half-brother of Jeongjo. But his Catholic wife and oldest daughter-in-law were given poison at the time of the 1801 Persecution of Catholics in Joseon; Euneon-gun also committed suicide on Ganghwa Island. He had three sons; Cheoljong was the third son of the third son, Jeongye-gun (全溪君). The family of Jeongye-gun farmed on a remote village on Ganghwa Island and lived quietly in fear of reprisal in order to continue the family line. The times were such that even royal family members were subjected to reprisals. Cheoljong was raised as a farmer and did not receive anything that resembled education until he was invited to become ruler at the age of 19.

Crown Prince Hyomyeong who was supposed to succeed Sunjo met a premature death, and Heonjong did not have any issue to inherit. The bloodline of the Joseon dynasty was already showing signs of having reached the end. But the ascension to the throne reaching as far as Yi Won-beom was completely unexpected. Yi Won-beom probably viewed Jeong Won-yong (鄭元容), the Head of the Privy Council, as a messenger of death when the latter went to meet the former under the command of Queen Sunwon as an elder vassal of the Joseon political world. It was said that Yi Won-beom curled into a ball and trembled in a corner of the room at that time. This was a great ordeal for one who lived the life of a common farmer in a remote village on Ganghwa since the time of his grandfather Euneon-gun. A historian recorded as follows about the scene at the time:

> First (Jeong Won-yong) told the head of Ganghwa Island to have a cart and a palanquin prepared, and together they visited the home of Jeongye-gun. Jeongye-gun had already passed away but his son lived in the farming village; the son was single yet and tilled the field and made straw sandals himself due to poverty. All family members became afraid and trembled when Won-yong and others delivered the unofficial order from the Dowager Queen Mother; they did not dare go with the messengers. Won-yong finally convinced them to accompany the messengers by telling of the earnest desire of the Dowager Queen Mother.

> - Bak Je-hyeong (朴齊炯), *Geunse joseon jeonggam* (近世朝鮮政鑑, Mirror for Modern Politics in Joseon), Vol. 1

Cheoljong ascended to the throne in 1849, but Dowager Queen Mother Sunwon acted as regent until 1851, followed by assistance from Kim Mun-geun, father of the queen of Cheoljong. Kim Mun-geun cemented the despotic system by appointing Kim Byeong-guk (金炳國), Kim Byeong-hak (金炳學), Kim Byeong-ik (金炳翼) and his son Kim Byeong-pil (金炳弼) of the Andong Kim clan as Head of Security, Academician, Left Chanseong, and Daegyo, respectively, during this period.[2]

Two more Catholic oppressions followed the 1801 Persecution of Catholics in Joseon in the first half of the 19th century: Catholic Persecution of 1839 (also known as Religious Persecution of Gihae) and Catholic Persecution of 1846 (also known as Religious Persecution of Byeong-o).

Missionary activities in Joseon hitherto had been managed by the ecclesiastical district of Beijing, but Pope Gregory XVI made the Joseon parish independent from the ecclesiastical district of Beijing in 1831 and put it under the management of the Paris Foreign Missions Society. Father Maubant in 1836, Father Chastan in 1837, and Bishop Imbert in 1838 snuck into Joseon from China by crossing the frozen Yalu River. These three French missionaries as well as Jeong Ha-sang (丁夏祥), his mother of the Yu clan, and almost 80 other believers died a martyr's death. There were many offspring left to carry on from the martyrs of the 1801 Persecution of Catholics in Joseon. Jeong Ha-sang was the son of Jeong Yak-jong, who was executed during the 1801 Persecution of Catholics.

Rear-Admiral Jean-Baptiste Thomas Cecille of the French Navy landed on Wehyeon Island (外煙島) off of Chungcheong Province in July 1846 with three French naval ships from Macao to deliver a letter of protest against the execution of the French missionaries. The letter was given to the Governor of Chungcheong Province to be forwarded to the central government of Joseon so that a response from the central government could be ready when the French naval ships came back the following year. Kim Dae-geon (金大建) was the first Joseon Catholic priest to be ordained under the auspices of Father Maubant in Macao in 1845; he snuck back into Joseon but was caught by Joseon authorities and executed along with 20-some faithful. This was the Catholic Persecution of 1846.

Sedo politics of the Andong Kim clan ended in 1863. Neighboring kingdoms of Japan and Qing China overcame the exclusion of

---

[2] Chanseong was a government post in the State Council and was in charge of all government officials. (S. Lee)

the West, and a movement to learn from the West began after some years of the Andong Kim clan's power in politics. Toward the end of the Bakufu period, Japan established an institution called Bansho Shirabesho in 1856, which was renamed Yosho Shirabesho in 1862 and again to Kaiseisho in 1863, to study about the West. The Self-Strengthening Movement began in Qing China in 1861, and Tongwen School was established to teach Western Learning in 1862. In Joseon, however, western religion and sciences were considered "evil learning" and the movement to purge heterodoxy permeated the world of Joseon thought.

Gyeongbok Palace Is Rebuilt but Private Academies Are Closed

During the 60-some years of turbulent times in the first half of the 19th century, the three successive kings Sunjo, Heonjong, and Cheoljong were not able to look after state affairs under *sedo* politics of the Andong Kim clan because they were all young and weak. All five sons of Cheoljong who was called in from a farming village on Ganghwa Island met an early demise, perhaps due to the unwholesome lifestyle within the palace, and succession to the throne became an issue when Cheoljong died without a successor. Ultimately, Myeongbok (命福), second son of Heungseon-gun (興宣君) Yi Ha-eung (李昰應, pen name is Seokpa 石坡), ascended to the throne in 1863 as the 26th king Gojong (r. 1863-1907). But Yi Ha-eung acted as regent under the title of Heungseon Daewon-gun because Gojong was only 12 years old at the time.

The Andong Kim clan had to exclude any royal family member with enough backbone to threaten the political power by banishing them or giving poison under royal command, but the Andong Kim clan was not able to comprehend the agenda of Yi Ha-eung. Yi Ha-eung foresaw the death of Cheoljong without a successor and behaved like a fool without any political aspirations. He would be ridiculed by the servants of the Andong Kim clan because he would go to the front gate of an Andong Kim house and shamelessly request money or keep company with libertines. In the meantime, he secretly approached Dowager Queen Jo (Queen Sinjeong), wife of Crown Prince Hyomyeong who met an early demise. She became the eldest person in the palace after the death of the queen of Sunjo of the Kim clan (Queen Sunwon), and as such held the power to designate the successor to Cheoljong.

Yi Ha-eung's acting was very effective; Dowager Queen Jo appointed the son of Yi Ha-eung as successor to Cheoljong by adopting Myeong-bok as the foster son of the deceased Crown Prince Hyomyeong. Euneon-gun and Eunsin-gun (恩信君) were both half-brothers of Jeongjo. Euneon-gun was the grandfather of Cheoljong, and Eunsin-gun was the grandfather of Daewon-gun, which made Cheoljong and Heungseon Daewon-gun second cousins due to the blood line of Euneon-gun → Jeongye-gun → Cheoljong and Eunsin-gun → Namyeon-gun → Heungseon-gun. Namyeon-gun became a foster son of Eunsin-gun because the latter died in exile on Jeju Island without a son to continue the line. Both royal families fell into a bad situation under *sedo* politics of the Andong Kim clan.

Libertine Heungseon Daewon-gun changed dramatically and appointed Yi Gyeong-ha (李景夏), a close friend during his libertine days, as Head of Security, thereby ruthlessly suppressing anyone who dared to oppose his political reforms. He dissolved *sedo* politics of the Andong Kim clan by advocating "balance among the four factions" during his regency of 10 years (1863-1873). Heungseon Daewon-gun overthrew central figures of the Andong Kim clan such as Chief State Councilor Kim Jwa-geun (金左根), Head of the Privy Council Kim Heung-geun (金興根), and Minister of Personnel Kim Byeong-ik and appointed Jo Du-sun (趙斗淳) as Chief State Councilor, Kim Byeong-hak as Second State Councilor, and Yu Hu-jo (柳厚祚) as Third State Councilor instead in 1866. Jo Du-sun was a central figure in the Pung'yang Jo clan, Dowager Queen Jo's family, but Yu Hu-jo was a descendant of Yu Seong-nyong and belonged to the Namin Faction, the political rival of the Noron Faction. Kang Ro (姜㳣) of the Bugin Faction and Han Gye-won (韓啓源) of the Namin Faction were appointed to the posts of Second State Councilor and Third State Councilor, respectively.

Permeation of Catholicism and trespassing of French and American warships on Ganghwa Island occurred during the Daewon-gun administration. In order to cope with this difficult foreign crisis, Daewon-gun created "balance among the four factions"; through this, he contrived for unity of decision within central politics by employing able men who belonged to factions (such as the Namin, Bugin, and Soron) that were excluded from the political world by the Noron Faction.

Smoothing over the antagonism and antipathy among the factions was not an easy issue that could be realized only with "balance among the four factions." This was because each faction had roots in private academies of various regions that played the role of providing manpower to factional strife in central politics. Private academies other than royally endowed private academies, in which the king personally wrote the name of the private academies on plaques, were established haphazardly in various regions. Historian Bak Je-hyeong described the mode of these private academies of the times as follows:

> At first, moral justice was discussed, but slowly they began to criticize politics of the royal court. Many people gathered their voices to say the same thing when one person led the criticism, and a nationwide appeal in writing was transmitted in a few weeks. This is called communication transmitted among the Confucian literati.
>
> • Mirror for Modern Politics in Joseon, Vol. 1

What was worse, private academies became a "holy ground" for the den of degenerate noblemen of good families, and the local government could not intervene.

> Wherever descendants of good families without government posts exist, atrocities are committed against commoners. But the worst are concentrated around the private academies. They demand funds with which to purchase materials for memorial rituals from the districts and counties by writing a document, putting

their seal on the document, and sending it. Descendants of good families without government posts as well as commoners are forced to open their purses in response to the content of the letter. Those who do not respond are forcefully taken to the private academies and threatened with severe punishment. The influence of the Hwayang-dong Academy (central academy of the Noron Faction where Song Si-yeol's ancestral tablet is enshrined) is so great that the letter from Hwayang-dong Academy is referred to as the reverent ink letter from Hwayang-dong. The lives of commoners become more destitute because they suffer hardships through avaricious and tyrannical government officials, after which they are further distressed by Confucian scholars of private academies; the commoners grind their teeth in their bitterness, but they can only stare at the sky.

- Mirror for Modern Politics in Joseon, Vol. 1

Originally, the general purport of private academies as educational facilities of the provinces was "to hold memorial rituals for ancient sages as the foundation for cultivating morale." But things came to such a state because too many private academies were established.

Daewon-gun first closed down the Mandong Tomb in Hwayang-dong, Gwesan-gun in Chungcheong Province in 1865 despite the protest of people. This tomb was a symbol of worshipping the powerful Ming, established by the literati according to the will of Song Si-yeol to commemorate Shenzong (Emperor Wanli) and Yizong (Emperor Chongzhen) of the Ming dynasty. The "faithful" of Ming China were deserted by the Chinese people but found root in Joseon. Daewon-gun left only 47 royally endowed private academies and ancestral shrines intact and closed 650-some private academies in 1871. Land and slaves that belonged to the private academies were confiscated to enrich the national treasury. The Hwayang-dong Academy mentioned in the excerpt above was the spiritual mainstay of the Noron Faction, which advocated "worshipping of the powerful Qing" along with the Mandong Tomb; it was closed despite being a royally endowed private academy.

The Noron Faction boasted of firm power nationally in the political world of the central government and among the civilian scholars not holding government posts in the days of the Daewon-gun regency. The uncommon determination of Daewon-gun can be inferred by his direct confrontation with the powerful Noron Faction. The reorganization of the private academies threatened the very foundation of each faction. As expected, Confucian literati rallied together by exchanging communication amongst themselves and by meeting in front of the palace to directly repeal the closing of the private academies. Daewon-gun was not moved at all and thundered as below:

> I will not accept even the resurrection of Confucius if it is harmful to the people. To say nothing of claiming to be the place for holding memorial rites for preceding Confucians of our kingdom, how can private academies become a den of thieves?

> - Mirror for Modern Politics in Joseon, Vol. 1

Daewon-gun commanded the policemen of the Police Bureau to chase the Confucians to the other side of the Han River. Descendants of good families without government posts who did not pay much attention to sovereign power and were very vocal under "weak ruler, strong vassals" trembled in front of the fierce authority of Daewon-gun.

Daewon-gun also implemented a tax reform that was welcomed by the people because it took away the special privileges enjoyed by the *yangban*. In the past, land tax evasion occurred in various regions where the *yangban* with special privileges would misappropriate land and the provincial government officials would be afraid to assess tax. Daewon-gun ordered an investigation into this, and assessed tax without making a distinction between *yangban* and commoners. The *gunpo* system existed to get commoners out of serving mandatory military term by accepting hemp cloth or cotton from those who desired to be excused from military service. The *yangban* were also excluded from this system. Daewon-gun changed this *gunpo* system to a *hopo* system where each family had to pay two *nyang* in tax regardless of whether *yangban* or commoner. The economic privileges enjoyed by the *yangban* were reduced through such tax reforms on the one hand, but the national finance became stronger on the other hand.

Reorganization of private academies and tax reform were intrepid reforms executed by a determined Daewon-gun who was not afraid to antagonize the greatly complaining *yangban* class. But complaints of the people focused against Daewon-gun due to the reconstruction of the Gyeongbok Palace, which could not be handled by the national treasury of the times and so placed a heavy burden on the people.

Gyeongbok Palace was the main palace symbolizing the Joseon dynasty; it was left in ruin after it burnt down during the invasion led by Toyotomi Hideyoshi. The task of reconstucting the symbol of the Joseon dynasty began in 1865 and was completed in 1868. Gyeongbok Palace would not have been reconstructed without the determination of Daewon-gun. The Office of Construction, which was established to manage the task of reconstructing, not only mobilized people from all over the kingdom, but it also collected donations for the reconstruction. The collection of donations gradually changed to "obligatory donations." Giant trees that were the objects of local folk beliefs and trees from forests protecting the burial grounds of descendants of prominent families without government posts were cut down and transported to the capital to be used as construction material. Indeed, the reconstruction of Gyeongbok Palace that integrated the quintessence of wooden architecture added to the magnificence of the scenery in the capital of Seoul, but resulted in earning the resentment of the people.

Choe Ik-hyeon (崔益鉉, pen name is Myeonam 勉庵, 1833-1906) directly opposed the authority of Daewon-gun in 1873. This was a showdown between two very stubborn heroes. Choe Ik-hyeon belonged to the Noron Faction; he denounced Daewon-gun for misgovernment by pointing out each item considered at fault and requested the punishment of Second State Councilor Kang Ro of the Bugin Faction and Third State Councilor Han Gye-won of the Namin Faction. Gojong was an adult of 22 at the time in 1873. Choe Ik-hyeon was banished to Jeju Island for confronting Daewon-gun, but he ultimately opened the way for the direct rule of Gojong and the retirement of Daewon-gun. Moreover, the Mandong Tomb was revived.

Sedo politics of the Yeoheung Min clan replaced that of the Andong Kim clan after Daewon-gun retired because Queen Myeongseong, consort of Gojong, appointed her clan members to important government posts. In the history of Joseon politics of the 19th century, Queens of the Andong Kim clan, Pung'yang Jo clan, and Yeoheung Min clan opened the way for male members of the clans to enter the political world. The fierce authority of Daewon-gun, who disliked politics dominated by the clan members of the queen, could not challenge the strength of the queen.

Events that occurred during the 10-year reign of Daewon-gun, such as the repulsion of French and American warships, the policy on hiring called "balance among the four factions," reorganization of private academies, and reconstruction of Gyeongbok Palace, could not have been handled by an ordinary politician. The direction of his reform policy in which the strong were suppressed and the weak were assisted left a strong impression on the people. The most conspicuous among his achievements was the fact that the cancer of factional politics in Joseon politics since the division of the Sarim Faction into Dong'in and Seoin Factions in 1757 ended with the overthrow of the despotic rule of the Andong Kim clan. But *sedo* politics of the Min clan began: "One abuse disappeared but is replaced by a new abuse." The dormant enmity among the various factions united with civilian official cliques and seethed below the surface, which later became a great obstacle to unity of the people in modern times. After Daewon-gun retired, the people became disappointed with *sedo* politics dominated by the Min clan and felt disillusioned with the weak countermeasures of the statesmen against foreign pressures; they thus desired Daewon-gun to return to politics. He should be remembered as a lucky adventurer who survived the turbulent storms of the latter half of the 19th century.

French and American Warships Invade Joseon

The Second Opium War (the Arrow Incident) of 1860 during which the British and French allies advanced from Tianjin to Beijing increased Joseon statesmen's feelings of being threatened by foreign powers as compared to the Opium War of 1840. The policy of Daewon-gun to strengthen sovereign power formed a double-sided coin with the policy of seclusion from western barbarians, a foreign threat.

Armed conflicts arose during the French Invasion of Ganghwa Island in 1866 (丙寅洋擾) by seven warships and the subsequent American Invasion of Ganghwa Island in 1871 (辛未洋擾) by five warships. Joseon already knew of the British and French allies invading Beijing through Joseon envoys to Yenching. Foreign aggression became the catalyst for the Self-Strengthening Movement in China, but Joseon opted for seclusion from western barbarians. Daewon-gun considered the Catholic faithful in Joseon to be in collusion with foreign threats of the West. Thus he executed a sweeping Catholic persecution in 1866 while searching for a coping method. Among those persecuted were nine of the 12 French missionaries who had been smuggled into Joseon; the remaining three missionaries fled to China. The French Invasion of Ganghwa Island in 1866 occurred in retaliation for the persecution of the French missionaries; the French warships landed on Ganghwa Island and demanded the opening of the ports by force but were driven away.

The reason for American warships invading Ganghwa Island was the burning of the U.S.S. General Sherman when it traveled up the Daedong River and neared Pyeong'yang in 1866. The American Invasion of Ganghwa Island in 1871 was to protest the burning of the General Sherman as well to request opening of the port. The American force that landed on Ganghwa Island was repulsed by hand-to-hand combat. Joseon was the first kingdom in East Asia to refuse to ports to French and American military powers.

The ideological weapon that destroyed the western cannons and warships in the two invasions was the doctrine of "defending orthodoxy and rejecting heterodoxy," i.e., protecting orthodox learning and excluding heterodox learning. Orthodox learning referred to "orthodox Confucianism" that linked Confucius → Mencius → Cheng-zi → Zhu Xi, whereas heterodox learning referred to Catholicism. In the 500-year Confucian history of Joseon, the definition of heterodoxy against "orthodox learning" differs according to each period. Buddhism and Daoism were heterodoxy in the beginning, and the Learning of Wang Yang-ming became heterodoxy in mid-Joseon after Yi Hwang rejected it. Catholicism became the main target of purges after it began to infiltrate Joseon in the latter half of the 18th century.

The mainstream of the doctrine of defending orthodoxy and rejecting heterodoxy in modern Joseon was the Hwaseo School with Yi Hang-no (李恒老, pen name is Hwaseo 華西, 1792-1868) at the head. As described before, Choe Ik-hyeon was one of the disciples of Yi Hang-no and opposed Daewon-gun. Yi Hang-no was a Noron Faction scholar of the Way who was living in a remote village in Yanggeun-gun, Gyeonggi Province, to focus on self-actualizing scholarship instead of learning for the sake of passing the civil service examination, when the French warships invaded Ganghwa Island in 1866.

The Joseon government divided into two camps, one "advocating war" and the other "advocating peace negotiations," when the "western barbarians" first challenged Joseon with military force. Thus it was decided to appoint Yi Hang-no as Royal Secretariat of Manufacturing and hear what he had to say. He declined the government post but sent a letter on the fundamentals of a countermeasure.

National opinion is divided into the extremes of advocating war or peace negotiations; our people claim that the western pirates must be attacked, and those who advocate peace negotiations with the western pirates are on the other side. The old way of dressing (a symbol of propriety) might be preserved if [decisions] are based on this (advocate war), but mankind will fall into the

433

world of beasts if [decisions] follow them (advocate peace negotiations).

- "Sadongbu seungji gyeomjinsohoeso" (辭同副承旨
    兼陳所懷疏), *Hwaseojip* (華西集,
    Collection of Works by Hwaseo)

The reason Yi Hang-no was against aggression was not "loyalty to
ruler and love of nation" to protect a kingdom or ruler, but to save
mankind by preserving "Confucian propriety." Why would [Joseon]
fall into a world of birds and beasts if a peace treaty with France
were signed? The logic was that Catholicism was a heterodox religion
with "no concern for father or ruler," and thus the foundation of
mankind in filial piety between father and son as well as loyalty
between ruler and vassals was denied, which is the same as a world of
birds and beasts. The debate on whether to handle western pirates
with "peace negotiations" or "war" was replaced by a showdown
between "humanity" (Confucianism) or "birds and beasts" (Catholicism).

What was the internal cause that gave rise to acts of aggression
by western pirates? Yi Hang-no found the cause in western products
"which are made of strange technology and excessive tricks." Rather,
persecution of Catholicism and repulsing aggressions against Joseon
by western powers were minor issues in comparison to the emphasis
put on "the advocacy of uprooting western products" as the fundamental countermeasure to the West. Thus he claimed the minds of
the people must be regulated so that they would reject western
products and not use them in all reaches of Seoul as well as the
remote regions. He emphasized that the king and the royal family
must first be a model because "the great foundation of everything
under Heaven and in the kingdom is in the mind of the ruler"
("Sagong jochampanso," 辭工曹參判疏, *Collection of Works by
Hwaseo*).

National opinion became united under the protest launched by
Yi Hang-no against peace negotiations. He claimed that "peace
negotiations = betrayal of nation," which was expressed well in the

contents of "epitaphs against peace negotiations" erected in strategic locations nationwide during the American Invasion of Ganghwa Island in 1871.

> Not fighting against the western barbarians' aggression is making peace. Advocating peace is selling the nation.
> — Be warned, our descendants throughout all ages. It is established in the year of *byeong-in* [1866] and erected in the year of *sinmi* [1871].

洋夷侵犯 非戰則和 主和賣國
— 戒我萬年子孫 丙寅作 辛未立

Hwaseo School Leads the Theory of Anti-Aggression and Anti-Modernity

The ideological basis for advocating the Learning of Master Zhu as the only scholarship was "orthodox teachings of Confucius and Mencius." It referred to the genealogy of the sages and the wise who transmitted the Confucian way, which, according to "Biography of Zhu Xi" (朱熹傳) in *History of Song*, stipulated that the orthodoxy of sagely learning was continued by Cheng-zi and Zhu Xi in the Song period after it was discontinued by the death of Mencius; it excluded the Han-Tang commentarial tradition despite it being part of Confucianism. Yi Hang-no described the orthodox teachings of Confucius and Mencius on learning and thought as follows:

> There was a current for conducting the Way from Yao [of Xia] and Shun [of Yin] to Zhou Gong, and there was a current for transmitting learning from Confucius to U-ong (尤翁, Song Si-yeol). Confucius is on a par with Yao and Shun, Mencius is on a par with Yu [of Zhou], Zhu Xi is on a par with the Duke of Zhou, and U-ong is on a par with Mencius.... The method of King Shun and Zhu Xi are the same in that the great King Shun utilized the doctrine of the mean well by assembling the words of

several people, and Zhu Xi compromised well by gathering the Hundred Schools of Thought. The actions of Mencius and U-ong are the same in that Mencius preserved Confucius by denying Yang Zhu and Mozi, whereas U-ong preserved Zhu Xi by excluding Hyu (Yun Hyu).

- "A-eon" (雅言), Collection of Works by Hwaseo, Vol. 12

Yi Hang-no claimed that orthodox Confucian teachings existed from the times of Yao and Shun to Duke of Zhou while orthodoxy of learning was transmitted from Confucius to Master Song (Song Si-yeol), but that Mencius defended Confucius from the likes of Yang Zhu and Mozi while Song Si-yeol protected Zhu Xi from Yun Hyu. Thus orthodox Confucian teachings and orthodoxy of learning from Confucius → Mencius → Zhu Xi → Master Song were to be preserved, while heterodoxy of Yang Zhu and Mozi, "defector" Yun Hyu, and Catholicism of "no father, no ruler" should be excluded. The anti-western theory of excluding things foreign as advocated by the Hwaseo School was directly linked to the advocacy of Song Si-yeol in excluding Qing and of Zhu Xi in excluding Jin.

To Song Si-yeol, both Qing and Jin were of barbaric Jurchen tribes in that the one forced Joseon to observe the propriety of serving a greater nation and the other was the cause of the downfall of Northern Song. The West was "the western barbarians" because it challenged Joseon with military might, which in itself was a barbaric act in that Joseon considered itself at the time to be "little China." Moreover, Meiji Japan was degraded to "barbaric Japan" because it overthrew the Tokugawa Bakufu with which Joseon had diplomatic relations and "became just like the West."

As such, the background for the thought on defending orthodoxy and rejecting heterodoxy was the concept of justification of "reverence for China and exclusion of all things foreign" where "China" referred to adherence to the Learning of Master Zhu as the only scholarship. It was similar to and yet different from the thought of being loyal to king and excluding foreigners as propounded at the end of the *Bakufu* period in Japan by the Mito School, which empha-sized the emperor as the core of national polity.[3]

Thus preserving the purity of "little China" in Joseon was a uni-versal mission that transcended the boundary of one nation or one ethnic group because "big China" had already become barbaric through the Jurchen conquest (Qing dynasty). Yi Hang-no ex-pounded on this as follows:

> The most apprehensive is confusion of the Way which might be brought on by the West. The one streak of bright energy between Heaven and earth is in our Joseon; how will the mind of the Heaven endure the destruction of this as well? We must hurry in adjusting our minds to be straight and in shedding light on the Way. The fate of the kingdom comes after these.

- "Yosun," Collection of Works by Hwaseo, Vol. 36

The Hwaseo School, represented by the disciples of Yi Hang-no such as Kim Pyeong-muk (金平默), Yu Jung-gyo (柳重敎), Choe Ik-hyeon, and Yu In-seok (柳麟錫), led the anti-aggression and anti-modern theory to defend the lonely fort of "little China"; Choe Ik-hyeon and Yu In-seok themselves became leaders of righteous troops and initiated the anti-Japanese righteous army movement. Call to arms for the troops was "sacrifice one's life to preserve one's virtue complete," which is from "Wei Ling Kung," *Analects of Confucius.*

> The determined scholar and the man of virtue will not seek to live at the expense of injuring their virtue. They will even sacrifice their lives to preserve their virtue complete.

"I will sacrifice the body, and choose righteousness" was another rallying cry representing their fundamental spirit; it meant the same as

---

[3] Mito School (or *Mitogaku* in Japanese) was a school of historical and Shinto studies in Japan. It was founded by Tokugawa Mitsukuni of the Mito clan. The Mito School emphasized respect for the imperial court and for the Shinto deities. (S. Lee)

"I will let life go, and choose righteousness" from "Gao Zi, Part I" of *The Works of Mencius.*

> I like life, and I also like righteousness. If I cannot keep the two together, I will let life go, and choose righteousness.

Chosen boto tobatsushi (朝鮮暴徒討伐誌, 1923, Chosenchusatsugun Shireibu), a secret document of Japanese military police, regarded the popular anti-Japanese righteous army movements toward the end of the Joseon dynasty simply as "riots," but in reality these were struggles and wars in which the patriots and the virtuous were sacrificing the body to achieve "virtue" and life to choose "righteousness."

Takahashi Toru, historian of thought and professor of Keijo Imperial University prior to World War II, reminisced about the motive for focusing on Joseon Confucianism as follows:

> Under the directive of the Government-General of Joseon, I visited the three southern provinces (Gyeongsang, Chungcheong, and Jeolla Provinces) in turn to investigate the movement of Confucians immediately after the annexation. I was surprised to see *Toegyejip* (Collection of Toegye's Works) on the desks of several leaders of the righteous army. This was the first step in studying Joseon Confucianism.

> - "Takahashi teisensei furya" (高橋亭先生譜略),
>   *Chosen Gakuho* (朝鮮学報), Vol. 14

Collection of Toegye's Works is of course a collection of writings by Yi Hwang, a great Confucian of the mid-Joseon dynasty. The sense of duty felt by the advocates of defending orthodoxy and rejecting heterodoxy that was represented in the form of taking up arms to protect the last stronghold of mankind called "little China" was truly heroic. But the tragedy in the advocacy of the Learning of Master Zhu as the only scholarship lies in the fact that it did not face facts of the changing world and reality; it only looked at things through the perspective of a filter called the Learning of Master Zhu from the

Song period. As such this thought was extremely anti-aggression but did not seem to offer any prospects for a future.

Attention on the Cannons of the West

The big difference in the reaction toward western impact between Joseon and Qing China or Japan was that the issue of modernizing "military power" was almost never raised as a national priority in Joseon despite the experiences of the two western invasions. Of course Joseon miraculously succeeded in fending off the two invasions, and it remains a mystery that no one raised the issue of the necessity for an in-depth study of French and American warships, cannons, western science, and the art of war based on "devices" and "military."

At the time, attention was paid solely to a statement made by Wei Yuan in "Chouhai" of *Illustrated Treatise on Nations across the Sea*, which was included in a letter from Kim Yun-sik (金允植) to a friend. In it, Wei Yuan claimed that "the exquisiteness of the cannons must be pursued rather than the majority of the military forces" to cope with the invading West from the ocean. The extent of assertion was that "it is advisable to 'copy and build' clever cannons, install them in strategic defensive locations, and repulse the western warships in coastal waters rather than adversely impact agricultural activities by mobilizing the majority of sturdy young men from farming villages" as the method for repulsing the western invasions ("Yangyosi dammoinseo," *Unyangjib*, Vol. 11).[4]

The defenders of orthodoxy and leaders of public opinion among the outdated dominant Confucian way of thinking of the times prided themselves in Joseon being "little China" because of preservation of the superiority of "the Way" over "devices" and of "literature" over "military." This was the traditional Joseon Confucian

---

[4] Kim Yun-sik is the author of *Unyangjib* (雲養集, Collected Works of Unyang), of which "Yangyosi dammoinseo" (洋擾時答某人書) is a part. (S. Lee)

thought on "encouragement of learning and discouragement of the military," which was why the only way to success in life was considered to be through the Erudite Examination of the civil service examination. There was no way for men with superior ability to apply for the Military Examination, and the situation was even worse for the Miscellaneous Examination due to the position below those of the Erudite and Military Examinations both.

Yi Ik, a master of the Silhak School, pointed out early on the following items in his criticism of the disabling practice of disdaining the military-official order when the scholar-official order and military-official order were both made up of *yangban*:

> I have always said that arts and literature are inferior to martial arts in today's world. Bows and arrows are useful in hunting wild animals or preventing robbers, but I cannot think of any use for documentary prose or poetic prose. Some people say documentary prose must be used in the diplomacy of serving a bigger nation, but there should not be a big obstacle in regular prose. How can the military be said to be inferior to literature? Military is met with contempt because people think arrows from foreigners can be fought off with a brush.

> • Foreword, "Mubyeon juui" (武辨注擬),
> Insignificant Explanations of Seongho

As Yi Ik subtly pointed out, public opinion based on the pen cannot prevent foreign invasions, even if vehement. But the doctrine of defending orthodoxy and rejecting heterodoxy was a doctrine of excluding foreigners based only on the pen without "the military."

Advocates of defending orthodoxy and rejecting heterodoxy showed minimal interest in the might of western devices and military forces perhaps due to the successful repulsion of the French fleet in 1866 and the American fleet in 1871. It was as if the invading nations were barbaric because they disdained "the Way" and "literature." Moreover, Yi Hang-no claimed prohibition of Catholicism or repelling western barbarians as unimportant side issues, and doing away with western goods as a counterplan to eradicate the root of all evils.

Yi Hang-no based his claim on "the principle." A summary of the debate on the study of the principle of human nature in the history of Joseon Confucian thought was examined in Chapter 15, but the debate there was whether the doctrine of the principle and material force as existentialism should be understood with the principle as the principal or material force as the principal. Yi Hang-no defined the doctrine of the principle and material force as "the principle is the master that commands material force, and material force is the utensil for holding the principle."

> Everything can be governed and everything under Heaven will be harmonious when the principle is the master and material force its messenger and when material force becomes upright because the principle is pure. But if material force is the master and the principle its effect and the principle hides because of the strength of material force, then everything will be confusion and everything under Heaven will be in danger. The slightest bit of disparity makes a difference of ten thousand *li*.[5]

> • A-eon, "Imcheon" (臨川),
> Collection of Works by Hwaseo

Yi Hang-no's position on the doctrine of the principle and material force was "the master is the principle and the guest is material force." Classification of these two was a fundamental issue linked directly to peace and turbulence under Heaven. What would happen if "the master is the principle and the guest is material force" was replaced with the mutual relationship of "the Way" and "device"?

> Fostering "the sage and the wise" is cultivating "the mind and the will," and cultivating "artisans" is cultivating "the form and the body." Both must be cultivated, but the point that the mind and

---

[5] *Li* is a measure of distance. 1 *li* is approximately 0.393 km. (S. Lee)

441

the will are high and big while the form and the body are low and small must be distinguished.

> • A-eon, "Jonjunghwa" (尊中華),
> *Collection of Works by Hwaseo*, Vol. 10

In other words, the relationship between the metaphysical "Way" and the physical "material force" and the hierarchical positions and the bigness and smallness will also be directly related to peace and turbulence if not clearly distinguished. Here, western products, especially manufacturing products, were not useful at all in everyday life, but rather bestirred thoughts of "ingenious devices and manu-facturing" which threw beautiful and good customs into confusion. This was the "honest poverty" of the thought of advocates defend-ing orthodoxy and rejecting heterodoxy.

> The fundamental of food is to curb hunger and nurse life, whereas *chunao* and *xiongfan* are insignificant and rather harmful to the fundamental.[6] The fundamental of a royal chamber is to block out the rain and wind, and beautiful and majestic palaces are insignificant and rather injurious to the fundamental.

> • A-eon, "Jonjunghwa" (尊中華),
> *Collection of Works by Hwaseo*, Vol. 10

The above excerpt shows Yi Hang-no's desertion of worldly fame and wealth in favor of concentrating solely on learning of the Way while secluding himself in a remote village. Thus he could not look idly by when the ways of the world from the palace to the distant borders became mesmerized by "ingenious devices and crafty things" and lost the foundation of life. In other words, western technology contradicted the correct way as "devices" and "crafts."

The origin of Confucianism was in denying human greed, and Confucian industrial policy was founded on "concentrating on the foundation and suppressing the insignificant." "The foundation" was

---

[6] *Chunao* and *xiongfan* are two of the eight delicacies in China. (S. Lee)

farming, and "the insignificant" was manufacturing and commerce in the saying, "farming is the greatest foundation in the world," Manufacturing and commerce brought harm to beautiful and good customs by stimulating extravagances and greed of man.

Bak Je-ga of the Bukhak School, however, criticized the suppression of asceticism of the insignificant and claimed that extravagance is instead a virtue in the late 18th century already.

> If the reasons for using extravagant things are not known, then the reasons for producing them are not known. The people will become poorer every day if the reasons for producing them are unknown. In general, fortunes are like water from a well. Water will fill up the well if used and dry up if unused. Thus female manufacturers will decline if satin clothes are not worn. Artistry will disappear if dented utensils are not disliked and craftsmanship is not considered important. Farming is in ruins because farming methods are lost, and commercial profits became stringent due to the loss of work.
>
> • Summary, "Sijeong" (市井),
> Discourse on Northern Learning

Confucian asceticism oppressed industrial and commercial development as well as disdained artisans and merchants who made a living in those fields. This was the cause of a Chonin culture of the metropolis in Japan not developing in Joseon.[7] There were many Buddhist monks and merchants among Japanese Confucians, but such personal history would have prevented Joseon people from becoming part of the descendants of good families without government posts. Hayashi Razan and Ito Jinsai are good examples of Japanese Confucians from humble backgrounds. The former was a monk but became a great Confucian during the Edo period, and the latter was a lumber merchant who later became a renowned Confucian scholar of the Ancient Learning School. Moreover, Ino Tadataka (1745-1818) was a merchant who sold alcoholic beverages and rice wholesale

---

[7] *Chonin* culture referred to merchant culture. (S. Lee)

before becoming the creator of the first accurate map of Japan entitled *Dainihon enkai yochi zenzu* (Maps of the Japanese Coastal Areas).

Farming, the basis of the original Confucian industrial policy, was restricted by harsh natural conditions which determined the lives of the people. That is why Confucianism based on physiocracy feared Heaven more, and a ritual for worshipping Heaven was an event that had to be performed by the sovereign, especially in rice-producing East Asian nations lying in the path of monsoons. Manufacturing and commerce free of such natural restrictions were trades that stimulated the wild curiosity and creativity of humanity held in rein by the tenets of the sage and the wise. If the industry of a nation were not led by manufacturing and commerce, the nation cannot enter modernization from a premodern system. The doctrine of defending orthodoxy and rejecting heterodoxy was a thought containing the duality of anti-modern and anti-invasion. The reason was that the door was closed to heterodox nations, trading with them was opposed, and attention to advanced technology was not paid in order to protect the purity of "Correct Learning."

The Door to the Nation Must Be Opened

At a time when anti-reconciliation with and exclusion of the West became the same thing in terms of the invasions of the French and American warships, reconciliation was advocated by Bak Gyu-su (朴珪壽, pen name is Hwanjae 瓛齋), grandson of Bak Ji-won, who led the Bukhak School.

The Seongho School of the Namin Faction disbanded after the 1801 Persecution of Catholics in Joseon. In contrast, the Bukhak School belonged to the Noron Faction. Bak Gyu-su entered the world of government bureaucracy immediately after passing the augmented examination in 1848 because he belonged to the genealogy of the Noron Faction. He was also a close boyhood friend of Crown Prince Hyomyeong who died at a young age. Bak Gyu-su was singled out by Queen Injo, widow of Crown Prince Hyomyeong, and became governor of Pyeong'an Province in 1866 after completing the elite course of the Office of Royal Decrees, Office of Special Advisors, and Office of Inspector General.

Bak Gyu-su led the burning of the U.S.S. General Sherman that traveled up the Daedong River without permission in 1866 and personally experienced the issue of how to cope with western impact surrounding the issue of handling this incident after the fact. He visited China twice as envoy to Yenching after the Second Opium War. He went on his first visit to China as Vice Ambassador of Courtesy Visit to Rehe in 1861 because Emperor Xian Feng fled to Rehe when the British and French forces invaded Beijing; he went to China a second time as Envoy of Congratulatory Message to Emperor Tongzhi in 1872. Thus not only did he observe the western impact in detail in China, but he also paid attention to the results of the Self-Strengthening Movement of China as a coping method during his second visit. This is the so-called period of "Tongzhi Restoration."

Bak Gyu-su commanded the burning of the U.S.S. General Sherman as the governor of the Pyeong'an Province in 1866. He also drafted diplomatic communiqués to the Board of Rites of Qing China as well as responses to America's questions on the American Invasion of Ganghwa Island in 1871 that had been instigated by American warships. The content of his communiqués justified the repulsion of American warships that invaded Joseon without authorization, as discussed in the royal court. For example, his statement below about the process of destroying American warships was contained in the diplomatic communiqués to the Board of Rites of Qing China.

> We will respond with goodwill if they (America) come to us with goodwill, and we will receive them with protocol if they come to us with protocol.

> - "Mi byeongseon jayoja," Collected Works of Hwanjae

The foreign relations of Joseon in serving a greater nation of China and in friendly relations with the neighboring nation of Japan were all based on "propriety." That is why the Ministry of Rites of the government was in charge of this. The standard for responding to foreign nations depended on the existence of "propriety" or lack thereof; the unauthorized invasion of American warships was an act "lacking propriety."

Bak Gyu-su presented this view from his official position based on the discussions in the royal court. As discussed above, the national opinion was united in that advocacy of peace was equivalent to selling out the nation. But his private view on this issue was to advocate reconciliation with the U.S. According to his personal view on "propriety," "propriety" does not belong exclusively to Confucian nations, but exists in various forms throughout the world. In his letter to his younger brother Bak Seon-su (朴瑄壽), he stated, "How can nations exist as nations without propriety in the universe for all eternity?" Rather, he was of the opinion that Joseon should be ashamed of being referred to as "the land of propriety in the East" by China.

Kim Yun-sik was a disciple of Bak Gyu-su and very close to him. He recollected the critical attitude of Bak Gyu-su toward the Joseon administrative "policy of closing its door and refusing reconciliation" in dealing with the U.S. when Bak Gyu-su wrote a draft of the diplomatic communiqués to the Board of Rites of Qing China. He further reminisced as below:

> I (Kim Yun-sik) was assisting the teacher. The teacher sighed and lamented as follows. "The conditions of the world are changing daily these days, and the confrontational state of various powerful nations in the East and the West resembles the Age of Spring and Autumn and the period of the Warring States. Tumultuous formation of alliances among the nations and conquering of each other are ceaseless. Our kingdom is small but must respond appropriately at all times in domestic policies as well as diplomacy to protect itself because it is in the center of Asia as was Zheng (鄭) in between Jin (晉) and Chu (楚). Otherwise, it is the Way of Heaven for the foolish and the weak to perish first. And who can

be blamed for this? I have heard that the U.S. is in the center of all kingdoms of the world, calls out the loudest for equality and resolves disputes the best, and is not motivated by the greed to expand its territory because its territory is the richest in the world. We should take the initiative to form diplomatic relations and an alliance with the U.S. even if it is silent on the subject to avoid the grief that might accompany isolation. How can refusing to do this be called a way to promote the kingdom?" This reveals that the diplomatic communiqués did not contain his own will.

- "Mi byeongseon jayoja," Collected Works of Hwanjae

Bak Gyu-su was of the position that "We should take the initiative to sign a treaty with the U.S. to open the port to avoid 'grief from isolation' even if the U.S. is silent on the subject." It seems clear that his view of the U.S. was based on observations of the Self-Strengthening Movement of China and information on western empires from China.

Kim Yun-sik, Kim Ok-gyun, Bak Yeong-hyo, Hong Yeong-sik, and Yu Gil-jun were disciples of Bak Gyu-su and members of the Modernization Faction, whereas Kim Pyeong-muk, Yu Jung-gyo, Choe Ik-hyeon, and Yu In-seok were members of the Hwaseo School which considered Yi Hang-no as the mainstream. As such, the Modernization Faction fiercely confronted the policy of seclusion and conservatism as promoted by the advocates defending orthodoxy and rejecting heterodoxy of the Hwaseo School by advocating the opening of the port externally and modernization internally. This was qualitatively different from the factional struggles fought until now because this opposition was linked to the confrontation of political lines involving integration of thoughts and politics of each faction.

20

Closed Kingdom to Open Kingdom

The Treaty of Ganghwa Island Is Signed after Japanese Warship Unyo Was Attacked

Daewon-gun took control over real power from 1863 to 1873 as regent and eliminated *sedo* politics of the Andong Kim clan as the in-laws of the king who had influenced Joseon politics for 60-some years in the first half of the 19th century. Thus he was very careful in the selection of a queen for Gojong to prevent the in-laws from political meddling. Gojong was wed to the daughter of Min Chi-rok (閔致祿) in 1866 after completing the three-year mourning for Cheoljong. She was Empress Myeongseong (明成皇后, 1851-1895) of the Min clan, and she was a year older than the 15-year-old Gojong at the time. Min Chi-rok was a maternal relative of the wife of Daewon-gun and lived in Yeoju-gun in Gyeonggi Province. He was a provincial *yangban* who had held the post of Cheomjeong. Daewon-gun was determined that the Yeoheung Min clan would not monopolize government authority as did the Andong Kim clan.

However, political domination by the king's in-laws in the form of the Yeoheung Min clan replaced that of the Andong Kim clan as soon as Gojong personally started to rule in 1873 because Queen Min with intelligence and strength of character appointed her relatives, such as Min Seung-ho (閔升鎬), Min Gyu-ho (閔奎鎬), Min Gyeom-ho (閔謙鎬), and Min Tae-ho (閔台鎬), in key positions. This was when the Min clan suddenly emerged as the major influence in the government in the latter half of the 19th century. Therefore

Daewon-gun, who did not welcome *sedo* politics, was adamantly opposed to Queen Min. Gojong continued to be swayed by the strong characters of both Daewon-gun and Queen Min.

In retrospect, *sedo* politics of the Andong Kim clan prior to the rule of Daewon-gun or of the Yeoheung Min clan following the rule of Daewon-gun lasted for 100 years from the death of Jeongjo in 1800, except for the 10-year term from 1863 to 1873 in which Daewon-gun ruled as regent. The fate of Joseon was already on the decline with the 20th century looming in sight.

The greatest diplomatic issue since Gojong personally began to rule was the recovery of diplomatic relations with the Meiji regime in Japan, which was a long-pending issue from the period of Daewon-gun. The restoration of monarchy occurred in Japan in 1867 after Tokugawa Yoshinobu, 15th general of Tokugawa Bakufu, returned the sovereignty to the Meiji emperor. In 1868, Japan sent a communiqué to Joseon to inform it of the change in the reign of government from the shogun of Tokugawa Bakufu to emperor of the Meiji government in accordance with the custom of the Edo period in which Joseon was informed of changes in the shogun.

The wording of the communiqué from Japan was unilaterally changed and at variance with the formality of the past Muromachi and Edo Bakufu periods in which Joseon and Japan observed the propriety of equal standing. Examples were such terminology as "emperor" (皇) to refer to the Meiji emperor and "imperial" (勅) to refer to his words in the communiqué to the Joseon king. These words had been used solely by the Chinese emperor to the Joseon king.

Joseon rejected this communiqué because it was seen as a one-sided attempt to place the Joseon king beneath the Japanese emperor after the Meiji Restoration instead of the previous relationship of an equal footing. Joseon confirmed that Japan had already become heterogeneous and "westernized," different from the friendly neighbor of the Edo period, through this process.

In order to overcome the complex issue of negotiating with Japan, the new government run by the Min clan banished Jeong

Hyeon-deok (鄭顯德) who held the post of Magistrate of Donglae, dismissed Kim Se-ho (金世鎬) who was the governor of Gyeong-sang Province, and executed Ahn Dong-jun (安東晙) who was in charge of diplomatic relations with Japan for suspicion of corruption. Ahn Dong-jun was a teacher in a village school in Busan.

Japan was wary of Joseon due to the stringent policy of seclusion from western barbarians during the rule of Daewon-gun, but its policy was changed to that of coercive diplomacy based on militaristic pressure when it saw the pliancy of Joseon toward Japan after the king began to rule personally. In May of 1875, Terashima Munenori as Secretary of the Ministry of Foreign Affairs received permission from Sanjo Sanetomi as Grand Minister of State and Iwakura Tonomi as Minister of the Right to reach an agreement with naval admiral Kawamura Sumiyoshi to negotiate for a solution on the show of force. Three Japanese warships, Kasuga, Unyo, and Daini Teibo were dispatched to the Joseon coast. The Ganghwa Island Incident (also known as Unyo Incident) of September 20 in the same year was provoked by this show of force.

Hyeon Seog-un was appointed as teacher of a village school in Busan after Ahn Dong-jun was executed. Unyo, Kasuga, and Daini Teibo reached port in Busan in May 1875, at which time the gunship showed off its military power while threatening the government officials and people of Busan and Donglae by firing cannons as practice with Hyeon Seog-un (玄昔運) and his party on board. Unyo returned to Nagasaki first, and under the pretext of studying the route to Niuzhuang in Qing China, advanced northward on the coast of the Yellow Sea and approached Ganghwa Island under the command of the Japanese navy. Secretary of the Ministry of Foreign Affairs Terashima later gave the excuse of approaching to "get something to drink" to the British minister in Japan, but this was a planned provocation. The Japanese government already knew of the precedence of fending off the French and American warships on Ganghwa Island.

The Unyo launched a counterattack against the fort on Ganghwa Island when the Ganghwa people attacked it on September 20, 1875; the Unyo also attacked Yeongjong Island. This was the so-called

Unyo Incident. In February of the following year, six Japanese warships led by Minister of Finance Kuroda Kiyotaka and Vice Minister of Finance Inoue Kaoru landed on Ganghwa Island to negotiate with Joseon representatives. This was typical gunship diplomacy of the great western powers. Shin Heon (申櫶: General of the Royal Brigade) and Yun Ja-seung (尹滋承: Minister of Rites) were the minister in charge of greeting foreigners and the vice minister in charge of greeting foreigners on behalf of Joseon, respectively.

Bak Gyu-su resigned from the political front line in 1874 after he served as Third State Councilor, but he still retained the right to participate in the State Council where policies of the highest level were discussed. The State Council, which was composed of preceding ministers and present ministers, was divided into anti-reconciliation and pro-reconciliation groups regarding Japan, but the minority was the pro-reconciliation group. Bak Gyu-su insisted on avoiding a clash of forces by not focusing on the improper wordings in accepting the document from the Japanese government, and on recovering the relationship of friendly neighbors on an equal footing based on the precedence from the Edo period from a perspective of reconciliation. His opinion was that the Japanese usage of the words "emperor" or "imperial" without agreement had nothing to do with other kingdoms, because Japan had imbued itself with "self-professed importance" from of old.

The negotiation for Ganghwa Island was carried out under the premise of the military defeat of Joseon following the Unyo Incident. Fortunately, errand runner Kang Wi and head of interpreter Oh Gyeong-seok (吳慶錫) participated as assistants to the minister on behalf of Joseon negotiators. These two held the same view as Bak Gyu-su in advocating reconciliation. These two provided progress reports on the negotiations to Bak Gyu-su, who in turn put all of his efforts to preventing another confrontation of force of arms due to a breakdown of negotiations by persuading the minister. Bak Gyu-su passed away in February of that year at the ripe old age of 70 following the signing of the Treaty of Ganghwa Island. The Treaty of Ganghwa Island was not an equitable treaty, as it was signed after the military defeat of Joseon.

Map of the region surrounding Ganghwa Island

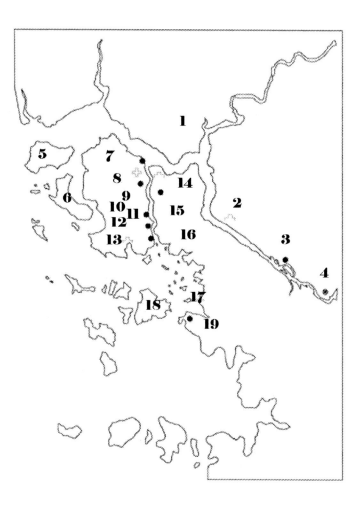

1. Imjin River
2. Haengju Mountain Fortress
3. Yanghwajin
4. Hanseong (Seoul)
5. Gyodong Island
6. Seongmo Island
7. Weolgotjin
8. Ganghwa Regional Government Office
9. Gapgotjin
10. Ganghwa Island
11. Gwangseongjin
12. Deokjinjin
13. Jeongjok Mountain Fortress
14. Munsu Mountain Fortress
15. Tongjinjin
16. Chojijin
17. Mulchi Island
18. Yeongjong Island
19. Jemul Port (Incheon)

The Enemy Must Be Contained by Another Enemy

What was the view of the Qing government on this issue of the suzerain state of Joseon when heated public debates were waged over Japan in Joseon? Joseon was a tributary state of China, but China could not interfere with the diplomatic relations with Japan because Joseon was traditionally "a kingdom with autonomy over church and state as well as decrees."

Yi Yu-won (李裕元) was dispatched to Beijing by the Joseon government as envoy for petitioning the Chinese emperor in 1875 in order to have the biological son of Queen Min (later to become Sunjong) invested as the Crown Prince. Gojong had an illegitimate son by a concubine of the Yi clan; the illegitimate son was named Wanhwa-gun (完和君) and was eight years older than the legitimate son. Queen Min could not shake off the suspicion of Daewon-gun pushing for his favorite older grandson Wanhwa-gun as the Crown Prince. The fated conflict between Daewon-gun and Queen Min arose from this, and the entrance of the Min clan into politics further aggravated the conflict.

Yi Yu-won opposed Daewon-gun because he sided with the Min clan. He sent a communiqué to Li Hongzhang (李鴻章, 1823-1901), Viceroyalty of Zhili and Minister of Beiyang, through Yongping Treasurer You Zhi-kai (游智開) when visiting Beijing as an envoy. In his response, Li Hongzhang only wrote of the situation of China foregoing "the policy of closing the door and of self-governing" and opening its door; he did not interfere in Joseon's relationship with Japan. But with this as a start, Li Hongzhang offered indirect advice to Yi Yu-won on foreign relations of Joseon when they exchanged personal letters.

Attention should be paid to the secret letter Li Hongzhang sent to Yi Yu-won in July of 1879 among several letters sent back and forth. Earlier in September 1872, Japan invested the king of the Ryukyu Islands with the Han prefecture, and Okinawa was turned into a Japanese prefecture. Moreover, Japan attacked Taiwan in 1874, using the murder of the Ryukyus in Taiwan as an excuse for attack. The Treaty of Ganghwa Island was signed with Joseon in 1876. Li Hongzhang was strongly distrustful of Japan because it had annexed the Ryukyu kingdom, invaded Taiwan, and advanced into Joseon to threaten the three provinces in northeastern China. The main content of the secret letter was the urging of a "strategy to use poison as an antidote to poison and to restrain the enemy with another enemy" by signing a treaty with western nations to hinder the Japanese unilateral advancement into the Korean peninsula.

> The strategy of attacking poison with poison and of using an enemy to restrain another enemy should be implemented now. Moreover, Japan should be restrained after treaties with various western nations are gradually signed.

- Materials on the History of Foreign Affairs in the Late
Qing Dynasty (清季外交史料,
Qingji waijiao shiliao in Ch.), Vol. 16

Of course the letters sent back and forth between the two statesmen reflected the inclinations of two governments, but Li Hongzhang as a statesman from the suzerain state gave indirect advice while respecting the domestic affairs and the autonomy of foreign affairs of Joseon.

Yi Yu-won was active in recovering diplomatic relations with Japan, but even he was not confident of following the recommendation of "signing treaties with various European nations." Pursuit of "signing treaties with various European nations" in the midst of strong criticism from advocates defending orthodoxy and rejecting heterodoxy surrounding the weak diplomatic relations with Japan was like pouring oil on top of a fire. Yi Yu-won had no option but to reject the advice of Li Hongzhang based on the reason that "I do not dare start a difficult fight." But Li Hongzhang did not give up the attempt to guide the foreign policy of Joseon toward "signing treaties with various European nations." The thing he was most concerned about was the return of Daewon-gun to Joseon politics because Daewon-gun was the leader of advocating seclusion from western barbarians.

Opening the Door to the West

The State Council of Joseon decided to sign a treaty to open the door to the U.S. due to the second visit made by Ambassador Kim Hong-jip to Japan in June to July of 1880. The main purpose of the visit was to revise a clause on the tariff of imported goods from Japan, which was missing in the Treaty of Ganghwa Island; the Japanese government, however, refused to negotiate with the excuse that it did not have authority from the king.

Kim Hong-jip visited various centers of civilization and enlightenment in Japan and then visited the delegation from Qing China to listen to Huang Zunxian, Qing Minister and Counselor in Japan, and He Ru-zhang, Secretary to the First Imperial Chinese Legation to Tokyo, about world affairs and domestic policies in Japan. Particular interest was paid to Chinese experiences in relation to Joseon adopting the policy of "signing treaties with various European nations." Huang Zunxian organized the discussions in *A Policy for Joseon* (私擬朝鮮策略). Kim Hong-jip submitted *A Policy for Joseon* to the king on his return to Joseon and reported the contents of his conversations with He Ru-zhang in detail.

A Policy for Joseon indicates the stand Joseon must take on diplomatic policy by pointing out the major threat to Joseon as not Japan but Russia, because Russia borders Joseon after its advancements into Siberia. It also stated that Joseon should be on close terms with China, maintain friendly relations with Japan, and form an alliance with the U.S. as a protective measure against Russia.

> Joseon must make haste to obstruct Russia with the most urgent measures today. What countermeasure can be utilized to defend Joseon against Russia? It is to expend effort on contriving to be self-reliant by being on close terms with China, maintaining friendly relations with Japan, and forming an alliance with the U.S.

Gojong asked the ministers of the Joseon government such as Chief State Councilor Yi Choe-eung (李最應) to give their opinions on *A Policy for Joseon*, and decided to open the door of Joseon first to the U.S. among various western nations on October 11, 1880. Thus this conference of senior statesmen was a turning point in that an open door policy to the West was adopted for the first time in the political thought of Joseon.

Therefore not only was *A Policy for Joseon* the stimulus for opening the door of Joseon to the western world for the first time via "an alliance with the U.S.," the report submitted by Kim Hong-jip as ambassador to Japan made the atmosphere amenable to "maintaining friendly relations with Japan." This could be seen in the dialogue between Gojong and Chief State Councilor Yi Choe-eung.

Gojong: The Japanese seem to be desirous of being on friendly terms without restraint, according to the ambassador to Japan.

Yi Choe-eung: I have heard the same thing, Your Majesty. We did not know their true feelings at the time of the visit by Kim Gi-su in the year of *byeongja* (first visit of Joseon ambassador to Japan in 1876), but [Japan's] goodwill was trusted because the reception was marked this time.

Gojong: There seems to some concern about Russia included in dialogues with the Japanese.

Yi Choe-eung: Your Majesty, Russia has grown very strong in recent days; China may not be able to control it.

Gojong: If China is such a case, then what of our kingdom?

Yi Choe-eung: That might have been the case at a banquet with Miyamoto Shoichi several years ago when the conversation was about Russia, but our people were suspicious of that. The real state of affairs are confirmed by the book (*A Policy for Joseon*) sent by a person from Qing China who is an acquaintance of the present ambassador to Japan.

Gojong: Let us assume that Russia is worth our concern; is the goodwill of the Japanese really their true intention?

Yi Choe-eung: Japan's reception of [Joseon's] ambassador to Japan and consideration for the interpreters and others in the party were different from the year of the *byeongja* (1876). This should be viewed as the real political situation, Your Majesty.

- September 8 of the 17th year of the reign of Gojong,
  Veritable Records of King Gojong

But because of the confrontation from the strong denunciation of Kim Hong-jip who brought *A Policy for Joseon* to Joseon and the resistance of the advocates defending orthodoxy and rejecting heterodoxy who considered the West as "evil learning," Tak Jeong-sik (卓挺植) was secretly dispatched to He Ru-zhang to request China to mediate negotiations with the U.S. He Ru-zhang presented "A Discussion on Joseon Foreign Policy" (主持朝鮮外交議) to the Ministry of Foreign Affairs in his native country on November 18, and the Ministry of Foreign Affairs of China commissioned Minister of Beiyang Li Hongzhang to negotiate the diplomatic relations of Joseon with the U.S.

Commodore Robert W. Shufeldt, who was authorized by the American government to negotiate a treaty of friendship with Joseon, stopped at Tianjin to impress Li Hongzhang to mediate the treaty with Joseon at the time Kim Hong-jip was visiting Japan. What was the reason for *A Policy for Joseon* urging Joseon to form an alliance especially with the U.S. among all western nations? In his conversation with Kim Hong-jip, Qing Minister He Ru-zhang urged that an opportunity for negotiating a treaty with the U.S. in Tianjin with Commodore Shufeldt must not be wasted.

> In my humble opinion, the matter with Russia is the most urgent. The U.S. is the only democratic nation among the nations in the world; it is rich and powerful as well. The U.S. likes to enter into friendly relations with all nations, and it does not conspire on behalf of its own advantages by insisting on trust. At this time the other party is requesting the opening of trade with Japan; the U.S. will happily agree to a treaty if the rough draft of Japan's revised treaty (Japan was preparing to negotiate for revision of the unequal treaties with Europe and the U.S.) is used as a model. If this plan is executed, all rights to a commercial treaty will be manipulated by this side because other nations that request a commercial treaty in the future must follow the precedence with the U.S. when signing a treaty. There is benefit in negotiating with all nations without loss. A golden opportunity must not be lost. There will be great loss if negotiations are attempted in a rush after troubles arise when the door is closed and signing of treaties denied.

> - July 21, at the legation of Qing China, "Daecheong heumsa pildam," *Records of Ambassador to Japan*

A Policy for Joseon was made out to be the "private opinions" of Huang Zunxian, however. This was due to the policy of avoiding direct involvement in the foreign policy of Joseon and following a policy of indirection in those days, as can be see in the secret letters from Li Hongzhang to Yi Yu-won.

According to the determination of the conference of senior statesmen of Joseon, Diplomatic Secretary Ma Jianzhong (馬建忠, 1845-1899) and Commodore Shufeldt negotiated on the practical aspects of the Joseon-American Treaty of Amity and Commerce on October 11, 1880, in Tianjin. This was done under the good offices of Li Hongzhang, and Kim Yun-sik and Eoh Yun-jung who were in Tianjin at the time provided advice. Ma Jianzhong was of the westernization faction; he studied abroad in France as commanded by Li Hongzhang and acted as the diplomatic secretary of Li Hongzhang upon returning to China.

The Joseon-American Treaty of Amity and Commerce was signed at Jemul Port on May 22, 1882, by Ambassador Shin Heon and Vice Ambassador Kim Hong-jip, representing Joseon, and Shufeldt representing the U.S., with Ma Jianzhong in attendance. Li Hongzhang was persistent in stipulating that Joseon was an autonomous state in domestic policies and foreign affairs, but stated in Clause 1 from the drafting of the treaty to the last that it had traditionally been a "vassal state." Shufeldt did not concede on this point. A compromise was ultimately reached where the treaty specifies that the treaty was made between the autonomous nations of Joseon and the U.S., but the Joseon government had to separately express to the U.S. of its status as a traditional "vassal state" of Qing China. In spite of this, negotiations with the U.S. that became the breakthrough in opening the door to the West occurred in Tianjin under the auspices of Li Hongzhang. The fact that it was signed in the presence of Ma Jianzhong spoke volumes about the anti-western theory of exclusionism of advocates defending orthodoxy and rejecting heterodoxy as well as the western allergy felt among the common *minjung* in Joseon.

Treaties to open the door were signed with Britain and Germany in November of 1883, Italy in June of 1884, and Russia in October of 1885 following the treaty with the U.S. A treaty with France was signed in June of 1886 due to continuous disputes surrounding the stipulation on the freedom to propagate missionary work based on the history of executed French missionaries prior to the opening of the door.

Lucius H. Foote was newly appointed to Seoul as American minister to Korea in May of 1883, the first diplomat from the western nations. He conveyed to Gojong the inclination of U.S. President Chester A. Arthur to welcome a delegation dispatched by Joseon. The response of Joseon to this was quick. Ambassador Min Yeong-ik (閔泳翊), Vice Ambassador Hong Yeong-sik, Lieutenants Seo Gwang-beom (徐光範), Yu Gil-jun, Choe Do-min (崔道敏), Ko Yeong-cheol (高永喆), Hyeon Gwang-taek (玄光澤), and Byeon Su (邊燧) as part of a goodwill mission visited the U.S., the land of "western barbarians," for the first time in Korean history.

The group of the Joseon envoy departed Incheon in July of 1883 and was joined by Percival Lowell in Tokyo as secretary through the introduction of the American Ambassador to Japan. Lowell was the author of the 1885 book entitled *Choson—the Land of the Morning Calm—a Sketch of Korea*. The group toured the U.S. for 40 days, but returned to Joseon at two separate times because the group had been divided. One group led by Min Yeong-ik returned to Joseon in May of 1884 by crossing the Atlantic Ocean to tour Europe, whereas the second group led by Hong Yeong-sik returned to Joseon in December of 1883 after crossing the Pacific Ocean and stopping in Japan.

Min Yeong-ik was the favorite nephew of Queen Min from her older brother Min Seung-ho. As such Min Yeong-ik was one of the most influential people in the Joseon court because he could influence Gojong through his aunt. Hong Yeong-sik and Seo Gwang-beom of the Modernization Faction expected Min Yeong-ik to join it after his visit to the western nations, but the expectation came to naught. It will be mentioned later, but Min Yeong-ik was injured in December in the Coup d'État of 1884 because he became a target of the Modernization Faction to be overthrown. Hong Yeong-sik was executed and Seo Gwang-beom fled to the U.S. after the failure of the Coup d'État. The likelihood of "the reform from top down" succeeding would have been great if Min Yeong-ik had supported the Modernization Faction after returning from his world tour.

460

Daewon-gun Returns to Politics after the Military Mutiny of 1882

Joseon transformed into "Joseon of the world" after the treaty to open the door to America was signed in May 1882 until 1886. This was a sudden change brought on by the international conditions of the times as opposed to the discontinuation of studies about the West after the 1801 Persecution of Catholics in Joseon. But the subordinate relationship with Qing as mentioned before became a big obstacle in the attempt of Joseon to develop autonomous diplomatic relations with the West.

Unlike the island kingdom of Japan that had an ocean between itself and China, Joseon was geopolitically a peninsular kingdom that was connected to China by land with a river in the north acting as a boundary. How much direct influence political changes in China had over Joseon can be seen clearly by recalling the situations of the transition of dynasties from Yuan to Ming and Ming to Qing in China as mentioned above.

Traditional diplomatic relations of "smaller kingdom serving a greater kingdom" with China that was a super power were effective in guaranteeing the security of the small kingdom of Joseon. But there remained such serious issues as how to change the traditionally subordinate relationship with China, how to reform the internal system of Joseon to cope with the rapid changes in international relations, and whether to adopt radical reforms or gradual improvements as the method for transformation after the transition in becoming "Joseon of the world." These were the reasons that attention had to be paid to the issue of the Modernization Faction which pursued independence from the subordinate relationship with Qing.

But the thick wall of the conservatives who schemed to survive through the subordinate relationship with Qing, as well as Qing China itself which supported the conservatives, blocked the Modernization Faction. The political world of Joseon was forced to make the most difficult decision in the history of party strife.

A great change occurred in the characteristics of the hitherto traditional subordinate relationship between Qing China and Joseon after Qing suppressed the Military Mutiny of 1882 in July of that year.[1] This incident provided an opportunity for Qing to become directly involved in domestic policies and diplomatic relations of Joseon for 12 years until the advent of the Sino-Japanese War. Qing China respected the autonomy of domestic policies and foreign relations of Joseon prior to this incident. During these 12 years, Joseon experienced great upheavals such as the Coup d'État of 1884 initiated by the Modernization Faction in December and the Dong-hak Peasants' War which began in February of 1894, which shook the foundation of the dynastic structure.

The Military Mutiny of 1882 derived from the discord between the old and new systems. In 1880, the Joseon government established a modern military unit called Special Skills Forces (別技軍) and gave it preferential treatment in comparison to the old military units of Palace Guards Garrison and Capital Guards Garrison. A Japanese military officer by the name of Horimoto Reizo was put in charge of instructing the Special Skills Forces. The members of the old military units received a portion of months of back pay in rice, but spoiled rice and sand that had been mixed in the rice became the direct cause of the military revolt of July 19, 1882.[2]

The rebelling soldiers attacked and destroyed the home of Min Gyeom-ho, who held the joint appointments of Minister of Military Affairs and high-level official of the Agency to Bestow Blessings. They lynched Heungin-gun (興寅君) Yi Choe-heung (1815-1882) and attempted to murder Queen Min by advancing into the royal palace; the poverty-stricken people of Seoul from Wangsim-li and Itaewon joined the riot. But Queen Min escaped to the home of Min

---

[1] Military Mutiny of 1882 is also known as the Soldiers' Riot of Imo in 1882. (S. Lee)

[2] It seems to have been a common enough practice in the Joseon period for a portion of the good rice to be taken out of each sack to line the pockets of the high ranking official(s) in charge, and rotten rice and sand to be mixed in to make the sacks of rice look full. (S. Lee)

Eung-sik (閔應植) in Chungju, Chungcheong Province, by disguising herself as a lady of the court. The murdered Heungin-gun Yi Choe-heung was the older brother of Heungseon Daewon-gun and was critical of the isolation policy. Yi Choe-heung presided over the conference of senior statesmen as Chief State Councilor in October of 1880, at which time the policy to open the door to America was determined.

Furthermore, the Japanese in Joseon, including Hanabusa Yoshimoto, barely escaped to Japan with the aid of a British ship, the HMS Flying Fish, when the rebelling soldiers and the mob made up of common people killed Horimoto Reizo who was in charge of instructing the Special Skills Forces and attacked the Japanese legation in Joseon. The Military Mutiny of 1882 contained anti-Japanese and anti-Min characteristics in that it opposed the infiltration of Japanese influence in Joseon and the regime of the Min clan that catered to it after the signing of the Treaty of Ganghwa Island. Gojong invested Daewon-gun with full authority in order to control the political confusion brought on by the rebelling soldiers. Thus Daewon-gun returned to politics nine years after his retirement in 1873. The Military Mutiny of 1882 signified victory for the advocates of seclusion from western barbarians.

China received the report on the military rebellion in Joseon through Li Shuchang (黎庶昌, 1837-1897), Chinese minister in Tokyo, Japan, on August 1 because China did not have a legation in Joseon at the time. Li Hongzhang, the Viceroyalty of Zhili and Minister of Beiyang, was on leave in Hefei, Anhui Province, at the time because his mother had passed away. Zhang Shu-sheng (張樹聲) was the acting administrator in his stead.

Zhang Shu-sheng dispatched Beiyang Naval Units under the command of Ding Ruchang to Joseon with Ma Jianzhong on board so that the actual conditions of Joseon could be understood. Based on this report, Qing took control over Joseon by suppressing the military rebellion and escorted Daewon-gun to China for his role in returning to politics at the invitation of the rebels.

It was August 20 by the time 3,000 Chinese soldiers of the six detachments of the Anhui Army led by Wu Changqing (吳長慶) on board the Beiyang Naval Units landed in Namyang Bay, which was one month after the military rebellion. Order had already been restored at the time by Daewon-gun. The Qing soldiers surrounded and attacked the regions of Wangsim-li and Itaewon where the rebelling soldiers lived, then beheaded the leaders of the military rebellion. Ma Jianzhong also arrested and transported Daewon-gun to Baoding in Tianjin; Daewon-gun had been opposed to Qing soldiers being stationed in Joseon.

Daewon-gun lived the life of an exile in Baoding for three years, from a month after his return to politics in August of 1882 to his return to Joseon in October of 1885. Li Hongzhang was able to maintain suzerainty over Joseon based on the 3,000 Chinese military force stationed in Joseon (1,500 troops were recalled to China in May of 1884 due to the Sino-French War). This situation continued until the Sino-Japanese War in 1894.

Opening the Door to Modernization

Joseon was 40 years behind China (Treaty of Nanjing in 1840) in opening ports and a door to the West; it was 28 years behind Japan (Kanagawa Treaty in 1854) in opening a door to the West, and 24 years behind (Ansei Treaties with five nations in 1858) in opening ports. In other words, the kingdom of Joseon protected the lonely stronghold of "little Confucian China" against Christian nations.

Bak Gyu-su died in February of 1877, but he expected the younger generations of disciples gathered around him since his retirement from the political arena in 1874 to carve out a new path after Joseon opened up. Those included Kim Yun-sik, Kim Ok-gyun, Bak Yeong-hyo, Hong Yeong-sik, Seo Gwang-beom, and Yu Gil-jun, who later formed the core of the Modernization Faction. The task after "opening the door" was that of taking a step further to "modernization," i.e., opening the way to modern reforms. The greatest ideological and political task faced by Joseon after opening up was how to overcome the conflict between "conservatism" and "modernization."

On December 4, 1884, radical progressives such as Kim Okgyun, Hong Yeong-sik, and Bak Yeong-hyo overthrew the conservative government and established a progressive reform government through a coup d'état; however, as was the case with the Military Mutiny of 1882, it was suppressed within three days by the Qing military. This was the Coup d'État of 1884.

The Modernization Faction had invited Inoue Kakugoro, a disciple of Fukujawa Yukichi, to create the first modern newspaper in Joseon on October 31, 1883, called the *Hanseong Weekly*. Kim Okgyun mentioned the following in the May 11, 1884 article on "Chidoyangnon" (治道略論, Summary of the Principle of Governance) that he wrote under his own name:

> The most urgent task of today is to employ able men, conserve available goods, suppress extravagance, and handle diplomatic relations well by overturning the seclusion policy throughout the kingdom. None of these must be missing, but it is more important to seek the Truth from facts rather than foolish opinions based on guesses. In other words, even one or two urgent tasks must be carried out, and grandiose plans that are distant from reality are nothing more than empty words. The forces of the world are currently changing rapidly in which steamships of all nations travel the ocean and battle lines cover the entire earth. Moreover, countless pieces of machinery have been invented by developing gold, silver, coal, and steel that make the everyday life of the people convenient. Political policies which each nation earnestly seek are 1) hygiene, 2) agriculture and sericulture, and 3) roads. These three cannot be violated, even by the sage and the wise of Asia, because they are models of governing a nation.

It is evident at a glance that the confrontation between the Conservative Faction and the Modernization Faction in modern Joseon was fundamentally different from hitherto party strife. Thus Bak Yeonghyo advocated as follows in "Geonbaekseo" (建白書, a document asserting his opinion in favor of modernization) that he sent to King Gojong in January of 1888 from his place of exile in Japan:

> Your Majesty's humble servant thought about the old days in our kingdom when the Seoin, Namin, Daebuk, and Sobuk Factions attacked, excluded, and murdered each other by condemning each other as traitors. Thereafter the Seoin Faction divided into Noron and Soron, and the cycle began again. But this can be referred to as "factions" because the factions of earlier times did not interfere greatly with national polity. The factions divided into self-reliance through pursuit of the new and reliance on traditional customs a few years ago. And Your Majesty's humble servants saw the urgency of the state of affairs and reached a point of committing a cruel atrocity (assassination of a senior minister) in our haste to plan for revival because we told ourselves that we could not waste time. But this should be called "a political party," because it was related to national polity in many ways. This humble servant is prostrate in wishing for Your Majesty to preserve the integrity of the kingdom and ease the lives of the people by distinguishing between right and wrong and protecting the party loyal to the kingdom. Trouble will brew otherwise.

According to Bak Yeong-hyo, traditional party strife was nothing more than mere factional disputes because it was not related to national polity. The confrontation between "the Conservative Faction that adhered to the old system and relied on the subordinate relationship with Qing" and "the Modernization Faction that was desirous of changing the old system and becoming independent of the subordinate relationship with Qing" was considered to be a confrontation between political parties "related to national polity." The world of Japanese history in older times regarded the party strife between the Conservative Faction and the Modernization Faction as a pre-modern factional dispute and viewed the Coup d'État of 1884 as a power struggle between the pro-Qing faction and the pro-Japanese faction. As a result of this turmoil, rash statements were made about factional dispute being the national characteristic of the Korean people.

The December Coup d'État of 1884 was in reality a confrontation between the Conservative Faction and the Modernization Faction on national polity reforms. Kim Ok-gyun was 34 and the eldest among the leaders of the Modernization Faction, Hong Yeong-sik was 30, Seo Gwang-beom was 26, and Bak Yeong-hyo was 24 at the time of the coup d'état. The Modernization Faction contained young people of the *yangban* class who had foresight, but unfortunately none of them was a skillful politician with latent influence.

Bae Cha-san (裴次山) critiqued *Mirror for Modern Politics in Joseon* mentioned above, and he commented as below about Daewon-gun:

> Modernization could not have been prevented and obstinacy could not have been preserved if the tiger-like authority of Daewon-gun did not exist, and, as well, [we] cannot move forward to modernization by transforming obstinacy in the future if Daewon-gun does not exist.

Kim Ok-gyun was visiting Japan when the Military Mutiny of 1882 occurred in July, and he rushed to return to Joseon to prevail on Daewon-gun who had returned to politics. But when he arrived in Incheon, Daewon-gun had already been taken to Baoding in Tianjin by the Qing military. His attitude toward Daewon-gun is below:

> The regent who is also the father of the king (Daewon-gun) is obstinate, but his administration is good and far-reaching. The regent must be convinced with all [our] might, because His Majesty the King is intelligent but lacks decisiveness.

> • *Collected Works of Kim Ok-gyun, Part 1*, compiled by Gogyun Commemoration Committee

The first clause of the political creed set forth by the Modernization Faction during the Coup d'État of 1884 was opposition to the suzerainty of Qing China. Below is the beginning of the clause:

Return Daewon-gun immediately to Joseon and abolish the formality of tributes.

Kim Ok-gyun met his death at the hands of an assassin by the name of Hong Jong-wu in Shanghai on March 28, 1894; to his dying day, he did not have an opportunity to meet with Daewon-gun.

Drive Qing Away by Approaching Russia

As mentioned above, the Joseon government entered into diplomatic relations with various western nations, beginning with the treaty signed with the U.S. to open the door to Joseon. As a result, the foreign relations of Joseon were dualistic in that the traditional subordinate relationship with Qing coexisted with international relations containing elements of international law. However, the problem was that the two systems did not coexist as separate entities; rather, the subordinate relationship with Qing hindered the autonomous diplomatic relations of Joseon with other signatory powers.

The December Coup d'État of 1884 aimed for independence from the subordinate relationship with Qing, but was crushed by the military intervention of Qing China. This was the reason for the Modernization Faction being referred to as "the Independence Party." Qing and Japanese troops withdrew from Joseon according to the Treaty of Tianjin signed between Qing and Japan after the Coup d'État of 1884. Secret diplomatic relations unfolded among those close to Gojong to "usher in Russia to usher out Qing" by approaching Russia, a third-party nation, to severe the subordinate relationship with Qing.

The issues were for Russia to protect Joseon if a military confrontation arose between Qing and Japan, and for inviting a Russian instructor to be in command of training 2,000 Joseon soldiers of the Four Barracks Command. The person chosen to play the behind-the-scenes role was Paul George von Moellendorff (穆鱗德, Chinese name is Mu Lin-de); he was appointed as the foreign relations advisor to the Joseon government by Li Hongzhang. Moellendorff was recalled to Beijing for his role in this.

To suppress the Joseon policy of "usher in Russia to usher out Qing," Li Hongzhang replaced the hitherto Minister of Trade Chen Shu-chang (陳樹裳) in August of 1885 with Yuan Shi-kai by appointing Yuan Shi-kai to the position of "Chinese Minister of Trade in Joseon" with great authority over internal affairs and foreign relations. Yuan Shi-kai not only led the Qing troops in suppressing the Military Mutiny of 1882 and the December Coup d'État of 1884, he was familiar with the internal affairs of Joseon as an "insider." He used the great authority bestowed on him by Li Hongzhang to foil the scheme to "usher in Russia" and also openly interfered in Joseon's foreign relations with the West in the nine years prior to the start of the Sino-Japanese War.

Li Hongzhang recalled Moellendorff back to China to prevent the Joseon government from approaching Russia and dispatched an American by the name of Owen N. Denny to Joseon as the replacement advisor of foreign relations in May of 1886. Denny, however, urged Joseon to execute diversified autonomic foreign relations and mediated its revolt against the exercise of Qing's suzerainty over Joseon through the team of Li Hongzhang and Yuan Shi-kai. Specifically, the Joseon government appointed Bak Jeong-yang (朴定陽) as Joseon minister in the U.S. and Jo Sin-hui (趙臣熙) as Joseon minister jointly in Britain, Germany, Russia, Italy, and France in June of 1887. Dispatching one minister to serve five European countries was linked with finances, but it also showed the greater importance put on diplomacy with the U.S.

As revealed above, Li Hongzhang played a leading role in the foreign relations of Joseon with the West, but the role played by Joseon was passive since Joseon signed the treaty to open the door to the U.S. in May of 1882. But for the first time in a long while, Joseon attempted to take the lead in foreign relations with the West by getting assistance from Denny who was knowledgeable about international law. Yuan Shi-kai reported this to Li Hongzhang and pressured the Joseon government to observe the principle of "dispatching [ministers] after submitting a consultative report" to the suzerain state.

Better relations between Joseon and the U.S. would have been a great threat to the suzerainty of Qing. After receiving the report from Yuan Shi-kai, Li Hongzhang acknowledged the dispatch of ministers to the U.S., but attached conditions after he found it impossible to prevent the dispatch. The conditions were that 1) the Joseon minister must report his arrival in the appointed country to the Qing legation there and a request to accompany visits to the U.S. Department of State must be made to the Qing minister in the U.S.; 2) the Joseon minister must follow the Qing minister when associating with foreigners during morning meetings and at official functions; and 3) the Joseon minister must first secretly consult with the Qing minister on important diplomatic matters. The Qing minister in the U.S. at the time was Zhang Yinhuan (張蔭桓). Whereas Bak Jeong-yang was granted plenary powers, Zhang Yinhuan was simply a resident minister. This was because the Joseon government considered diplomatic relations with the U.S. as especially important among western nations.

As mentioned before, Li Hongzhang attempted to stipulate the point that Joseon was a vassal state of Qing when he mediated the signing of the treaty between Joseon and the U.S., but was refused by the American representative Commodore Shufeldt. The three conditions to be carried out by Bak Jeong-yang were an attempt to realize the subordinate relationship between Qing and Joseon in the diplomatic relations of Joseon with the U.S.

Bak Jeong-yang, however, ignored these conditions and visited Secretary of State Bayard by himself after arriving in the U.S., and presented his credentials to U.S. President Grover Cleveland in January of 1888 with the assistance of Secretary of State Bayard. Bak Jeong-yang had to return to Joseon in 1889, because Li Hongzhang threatened via Yuan Shi-kai to ask the Joseon king to account for the "offense of violating the conditions" after receiving a report on this incident from Zhang Yinhuan. Jo Sin-hui had to return to Joseon from Hong Kong before he had even set foot in Europe.

Joseon May Send Tributes but Is an Independent State

Yuan Shi-kai and Denny were fierce antagonists in Joseon politics because Yuan Shi-kai not only interfered with the foreign policies of Joseon with western nations but he also schemed to dethrone Gojong. Denny, as a scholar of law, published "China and Korea" (1888, Shanghai), in which he attacked the "doctrine of dependent state" of Qing by quoting *Elements of International Law* and opinions of international lawyers. His main point was that although Joseon was "a tributary state" of Qing, it was clearly an independent nation, not a "dependent country" whose sovereignty was restricted.

Moellendorff, having been recalled to Beijing, sided with Li Hongzhang in his rebuttal to the claim of Denny; Moellendorff stated that Denny's opinion ignored the traditional historical relationship between Joseon and Qing (Reply to Mr. O. N. Denny's Pamphlet entitled, "China and Korea"). Denny ultimately resigned his role as foreign relations advisor in 1890 and returned to the U.S.

Yu Gil-jun also claimed that the relationship of a nation that sends tributes and a nation that receives tributes did not signify the negation of the independence of the sender. He had been studying in the U.S. after participating in the goodwill mission there in 1883, but he was put under house arrest in the private residence of Chief of Police Han Gyu-seol (韓圭卨) when he returned to Joseon after the Coup d'État of 1884. While under house arrest, he wrote *Seoyu gyeonmun* (西遊見聞, Observations on a Journey to the West), in which he made the following claim:

> The ruler of a strong nation is a ruler, and so is the ruler of a weak nation a ruler. There cannot be any difference between the two in that they both occupy the throne of their respective nation, and they both exercise their authority to the maximum to enforce policies and supervise rules. Is it then appropriate for a vassal (referring to Yuan Shi-kai) who administers policies and rules of the other nation to struggle for equal propriety with the ruler who promulgates and supervises rules of this nation? It can be said that this is the highest form of indiscretion and irreverence.

- "Banggugui gwolli" (Rights of a Nation),
  Observations on a Journey to the West 3

The Joseon government was opposed to the interference of Qing over autonomy on foreign relations on the one hand while being forced to rely on the suzerainty of Qing in order to overcome the crisis faced by the dynastic system on the other hand. "Donghak" (Eastern Learning) was considered a cult by the Joseon government but was a popular religion of the people. As such, it spread extensively throughout the Jeolla region, which was the greatest breadbasket in Joseon, and the peasants ultimately began an armed revolt in February 1894. Peasants who began the revolt in Gobu of Jeolla Province quickly gathered power and defeated government troops dispatched to the area. On May 31, the peasant army entered Jeonju Castle where the office of the Jeolla governor was located, and submitted "Administrative Reform Proposals" to the government in a commanding manner. The leader of the peasant army was Jeon Bong-jun (全琫準, 1856-1895).

The government became divided on whether to placate with domestic administrative reforms or to call in the Qing army to suppress the revolt. Min Yeong-jun (閔泳駿), the most powerful politician among the in-laws of the king, led the side of borrowing the military power of the Qing army. Yuan Shi-kai thought this to be a golden opportunity to cement the subordinate relationship between Qing and Joseon. Minister of Military Affairs Min Yeong-jun conspired with Yuan Shi-kai to convince Gojong, and sent a request to Qing China for troops to be dispatched to Joseon. This provided the Japanese army with an excuse to dispatch troops to Joseon as well, which developed into the Sino-Japanese War.

The Peasants' War itself came under control after a peace treaty was signed in Jeonju on June 10 after the "Administrative Reform Proposals" submitted by the peasants was accepted by the Joseon government. But the Qing troops arrived in Asan, Chungcheong Province, while the Japanese troops landed in Incheon and Seoul almost simultaneously; the war began again in August 1. Yuan Shi-kai fled to China before the war raged again.

The logic inherent in the doctrine of borrowing the military power of the Qing army was based on the premodern subordinate relationship of the suzerain state saving the vassal state from crisis. *Sedo* politics dominated by the Min clan suppressed the Military Mutiny of 1882 in July, and the Coup d'État of 1884 in December by relying on the suzerainty of Qing China. The Min clan attempted to suppress the peasant army and preserve the privilege of the clan with the assistance of the Qing troops, but this became the cause of the Sino-Japanese War. The exercising of suzerainty by Qing backed by military might blocked the way for Joseon to resolve internal contradictions with autonomous domestic administrative reforms.

A Policy for Joseon urged Joseon to "be on close terms with China" and to "maintain friendly relations with Japan" as a defensive mechanism against the threat of Russia in the north. But that effort came to naught due to the fight for supremacy over Joseon between Qing and Japan. As a result, an attempt was made to get Russia involved to remove the interference of both Qing and Japan, but that attempt failed also.

21

At the Crossroads of Conservatism and Modernization

Modernization Thought in Confucianism

Bak Yeong-hyo, one of the leaders of the Modernization Faction, claimed in "Geonbaekseo" of 1888 that the December Coup d'État of 1884 was a coup that arose as the result of confrontation between the two political parties on "reliance on traditional customs" by the Conservative Faction and "self-reliance through pursuit of the new" by the Modernization Faction. The backgrounds of the leading members of the Modernization Faction were just as good as the leaders of the Conservative Faction in that they were from renowned *yangban* families and had attained Confucian refinements. For example, Bak Yeong-hyo was the son-in-law of Cheoljong who preceded Gojong as king of Joseon, Hong Yeong-sik was the son of Chief State Councilor Hong Sun-mok (洪淳穆), and Kim Ok-gyun was an elite who passed the civil service examination with the highest score. The only difference was that the leaders of the Modernization Faction were all a young generation of *yangban*. Then what was the understanding of the relationship between modernization thought (also known as enlightenment thought) and Confucianism?

In "Geonbaekseo," Bak Yeong-hyo revealed "eight urgent issues of today" as the tasks confronting reform in Joseon. The gist of Clause 1 on "conditions of the world" is below.

A nation cannot sustain itself without the ability for self-reliance and self-respect because the weak are preyed upon by the strong in today's world despite elements of international law and fair moral principles. Europeans pay lip service to public law and fair moral principles, but they are gradually encroaching upon the Asian nations with their minds full of the aggressive greed of a tiger. Is the reason for Asia being encroached upon by Europe indeed due to racial inferiority of Asians in comparison to Europeans? That is not so. The divine energy of all under Heaven is concentrated in Asia, and as such, Confucianism, Buddhism, Christianity, and Mohammedanism originated from Asia. If such is the case, why was the office of such divine energy conceded to Europe and the U.S.?

> In general, this is due to the governments of all nations considering their people as serfs and not leading them through benevolence, righteousness, propriety, and knowledge or teaching them with literary accomplishments in general.... This is the fault of the government and not of the people.

The reason for the decline of Confucianism was mentioned in Clause 6: "Administer the fundamentals by teaching skills and virtue as well as arts and literature to the people."

> Culture declined and customs deteriorated in recent times. Appreciating extravagant prose and copying passages were considered important without knowing the original meaning of investigation of things and cultivation of knowledge. The kingdom was destroyed because unenlightened and corrupt Confucians were called great scholars and became great ranking officials if they were able to write prosy sentences and memorize the Four Books and Three Confucian Classics as well as books by the Hundred Schools of Thought. This is the cause of the decline of all nations in Asia.... Thus it is this servant's foolish thought that "learning, regardless of whether eastern or western, must put practical application first and extravagant prose last." Practical application is equivalent to a tangerine and extravagance of prose is similar to its aroma. The aroma arises from the tangerine; how can the tangerine arise from the aroma? If the substance is thrown away and the external splendor is adopted, it will result in a trend where the outer coverings look good but the scholarship of investigating things so as to thoroughly understand the princi-

ple and of governing the nation through self-cultivation become superfluous.

In sum, eastern and western learning do not contradict each other; rather, they are both rooted in "practical application." The foundation of Confucianism also lies in "investigating things so as to thoroughly understand the principle and governing the nation through self-cultivation," but Confucianism declined because the foundation was thrown away in favor of extravagant prose. "Investigating things so as to thoroughly understand the principle" is natural science, whereas "governing the nation through self-cultivation" is ethics and politics. In contrast to Fukujawa Yukichi who considered Confucianism as anti-enlightenment, the enlightenment thought of Joseon considered Confucianism to have flexibly developed Confucian thought to coincide with a new era.

More important is the inclusiveness of religious freedom instead of understanding Confucianism and Christianity as being contradictory.

> Moreover, religion is the foundation of enlightenment in that the populace relies on it. Thus the nation will decline if religion becomes weak, and the nation will flourish if religion is sound. The soundness of Confucianism made China strong in the olden days, transmission of Buddhism made India and several eastern nations strong as well, and the soundness of Mohammedanism made many countries west of China and Turkey stronger.... But there is a time for everything, and might cannot force it. Thus religion must be left in the hands of the populace; the government must not interfere. Religious disputes have agitated the minds of the people and have brought destruction to nations and been injurious to people's lives from of old. This must be used as a mirror.

In other words, freedom of religion must be allowed and selection of religion must be left up to the populace because all religions, whether Confucianism or Christianity, were "the foundation of enlightenment." Rather, Bak Yeong-hyo warned of the possible danger of government intervention inducing religious war. We can clearly see that this was fundamentally different from the thinking of defending orthodoxy and rejecting heterodoxy, which assumes that Confucianism was the only "true learning" and Christianity was "evil learning."

As an additional remark, the meaning of "enlightenment" was understood in a Confucian way in Joseon, which was different from the "civilization and enlightenment" of Japan. Joseon understood "enlightenment" to be a contraction of "modernization based on material development and cultivation of cultured people," which was a combination of "material development and cultivation" in the "Great Appendix" (繫辭傳, *Xicichuan* in Ch.) of *Book of Changes,* and "cultivation of new customs through changing the people with the new" in Chapter 1, "Record of Studies" (學記, *Xueji* in Ch.) of *Book of Rites.*

Bak Yeong-hyo laid the foundation of eastern and western learning in "practical application" as revealed in "Geonbaekseo" mentioned above. This is a trend that did not concern itself as to whether the learning was eastern or western as long as it was useful in "practical application." He enumerated specific thoughts on educational reform to cultivate able men with practical skills in Clause 6 of "Geonbaekseo." Its contents contained an aspect which fundamentally negated the Confucian education perpetuated for hundreds of years to pass the civil service examination. The following is an organized summary of that:

① Establish primary and normal schools, and educate all boys and girls over the age of six.

② Establish schools for adults in their prime and translate books on politics, finance, domestic and international law, history, geography, and arithmetic in Chinese characters or *han'geul* to teach the young among the populace or scholars in their prime who are chosen from throughout the kingdom.[1] Employ them as scholar-officials after they take the examination of the past in anticipation of their scholastic achievements.[2]

---

[1] This is an imitation of Hodang (湖堂); it was very beneficial.

[2] Hodang refers to Dokseodang for which talented civilian officials were

③ Priority should be given to national history, language, and literature when teaching the populace.[3]

④ Teach the populace about law, finance, politics, medicine, investigation of principles, and other accomplishments by hiring foreigners.

⑤ Build many printing shops by minting printing types and creating paper to make books widely available.[4]

⑥ Increase the knowledge of the populace by building museums.

⑦ Make the populace or educated men realize their narrow-mindedness by authorizing lectures at assemblies from time to time.

⑧ Teach the languages of various nations in the East and West to facilitate exchange.

⑨ Establish rules so that the populace can be authorized to establish newspaper companies for the printing and publishing of newspapers.[5]

---

selected and given a break from their duties to study in a mountain temple from the eighth year of the reign of Sejong (1426) in the early Joseon period. The name was later changed to Hodang. (Ha Woo-bong)

[3] The populace considered Qing China important as the foundation and did not know the authentic precedent of their own kingdom, because they were taught Qing history and writing but not the history and writing of their own kingdom. This is like discarding the means and accepting the end.

[4] The populace could not learn even if they wanted to due to lack of books. An enlightened kingdom has plenty of books. What is envious about Japan is that there are many books as well as students and schools in Japan because the price of paper is low and many printing types are used in printing.

[5] A newspaper will discuss affairs of the royal court, announce official orders, and mention new items that draw the public's attention, such as course of action of government officials, conditions of foreign nations, cultural ups and downs, good and bad harvests, rise and fall of prices, ups and downs in trade, civilian manufacturing, births and deaths, strange occurrences and stories; pictures are attached to clarify things. Circumstances of the people are also treated as things are treated. Thus there is nothing better to broaden the views and provide information to the

⑩ Authorize religions without question, and leave them to the freedom of the believers. Refusing permission to authorize construction of a place of worship might incur calamity.

To achieve modernization, an educational reform that systematically cultivated able men who would be in charge of each field must be executed first. The Modernization Faction must take power away from the Conservative Faction in order to liberate the younger generations of Joseon people from the officialdom of impractical Confucian education. But the December Coup d'État of 1884 ended in failure.

The year 1884 corresponded to the 17th year of Meiji in Japan. There was a feeling of repenting over missing an opportunity, but there was the possibility of Joseon achieving modernization effectively in a short period by learning from the trials and errors experienced by Japan during the process of "civilization and enlightenment." In addition, Joseon was of an appropriate size to achieve such a rapid reform because the territory was not large and there was not the complication of different ethnic groups.

The educational reform was not implemented during the Coup d'État of 1884 but was implemented instead from July 1894 to February 1896 during the execution of the Gabo Reform Movement of 1894. But even that ended unsuccessfully due to resistance and counterattack by the Conservative Faction. There was great significance in the failure of the reform plan to take hold during the ten-year period from the Coup d'État of 1884 to the start of the Gabo Reform Movement of 1894. Everything was a race against time.

Civil Service Examination System Is Abolished and Schools Established

The form of education during the 500-some years of the Joseon dynasty was Chinese literature, and the content was Confucian in

---

populace than this. In Europe and the U.S., the extent of enlightenment is compared these days by the number of available newspapers.

nature. It created many illiterate people before they even began to study the Four Books and Five Confucian Classics due to the difficulty of Chinese characters. The Korean alphabet was disdained as the written characters for women and monks. The most significant slogan advanced by the Modernization Faction was that the abolition of the cliques of civilian officials and of regions would realize equality of the populace because the cliques of civilian officials and of region were obstacles in unifying the people. For example, this issue was also included as one of the reform platforms of the December Coup d'État of 1884.

> Employ able men based on talent by abolishing cliques of civilian officials and offering equal rights to the populace.

Ten years after the failure of the Coup d'État of 1884, a coalition of the moderate and the radical reformists of the Modernization Faction started the Gabo Reform Movement in July of 1894. The core of the moderate reformists included Kim Hong-jip, Kim Yun-sik, Eoh Yun-jung, and Yu Gil-jun, while radical reformists included Bak Yeong-hyo who fled to Japan and Seo Gwang-beom who fled to the U.S. after the failed Coup d'État of 1884. A conflict naturally arose as to whether to pursue moderate or radical reforms. The leader of the Coup d'État of 1884 was assassinated in March of the same year.

The last clause of the 14 Clauses of the Great Plan announced by Gojong at the ancestral temple of the royal family on January 7, 1895, contained the following information:

> Cliques of civilian officials and of regions will not be related to employing of men; engage men of ability from far and wide by searching for men of virtue from far and wide.

Cliques of civilian officials and of regions were the worst legacy of the Sarim Faction's factional disputes. People are still strongly conscious of traditional cliques of civilian officials and of regions even today, 100 years after the Joseon dynasty. The political map of Korea still shows that except for Seoul and its outlying areas where people from all over the peninsula have congregated, people in the Gyeong-sang Provinces, Jeolla Provinces, and Chungcheong Provinces are especially conscious of regional cliques. Even the violent democratic movements in Korea in the past could not overcome the thick wall of regional cliques.

However that may be, the civil service examination system was abolished and the Bureau of Scrutiny Ordinance was adopted in August of 1894. There were two stages of examination according to it: regular and special. The regular examination included subjects on Korean literature, Chinese literature, document copying, arithmetic, domestic politics, and international state of affairs. The special examination was for those who passed the regular examination and was geared toward finding out whether the applicants were appropriate for specific fields.

Through this reform Confucianism and politics became segregated, and the civil service examination, which had continued from the ninth year of the reign of Gwangjong (958) in the Goryeo period, was abolished. Educational system reform was executed to allow opportunity for learning without relation to cliques of civilian officials or of regions. Gojong announced three main principles of education in a royal decree in February 1895, in which learning "in name only" was discarded in favor of learning for "practical application."

Our intent today is to present the main principles of education herewith. Learning in name only must be discarded in favor of practical application.

First is moral education. The essence of customs should be prevented from chaos by practicing the five human relationships with moral obligations. Instill civic morality to maintain world order and increase happiness of the society.

Second is cultivation of the body. Motion must be always diligent, not crave laziness and not avoid hardships. Enjoy happiness with health and without illness by building your muscles and strengthening your physique.

Third is cultivation of knowledge. Gain knowledge from things, thoroughly investigate the principle, and do your utmost to distinguish likes and dislikes, right and wrong, and advantages and disadvantages without creating a boundary between mine and what belongs to others. Study deeply and be well versed; do not pursue personal gain, but instead pursue public gain.

These three are the main principles of education.

This royal edict on education presented a philosophy of education containing a union of moral education, cultivation of the body, and cultivation of knowledge. The Ministry of Education established the Bureau of Normal Education to manage primary schools and normal school for the fostering of teachers, and the Bureau of Specialized Education to manage normal schools, vocational schools, foreign language schools, and specialized schools.

There was a need for people who had received higher education in each field if the Gabo Reform Movement of 1894 were to be successful. Thus Fukujawa Yukichi of Keio University was commissioned to "teach foreign students," and 114 students were sent to Japan to study abroad in May 1895. Yu Gil-jun and Yu Jeong-su (柳定秀), attendants of Eoh Yun-jung, enrolled at Keio University established by Fukujawa Yukichi, and Yun Chi-ho (尹致昊, 1865-1945) studied at Dojinsha College established by Nakamura Masanao when a Joseon inspection team to Japan (also known as "gentlemen's sightseeing group") visited Japan in 1881 to learn the advancements of Japanese society.[6] Approximately 50 students studied abroad in Japan due to the efforts of the Modernization Faction until the December Coup d'État of 1884. The Joseon government summoned students studying in Japan back to Joseon after the failed Coup d'État of 1884 because of the fear that political refugees in Japan such as Kim Ok-gyun and Bak Yeong-hyo might initiate contact with the students. Additional students were not sent to Japan for 10 years until the Gabo Reform Movement of 1894. Lack of able men to be in charge of the practical side of the Gabo Reform Movement was an aftermath of this.

---

[6] The "gentlemen's sightseeing group" was a group of Joseon government officials dispatched to Japan in 1881 to learn the advancements made by Japanese society. (S. Lee)

Many linked Fukujawa Yukichi with his presentation of "Away from Asia" in March 1885 and emphasized his policy of aggression after the Coup d'État of 1884. But to the Joseon Modernization Faction, he was the greatest Japanese collaborator even before the Coup d'État of 1884. Eoh Yun-jung and Yu Gil-jun became closely acquainted with Fukujawa Yukichi during a visit to Japan as part of the 1881 inspection team; Yu Gil-jun later became the first Joseon student to study at Keio University.

Modern theological schools were established in Joseon prior to the Gabo Reform Movement of 1894. One of these was Yugyeong Public School, which was established in September 1886. Educational contents were very limited; its character was closer to a type of English language school taught by H. B. Hulbert and two other American missionaries. Other Christian schools established by American missionaries included Pai Chai Hakdang established in 1885 and Ehwa Hakdang established in 1886 for women. American missionaries adopted a method of transmitting Christianity under the pretext of "medical treatment and education" activities in the late 1880s in order to avoid conflict with Confucianism. These schools, of course, were not just theological schools; they taught normal education based on the Christian spirit.[7]

It is no exaggeration to say that the first step toward modern education in Korea was pioneered by American missionaries. As a result, "allergies toward western barbarians" that considered western religion or learning as evil learning were alleviated, and a breath of fresh air came into the spiritual world of Koreans which was firmly Confucian. The conclusion of the educational reform was the Gabo Reform Movement of 1894.

The Gabo Reform Movement of 1894 abolished the hitherto exclusive Confucian education and institutionally established modern education to cultivate able men for "practical application." But educational reform was put on hold because the Kim Hong-jip cabinet was overturned and the Conservative regime revived in

---

[7] "Normal education" is the term used in the olden days to refer to what is now called elementary education. (S. Lee)

February 1896, one year after Gojong announced the royal edict on education.

Modern education in Korea took root among the people when the Japanese invasion became earnest in the late 1900s after the Russo-Japanese War. One of the national salvation movements through education that unfolded in this period was the establishment of private schools for grooming leaders of future generations in various regions as part of the *minjung* movement. The Department of Education of the current Korean government could verify that there were 2,250 private schools in contrast to 81 public government schools and 65 public schools among a total of 2,396 schools immediately before the annexation in July 1910.

There was still the sense of the turning point from Confucian education to modern education having occurred too late. Under the rule of the Japanese Resident-General in Korea which had already begun in February 1906, all trace of Korean sovereignty disappeared. Even in the field of education, a Japanese vice minister seized command of real power in the Department of Education in Korea and regulated the founding of private schools as well as interfering with the contents of education. Thus the new style of education under the rule of the Japanese Resident-General in Korea did not foster autonomous modernization; rather, it performed the role of guiding in the direction of colonization.

Regicide of Queen Min and the Downfall of the Kim Hong-jip Cabinet

The traditional subordinate relationship between Joseon and Qing China came to an end due to the Gabo Reform Movement of 1894 that began in July. Gojong delivered the following royal edict to all civilian and military officials in front of the ancestral temple of the royal family in January 1895:

> Sever all thoughts of obeying Qing China and firmly build the foundation for autonomy.

This was Clause 1 of the 14 Clauses of the Great Plan. But the Gabo Reform Movement of 1894 itself was possible because the bond between the Conservative Faction in Joseon and Qing China was severed after Japan won the Sino-Japanese War. But the national sovereignty was hitherto able to limp along under the umbrella of a subordinate relationship with Qing China despite great restrictions imposed on it.

Japan was watching for an opportunity toward Joseon, and with the vacuum created after Joseon became independent of the subordinate relationship with Qing China, Japan started to interfere with the domestic policies of Joseon. This is like having a tiger at the front door and a wolf at the back door. This was when Russia emerged as a power to counter Japan. Immediately following the signing of the Treaty of Shimonoseki, Russia, France, and Germany requested Japan to return the Liaoning province to Qing on April 23, 1895. Qing had been forced to cede the Liaoning province to Japan in the Treaty of Shimonoseki. This was the so-called "Triple Intervention."

Japanese policy toward Joseon was that of a "protectorate state" after the Sino-Japanese War. Japan attempted to advance the plan for Joseon from a "protectorate" to an "annexed nation" after the end of the Sino-Japanese war by moving the plan forward by 10 years after the Russo-Japanese War. But Russia, which led the Triple Intervention, became an obstacle to this plan. Within the Joseon government was a movement to bring in Russian intervention to remove Japanese meddling; Japan was under the impression that Queen Min was behind it.

The Japanese minister in Joseon at the time was Inoue Kaoru, a senior statesman of Japan; he left his post in August 1895 for having failed to segregate the Joseon government from Russia. Miura Goro (1846-1926) of the Choshu clan and a retired army lieutenant general succeeded Inoue Kaoru at the Japanese legation in Joseon. He attempted to eliminate Queen Min by bringing her archenemy Daewon-gun who had retired to Gongdeok-li in the suburb of Seoul, back into politics. He pretended on the surface to confine himself in the Office of the Japanese Resident-General deeply wrapped up in copying Chinese Classics, but in reality he secretly maneuvered to hand political power over Joseon to Daewon-gun with only a small number of very close co-conspirators and pursued a plan to mobilize assassins. Queen Min was assassinated on October 8.

On October 3, right before the Queen's assassination, Miura Goro held a secret meeting with his co-conspirators Sugimura Fukashi and Okamoto Ryunosuke, Secretary of the Japanese Legation in Joseon and Advisor to the Department of the Royal Household. They decided on a scenario in which Japanese troops would advance into the palace as if to allay the disturbance when "a struggle between the supporters of Daewon-gun and supporters of Queen Min" would arise ("Japanese Court of Preliminary Inquiries," Hiroshima Court). The Japanese troops would be the main force, but the Military Training Division of Joseon would join the assassination effort. There were two different Joseon troops in Seoul, the Palace Guard Regiment led by an American instructor and the Military Training Division led by a Japanese instructor. The Joseon government was discussing the issue of disbanding the pro-Japanese Military Training Division. It was easier to make things look as if the disturbance arose from an internal discord between the Palace Guard Regiment and the Military Training Division.

Japanese troops led by military officer Lieutenant Colonel Minase Yukihiko, joined by Japanese groups and the Military Training Division of Joseon, escorted Daewon-gun and advanced into Gyeongbok Palace at dawn on October 8. Part of the Japanese group stormed into Okhoru Pavilion, the royal chamber of Queen Min in Geoncheong Palace, dragged her out of her chamber, cut her down with swords, doused her body with kerosene, and set the body on fire. This left Joseon as an independent nation in name only as it did not have enough military power to defend the palace, which was the heart of the kingdom. This assassination of Queen Min was witnessed by General Dye, an American in charge of training the Palace Guard Regiment, and a Russian electrical engineer by the name of Sabatin. The U.S. Minister Horace N. Allen and the Russian Minister Karl Waeber rushed to the Japanese legation in Joseon to demand an explanation after hearing of this incident from General Dye and Sabatin, which raised an international diplomatic outrage.

The Japanese government quickly dispatched Japanese Foreign Minister Kobayashi Jutaro to Joseon for the purpose of sending Miura Goro and 47 other conspirators in the assassination under guard to Hiroshima where they were detained to keep them from talking. All of them were found not guilty at the trial held on January 20 of the following year and freed for lack of evidence. A nonfiction book entitled *Assassination of Queen Minbi* (*Minbi ansatsu* in Japanese, 1988, Shinchosha) provides a complete picture of the assassination, which has shocked many Japanese readers.

Unknown men going into the quarters reserved only for women was considered a depraved act that went against good sense even in the households of commoners in Joseon where "distinction between the two genders" was strictly adhered to. It was an unthinkable outrage for Miura Goro who served as president of Gakushuin (the university in charge of educating the royal family and peers of Japan) in 1888 to head this investigation. The truth is still unknown as to whether the Japanese government gave tacit consent to the assassination by appointing a savage diplomatic novice without any backbone to the post of Japanese Minister in Joseon or if the assassination was his arbitrary decision.

Whatever the case may be, the conspirators who were sent under guard to Japan were surrounded by the "scene of welcoming victorious returning troops" and treated as national heroes when they landed in Port Ujina. Miura Goro reminisced as follows on his way to Tokyo after his release from prison.

> I received an invitation to a welcoming reception of a supporter as soon as I was released from prison. I returned by train, and I heard cheers wherever I went.

Gojong was shocked by the assassination of the queen by the Japanese invading the palace. He escaped from Gyeongbok Palace and fled to the Russian legation on February 11, 1896, to avoid evil influences. There he commanded the arrest and punishment of the pro-Japanese Kim Hong-jip cabinet. Thus the Gabo Reform Movement of 1894 failed after 18 months without a chance for the results of the reform movement to settle. The Kim Hong-jip cabinet fell because it was unjustly blamed for the assassination of Queen Min; the Modernization Faction dispersed because the key figures of the Gabo Reform Movement of 1894 such as Kim Hong-jip and Eoh Yun-jung were killed, Kim Yun-sik was exiled to Jeju Island, and Yu Gil-jun sought refuge in Japan. This was the second blow to the Modernization Faction following the failure of the December Coup d'État of 1884.

Russia and Japan Fight in the Heart of Korea

Interference from Qing China was removed based on "usher in Russia to usher out Qing" after the Coup d'État of 1884. Russia was approached after the Russo-Japanese War to remove interference from Japan based on "bring in Russian intervention to remove Japanese meddling." Gojong resided in the Russian legation for a year before returning to Gyeong'un Palace (also known as Deoksu Palace) in February 1897 instead of going to Gyeongbok Palace where Queen Min was assassinated. A road leading to the U.S. legation and the Russian legation in Joseon was kept open at the rear gate. For the reign, he declared a unique name called "*gwangmu*" (Martial Brilliance) in August and assigned 1897 as the first year of the reign of *gwangmu*, and observed the formality of an independent empire by changing the title of king to emperor as well as the name of the kingdom to "Daehan Jeguk" (the Great Han Empire) in October. Joseon became completely independent from the subordinate relationship with China through this "renaming of the nation and the reign." The Qing government accordingly appointed Inspector-General Xu Shou-peng as Chinese Minister in Korea.

The fate of Korea was now in the hands of Russia and Japan. The conflict between Russia and Japan over supremacy in Manchuria and Korea escalated gradually when Qing China withdrew from Korea after losing the Sino-Japanese War.

The two countries officially declared war on February 10, 1904. Japanese fleets sank a Russian cruiser and gunboats two days earlier on February 8. A day later, an advance party of some 2,000 Japanese soldiers from the 12th Division landed in Incheon and advanced into

Seoul. It goes without saying that Incheon and Seoul comprised the heart of Korea. Japanese troops captured these two regions without much resistance. Reinforcements for the 12th Division and the 1st Army led by Commander Kuroki Tamemoto in addition to the advance party rendezvoused in Korea to march northward.

The Joseon government declared neutrality on January 23 when faced with the crisis of military conflict between Russia and Japan. But in order to adhere to neutrality and stop the military conflict, Joseon needed to have the ability to defend itself in driving out the encroaching armies or appeal to world powers that supported neutrality. Joseon had to be able to defend Incheon and Seoul, the heart of Joseon, to initiate diplomatic activities to garner international support. Foreign relations without military power are useless. Japanese forces took over Incheon and Seoul without any resistance on February 8 and 9 before Russia and Japan officially declared war. Moreover, the Korean government was forced by the overwhelming Japanese troops to sign the Protectorate Treaty of 1904 between Korea and Japan. Article 4 of the treaty is below:

> In case the welfare of the Imperial House of Korea or the territorial integrity of Korea is endangered by aggression of a third power or internal disturbances, the Imperial Government of Japan shall immediately take such necessary measures as circumstances require, and in such case the Imperial Government of Korea shall give full facilities to promote the actions of the Imperial Japanese Government. The Imperial Government of Japan may, for the attainment of the above-mentioned object, occupy when the circumstances require such places as may be necessary from strategic points of view.

Korea became a hostile nation to Russia because Korea had to acknowledge unrestricted occupation of Japanese forces in Korea and provided military bases according to this protectorate treaty. This was the first step toward "annexation" of August 1910 in that this led to the First Korea-Japan Agreement in August 1904, the Second Korea-Japan Agreement in November 1905, and the Third Korea-Japan Agreement in July 1907.

The idea to bring in Russian intervention to remove Japanese meddling not only failed, but the announcement of neutrality in the face of military conflict between Russia and Japan came to naught in the face of overwhelming Japanese military force. This could only be said to be a grim conclusion to the Confucian civil administration that created a military vacuum in Korea by neglecting modernization of the Korean military troops in the contentedness under the umbrella of a subordinate relationship with Qing China. Japan removed Qing China and Russia from the Korean peninsula after the Sino-Japanese War and the Russo-Japanese War in order to realize "the theory on conquering Korea" (*seikan ron* in Japanese history) since the early Meiji period. Korea could no longer independently withstand the Japanese invasion.

Choe Ik-hyeon, Leader of Anti-Japanese Righteous Army

The thought of Choe Ik-hyeon on defending orthodoxy and rejecting heterodoxy was discussed in Chapter 19. After the conclusion of the Russo-Japanese War, Korea was divested of the right to execute foreign policy and became a "protectorate" under the Japanese Resident-General Ito Hirobumi based on the Second Korea-Japan Agreement in November 1905.

The anti-Japanese Righteous Army movement spread among Korean people of all classes throughout various regions of Korea due to the outcry of Confucian scholars. Fierce militant wars were waged between the anti-Japanese Righteous Army and a union of Japanese military troops, military police, and police.

Choe Ik-hyeon was already 74 and a senior member of the Hwa-seo School when he was invited by the literati to be the leader of the Righteous Army in June of 1906 in Sunchang, North Jeolla Province. Therefore the person who commanded the Righteous Army in reality was Yim Byeong-chan (林炳瓚), magistrate of Nagan. His thought on becoming involved in the anti-Japanese Righteous Army movement can be viewed by examining "Letter to the Japanese Government" presented before the formation of the Righteous Army.

Alas, to love a loyal vassal of the nation is called nature, and having faith and doing one's duty is called the Way. Man will certainly die without this nature, and a nation will fall without this Way. This is not an ordinary story or lecture of a stubborn old man. Many nations may struggle for the modern, but they cannot become self-reliant in the world by discarding these.

- "To the Japanese Government" (寄日本政府), *Myeonamjib* (勉庵集, Collected Works of Myeonam), Vol. 16

He was adamantly against the signing of the Treaty of Ganghwa Island in February 1876. With an ax in hand, he knelt in front of the Gwanghwa Gate that is in front of Gyeongbok Palace, and after saying that "this is the crossroad between culture and barbarism," appealed to the king to cut his throat if his protest were not accepted. Below is another section of the letter mentioned above:

But the tide of the world is different from the olden days in that the advent of western powers in the East cannot be stopped single-handedly. It is known to everyone that Korea, Qing China, and Japan must come together to preserve the general situation in the East, and this was also my desire. I do not necessarily believe your nation by all means; I have lived in seclusion for 20 years and determined not to air my opinions on current affairs because I was not desirous of causing damage to the friendly relations between the two nations.

He had observed Japan's movements against Korea from the signing of the Treaty of Ganghwa Island and rang an alarm bell on the upcoming downfall because Japan "did not keep faith and was disloyal" rather than acting with "faith and righteousness."

I am convinced my opinion is correct because your nation in recent years has acted without faith and righteousness. I have uncovered that your nation, although strong now, will eventually fall, which will lead to unrestrained chaos in the East. I will first expound on the crime committed by your nation in not keeping faith and being disloyal, followed by the reason for your nation's fall and chaos in the East.

He enumerated "the 16 crimes in not keeping faith and being disloyal" committed by Japan since the Treaty of Ganghwa Island as follows toward the conclusion of his letter:

> In truth, the situation of the world is such that the ability of the three nations of the East to preserve themselves is questionable even with combined efforts like the three legs of a tripod. But they are envious of each other, harbor grudges, and have become enemies. Why would the western powers leave your nation alone when she, in her hasty and unreasonable act, does not intend to love her own allies? As such, your nation's downfall is near at hand, and the calamity of the collapse of the East as a whole will come soon. Your nation cannot escape the crime of bringing calamity to the East. This is why I say, "your nation may be strong, but it will eventually fall." Going back to the fundamentals is the only strategy indeed to benefit your nation. The way to go back to the fundamentals is to be faithful and respect loyalty.

To summarize the above, the three nations of East Asia must unify and resist the invasion of European and American superpowers in order to preserve each nation. But the three nations of East Asia became enemies due to the actions of Japan in not keeping faith and being disloyal. Asia will not be able to avoid falling one after the other in the face of European and American superpowers. The fall of Japan was predicted to be close at hand as well.

Yim Byeong-chan applied Confucian reasoning to clearly predict the process of Japan's downfall from the "annexation of Korea" in August 1910 to the Manchurian Incident (also known as the Mukden Incident) in September 1931, the Second Sino-Japanese War in July 1937, and further, the Pacific War in December 1941.

But Choe Ik-hyeon and his disciple Yim Byeong-chan were sent to Tsushima Island and exiled to Izuhara on Tsushima after the Righteous Army they led was defeated in the early battle fought in Sunchang. He refused to eat the grain given by the enemy and, requesting Yim Byeong-chan to deliver the joint appeal to the Joseon king, died on November 17, 1906, at the age of 74. His life was a model of sacrificing a life for righteousness.

The Wang Yang-ming School as a Union of Knowledge and Practice Is Behavioral Philosophy

The history of thought in Korea naturally faced ideological pluralism within internationalization after the opening of the door. Advocates defending orthodoxy and rejecting heterodoxy were still adamant about the Learning of Master Zhu as the only scholarship, but adaptability inherent in Confucianism surfaced in the form of modernization thought, Christianity, Buddhism, and Eastern Learning (which later changed to Cheondo Religion, or Religion of the Heavenly Way), which was considered heterodoxy by Confucians.

Thus it became impossible to oppress thought or religion that contradicted or transcended the Learning of Master Zhu as something that "disturbs and behaves contrary to the Confucian tenets." The Cheng-Zhu School, Liu-Wang School, and philologico-bibliographical study converged on the point of being the Way of Confucius and Mencius. But the outstanding characteristic of Joseon Confucianism was that the Learning of Master Zhu as the only scholarship was practiced only in Joseon and not in other Confucian cultures. The Yeongnam School and the Giho School, two main factions that were opposed to each other in the Joseon Confucian world, agreed on the issue of the Learning of Master Zhu as the only scholarship (See Ch. 15).

As mentioned earlier, the Yeongnam School would not follow the Liu-Wang School because Yi Hwang rejected the Liu-Wang School. A Confucian who was opposed to or transcended Zhu Xi was stigmatized and oppressed as "one who disturbs and behaves contrary to the Confucian tenets" in the days of Song Si-yeol of the Giho School (See Ch. 17). A Confucian who deviated from the Learning of Master Zhu was oppressed and excluded completely from politics, especially when the Seoin and the Noron Factions of the lineage of Song Si-yeol held political power for a long time. This was cliquishness based on school and faction.

Such extreme ideological exclusionism by advocates of the Learning of Master Zhu in Joseon led to a more extreme form of seclusion policy, more so than the Confucian cultures of China or Japan. Bak Eun-sik (朴殷植, pen name is Baegam 白巖, 1859-1925) criticized the ideological rigidity and impracticality of utter devotion to the Learning of Master Zhu, which could not cope with the shock of international situations, and pushed to reform the Confucian world through the Wang Yang-ming School in the late Joseon dynasty.

As the editor-in-chief of *Daehan maeil sinbo* (The Korea Daily News) in the late Joseon period, not only did Bak Eun-sik defend the rights of Joseon and attempt to improve civil rights through journalistic activities, but also advocated the reform of the Confucian world through the Wang Yang-ming School by presenting "Yugyo gusinnon" (儒敎求新論, Toward a New Confucianism) in *Seobuk hakhoe wolbo* (西北學會月報, North and West Educational Association Monthly), Vol. 10. He criticized wholehearted devotion to the Learning of Master Zhu as below in this article:

> The tenets handed down by preceding scholars who have been respected as authorities on Confucianism throughout the kingdom during the past 600 years were all of the Learning of Master Zhu. Anyone who advocated any other doctrine beside that of the Learning of Master Zhu would gain the reputation of one who disturbs and behaves contrary to the Confucian tenets, and would be excluded by other Confucians as a heretic. Thus no other schools could exist except the Learning of Master Zhu.

Moreover, he pointed out three problems with the hitherto Joseon Confucian world and proposed a reform plan.

First, the spirit of the Confucian schools was focused only around the sovereign, and it lacked the spirit to be transmitted to the people and society. Despite the fact that distributing knowledge to the people was the basis of Confucianism from the perspective of the meaning of "great unity" of Confucius and the doctrine of "the people are the foundation" of Mencius, it was not being carried out. Thus the teaching of Mencius on "people are important" must be transmitted to the people and society.

494

Second, the Way of Confucianism of the times was disengaged from the intent to save, such as "think of changing the world" of Confucius, "convert mankind to the Buddhist scriptures" of Buddha, and "sacrifice oneself for the benefit of others" of Christianity.

Third, the "handy and simple" Wang Yang-ming School was more suitable for the limited knowledge of man than the "chaotic and careless" Learning of Zhu Xi in this era during which various sciences had developed.

> The Learning of Zhu Xi and the Wang Yang-ming School are both from Confucius and Mencius. Which one should we select? Scholars of succeeding generations must be led by the Wang Yang-ming School in order not to lose the transmission of the Way of Confucius and Mencius.

Why is the Learning of Zhu Xi "chaotic and careless" while the Wang Yang-ming School is "handy and simple"? He compared the two below:

> In short, the difference between the schools of Zhu Xi and Wang Yang-ming lies in that the interpretation of *gyeongmul chiji* (*gewu zhizhi* in Ch.) is not the same. In general, *gyeongmul* for Zhu Xi is the study of things while it is an extension of innate knowledge for Wang.

> - "Hangmunui jillineun uisimhaneun geoseseobuteo guhara" (Search for the Truth of Learning from the Doubtful), *Bageunsik jeonseo* (Complete Works of Bak Eun-sik)

Wang Yang-ming originally studied the Learning of Master Zhu, but he began to question the doctrine of "nature is the principle" advocated by Zhu Xi and claimed that "the mind is the principle," wherein the mind is a union of human nature and spirit. He also realized that the mind was self-sufficient and did not need to be supplemented by studying the principle of the externally existing thing. This was "the great realization obtained while in Longchang" at the age of 37.

Moreover, he was critical of the doctrine of "investigation of things and cultivation of knowledge" by Zhu Xi in which knowledge was achieved only when the principle of the mind inherent in man and the principle of external things suddenly penetrated each other; he advocated "extension of innate knowledge" as the basic tenet of the Wang Yang-ming School after realizing that "*ji*" (knowledge) in "*chiji*" (*zhizhi* in Ch.) was the innate knowledge that everyone is born with. Mencius said the following:

> Man can do [a task] well without learning because of innate ability, and know without thinking because of innate knowledge.

> - "Jin Xin," Part I, The Works of Mencius

In other words, "innate knowledge" was something that is inherent and with which all are born, Confucians and commoners alike. The state of a sage could be achieved by cultivating "innate knowledge" by eliminating personal feelings and greed that block it. In effect, knowledge and practice cannot be divided as Zhu Xi claims if "the Way of the sage is within my mind" is viewed from the perspective of "the mind is the principle." Wang Yang-ming stated this as follows:

> Knowledge and practice are divided into two because the principle is sought outside of the mind. Seeking the principle from within the mind is the teaching of the integration of knowledge and practice as stated in the teaching of Confucius.

> - "Daren lunxueshu" (答人論學書), *Record of Instructions*

Therefore, the Way of the "extension of innate knowledge" was not limited to the Confucians who devoted their lives to reading the books of the sage and the wise, but was open to all people. Bak Eun-sik called the Wang Yang-ming School "handy and simple" for this reason. The Learning of Master Zhu of "first realize the principle by studying widely, and then practice the principle" was indeed speculative, whereas the Wang Yang-ming School of "integration of knowledge and practice" was a markedly behavioral philosophy. There was no time to indulge in speculations when the fate of the people was approaching without fail.

Bak Eun-sik Cries for Confucian Reform through the Daedong Religion

Bak Eun-sik was of course a Confucian. He advocated for the Confucian reform movement based on "handy and simple" Wang Yang-ming School instead of "chaotic and careless" Learning of Master Zhu in order for Korean Confucianism to survive into the new era. That was the Daedong Religion (Great Unity) of 1909, which appeared in the form of *Wangyangmyeong silgi* (王陽明實記, History of Wang Yang-ming). He summarized the tenet of Great Unity as follows:

> What is the tenet of Great Unity? The mind of the sage is to make the universe into one body. This is not intentional; the essence of virtue is thus. Why is this? Material force of Heaven and earth is my material force, material force received by all things is also received by me. Material force is already one and the same, and thus the principle bestowed cannot be from a different location.

> - "Gongbuja tansin ginyeomhoe gangyeon" (Lecture at the Commemoration of the Birth of Master Kong), *Hwanjae*, Vol. 2

Wang Yang-ming explained the virtue of the myriad things as one body based on "extension of innate knowledge" in *Inquiry on the Great Learning* (大學問), which criticized *Daxue huowen* (大學或問) by Zhu Xi.

The great man considers Heaven and earth and the myriad things as one body. He regards the world as one family and China as one person. Those who distinguish between the self and others because they have different forms are small men. A great man regards Heaven, earth, and the myriad things as one body not because he deliberately does so. His virtuous nature is naturally thus, and he is one with Heaven, earth, and the myriad things. This is true not only of the great man; even the mind of the small man is the same, but the small man makes his mind small.

The thought of "Great Unity" was originally the thought of "the whole world belongs to all people" from "Great Harmony is achieved when the Great Principle prevails" in "Li Yun" of *Record of Rites*. Thus "the great man considers the world as one family and China as one person" originated from here, and this was developed further by Wang Yang-ming's virtue as the unity of the myriad things and the body.

Bak Eun-sik advocated the Great Unity Religion in 1909. He attempted to build a subject that would oppose Japanese annexation based on national unity through the doctrine of the unity of the myriad things and the body of the Wang Yang-ming School in order to recover the national sovereignty lost under the "protectorate" of Ito Hirobumi, first Japanese Resident-General in Korea. But Korea was annexed to Japan on August 22, 1910, and sank to the status of a colony. He fled to China and wrote *Hanguk tongsa* (韓國痛史, The Tragic History of Korea) and *Hanguk dongnip undongji hyeolsa* (韓國獨立運動之血史, The Bloody History of the Korean Independence Movement).

Bak Eun-sik was convinced that the nation would ultimately recover independence as long as the national "spirit" was intact even if the "body," or nation, had fallen. *The Tragic History of Korea* is the history of a fallen nation that included his personal experience from 1864 to 1911. The following paragraph is part of the conclusion in the book:

Diplomatic relations, national studies, national language, national literature, and national history belong to the spirit, and money and grains, military troops, moats, ships, and equipment belong to the body. Realizing the spirit is not determined by the existence of the body. Thus the nation will not disappear if the religion and history of the nation are not forgotten. Alas, is the spirit of Korea already dead? Does the so-called spirit exist or not?

"The body" is corporeal material strength, i.e., economic and military powers. Metaphysical "spirit" cannot be destroyed by any material power. Bak Eun-sik wrote *The Tragic History* and *The Bloody History* as the history of "spirit" because he considered raising the "national" spirit and resisting the policy of national obliteration as indeed the way to recover independence.

Index

Homa & Sekey Books Titles on Korea (1)

East and West: Fusion of Horizons
By Kwang-Sae Lee, Kent State University
ISBN 1931907269, Order No 1030, 6 x 9, Hardcover, $59.95, £35.00
ISBN 1931907331, Order No 1041, 6 x 9, Paperback, $34.95, £22.00
Philosophy/Culture/Comparative Studies, 2006, xii, 522pp

A Topography of Confucian Discourse: Politico-philosophical Reflections on Confucian Discourse since Modernity
By Lee Seung-hwan, Korea University
ISBN 1931907277, Order No 1031, 6 x 9, Hardcover, $49.95, £30.00
ISBN 193190734X, Order No 1042, 6 x 9, Paperback, $29.95, £19.00
History/Culture/Philosophy, 2006, xii, 260pp

Developmental Dictatorship and the Park Chung-hee Era: The Shaping of Modernity in the Republic of Korea
Edited by Lee Byeong-Cheon, Kangwon National University
ISBN 1931907285, Order No 1032, 6 x 9, Hardcover, $54.95, £32.00
ISBN 1931907358, Order No 1043, 6 x 9, Paperback, $32.95, £20.00
History/Politics, 2006, xviii, 384pp

The Gwangju Uprising: The Pivotal Democratic Movement That Changed the History of Modern Korea
By Choi Jung-woon, Seoul National University
ISBN 1931907293, Order No 1033, 6 x 9, Hardcover, $49.95, £31.00
ISBN 1931907366, Order No 1044, 6 x 9, Paperback, $29.95, £19.00
History/Politics, 2006, xx, 326pp

The Land of Scholars: Two Thousand Years of Korean Confucianism
By Kang Jae-Un
ISBN 1931907307, Order No 1034, 6 x 9, Hardcover, $59.95, £35.00
ISBN 1931907374, Order No 1045, 6 x 9, Paperback, $34.95, £22.00
History/Culture/Philosophy, 2006, xxx, 516pp

Korea's Pastimes and Customs: A Social History
By Lee E-Wha. 16 pages of color photos. B&W illustrations throughout.
ISBN 1931907382, Order No 1035, 6 x 9, Paperback, $29.95, £21.00
History/Culture, 2006, x, 264pp

Homa & Sekey Books Titles on Korea (2)

A Love Song for the Earnest: Selected Poems of Shin Kyungrim
ISBN: 1931907390, Order No 1037, 5 ½ x 8 ½, Paperback
Poetry, $11.95, 2006

Cracking the Shell: Three Korean Ecopoets
By Seungho Choi, Chiha Kim, and Hyonjong Chong
ISBN: 1931907404, Order No 1038, 5 ½ x 8 ½, Paperback
Poetry, $12.95, 2006

Sunrise over the East Sea: Selected Poems of Park Hi-jin
ISBN: 1931907412, Order No 1039, 5 ½ x 8 ½, Paperback
Poetry, $10.95, 2006

Fragrance of Poetry: Korean-American Literature.
Ed. by Yearn Hong Choi, Ph.D., 5 ½ x 8 ½, Paperback, 108pp
ISBN: 1931907226, Order No. 1027, **Poetry**, $13.95, 2005

A Floating City on the Water: A Novel by Jang-Soon Sohn
ISBN: 1931907188, Order No: 1025, 5½ x 8½, Paperback, 178pp
Fiction, $14.95, 2005

Korean Drama Under Japanese Occupation:
Plays by Ch'i-jin Yu & Man-sik Ch'ae, 5½ x 8½, Paperback, 178pp
ISBN: 193190717X, Order No: 1026, **Drama**, $16.95, 2004

The Curse of Kim's Daughters: A Novel By Park Kyong-ni
ISBN: 1931907102, Order No: 1018, 5½ x 8½, Paperback, 299pp
Fiction, $18.95, 2004

I Want to Hijack an Airplane: Selected Poems of Kim Seung-Hee
ISBN: 1931907137, Order No: 1021, 5½ x 8½, Paperback, 208pp
Poetry, $15.95, 2004

Flowers in the Toilet Bowl: Selected Poems of Choi Seungho
ISBN: 1931907110, Order No: 1022, 5½ x 8½, Paperback, 112pp
Poetry, $12.95, 2004

Drawing Lines: Selected Poems of Moon Dok-su
ISBN: 1931907129, Order No: 1023, 5½ x 8½, Paperback, 112pp
Poetry, $11.95, 2004

What the Spider Said: Poems of Chang Soo Ko
ISBN: 1931907145, Order No: 1024, 5½ x 8½, Paperback, 96pp
Poetry, $10.95, 2004

Surfacing Sadness:
A Centennial of Korean-American Literature 1903-2003
Ed. by Yearn Hong Choi, Ph.D & Haeng Ja Kim
ISBN: 1931907099, Order No: 1017, 6 x 9, Hardcover, 224pp
Asian-American Studies/Literature, $25.00, 2003

Father and Son: A Novel by Han Sung-won,
ISBN: 1931907048, Order No: 1010, 5½ x 8½, Paperback, 285pp, 2002,
Fiction, $17.95

Reflections on a Mask: Two Novellas by Ch'oe In-hun.
ISBN: 1931907056, Order No: 1011, 5½ x 8½, Paperback, 258pp, 2002,
Fiction, $16.95

Unspoken Voices: Selected Short Stories by Korean Women Writers
By Park Kyong-ni, et al.
ISBN: 1931907064, Order No: 1012, 5½ x 8½, Paperback, 266pp, 2002,
Fiction, $16.95

The General's Beard: Two Novellas by Lee Oyoung,
ISBN: 1931907072, Order No: 1013, 5½ x 8½, Paperback, 182pp, 2002,
Fiction, $14.95

Farmers: A Novel by Lee Mu-young,
ISBN: 1931907080, Order No: 1014, 5½ x 8½, Paperback, 216pp, 2002,
Fiction, $15.95

www.homabooks.com

Ordering Information: Within U.S.: $5.00 for the first item, $1.50 for each additional item. **Outside U.S.:** $10.00 for the first item, $5.00 for each additional item. All major credit cards accepted. You may also send a check or money order in U.S. fund (payable to Homa & Sekey Books) to: Orders Department, Homa & Sekey Books, 138 Veterans Plaza, P. O. Box 103, Dumont, NJ 07628 U.S.A. Tel: 800-870-HOMA, 201-261-8810; Fax: 201-261-8890, 201-384-6055; Email: info@homabooks.com

Printed in the United States
39606LVS00003B/55-153